ADDING
+ IT
UP

HELPING CHILDREN LEARN MATHEMATICS

Mathematics Learning Study Committee

Jeremy Kilpatrick, Jane Swafford,
and Bradford Findell, editors

Center for Education
Division of Behavioral and Social Sciences and Education
National Research Council

National Academy Press
Washington, DC

NATIONAL ACADEMY PRESS   2101 Constitution Avenue, N.W.   Washington, DC 20418

NOTICE: The project that is the subject of this report was approved by the Governing Board of the National Research Council, whose members are drawn from the councils of the National Academy of Sciences, the National Academy of Engineering, and the Institute of Medicine. The members of the committee responsible for the report were chosen for their special competences and with regard for appropriate balance.

This study was supported by Contract/Grant No. ESI-9816818 between the National Academy of Sciences and the U.S. Department of Education and the National Science Foundation. Any opinions, findings, conclusions, or recommendations expressed in this publication are those of the author(s) and do not necessarily reflect the views of the organizations or agencies that provided support for the project.

Library of Congress Cataloging-in-Publication Data

Adding it up : helping children learn mathematics / Jeremy Kilpatrick,
Jane Swafford, and Bradford Findell, editors.
    p. cm.
Includes bibliographical references and index.
  ISBN 0-309-06995-5 (hardcover)
  1. Mathematics—Study and teaching (Elementary)—United States. 2.
Mathematics—Study and teaching (Middle school)—United States. I.
Kilpatrick, Jeremy. II. Swafford, Jane. III. Findell, Bradford.
  QA135.5 .A32 2001
  372.7—dc21
                        2001001734

Suggesed citation:
National Research Council. (2001). *Adding it up: Helping children learn mathematics.* J. Kilpatrick, J. Swafford, and B. Findell (Eds.). Mathematics Learning Study Committee, Center for Education, Division of Behavioral and Social Sciences and Education. Washington, DC: National Academy Press.

Additional copies of this report are available from National Academy Press, 2101 Constitution Avenue, N.W., Lockbox 285, Washington, DC 20055; (800) 624-6242 or (202) 334-3313 (in the Washington metropolitan area); Internet, http://www.nap.edu

Printed in the United States of America.

THE NATIONAL ACADEMIES

National Academy of Sciences
National Academy of Engineering
Institute of Medicine
National Research Council

The **National Academy of Sciences** is a private, nonprofit, self-perpetuating society of distinguished scholars engaged in scientific and engineering research, dedicated to the furtherance of science and technology and to their use for the general welfare. Upon the authority of the charter granted to it by the Congress in 1863, the Academy has a mandate that requires it to advise the federal government on scientific and technical matters. Dr. Bruce M. Alberts is president of the National Academy of Sciences.

The **National Academy of Engineering** was established in 1964, under the charter of the National Academy of Sciences, as a parallel organization of outstanding engineers. It is autonomous in its administration and in the selection of its members, sharing with the National Academy of Sciences the responsibility for advising the federal government. The National Academy of Engineering also sponsors engineering programs aimed at meeting national needs, encourages education and research, and recognizes the superior achievements of engineers. Dr. Wm. A. Wulf is president of the National Academy of Engineering.

The **Institute of Medicine** was established in 1970 by the National Academy of Sciences to secure the services of eminent members of appropriate professions in the examination of policy matters pertaining to the health of the public. The Institute acts under the responsibility given to the National Academy of Sciences by its congressional charter to be an adviser to the federal government and, upon its own initiative, to identify issues of medical care, research, and education. Dr. Kenneth I. Shine is president of the Institute of Medicine.

The **National Research Council** was organized by the National Academy of Sciences in 1916 to associate the broad community of science and technology with the Academy's purposes of furthering knowledge and advising the federal government. Functioning in accordance with general policies determined by the Academy, the Council has become the principal operating agency of both the National Academy of Sciences and the National Academy of Engineering in providing services to the government, the public, and the scientific and engineering communities. The Council is administered jointly by both Academies and the Institute of Medicine. Dr. Bruce M. Alberts and Dr. Wm. A. Wulf are chairman and vice chairman, respectively, of the National Research Council.

MATHEMATICS LEARNING STUDY COMMITTEE

JEREMY KILPATRICK, *Chair*, University of Georgia
DEBORAH LOEWENBERG BALL, University of Michigan
HYMAN BASS, University of Michigan
JERE BROPHY, Michigan State University
FELIX BROWDER, Rutgers University
THOMAS P. CARPENTER, University of Wisconsin–Madison
CAROLYN DAY, Dayton Public Schools
KAREN FUSON, Northwestern University
JAMES HIEBERT, University of Delaware
ROGER HOWE, Yale University
CAROLYN KIERAN, University of Quebec, Montreal
RICHARD E. MAYER, University of California, Santa Barbara
KEVIN MILLER, University of Illinois, Urbana-Champaign
CASILDA PARDO, Albuquerque Public Schools
EDGAR ROBINSON, Exxon Mobil Corporation (Retired)
HUNG-HSI WU, University of California, Berkeley

NATIONAL RESEARCH COUNCIL STAFF

JANE SWAFFORD, *Study Director*
BRADFORD FINDELL, *Program Officer*
GAIL PRITCHARD, *Program Officer*
SONJA ATKINSON, *Administrative Assistant*

SPECIAL OVERSIGHT COMMISSION FOR THE MATHEMATICS LEARNING STUDY

RONALD L. GRAHAM, *Chair*, University of California, San Diego
DEBORAH LOEWENBERG BALL, University of Michigan
IRIS CARL, Houston Independent School District
THOMAS P. CARPENTER, University of Wisconsin–Madison
CHRISTOPHER CROSS, Council for Basic Education
RONALD DOUGLAS, Texas A&M University
ROGER HOWE, Yale University
LYNNE REDER, Carnegie Mellon University
HAROLD STEVENSON, University of Michigan
PHILLIP URI TREISMAN, University of Texas, Austin

REVIEWERS

This report has been reviewed in draft form by individuals chosen for their diverse perspectives and technical expertise, in accordance with procedures approved by the National Research Council's Report Review Committee. The purpose of this independent review is to provide candid and critical comments that will assist the institution in making its published report as sound as possible and to ensure that the report meets institutional standards for objectivity, evidence, and responsiveness to the study charge. The review comments and draft manuscript remain confidential to protect the integrity of the deliberative process. We wish to thank the following individuals for their participation in the review of this report:

JOHN ANDERSON, Carnegie Mellon University
RICHARD A. ASKEY, University of Wisconsin–Madison
ARTHUR BAROODY, University of Illinois, Urbana-Champaign
GUNNAR CARLSSON, Stanford University
JERE CONFREY, University of Texas
JOHN DOSSEY, Illinois State University
JEAN-CLAUDE FALMAGNE, University of California, Irvine
HERBERT GINSBURG, Columbia University
KENNETH KOEDINGER, Carnegie Mellon University
CAROLYN MAHER, Rutgers University
ALFRED MANASTER, University of California, San Diego
BETHANY RITTLE-JOHNSON, Carnegie Mellon University

MARIA SANTOS, San Francisco Unified School District
PATRICK THOMPSON, Vanderbilt University
ZALMAN USISKIN, University of Chicago

Although the reviewers listed above have provided many constructive comments and suggestions, they were not asked to endorse the conclusions or recommendations nor did they see the final draft of the report before its release. The review of this report was overseen by Ronald L. Graham, University of California, San Diego, and Patrick Suppes (NAS), Stanford University. Appointed by the National Research Council, they were responsible for making certain that an independent examination of this report was carried out in accordance with institutional procedures and that all review comments were carefully considered. Responsibility for the final content of this report rests entirely with the authoring committee and the institution.

ACKNOWLEDGMENTS

Adding It Up is the product of an 18-month project in which 16 individuals with diverse backgrounds, as a committee, reviewed and synthesized relevant research on mathematics learning from pre-kindergarten through grade 8. We had the good fortune of working with a number of people outside the committee who shared our enthusiasm for this project, and we are indebted to them for the intellectual insights and support that they provided.

At a time when mathematics education issues have reached a critical point, both publicly and politically, it has become clear that our nation has a responsibility to provide guidance and leadership in answering questions about how to improve mathematics learning for all students. We would like to thank our sponsors, the National Science Foundation and the U.S. Department of Education, for their foresight in providing a timely opportunity to move the debate forward. In particular, we thank Janice Earle, from the National Science Foundation; Patricia O'Connell Ross, from the U.S. Department of Education; and Judy Wurtzel and Linda Rosen, both formerly with the U.S. Department of Education, for their constant support and interest in this study.

During the information-gathering phase of our work, a number of people made presentations to the committee on various topics pertaining to mathematics learning. We benefited greatly from their stimulating presentations and extend our thanks to Jo Boaler, Stanford University, School of Education; Douglas Carnine, University of Oregon, National Center to Improve the Tools of Educators; Paul Clopton, Mathematically Correct; Megan Franke, University of California, Los Angeles, Graduate School of Education and Information Studies; and Judith Sowder, San Diego State University, Center for Research in Mathematics and Science Education. Additionally, we would like to thank

Steven Stahl and Donna Alvermann, University of Georgia, and Susan Burns, George Mason University, for providing us with insights about the parallels between mathematics and reading. And we are grateful to Carne Barnett, WestEd Regional Education Laboratory; Deborah Schifter, Education Development Center; Patricia Campbell, University of Maryland, Center for Mathematics Education; Anne Morris, University of Delaware, School of Education; and Mary Kay Stein, University of Pittsburgh, Learning Research and Development Center; for providing information about specific programs in elementary mathematics or teacher development.

We also wish to acknowledge the people who provided informative commissioned papers that expanded and enhanced our collective thinking. In particular, we appreciate the work of Rolf Blank, Council of Chief State School Officers; Graham Jones, Cynthia Langrall, and Carol Thornton, Illinois State University; Gloria Ladson-Billings and Richard Lehrer, University of Wisconsin–Madison; and Denise Mewborn, University of Georgia. We also thank Douglas McLeod and Judith Sowder, San Diego State University, and Les Steffe, University of Georgia, for their assistance with research reviews for specific topics on which we had questions.

While writing the final draft of this report, we commissioned several chapter reviews that strengthened our research synthesis and focused our prose. Many thanks to Kathleen Cramer, University of Minnesota; James Kaput, University of Massachusetts–Dartmouth; Mary Lindquist, Columbus State University; Thomas Post, University of Minnesota; and Edward Rathmell, University of Northern Iowa.

While the individuals listed above have provided many constructive comments and suggestions, responsibility for the final content of this report rests solely with the authoring committee and the National Research Council.

Finally, we would like extend our sincere thanks to several individuals within the National Research Council and in other places who made significant contributions to our work: Rodger Bybee, former Executive Director for the Center, and Patrice Legro, former Division Director for Special Projects, for providing the initial impetus for this project and getting it off to a strong start; Gail Pritchard, Program Officer, for keeping us on the straight and narrow in complying with the myriad of NRC policies and procedures; Bradford Findell, Program Officer, for researching, drafting, and editing many sections of the report; Michael J. Feuer, Executive Director for the Center for Education (CFE), for providing key advice; Kirsten Sampson Snyder, Reports Officer for CFE, for guiding us through the report review process; Steve Olson and Yvonne Wise, for providing editorial assistance; Sally Stanfield, National

Academy Press, for making our report look so nice; Lynn Geiger and Gooyeon Kim, doctoral students at the University of Georgia, for assisting the chair in his work on this report; Mark Hoover, doctoral student at the University of Michigan, for helping on some early drafts of chapters; and Todd Grundmeier, graduate student at the University of New Hampshire, for tracking down most of our references and verifying them for appropriateness and accuracy. Lastly, we would like to express our appreciation to Sonja Atkinson, Administrative Assistant, whose agility in managing the complex arrangements, attention to detail, and cheerful attitude made our work much easier and our time together more enjoyable.

Jeremy Kilpatrick, *Chair*
Jane Swafford, *Study Director*
Mathematics Learning Study Committee

PREFACE

Public concern about how well U.S. schoolchildren are learning mathematics is abundant and growing. The globalization of markets, the spread of information technologies, and the premium being paid for workforce skills all emphasize the mounting need for proficiency in mathematics. Media reports of inadequate teaching, poorly designed curricula, and low test scores fuel fears that young people are deficient in the mathematical skills demanded by society.

Such concerns are far from new. Over a century and a half ago, Horace Mann, secretary of the Massachusetts State Board of Education, was dismayed to learn that Boston schoolchildren could answer only about a third of the arithmetic questions they were asked in a survey. "Such a result repels comment," he said. "No friendly attempt at palliation can make it any better. No severity of just censure can make it any worse." In 1919, when part of the survey was repeated in school districts around the country, the results for arithmetic were even worse than they had been in 1845. Apparently, there has never been a time when U.S. students excelled in mathematics, even when schools enrolled a much smaller, more select portion of the population. Over the last half-century, however, mathematics achievement has become entangled in urgent national issues: building military and industrial strength during the Cold War, maintaining technological and economic advantage when the Asian tigers roared, and most recently, strengthening public education against political attacks. How well U.S. students are learning mathematics and what should be done about it are now matters for every citizen to ponder. And one hears calls from many quarters for schools, teachers, and students to boost their performance.

During the new math era of the mid-1950s to mid-1970s, reformers emphasized changes in the mathematics curriculum; today's reformers want changes in mathematics teaching and assessment as well. In the mathematician E.G. Begle's laconic formulation, the problem is no longer so much teaching better mathematics as it is teaching mathematics better. Almost everyone today agrees that elementary and middle school mathematics should not be confined to arithmetic but should also include elements from other domains of mathematics, such as algebra, geometry, and statistics. There is much less consensus, however, on how these elements should be organized and taught. Different people urge that school mathematics be taken in different directions.

A claim used to advocate movement in one direction is that mathematics is bound by history and culture, that students learn by creating mathematics through their own investigations of problematic situations, and that teachers should set up situations and then step aside so that students can learn. A countervailing claim is that mathematics is universal and eternal, that students learn by absorbing clearly presented ideas and remembering them, and that teachers should offer careful explanations followed by organized opportunities for students to connect, rehearse, and review what they have learned. The trouble with these claims is not that one is true and the other false; it is that both are incomplete. They fail to capture the complexity of mathematics, of learning, and of teaching.

Mathematics is at the same time inside and beyond culture; it is both timely and timeless. The theorem attributed to Pythagoras was known in various forms in the civilizations of ancient Babylon and China, and it is still true the world over today even though systems of geometry now exist in which it does not hold. Mathematics is invented, and it is discovered as well. Students learn it on their own, and they learn it from others, most especially their teachers. If students are to become proficient in mathematics, teaching must create learning opportunities both constrained and open. Mathematics teaching is a difficult task under any circumstances. It is made even more complicated and challenging when teachers are paying attention simultaneously, as they should, to the manifold paths mathematics learning can take and to the multifaceted nature of mathematics itself.

In this report, we have attempted to address the conflicts in current proposals for changing school mathematics by giving a more rounded portrayal of the mathematics children need to learn, how they learn it, and how it might be taught to them effectively. In coming up with that portrayal, we have drawn on the research literature as well as our experience and judgment.

Early on, we decided to concentrate primarily on the mathematics of numbers and their operations—for reasons spelled out in chapter 1. We wanted readers to understand that we were using the topic to illustrate what might be done throughout the curriculum. Nonetheless, we recognize the ease with which some may conclude that attention equals advocacy, that we think arithmetic must constitute the mathematics curriculum from pre-kindergarten to eighth grade. Such a conclusion would be wrong: The emphasis on numbers and operations in the research literature and the even greater emphasis in this report say nothing about what the emphasis should be in school. We support a comprehensive curriculum that draws on many domains of mathematics.

The mathematician George Pólya, poking fun at the new math textbooks being assembled by platoons of mathematicians and teachers, once proposed a mock word problem something like the following: If one person can write a book in 12 months, how many months will 30 people need? Producing the present book in 18 months demanded something other than proportional reasoning; it took a superb committee of talented, dedicated people. The committee members were truly diverse, with different sorts of expertise. None of us knew all the others before we began. We brought many views, some opposing, on the issues before us. Yet we set to work immediately to develop a report we could all support, eventually meeting eight times from January 1999 to June 2000. Small groups of two or three met occasionally between committee meetings to draft sections of the report, and we engaged in countless e-mail exchanges to work out thorny details. The process worked because each of us valued the others' opinions, we listened to one another thoughtfully and respectfully, and we worked hard together to reach our common goal.

No matter how many months more or less than 18 it might have taken, none of us could have written this report alone. Whatever merits it has lie not only in the messages it contains but also in how it was produced. We offer the report in the hope that it will enable others to address the problems of school mathematics in a more balanced, informed way than is common today and in the same spirit we had of cooperation and mutual regard.

Jeremy Kilpatrick, *Chair*
Mathematics Learning Study Committee

TABLE OF CONTENTS

ADDING
+ IT

UP

EXECUTIVE SUMMARY

Mathematics is one of humanity's great achievements. By enhancing the capabilities of the human mind, mathematics has facilitated the development of science, technology, engineering, business, and government. Mathematics is also an intellectual achievement of great sophistication and beauty that epitomizes the power of deductive reasoning. For people to participate fully in society, they must know basic mathematics. Citizens who cannot reason mathematically are cut off from whole realms of human endeavor. Innumeracy deprives them not only of opportunity but also of competence in everyday tasks.

The mathematics students need to learn today is not the same mathematics that their parents and grandparents needed to learn. When today's students become adults, they will face new demands for mathematical proficiency that school mathematics should attempt to anticipate. Moreover, mathematics is a realm no longer restricted to a select few. *All young Americans must learn to think mathematically, and they must think mathematically to learn.*

Adding It Up: Helping Children Learn Mathematics is about school mathematics from pre-kindergarten to eighth grade. It addresses the concerns expressed by many Americans, from prominent politicians to the people next door, that too few students in our elementary and middle schools are successfully acquiring the mathematical knowledge, the skill, and the confidence they need to use the mathematics they have learned. Moreover, certain segments of the U.S. population are not well represented among those who do succeed in school mathematics.

All young Americans must learn to think mathematically, and they must think mathematically to learn.

The mathematics curriculum during the preschool, elementary school, and middle school years has many components. But at the heart of mathematics in those years are concepts of number and operations with numbers—the mathematical domain of *number*. In this report, much of our attention is given to issues associated with teaching and learning about number in prekindergarten through eighth-grade mathematics. Many controversies over the teaching of mathematics center on the understanding and use of numbers. The learning of concepts associated with number also has been more thoroughly investigated than the learning of other parts of the mathematics curriculum. And much of the rest of the mathematics curriculum, some of which we do address, is intertwined with number concepts.

Number is a rich, many-sided domain whose simplest forms are comprehended by very young children and whose far reaches are still being explored by mathematicians. Proficiency with numbers and numerical operations is an important foundation for further education in mathematics and in fields that use mathematics. Because much of this report attends to the learning and teaching of number, it is important to emphasize that our perspective is considerably broader than just computation. First, numbers and operations are abstractions—ideas based on experience but independent of any particular experience. Communication about numbers, therefore, requires some form of external representation, such as a graph or a system of notation. The usefulness of numerical ideas is enhanced when students encounter and use multiple representations for the same concept. Second, the numbers and operations of school mathematics are organized as number systems, such as the whole numbers, and the regularities of each system can help students learn with understanding. Third, numerical computations require algorithms—step-by-step procedures for performing the computations. An algorithm can be more or less useful to students depending on how it works and how well it is understood. And finally, the domain of number both supports and is supported by other branches of mathematics, including algebra, measure, space, data, and chance. Our decision to address the domain of number was a pragmatic one; in no way does it imply that the elementary and middle school curriculum should be limited to arithmetic.

> Our decision to address the domain of number was a pragmatic one; in no way does it imply that the elementary and middle school curriculum should be limited to arithmetic.

About This Report

The Committee on Mathematics Learning was established by the National Research Council at the end of 1998. It was formed at the request of the Division of Elementary, Secondary, and Informal Education in the

National Science Foundation's Directorate for Education and Human Resources and the U.S. Department of Education's Office of Educational Research and Improvement. The sponsors were concerned about the shortage of reliable information on the learning of mathematics by schoolchildren that could be used to guide best practice in the early years of schooling. More specifically, the committee was given the following charge:

- To synthesize the rich and diverse research on pre-kindergarten through eighth-grade mathematics learning.
- To provide research-based recommendations for teaching, teacher education, and curriculum for improving student learning and to identify areas where research is needed.
- To give advice and guidance to educators, researchers, publishers, policy makers, and parents.

We based our conclusions in this report on a careful review of the research literature on mathematics teaching and learning. Many educational questions, however, cannot be answered by research. Choices about the mathematics curriculum and the methods used to bring about that curriculum depend in part on what society wants educated adults to know and be able to do. Research can inform these decisions—for example, by demonstrating what knowledge, skills, and abilities employees need in the workplace. But ideas about what children need to know also depend on value judgments based on previous experience and convictions, and these judgments often fall outside the domain of research.

Once the learning objectives for mathematics education have been established, research can guide decisions about how to achieve these objectives. In preparing this report, we sought research that is *relevant* to important educational issues, *sound* in shedding light on the questions it sets out to answer, and *generalizable* in that it can be applied to circumstances beyond those of the study itself. We also looked for multiple lines of research that *converge* on a particular point and fit well within a larger network of evidence. Because studies that touch on a key question and yield unequivocal findings are rare in educational research, we have sought to point out when we have used professional judgment and reasoned argument to make connections, note patterns, and fill in gaps. In the final chapter of the report, we have also called for additional research in areas where it could improve educational practice.

The State of School Mathematics
in the United States

One area in which the research evidence is consistent and compelling concerns weaknesses in the mathematical performance of U.S. students. State, national, and international assessments conducted over the past 30 years indicate that, although U.S. students may not fare badly when asked to perform straightforward computational procedures, they tend to have a limited understanding of basic mathematical concepts. They are also notably deficient in their ability to apply mathematical skills to solve even simple problems. Although performance in mathematics is generally low, there are signs from national assessments that it has been improving over the past decade. In a number of schools and states, students' mathematical performance is among the best in the world. The evidence suggests, however, that many students are still not being given the educational opportunities they need to achieve at high levels.

In comparison with the curricula of countries achieving well on international comparisons, the U.S. elementary and middle school mathematics curriculum has been characterized as shallow, undemanding, and diffuse in content coverage. U.S. mathematics textbooks cover more topics, but more superficially, than their counterparts in other countries do. Despite efforts over the last half-century to set higher learning goals for U.S. school mathematics and to provide new instructional materials and better assessments, most students in grades pre-K to 8 encounter a rather shallow curriculum. The instruction they are given continues to emphasize the execution of paper-and-pencil skills in arithmetic through demonstrations of procedures followed by repeated practice.

> Most students in grades pre-K to 8 encounter a rather shallow curriculum.

To ensure that students are meeting standards, states and districts have, during the past decade or so, mandated a variety of assessments in mathematics, many with serious consequences for students, teachers, and schools. Although intended to ensure that all students have an opportunity to learn mathematics, some of these assessments are not well aligned with the curriculum. Those that were originally designed to rank order students, schools, and districts seldom provide information that can be used to improve instruction.

The preparation of U.S. preschool to middle school teachers often falls far short of equipping them with the knowledge they need for helping students develop mathematical proficiency. Many students in grades pre-K to 8 continue to be taught by teachers who may not have appropriate certification at that grade and who have at best a shaky grasp of mathematics.

Mathematical Proficiency

Our analyses of the mathematics to be learned, our reading of the research in cognitive psychology and mathematics education, our experience as learners and teachers of mathematics, and our judgment as to the mathematical knowledge, understanding, and skill people need today have led us to adopt a composite, comprehensive view of successful mathematics learning. Recognizing that no term captures completely all aspects of expertise, competence, knowledge, and facility in mathematics, we have chosen *mathematical proficiency* to capture what we think it means for anyone to learn mathematics successfully. Mathematical proficiency, as we see it, has five strands:

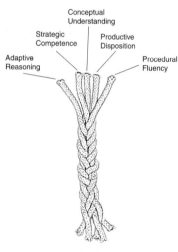

- *conceptual understanding*—comprehension of mathematical concepts, operations, and relations
- *procedural fluency*—skill in carrying out procedures flexibly, accurately, efficiently, and appropriately
- *strategic competence*—ability to formulate, represent, and solve mathematical problems
- *adaptive reasoning*—capacity for logical thought, reflection, explanation, and justification
- *productive disposition*—habitual inclination to see mathematics as sensible, useful, and worthwhile, coupled with a belief in diligence and one's own efficacy.

Intertwined Strands of Proficiency

The most important observation we make about these five strands is that they are interwoven and interdependent. This observation has implications for how students acquire mathematical proficiency, how teachers develop that proficiency in their students, and how teachers are educated to achieve that goal.

The Mathematical Knowledge Children Bring to School

Children begin learning mathematics well before they enter elementary school. Starting from infancy and continuing throughout the preschool period, they develop a base of skills, concepts, and misconceptions. At all ages, students encounter quantitative situations outside of school from which they learn a variety of things about number. Their experiences include, for example, noticing that a sister received more candies, counting the stairs between the first and second floors of an apartment, dividing a cake so everyone gets the same amount, and figuring out how far it is to the bus stop.

By the time children reach kindergarten, many of them can use their counting skills to solve simple problems that call for adding, subtracting, multiplying, or dividing. It is only when they move beyond what they understand informally—to the base-10 system for teens and larger numbers, for example—that their fluency and strategic competencies falter. Young children also show a remarkable ability to formulate, represent, and solve simple mathematical problems and to reason and explain their mathematical activities. They are positively disposed to do and to understand mathematics when they first encounter it. For the preschool child, the strands of mathematical proficiency are especially closely knit.

Although most U.S. children enter school with a basic understanding of number, their knowledge is limited to small whole numbers and heavily influenced by the context in which the numbers appear. Furthermore, not all children enter school with the informal understanding of number assumed by the elementary school curriculum.

Developing Proficiency with Whole Numbers

Whole numbers are the easiest numbers to understand and use. In the early grades, children begin by solving numerical problems using methods that are intuitive and concrete. They then proceed to methods that are more problem independent, mathematically sophisticated, and reliant on standard symbolic notation. Some form of this progression is seen in each operation for both single-digit and multidigit numbers.

For most of a century, learning single-digit arithmetic—the sums and products of single-digit numbers and their companion differences and quotients (e.g., $5 + 7 = 12$, $12 - 5 = 7$, $12 - 7 = 5$ and $5 \times 7 = 35$, $35 \div 5 = 7$, $35 \div 7 = 5$)—has been characterized in the United States as "learning basic facts," and the emphasis has been on memorizing those facts. Acquiring proficiency in single-digit arithmetic, however, involves much more than memorizing. Even in the early grades, students choose adaptively among different procedures, depending on the numbers involved and the context. We use the term *basic number combinations* to highlight the relational character of this knowledge.

For addition and subtraction, many children follow a well-documented progression of procedures. Counting becomes abbreviated and rapid, and students begin to use properties of arithmetic to simplify their computation. Basic multiplication and division combinations are more of a challenge. Learning these combinations seems to require much specific pattern-based knowledge that needs to be orchestrated into accessible and rapid-enough procedures. When given instruction that emphasizes thinking strategies, children are able to develop the strands of proficiency in a unified manner.

Learning to use algorithms for computation with multidigit numbers is an important part of developing mathematical proficiency. Algorithms are procedures that can be executed in the same way to solve a variety of problems arising from different situations and involving different numbers. Children can and do devise algorithms for carrying out multidigit arithmetic, using reasoning to justify their inventions and developing confidence in the process. A variety of instructional approaches (using physical materials, special counting activities, and mental computation) are effective in helping students learn multidigit arithmetic by focusing on the base-ten structure and encouraging students to use algorithms that they understand. Physical materials are not automatically meaningful to students, however, and need to be connected to the situations being modeled. Because of its conciseness, the base-ten place-value system takes time to master. Full understanding of the system, however, is not required before students begin to learn multidigit algorithms—the two can be developed in tandem. The learning of whole number arithmetic demands that attention be given to developing all strands of proficiency in concert, emphasizing no strand at the expense of the others.

> When given instruction that emphasizes thinking strategies, children are able to develop the strands of proficiency in a unified manner.

Developing Proficiency with Rational Numbers

In grades pre-K to 8, the rational numbers present a major challenge, in part because rational numbers are represented in several ways (e.g., common fractions and decimal fractions) and used in many ways (e.g., as parts of regions and sets, as ratios, as quotients). There are numerous properties for students to learn, including the significant fact that the two numbers that compose a common fraction (numerator and denominator) are related through multiplication and division, not addition.

Students' informal notions of partitioning, sharing, and measuring provide a starting point for building the concept of rational number. Young children appreciate the idea of "fair shares," and they can use that understanding to partition quantities into equal parts. In some ways, sharing can play the role for rational numbers that counting does for whole numbers.

As with whole numbers, the written notations and spoken words used for decimal and common fractions contribute to—or at least do not help correct—the many kinds of errors students make with them. Furthermore, many students do not understand the meanings of and connections between the various symbols for rational numbers when they are asked to compute with them, which creates barriers to developing the strands of proficiency in an integrated fashion.

Proportions are statements that two ratios are equal. Understanding and working with the relationships in a situation involving proportions is called *proportional reasoning* and has been described as the capstone of elementary school arithmetic. Proportional reasoning is sophisticated and complex; it needs to develop over many years. Students need to have a solid understanding of proportional situations and be able to reason about them informally before formal procedures are introduced.

Developing Proficiency Beyond Number

Many students have difficulties making the transition from school arithmetic to school algebra—with its symbolism, equation solving, and emphasis on relationships among quantities. Recent calls of "algebra for all" have increased the number of students making the transition and therefore the number encountering obstacles. Over the past two decades, much has been learned about the nature of students' difficulties in algebra. Various innovative approaches to beginning algebra, many using computational tools, have been investigated. At the same time, modifications of elementary school mathematics have been developed and studied that are aimed at introducing the notions of algebra earlier. These new approaches offer considerable promise for avoiding the difficulties many students now experience.

Just as the elementary and middle school mathematics curriculum should prepare students for the study of algebra, so it should also include attention to other domains of mathematics. Students need to learn to make and interpret measurements and to engage in geometric reasoning. They also need to gather, describe, analyze, and interpret data and to use elementary concepts from probability. Instruction that emphasizes more than a single strand of proficiency has been shown to enhance students' learning about space and measure and shows considerable promise for helping students learn about data and chance.

Teaching for Mathematical Proficiency

Effective teaching—teaching that fosters the development of mathematical proficiency over time—can take a variety of forms, each with its own possibilities and risks. All forms of instruction can best be examined from the perspective of how teachers, students, and content interact in contexts to produce teaching and learning. The effectiveness of mathematics teaching and learning is a function of teachers' knowledge and use of mathematical content, of teachers' attention to and work with students, and of students' engagement in and use of mathematical tasks. Effectiveness depends on *enactment*, on the mutual and interdependent interaction of the three elements—mathematical content, teacher, students—as instruction unfolds. The quality of instruction depends, for example, on whether teachers select cognitively demanding tasks, plan the lesson by elaborating the mathematics that the students are to learn through those tasks, and allocate sufficient time for the students to engage in and spend time on the tasks. Effective teachers have high expectations for their students, motivate them to value learning activities, can interact with students with different abilities and backgrounds, and can establish communities of learners. A teacher's expectations about students and the mathematics they are able to learn can powerfully influence the tasks the teacher poses for the students, the questions they are asked, the time they have to respond, and the encouragement they are given—in other words, their opportunities and motivation for learning. How the students respond to the opportunities the teacher offers then shapes how the teacher sees their capacity and progress, as well as the tasks they are subsequently given.

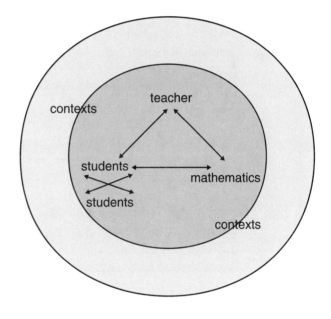

The quality of instruction also depends on how students engage with learning tasks. Students must link their informal knowledge and experience to mathematical abstractions. Manipulatives (physical objects used to represent mathematical ideas), when used well, can provide such links. The use of calculators can enhance students' conceptual understanding, and practice can help them make automatic those procedures they understand. Although much is known about characteristics of effective instruction, research on teaching has often been restricted to describing isolated fragments of teaching and learning rather than examining continued interactions among the teacher, the students, and the mathematical content.

Developing Proficiency in Teaching Mathematics

Proficiency in teaching mathematics is related to effectiveness: consistently helping students learn worthwhile mathematical content. It also entails versatility: being able to work effectively with a wide variety of students in different environments and across a range of mathematical content. Despite the common myth that teaching is little more than common sense or that some people are just born teachers, effective teaching practice can be learned. Just as mathematical proficiency itself involves interwoven strands, teaching for mathematical proficiency requires similarly interrelated components: *conceptual understanding* of the core knowledge of mathematics, students, and instructional practices needed for teaching; *procedural fluency* in carrying out basic instructional routines; *strategic competence* in planning effective instruction and solving problems that arise while teaching; *adaptive reasoning* in justifying and explaining one's practices and in reflecting on those practices; and a *productive disposition* toward mathematics, teaching, learning, and the improvement of practice.

Effective programs of teacher preparation and professional development help teachers understand the mathematics they teach, how their students learn that mathematics, and how to facilitate that learning. In these programs, teachers are not given prescriptions for practice or readymade solutions to teaching problems. Instead, they adapt what they are learning to deal with problems that arise in their own teaching.

Recommendations

> The overriding premise of our work is that throughout the grades from pre-K through 8 all students can and should be mathematically proficient.

As a goal of instruction, mathematical proficiency provides a better way to think about mathematics learning than narrower views that leave out key features of what it means to know and be able to do mathematics. It takes time for proficiency to develop fully, but in every grade in school, students can demonstrate mathematical proficiency in some form. **The overriding premise of our work is that throughout the grades from pre-K through 8** *all students can and should be mathematically proficient.*

School mathematics in the United States does not now enable most students to develop the strands of mathematical proficiency in a sound fashion. Proficiency for all demands that fundamental changes be made concurrently in curriculum, instructional materials, assessments, classroom practice, teacher preparation, and professional development. These changes will require continuing, coordinated action on the part of policy makers, teacher educators, teachers, and parents. Although some readers may feel that substantial advances are already being made in reforming mathematics teaching and learning, we find real progress toward mathematical proficiency to be woefully inadequate.

These observations lead us to five principal recommendations regarding mathematical proficiency that reflect our vision for school mathematics. The full report augments these five with specific recommendations that detail policies and practices needed if all children are to become mathematically proficient.

- **The integrated and balanced development of all five strands of mathematical proficiency (conceptual understanding, procedural fluency, strategic competence, adaptive reasoning, and productive disposition) should guide the teaching and learning of school mathematics. Instruction should not be based on extreme positions that students learn, on one hand, solely by internalizing what a teacher or book says or, on the other hand, solely by inventing mathematics on their own.**

One of the most serious and persistent problems facing school mathematics in the United States is the tendency to concentrate on one strand of proficiency to the exclusion of the rest. For too long, students have been the victims of crosscurrents in mathematics instruction, as advocates of one learning goal or another have attempted to control the mathematics to be taught and tested. We believe that this narrow and unstable treatment of mathematics is, in part, responsible for the inadequate performance that U.S. students display on national and international assessments. Our first recommendation is that these crosscurrents be resolved into an integrated, balanced treatment of all strands of mathematical proficiency at every point in teaching and learning.

Although we endorse no single approach, we contend that instruction needs to configure the relations among teachers, students, and mathematics in ways that promote the development of mathematical proficiency. Under this view, significant instructional time is devoted to developing concepts and methods, and carefully directed practice, with feedback, is used to support learning. Discussions build on students' thinking. They attend to relationships between problems and solutions and to the nature of justification and mathematical argument. All strands of proficiency can grow in a coordinated, interactive fashion.

• Teachers' professional development should be high quality, sustained, and systematically designed and deployed to help all students develop mathematical proficiency. Schools should support, as a central part of teachers' work, engagement in sustained efforts to improve their mathematics instruction. This support requires the provision of time and resources.

Improving students' learning depends on the capabilities of classroom teachers. Although children bring important mathematical knowledge with them to class, most of the mathematics they know is learned in school and depends on those who teach it to them. Teachers cannot automatically know how to teach more effectively. Learning to teach well cannot be accomplished once and for all in a preservice program; it is a career-long challenge.

As we have indicated, proficiency in mathematics teaching has parallels to proficiency in mathematics. Unfortunately, just as students' opportunities to learn mathematics effectively have been insufficient, so have teachers' opportunities to learn more about mathematics, students' learning and thinking, and their teaching practice. Regular time needs to be provided for teachers to continue their professional development, conferring with one another about common problems and working together to develop their teaching proficiency. They need access to resources and expertise that will assist them in improving their instruction, including access to mathematics specialists in every elementary school. If the United States is serious about improving students' mathematics learning, it has no choice but to invest in more effective and sustained opportunities for teachers to learn.

• The coordination of curriculum, instructional materials, assessment, instruction, professional development, and school organization around the development of mathematical proficiency should drive school improvement efforts.

Piecemeal efforts aimed at narrow learning goals have failed to improve U.S. students' learning. The development of mathematical proficiency provides a broad, compelling goal around which all parts of the educational community can rally. If even one sector of that community lags behind, it can thwart the development of mathematical proficiency.

The school mathematics curriculum needs to be organized within and across grades to support, in a coordinated fashion, all strands of mathematical proficiency. Programs at all grades should build on the informal knowledge children bring to school. An integrated approach should be taken to the development of proficiency with whole numbers, integers, and rational numbers to ensure that all students in grades pre-K to 8 can use the numbers fluently and flexibly to solve challenging but accessible problems. Students should also understand and be able to translate within and across the various common representations for numbers.

A major focus of the study of number should be the conceptual bases for the operations and how they relate to real situations. For each operation, all students should understand and be able to carry out an algorithm that is general and efficient. Before they get to the formal study of algebra, they already should have had numerous experiences in representing, abstracting, and generalizing relationships among numbers and operations with numbers. They should be introduced to these algebraic ways of thinking well before they are expected to be proficient in manipulating algebraic symbols. They also need to learn concepts of space, measure, data, and chance in ways that link these domains to that of number.

Materials for instruction need to develop the core content of school mathematics in depth and with continuity. In addition to helping students learn, these materials should also support teachers' understanding of mathematical concepts, of students' thinking, and of effective pedagogical techniques. Mathematics assessments need to enable and not just gauge the development of proficiency. All elements of curriculum, instruction, materials, and assessment should be aligned toward common learning goals.

Every school should be organized so that the teachers are just as much learners as the students are. The professional development activities in which teachers of mathematics are engaged need to be focused on mathematical proficiency. Just as mathematical proficiency demands the integrated, coordinated development of all strands, so the enhancement of each student's opportunities to become proficient requires the integrated, coordinated efforts of all parts of the educational community.

• **Efforts to improve students' mathematics learning should be informed by scientific evidence, and their effectiveness should be evaluated systematically. Such efforts should be coordinated, continual, and cumulative.**

Steady and continuing improvements in students' mathematics learning can be made only if decisions about instruction are based on the best available information. As new, systematically collected information becomes available, better decisions can be made, and mathematics instruction should gradually but steadily become more effective. Unfortunately, too many new programs are tried but then abandoned before their effectiveness has been well tested, and lessons learned from program evaluations are often lost. Without high-quality, cumulative information, the system of school mathematics cannot learn.

- **Additional research should be undertaken on the nature, development, and assessment of mathematical proficiency.**

We are convinced that the goal of mathematical proficiency for all students is the right goal. Not surprisingly, however, much of the research on mathematics teaching and learning has been conducted to address narrower learning goals, since shifting, relatively narrow goals have been the norm. Although we have interpreted much of that research for this report, extensive work remains to refine and elaborate our portrayal of mathematical proficiency. In many places, our conclusions are tentative, awaiting better evidence.

We urge researchers concerned with school mathematics to frame their questions with a view to the goal of developing mathematical proficiency for all students. Evidence from such research, together with information from evaluations of current and future programs of curriculum and professional development, will enable the United States to make the genuine, lasting improvements in school mathematics learning that have eluded it to date.

Conclusion

The goal of mathematical proficiency is an extremely ambitious one. In fact, in no country—not even those performing highest on international surveys of mathematics achievement—do all students display mathematical proficiency as we have defined it in this report. The United States will never reach this goal by continuing to tinker with the controls of educational policy, pushing one button at a time. Instead, systematic modifications will need to be made in how the teaching and learning of mathematics commonly proceed, and new kinds of support will be required. At all levels of the U.S. educational system, the formulation and implementation of policies demands sustained, focused attention to school mathematics. We hope this report will be the basis for innovative, comprehensive, long-term policies that can enable every student to become mathematically proficient.

1

LOOKING AT MATHEMATICS
AND LEARNING

Children today are growing up in a world permeated by mathematics. The technologies used in homes, schools, and the workplace are all built on mathematical knowledge. Many educational opportunities and good jobs require high levels of mathematical expertise. Mathematical topics arise in newspaper and magazine articles, popular entertainment, and everyday conversation.

Mathematics is a universal, utilitarian subject—so much a part of modern life that anyone who wishes to be a fully participating member of society must know basic mathematics. Mathematics also has a more specialized, esoteric, and esthetic side. It epitomizes the beauty and power of deductive reasoning. Mathematics embodies the efforts made over thousands of years by every civilization to comprehend nature and bring order to human affairs.

These dual aspects of mathematics, the practical and the theoretical, have earned the subject a place at the center of education throughout history. Even simple systems for counting have to be passed on to the next generation. Every literate society has needed people who knew how to read the heavens and measure the earth. Farmers have wanted to calculate crop production, and merchants to record their transactions.

As mathematics became more formal and abstract in the hands of the ancient Greeks, it also became enshrined among the liberal arts. The mastery of its forms of reasoning became a hallmark of the educated person. Its study was seen as bringing the discipline of logical thinking to the apprentice scholar.

Despite the value of mathematics as a model of deductive reasoning, the teaching of mathematics has often taken quite a different form. For centuries, many students have learned mathematical knowledge—whether the rudiments of arithmetic computation or the complexities of geometric theorems—without much understanding.[1] Of course, many students tried to make whatever sense they could of procedures such as adding common fractions or multiplying decimals. No doubt many students noticed underlying regularities in the computations they were asked to perform. Teachers who themselves were skilled in mathematics might have tried to explain those regularities. But mathematics learning has often been more a matter of memorizing than of understanding.

Today it is vital that young people understand the mathematics they are learning. Whether using computer graphics on the job or spreadsheets at home, people need to move fluently back and forth between graphs, tables of data, and formulas. To make good choices in the marketplace, they must know how to spot flaws in deductive and probabilistic reasoning as well as how to estimate the results of computations. In a society saturated with advanced technology, people will be called on more and more to evaluate the relevance and validity of calculations done by calculators and more sophisticated machines. Public policy issues of critical importance hinge on mathematical analyses.

Citizens who cannot reason mathematically are cut off from whole realms of human endeavor. Innumeracy deprives them not only of opportunity but also of competence in everyday tasks. *All young Americans must learn to think mathematically, and they must think mathematically to learn.* The overriding premise of our work is that throughout the grades from pre-K through 8 all students should learn to think mathematically.

Helping all students learn to think mathematically is a new and ambitious goal, but the circumstances of modern life demand that society embrace it. Equal opportunity in education and in the workplace requires that mathematics be accessible to all learners. The growing technological sophistication of everyday life calls for universal facility with mathematics. For the United States to continue its technological leadership as a nation requires that more students pursue educational paths that enable them to become scientists, mathematicians, and engineers.

The research over the past two decades, much of which is synthesized in this report, convinces us that all students can learn to think mathematically. There are instances of schools scattered throughout the country in which a high percentage of students have high levels of achievement in mathematics. Further, there have also been special interventions in disadvantaged schools whereby students have made substantial progress. More is now known about

The overriding premise of our work is that throughout the grades from pre-K through 8 all students should learn to think mathematically.

how children learn mathematics and the kinds of teaching that supports that learning. Research continues to expand our understanding of the teaching-learning process. All of this taken together makes us believe that our goal is in large measure achievable.

Mathematics and Reading

A comparison of mathematics with reading leads to several important observations. First, competence in both domains is important in determining children's later educational and occupational prospects. Children who fail to develop a high level of skill in either one are precluded from the most interesting and rewarding careers. As a recent report on reading from the National Research Council put it, "To be employable in the modern economy, high school graduates need to be more than merely literate. They must be able to read challenging material, to perform sophisticated computations, and to solve problems independently."[2]

Second, there are important similarities as well as differences in the problems children face in developing competence in reading and mathematics. Understanding the common features of reading development and mathematical development is as important as understanding the special characteristics of learning in each domain.

Finally, international comparisons suggest that U.S. schools have been relatively successful in developing skilled reading, with improvements in both instruction and achievement occurring in a large number of schools.[3] Unfortunately, the same cannot be said of mathematics. International comparisons discussed in the next chapter suggest that by eighth grade the mathematics performance of U.S. children is well below that of other industrialized countries. Furthermore, this performance has been relatively low in a variety of comparisons conducted at intervals over several decades. The organizational and instructional factors that U.S. schools have used in developing skilled reading performance may be equally important in improving the learning of mathematics. Learning to read and developing mathematical proficiency both rest on a foundation of concepts and skills that are acquired by many children before they leave kindergarten. In the case of reading, children are expected to enter school with a basic understanding of the sound structure of their native language, a conscious awareness of the units (phonemes) that are represented by an alphabetic writing system, and skill in handling basic language concepts. Likewise in mathematics, students should possess a toolkit of basic mathematical concepts and skills when they enter first grade. (These are reviewed in chapter 5.) In both reading and mathematics, some children enter school without the knowledge and experience that school instruction presumes they possess. In both domains, there is evidence that early intervention can prevent full-blown problems in school.[4]

For both reading and mathematics, children's performance at the end of elementary school is an important predictor of their ultimate educational success. If they have not mastered certain basic skills, they can expect problems throughout their schooling and later. Research on reading indicates that all but a very small number of children can learn to read proficiently, though they may learn at different rates and may require different amounts and types of instructional support. Furthermore, experiences in pre-kindergarten and the early elementary grades serve as a crucial foundation for students' emerging proficiency. Similar observations can be made for mathematics.

For example, nearly all second graders might be expected to make a useful drawing of the situation portrayed in an arithmetic word problem as a step toward solving it. Representing numbers by means of a drawing is a task that few children find difficult. Other tasks, however, depend much more heavily on children's knowledge and experience. For example, in Roman numerals, the value of V is five regardless of where it is located in the numeral, whether IV, VI, or VII. The Hindu-Arabic numerals used in everyday life are different; a digit's value depends on the place it occupies. For example, the 5 in 115 denotes five, whereas in 151 it denotes fifty, and in 511, five hundred. Also, a special symbol, 0, is used to hold a place that would otherwise be unoccupied. Although adults may view this place-value system as simple and straightforward, it is actually quite sophisticated and challenging to learn (see chapters 5 and 6).

To make progress in school mathematics, children must understand Hindu-Arabic numerals and be able to use them fluently. But the children in, say, a second-grade class can be expected to differ considerably in the rate at which they grasp place value. It is a complex system of representation that functions almost like a foreign language that a child is learning to use and simultaneously using to learn other things. Much of school mathematics has this mutually dependent quality. Abstractions at one level are used to develop abstractions at a higher level, and abstractions at a higher level are used to gain insights into abstractions at a lower level.

To ensure that students having reading difficulties get prompt and effective assistance outside the regular school program, the reading community has developed a variety of intervention programs designed to address the problems students are having and to bring them back rapidly into the regular program.[5] Although there is much "remediation" done as part of school mathematics instruction in grades K to 8 and beyond, there are not nearly so many supplementary interventions in mathematics as there are in reading. There is very little in the way of "mathematics recovery" that provides early targeted enrichment in mathematics to help students overcome special difficulties.

One difference between reading and mathematics is that, after a certain point, reading requires little explicit instruction: Once children have acquired basic principles and skills for reading, they use those skills in the service of other activities, to learn about history, literature, or mathematics, for example. Their skills can always be polished and instruction given on interpreting a text, but they need no further explanations and demonstrations of reading by others. Furthermore, they practice and develop their reading throughout their lives, both inside and outside of school. As is the case for reading, students develop some basic concepts and practices in mathematics outside of school, but a new and unfamiliar topic in mathematics—say, the division of fractions—usually cannot be fully grasped without some assistance from a text or a teacher.

Reading uses a core set of representations. In U.S. schools, the English alphabetic writing system, once learned, enables the student to read and decode any English sentence, although of course not necessarily to understand its meaning. Graphs, pictures, and signs also need to be read, but the core symbols are the alphabet.

Mathematics, in contrast, has many types and levels of representation. In fact, mathematics can be said to be *about* levels of representation, which build on one another as the mathematical ideas become more abstract. For example, the increasing focus on algebra during the school years builds facility with more abstract levels of representation.

Another characteristic of learning to read is the vast variation among children in their exposure to literature outside of school, as well as in the amount of time they spend reading. Studies on the development of reading[6] have shown that variations in children's reading skill are associated with large differences in reading experience. Children at the 80th percentile in reading level were estimated to average more than 20 times as much reading per day as children at the 20th percentile.[7]

Similar data are not available for mathematics, but differences in the amount of time spent doing mathematics are likely to be less than for reading. This suggests that direct school-based instruction may play a larger part in most children's mathematical experience than it does in their reading experience. If so, the consequences of good or poor mathematics instruction may have an even greater effect on children's proficiency than is the case with reading.

An important recent change in American education is the increased emphasis on ensuring that all children achieve a basic level of competence in reading during the course of elementary school. Success in school also depends on establishing good mathematical competence in the early elementary grades, yet mathematics instruction has not received the same sustained emphasis. Schools generally lack a mathematics specialist corresponding to the reading specialists who provide instruction and assist children having difficulties with the subject. Many school districts have revised their schedules and their curriculum programs to ensure that adequate reading instruction is given in the elementary grades; mathematics instruction has yet to receive similar attention. The recommendations we give at the end of this report attempt to take into account the progress made in homes and at school in achieving reading proficiency.

Looking at Mathematics

The mathematics to which U.S. schoolchildren are exposed from pre-school through eighth grade has many aspects. However, at the heart of pre-school, elementary school, and middle school mathematics is the set of concepts associated with the term *number*.[8] Children learn to count, and they learn to keep track of their counting by writing numerals for the natural numbers. They learn to add, subtract, multiply, and divide whole numbers, and later in elementary school they learn to perform these same operations with common fractions and decimal fractions. They use numbers in measuring a variety of quantities, including the lengths, areas, and volumes of geometric figures. From various sources, children collect data that they learn to represent and analyze using numerical methods. The study of algebra begins as they observe how numbers form systems and as they generalize number patterns.

We have focused much of this report on the domain of number. Most of the controversy over how and what mathematics should be taught in elementary and middle school revolves around number. Should children learn computational methods before they understand the concepts involved? Should they be introduced to standard algorithms for arithmetic computation, or should they be encouraged to develop their own algorithms first? How much time should be spent learning long division or how to add common fractions? Should decimals be introduced before or after fractions? How proficient do children need to be at paper-and-pencil arithmetic before they are taught algebra or geometry? Such questions are controversial partly because they touch on the third R—arithmetic—that parents want their children to master, and also because they deal with topics on which reformers have taken some of their strongest stands in opposition to current practice.

Furthermore, much more research has been conducted in the domain of number than in most other areas of the mathematics curriculum. For most controversial questions involving number, at least some related research is available, and many of these questions have been studied extensively.

Our attention to number and operations is certainly not meant to imply that the elementary and middle school curriculum is or should be limited to number. Mathematics is a broad discipline, and children need to learn about its many aspects. Although the amount of research that is available is less, we have also reviewed what is known from research about how students develop proficiency with some of the central concepts of measurement, geometry, descriptive statistics, and probability. Further, we have reviewed the research on beginning algebra learning. Nevertheless, our review of the research on mathematics learning paints an incomplete picture of the nature of mathematics, even elementary and middle school mathematics. Many facets of the discipline are not covered or not covered adequately by the research or our review. Further, our review does not capture the many connections both between various topics in mathematics and between mathematics and its uses in the world around us. Hence, in describing what is known about how children learn mathematics, we are not indirectly prescribing what mathematics children should learn.

> In describing what is known about how children learn mathematics, we are not indirectly prescribing what mathematics children should learn.

Nature of the Evidence

For every generation of students, the mathematics curriculum and the methods used to deliver that curriculum are products of many choices. Some of these choices reflect the fact that the volume of knowledge in any subject greatly exceeds the time available for teaching it. Decisions always must be made as to what topics to teach and how much time to spend on them.

Choices about the teaching and learning of mathematics also depend on what society wants educated adults to know. Questions of what needs to be taught are essentially questions of what knowledge is most preferred. Research can inform these decisions—for example, studies of modern workplaces can reveal what mathematics employees most need to know.[9] However, ideas about what children today need to know also depend on value judgments based on previous experience and convictions, and these judgments often fall outside the domain of research.

Once choices have been made regarding the mathematics that students should know, the goals for instruction can be framed. The available evidence from research can be used to analyze the feasibility of the goals as well as to contribute to decisions about how to help children achieve them. The task then becomes, first, to identify the research that can be used to inform these analyses and decisions and, second, to figure out how best to use that research.

The experience that people know and understand best is their own. To establish policies for school mathematics, however, it is essential to look beyond one's own experience to the evidence obtained through a systematic examination of what others have seen and reported.

Some of this evidence is analytical or conceptual, such as analyses of mathematical representations and strategies. This research might describe and categorize mathematical situations, analyze attributes of mathematical representations, or design conceptual supports to increase student learning. The value of this research depends on the strength of its analytical framework and its accessibility to others.

Other evidence is more empirical. The essence of empirical research is that evidence has been gathered and analyzed in a systematic, focused way so as to address a clearly formulated question. Researchers make public the assumptions they have made and the methods they have used to gather and analyze their data. They explain how their conclusions follow from a careful analysis of those data. They report their methods and findings in a way that makes informed critique possible. In many cases—though not all—adherence to these methods allows others to repeat their work.

Some empirical studies are largely descriptive. They can illuminate how learning occurs under various conditions, suggest what the learner brings to the teaching situation, or describe how the learner understands what is being taught. Some studies portray relationships. They can suggest how differences in conditions under which learning occurs might be related to differences in what is learned. Other studies are experimental. Through the manipulation of learning conditions, they can suggest how changes in those conditions might cause changes in learning.

Whether a study is a tightly controlled experiment or an observation of a single child's performance, it can be of high or low quality. Box 1-1 describes several determinants of quality in research. In turn, the quality of the evidence determines the level of confidence with which a conclusion, observation, or recommendation is made.

In addition, no single study can provide conclusive evidence on broad educational issues. It is therefore necessary to look at as many studies as

Box 1-1

The Quality of Research Studies

Several indicators of quality must be evaluated in assessing studies of mathematics education. This report is based on research that meets standards of relevance, soundness, and generalizability.

Relevance

A research study is relevant if it addresses or produces data that speak to any of a number of components of mathematics learning. The teaching and learning of mathematics involve both desired goals and various mental processes. These goals and processes include the content to be learned, materials for teaching, activities undertaken by teachers and students to promote learning, and assessment of what has been learned. Teaching and learning also take place in a social context ranging from the classroom to the nation as a whole. Teaching and learning depend not only on teachers and students but also on support from a variety of enablers: policy makers, teacher educators, publishers, researchers, administrators, and others.

A relevant study of mathematics learning might, for example, lead to a sharper understanding of desired learning processes and outcomes. It might reveal features of good practice or evaluate tradeoffs among various educational alternatives.

Soundness

The soundness of a research study concerns the extent to which the study supplied the data needed to address the research question. A study's soundness therefore depends on the suitability of the methods used to achieve the results obtained. Were the groups of participants adequate in size and composition, or were they biased or limited in some fashion? Did the methods generate credible, reliable, and valid data? Were the methods specified so that they could be repeated? Was the data analysis appropriate to the methods, carefully conducted, replicable, and penetrating? Was the data presentation clear and complete? Were the conclusions warranted by the results and appropriately qualified?

Generalizability

The generalizability of a study concerns the extent to which its findings can be applied to circumstances beyond those of the study itself. Was the class typical in size and composition? Were the time allocated to mathematics and the materials and equipment used in the study characteristic of today's mathematics instruction? Did the conditions of the study depart from those of an ordinary classroom? Were the teachers or students somehow anomalous?

possible that are relevant to a particular question. The confidence with which an observation, conclusion, or recommendation is made is increased when all the relevant evidence supports the same point. This feature of convergence is reinforced when the evidence has been collected in different places, under different circumstances, and by different researchers working independently.

In particular, findings should stand up across different groups of students and teachers, and ideally they should have been obtained using different methods for gathering data. Findings also should fit well within a larger network of evidence that makes good common and theoretical sense. Determining the degree of convergence in existing evidence demands discrimination and judgment. It cannot be ascertained simply by tallying studies.

One problem in weighing the evidence on a given issue in education is that a fully convergent database that speaks directly to the issue and yields unequivocal findings is seldom, if ever, available. The findings from experimental studies of mathematics learning often conflict. Data from non-experimental studies of relationships generally are ambiguous with respect to causality. Descriptive data can help frame an issue but usually do not address the question of which processes might lead to which learning outcomes. Ostensibly comparable studies can differ in key features, making it difficult to decide whether the data are really comparable. Much of the evidence is still in the form of demonstrations that selected children can learn certain topics in certain ways, and large-scale studies have not yet been done.

All these factors require that the research evidence be interpreted. Arguments and recommendations have to be constructed by drawing on professional judgment. Inductive reasoning must be used to make connections among studies, note patterns, fill in gaps, and attempt to explain why contradictory findings should be ignored or downplayed. We have sought to identify in this report conclusions that depend on such interpretations of the available evidence.

The Role of Research in Improving School Mathematics

A premise of this report is that sound research can help guide the design of effective mathematics instruction. Yet research cannot be the only basis for making instructional decisions in mathematics. First, as we stated earlier, research, by itself, cannot tell educators which of their learning goals are most important or how they should set priorities. Only after such goals have been established can research generate information to help educators decide whether goals are feasible and, if so, how to accomplish them. In short, instructional decisions, as well as the research supporting them, must be guided by values.

Second, decisions about how to help students reach learning goals can never be made with absolute certainty. As the famous American psychologist William James noted at the end of the nineteenth century, psychology's description of "the elements of the mental machine . . . and their workings"[10] does not translate directly into a prescription for educational practice. James warned: "You make a great, a very great mistake, if you think that psychology, being the science of the mind's laws, is something from which you can deduce definite programmes and schemes and methods of instruction for immediate schoolroom use."[11] Education is an applied field: no matter what the state of theoretical knowledge from psychology or elsewhere, the conditions of practice make the success of any procedure contingent. Just as a doctor cannot be 100 percent sure that this operation will cure that patient, or an engineer that this design cannot fail, so a teacher cannot know exactly what approach will work with a particular student or class. Decisions about procedures can be made with greater confidence when high-quality empirical evidence is available, but decisions about educational practice always require judgment, experience, and reasoned argument, as well as evidence.

Third, the research base for mathematics learning is diverse in the methods used and contains diverse kinds of results. For example, observational methods—including clinical interviews with students—are faithful to actual conditions and environments. But they may have trouble controlling irrelevant variables that might have been responsible for the results. It can be challenging to draw scientifically sound conclusions from a selected set of observations. In contrast, experimental methods—including studies comparing an experimental and control group—establish stronger bases for drawing conclusions, although even these conclusions have important limitations and qualifications. Experimental control is a challenge because the classroom teaching of mathematics constitutes a system of mutually dependent elements that cannot easily be disentangled so that each element can be controlled. Experimental rigor often requires narrowing one's focus to a single feature of an instructional method or to a limited amount of mathematical content. Furthermore, evidence that an instructional method produced a certain result in a controlled situation does not guarantee that it would produce the same result in a situation when, for example, different mathematical content were being taught or the students had different backgrounds and experience. There are pros and cons for each methodological approach, and we believe that the greatest progress is made when together they offer converging evidence, that is, a coherent picture of how mathematics learning occurs. The interpretation and use of research always require a search for commonalities in evidence from diverse sources.

Finally, most published studies in education confirm the predictions made by the investigators. Information obtained from research therefore is particularly useful when it goes beyond the sought-after effects. The interpretation and use of such information require an examination of the conditions under which the effects were obtained and other possible effects. For example, the students in the groups under investigation may have met other learning goals than those targeted by the instructional methods.

> **High-quality research should play a central role in any effort to improve mathematics learning.**

In summary, high-quality research should play a central role in any effort to improve mathematics learning. That research can never provide prescriptions, but it can be used to help guide skilled teachers in crafting methods that will work in their particular circumstances. For many important issues in mathematics education, the body of evidence is simply too thin at present to warrant a comprehensive synthesis. Where convergent evidence is not available, we have attempted in this report to suggest the sorts of evidence that would be needed for good inferences to be drawn.

About This Report

The Committee on Mathematics Learning was created at the request of the Division of Elementary, Secondary, and Informal Education in the National Science Foundation's Directorate for Education and Human Resources and the U.S. Department of Education's Office of Educational Research and Improvement. The sponsors were concerned about the shortage of reliable information on the learning of mathematics by schoolchildren that could be used to guide best practice in the early years of schooling.

The charge to the committee lists three goals:

1. To synthesize the rich and diverse research on pre-kindergarten through eighth-grade mathematics learning.

2. To provide research-based recommendations for teaching, teacher education, and curriculum for improving student learning and to identify areas where research is needed.

3. To give advice and guidance to educators, researchers, publishers, policy makers, and parents.

Additionally, the committee was charged with describing the context of the study with respect to what is meant by successful mathematics learning, what areas of mathematics are important as foundations in grades pre-K-8 for building continued learning, and the nature of evidence and the role of research in influencing and informing education practice, programs, and policies.

The goals for the study cover a broad grade span and a number of different facets of mathematics education—learning, teaching, teacher education, and curriculum. Further, the report is to provide guidance to a diverse audience. The complexity of the task and the time constraints imposed led the committee to make some judicious choices and decisions. First, as indicated earlier, we chose to focus primarily on the domain of number in order to make our task manageable and to present findings on the area of mathematics of most interest to our audience. Second, because we could not assume a common background, necessary background had to be included in the report. Finally, we decided to limit the detail reported on individual studies in order to make the report more accessible.

To meets its charge, the committee conducted an extensive examination of the research literature relevant to the learning of mathematics in the pre-kindergarten through eighth-grade years. We did not review other bodies of literature that have an impact on learning such as textbooks, curriculum projects, assessments, and standards documents. In reviewing the research, we asked ourselves what promising changes in practice the evidence suggests and what else needs to be known to improve practice. We then concluded how teaching, curricula, and teacher education should change to improve mathematics learning in these critical years.

In chapter 2, we describe the current status of mathematics curricula, teaching practices, assessments, and student achievement. In response to the charge to describe what areas of mathematics are important, chapter 3 outlines the domain of number and discusses what it means to learn about number in the pre-kindergarten to eighth-grade years. Chapter 4 details the strands of what we refer to as "mathematical proficiency," which we have established as what is meant by successful mathematics learning in the elementary school and middle school years.

Chapters 5, 6, 7, and 8 then present a portrait of mathematics learning that spans the grade levels considered in this report. Chapter 5 considers what students learn outside school and bring with them to the formal study of mathematics. Chapter 6 describes the process by which students acquire mathematical proficiency with whole numbers, and chapter 7 addresses proficiency with other number systems. Chapter 8 describes the process by which students achieve proficiency in domains other than number, including beginning algebra, measurement and geometry, and statistics and probability.

Chapters 9 and 10 focus on the teaching of mathematics. Chapter 9 describes what we know from research about teaching for mathematical proficiency. Chapter 10 discusses what it means to be a proficient teacher of mathematics and describes the kinds of experiences teachers need to develop this proficiency.

Finally, chapter 11 presents the committee's recommendations for teaching practices, curricula, and teacher education, offering some suggestions for parents, educators, and others. Chapter 11 also recommends the various types of research needed if both practice and policy are to be improved.

Notes

1. Butts, 1955, p. 454; Cubberley, 1920, pp. 17, 235; Kouba and Wearne, 2000; Thorndike, 1922.
2. Snow, Burns, and Griffin, 1998, p. 20. The case for critical reading skill and literacy by adolescence is addressed by Moore, Bean, Birdyshaw, and Rycik, 1999.
3. Binkley and Williams, 1996; Elley, 1992.
4. Fuson, Smith, and Lo Cicero, 1997; Griffin, Case, and Siegler, 1994; Snow, Burns, and Griffin, 1998.
5. One well-known program is called Reading Recovery (see Snow, Burns, and Griffin, 1998, pp. 255–258), which is designed for the lowest fifth of a first-grade class. In that program, the teacher, who has received extensive instruction in the reading process and its implications for teaching, notes an individual child's literacy strategies and knowledge and then engages the child in a structured series of activities. Each child is tutored individually for a half hour a day for up to 20 weeks.
6. Wagner and Stanovich, 1996.
7. Anderson, Wilson, and Fielding, 1988.
8. See chapter 2 for data on the level of instructional emphasis fourth- and eighth-grade teachers reported giving to number and operations.
9. See, for example, the SCANS study (U.S. Department of Labor, Secretary's Commission on Achieving Necessary Skills, 1991).
10. James, 1899/1958, p. 26.
11. James, 1899/1958, p. 23.

References

Anderson, R. C., Wilson, P. T., & Fielding, L. G. (1988). Growth in reading and how children spend their time outside of school. *Reading Research Quarterly, 23,* 285–303.

Binkley, M., & Williams, T. (1996). *Reading literacy in the United States: Findings from the IEA Reading Literacy Study* (NCES-96-258). Washington, DC: National Center for Education Statistics. Available: http://nces.ed.gov/spider/webspider/96258.shtml. [July 10, 2001].

Butts, R. F. (1955). *A cultural history of Western education.* New York: McGraw-Hill.

Cubberley, E. P. (1920). *The history of education.* Boston: Houghton Mifflin.

Elley, R. (1992). *How in the world do students read?* The Hague, The Netherlands: International Association for the Evaluation of Educational Achievement.

Fuson, K. C., Smith, S. T., & Lo Cicero, A. M. (1997). Supporting Latino first graders' ten-structured thinking in urban classrooms. *Journal for Research in Mathematics Education, 28,* 738–766.

Griffin, S., Case, R., & Siegler, R. S. (1994). Rightstart: Providing the central conceptual prerequisites for first formal learning of arithmetic to students at risk for school failure. In K. McGilly (Ed.), *Classroom lessons: Integrating cognitive theory and classroom practice.* Cambridge, MA: MIT Press/Bradford Books.

James, W. (1958). *Talks to teachers.* New York: Norton. (Original work published 1899)

Kouba, V. L., & Wearne, D. (2000). Whole number properties and operations. In E. A. Silver & P. A. Kenney (Eds.), *Results from the seventh mathematics assessment of the National Assessment of Educational Progress* (pp. 141–161). Reston, VA: National Council of Teachers of Mathematics.

Moore, D. W., Bean, T. W., Birdyshaw, D., & Rycik, J. A. (1999). *Adolescent literacy: A position statement for the Commission on Adolescent Literacy of the International Reading Association.* Newark, DE: International Reading Association. Summary available: http://www.reading.org/pdf/1036.pdf. [July 19, 2001].

Snow, C. E., Burns, M. S., & Griffin, P. (Eds.). (1998). *Preventing reading difficulties in young children.* Washington, DC: National Academy Press. Available: http://books.nap.edu/catalog/6023.html.

Thorndike, E. L. (1922). *The psychology of arithmetic.* New York: Macmillan.

Wagner, R. K., & Stanovich, K. E. (1996). Expertise in reading. In K. A. Ericsson (Ed.), *The road to excellence: The acquisition of expert performance in the arts and sciences, sports, and games* (pp. 189-225). Mahwah, NJ: Erlbaum.

U.S. Department of Labor, Secretary's Commission on Achieving Necessary Skills. (1991). *What work requires of schools: A SCANS report for America 2000.* Washington, DC. Author. (ERIC Document Reproduction Service No. ED 332 054).

2

THE STATE OF SCHOOL MATHEMATICS IN THE UNITED STATES

The U.S. system for teaching children mathematics is large, is complex, and has numerous components. Children's mathematical achievement, however, is ultimately determined and constrained by the opportunities they have had to learn. Those opportunities are determined by several major components of school mathematics. The curriculum contains *learning goals* spelling out the mathematics to be studied. It also includes *instructional programs and materials* that organize the mathematical content, together with *assessments* for determining what has been learned. In addition, and of primary importance, it is through *teaching* that students encounter the mathematical content afforded by the curriculum.

In every country, the complex system of school mathematics is situated in a cultural matrix. Mathematics teaching is not the same in the United States as in, say, Japan or Germany,[1] and the curricula are different as well.[2] Countries differ in such global characteristics as the centralization of educational policies, the organization and types of schools, and the success of efforts to provide universal access to education. The status of teachers in the society, the composition and mobility of the student population, and the extent to which external examinations determine one's life chances all constrain the ways in which mathematics is taught and learned. Countries also differ in more specific ways: parents, teachers, and students have different beliefs about the value of hard work and the importance of mathematics for one's education; whether and how students are grouped for mathematics instruction varies; mathematics textbooks are written, distributed, and used in diverse ways; and there is variation in the prevalence of tutors or special schools to coach students for mathematics tests. Each country provides a unique setting for school mathematics, one that very much determines how students are taught, what they learn, how successful they are, and how satisfied society is with the products of the system.

Education in the United States is marked by a diverse, mobile population of students and teachers, a variety of organizational structures, and minimal centralized control over policies and practices. The U.S. system of school mathematics has evolved over several centuries in accordance with these characteristics. Not only do the components of the U.S. system differ from those of other countries, but they are organized and operate differently. To understand the possibilities for improving children's learning of mathematics, one needs a sense of how the elements of U.S. school mathematics currently function.

In the past half century, a number of research studies have examined differences in the mathematics learned by students in various educational systems. Some of these studies have also looked at various features of the systems that might help researchers understand and interpret the pattern of results. To date, the most comprehensive study to be analyzed in detail has been the Third International Mathematics and Science Study (TIMSS), which was conducted in the mid-1990s. Over 40 countries participated in TIMSS. Tests in science and mathematics, as well as questionnaires about their studies and their beliefs, were given to students midway through elementary school (grade 4 in the United States), midway through lower secondary school (U.S. grade 8), and at the end of upper secondary school (U.S. grade 12). Questionnaires about beliefs, practices, and policies were also given to these students' teachers and school administrators. Unique features of TIMSS included an extensive examination of textbooks and curriculum guides from many of the participating countries, a video study of eighth-grade mathematics classes in three countries, and case studies of educational policies in those three countries.

The results from TIMSS have been widely reported in the media, catching the attention of politicians, policy makers, and the general public. Many people have compared various practices, programs, and policies in the United States with those of high-achieving countries. Such comparisons are interesting but at best can only be suggestive of the sources of achievement differences. TIMSS provides no evidence that a single practice—say, the amount of homework assigned, the particular textbook used, or how periods of mathematics instruction are arranged during the school day—is responsible for higher mathematics test scores in one country than in another. The countries

> To understand the possibilities for improving children's learning of mathematics, one needs a sense of how the elements of U.S. school mathematics currently function.

participating in TIMSS vary in many respects—educationally, socially, economically, historically, culturally—and in each of those respects, they vary along many different dimensions. In the absence of more evidence than TIMSS can provide, one cannot select one practice and claim that if it were changed to be more like that of high-scoring countries, scores in the United States would rise.[3] Studies like TIMSS can at best generate conjectures that need to be tested in the complex system of school mathematics that exists in any county. In this report, we use data from TIMSS and other international studies to help describe practice and performance in the United States—sometimes in contrast to that of other countries but never assuming a simple causal relation between a specific practice and performance.

This chapter is intended primarily to give an overall picture of U.S. mathematics education, describing the experiences and achievement of most students. But it should be emphasized that U.S. education is quite diverse, partly because of an unequal distribution of needs and resources, and partly because of the principle of local control. Thus, this chapter also attempts to describe that diversity, particularly with respect to student achievement.

In this chapter, we first take up in turn four central elements of school mathematics—learning goals, instructional programs and materials, assessment, and teaching—discussing the current status of each in the United States. We then examine the preparation and professional development of U.S. teachers of mathematics. Finally, we look at a major indicator of the health of the whole system, student achievement results, both across time and internationally.

Learning Goals

The U.S. Constitution leaves to the separate states the responsibility for public education. State and local boards of education have the authority to determine the mathematics that students learn as well as the conditions under which they learn it. Many state boards of education have created curriculum standards and frameworks, and some have specified criteria that educational materials (principally textbooks) must meet if they are to be approved. Thus, each state can, in principle, specify quite different goals for learning mathematics at each grade level, and each local district can make adjustments as long as they fall within the state guidelines.

A major effort to set comprehensive learning goals for school mathematics at the national level was undertaken in 1989 by the National Council of Teachers of Mathematics (NCTM) with the release of *Curriculum and Evalu-*

ation Standards for School Mathematics.[4] The document outlined and illustrated goals in the form of standards to be met by school mathematics programs. It called for a broadened view of mathematics and its teaching and learning, emphasizing the development of students' "mathematical power" alongside more traditional skill and content goals. The NCTM later produced *Professional Standards for Teaching Mathematics*[5] and *Assessment Standards for School Mathematics.*[6] Beginning in 1995, it embarked on a process to revise all three documents, resulting in *Principles and Standards for School Mathematics,*[7] which was released in April 2000.

Although none of the NCTM documents established national standards for school mathematics in an official sense, much of the activity in U.S. mathematics education since 1989 has been based on or informed by the ideas in those documents. Many school mathematics textbooks claim to be aligned with the NCTM standards, and 13 curriculum projects were funded by the National Science Foundation to produce materials for elementary, middle, or high school that embodied the ideas expressed in the standards documents.[8] The NCTM standards of 1989 launched the so-called standards movement, with standards for other school subjects appearing over the following decade.[9] In 1994 the reauthorization of Title I of the Elementary and Secondary Education Act furthered boosted the movement. Title I provides supplemental financial assistance to local educational agencies to improve teaching and learning in schools with high concentrations of children from low-income families. The reauthorization "requires states to develop challenging standards for performance and assessments that measure student performance against the standards."[10] It should also be noted that *A Nation at Risk*, America 2000, and Goals 2000 (under Presidents Reagan, Bush, and Clinton, respectively) all called for higher, measurable standards in education.[11]

As of 1999, 49 states reported having content standards in mathematics and several states were in the process of revising their standards.[12] These standards (sometimes called curriculum frameworks) describe what students should know and be able to do in mathematics. Most of the state standards reflect the 1989 NCTM standards and either repeated verbatim or were adapted from the document. Early versions of these state standards were organized into grade clusters (e.g., grades K-4), but some states (e.g., California, Texas, North Carolina, and Virginia) have recently developed grade-by-grade standards.[13]

Current state standards and curriculum frameworks vary considerably in their specificity, difficulty, and character, as illustrated by the widely divergent ratings they received in three reviews conducted by the American Federation of Teachers, the Fordham Foundation, and the Council for Basic Education.[14] The conflicting reports have created confusion among parents, teachers, and policy makers alike. According to one analysis of the reviews:

> While . . . multiple analyses of state standards are better than no analyses, the grade differentials among the three reports are confounding—enough so to make state leaders either throw up their hands in utter bewilderment or embrace a high mark and ignore the others. Both responses threaten to defeat the very purpose of the reports. For example, Florida received a D from one appraiser and the equivalent of an A from another in mathematics. In both English and mathematics, Michigan received an F from one appraiser and a B-plus from another.[15]

Often missing from the public discussion of such reports are the processes and criteria that gave rise to the ratings, which has only added to the confusion.

Some caveats about standards deserve mention. First, most groups charged with developing standards for a school subject have strong expectations for learning in that subject. They may spend more time devising the standards than checking the feasibility of achieving them in the time available for learning. One analysis of standards for 14 subjects found that it would take nine additional years of schooling to achieve them all.[16] Thus, it is important that states and districts avoid long lists that are not feasible and that would contribute to an unfocused and shallow mathematics curriculum.

Second, when grade bands (e.g., grades pre-K–2) are used in specifying standards, it is important to clarify that each goal does not have to be addressed at every grade in a band. Such redundancy again contributes to the dissipation of learning efforts and interferes with the acquisition of proficiency.

Third, states and districts need to decide what they will do when students do not meet grade-level goals. Children enter school with quite different levels of mathematical experience and knowledge. Some need additional learning time and support for learning if they are to meet the goals. As schools shift to standards-based mathematics curricula for grades pre-K to 8 with challenging grade-level goals, thorny questions arise as to whether and how special accommodations will be made for some students and what criteria will be imposed for promotion to the next grade.

A recent comparative analysis of mathematics assessments given to U.S. and Japanese eighth graders revealed some striking differences in the expectations held for each group, with much lower expectations in the United States. The author concluded by pointing to the need for grade-level goals:

To achieve the coherence and focus observed in the Japanese materials, the *Curriculum and Evaluation Standards for School Mathematics* need to be further extended to provide grade level guidance about focus and primary activities for given years. This step to achievement and delivery standards for school mathematics is *curricularly achievable* within the framework outlined by the NCTM content standards. Whether it is *politically acceptable* or *systematically implementable* are larger and more volatile questions.[17]

On balance, we see the efforts made since 1989 to develop standards for teaching and learning mathematics as worthwhile. Many schools have been led to rethink their mathematics programs, and many teachers to reflect on their practice. Nonetheless, the fragmentation of these standards, their multiple sources, and the limited conceptual frameworks on which they rest have not resulted in a coherent, well-articulated, widely accepted set of learning goals for U.S. school mathematics that would detail what students at each grade should know and be able to do. Part of our purpose in this report is to present a conceptual framework for school mathematics that could be used to move the goal-setting process forward.

Instructional Programs and Materials

Learning goals are inert until they are translated into specific programs and materials for instruction. What is actually taught in classrooms is strongly influenced by the available textbooks because most teachers use textbooks as their primary instructional materials.[18] As of 1998, 12 states—including the very large markets of California and Texas—had policies in which the state either chose the materials that students would use or drew up a list of textbooks and materials from which districts had to choose, though sometimes only if they wanted to use state funds for the purchase. Another seven states recommended materials for use.[19]

Surveys of U.S. teachers have consistently shown that nearly all their instructional time is structured around textbooks or other commercially produced materials, even though teachers vary substantially in the extent to which they follow a book's organization and suggested activities.[20] In 1980 one researcher maintained that the chalkboard and printed textbooks were the predominant instructional media in mathematics classes,[21] a verdict substantiated by recent data from the National Assessment of Educational Progress (NAEP). Responding to a questionnaire in 1996, teachers of three fifths of the fourth graders and of almost three fourths of the eighth graders in the

NAEP sample said that they used the mathematics textbook almost every day.[22] Observational studies of elementary school classrooms, however, reveal that at least some teachers pick and choose from the mathematics textbook even as they follow its core content.[23]

The American textbook system is notable for being heavily market driven. In that market, publishers must contend with multiple and sometimes contradictory specifications:

> If we lived in a country with one national curriculum, then textbook publishers could compete with each other in the effort to produce a book that would best mirror that one curriculum. But we are not such a country. Instead, we have dozens of powerful ministries of education issuing undisciplined lists of particulars that publishers must include in the textbooks. Since publishers must sell in as many jurisdictions as possible in order to turn a profit, their books must incorporate this melange of test-oriented trivia, pedagogical faddism, and inconsistent social messages.[24]

To be sold nationwide, a textbook needs to include all the topics from the standards and curriculum frameworks of at least those influential states that officially adopt lists of approved materials. Consequently, the major U.S. school mathematics textbooks, which collectively constitute a de facto national curriculum, are bulky, address many different topics, and explore few topics in depth.

In comparison with the curricula of countries achieving well on international comparisons, the U.S. elementary and middle school mathematics curriculum has been characterized as superficial, "underachieving," and diffuse in content coverage.[25] Successful countries tend to select a few critical topics for each grade and then devote enough time to developing each topic for students to master it. Rather than returning to the same topics the following year, they select new, more advanced topics and develop those in depth. In the United States, not a single topic in the grade pre-K to 8 mathematics curriculum is seen as the province of one grade, to be learned there once and for all. Instead, topics such as multidigit computations are distributed over several years, with one digit added to the numbers each year. Students invariably spend considerable time on topics they encountered in the previous grade.[26] At the beginning of each year and of each new topic, numerous lessons are devoted to teaching what was not learned or was learned inadequately the year before. Because the curriculum is consequently so crowded, depth is seldom achieved, and mastery is deferred. Not surprisingly, international curriculum analyses have found that U.S. mathematics textbooks cover more topics, but more superficially, than do their counterparts in other countries.[27]

The massive amount of review created by the inadvertent de facto curriculum set by textbooks wastes learning time and may bore those students who have already mastered the content. Such constant review is also counterproductive. It is much easier to help students build correct mathematical methods at the start than to correct errors that have been learned and practiced for a year or more. As the following chapters show, the lack of concentrated attention to core topics militates against powerful learning.

Further attributes of this de facto curriculum also are problematic. For example, even with their supplementary materials, many textbooks fail to discuss student strategies or progressions in student thinking. They also frequently omit explanations of mathematical processes. Further, decorative artwork with little connection to textbook content sometimes confuses or distracts students.[28] Research indicates that students can learn more mathematics than is usually offered them in the early grades, so the U.S. elementary school mathematics curriculum could be made more challenging. If the curriculum of the early grades were more ambitious, and if instruction were focused on mastery of topics rather than unwarranted review, teachers of the middle and upper grades could concentrate on teaching core grade-level topics more thoroughly.

The short timelines between the formulation of state learning goals and the selection of textbooks create a textbook production schedule that seldom permits both consultation of research about student learning and field testing followed by revision based on actual use in schools.[29] Most students today are using materials that were produced under heavy (perceived or actual) market constraints. In contrast, some recent school curriculum development projects that were supported by the National Science Foundation built research and pilot testing into their design.

An expert panel convened by the Department of Education recently evaluated materials from these NSF-funded projects as well as from other programs. The panel labeled some curriculum programs as "exemplary" and others as "promising" based on a review process that examined evidence of the programs' effectiveness.[30] Almost immediately, the panel's conclusions were called into question.[31] Just as with ratings of standards, evaluations of curriculum materials have led to divergent ratings depending on the group doing the evaluating.[32]

In some countries, including England, France, Hong Kong, Singapore, and the Netherlands, there are permanent national centers or institutes that conduct multi-year research and curriculum development efforts in school mathematics. In the United States, the government has funded both a research center for mathematics learning at a single institution and projects to develop materials for teaching and learning mathematics at a number of other institutions.[33] Typically, the curriculum development programs have required, as part of the project, both pilot testing of the materials while they are under development and the collection of evidence on the effectiveness of the materials, once developed. In some cases, the evaluation studies have been only perfunctory and the evidence gathered of poor quality. In others the support has resulted in sustained research-based curriculum development that systematically uses evidence as to what U.S. students can learn.[34] Such a development program can be interactive, with improved learning materials yielding improved student learning that, in turn, yields improved and even-more-ambitious learning materials.

Developing teachers' capacity to acquire and use good instructional materials is also a problem. Textbook selection processes can be overwhelming. Committee members usually do not have time to examine carefully the continuity of treatment of topics or the depth and clarity of the conceptual development facilitated by the materials. Instead, their focus is often on superficial features such as the appearance of the materials and whether all goals on a checklist are addressed. The problems created by checklists are especially keen in states and local districts with large numbers of specified special criteria. Failure to meet even a few of these criteria can eliminate an otherwise strong program.[35]

The methods used in the United States in the twentieth century for producing school mathematics textbooks and for choosing which textbooks and other materials to use are not sufficient for the goals of the twenty-first century. The nation must develop a greater capacity for producing high-quality materials and for using effectively those that are produced. In subsequent chapters, we cite research on children's learning that can guide that production and use.

Assessments

In general, assessments of children's mathematics learning fall into two categories: internal and external. Internal assessments are those used by teachers in monitoring and evaluating their students' progress and in making instructional decisions. Such assessments range from the informal questions a teacher might ask about a student's work to an end-of-year examination. They arise from the teaching-learning process in the classroom. External assessments, in contrast, come from outside, from projects gathering comparative research data or mandated by state or local districts as part of their evaluation programs.

Relative to the vast literature on external assessments and their results, little up-to-date information is available on how U.S. teachers conduct internal assessments in mathematics, particularly those activities such as classroom questioning, quizzes, projects, and informal observations. Even less attention appears to have been paid to how teachers' assessments might help improve mathematics learning. According to one analysis, "Aside from teacher-made classroom tests, the integration of assessment and learning as an interacting system has been too little explored."[36]

As part of the 1996 NAEP mathematics assessment, teachers responded to several questions about their testing practices.[37] Fourth graders were usually tested in mathematics once or twice a month, with about a third being tested once or twice a week. More frequent testing was associated with lower achievement.[38] Eighth graders were somewhat more likely to be tested weekly. At both grades, teachers appeared to be responding to calls arising from the standards movement for less multiple-choice testing in favor of tests on which students supply written responses.[39] Multiple-choice testing is still prevalent, however, stimulated perhaps by the increased number of such tests provided by publishers to accompany their textbooks. Two thirds of fourth and eighth graders had teachers who reported that they used multiple-choice tests to assess students' progress at least once or twice a year, most as often as once or twice a month.[40] In part, teachers are attempting to prepare students for external assessments by using multiple-choice items on their own tests.

The form of multiple-choice test items appears not to be as big a problem as the nature of the items and the conditions under which they are typically administered in the United States. An examination given to a national sample of eighth graders in Japan as part of a Special Study on Essential Skills in Mathematics was composed entirely of multiple-choice items, yet it was judged substantially more challenging than the 1992 NAEP mathematics assessment given to U.S. eighth graders, which contained both multiple-choice items and items on which students had to write either a brief or lengthy response.[41] The difference was that the Japanese exam contained about half as many items as the U.S. exam; the items were longer, demanded more reading and analysis, and were more focused on strategies for problem solving.

Exhortations to change assessments, whether internal or external, clearly need to focus on more than just item format. In the remainder of this section, we examine current external assessment practices and results.

In recent years, largely because of language in the reauthorization of Title I, many states have designed and implemented their own assessments, usually aligned with newly developed state standards or curriculum frameworks. Many of these assessments are intended to have *high stakes*. They may have financial or other consequences for districts, schools, teachers, or individual students. In some cases, promotion or even a high school diploma may depend on a student achieving a passing score. As of 1998, 48 states and the District of Columbia had instituted testing programs, typically at grades 4, 8, and 11, and usually in mathematics, language arts, science, and technology.[42]

Many states report the results of their high-stakes assessments by school or by district to identify places that are most in need of improvement. The states' responses to those results vary. Some states have the authority to close, take over, or "reconstitute" a failing school. To date, only a few states have ever used such sanctions.[43] Florida awards additional funds to schools that perform near the bottom and also to schools that perform near the top.[44] When schools or districts with poor results do not show sufficiently rapid improvement, some states revoke accreditation, close down the school, seize control of the school, or grant vouchers so that students may choose to enroll elsewhere.

Currently, 19 states require that in order to graduate from high school, students must pass a mandated assessment, and several other states are phasing in such a requirement.[45] In TIMSS, countries with rigorous assessments at the end of secondary education outperformed other countries at a comparable level of economic development; such assessments, however, were probably not the most important determinant of achievement levels.[46] In response to calls for an end to social promotion, some states and districts have begun requiring grade-level mastery tests for promotion, typically in grades 4 and 8. Interestingly, there is some evidence to suggest that there is an almost inverse relationship between statewide testing policies and students' mathematics achievement:

> Among the 12 highest-scoring states in 8th grade mathematics in 1996, . . . none had mandatory statewide testing programs in place during the 1980s or early 1990s. Only two of the top 12 states in the 4th grade mathematics had statewide programs prior to 1995. By contrast, among the 12 lowest-scoring states, . . . 10 had extensive student testing programs in place prior to 1990, some of which were associated

with highly specified state curricula and an extensive menu of rewards and sanctions.[47]

Of course, this relationship does not imply that simply easing statewide test policies would improve achievement.

To give teachers, students, parents, and other caregivers sufficient time to prepare for high-stakes assessments, states typically administer them for several years before the consequences take effect. During these trial runs, the failure rates are sometimes alarmingly high. In Arizona, for example, only 1 in 10 sophomores passed the mathematics test first given in the spring of 1999. That same spring, only 7% of Virginia schools were able to achieve a 70% passing rate, which was to become the condition for accreditation in 2007. In response to these results, some states have begun to relax their expectations, reconsider the test, or withdraw it altogether. Wisconsin, for example, yielded to pressure from parents and withdrew its high school graduation test. Massachusetts and New York set lower passing scores for their exams.[48]

Most states report the level of student results on their assessments by setting so-called cut scores to define categories with such labels as *advanced, proficient, needs improvement,* and *failing,*[49] terms similar to those used in NAEP: *advanced, proficient,* and *basic.* When results on state assessments are compared with the state results in NAEP, the proportions of students reaching the proficient level are often higher.[50] Some researchers, politicians, and policy makers have concluded from this discrepancy that most state tests do not reflect sufficiently high expectations.[51] Others argue instead that minimum competence and high expectations are different goals that cannot be measured by the same assessment and certainly not with the same cut scores. Thus, the results appear discrepant because the same categories are used to describe performance on assessments with very different goals.

Many states and school districts use standardized tests[52] (which may or may not coincide with the state assessments discussed above) to assess how their students are achieving. Commercially published standardized mathematics achievement tests are quite variable in the topics they cover and in the proportion of these topics emphasized at each grade level.[53] The tests frequently are not aligned with the teaching materials used in a district or even with the goals of the district. This misalignment further dilutes teaching efforts, as teachers must add to their long list of goals coverage of the major topics emphasized on a specific standardized test.

Standardized tests can have other negative consequences. The word *standardized* is likely to carry certain connotations: that such a test is more objective than other instruments, that it contains mostly grade-level items, that it was developed or sanctioned by experts in the domain, that it reflects important learning goals in a balanced way, and that it represents and assesses what students know about the content that the state or district has prescribed for that grade level. In fact, many standardized tests have few or none of these characteristics.[54]

Most standardized tests might be called "comparison" tests because their function is to rank order students, schools, and districts or to compare them with another group that was selected as typical. Items are chosen to range widely in difficulty in part to disperse students' scores. That range allows for half the students to be classified as "below average" and the other half as "above average." The tests do not include many items that only a few students get right or that only a few get wrong, because such items do not help distinguish among students.[55] The omission of these items may mean that some important aspects of mathematics that students have or have not learned are not tested. For tests designed for making comparisons, however, the omission is necessary.

In contrast, if the purpose of a test is to assess whether students have met specific goals, test designers can choose items to span the important mathematics to be learned. When the goal is to determine students' proficiency with grade-level topics, the cut scores are then set to indicate various levels of proficiency. Students and teachers know where to aim their efforts, and students can study for the test with the goals in mind. If the students have learned well, large proportions of them can achieve high proficiency, and there is no need to label half of them as below average (or even to rank them at all). Standardized tests have traditionally been kept secret so that questions can be reused. In recent years, this practice has come under fire. If students are to reach publicly accepted standards, the argument goes, they need to know what type of performance will be expected of them.[56] They should have an opportunity to learn the mathematical content and processes on which they will be examined. At the same time, they need to become familiar with the instructions, the organization of the assessment, and the format of the items, so that such nonmathematical considerations do not prevent them from showing what they know. Legally and ethically, when the stakes are high, students should be provided with sample assessments or at least sample items that are representative of the actual assessments.[57]

The movement over the past four decades to hold schools accountable for students' performance has resulted in increased high-stakes testing of "minimum competency" in mathematics and other subjects. Many states give competency tests at several grade levels, including high school exit exams. Performance on the mathematics portions of such tests has often been con-

If the purpose of a test is to assess whether students have met specific goals, test designers can choose items to span the important mathematics to be learned.

siderably below what was anticipated or desired. Many districts meanwhile have continued to use standardized comparison tests that were not necessarily aligned with their textbooks, their state goals, or their state competency tests. The combination of standardized comparison tests and state competency tests can overwhelm teachers, who have to prepare students for two kinds of high-stakes tests about which they often know very little.

State competency tests in mathematics are often given first at a grade level at which many students are already far behind and likely to have difficulty catching up. If such tests are to be used, they need to be accompanied in earlier grades—and throughout all grades—by other assessments that would enable teachers to make their instruction more effective. In particular, such assessments could identify students who are not achieving and need special help so that they do not fall further behind. This linking of assessment to instructional efforts is consistent with the recent NRC report *Testing, Teaching, and Learning*,[58] which focuses on recommendations for Title I students. Two of the central recommendations of that report concerning assessment and instruction are as follows:

- Teachers should administer assessments frequently and regularly in classrooms for the purpose of monitoring individual students' performance and adapting instruction to improve their performance. (p. 47)

- Teachers should monitor the progress of individual children in grades pre-K-3 to improve the quality and appropriateness of instruction. Such assessments should be conducted at multiple points in time, in children's natural settings, and should use direct assessments, portfolios, checklists, and other work sampling devices. The assessments should measure all domains of children's development, particularly social development, reading, and mathematics. (p. 53)

The current national focus on standards-based testing is a definite improvement on the past focus on comparison testing. But standards-based assessment needs to be accompanied by a clear set of grade-level goals so that teachers, parents, and the whole community can work together to help all children in a school achieve those goals. (And the goals need to aim at more than skills, as we argue in chapter 4.) Continuing informal assessments throughout the year can help teachers adjust their teaching and identify students who need additional help. More such help might be available if money formerly spent on comparison testing were reallocated to help children learn.

Teaching

Even with high standards, exemplary textbooks, and powerful assessments, what really matters for mathematics learning are the interactions that take place in classrooms. The literature on mathematics education, perhaps surprisingly, contains little reliable data about those interactions. Most of the available research evidence consists of reports by teachers of their practice, but an increasing amount comes from systematic observations of lessons. The discussion in this section addresses both types of evidence.

Reported Practices

The emphasis in U.S. elementary and middle school mathematics teaching seems to be predominantly on number and operations. Teachers of 93% of the fourth graders and 88% of the eighth graders in the 1996 NAEP mathematics assessment reported that they gave the topic "a lot" of instructional emphasis.[59] At grade 8, algebra also received a lot of emphasis (for 57% of the students), but that was the only other curriculum strand to receive much attention. Fourth-grade teachers reported giving considerable emphasis to facts, concepts, skills, and procedures (over 90% of the students got "a lot"), with less emphasis on reasoning processes (52%) and even less attention to communication (38%). Eighth-grade teachers' responses followed a similar pattern, with somewhat less attention to facts, concepts, skills, and procedures (79%). In a recent study comparing schools participating in state initiatives in mathematics and science with schools not involved in such initiatives, elementary school teachers in the initiatives schools spent significantly more time than their counterparts on reasoning and problem-solving activities.[60]

For decades, mathematics educators have been exhorting teachers to allow children to use *manipulatives*—counting blocks, geometric shapes, and other objects—to support their thinking. The use of manipulatives, however, is not a common classroom practice. In 1996, teachers of 27% of the fourth graders in NAEP reported that their students used counting blocks and geometric shapes at least once a week; 74% used them at least once a month, leaving 26% who seldom if ever used them. Teachers of 8% of the eighth graders said that their students used such manipulatives at least once a week, and teachers of more than half the students reported essentially no use. Data were not available on how this use was connected to mathematical ideas, words, and notations.

Materials such as rulers and calculators are apparently used much more frequently than manipulatives in mathematics teaching. Teachers of almost half the fourth graders in the 1996 NAEP sample reported that their students used rulers or related tools at least once a week, and teachers of 95% of the fourth graders reported frequencies of at least once a month. Teachers of a quarter of the eighth graders reported that their students used objects such as rulers at least once a week, and teachers of almost 80% said their students used them at least once a month.

Eighth-grade teachers reported considerably greater use of calculators in their teaching than fourth-grade teachers did. Teachers of over half of the eighth graders in the 1996 NAEP sample reported that their students used calculators almost every day, and teachers of less than a tenth claimed never or hardly ever to use calculators. Teachers of less than a third of the fourth graders, in contrast, said their students used a calculator in class at least once a week, teachers of only 5% said almost every day, and teachers of more than a quarter said never or hardly ever. Eighth graders enrolled in algebra were reported to use calculators more frequently than those in prealgebra or eighth-grade mathematics, and at both grades 4 and 8 the reported frequency of calculator use increased from 1992 to 1996.

The teachers of about a quarter of the 1996 NAEP sample at both grades 4 and 8 reported that their students worked in small groups or with a partner almost every day, and teachers of more than 90% of the students had them working that way at least once a month. Teachers of about a third of each sample said that at least once a week their students wrote a few sentences about how to solve a mathematics problem, but teachers of another third said their students never or hardly ever wrote up their solutions. Few students at either grade wrote reports or worked on projects more than once a week, and teachers of about two thirds said their students hardly ever did project work. For nearly half of the eighth graders and more than a third of the fourth graders, their teachers reported that almost every day they had students discuss solutions with one another, and teachers of almost all students held such discussions at least once a month. According to these survey data, standards-based efforts to increase attention to realistic mathematics problems may be having some effect:

> In 1996, substantial proportions of students from grades 4 and 8 were working and discussing mathematics that reflected real-life situations at least "once or twice a week." Teachers of 29 percent of fourth-grade students reported that their students did this "almost every day," while teachers of 45 percent reported that their students did this "once or twice a week."

The percentages were similar for eighth-grade students: teachers of 27 percent reported that students worked and discussed mathematics problems that reflected real-life situations "almost every day," and teachers of 47 percent reported working and discussing these types of problems "once or twice a week."[61]

As part of the 1996 NAEP, teachers were asked about their knowledge of the 1989 NCTM standards. The teachers of 46% of the fourth graders professed little or no knowledge of the standards, and only 5% of the fourth graders had teachers who indicated that they were very knowledgeable. In contrast, only 19% of the eighth graders had teachers who claimed to have little or no knowledge of the standards, and 16% had teachers claiming to be very knowledgeable.[62]

The accuracy of teachers' self-reports of their practice can of course be questioned. Teachers have their own meanings for what they do. For example, in a recent survey of 85 elementary school teachers in two districts, 93% said that they were using cooperative learning, a practice in which students are grouped for instruction, are assigned roles in the group, work together on a task, are each assessed on their performance, are each held accountable for contributing to the work, and, in some versions, are taught skills for working together, promote each other's contributions, and work collectively to improve their effectiveness.[63] Interviews with 21 of the teachers who had indicated they were using cooperative learning (17 of whom said they used it for mathematics) revealed that all but one had their own version of the practice, which they distinguished from the "more formal" version. Primarily, they almost never attempted to make sure that individual students were held accountable for contributing to the work. From their own descriptions, the majority of the teachers were using a form of cooperative learning that differed substantially from the forms described in the literature by the researchers who had developed the practice. Similar discrepancies have been documented between teachers' reports of implementation of other reform practices and the observation of those practices in their video lessons.[64]

Overall, teachers' reports give at best a mixed picture of mathematics teaching in U.S. elementary and middle schools: heavy attention to traditional content accompanied by modest and possibly idiosyncratic use of practices endorsed by advocates of standards-based instruction. Regardless of how teachers are interpreting these practices, most do appear to be at least somewhat aware of recent proposals for change. Self-report data address isolated practices only, however; observational data are needed if one is to get a sense of how lessons are organized and conducted.

Observed Lessons

For more than a century, observers have been looking into classrooms and emerging with descriptions of how U.S. teachers teach.[65] What is most striking in these observers' reports is that the core of teaching—the way in which the teacher and students interact about the subject being taught—has changed very little over that time. The commonest form of teaching in U.S. schools has been called *recitation*.[66] Recitation means that the teacher leads the class of students through the lesson material by asking questions that can be answered with brief responses, often one word. The teacher acknowledges and evaluates each response, usually as right or wrong, and asks the next question. The cycle of question, response, and acknowledgment continues, often at a quick pace, until the material for the day has been reviewed. New material is presented by the teacher through telling or demonstrating. After the recitation part of the lesson, the students often are asked to work independently on the day's assignment, practicing skills that were demonstrated or reviewed earlier. U.S. readers will recognize this pattern from their own school experience because it has been popular in all parts of the country, for teaching all school subjects.

Although there are some differences in the way different subjects are taught,[67] the description of recitation teaching is consistent with more recent descriptions of mathematics lessons. In the mid-1970s, the National Science Foundation funded a set of studies on classroom practice, including a national survey of teaching practices[68] and a series of case studies.[69] After observing a number of mathematics classrooms, one researcher said:

> In all math classes I visited, the sequence of activities was the same. First, answers were given for the previous day's assignment. The more difficult problems were worked by the teacher or a student at the chalkboard. A brief explanation, sometimes none at all, was given of the new material, and problems were assigned for the next day. The remainder of the class was devoted to working on the homework while the teacher moved about the room answering questions. The most noticeable thing about math classes was the repetition of this routine.[70]

The findings for the full set of case studies are not easily summarized because there were some substantial differences between teachers, but a commissioned synthesis noted that the most common pattern in mathematics classrooms was "extensive teacher-directed explanation and questioning followed by student seatwork on paper-and-pencil assignments."[71]

At about the same time, the National Advisory Committee on Mathematical Education (NACOME) commissioned a study of elementary school mathematics instruction. Their report was entirely consistent with that of the National Science Foundation studies. In fact, NACOME expressed some concern that teaching had changed so little over the previous 10 to 15 years, a time of concentrated curriculum development in mathematics. The NACOME report's concluding remarks reviewed the committee's findings:

> The median [elementary school] classroom is self-contained. The mathematics period is about 43 minutes long, and about half of this time is written work. A single text is used in whole-class instruction. The text is followed fairly closely.... Teachers are essentially teaching the same way they were taught in school.[72]

The most extensive look into mathematics classrooms around the United States was conducted in 1995: the video study component of TIMSS.[73] The TIMSS Video Study marked the first time that a nationally representative sample of classrooms was selected for study and that a sample of lessons was videotaped. The videotapes revealed classroom instruction that resembled the instruction described in earlier reports. Apparently, U.S. teachers are continuing to teach mathematics in the same way their predecessors taught.

The TIMSS videotapes allowed researchers to take a much more detailed look at common classroom practice than any earlier study had provided, and the availability of tapes from Germany and Japan permitted some contrasting descriptions. The full sample included 81 eighth-grade mathematics lessons in the United States, 100 such lessons in Germany, and 50 lessons in Japan.

Reports from parents and in the popular press as to how U.S. children are being taught today suggest that some teachers have their students investigating mathematical ideas almost entirely on their own, whereas others are carefully explaining those ideas and providing lots of practice. It is tempting to conclude, therefore, that methods of teaching mathematics are highly variable within the United States. In fact, the TIMSS Video Study clearly shows that such differences are quite small compared with the substantial differences that exist between countries. Each country appears to have its own dominant style of mathematics teaching.[74]

In the videotaped lessons from the United States, a typical lesson begins by checking homework or engaging in a warm-up activity. The teacher then presents a few sample problems and demonstrates how to solve them. This part of the lesson is often conducted in recitation fashion, with the teacher asking fill-in-the-blank questions as the procedures are shown. Seatwork is assigned, and students complete exercises like those they have been shown. The teacher often ends the lesson by checking some of the seatwork problems and assigning similar problems for homework.

Typical lessons in Germany and Japan contain many of the same components, but the components are arranged differently and aim at different goals. For example, most lessons in all three countries include an early segment in which the teacher presents one or more problems for the day. But that activity has a different purpose in each country. In Germany, presenting the problem initiates a relatively lengthy development of advanced solution techniques. The teacher guides, through questioning, the process of solving the problem, which is often quite challenging. In Japan, presenting the carefully chosen problem sets the stage for the students to work, individually and in groups, on developing solution procedures that they then report to the class. About half the time, the procedures are expected to be original constructions. As described above, presenting problems in the United States leads to students practicing procedures that have been demonstrated by the teacher.

The different patterns of teaching generated a set of findings that illustrated the dramatic differences in classroom practice across the three countries. For example, 78% of the mathematical topics in the U.S. lessons contain concepts that were stated by the teacher rather than developed through examples or explanations. In contrast, that practice occurred for 23% of the concepts in Germany and only 17% in Japan; at least some of the concepts from the remaining topics in these countries were developed and elaborated in some way.[75] Moreover, the quality of the mathematical content of the U.S. lessons was independently rated as being much lower than that of the German and Japanese lessons.[76]

The descriptions from the TIMSS Video Study match other reports of classroom practice in mathematics. For example, a 1998 report to the California State Board of Education summarizes the conventional method of mathematics teaching in the United States, often used as the control treatment in experimental studies of new teaching approaches.[77] The summary divides the conventional method into two phases. In the first phase, the teacher demonstrates, often working one to four problems, and the students observe passively; in the second phase, the students work independently, with the teacher possibly monitoring their work and giving feedback.

That description might easily have been written to describe U.S. mathematics lessons in 1900. Mathematics teaching in the United States clearly has not changed a great deal in a century. It continues to emphasize the execution of paper-and-pencil skills through demonstrations of procedures and repeated practice.

Teacher Preparation, Certification, and Professional Development

A bachelor's degree and a teaching certificate are required to teach in most public schools in the United States. Teaching certificates are granted by states, usually based on the completion of specific undergraduate coursework and field experience in schools. Some states also require that candidates pass an examination. A teaching certificate from one state is occasionally honored across state lines; states without reciprocity of certification commonly offer a provisional certificate to out-of-state teachers until they have met all the requirements. Some states also offer alternative routes to certification for prospective teachers with a bachelor's degree but lacking some of the requisite coursework or field experience.

Programs of teacher education have traditionally separated knowledge of mathematics from knowledge of pedagogy by offering separate courses in each.[78] A common practice in university-based programs has been for prospective teachers to take courses in mathematics from the mathematics department and courses in pedagogy from the college or department of education, which is where they also get field experience and do supervised teaching practice. The standards for both types of courses have, in recent years, been influenced by reports such as *A Call for Change*,[79] which listed expectations for the mathematics courses required in teacher preparation, and the *Professional Standards for Teaching Mathematics*,[80] which concentrated more on issues of pedagogy.

Nationally, two-year colleges have been urged to play a larger role in recruiting future elementary and middle school teachers and providing college-level mathematics courses for them.[81] At the same time, universities are exploring different ways of connecting courses on mathematics content and pedagogy and on giving students earlier and more intensive experience in school mathematics classes. Some recent programs have attempted to bring content and pedagogy together in both teacher preparation and professional development by considering the actual mathematical work of teaching.[82]

Although states have long set such requirements for teachers seeking certification, some have recently begun to impose higher standards for the knowledge teachers should have to teach children at a given age or grade level, requiring teachers to take specified courses and to pass assessments of their subject matter knowledge.[83] There is considerable variation across states as to how rigorous these requirements are. As of 1998, 31 states reported having standards for teacher certification, although in several the standards were not yet in effect. In 12 of the 31, there were specific standards for mathematics. Six other states were still developing standards.[84]

To be certified to teach elementary school, only 12 states require a minimum number of credits in mathematics (from 6 to 12 semester hours). The other states either specify a total number of credits drawn from five to eight fields (often with a major in one of the fields), impose their own standards rather than specifying courses, require a minimum number of credits in one unspecified field, or require the completion of an approved teacher education program. Thirty-seven states grant middle school certification, and the requirements fall into categories similar to those for elementary school. Eight of those states require a minimum number of credits in mathematics to teach in middle school (from 6 to 21 semester hours).

A highly influential report on the reform of teacher education was issued in 1986 by the Holmes Group, later the Holmes Partnership, a consortium of major research universities.[85] The report recommended that prospective teachers get a solid grounding in academic subjects as undergraduates, learning pedagogy as postgraduates. The report also encouraged the development of so-called professional development schools and other forms of cooperative partnerships between schools and universities. In part because of the Holmes report, some 300 schools of education created programs that went beyond the traditional four-year degree programs, included more study of subject matter, and gave more clinical training in schools.[86] Also, during the 1990s, more states began to require new teachers to have an undergraduate or graduate major in an academic subject they would be teaching rather than a major in education. As of 1998, 21 states required a major in the teaching field, and another 10 required either a major or a minor. In most states the requirement applies to teachers applying for middle or secondary certification, which usually cover grades 7 to 12. In four states an academic major is required for teachers at all grades K to 12.

In line with the trend toward more mandated assessments of students, as of 1998, 38 states required that prospective teachers pass an assessment, sometimes to be admitted to a program and other times after completing the program but before certification. Almost all of these states assess new teachers' "basic skills," and most of the others also assess "professional knowledge of teaching," "subject matter knowledge" (e.g., mathematics), or both. Eight states use portfolio assessment, with some requiring the portfolio at the end of preservice education and others requiring it during the first or second year of teaching. Thirteen states require classroom observation as part of the assessment for certification.

Despite the establishment of these increased standards, there is wide variation in the extent to which they are enforced:

> Whereas some states do not allow districts to hire unqualified teachers, others routinely allow the hiring of candidates who have not met their standards, even when qualified teachers are available. In Wisconsin and eleven other states, for example, no new elementary or secondary teachers were hired without a license in their field in 1994. By contrast, in Louisiana, 31% of new entrants were unlicensed and another 15% were hired on substandard licenses. At least six other states allowed 20% or more of new public school teachers to be hired without a license in their field.[87]

Of the 26 states reporting data in 1998 on the certification of their teachers at grades 7 and 8, only 6 states reported that 90% or more of these teachers were certified in mathematics, and only 10 states reported that more than 80% were certified. In response to urgent needs for teachers, states often issue so-called emergency credentials that bypass their own requirements. These credentials typically require only a bachelor's degree and enrollment in an approved program leading to some form of alternative certification. Many districts respond to the need for mathematics and science teachers by assigning teachers to teach outside their field.[88]

The evidence is mixed as to whether relatively fewer teachers are teaching outside their field today than a decade ago; data from different sources yield different numbers and contrasting evidence of change. In the 1996 NAEP mathematics assessment, teachers of 81% of the eighth graders in the sample reported that they were certified in mathematics, and the corresponding figure for fourth graders was 32%. Those numbers were not significantly different from what teachers had reported in 1992.[89] In contrast, the Council of Chief State School Officers reported in 1998 that 72% of all mathematics teachers at grades 7 and 8 in the 26 states providing data were reported as certified, 22% as not certified, and the remainder as having elementary school certification. In a corresponding survey in 1994, the percentage of certified teachers at those grades had been only 54, a significantly smaller number.[90] In other words, to judge by teachers' own reports, the situation has not changed, but to judge by reports from the states, it has improved at grades 7 and 8.

In the 1996 NAEP mathematics assessment, teachers were asked how many hours of professional development they had received in the previous 12 months. Nationally, 28% of the fourth graders in the sample had teachers who had received 16 or more hours of professional development in mathematics; for eighth graders, the percentage was 48. In 16 states, over half the eighth graders were taught by mathematics teachers who had received that much professional development.[91]

The number of states requiring that teachers participate in professional development activities for renewal of certification has been on the increase over the past decade. Currently, only Hawaii, Illinois, New Jersey, New Mexico, and New York do not have a policy on professional development for renewing certification. In half the states the policy is 6 semester credits every five years. Several states have higher requirements. North Carolina requires 15 credits every five years, and in Oregon, teachers must earn 24 quarter hours in their first three years of teaching.[92]

In an effort to encourage teachers to extend their professional development efforts, 30 states have adopted incentives for teachers certified by the National Board for Professional Teaching Standards, such as portability of certification, certification renewal, fee supports, and pay supplements.[93] Standards for National Board certification are available in mathematics for teachers of students ages 11 to 15. Certification at the elementary school level is general. Teachers seeking a certificate must submit a portfolio documenting their classroom practice and must go to an assessment center for a one-day series of exercises in which they demonstrate their knowledge of mathematical content and analyze student work.

There is a growing body of evidence suggesting that states and local districts "interested in improving student achievement may be well-advised to attend, at least in part, to the preparation and qualifications of the teachers they hire and retain in the profession."[94] A qualitative and quantitative analysis of data from a 50-state survey of policies, state case study analyses, the 1993-94 Schools and Staffing Surveys, and NAEP identified the percentage of teachers with full certification and a major in the field they teach as a strong and consistent predictor of student achievement in mathematics, considerably stronger than such factors as class sizes, pupil-teacher ratios, state per-pupil spending, or teachers' salaries.[95] This link between teacher qualification and student achievement raises the question of how good that achievement is.

Achievement

Since the early 1970s, a series of national and international assessments have provided a reasonably consistent picture of U.S. students' achievement in mathematics. As one analysis of these assessments puts it, the results "evoke both a sense of despair and of hope."[96] The despair comes from the generally low level of performance, the hope from signs that performance in some areas of mathematics and by some groups of students has been improving over the last decade.

The many mathematics assessments conducted since 1973 by NAEP demonstrate that student performance at each of the grade levels assessed is considerably below what mathematics teachers and the public would prefer. Since 1990, NAEP has included two separate components for mathematics: main NAEP and long-term trend NAEP. The long-term trend assessments use the same sets of questions first used in 1973, allowing comparison across time. The main assessments reflect more contemporary educational objectives and are used to collect both national and state data, including contextual data such as teaching practices, some of which are reported earlier in this chapter.[97] Except when we refer explicitly to the long-term trend assessments, the data reported here are from the main assessments.

In the 1996 mathematics assessment—the most recent main assessment to be thoroughly analyzed—across grades 4, 8, and 12, roughly 35% of the students were below the basic level of achievement and another 45% or so were at that level, which is defined as denoting "partial mastery of knowledge and skills that are fundamental for proficient work." In the same assessment, 21% of fourth graders and 24% of eighth graders were at or above the "proficient" level, where proficiency is defined as students having "demonstrated competency over challenging subject matter" and being "well prepared for the next level of schooling." Only 2% and 4% of fourth-grade and eighth-grade students, respectively, were doing advanced work significantly "beyond proficient grade-level mastery."[98]

Although overall levels of achievement are low, the main NAEP assessments in the 1990s revealed significant gains.[99] The gains between 1990 and 1996 have been estimated to be about one grade level.[100] According to the NAEP long-term trend, mathematics achievement improved between 1973 and 1996 at both the fourth-grade and eighth-grade levels.[101] Performance improved even more sharply from 1973 to 1996 among black and Hispanic students.[102] Although the gap between black students and white students had narrowed through the 1980s, it widened between 1990 and 1999, especially among students of the best-educated parents.[103] This disparity represents a serious challenge to U.S. education. In 1994, NAEP began collecting information on participation in Title I programs, programs designed to help disadvantaged students, and in 1996 on eligibility for free or reduced-priced lunches. At both grades 4 and 8, students who participated in Title I programs and students who were eligible for free or reduced-priced lunches scored lower than their nonparticipating or noneligible classmates.[104] The low mathematics achievement of poor children is embedded in the larger social issues of poverty and poses another serious challenge to U.S. education.

International comparisons of mathematics achievement demonstrate many of the same findings as the NAEP results. On several international mathematics assessments conducted since the 1970s, the overall performance of U.S. students has lagged behind the performance of students in other countries. In TIMSS, U.S. fourth graders performed above the international average of the 26 participating countries at fourth grade but still significantly below the levels of the top-performing countries. U.S. eighth graders performed slightly below the international average in mathematics among the 41 participating countries.

As this volume went to press, the results of TIMSS-R (Third International Mathematics and Science Study-Repeat), the 1999 version of TIMSS, had just been released. Between 1995 and 1999, there was no significant change in the mathematics achievement of U.S. eighth graders. Furthermore, the eighth graders in 1999, who compared quite well internationally in 1995 as fourth graders, were very much like the 1995 eighth graders, performing near the international average.[105]

One way to quantify U.S. students' performance is in terms of the average number of points they scored on the 1995 TIMSS assessment. Each student answered a subset of the TIMSS questions, and an average score was calculated for each question, with some questions worth more than one point. The U.S. fourth graders scored, on average, 71 out of the 113 points available on the TIMSS achievement test, which contained 102 questions.[106] That was about 4 points above the performance across all 26 countries, but it was 11 to 15 points below the performance of students in the top four countries (Singapore, Korea, Japan, and Hong Kong) and was in a band of performance comparable with that found in the Czech Republic, Ireland, and Canada. In the assessment of eighth graders, U.S. students scored, on average, 86 points out of the 162 available on the 151 TIMSS items, which was 3 points below the 41-country average. Students in the four top-scoring countries—Singapore, Japan, Korea, and Hong Kong—scored, on average, between 113 and 128 points.[107]

The performance of U.S. students in TIMSS differed markedly across core domains of mathematics. U.S. performance was above the international average on data representation, analysis, and probability and not significantly different from the international average on fractions, number sense, and algebra. Performance was below the international average on geometry, measurement, and proportionality.[108] For example, U.S. eighth graders had much weaker abilities, overall, than their counterparts in other countries to conceptualize measurement relationships, perform geometric transformations, and engage in other complex mathematical tasks. These kinds of abilities are among the learning goals called for by national documents setting forth standards and benchmarks for school mathematics and by many sets of state standards, indicating that many U.S. students are not now achieving the objectives of those standards.[109]

Interestingly, the variance of U.S. scores in the TIMSS results was not markedly greater than in other countries. There was, however, considerable variability in scores between states. A study linking state NAEP scores at grade 8 with TIMSS scores showed that the top-scoring states on NAEP performed quite well internationally, with only 6 of 41 countries scoring significantly higher. In contrast, low-scoring states scored significantly higher than as few as 3 of 41 countries.[110] These results suggest that national averages may miss important aspects of U.S. mathematics education.

Even state averages do not tell the whole story, however. A consortium of districts in suburban Chicago participated in TIMSS so that they might be treated as a country in the analysis. Their performance was exceptional on the mathematics assessments at both grades 4 and 8, with only Singapore scoring significantly higher. Although some of their success is clearly attributable to being relatively wealthy districts, socioeconomic factors explained only 25% of the differences in scores at fourth grade and 50% of the differences in scores at eighth grade.[111]

More generally, variance in student scores was strongly linked to the specific classes a student took (for example, regular mathematics versus algebra in middle school or junior high) and to differences among schools. In particular, 64% of the variance in U.S. student mathematics achievement at eighth grade can be explained by differences between schools or classes. In Japan, in contrast, only 7% of the variance in student mathematics achievement was between schools or classes.[112] These findings suggest that many U.S. students are not being given the educational opportunities they need to achieve at high levels.[113]

Coordinating Improvement Efforts

In the late 1850s, the city of Chicago started a massive project to replace its dirt (and often mud) streets with a more permanent road and sidewalk system. The city had to raise the roadbed substantially and lift the existing buildings so that they were level with the new sidewalks. The zenith of this undertaking was the lifting of the Tremont Hotel in 1858, organized by George Pullman. While hotel patrons ate breakfast, Pullman's crew of 1,200 men carefully turned some 5,000 jackscrews to raise the building evenly.

Improving the U.S. system of school mathematics demands not simply effort but coordination.

As with raising the Tremont Hotel, improving the U.S. system of school mathematics demands not simply effort but coordination. Although many individuals have worked diligently over the past several decades to change the ways in which mathematics is taught and learned, the evidence clearly indicates that considerable improvement is still necessary. Across the country, schools and teachers face the substantial challenge of providing all children with the opportunity to become mathematically proficient. Much of the difficulty in meeting that challenge arises because the effort to date has not been concerted. The U.S. system of school mathematics cannot be made to operate better by fixing one tiny piece at a time; it requires a thorough, methodical overhaul.[114]

It requires a thorough, methodical overhaul.

Authority in the U.S. system is widely dispersed, with states, districts, the federal government, textbook and test publishers, professional and political organizations, teachers, and parents and other caregivers each trying to exercise control of the part of the system within their purview. We urge, therefore, all who are attempting to improve mathematics learning in grades pre-K to 8 to reflect on the observations made in this report and to consider how they might connect and coordinate their efforts with those of others.

In subsequent chapters we set forth important research, theory, and organizing principles intended to ground future efforts in fact and principled argument, to make assumptions more explicit, and to bring greater coherence to the system. We would like to see an independent group of recognized standing conduct continuing, ongoing assessment of the progress made over the coming years in meeting the goal of mathematical proficiency for all U.S. schoolchildren. Such an assessment would help enormously in the coordination of efforts to make school mathematics a better functioning system for everyone.

Before considering the issues of learning and teaching that contribute to the development of mathematical proficiency, we devote the next chapter to considering the mathematical landscape upon which our later analyses are built. To understand how it is that students become proficient and the challenges they face in doing so, it is important to understand the mathematics with which they are engaged. Because we have chosen to focus on proficiency with number, chapter 3 lays out the mathematics of number.

Notes

1. Robitaille, 1997; Stigler and Hiebert, 1999; U.S. Department of Education, 1998b, 1999a, 1999b.
2. Howson, 1995; Schmidt, McKnight, and Raizen, 1997.
3. An analysis of data from the Second International Mathematics Study (SIMS) examined features such as time for mathematics instruction, class size, and teacher preparation, and other instructional variables and concluded that none of them alone could explain differences in achievement across countries (McKnight, Crosswhite, Dossey, Kifer, Swafford, Travers, and Cooney, 1987).
4. National Council of Teachers of Mathematics, 1989.
5. National Council of Teachers of Mathematics, 1991.
6. National Council of Teachers of Mathematics, 1995.
7. National Council of Teachers of Mathematics, 2000.
8. See http://www.edc.org/mcc/currcula.htm for information on the 13 NSF projects.
9. See Jennings, 1998. In making the case for national standards and describing the background behind the movement, Ravitch, 1995, emphasizes that when the president and the governors established national education goals in 1990, mathematics was the only subject matter for which "educators were ready to say what children should learn and teachers should teach" (p. 121).
10. Elmore and Rothman, 1999, p. 1.
11. *A Nation at Risk*: National Commission on Excellence in Education, 1983; America 2000: U.S. Department of Education, 1991; Goals 2000: U.S. Department of Education, 1998a.
12. Blank, Manise, and Brathwaite, 2000, pp. viii–xi. See also Orlofsky and Olson, 2001.
13. See the individual state reports in Raimi and Braden, 1998.
14. Fordham Foundation, 1997–98; Gandal, 1997; Joftus and Berman, 1998; Raimi and Braden, 1998; for an analysis of the divergence across the three sets of ratings, see Camilli and Firestone, 1999.
15. Pimentel and Arsht, 1998.
16. Marzano, Kendall, and Gaddy, 1999.
17. Dossey, 1997, p. 40.
18. McKnight, Crosswhite, Dossey, Kifer, Swafford, Travers, and Cooney, 1987, p. 74; Suydam, 1985; Tyson and Woodward, 1989; Woodward and Elliott, 1990.
19. Council of Chief State School Officers, 1998.
20. Woodward and Elliot, 1990; Tyson and Woodward, 1989. The observations in this paragraph are based on a review by Grouws and Cebula, 2000.
21. Fey, 1980.
22. Grouws and Smith, 2000.

23. Schwille, Porter, Belli, Floden, Freeman, Knappen, Kuhs, and Schmidt, 1983; Stodolsky, 1988; Sosniak and Stodolsky, 1993.

24. Tyson-Bernstein, 1988, p. 7.

25. Fuson, Stigler, and Bartsch, 1988; McKnight, Crosswhite, Dossey, Kifer, Swafford, Travers, and Cooney, 1987; McKnight and Schmidt, 1998; Peak, 1996.

26. Flanders, 1987; Fuson, Stigler, and Bartsch, 1988; Schmidt, McKnight, and Raizen, 1997.

27. Fuson, Stigler, and Bartsch, 1988; Schmidt, McKnight, Cogan, Jakwerth, and Houang, 1999; Schmidt, McKnight, and Raizen, 1997.

28. Levin, 1989; Levin and Mayer, 1993; Mayer, 1993.

29. Reys, 2000.

30. U.S. Department of Education, Mathematics and Science Expert Panel, 1999.

31. Mathematically Correct, 2000.

32. American Association for the Advancement of Science, 2000a, 2000b; Clopton, McKeown, McKeown, and Clopton, 2000a, 2000b.

33. The current center is the National Center for Improving Student Learning and Achievement in Mathematics and Science at the University of Wisconsin-Madison. For information on currently funded projects, see http://forum.swarthmore.edu/mathed/curriculum.dev.html. [July 20, 2001].

34. For example, the University of Chicago School Mathematics project and the Mathematics in Context project at the University of Wisconsin.

35. Tyson-Bernstein, 1988, pp. 17–36.

36. Glaser and Silver, 1994, p. 403.

37. Mitchell, Hawkins, Jakwerth, Stancavage, and Dossey, 1999, pp. 260–264.

38. Mitchell, Hawkins, Jakwerth, Stancavage, and Dossey, 1999, p. 261. Moderate testing is associated with higher achievement even when controlling for socioeconomic factors. See Mullis, Jenkins, and Johnson, 1994, p. 61.

39. For a discussion of these calls, see Elmore and Rothman, 1999.

40. Mitchell, Hawkins, Jakwerth, Stancavage, and Dossey, 1999, p. 262.

41. Dossey, 1997, p. 37.

42. Council of Chief State School Officers, 1998.

43. Jerald, Curran, and Boser, 1999, p. 81. See Education Commission of the States, 2000, for a thorough description of state policies and actions.

44. Sandham, 1999.

45. Gehring, 2000.

46. Bishop, 1997.

47. Darling-Hammond, 1999, p. 33.

48. Steinberg, 1999.

49. This terminology was part of the Title I law; Elmore and Rothman, 1999.

50. Archer, 1997.

51. Musick, 1997.

52. Standardized tests are tests that are "administered and scored under conditions uniform to all students" (U.S. Congress, Office of Technology Assessment, 1992, p. 5).

53. Romberg and Wilson, 1992.

54. Rothman, 1995; U.S. Congress, Office of Technology Assessment, 1992, chap. 6.
55. Anastasi, 1988; Crocker, and Algina, 1986.
56. Rothman, 1995, p. 5.
57. Heubert and Hauser, 1998; Pullin, 1993.
58. Elmore and Rothman, 1999.
59. Except for the data on teachers' knowledge of the 1989 NCTM standards, the remaining data in this section are taken from Mitchell, Hawkins, Jakwerth, Stancavage, and Dossey, 1999.
60. Council of Chief State School Officers, 2000, p. 10.
61. Mitchell, Hawkins, Jakwerth, Stancavage, and Dossey, 1999, pp. 251–252.
62. Hawkins, Stancavage, and Dossey, 1998, p. 41.
63. Antil, Jenkins, Wayne, and Vadasy, 1998.
64. Stigler and Hiebert, 1999, pp. 104-106.
65. Cuban, 1993; Hoetker and Ahlbrand, 1969.
66. Hoetker and Ahlbrand, 1969; Tharp and Gallimore, 1988.
67. Stodolsky, 1988.
68. Weiss, 1978.
69. Stake and Easley, 1978.
70. Welch, 1978, p. 6.
71. Fey, 1979, p. 494.
72. National Advisory Committee on Mathematical Education, 1975, p. 77.
73. Stigler, Gonzales, Kawanaka, Knoll, and Serrano, 1999.
74. Stigler and Hiebert, 1999.
75. Stigler and Hiebert, 1999, p. 61.
76. Stigler and Hiebert, 1999, p. 57.
77. Dixon, Carnine, Kameenui, Simmons, Lee, Wallin, and Chard, 1998a, 1998b.
78. Swafford, 1995.
79. Leitzel, 1991.
80. National Council of Teachers of Mathematics, 1991.
81. Raychowdhury, 1998.
82. See, for example, National Research Council, 2001; Conference Board of the Mathematical Sciences, 2000. See Ferrini-Mundy and Findell, 2001, for a discussion of the principles behind these and other approaches to improving the connection between the mathematical education of teachers and the mathematics used in classrooms.
83. See http://www.ccsso.org/intasc.html [July 20, 2001] for information on model standards and assessments of beginning teachers promoted by the Interstate New Teacher Assessment and Standards Consortium.
84. Council of Chief State School Officers, 1998. Unless otherwise indicated, the data on certification come from this document.
85. Holmes Group, 1986.
86. Darling-Hammond, 1997.
87. Darling-Hammond, 1999, p. 15.
88. Blank and Langeson, 1999, p. 66.

89. Hawkins, Stancavage, and Dossey, 1998, p. 19.
90. Blank and Langeson, 1999, p. 64.
91. Blank and Langeson, 1999, p. 73.
92. Council of Chief State School Officers, 1998, p. 26.
93. Jerald, Curran, and Boser, 1999, p. 116. For information on the National Board for Professional Teaching Standards, see http://www.nbpts.org [July 20, 2001] or Kelly, 1995.
94. Darling-Hammond, 1999, pp. 38–39.
95. Darling-Hammond, 1999, p. 29.
96. Dossey and Mullis, 1997, p. 20.
97. Campbell, Voelkl, and Donahue, 2000.
98. Reese, Miller, Mazzeo, and Dossey, 1997, p. 53.
99. Reese, Miller, Mazzeo, and Dossey, 1997.
100. Dossey, 2000, p. 31.
101. Campbell, Voelkl, and Donahue, 2000.
102. Campbell, Voelkl, and Donahue, 2000, p. 62–64. See also Secada, 1992; Silver, Strutchens, and Zawojewski, 1997; Strutchens and Silver, 2000.
103. Zernike, 2000.
104. Reese, Miller, Mazzeo, and Dossey, 1997, pp. 38–39.
105. U.S. Department of Education, 2000b.
106. The values in the text are computed from Mullis, Martin, Beaton, Gonzalez, Kelly, & Smith, 1997, p. B-3. For similar discussions, see National Research Council, 1999a, p. 21; National Council of Teachers of Mathematics, 1997.
107. The values in the text are computed from Beaton, Mullis, Martin, Gonzalez, Kelly, & Smith, 1996, p. B-3. For similar discussions, see National Research Council, 1999a, p. 21; National Council of Teachers of Mathematics, 1996.
108. U.S. Department of Education, 2000a.
109. National Research Council, 1999a, p. 27; Wilson and Blank, 1999, pp. 2–3.
110. National Education Goals Panel, 1998.
111. Kimmelman, Kroeze, Schmidt, van der Ploeg, McNeely, and Tan, 1999.
112. Martin, Mullis, Gregory, Hoyle, and Shen, in press. The Second International Mathematics Study produced similar results (McKnight, Crosswhite, Dossey, Kifer, Swafford, Travers, and Cooney, 1987, pp. 108–109).
113. National Research Council, 1999a, p. 20.
114. The National Research Council, 1999b, put forward a Strategic Education Research Program that aims to coordinate improvement efforts through networks of committed education researchers, practitioners, and policy makers.

References

American Association for the Advancement of Science. (2000a). *Algebra for all—Not with today's textbooks, says AAAS* [On-line]. Available: http://www.project2061.org/newsinfo/press/r1000426.htm. [July 10, 2001].

American Association for the Advancement of Science. (2000b). *Middle grades mathematics textbooks: A benchmarks-based evaluation* [On-line]. Available: http://www.project2061.org/matheval/default.htm. [July 10, 2001].

Anastasi, A. (1988). *Psychological testing.* New York: Macmillan.

Antil, L. R., Jenkins, J. R., Wayne, S. K., & Vadasy, P. F. (1998). Cooperative learning: Prevalence, conceptualizations, and the relation between research and practice. *American Educational Research Journal, 35,* 419–454.

Archer, J. (1997, January 15). States struggle to ensure data make the grade. *Education Week* [On-line]. Available: http://www.edweek.com/ew/1997/16data.h16. [July 10, 2001].

Beaton, A. E., Mullis, I. V. S., Martin, M. O., Gonzalez, E. J., Kelly, D. L., & Smith, T. A. (1996). *Mathematics achievement in the middle school years: IEA's Third International Mathematics and Science Study (TIMSS).* Chestnut Hill, MA: Boston College.

Bishop, J. H. (1997). The effect of national standards and curriculum-based exams on achievement. *American Economic Review, 87,* 260–264.

Blank, R. K., & Langeson, D. (1999). *State indicators of science and mathematics education 1999: State-by-state trends and new indicators from the 1997–98 school year.* Washington, DC: Council of Chief State School Officers. Available: http://www.ccsso.org/SciMathIndicators99.html. [July 10, 2001].

Blank, R. K., Manise, J., & Brathwaite, B. C. (2000). *State education indicators with a focus on Title I: 1999.* Washington, DC: Council of Chief State School Officers. Available: http://www.ccsso.org/99Indicators.html. [July 10, 2001].

Camilli, G., & Firestone, W. A. (1999). Values and state ratings: An examination of the state-by-state education indicators in Quality Counts. *Educational Measurement: Issues and Practice, 18*(4), 17–25.

Campbell, J. R., Voelkl, K. E., & Donahue, P. L. (2000). *NAEP 1996 trends in academic progress* (NCES 97-985r). Washington, DC: National Center for Education Statistics. Available: http://nces.ed.gov/spider/webspider/97985r.shtml. [July 10, 2001].

Clopton, P., McKeown, E. H., McKeown, M., & Clopton, J. (2000a). *Mathematically correct Algebra 1 reviews* [On-line]. Available: http://www.mathematicallycorrect.com/algebra.htm. [July 10, 2001].

Clopton, P., McKeown, E., McKeown, M., & Clopton, J. (2000b). *Mathematically correct mathematics program reviews for grades 2, 5, and 7* [On-line]. Available: http://www.mathematicallycorrect.com/books.htm. [July 10, 2001].

Conference Board of the Mathematical Sciences. (2000, September). *CBMS Mathematical Education of Teachers Project draft report* [On-line]. Available: http://www.maa.org/cbms/metdraft/index.htm. [January 3, 2001].

Council of Chief State School Officers. (2000). *Using data on enacted curriculum in mathematics & science.* Washington, DC: Author. Available: http://www.ccsso.org/pdfs/finalsummaryreport.pdf. [July 10, 2001].

Council of Chief State School Officers, State Education Assessment Center. (1998). *Key state education policies on K-12 education.* Washington, DC: Author. Available: http://publications.ccsso.org/ccsso/publication_detail.cfm?PID=187. [July 10, 2001].

Crocker, L., & Algina, J. (1986). *Introduction to classical and modern test theory.* New York: CBS College Publishing.

Cuban, L. (1993). *How teachers taught: Constancy and change in American classrooms, 1890– 1990* (2nd ed.). New York: Teachers College Press.

Darling-Hammond, L. (1997). *The right to learn: A blueprint for creating schools that work.* San Francisco: Jossey-Bass.

Darling-Hammond, L. (1999, December). *Teacher quality and student achievement: A review of state policy evidence.* Seattle: Center for the Study of Teaching and Policy. Available: http://depts.washington.edu/ctpmail/ or http://olam.ed.asu.edu/epaa/v8n1/. [July 10, 2001].

Dixon, R. C., Carnine, D. W., Kameenui, E. J., Simmons, D. C., Lee, D.-S., Wallin, J., & Chard, D. (1998a). *Report to the California State Board of Education: Review of high quality experimental mathematics research.* Eugene, OR: National Center to Improve the Tools of Educators. Available: http://idea.uoregon.edu/~ncite/documents/math/ math.html. [July 10, 2001].

Dixon, R. C., Carnine, D. W., Kameenui, E. J., Simmons, D. C., Lee, D.-S., Wallin, J., & Chard, D. (1998b). *Report to the California State Board of Education: Review of high quality experimental research. Executive summary.* Eugene, OR: National Center to Improve the Tools of Educators. Available: http://idea.uoregon.edu/~ncite/documents/ math/math.html. [July 10, 2001].

Dossey, J. A. (1997). *Essential skills in mathematics: A comparative analysis of American and Japanese assessments of eighth-graders* (NCES 97-885). Washington, DC: National Center for Education Statistics. Available: http://nces.ed.gov/spider/webspider/97885.shtml. [July 10, 2001].

Dossey, J. A. (2000). The state of NAEP mathematics findings. In E. A. Silver & P. A. Kenney (Eds.), *Results from the seventh mathematics assessment of the National Assessment of Educational Progress* (pp. 23–43). Reston, VA: National Council of Teachers of Mathematics.

Dossey, J. A., & Mullis, I. V. S. (1997). NAEP Mathematics—1990–1992: The national, trial state, and trend assessments. In P. A. Kenney & E. A. Silver (Eds.), *Results from the sixth mathematics assessment of the National Assessment of Educational Progress* (pp. 17– 32). Reston, VA: National Council of Teachers of Mathematics.

Education Commission of the States. (August 2000). *State takeovers and reconstitutions* (Policy Brief 1359). Denver: Author. Available: http://www.ecs.org/clearinghouse/ 13/59/1359.htm. [July 10, 2001].

Elmore, R. F., & Rothman, R. (Eds.). (1999). *Teaching, testing, and learning: A guide for states and school districts.* Washington, DC: National Academy Press. Available: http:// books.nap.edu/catalog/9609.html. [July 10, 2001].

Ferrini-Mundy, J., & Findell, B. (2001). The mathematical education of prospective teachers of secondary school mathematics: Old assumptions, new challenges. In *CUPM discussion papers about mathematics and the mathematical sciences in 2010: What should students know?* (pp. 31–41). Washington, DC: Mathematical Association of America. Available: http://www.maa.org/news/cupm_text.html. [July 10, 2001].

Fey, J. T. (1979). Mathematics teaching today: Perspectives from three national surveys. *Mathematics Teacher, 72,* 490–504.

Fey, J. T. (1980). Mathematics education research on curriculum and instruction. In R. J. Shumway (Ed.), *Research in mathematics education* (pp. 388–432). Reston, VA: National Council of Teachers of Mathematics.

Flanders, J. R. (1987). How much of the content in mathematics textbooks is new? *Arithmetic Teacher, 35*(1), 18–23.

Fordham Foundation. (1997-1998). *Evaluation of state standards for math, English, science and history.* Washington, DC: Author.

Fuson, K. C., Stigler, J., & Bartsch, K. (1988). Brief report: Grade placement of addition and subtraction topics in Japan, mainland China, the Soviet Union, Taiwan, and the United States. *Journal for Research in Mathematics Education, 19*, 449–456.

Gandal, M. (1997). *Making standards matter: An annual fifty-state report on efforts to raise academic standards.* Washington, DC: American Federation of Teachers.

Gehring, J. (2000, February 2). "High stakes" exams seen as test for voc. ed. *Education Week* [On-line]. Available: http://www.edweek.org/ew/ewstory.cfm?slug=21voctest.h19. [July 10, 2001].

Glaser, R., & Silver, E. A. (1994). Assessment, testing, and instruction: Retrospect and prospect. In L. Darling-Hammond (Ed.), *Review of research in education* (vol. 20, pp. 393–419). Washington, DC: American Educational Research Association.

Grouws, D. A., & Cebulla, K. J. (2000). Elementary and middle school mathematics at the crossroads. In T. L. Good (Ed.), *American education: Yesterday, today, and tomorrow* (Ninety-ninth Yearbook of the National Society for the Study of Education, Part 2, pp. 209–255). Chicago: University of Chicago Press.

Grouws, D. A., & Smith, M. A. (2000). NAEP findings on the preparation and practices of mathematics teachers. In E. A. Silver & P. A. Kenney (Eds.), *Results from the seventh mathematics assessment of the National Assessment of Educational Progress* (pp. 107-139). Reston, VA: National Council of Teachers of Mathematics.

Hawkins, E. F., Stancavage, F. B., & Dossey, J. A. (1998). *School policies and practices affecting instruction in mathematics* (NCES 98-495). Washington, DC: National Center for Education Statistics. Available: http://nces.ed.gov/spider/webspider/98495.shtml. [July 10, 2001].

Heubert, J. P., & Hauser, R. M. (Eds.). (1998). *High stakes: Testing for tracking, promotion, and graduation.* Washington, DC: National Academy Press. Available: http://books.nap.edu/catalog/6336.html. [July 10, 2001].

Hoetker, J., & Ahlbrand, W. (1969). The persistence of the recitation. *American Educational Research Journal, 6*, 145–167.

Holmes Group. (1986). *Tomorrow's teachers.* East Lansing, MI: Author. (ERIC Document Reproduction Service No. ED 270 454).

Howson, G. (1995). *Mathematics textbooks: A comparative study of grade 8 texts* (TIMSS Monograph No. 3). Vancouver: Pacific Educational Press.

Jennings, J. F. (1998). *Why national standards and tests? Politics and the quest for better schools.* Thousand Oaks, CA: Sage Publications.

Jerald, C. D., Curran, B. K., & Boser, U. (1999, January 11). The state of the states [Quality Counts '99]. *Education Week*, pp. 106–123. Available: http://www.edweek.org/sreports/qc99/states/indicators/in-intro.htm. [July 10, 2001].

Joftus, S., & Berman, I. (1998). *Great expectations? Defining and assessing rigor in state standards for mathematics and English language arts.* Washington, DC: Council for Basic Education.

Kelly, J. A. (1995). The National Board for Professional Teaching Standards: Making professional development "professional." In I. M. Carl (Ed.), *Prospects for school mathematics* (pp. 202–215). Reston, VA: National Council of Teachers of Mathematics.

Kimmelman, P., Kroeze, D., Schmidt, W., van der Ploeg, A., McNeely, M., & Tan, A. (1999). *A first look at what we can learn from high performing school districts: An analysis of TIMSS data from the First in the World Consortium.* Jessup, MD: U.S. Department of Education.

Leitzel, J. R. C. (Ed.). (1991). *A call for change: Recommendations for the mathematical preparation of teachers of mathematics* (MAA Reports, vol. 3). Washington, DC: Mathematical Association of America.

Levin, J. R. (1989). A transfer-appropriate processing perspective of pictures in prose. In H. Mandl & J. R. Levin (Eds.), *Knowledge acquisition from text and pictures* (pp. 83–100). Amsterdam: Elsevier.

Levin, J. R., & Mayer, R. E. (1993). Understanding illustrations in text. In B. K. Britton, A. Woodward, & M. Binkley (Eds.), *Learning from textbooks: Theory and practice* (pp. 95–113). Hillsdale, NJ: Erlbaum.

Martin, M. O., Mullis, I. V. S., Gregory, K. D., Hoyle, C. D., & Shen, C. (in press). *Effective schools in science and mathematics: IEA's Third International Mathematics and Science Study.* Chestnut Hill, MA: Boston College.

Marzano, R. J., Kendall, J. S., & Gaddy, B. B. (1999). *Essential knowledge: The debate over what American students should know.* Aurora, CO: Mid-Continent Research for Education and Learning.

Mathematically Correct. (2000). *Open letter on the Department of Education's list of programs* [On-line]. Available: http://mathematicallycorrect.com/nation.htm#doesham.

Mayer, R. E. (1993). Illustrations that instruct. In R. Glaser (Ed.), *Advances in instructional psychology* (vol. 4, pp. 253–284). Hillsdale, NJ: Erlbaum.

McKnight, C. C., Crosswhite, F. J., Dossey, J. A., Kifer, E., Swafford, J. O., Travers, K. T., & Cooney, T. J. (1987). *The underachieving curriculum: Assessing U.S. school mathematics from an international perspective.* Champaign, IL: Stipes Publishing.

McKnight, C. C., & Schmidt, W. H. (1998). Facing facts in U.S. science and mathematics education: Where we stand, where we want to go. *Journal of Science Education and Technology, 7*(1), 57–76.

Mitchell, J. H., Hawkins, E. F., Jakwerth, P. M., Stancavage, F. B., & Dossey, J. A. (1999). *Student work and teacher practices in mathematics* (NCES 1999-453). Washington, DC: National Center for Education Statistics. Available: http://nces.ed.gov/spider/webspider/1999453.shtml. [July 10, 2001].

Mullis, I. V. S., Jenkins, F., & Johnson, E. G. (1994). *Effective schools in mathematics: Perspectives from the NAEP 1992 assessment* (NCES 94-701). Washington, DC: National Center for Education Statistics.

Mullis, I. V. S., Martin, M. O., Beaton, A. E., Gonzalez, E. J., Kelly, D. L., & Smith, T. A. (1997). *Mathematics achievement in the primary school years: IEA's Third International Mathematics and Science Study (TIMSS).* Chestnut Hill, MA: Boston College.

Musick, M. (1997). *Setting education standards high enough.* Atlanta: Southern Regional Education Board. Available: http://www.sreb.org/main/highschools/accountability/settingstandardshigh.asp. [July 10, 2001].

National Advisory Committee on Mathematical Education. (1975). *Overview and analysis of school mathematics, grades K-12.* Washington, DC: Conference Board of the Mathematical Sciences.

National Commission on Excellence in Education. (1983). *A nation at risk: The imperative for educational reform.* Washington, DC: U.S. Government Printing Office. Available: http://www.ed.gov/pubs/NatAtRisk/. [July 10, 2001].

National Council of Teachers of Mathematics. (1989). *Curriculum and evaluation standards for school mathematics.* Reston, VA: Author. Available: http://standards.nctm.org/Previous/CurrEvStds/index.htm. [July 10, 2001].

National Council of Teachers of Mathematics. (1991). *Professional standards for teaching mathematics.* Reston, VA: Author. Available: http://standards.nctm.org/Previous/ProfStds/index.htm. [July 10, 2001].

National Council of Teachers of Mathematics. (1995). *Assessment standards for school mathematics.* Reston, VA: Author. Available: http://standards.nctm.org/Previous/AssStds/index.htm. [July 10, 2001].

National Council of Teachers of Mathematics. (1996). *U.S. mathematics teachers respond to the Third International Mathematics and Science Study: Grade 8 results* [On-line]. Available: http://www.nctm.org/news/releases/timss_eighth_grade.htm. [July 10, 2001].

National Council of Teachers of Mathematics. (1997). *U.S. mathematics teachers respond to the Third International Mathematics and Science Study: Grade 4 results* [On-line]. Available: http://www.nctm.org/news/releases/timss-4th-pg01.htm. [July 10, 2001].

National Council of Teachers of Mathematics. (2000). *Principles and standards for school mathematics.* Reston, VA: Author. Available: http://standards.nctm.org/document/index.htm. [July 10, 2001].

National Education Goals Panel. (1998). *Mathematics and science achievement state by state, 1998.* Washington, DC: Government Printing Office. Available: http://www.negp.gov/reports/goal3_98.htm. [July 10, 2001].

National Research Council. (1999a). *Global perspectives for local action: Using TIMSS to improve U.S. mathematics and science education.* Washington, DC: National Academy Press. Available: http://books.nap.edu/catalog/9605.html. [July 10, 2001].

National Research Council. (1999b). *Improving student learning: A strategic plan for education research and its utilization.* Washington, DC: National Academy Press. Available: http://books.nap.edu/catalog/6488.html. [July 10, 2001].

National Research Council. (2001). *Knowing and learning mathematics for teaching: Proceedings of a workshop.* Washington, DC: National Academy Press. Available: http://books.nap.edu/catalog/10050.html. [July 10, 2001].

Orlofsky, G. F., & Olson, L. (2001, January 11). The state of the states [Quality Counts 2001]. *Education Week*, pp. 86-88. Available: http://www.edweek.com/sreports/qc01/articles/qc01story.cfm?slug=17states.h20. [July 10, 2001].

Peak, L. (1996). *Pursuing excellence: A study of U.S. eighth-grade mathematics and science teaching, learning, curriculum, and achievement in an international context.* Washington, DC: National Center for Educational Statistics. Available: http://nces.ed.gov/spider/webspider/97198.shtml. [July 10, 2001].

Pimentel, S., & Arsht, L. A. (1998, November 11). Don't be confused by the rankings; focus on results. *Education Week* [On-line]. Available: http://www.edweek.org/ew/1998/11arsht.h18. [July 10, 2001].

Pullin, D. C. (1993). Legal and ethical issues in mathematics assessment. In Mathematical Sciences Education Board, *Measuring what counts: A conceptual guide for mathematics assessment* (pp. 201–223). Washington, DC: National Academy Press. Available: http://books.nap.edu/catalog/2235.html. [July 10, 2001].

Raimi, R. A., & Braden L. S. (1998). *State mathematics standards: An appraisal of math standards in 46 states, the District of Columbia, and Japan* (Fordham Report 2, No. 3). Washington, DC: Fordham Foundation. Available: http://www.edexcellence.net/standards/math/math.htm. [July 10, 2001].

Ravitch, D. (1995). *National standards in American education: A citizen's guide.* Washington, DC: Brookings Institution.

Raychowdhury, P. N. (Ed.). (1998). The integral role of the two-year college in the science and mathematics preparation of prospective teachers [Special issue]. *Journal of Mathematics and Science: Collaborative Explorations, 1*(2).

Reese, C. M., Miller, K. E., Mazzeo, J., & Dossey, J. A. (1997). *NAEP 1996 mathematics report card for the nation and the states* (NCES 97-488). Washington, DC: National Center for Education Statistics. Available: http://nces.ed.gov/spider/webspider/97488.shtml. [July 10, 2001].

Reys, R. R. (2000). Letter to the editor. *Journal for Research in Mathematics Education, 31,* 511–512.

Robitaille, D. F. (Ed.). (1997). *National contexts for mathematics and science education: An encyclopedia of the education systems participating in TIMSS.* Vancouver, Canada: Pacific Educational Press.

Romberg, T. A., & Wilson, L. D. (1992). Alignment of tests with the standards. *Arithmetic Teacher, 40*(1), 18–22.

Rothman, R. (1995). *Measuring up: Standards, assessment, and school reform.* San Francisco: Jossey-Bass.

Sandham, J. L. (1999, July 14). In first for states, Florida releases graded "report cards" for schools. *Education Week* [On-line]. Available: http://edweek.org/ew/1999/42fla.h18. [July 10, 2001].

Schmidt, W. H., McKnight, C. C., Cogan, L. S., Jakwerth, P. M., & Houang, R. T. (1999). *Facing the consequences: Using TIMSS for a closer look at mathematics and science education.* Dordrecht: Kluwer.

Schmidt, W. H., McKnight, C. C., & Raizen, S. A. (1997). *A splintered vision: An investigation of U.S. science and mathematics education.* Dordrecht: Kluwer.

Schwille, J., Porter, A., Belli, G., Floden, R., Freeman, D., Knappen, L., Kuhs, T., & Schmidt, W. (1983). Teachers as policy brokers in the content of elementary school mathematics. In L. S. Shulman & G. Sykes (Eds.), *Handbook of teaching and policy* (pp. 370–391). New York: Longman.

Secada, W. G. (1992). Race, ethnicity, social class, language, and achievement in mathematics. In D. Grouws (Ed.), *Handbook of research on mathematics teaching and learning* (pp. 623–660). New York: Macmillan.

Silver, E. A., Strutchens, M. E., & Zawojewski, J. S. (1997). NAEP findings regarding race/ethnicity and gender: Affective issues, mathematics performance, and instructional context. In P. A. Kenney & E. A. Silver (Eds.), *Results from the sixth mathematics assessment of the National Assessment of Educational Progress* (pp. 33–59). Reston, VA: National Council of Teachers of Mathematics.

Sosniak, L. A., & Stodolsky, S. S. (1993). Teachers and textbooks: Materials use in four fourth-grade classrooms. *Elementary School Journal, 93*, 249–275.

Stake, R., & Easley, J. (Eds.). (1978). *Case studies in science education.* Urbana: University of Illinois.

Steinberg, J. (1999, December 3). Academic standards eased as a fear of failure spreads. *The New York Times*, p. A1.

Stigler, J. W., Gonzales, P., Kawanaka, T., Knoll, S., & Serrano, A. (1999). *The TIMSS Videotape Classroom Study: Methods and findings from an exploratory research project on eighth-grade mathematics instruction in Germany, Japan, and the United States.* Washington, DC: National Center for Education Statistics. Available: http://nces.ed.gov/timss. [July 10, 2001].

Stigler, J. W., & Hiebert, J. (1999). *The teaching gap: Best ideas from the world's teachers for improving education in the classroom.* New York: Free Press.

Stodolsky, S. S. (1988). *The subject matters: Classroom activity in math and social studies.* Chicago: University of Chicago Press.

Strutchens, M. E., & Silver, E. A. (2000). NAEP findings regarding race/ethnicity: Students' performance, school experiences, and attitudes and beliefs. In E. A. Silver & P. A. Kenney (Eds.), *Results from the seventh mathematics assessment of the National Assessment of Educational Progress* (pp. 45–72). Reston, VA: National Council of Teachers of Mathematics.

Suydam, M. N. (1985). *Research in instructional materials for mathematics* (ERIC/SMEAC Special Digest No. 3). Columbus, OH: ERIC Clearinghouse for Science, Mathematics, and Environmental Education.

Swafford, J. O. (1995). Teacher preparation. In I. M. Carl (Ed.), *Prospects for school mathematics* (pp. 157–174). Reston, VA: National Council of Teachers of Mathematics.

Tharp, R. G., & Gallimore, R. (1988). *Rousing minds to life: Teaching, learning, and schooling in social context.* New York: Cambridge University Press.

Tyson, H., & Woodward, A. (1989). Why students aren't learning very much from textbooks. *Educational Leadership, 47*, 14–17.

Tyson-Bernstein, H. (1988). *A conspiracy of good intentions: America's textbook fiasco.* Washington, DC: Council for Basic Education.

U.S. Congress, Office of Technology Assessment. (1992, February). *Testing in American schools: Asking the right questions* (OTA-SET-519). Washington, DC: U.S. Government Printing Office.

U.S. Department of Education. (1991). *America 2000: An education strategy.* Washington, DC: U.S. Government Printing Office.

U.S. Department of Education. (1998a). *Goals 2000: Reforming education to improve student achievement.* Washington, DC: U.S. Government Printing Office. Available: http://www.ed.gov/pubs/G2KReforming/. [July 10, 2001].

U.S. Department of Education. (1998b). *The educational system in Japan: Case study findings.* Washington, DC: U.S. Government Printing Office. Available: http://www.ed.gov/pubs/JapanCaseStudy/. [July 10, 2001].

U.S. Department of Education. (1999a). *The educational system in Germany: Case study findings.* Washington, DC: U.S. Government Printing Office. Available: http://www.ed.gov/pubs/GermanCaseStudy/. [July 10, 2001].

U.S. Department of Education. (1999b). *The educational system in the United States: Case study findings*. Washington, DC: U.S. Government Printing Office. Available: http://www.ed.gov/pubs/USCaseStudy/. [July 10, 2001].

U.S. Department of Education, Mathematics and Science Expert Panel. (1999). *Exemplary and promising mathematics programs*. Washington, DC: Author. Available: http://www.enc.org/professional/federalresources/exemplary/. [July 10, 2001].

U.S. Department of Education, National Center for Education Statistics. (2000a). *Mathematics and science in the eighth grade: Findings from the Third International Mathematics and Science Study*. Washington, DC: U.S. Government Printing Office. Available: http://nces.ed.gov/timss/. [July 10, 2001].

U.S. Department of Education, National Center for Education Statistics. (2000b). *Pursuing excellence: Comparisons of international eighth-grade mathematics achievement from a U.S. perspective, 1995 and 1999* (NCES 2001-028) by P. Gonzalez, C. Calsyn, L. Jocelyn, K. Mak, D. Kastberg, S. Arafeh, T. Williams, W. Tsen. Washington, DC: U.S. Government Printing Office. Available: http://nces.ed.gov/timss/. [July 10, 2001].

Weiss, I. (1978). *Report of the 1977 National Survey of Science, Mathematics, and Social Studies Education*. Research Triangle Park, NC: Research Triangle Institute.

Welch, W. (1978). Science education in Urbanville: A case study. In R. Stake & J. Easley (Eds.), *Case studies in science education* (pp. 5-1–5-33). Urbana: University of Illinois.

Wilson, L. D., & Blank, R. K. (1999). *Improving mathematics education using results from NAEP and TIMSS*. Washington, DC: Council of Chief State School Officers. Available: http://publications.ccsso.org/ccsso/publication_detail.cfm?PID=212. [July 10, 2001].

Woodward, A., & Elliot, D. L. (1990). Textbook use and teacher professionalism. In *Textbooks and schooling in the United States* (Eighty-ninth Yearbook of the National Society for the Study of Education, Part 1, pp. 178–193). Chicago: University of Chicago Press.

Zernike, K. (2000, August 25). Gap widens again on tests given to blacks and whites: Disparity widest among the best educated. *The New York Times*, p. A14.

3

NUMBER:
WHAT IS THERE TO KNOW?

Seven. What is seven? Seven children; seven ideas; seven times in a row; seventh grade; a lucky roll in dice; seven yards of cotton; seven stories high; seven miles from here; seven acres of land; seven degrees of incline; seven degrees below zero; seven grams of gold; seven pounds per square inch; seven years old; finishing seventh; seven thousand dollars of debt; seven percent alcohol; Engine No. 7; The Magnificent Seven. How can an idea with one name be used in so many different ways, denoting such various senses of quantity? Consider how different a measure of time (seven years) is from one of temperature (seven degrees), how different a measure of length (seven meters) is from a count (seven children), and how different either of these is from a position (finishing seventh or being in seventh grade). Even within measures, some are represented as ratios (seven pounds per square inch, seven percent alcohol) and others as simple units (seven miles, seven liters). Although normally taken for granted, it is remarkable that seven, or any number, can be used in so many ways. That versatility helps explain why number is so fundamental in describing the world.

> Its versatility helps explain why number is so fundamental in describing the world.

This chapter surveys the domain of number. It was developed in part in response to the charge to the committee to describe the context of the study with respect to the areas of mathematics that are important as foundations in grades pre-K to 8 for building continued learning. The intent of this chapter is essentially mathematical; learning and teaching are treated elsewhere. The chapter does not set forth a curriculum for students but instead provides a panoramic view of the territory on which the numerical part of the school curriculum is built. Nor is the chapter intended as a curriculum for teachers. Instead, it identifies some of the crucial ideas about number that we think teachers should know. Many of these ideas are treated in more detail in textbooks intended for prospective elementary school teachers.

A major theme of the chapter is that numbers are ideas—abstractions that apply to a broad range of real and imagined situations. Operations on numbers, such as addition and multiplication, are also abstractions. Yet in order to communicate about numbers and operations, people need representations—something physical, spoken, or written. And in order to carry out any of these operations, they need algorithms: step-by-step procedures for computation. The chapter closes with a discussion of the relationship between number and other important mathematical domains such as algebra, geometry, and probability.

Number Systems

At first, school arithmetic is mostly concerned with the *whole numbers*: 0, 1, 2, 3, and so on.[1] The child's focus is on counting and on calculating—adding and subtracting, multiplying and dividing. Later, other numbers are introduced: negative numbers and rational numbers (fractions and mixed numbers, including finite decimals). Children expend considerable effort learning to calculate with these less intuitive kinds of numbers. Another theme in school mathematics is measurement, which forms a bridge between number and geometry.

Mathematicians like to take a bird's-eye view of the process of developing an understanding of number. Rather than take numbers a pair at a time and worry in detail about the mechanics of adding them or multiplying them, they like to think about whole classes of numbers at once and about the properties of addition (or of multiplication) as a way of combining pairs of numbers in the class. This view leads to the idea of a *number system*. A number system is a collection of numbers, together with some operations (which, for purposes of this discussion, will always be addition and multiplication), that combine pairs of numbers in the collection to make other numbers in the same collection. The main number systems of arithmetic are (a) the *whole numbers*, (b) the *integers* (i.e., the positive whole numbers, their negative counterparts, and zero), and (c) the *rational numbers*—positive and negative ratios of whole numbers, except for those ratios of a whole number and zero.

Thinking in terms of number systems helps one clarify the basic ideas involved in arithmetic. This approach was an important mathematical discovery in the late nineteenth and early twentieth centuries. Some ideas of arithmetic are fairly subtle and cause problems for students, so it is useful to have a viewpoint from which the connections between ideas can be surveyed.

The Whole Numbers

One of the starting points of arithmetic is counting. Children can find out how many objects are in a collection by counting them: one, two, three, four, five. They also need zero to say that there is not any of some type of thing.[2]

Addition arises to simplify counting. When children join two collections, instead of recounting all the objects in the combined set, they add the numbers of objects in each of the original sets. (I have five apples, and Dave has three apples. How many apples do we have together?) Multiplication provides a further shortcut when children want to add many copies of the same number. (I have 10 boxes of cookies, with 12 cookies in each box. How many cookies do I have?) The whole numbers, with the two operations of addition and multiplication, form the *whole number system*, the most basic number system.

It is important to take note that, although the whole numbers with their operations are very familiar, they are already abstract. Although counting is usually done with some particular kind of things (apples or cats or dollars), arithmetic can be independent of the things counted. Five apples plus three apples makes eight apples; five cats plus three cats makes eight cats; five dollars plus three dollars makes eight dollars. (A word of caution: when adding, you must combine units of the same kind: five dollars plus three cats does not make eight of anything in particular.) This independence of the results from whatever is being counted leads to the abstract operation called addition. It is similar with multiplication. Note that the abstract nature of the arithmetic operations is exactly what makes them useful. If addition of apples, of cats, and of dollars each required its own peculiar set of rules, people would probably have no general concept of addition, just ideas about combining each type of object in its own individual way. Mathematics itself might not exist. Certainly, it would require a lot more work.

Appropriate to the abstract nature of arithmetic, each operation has several concrete interpretations. We introduced addition by means of its interpretation in terms of combining sets of like objects. Other interpretations are often used. One is the joining of segments of various lengths. If Jane has a rod 3 inches long, and another rod 5 inches long, she can lay them end to end (or perhaps even attach them together) to get a rod 8 inches long.

This interpretation may seem the same, or almost the same, as the combining-sets interpretation. Indeed, it must be somewhat similar, since it is a representation of addition. But it differs in perhaps subtle ways. For example, inches can be subdivided into parts, which are hard to tell from the wholes, except that they are shorter; whereas it is painful to cats to divide

Although the whole numbers with their operations are very familiar, they are already abstract.

them into parts, and it seriously changes their nature. Thus, joining rods will support an extension of arithmetic into fractional quantities much more easily than counting cats will.

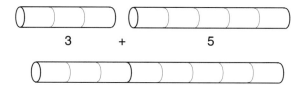

Similarly, multiplication has multiple interpretations. We introduced it as adding the same number many times. The set-combination interpretation of multiplication would be to combine several essentially identical collections, such as the packages of cookies mentioned above. If you think of addition in terms of joining rods, then multiplication would amount to joining several rods of the same length end to end. Thus, 4 × 6 can be visualized by laying four rods of length six end to end, where you can think of each rod as a little row of boxes. A more compact way to arrange the rods would be to lay them side by side rather than end to end. This arrangement produces an array of four rows of boxes with six boxes in each row, which may be called a *rectangular array interpretation* of multiplication. When the rods have height one, there is an added benefit: The array looks like a rectangle of boxes, and the area of the rectangle (measured in box areas) is just 4 × 6. This is the *area interpretation* of multiplication.

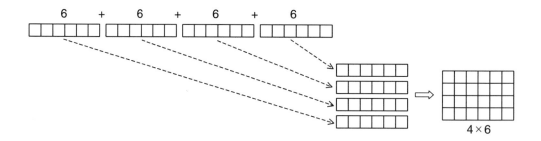

The multiple interpretations of the basic operations is symptomatic of a general feature of mathematics—the tension between abstract and concrete.[3] This tension is a fundamental and unavoidable challenge for school mathematics. On the one hand, as we indicated above, the abstractness of mathematics is an important reason for its usefulness: A single idea can apply in many circumstances. On the other hand, it is difficult to learn an idea in a purely abstract setting; one or another concrete interpretation must usually be used to make the idea real. But having been introduced to a mathematical concept by means of one interpretation, children then need to pry it away from *only* that interpretation and take a more expansive view of the abstract idea. That kind of learning often takes time and can be quite difficult. Sometimes the way in which a concept is first learned creates obstacles to learning it in a more abstract way. At other times, overcoming such obstacles seems to be a necessary part of the learning process.

Properties of the Operations

Experience with the operations of addition and multiplication leads to the observation of certain regularities in their behavior. For example, it does not matter in what order two numbers are added. If I dump a basket of three apples into a basket with five apples already in it, there will be eight apples in the basket; and if I dump the basket of five apples into the basket with three, I will also have eight. Thus $5 + 3 = 8 = 3 + 5$. The similar fact is true for any two numbers. Thus, I know that $83,449 + 173,248,191 = 173,248,191 + 83,449$ without actually doing either addition. I have used what is known as the *commutative law* of addition.

When three numbers are to be added, there are several options. To add 1 and 2 and 3, I can add 1 and 2, giving 3, and then add the original 3 to this, to get 6. Or I can add 1 to the result of adding the 2 and the 3. This process again gives 6. These two ways of adding give the same final answer, although the intermediate steps look quite different:

$$(1 + 2) + 3 = 3 + 3 = 6 = 1 + 5 = 1 + (2 + 3).$$

This statement of equality uses what is known as the *associative law*. Again, it holds for any three numbers. I know that

$$(83,449 + 173,248,191) + 417 = 83,449 + (173,248,191 + 417)$$

without doing either sum.

The commutative and associative laws in combination allow tremendous freedom in doing arithmetic. If I want to add three numbers, such as 1, 2, and 3, there are potentially 12 ways to do it:

$(1 + 2) + 3$	$(2 + 1) + 3$	$(1 + 3) + 2$	$(3 + 1) + 2$	$(2 + 3) + 1$	$(3 + 2) + 1$
$1 + (2 + 3)$	$2 + (1 + 3)$	$1 + (3 + 2)$	$3 + (1 + 2)$	$2 + (3 + 1)$	$3 + (2 + 1)$

Commutativity and associativity guarantee that all 12 ways of doing this sum give the same answer—so it does not matter which one I do. (For adding four numbers, there are 120 (!) conceivable different schemes, all of which again give the same result.) This flexibility is very useful when students do computations. For example, $1 + 8$ can be found by thinking of it as $8 + 1$ and then just recalling the next whole number after 8. The standard procedures for doing multidigit arithmetic also heavily exploit commutativity and associativity. However, the flexibility permitted by these rules also greatly increases the challenges of teaching arithmetic. When there are several ways to do a calculation, it is virtually certain that students will produce the answer more than one way. A teacher must therefore have a sufficiently flexible knowledge of arithmetic to evaluate the various student solutions, to validate the correct ones, and to correct errors productively.

The commutative and associative laws also hold for multiplication (see Box 3-1). The commutativity of multiplication by 2 is also reflected in the equivalence of the two definitions of even number typically offered by children. The "fair share" definition says that a number is even if it can be divided into two equal parts with nothing left over (which may be written as $2 \times m$); the "pairing" definition says that a number is even if it can be divided into pairs with nothing left over ($m \times 2$).

In addition to these two laws for each operation, there is a rule, known as the distributive law, connecting the two operations. It can be written symbolically as $a \times (b + c) = a \times b + a \times c$.

An example would be $2 \times (3 + 4) = 2 \times 7 = 14 = 6 + 8 = 2 \times 3 + 2 \times 4$. A good way to visualize the distributive law is in terms of the area interpretation of multiplication. Then it says that if I have two rectangles of the same height, the sum of their areas is equal to the area of the rectangle gotten by joining the two rectangles into a single one of the same height but with a base equal to the sum of the bases of the two rectangles:

The basic properties of addition and multiplication of whole numbers are summarized in Box 3-1.

Box 3-1

Properties of the Arithmetic Operations

Commutativity of addition. The order of the two numbers does not affect their sum: $3 + 5 = 8 = 5 + 3$. In general, $m + n = n + m$.

$$3 + 5 \qquad\qquad\qquad 5 + 3$$

Associativity of addition. When adding three (or more) numbers, it does not matter whether the first pair or the last pair is added first: $(3 + 5) + 4 = 8 + 4 = 12 = 3 + 9 = 3 + (5 + 4)$. In general, $(m + n) + p = m + (n + p)$.

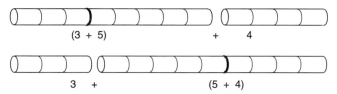

$$(3 + 5) \qquad\qquad + \qquad 4$$

$$3 \qquad + \qquad\qquad (5 + 4)$$

Commutativity of multiplication. The order of the two numbers does not affect their product: 5×8 produces the same answer as 8×5. In general, $m \times n = m \times n$.

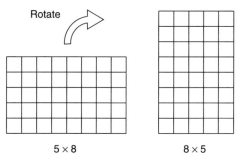

$$5 \times 8 \qquad\qquad\qquad 8 \times 5$$

Associativity of multiplication. When multiplying three or more numbers, it does not matter whether the first pair or the last pair is multiplied first: $3 \times (5 \times 4)$ is the same as $(3 \times 5) \times 4$. In general, $(m \times n) \times p = m \times (n \times p)$.

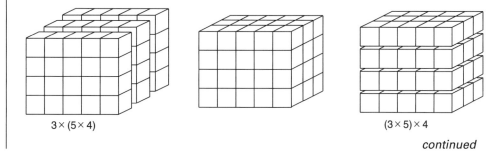

$$3 \times (5 \times 4) \qquad\qquad\qquad (3 \times 5) \times 4$$

continued

Box 3-1 Continued

Distributivity of multiplication over addition. When multiplying a sum of two numbers by a third number, it does not matter whether you find the sum first and then multiply or you first multiply each number to be added and then add the two products: $4 \times (3 + 2) = (4 \times 3) + (4 \times 2)$. In general, $m \times (n + p) = (m \times n) + (m \times p)$.

$$
\begin{array}{ccc}
\nabla\ \nabla\ \nabla\ \square\ \square & \nabla\ \nabla\ \nabla & \square\ \square \\
\nabla\ \nabla\ \nabla\ \square\ \square & \nabla\ \nabla\ \nabla & \square\ \square \\
\nabla\ \nabla\ \nabla\ \square\ \square & \nabla\ \nabla\ \nabla & \square\ \square \\
\nabla\ \nabla\ \nabla\ \square\ \square & \nabla\ \nabla\ \nabla & \square\ \square \\
4 \times (3 + 2) \qquad = & (4 \times 3) \quad + & (4 \times 2)
\end{array}
$$

Question: Is subtraction commutative?

Answer: No. For example, $6 - 2 = 4$, but $2 - 6 = -4$.

Question: Is subtraction associative?

Answer: No. For example, $(7 - 4) - 2 = 3 - 2 = 1$, but $7 - (4 - 2) = 7 - 2 = 5$.

Subtraction and Division

So far we have talked only about addition and multiplication. It is traditional, however, to list four basic operations: addition and subtraction, multiplication and division. As implied by the usual juxtapositions, subtraction is related to addition, and division is related to multiplication. The relation is in some sense an inverse one. By this, we mean that subtraction undoes addition, and division undoes multiplication. This statement needs more explanation.

Just as people sometimes want to join sets, they sometimes want to break them apart. If Eileen has eight apples and eats three, how many does she have left? The answer can be pictured by thinking of eight apples as composed of two groups, a group of five apples and a group of three apples. When the three are taken away, the five are left. In this solution, you think of eight as $5 + 3$, and then when you subtract the three, you are again left with five. Thus subtracting three undoes the implicit addition of three and leaves you with the original amount. It is the same no matter what amount you start with: 5 + 3 – 3 = 5; 9 + 3 – 3 = 9; 743 + 3 – 3 = 743. More formally, subtracting 3 is the *inverse* of adding 3.

It is similar with division and multiplication. Just as people sometimes want to form sets of the same size into one larger set, they sometimes want to break up a large set into equal-sized pieces. If you think of 15 as 5 × 3, then when you divide 15 by 3, you are again left with 5. Thus division by 3 undoes implicit multiplication by 3 and leaves you with the original amount. It is the same no matter what amount you start with: 5 × 3 ÷ 3 = 5; 9 × 3 ÷ 3 = 9; 743 × 3 ÷ 3 = 743. More formally, dividing by 3 is the *inverse* of multiplying by 3.

Two interpretations of division deserve particular mention here. If I have 20 cookies, and want to sort them into 5 bags, how many go in each bag? This is the so-called sharing model of division because I know in how many ways the cookies are to be shared. I can find the answer by picturing the 20 cookies arranged in 5 groups of 4 cookies, which will be the contents of 1 bag. If the cookies originally came out of 5 bags of 4 each, when I put them back into those bags, I will again have 4 in each. Thus, division by 5 undoes multiplication by 5, or division by 5 is the inverse of multiplication by 5. The picture below shows the sharing model for this situation.

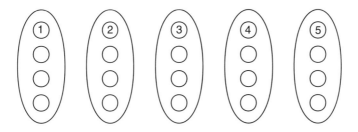

Sharing 20 cookies among 5 bags

To think about 20 ÷ 5, you could also use the measurement model: If I have 20 cookies that are to be packaged in bags of 5 each, how many bags will I get? In the sharing model (also called the partitioning model or partitive division), you know the number of groups and seek the number in a group. In the measurement model (also called quotative division), you know the size of the groups and seek the number of groups. The circled numbers in the figures above and below illustrate a crucial difference between the two models: the order in which the cookies are placed in bags. In the sharing model, the cookies are dealt into the bags one at a time; in the measurement model, the cookies are counted out by complete bags. When you deal with actual cookies, the processes are quite different, but abstractly they are both 20 ÷ 5. Note that because multiplication is commutative, 5 bags of 4 cookies each is the same total number of cookies as 4 bags of 5 cookies each. Eventually students come to see the two kinds of division as interchangeable and use whichever model helps them with a particular division problem.

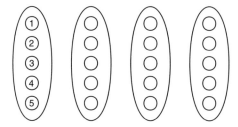

Measuring 20 cookies into bags of 5 each

Subtraction and the Integers

We might summarize the story so far by saying that there are two pairs of operations—addition and subtraction, and multiplication and division—and these are inversely related in the sense described above. However, this summary would not quite be correct. In fact, subtraction is not actually an operation on whole numbers in the same sense that addition is. You can add *any* pair of whole numbers together, and the result is again a whole number. Sometimes, however, you cannot subtract one whole number from another. If I have three apples, and Bart asks for five, I can't give them to him. I just don't have five apples. If I'm really supposed to give him five apples (maybe he left five apples in my care, I ate two, and then he came back to reclaim his apples), then I am in trouble. This situation can be described by using negative numbers: I have negative-two apples, meaning that after I give Bart all the apples I have, I still owe him two. What is happening mathematically is that I have bumped up against a subtraction problem, 3 – 5, for which there is no solution (in whole numbers). Mathematicians respond by inventing a solution for it, and they call the solution -2.

Thus, the desire to describe solutions for certain "impossible" subtraction problems leads to the invention of new numbers, the negative integers.[4] Thanks to the negative integers, you can solve *all* whole number subtraction problems. But your problems are not over. You soon find that you cannot be content simply to admire these new creations. You get into situations in which you want to do arithmetic with them also. If I owe Bart two apples and I owe Teresa four apples, how many apples do I owe all together—that is, what is (-2) + (-4)? If on Monday I get into a situation that leaves me two apples short and this happens again on Tuesday and Wednesday, how many apples short am I then—that is, what is 3 × (-2)? Besides enlarging their idea of number, people have had to extend the arithmetic operations to this new larger class of numbers. They have needed to create a new, enlarged *number system*. The new system, encompassing both positive and negative whole numbers, is called the *integers*.

How do people decide what arithmetic in this extended system is (or should be)? How do they create recipes for adding and multiplying integers, and what are the properties of these extended operations? They have two guides: (a) intuition and (b) the rules of arithmetic, as described above and in Box 3-1. Fortunately, the guides agree.

Consider first the intuitive approach: Think hard about a lot of different cases and decide what is the right way to add and multiply in each one. To use intuition, you need to think in terms of some concrete interpretation of arithmetic. The yield of financial transactions is a good one for these purposes. Here negative amounts are money you owe, and positive amounts are money that you have or are owed by someone else. If you owe $2 to Joan and $3 to Sammy, then you owe $5 to the two of them together. So (-2) + (-3) = -5. If you owe $2 to three people, then you owe $6, so 3 × (-2) = -6. If you have a debt of $2 and someone takes it away, you have gained $2. So -(-2) = 2. If someone takes three $2 debts away from you, the amount you owe is then $6 less than before, which means you have $6 more. Therefore (-3) × (-2) = 6. Continuing in this way, you can puzzle out what the sum, difference, or product of any two integers should be. The trouble with this approach is that it is somewhat contrived and depends upon making decisions about how to interpret each case in the particular context.[5]

Another approach[6] is to use an exploratory method to reason how the operations should extend from the whole numbers. By extending the patterns in the table below, you find that (-3) × (-2) = 6, just as was shown above in context.

$3 + 2 = 5$	$3 - 2 = 1$	$3 \times 2 = 6$	$(-3) \times 2 = -6$
$3 + 1 = 4$	$3 - 1 = 2$	$3 \times 1 = 3$	$(-3) \times 1 = -3$
$3 + 0 = 3$	$3 - 0 = 3$	$3 \times 0 = 0$	$(-3) \times 0 = 0$
$3 + (-1) =$	$3 - (-1) =$	$3 \times (-1) =$	$(-3) \times (-2) =$
$3 + (-2) =$	$3 - (-2) =$	$3 \times (-2) =$	$(-3) \times (-2) =$

By means of somewhat lengthy reasoning, you can find out how to do arithmetic with integers. But are the regularities observed about the whole number system (the rules in Box 3-1) still valid? Going through the cases again will show that they are. So not only has the number system been extended from the whole numbers to all integers, but the arithmetic in the larger system looks very similar to arithmetic in the original one in the sense that these laws are still valid.

Moreover, there are some new notable regularities that describe how the new numbers are related to the original ones. These are summarized in Boxes 3-2 and 3-3.

Something much more dramatic is also true. One can show that, if the goal is to extend addition and multiplication from the whole numbers to the integers in such a way that the laws of arithmetic of Boxes 3-1 and 3-2 remain true, then *there is only one way to do it*. And the rules in Box 3-3 describe how it has to work. Recipes laboriously constructed by means of some sort of concrete interpretation of negative numbers are all completely dictated by this short list of rules of arithmetic. This uniqueness is a striking exhibition of the power of these rules—that they capture in a few general statements a large chunk of people's intuition about arithmetic. The extension of whole numbers to integers is an example of the axiomatic method in mathematics: basing a mathematical system on a short list of key properties. Its most famous success is the *Elements* of Euclid for plane geometry. Since Euclid's time, axiomatic schemes have been constructed to cover most areas of mathematics.

Another rather striking thing has happened during this extension from whole numbers to (all) integers. The reason for making the extension was to

> The extension of whole numbers to integers is an example of the axiomatic method in mathematics: basing a mathematical system on a short list of key properties.

Box 3-2

Additional Properties of Addition

Additive identity. Adding zero to any number gives that number. For example, $3 + 0 = 3$ and $0 + 3 = 3$. In general, $m + 0 = m$, and $0 + m = m$.

Additive inverse. Every number has an additive inverse, also called an opposite. The opposite is the unique number that, when added to that number, gives zero. For example, the opposite of 3 is -3 because $3 + -3 = 0$; the opposite of -4 is 4 because $-4 + 4 = 0$. In general, $-s$ is the unique solution m for $s + m = 0$.

Box 3-3

Consequences of the Basic Properties: Formulas for the Arithmetic of Negation

Subtraction and negation. Subtracting a number is the same as adding its opposite. For example, $5 - 3 = 5 + (-3)$ and $5 - (-2) = 5 + 2$. In general, $s - t = s + (-t)$.

Multiplication and negation. Negation is the same as multiplication by -1. For example, $-3 = (-1) \times 3$ and $2 = (-1) \times (-2)$. In general, $-s = (-1) \times s$.

Opposite of opposite. The opposite of the opposite of a number is the number itself. For example, $-(-3) = 3$. In general, $-(-s) = s$.

be able to solve subtraction problems. Now, in the integers, subtraction is a true operation in the sense that you can subtract any integer from any other. As described in the rule on additive inverses in Box 3-2, for every integer, there is another integer, called its *opposite* or *additive inverse*, that counterbalances it: the two sum to zero. Thus $2 + (-2) = 0$, and $-84 + 84 = 0$. The second equation means that $-(-84) = 84$ and leads to the rule on subtraction and negation in Box 3-3, which says that *subtracting an integer gives the same result as adding its additive inverse.* Thus $2 - 3 = 2 + (-3)$, and $24 - (-7) = 24 + (-(-7))$, which is equal to $24 + 7 = 31$. Thus, at least on a conceptual level, subtraction is merged into addition, and you really only need to have the single operation of addition to capture all the arithmetic of addition and subtraction. As soon as subtraction is made into a true operation by extending the whole numbers to the integers, you also get additive inverses, which allows you to subordinate subtraction to addition. This sort of simplification illustrates a kind of mathematical elegance: Two ideas that seemed different can be subsumed under one bigger idea. As we show below, the analogous thing happens to division when you construct rational numbers. That subordination is the best justification for why mathematicians talk about only the two operations of addition and multiplication when discussing number systems, and not all four operations recognized in school arithmetic.

Division and Fractions

Forgetting for a moment the triumph with integers, return to the whole numbers and the problem of division. Here the situation is in some sense much more complicated than for subtraction. You can subtract in whole numbers about half the time. However, division of one whole number by another rarely comes out even. If I have eight apples and want to share them equally with Carl and Maria (the three of us), I either have to leave two apples out of the division or have to cut them in pieces. The desire to solve this kind of problem leads to new numbers, the *positive rational numbers*. These are usually written as fractions (here we allow improper fractions, such as $\frac{12}{5}$, in which the numerator is larger than the denominator), and each one is a solution to a division problem for integers. For example, $\frac{2}{3}$ is the number you get when you divide 2 into 3 equal parts. In other words, $\frac{2}{3}$ is by definition the number such that $3 \times \frac{2}{3} = 2$. Although this definition suffices to specify fractions as mathematical objects, fractions have many concrete interpretations. We refer the reader to the section "Discontinuities in Proficiency" in chapter 7 for a list of such interpretations.

Again, having introduced these new numbers, you find yourself needing to do arithmetic with them. If I get half an apple from Bart and two thirds of an apple from Teresa, how many apples do I have? If I have $1\frac{3}{4}$ boxes of marbles, and I want to put them in boxes half as large, how many of the small boxes will that make? By figuring out the answers to these questions, you turn the positive rational numbers (along with zero) into a number system, with operations of addition and multiplication extending the old operations on whole numbers. This feat is difficult technically and conceptually. The arithmetic of, and even developing meanings for, fractions is one of the stumbling blocks of the pre-K to grade 8 mathematics curriculum.[7]

Nevertheless, if you go through the effort of constructing the arithmetic of positive rational numbers by considering various cases and using some sort of concrete model, as with the integers, you find that it can be done. At the end of your labors, being a mathematician, you survey the new system and ask whether the marvelous rules of Box 3-1 still hold. They do! Moreover, there are some further regularities, analogous to the rules of Box 3-2, that relate the new numbers to the old. The new rules for multiplication are listed in Box 3-4.

The analogy with the construction of the integers is remarkable, with multiplication replacing addition, and division replacing subtraction. First, the arithmetic in the laboriously constructed new system is entirely determined by the rules of Boxes 3-1 to 3-4. This means that for the formulas of adding, multiplying, and dividing (positive) rational numbers, as described in Box 3-5, there really was no choice: That is the only way to do it and preserve the rules.[8] Furthermore, although the new system was created to allow divi-

Box 3-4

Additional Properties of Multiplication

Multiplicative identity. Multiplying a number by 1 gives that number: 5 x 1 = 5 and 1 x 5 = 5. In general, *m* x 1 = *m* and 1 x *m* = *m*.

Multiplicative inverse. Every number other than 0 has a multiplicative inverse, also called a reciprocal. The reciprocal is the unique number that, when multiplied by that number, gives 1. For example, the reciprocal of 3 is $\frac{1}{3}$ because 3 x $\frac{1}{3}$ = 1; the reciprocal of $\frac{5}{8}$ is $\frac{8}{5}$ because $\frac{5}{8}$ x $\frac{8}{5}$ = 1. In general, for *s* not zero, $\frac{1}{s}$ is the unique solution *m* of *s* x *m* = 1.

sion, once you have it, you see that in some sense division is no longer necessary. In enabling division you have created a system in which every (nonzero) number has a *multiplicative inverse* or *reciprocal*. In this system, division by a number (other than zero) is accomplished by multiplying by its reciprocal, which is the source of the "invert and multiply" rule for dividing fractions.

The Rational Numbers

You have seen how a desire to solve subtraction problems with no solutions in whole numbers leads to the construction of the integers. In a very similar way, the desire to solve division problems with no solutions in whole numbers leads to the construction of the positive rational numbers (along with zero). But neither of these number systems does it all: There are some integers that will not divide a given integer, and there are some positive rational numbers that cannot be subtracted from a given positive rational number (and still remain within the system). Thus, if you want to be able to always do both operations (except dividing by zero), you have to extend these systems further: You have to annex reciprocals to the integers, and you have to annex negatives to the positive rationals.

That process involves a lot more work. The end result, however, is as elegant as one could wish. It turns out that either procedure produces a system in which all operations are possible, with additive inverses for all numbers and multiplicative inverses for all numbers except zero. In this system, subtraction of a number becomes addition of its additive inverse, and division by a number becomes multiplication by its multiplicative inverse. The

Box 3-5

Consequences of the Basic Properties: Formulas for the Arithmetic of Fractions

Fraction notation. The fractions 3/2 and $\frac{3}{2}$ are alternative ways of writing $3 \div 2$. For numbers m and n, with m not 0, both n/m and $\frac{n}{m}$ denote $n \div m$. These are not defined when $m = 0$.

Reciprocal of reciprocal. The reciprocal of the reciprocal of a number is the number itself. For example, $\frac{1}{\frac{1}{5}} = 5$ and $\frac{1}{\frac{1}{\frac{2}{3}}} = \frac{2}{3}$. In general, for m and n not 0,

$$\frac{1}{\frac{1}{\frac{n}{m}}} = \frac{n}{m}$$

Equality. For m and s not zero, $\frac{n}{m} = \frac{t}{s}$ is true exactly when $n \times s = m \times t$.

Addition of fractions. Adding fractions requires that they have a common denominator, which often requires conversion to equivalent fractions. When fractions have a common denominator, their sum is the fraction whose numerator is the sum of their numerators and whose denominator is the common denominator.

For example, $\frac{2}{3} + \frac{4}{5} = \frac{2 \times 5}{3 \times 5} + \frac{4 \times 3}{5 \times 3} = \frac{(2 \times 5) + (4 \times 3)}{3 \times 5} = \frac{22}{15}$.

In general, for m and s not zero, $\frac{n}{m} + \frac{t}{s} = \frac{n \times s}{m \times s} + \frac{t \times m}{s \times m} = \frac{(n \times s) + (t \times m)}{m \times s}$.

Multiplication of fractions. The product of two fractions is the fraction whose numerator is the product of their numerators and whose denominator is the product of their denominators. For example, $\frac{2}{3} \times \frac{5}{7} = \frac{2 \times 5}{3 \times 7} = \frac{10}{21}$.

In general, for m and s not zero, $\frac{n}{m} \times \frac{t}{s} = \frac{n \times t}{m \times s}$.

Division of fractions. Dividing by a fraction is the same as multiplying by its reciprocal. For example, $\frac{2}{3} \div \frac{5}{7} = \frac{2}{3} \times \frac{7}{5} = \frac{2 \times 7}{3 \times 5} = \frac{14}{15}$. In general, for m, s, and t not zero, $\frac{n}{m} \div \frac{t}{s} = \frac{n}{m} \times \frac{s}{t} = \frac{n \times s}{m \times t}$.

rules in Boxes 3-1 to 3-5 all hold. In both systems, all arithmetic is determined by these rules.

Finally, the two procedures actually produce the same system. The end result is essentially the same, whether one first annexes the negatives and then the fractions, or the other way around. The hard part is making sure that you can actually do it—that there really is a system in which you can add, subtract, multiply, and divide, and where all the rules work in harmony to tell you how to do it. Mathematicians call this system the *rational numbers*.

Arithmetic into Geometry—The Number Line

The rational numbers are harder to visualize than the whole numbers or even the integers, but there is a picture that lets you think about rational numbers geometrically. It lets you interpret whole numbers, negative numbers, and fractions all as part of one overall system. Furthermore, it provides a uniform way to extend the rational number system to include numbers such as π and $\sqrt{2}$ that are not rational;[9] it provides a link between arithmetic and geometry; and it paves the way for analytic geometry, which connects algebra and geometry. This conceptual tool is called the *number line*. It can be seen in a rudimentary way in many classrooms, but its potential for organizing thinking about number and making connections with geometry seems not to have been fully exploited. Finding out how to realize this potential might be a profitable line of research in mathematics education.

The number line is simply a line, but its points are labeled by numbers. One point on the line is chosen as the origin. It is labeled 0. Then a positive direction (usually to the right) is chosen for the line. This choice amounts to specifying which side of the origin will be the positive half of the line; the other side is then the negative half. Finally, a unit of length is chosen. Any point on the line is labeled by its (directed) distance from the origin measured according to this unit length. The point is labeled positive if it is on the positive half of the line and as negative if it is on the negative half. The integers, then, are the points that are a whole number of units to the left or the right of the origin. Part of the number line is illustrated below, with some points labeled.[10]

> The potential for organizing thinking about number and making connections with geometry seems not to have been fully exploited.

Rational numbers fit into this scheme by dividing up the intervals between the integers. For example, $\frac{1}{2}$ goes midway between 0 and 1, and $\frac{3}{2}$ goes midway between 1 and 2. The numbers $\frac{1}{3}$ and $\frac{2}{3}$ divide the interval from 0 to 1 into three parts of equal length, and the numbers $\frac{7}{3} = 2\frac{1}{3}$ and $\frac{8}{3} = 2\frac{2}{3}$ divide the interval between 2 and 3 similarly. If you locate fractions with different denominators on the line, they may appear to be arranged somewhat irregularly.

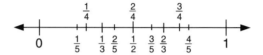

However, if you fix a denominator, and label all points by numbers with that fixed denominator, then you get an evenly spaced set, with each unit interval divided up into the same number of subintervals. Thus all rational numbers, whatever their denominators, have well-defined places on the number line. In particular, decimals with one digit to the right of the decimal point partition each unit interval on the number line into subintervals of length $\frac{1}{10}$, and decimals with two digits to the right of the decimal point refine this to intervals of length $\frac{1}{100}$, with 10 of these fitting into each interval of length $\frac{1}{10}$. See Box 3-6.

Box 3-6

The Number System of Finite Decimals

Although they are not usually singled out explicitly, the finite decimals, such as 3, -104, 21.6, 0.333, 0.0125, and 3.14159, form a number system in the sense that you can add them and multiply them and get finite decimals. You can also subtract finite decimals, but you cannot always divide them. For example, $\frac{1}{3}$ cannot be exactly represented as a finite decimal, although it can be approximated by 0.333. The finite decimal system is intermediate between the integers and the rational numbers.

The advantage of working with finite decimals rather than all the rational numbers is that the usual arithmetic for integers extends almost without change. The only complication is that one must keep track of the decimal point. (This seemingly small complication is actually a large conceptual leap.) For example,

```
                                  104
                               × .333
          3.14159                 312
        +  .0125                 312
          3.15409               312
                               34.632
```

The finite decimal system does allow division by 10 (and by its divisors, 2 and 5), and it may be characterized as the smallest number system containing the integers and allowing division by 10. Indeed, another way of representing finite decimals is as rational numbers with denominators that are powers of 10. For example, $21.6 = 216/10$ and $0.0125 = 125/10,000$.

It may not seem a huge gain to be able to divide by 10. What is the point of enlarging the system of integers to the system of finite decimals? It is that arithmetic can remain procedurally similar to the arithmetic of whole numbers, and yet finite decimals can be arbitrarily small and, as a consequence, can approximate any number as closely as you wish. This process is best illustrated by using the number line.

The integers occupy a discrete set of points on the number line, each separated from its neighbors on either side by one unit distance:

The finite decimals with at most one digit to the right of the decimal point label the positions between the integers at the division points:

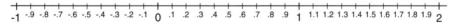

If you allow two digits to the right of the decimal point, these tenths are further subdivided into hundredths.

As you can see, space between these numbers is already rather small. It would be very difficult to draw a picture of the next division, defined by decimals with three digits to the right of the decimal point. Nonetheless, you can imagine this subdivision process continuing on and on, giving finer and finer partitions of the line.

continued

Box 3-6 Continued

Geometrically, the digits in a decimal representation can be viewed as being parts of an "address" of the number, with each successive digit locating it more and more accurately. Thus if you have the decimal 1.41421356237, the integer part tells you that the number is between 1 and 2. The first decimal place tells you that the number is between 1.4 and 1.5. The next place says that the number is between 1.41 and 1.42. The first decimal place specifies the number to within an interval of $\frac{1}{10}$. The second decimal place specifies the number to within an interval of length $\frac{1}{100}$, and so on.

If you think of it in this way, you can imagine applying this "address system" to any number, not just finite decimals. For finite decimals the procedure would effectively stop, with all digits beyond a given point being zero. With a number that is not a finite decimal, the process would go on forever, with each successive digit giving the number 10 times more precision. Thus, the finite decimals give you a systematic method for approximating *any* number to *any* desired accuracy. In particular, although the reciprocal of an integer will not usually be a finite decimal, you can approximate it by a finite decimal. Thus, $\frac{1}{3}$ is first located between 0 and 1, then between 0.3 and 0.4, then between 0.33 and 0.34, and so on.

But once you have started allowing approximation, there is no need or reason to restrict yourself to rational numbers. All numbers on the number line—even those that are not rational—can be approximated by finite decimals. For example, the number $\sqrt{2}$ is approximately 1.41421. Expanding the rational number system to include all numbers on the number line brings you to the *real number system*. Finite decimals give you access to arbitrarily accurate approximate arithmetic for all real numbers. That is one reason for their ubiquitous use in calculators.

NOTE: The finite decimals, also called decimal fractions, were first discussed by Stevin, 1585/1959.

The potential of the number line does not stop at providing a simple way to picture all rational numbers geometrically. It also lets you form geometric models for the operations of arithmetic. These models are at the same time more visual and more sophisticated than most interpretations. Consider addition. We have already mentioned that one way to interpret addition of whole numbers is in terms of joining line segments. Now you can refine that interpretation by taking a standard segment of a given (positive) length to be the segment of that length with its left endpoint at the origin. Then the right endpoint will lie at the point labeled by the length of the segment. To encompass negative numbers, you must give your segments more structure. You must provide them with an *orientation*—a beginning and an end, a head and a tail. These oriented segments may be represented as arrows. The positive numbers are then represented by arrows that begin at the origin and end at the positive number that gives their length. Negative numbers are represented by arrows that begin at the origin and end at the negative number. That way, 4 and -4, for example, have the same length but opposite orientation. (*Note:* For clarity, arrows are shown above rather than on the number line.)

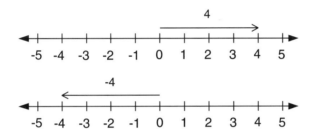

Suppose I want to compute 4 + 3 on the number line. It is difficult to add the arrows when they both begin at the origin:

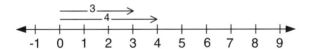

But the arrows may be moved left or right, as needed, as long as they maintain the same length and orientation. To add the arrows, I move the second arrow so that it begins at the end of the first arrow.

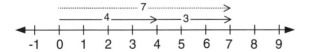

The result of the addition is an arrow that extends from the beginning of the first arrow to the end of the second arrow.

This geometric approach is quite general: It works for negative integers and rational numbers, although in the latter case it is hard to interpret the answer in simple form without dividing the intervals according to a common denominator.

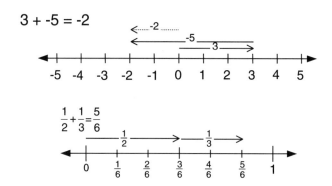

$3 + -5 = -2$

$$\frac{1}{2} + \frac{1}{3} = \frac{5}{6}$$

Another method (see below) for illustrating addition on the number line is simpler because it uses only one arrow. The method is more subtle, how-ever, because it requires that some numbers be interpreted as points and others as arrows.

$4 + 3 = 7$

Interpret the first number as a point and the second number as an arrow. Position the beginning of the arrow at the point. The result of the addition is given by the point at the end of the arrow.

$3 + -5 = -2$

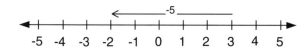

Numbers on the number line have a dual nature: They are simultaneously points and oriented segments (which we represent as arrows). A deep under-standing of number and operations on the number line requires flexibility in using each interpretation. A principal advantage to this shorthand method for addition is that it supports the idea that adding 3, for example, amounts to moving the line (translating) three units to the right. By similar reasoning, adding -5 amounts to translating five units to the left. In general, adding any number may be interpreted as a translation of the line. The size of the trans-lation depends on the size of the number, and the direction of the translation depends on its sign (i.e., positive or negative).

Multiplication on the number line is subtler than addition. Multiplica-tion by whole numbers, however, may be interpreted as repeated addition:

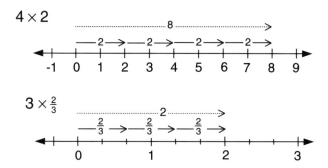

In what way does multiplication transform the line? Multiplication by 4, for example, stretches the line so that all points are four times as far from the origin as they previously were, given a constant unit. Division by 4 (or multiplication by $\frac{1}{4}$) reverses this process, thereby shrinking the line. Then multiplication by $\frac{3}{5}$, for example, may be interpreted as stretching by a factor of 3 and then shrinking by a factor of 5. Multiplication by -1 takes positive numbers to their negative counterparts and vice versa, which amounts to flipping the line about the origin.

These geometric interpretations of addition and multiplication as transformations of the line are quite sophisticated despite their pictorial nature. Nonetheless, these interpretations are important because they provide a way to picture the differences between addition and multiplication. Furthermore, the interpretations provide links between number, algebra, geometry, and higher mathematics.

Nested Systems of Numbers

While the number line gives a faithful geometric picture of the real number system, it does not make it easy to see geometrically the expansion of the number systems from whole numbers to integers to rationals, with each system contained in the next. The schematic picture in Box 3-7 illustrates how the number systems are related as sets. In the center is zero, surrounded on the right by the positive whole numbers and on the left by their negative counterparts. Together they form the integers. In the next larger circle are the rationals, which include the integers as a subset. In elementary school, children begin with the right half of the innermost circle (the whole numbers) and then learn about the right half of the next larger circle (nonnegative rationals). In the middle grades, the two circles are completed with the introduction of integers and negative rationals. In the late middle grades or high school, rationals are augmented to form real numbers.

Box 3-7

The Real Number System and Its Subsystems

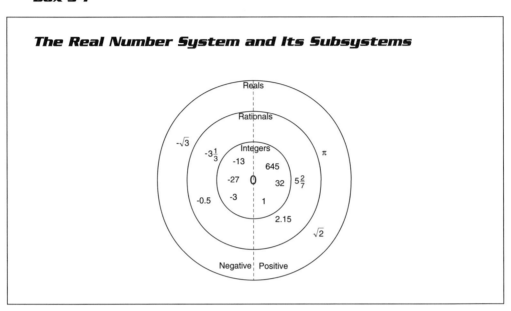

The number systems that have emerged over the centuries can be seen as being built on one another, with each new system subsuming an old one. This remarkable consistency helps unify arithmetic. In school, however, each number system is introduced with distinct symbolic notations: negation signs, fractions, decimal points, radical signs, and so on. These multiple representations can obscure the fact that the numbers used in grades pre-K through 8 all reside in a very coherent and unified mathematical structure—the number line.

Representations

In this chapter we are concerned primarily with the physical representations for number, such as symbols, words, pictures, objects, and actions.[11] Physical representations serve as tools for mathematical communication, thought, and calculation, allowing personal mathematical ideas to be externalized, shared, and preserved.[12] They help clarify ideas in ways that support reasoning and build understanding. These representations also support the development of efficient algorithms for the basic operations.[13]

Mathematics requires representations. In fact, because of the abstract nature of mathematics, people have access to mathematical ideas only through the representations of those ideas.[14] Although on its surface school mathematics may seem to be about facts and procedures, much of the real intellectual work in mathematics concerns the interpretation and use of representations of mathematical ideas.[15] The discussion of number systems above, for example, would have been impossible without the use of a variety of representations of numbers and operations.

Mathematical ideas are essentially metaphorical.[16] The section on number systems made liberal use of metaphors, including the following:

- number as collection, number as a point on a line, number as an arrow
- addition as joining, multiplication as area
- fraction as partitioning, fraction as piece, and fraction as number.

It has been argued that in mathematics "*a new concept is the product of a cross-breeding between several metaphors rather than of a single metaphor.*"[17] This claim suggests that having multiple metaphors is a necessary condition for a concept to be meaningful.

Because many mathematical representations are suggestive of the corresponding metaphors, mathematical ideas are enhanced through multiple representations, which serve not merely as illustrations or pedagogical tricks but form a significant part of the mathematical content and serve as a source of mathematical reasoning. Even the numeral "729" is a representation that embodies a significant amount of mathematical thinking and interpretation.

> Mathematical ideas are enhanced through multiple representations.

Numbers may be represented as physical objects, schematic pictures, words, or abstract symbols. For example, the number *five* may be represented by collections of physical objects, such as five blocks or five beads, by means of schematic (iconic) pictures like ⧎⧎ or ├─┼─┼─┼─┤, or by abstract symbols like 5 or V.

Operations can also be represented. In this chapter, for example, addition is represented by combining plates of cookies, by joining segments, and by symbolic expressions such as $3 + 5$. Similarly, we represent multiplication as repeated addition, as area, and symbolically as 4×6. There is an inherent ambiguity in the symbolic notation for operations that is both useful and difficult to grasp: the expression $3 + 5$, for example, simultaneously represents a process (an addition operation) and the result of that process (the number 8). For division this distinction is sometimes made through different notations (e.g., $164 \div 17$ and $164/17$), but in practice, these are often used as synonyms.[18]

When a child combines a plate of three cookies with a plate of five cookies, he or she could use $3 + 5$ as a representation of the physical situation. Conversely, given the symbolic expression $3 + 5$, the child could represent the mathematical idea by using plates of cookies. Whether the symbols represent the concrete objects or vice versa depends upon where the child starts. Both symbols and objects, however, represent a mathematical idea that is independent of the particular representation used.

The remainder of this section considers one particular representation system for numbers, the decimal place-value system, which is a significant human achievement. It should be emphasized, however, that representation systems arise out of human activity, and much mathematical insight can be gained by considering the genesis and development of the representation systems of the Egyptians, the Babylonians, the Mayans, or other cultures. Our intent here is more modest: to describe issues of mathematical representation by focusing on the representation system that is the major focus of school mathematics. It should also be emphasized that a representation system discussed previously, the number line, also deserves significant attention. In fact, the main unifying and synthesizing point of the previous section was that the number systems of school mathematics, which remain often fragmented and disjointed in the perceptions conveyed by school curricula, are in fact all subsystems of a single system, which has a geometric model that is the foundation of later analysis and geometry.

Grouping and Place Value

To use numbers effectively, to speak about them, or to manipulate them requires that they have names. Modern societies use decimal place-value notation in daily life and commerce. With just 10 symbols—0, 1, 2, . . . , 9— any number, no matter how big or small in magnitude, can be represented. For example, there are roughly 300,000,000 people in the United States. Or the diameter of the nucleus of an atom of gold is roughly 0.00000000034 centimeters. The decimal system is versatile and simple, although not necessarily obvious or easily learned. The decimal place-value system is one of the most significant intellectual constructs of humankind, and it has played a decisive role in the development of mathematics and science.

Over the centuries, various notational systems have been invented for naming numbers. To represent numbers symbolically, the ancient Hindus developed a numeration system that is based on the principles of *grouping*[19] and *place value*, and that forms the basis for our numeration system today. In this system, objects are grouped by tens, then by tens of tens (hundreds), and so on. Hence, this numeration system is a base-10 or *decimal* system. These are nontrivial ideas that took humankind many centuries to invent and refine.

Early versions of these ideas were present in Roman numerals, for example, where 729 would be represented as DCCXXIX (D = 500, C = 100, X = 10, and I = 1). Although Roman numerals use grouping by tens and the interpretation of a numeral depends to some extent on the placement of the symbols,[20] they do not at all constitute a place-value system. Also, the system of Roman numerals is ad hoc, in the sense that each new grouping requires a new symbol, so it is strictly limited in extent. A crucial steppingstone in the development of place-value notation was the idea of using a separate symbol to denote zero, which could then be used as a placeholder when necessary. This invention allows the same symbols to be used over and over to describe larger and larger groups.

Since the grouping is by tens, only 10 symbols, the digits 0 through 9, are needed to indicate how many groups there are of a particular size. In a numeral the size of the group depends on the place that the digit appears in the numeral. Thus, in 729 the "7" represents seven hundreds, whereas in 174 the "7" means seven tens.

Some pictorial and physical representations can be helpful in understanding the decimal place-value system. Special blocks, called *base-10 blocks*, for example, can be used to develop and support an understanding of the importance of tens and hundreds and the meaning of the various digits. The number 729 is pictured with base-10 blocks below.

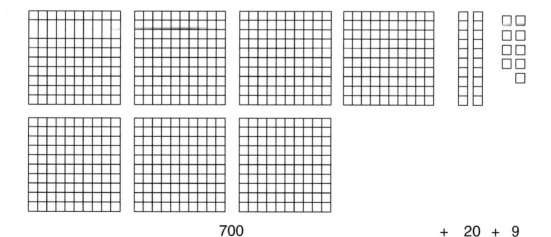

700   + 20 + 9

The composition of 729 shown above might be expressed symbolically as follows:

$$729 = 700 + 20 + 9$$
$$= (7 \times 100) + (2 \times 10) + (9 \times 1)$$
$$= (7 \times 10^2) + (2 \times 10) + (9 \times 1)$$

The symbol 10^2 means 10×10. In this case, 2 is called the *exponent*, and 10^2 is 10 to the second *power.* Making the meaning of the digits explicit in a larger number requires the use of higher powers of 10. For example,

$$39,406 = (3 \times 10,000) + (9 \times 1,000) + (4 \times 100) + (0 \times 10) + 6$$
$$= (3 \times 10^4) + (9 \times 10^3) + (4 \times 10^2) + (0 \times 10) + (6 \times 1)$$

A number in the decimal system is the sum of the products of each digit and an appropriate power of 10, where the power in question corresponds to the position of the digit.

The system is general enough to represent any whole number, no matter how large.[21] Furthermore, it is quite concise, requiring only nine digits to represent the population of the United States, and only 10 digits to represent the population of the entire earth. This conciseness, however, presents a challenge to young learners as they try to understand this compact notational system.

Extending the decimal system to the right of the decimal point is accomplished by analogy. As you move to the left, the value of the place is multiplied by 10: 1, 10, 100, 1,000, and so on. As you move to the right, this sequence is reversed, so that the value is divided by 10. Continuing past the units (ones) place and over the decimal point, you continue dividing by 10, to reach places for tenths, hundredths, thousandths, and so on. A rational number such as $\frac{3}{8}$, therefore, is written as 0.375, in perfect analogy with the notation for whole numbers: The number is the sum of the product of each digit to the right of the decimal point with the appropriate *reciprocals* (see Box 3-4) of powers of 10.

$$\frac{3}{8} = .375$$
$$= .3 + .07 + .005$$
$$= \left(3 \times .1\right) + \left(7 \times .01\right) + \left(5 \times .001\right)$$
$$= \left(3 \times \frac{1}{10}\right) + \left(7 \times \frac{1}{100}\right) + \left(5 \times \frac{1}{1000}\right)$$
$$= \left(3 \times \frac{1}{10}\right) + \left(7 \times \frac{1}{10^2}\right) + \left(5 \times \frac{1}{10^3}\right)$$

The values of the digits are sometimes shown in a place-value chart, in which 5620.739 might be represented as follows:

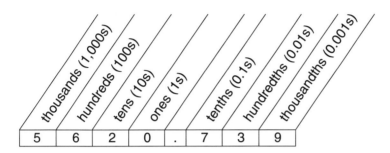

Because the reciprocals of powers of 10 become smaller in magnitude as their exponents get larger in absolute value, such decimal representations can describe quantities that are arbitrarily small. Consequently, any positive number, no matter how small in magnitude, can be represented by a decimal.

Choosing and Translating Among Representations

To represent numbers that are not whole numbers, one could choose a fractional rather than a decimal representation. Representational choices are much broader, however, than whether to use decimals or fractions. In the previous section, for example, we used points and arrows on the number line to indicate fractions, integers, and operations on integers. Fractional values are often represented with pictures, and relationships between quantities are often represented with graphs or tables. Communicating about mathematical ideas, therefore, requires that one choose representations and translate among them. Such choices depend on balancing such characteristics as the following:

- **Transparency.** How easily can the idea be seen through the representation? Base-10 blocks, for example, are more transparent than a number line for understanding the decimal notation for whole numbers, whereas the decimal numerals themselves are not at all transparent.

- **Efficiency.** Does the representation support efficient communication and use? Is it concise? Symbolic representations are more efficient than base-10 blocks.

• **Generality.** Does the representation apply to broad classes of objects? Finger representations are not general. The number line is quite general, allowing the representation of counting numbers, integers, rationals, and reals. If digits on both sides of the decimal point are included, the decimal place-value representation of numbers is completely general in the sense that any number may be so represented.

• **Clarity.** Is the representation unambiguous and easy to use? Representations should be clear and unambiguous, but that is often established by convention—how the representation is commonly used. (See Box 3-8.)

Box 3-8

Clarity of Representations

For simplicity of use, representations should be as clear and unambiguous as possible. Much of that clarity is not inherent in the representation, however, but is established through convention. For example, the expression $3 + 4 \times 5$ is ambiguous on its face because there is no explicit indication of whether to perform the multiplication or the addition first.* One might be tempted to proceed simply from left to right. The conventional order of operations, however, dictates that multiplication and division precede addition and subtraction, so $3 + 4 \times 5$ is evaluated as $23 = 3 + (4 \times 5)$ and not $35 = (3 + 4) \times 5$. In the middle grades and high school, as algebraic symbolism is introduced, the letter x and the multiplication symbol $\times$ can be confused, especially in written (rather than typeset) work. This ambiguity is solved in part by omitting multiplication signs, using parentheses or juxtaposition instead. Thus, xy means x times y, and $5(3)$ means 5 times 3.

But that practice creates another ambiguity. In the notation for mixed numbers, $3\frac{2}{5}$ means $3+\frac{2}{5}$. It does not mean $3\times\frac{2}{5}$. Furthermore, juxtaposing symbols to indicate multiplication creates confusion in high school mathematics with the introduction of function notation, where $f(4)$ looks like multiplication but instead means the output of the function f when the input value is 4. The ambiguities of such standard notations can interfere with learning if they are not acknowledged, explained, developed, and understood.

---

*Try a few different calculators. Scientific calculators typically perform the multiplication first, but simpler "four-function" calculators usually perform the addition first.

- **Precision.** How close is the representation to the exact value? Graphs are usually not very precise. With enough digits to the right of the decimal point, decimal representation can be as precise as desired.

Consider the following representations for one-half:

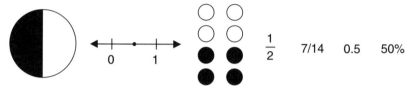

$$\frac{1}{2} \qquad 7/14 \qquad 0.5 \qquad 50\%$$

And one-half is the simplest fraction. Much more is involved in understanding and translating among representations of $\frac{13}{40}$, or rational numbers more generally. (See Box 3-9 for an example.)

Box 3-9

Translating Among Representations: An Example

Perhaps the deepest translation problem in pre-K to grade 8 mathematics concerns the translation between fractional and decimal representations of rational numbers. Successful translation requires an understanding of rational numbers as well as decimal and fractional notation—each of which is a significant and multifaceted idea in its own right. In school, children learn a standard way of converting a fraction such as $\frac{3}{8}$ to a decimal by long division.

The first written step of the long division is dividing 30 tenths by 8. After three divisions, the process stops because the remainder is zero. The quotient obtained, 0.375, is said to be a finite (or terminating) decimal because the number of digits is finite.

$$
\begin{array}{r}
.375 \\
8\,\overline{)3.000} \\
2\,4 \\
\hline
60 \\
56 \\
\hline
40 \\
40 \\
\hline
0
\end{array}
\qquad\qquad
\begin{array}{r}
.285714 \\
7\,\overline{)2.000000} \\
14 \\
\hline
60 \\
56 \\
\hline
40 \\
35 \\
\hline
50 \\
49 \\
\hline
10 \\
7 \\
\hline
30 \\
28 \\
\hline
2
\end{array}
$$

continued

Box 3-9 Continued

The long division of 2 ÷ 7 is more complicated. The remainder at the seventh step is 2, which is where the first step began. Because there will always be another 0 to "bring down" in the next place, the sequence of remainders (2, 6, 4, 5, 1, 3) will repeat, as will the digits 285714 in the quotient. Thus, $\frac{2}{7} = 0.\overline{285714}$, a repeating decimal, where the horizontal bar is used to indicate which digits repeat.

The process of using long division to obtain the decimal representation of a fraction will always be like one of the above cases: Either the process will stop or it will cycle through some sequence of remainders. So the decimal representation of a rational number must be either a repeating or a terminating decimal. Thus a nonrepeating decimal cannot be a rational number and there are many such numbers, such as π and $\sqrt{2}$.

---

*In the process of converting a fraction to a decimal, all remainders must be less than the denominator of the fraction. Because the list of possible remainders is finite, and because each subsequent step is always the same (brings down a 0, etc.), the remainders must eventually repeat. The fraction 2/7 had six remainders (the maximum) and repeated in six digits. Other examples: 1/11 repeats in two digits, 1/13 repeats in six digits, and 1/17 repeats in 16 digits.

Understanding a mathematical idea thoroughly requires that several possible representations be available to allow a choice of those most useful for solving a particular problem. And if children are to be able to use a multiplicity of representations, it is important that they be able to translate among them, such as between fractional and decimal notations or between symbolic representations and the number line or pictorial representations.

Algorithms

Addition is an idea—an abstraction from combining collections of objects or from joining lengths. Carrying out the addition of two numbers requires a strategy that will lead to the result. For single-digit numbers it is reasonable to use or imagine blocks or cookies, but for multidigit numbers you need something more efficient. You need algorithms.

An algorithm is a "precisely-defined sequence of rules telling how to produce specified output information from given input information in a finite number of steps."[22] More simply, an algorithm is a recipe for computation.[23] Most people know algorithms for doing addition, subtraction, multiplication, and division with pencil and paper. There are many such algorithms, as well as others that do not use pencil and paper. Years ago many people knew algorithms for computation on fingers, slide rules, and abacuses. Today, calculators and computer algorithms are widely used for arithmetic. (Indeed, a defining characteristic of a computational algorithm is that it be suitable for implementation on a computer.) And in fact, most of algebra, calculus, and even more advanced mathematics may now be done with computer programs that perform calculations with symbols.

When confronted with a need for calculation, one must choose an algorithm that will give the correct result and that can be accomplished with the tools available. Algorithms depend upon representations. (Note, for example, that algorithms for fractions are different from algorithms for decimals.) And as was the case for representations, choosing an algorithm benefits from consideration of certain characteristics: *transparency*, *efficiency*, *generality*, and *precision*. The more transparent an algorithm, the easier it is to understand, and a child who understands an algorithm can reconstruct it after months or even years of not using it. The need for efficiency depends, of course, on how often an algorithm is used. An additional desired characteristic is *simplicity* because simple algorithms are easier to remember and easier to perform accurately. Again, the key is finding an appropriate balance among these characteristics because, for example, algorithms that are sufficiently general and efficient are often not very transparent. It is worth noting that pushing buttons on a calculator is the epitome of a nontransparent algorithm, but it can be quite efficient. In Box 3-10, we show some examples of algorithms with various qualities.

Algorithms are important in school mathematics because they can help students understand better the fundamental operations of arithmetic and important concepts such as place value and also because they pave the way for learning more advanced topics. For example, algorithms for the operations on multidigit whole numbers can be generalized (with appropriate modifications) to algorithms for corresponding operations on polynomials in algebra, although the resulting algorithms do not look quite like any typical multiplication algorithms but rather are based upon the idea behind such algorithms: computing and recording partial products and then adding. The polynomial multiplication illustrated below, for example, is somewhat like multiplication

An algorithm is a recipe for computation.

of whole numbers, but the relationship is hard to see, mostly because there is no "carrying," from the x to the x^2 term, for example. The expanded method below shows the relationship a bit more clearly.

Multiplication	Expanded method	Multiplying polynomials

$$
\begin{array}{lll}
\text{Multiplication} & \text{Expanded method} & \text{Multiplying polynomials} \\
\end{array}
$$

Multiplication:
$$
\begin{array}{r}
23 \\
\times 15 \\
\hline
115 \\
23 \\
\hline
345
\end{array}
$$

Expanded method:
$$
\begin{array}{rll}
23 & = & 20 + 3 \\
\times 15 & = & 10 + 5 \\
\hline
 & & 100 + 15 \\
 & 200 + & 30 \\
\hline
 & 200 + & 130 + 15 = 345
\end{array}
$$

Multiplying polynomials:
$$
\begin{array}{rl}
2x & + 3 \\
x & + 5 \\
\hline
10x & + 15 \\
2x^2 + 3x & \\
\hline
2x^2 + 13x & + 15
\end{array}
$$

Box 3-10

Examples of Algorithms

The decimal place-value system allows many different algorithms for the four main operations. The following six algorithms for multiplication of two-digit numbers were produced by a class of prospective elementary school teachers. They were asked to show how they were taught to multiply 23 by 15:

$$
\begin{array}{r}
23 \\
\times 15 \\
\hline
115 \\
23 \\
\hline
345
\end{array}
\qquad
\begin{array}{r}
23 \\
\times 15 \\
\hline
45 \\
30 \\
\hline
345
\end{array}
\qquad
\begin{array}{r}
23 \\
\times 15 \\
\hline
15 \\
100 \\
30 \\
200 \\
\hline
345
\end{array}
$$

$$
\begin{array}{l}
23 \times 15 \\
23 \times 30 = 690 \\
\quad\quad \div 2 = 345
\end{array}
\qquad
\begin{array}{l}
23 \times 10 = 230 \\
23 \times\ \ 5 = 115 \\
\hline
\quad\quad\quad\ 345
\end{array}
$$

In Method 6, sometimes called lattice multiplication,* the factors are written across the top and on the right, the products of the pairs of digits are put into the cells (for example, 15 is written $\boxed{{}^1\!\diagup_5}$), and the numbers in the diagonals are added to give the product underneath.

Note that all of these algorithms produce the correct answer. All except Method 4 are simply methods for organizing the four component multiplications and

---

*The method is also called *gelosia multiplication* and is related to the method of Napier's rods or bones, named after the Scottish mathematician John Napier (1550–1617).

adding. The algorithms can be verified by decomposing the factors according to the values of their digits (in this case, 23 = 20 + 3 and 15 = 10 + 5) and using the distributive law in one of several ways:

$$23 \times 15 = 23 \times (10 + 5)$$

$$= 23 \times 10 + 23 \times 5 \qquad \text{Methods 1 and 5}$$

$$= 230 + 115$$

$$23 \times 15 = (20 + 3) \times 15$$

$$= 20 \times 15 + 3 \times 15 \qquad \text{Method 2}$$

$$= 300 + 45$$

$$23 \times 15 = (20 + 3) \times (10 + 5)$$

$$= 20 \times 10 + 20 \times 5 + 3 \times 10 + 3 \times 5 \qquad \text{Methods 3 and 6}$$

$$= 200 + 100 + 30 + 15$$

A more compelling justification uses the area model of multiplication. If the sides of a 23 × 15 rectangle are subdivided as 20 + 3 and 10 + 5, then the area of the whole rectangle can be computed by summing the areas of the four smaller rectangles.

	20	3
5	100	15
10	200	30

Note the correspondence between the areas of the four smaller rectangles and the partial products in Method 3. With more careful examination, it is possible to see the same four partial products residing in the four cells in Method 6. (The 2 in the upper left cell, for example, actually represents 200.) Methods 1,

continued

Box 3-10 Continued

2, and 5 differ from these only in that they record the areas for one pair of these rectangles at a time.

Any of the methods—and, in fact, any of the four justifications that followed—could serve as the standard algorithm for the multiplication of whole numbers because they are all general and exact. Mathematically, these methods are essentially the same, differing only in the intermediate products that are calculated and how they are recorded.

These methods, however, are quite different in transparency and efficiency. Methods 3 and 5 and the area model justification are the most transparent because the partial products are all displayed clearly and unambiguously. The three justifications using the distributive law also show these partial products unambiguously, but some of the transparency is lost in the maze of symbols. Methods 1 and 2 are the most efficient, but they lack some transparency because the 23 and the 30 actually represent 230 and 300, respectively.

Method 4 takes advantage of the fact that doubling the factor 15 gives a factor that is easy to use. It is quite different from the others. For one thing, the intermediate result is larger than the final answer. This method can also be shown to be correct using the properties of whole numbers, since multiplying one factor by 2 and then dividing the product by 2 has no net effect on the final answer. The usefulness of Method 4 depends on the numbers involved. Doubling 15 gives 30, and 23×30 is much easier to calculate mentally than 23×15. Using this method to find a product like 23×17, on the other hand, would require first calculating 23×34, which is no easier than 23×17. Clearly this method, although completely general, is not very practical. For most factors, it is neither simple nor efficient.

Building Blocks

The preceding sections have described concepts in the domain of number that serve as fundamental building blocks for the entire mathematics curriculum. Other fundamental ideas—such as those about shape, spatial relationships, and chance—are foundational as well. Students do not need to, and should not, master all the number concepts we have described before they study other topics. Rather, number concepts should serve to support mathematics learning in other domains as students are introduced to them, and, conversely, these other domains should support students' growing understanding of number.

Number is intimately connected with geometry, as illustrated in this chapter by our use of the number line and the area model of multiplication. Those same models of number can, of course, arise when measurement is introduced in geometry. The connection between number and algebra is illustrated in the chapter by our use of algebra to express properties of number systems and other general relationships between numbers. The links from number to geometry and to algebra are forged even more strongly when students are introduced to the coordinate plane, in which perpendicular number lines provide a system of coordinates for each point—an idea first put forward by the French mathematician and philosopher René Descartes (1596–1650), although he did not insist that the number lines were perpendicular. Number is also essential in data analysis, the process of making sense of collections of numbers. Using numbers to investigate processes of variation, such as accumulation and rates of change, can provide students with the numerical underpinnings of calculus.

Some of the manifold connections and dependencies between number and other mathematical domains may be illustrated by the so-called handshake problem:

> *If eight people are at a party and each person shakes hands exactly once with every other person, how many handshakes are there?*

This problem appears often in the literature on problem solving in school mathematics, probably because it can be solved in so many ways. Perhaps the simplest way of getting a solution is just to count the handshakes systematically: The first person shakes hands with seven people; the second person, having shaken the first person's hand, shakes hands with six people whose hands he or she has not yet shaken; the third person shakes hands with five people; and so on until the seventh person shakes hands with only the eighth person. The number of handshakes, therefore, is $7 + 6 + 5 + 4 + 3 + 2 + 1$, which is 28.

This method of solution can be generalized to a situation with any number of people, which is what a mathematician would want to do. For a party with 20 people, for example, there would be
$19 + 18 + 17 + 16 + 15 + 14 + 13 + 12 + 11 + 10 + 9 + 8 + 7 + 6 + 5 + 4 + 3 + 2 + 1$
handshakes, but the computation would be more time consuming. Because mathematicians are interested not only in generalizations of problems but also in simplifying solutions, it would be nice to find a simple way of adding the numbers. In general, for $m + 1$ people at a party, the number of handshakes would be the sum of the first m counting numbers:[24]

$$1 + 2 + \ldots + m.$$

Numbers that arise in this way are called *triangular numbers* because they may be arranged in triangular formations, as shown below.

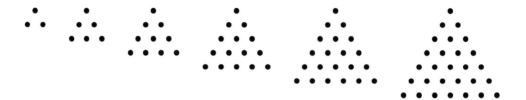

Therefore, 3, 6, 10, 15, 21, and 28 are all triangular numbers. This is a geometric interpretation, but can geometry be used to find a solution to the handshake problem that would simplify the computation?

One way to approach geometrically the problem of adding the numbers from 1 to *m* is to think about it as a problem of finding the area of the side of a staircase. The sum $1 + 2 + 3 + 4 + 5 + 6 + 7$, for example, would then be seen as a staircase of blocks in which each term is represented by one layer, as in the diagram on the left below. The diagram on the right below includes a second copy of the staircase, turned upside down. When the two staircases are put together, the result is a 7×8 rectangle, with area 56. So the area of the staircase is half that, or 28. This reasoning, although specific, supports a general solution for the sum of the whole numbers from 1 to *m*: $m(m + 1)/2$.

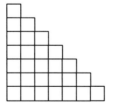 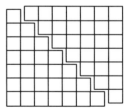

A closely related numerical approach to the problem of counting hand-shakes comes from a story told of young Carl Friedrich Gauss (1777–1855), whose teacher is said to have asked the class to sum the numbers from 1 to 100, expecting that the task would keep the class busy for some time. The story goes that almost before the teacher could turn around, Gauss handed in his slate with the correct answer. He had quickly noticed that if the numbers to be added are written out and then written again below but in the opposite order, the combined (double) sum may be computed easily by first adding the pairs of numbers aligned vertically and then adding horizontally. As can be seen below, each vertical sum is 101, and there are exactly 100 of them. So the double sum is 100×101, or 10,100, which means that the desired sum is half that, or 5050.

$$
\begin{array}{cccccccccccccc}
100 & + & 99 & + & 98 & + & L & + & 3 & + & 2 & + & 1 \\
1 & + & 2 & + & 3 & + & L & + & 98 & + & 99 & + & 100 \\
\hline
101 & + & 101 & + & 101 & + & L & + & 101 & + & 101 & + & 101
\end{array}
$$

For the original handshake problem, which involves the sum of the blocks in the staircase above, that means taking the double sum 7×8, or 56, and halving it to get 28.

The handshake problem can be approached by bringing in ideas from other parts of mathematics. If the people are thought of as standing at the vertices of an eight-sided figure (octagon), then the question again becomes geometric but in a different way: How many segments (sides and diagonals) may be drawn between vertices of an octagon? The answer again is 28, as can be verified in the picture below.

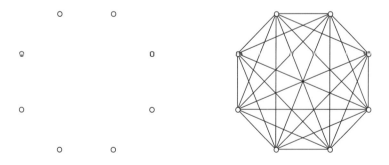

As often happens in mathematics, connections to geometry provide a new way of approaching the problem: Each vertex is an endpoint for exactly 7 segments, and there are 8 vertices, which sounds like there ought to be $7 \times 8 = 56$ segments. But that multiplication counts each segment twice (once for each endpoint), so there are really half as many, or 28, segments.

In still another mathematical domain, combinatorics—the study of counting, grouping, and arranging a finite number of elements in a collection—the problem becomes how to count the number of ways to choose two items (people shaking hands) from a collection of eight elements. For example, in how many ways can a committee of two be chosen from a group of eight people? This is the same as the handshake problem because each committee of two corresponds to a handshake. It is also the same as the octagon problem because each committee corresponds to a segment (which is identified by its two endpoints).

A critically important mathematical idea in the above discussion lies in noticing that these are all the same problem in different clothing. It also involves solving the problem and finding a representation that captures its key features. For students to develop the mathematical skill and ability they need to understand that seemingly different problems are just variations on the same theme, to solve the problem once and for all, and to develop and use representations that will allow them to move easily from one variation to another, the study of number provides an indispensable launching pad.

Key Ideas About Number

In this chapter, we have surveyed the domain of number with an eye toward the proficiency that students in grades pre-K to 8 need for their future study of mathematics. Several key ideas have been emphasized. First, numbers and operations are abstractions—ideas based on experience but independent of any particular experience. The numbers and operations of school mathematics are organized as number systems, and each system provides ways to consider numbers and operations simultaneously, allowing learners to focus on the regularities and the structure of the system. Despite different notations and their separate treatment in school, these number systems are related through a process of embedding one system in the next one studied. All the number systems of pre-K to grade 8 mathematics lie inside a single system represented by the number line. Second, all mathematical ideas require representations, and their usefulness is enhanced through multiple representations. Because each representation has its advantages and disadvantages, one must be able to choose and translate among representations. The number line and the decimal place-value system are important representational tools in school mathematics, but students should have experience with other useful interpretations and representations, which also are important parts of the content. Third, calculation requires algorithms, and once again there are choices to make because each algorithm has advantages and disadvantages. And finally, the domain of number both supports and is supported by other branches of mathematics. It is these connections that give mathematics much of its power. If students are to become proficient in mathematics by eighth grade, they need to be proficient with the numbers and operations discussed in this chapter, as well as with beginning algebra, measure, space, data, and chance—all of which are intricately related to number.

Notes

1. Some authors (see, e.g., Russell, 1919, p. 3; Freudenthal, 1983, pp. 77ff) call these the natural numbers. We are adopting the common usage of the U.S. mathematics education literature, in which the natural numbers begin 1, 2, 3, and so on, and the whole numbers include zero.

2. The recognition that zero should be considered a legitimate number—rather than the absence of number—was an important intellectual achievement in the history of mathematics. Zero (as an idea) is present in the earliest schooling, but zero (as a number) is a significant obstacle for some students and teachers. "Zero is nothing," some people say. "How can we ask whether it is even or odd?"

3. "To criticize mathematics for its abstraction is to miss the point entirely. *Abstraction is what makes mathematics work.* If you concentrate too closely on too limited an application of a mathematical idea, you rob the mathematician of his [or her] most important tools: analogy, generality, and simplicity" (Stewart, 1989, p. 291).

4. Although negative numbers are quite familiar today, and part of the standard elementary curriculum, they are quite a recent development in historical terms, having become common only since the Renaissance. Descartes, who invented analytic geometry and after whom the standard Cartesian coordinate system on the plane is named, rejected negative numbers as impossible. (His coordinate axes had only a positive direction.) His reason was that he thought of numbers as quantities and held that there could be no quantity less than nothing. Now, however, people are not limited to thinking of numbers solely in terms of quantity. In dealing with negative numbers, they have learned that if they think of numbers as representing movement along a line, then positive numbers can correspond to movement to the right, and negative numbers can represent movement to the left. This interpretation of numbers as *oriented* length is subtly different from the old interpretation in terms of quantity, which would here be *un*oriented length, and gives a sensible and quite concrete way to think about these numbers that Descartes thought impossible.

5. Freudenthal, 1983, suggests that "negative numbers did not really become important until they appeared to be indispensable for the permanence of expressions, equations, formulae in the 'analytic geometry'" (p. 436). "Later on arguments of content character were contrived . . . although some of them are not quite convincing (positive-negative as capital-debt, gain-loss, and so on)" (p. 435).

6. See Freudenthal, 1983, p. 435.

7. Although rational numbers seem to present more difficulties for students than negative integers, historically they came well before. The Greeks were comfortable

with positive rational numbers over 2000 years before negative numbers became accepted. See also Behr, Harel, Post, and Lesh, 1992.

8. The rules are in a sense guided by the fractional notation, *a/b*. In other notational systems, such as decimal representation, the rules will look somewhat different, although they will be equivalent.

9. These numbers (and many others) are not rational because they cannot be expressed as fractions with integers in the numerator and denominator.

10. In the number-line illustrations throughout this chapter, the portion displayed and the scale vary to suit the intent of the illustration. That is reasonable not just because one can imagine moving a "lens" left and right and zooming in and out, but also because the ideas are independent of the choice of origin and unit.

11. Bruner, 1966 (pp. 10–11), suggests three ways of transforming experience into models of the world: enactive, iconic, and symbolic representations. Enactively, addition might be the action of combining a plate of three cookies with a plate of five cookies; iconically, it might be represented by a picture of two plates of cookies; symbolically, it might be represented as 5 cookies plus 3 cookies, or merely 5 + 3.

12. Greeno and Hall, 1997.

13. Pimm, 1995, suggests that people seek representational systems in which they can operate on the symbols as though the symbols were the mathematical objects.

14. Duvall, 1999.

15. Kaput, 1987, argues that much of elementary school mathematics is not about numbers but about a particular representational system for numbers. See Cuoco, 2001, for detailed discussions of various ways representations come into play in school mathematics.

16. See Lakoff and Núñez, 1997, and Sfard, 1997, for detailed discussion of the metaphoric nature of mathematics.

17. Sfard, 1997, p. 36, emphasis in original.

18. "I remember as a child, in fifth grade, coming to the amazing (to me) realization that the answer to 134 divided by 29 is 134/29 (and so forth). What a tremendous labor-saving device! To me, '134 divided by 29' meant a certain tedious chore, while 134/29 was an object with no implicit work. I went excitedly to my father to explain my discovery. He told me that of course this is so, *a/b* and *a* divided by *b* are just synonyms. To him it was just a small variation in notation" (Thurston, 1990, p. 847).

19. Grouping is a common approach in measurement activities. For example, in measuring time, there are 60 seconds in a minute, 60 minutes in an hour, 24 hours in a day, approximately 30 days in a month, 12 months in a year, and so on. For distance, the customary U.S. system uses inches, feet, yards, and miles, and the metric system uses centimeters, meters, and kilometers.

20. For example, IX means nine (that is, one less than ten), whereas XI means eleven (one more than ten).

21. This generality was a significant accomplishment. In the third century B.C. in Greece, with its primitive numeration system, a subject of debate was whether there even existed a number large enough to describe the number of grains of sand in the universe. The issue was serious enough that Archimedes, the greatest mathematician

of classical times, wrote a paper in the form of a letter to the king of his city explaining how to write such very large numbers. Archimedes, however, did not go so far as to invent the decimal system, with its potential for extending indefinitely.

22. Knuth, 1974, p. 323.

23. Steen, 1990. See Morrow and Kenney, 1998, for more perspectives on algorithms.

24. The ellipsis points "..." in the expression are a significant piece of abstract mathematical notation, compactly designating the omission of the terms needed (to reach m, in this case).

References

Behr, M. J., Harel, G., Post, T., & Lesh, R. (1992). Rational number, ratio, and proportion. In D. A. Grouws (Ed.), *Handbook of research on mathematics teaching and learning* (pp. 296–333). New York: Macmillan.

Bruner, J. S. (1966). *Toward a theory of instruction.* Cambridge, MA: Belknap Press.

Cuoco, A. (Ed.). (2001). *The roles of representation in school mathematics* (2001 Yearbook of the National Council of Teachers of Mathematics). Reston, VA: NCTM.

Duvall, R. (1999). Representation, vision, and visualization: Cognitive functions in mathematical thinking. Basic issues for learning. In F. Hitt & M. Santos (Eds.), *Proceedings of the twenty-first annual meeting of the North American Chapter of the International Group for the Psychology of Mathematics Education* (vol. 1, pp. 3–26). Columbus, OH: ERIC Clearinghouse for Science, Mathematics, and Environmental Education. (ERIC Document Reproduction Service No. ED 433 998).

Freudenthal, H. (1983). *Didactical phenomenology of mathematical structures.* Dordrecht, The Netherlands: Reidel.

Greeno, J. G., & Hall, R. (1997). Practicing representation: Learning with and about representational forms. *Phi Delta Kappan, 78,* 1–24. Available: http://www.pdkintl.org/kappan/kgreeno.htm. [July 10, 2001].

Kaput, J. (1987). Representation systems and mathematics. In C. Janvier (Ed.), *Problems of representation in the teaching and learning of mathematics* (pp. 19–26). Hillsdale, NJ: Erlbaum.

Knuth, D. E. (1974). Computer science and its relation to mathematics. *American Mathematical Monthly, 81,* 323–343.

Lakoff, G., & Núñez, R. E. (1997). The metaphorical structure of mathematics: Sketching out cognitive foundations for a mind-based mathematics. In L. D. English (Ed.), *Mathematical reasoning: Analogies, metaphors, and images* (pp. 21–89). Mahwah, NJ: Erlbaum.

Morrow, L. J., & Kenney, M. J. (Eds.). (1998). *The teaching and learning of algorithms in school mathematics* (1998 Yearbook of the National Council of Teachers of Mathematics). Reston, VA: NCTM.

Pimm, D. (1995). *Symbols and meanings in school mathematics.* London: Routledge.

Russell, B. (1919). *Introduction to mathematical philosophy.* New York: Macmillan.

Sfard, A. (1997). Commentary: On metaphorical roots of conceptual growth. In L. D. English (Ed.), *Mathematical reasoning: Analogies, metaphors, and images* (pp. 339–371). Mahwah, NJ: Erlbaum.

Steen, L. (1990). Pattern. In L. Steen (Ed.), *On the shoulders of giants: New approaches to numeracy* (pp. 1(10). Washington, DC: National Academy Press. Available: http://books.nap.edu/catalog/1532.html. [July 10, 2001].

Stevin, S. (1959). On decimal fractions (V. Sanford, Trans). In D. E. Smith (Ed.), *A source book in mathematics* (pp. 20–34). New York: Dover. (Original work published 1585)

Stewart, I. (1989). *Does God play dice? The mathematics of chaos.* Oxford, England: Blackwell.

Thurston, W. P. (1990). Mathematical education. *Notices of the American Mathematical Society, 37,* 844–850.

4

THE STRANDS OF MATHEMATICAL PROFICIENCY

During the twentieth century, the meaning of successful mathematics learning underwent several shifts in response to changes in both society and schooling. For roughly the first half of the century, success in learning the mathematics of pre-kindergarten to eighth grade usually meant facility in using the computational procedures of arithmetic, with many educators emphasizing the need for skilled performance and others emphasizing the need for students to learn procedures with understanding.[1] In the 1950s and 1960s, the new math movement defined successful mathematics learning primarily in terms of understanding the structure of mathematics together with its unifying ideas, and not just as computational skill. This emphasis was followed by a "back to basics" movement that proposed returning to the view that success in mathematics meant being able to compute accurately and quickly. The reform movement of the 1980s and 1990s pushed the emphasis toward what was called the development of "mathematical power," which involved reasoning, solving problems, connecting mathematical ideas, and communicating mathematics to others. Reactions to reform proposals stressed such features of mathematics learning as the importance of memorization, of facility in computation, and of being able to prove mathematical assertions. These various emphases have reflected different goals for school mathematics held by different groups of people at different times.

Our analyses of the mathematics to be learned, our reading of the research in cognitive psychology and mathematics education, our experience as learners and teachers of mathematics, and our judgment as to the mathematical knowledge, understanding, and skill people need today have led us to adopt a composite, comprehensive view of successful mathematics learning. This view, admittedly, represents no more than a single committee's consensus. Yet our various backgrounds have led us to formulate, in a way that we hope others can and will accept, the goals toward which mathematics learning should be aimed. In this chapter, we describe the kinds of cognitive changes that we want to promote in children so that they can be successful in learning mathematics.

Recognizing that no term captures completely all aspects of expertise, competence, knowledge, and facility in mathematics, we have chosen *mathematical proficiency* to capture what we believe is necessary for anyone to learn mathematics successfully. Mathematical proficiency, as we see it, has five components, or *strands:*

- *conceptual understanding*—comprehension of mathematical concepts, operations, and relations
- *procedural fluency*—skill in carrying out procedures flexibly, accurately, efficiently, and appropriately
- *strategic competence*—ability to formulate, represent, and solve mathematical problems
- *adaptive reasoning*—capacity for logical thought, reflection, explanation, and justification
- *productive disposition*—habitual inclination to see mathematics as sensible, useful, and worthwhile, coupled with a belief in diligence and one's own efficacy.

The five strands are interwoven and interdependent in the development of proficiency in mathematics.

These strands are not independent; they represent different aspects of a complex whole. Each is discussed in more detail below. The most important observation we make here, one stressed throughout this report, is that *the five strands are interwoven and interdependent in the development of proficiency in mathematics* (see Box 4-1). Mathematical proficiency is not a one-dimensional trait, and it cannot be achieved by focusing on just one or two of these strands. In later chapters, we argue that helping children acquire mathematical proficiency calls for instructional programs that address all its strands. As they go from pre-kindergarten to eighth grade, all students should become increasingly proficient in mathematics. That proficiency should enable them to cope with the mathematical challenges of daily life and enable them to continue their study of mathematics in high school and beyond.

The five strands provide a framework for discussing the knowledge, skills, abilities, and beliefs that constitute mathematical proficiency. This frame-

Box 4-1

Intertwined Strands of Proficiency

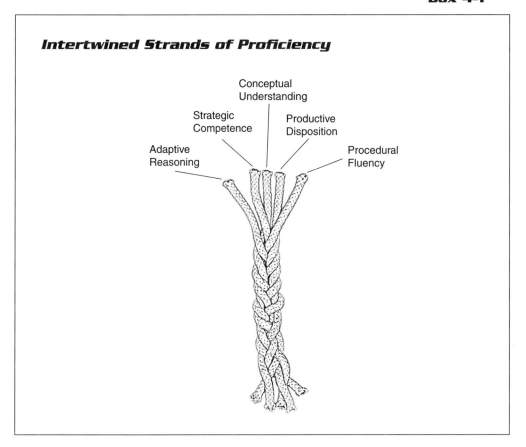

work has some similarities with the one used in recent mathematics assessments by the National Assessment of Educational Progress (NAEP), which features three mathematical abilities (conceptual understanding, procedural knowledge, and problem solving) and includes additional specifications for reasoning, connections, and communication.[2] The strands also echo components of mathematics learning that have been identified in materials for teachers. At the same time, research and theory in cognitive science provide general support for the ideas contributing to these five strands. Fundamental in that work has been the central role of mental representations. How learners represent and connect pieces of knowledge is a key factor in whether they will understand it deeply and can use it in problem solving. Cognitive scientists have concluded that competence in an area of inquiry depends upon knowledge that is not merely stored but represented mentally and organized (connected and structured) in ways that facilitate appropriate retrieval and application. Thus, learning with understanding is more powerful than simply memorizing because the organization improves retention, promotes fluency, and facilitates learning related material. The central notion that strands of competence must be interwoven to be useful reflects the finding that having a deep understanding requires that learners connect pieces of knowledge, and that connection in turn is a key factor in whether they can use what they know productively in solving problems. Furthermore, cognitive science studies of problem solving have documented the importance of adaptive expertise and of what is called *metacognition:* knowledge about one's own thinking and ability to monitor one's own understanding and problem-solving activity. These ideas contribute to what we call strategic competence and adaptive reasoning. Finally, learning is also influenced by motivation, a component of productive disposition.[3]

Although there is not a perfect fit between the strands of mathematical proficiency and the kinds of knowledge and processes identified by cognitive scientists, mathematics educators, and others investigating learning, we see the strands as reflecting a firm, sizable body of scholarly literature both in and outside mathematics education.

Conceptual Understanding

Conceptual understanding refers to an integrated and functional grasp of mathematical ideas. Students with conceptual understanding know more than isolated facts and methods. They understand why a mathematical idea is important and the kinds of contexts in which is it useful. They have organized their knowledge into a coherent whole, which enables them to learn new ideas by connecting those ideas to what they already know.[4] Conceptual understanding also supports retention. Because facts and methods learned with understanding are connected, they are easier to remember and use, and they can be reconstructed when forgotten.[5] If students understand a method, they are unlikely to remember it incorrectly. They monitor what they remember and try to figure out whether it makes sense. They may attempt to explain the method to themselves and correct it if necessary. Although teachers often look for evidence of conceptual understanding in students' ability to verbalize connections among concepts and representations, conceptual understanding need not be explicit. Students often understand before they can verbalize that understanding.[6]

> *Conceptual understanding refers to an integrated and functional grasp of mathematical ideas.*

A significant indicator of conceptual understanding is being able to represent mathematical situations in different ways and knowing how different representations can be useful for different purposes. To find one's way around the mathematical terrain, it is important to see how the various representations connect with each other, how they are similar, and how they are different. The degree of students' conceptual understanding is related to the richness and extent of the connections they have made.

For example, suppose students are adding fractional quantities of different sizes, say $\frac{1}{3} + \frac{2}{5}$. They might draw a picture or use concrete materials of various kinds to show the addition. They might also represent the number sentence $\frac{1}{3} + \frac{2}{5} = ?$ as a story. They might turn to the number line, representing each fraction by a segment and adding the fractions by joining the segments. By renaming the fractions so that they have the same denominator, the students might arrive at a common measure for the fractions, determine the sum, and see its magnitude on the number line. By operating on these different representations, students are likely to use different solution methods. This variation allows students to discuss the similarities and differences of the representations, the advantages of each, and how they must be connected if they are to yield the same answer.

Connections are most useful when they link related concepts and methods in appropriate ways. Mnemonic techniques learned by rote may provide connections among ideas that make it easier to perform mathematical operations, but they also may not lead to understanding.[7] These are not the kinds of connections that best promote the acquisition of mathematical proficiency.

Knowledge that has been learned with understanding provides the basis for generating new knowledge and for solving new and unfamiliar problems.[8] When students have acquired conceptual understanding in an area of mathematics, they see the connections among concepts and procedures and can give arguments to explain why some facts are consequences of others. They gain confidence, which then provides a base from which they can move to another level of understanding.

With respect to the learning of number, when students thoroughly understand concepts and procedures such as place value and operations with single-digit numbers, they can extend these concepts and procedures to new areas. For example, students who understand place value and other multidigit number concepts are more likely than students without such understanding to invent their own procedures for multicolumn addition and to adopt correct procedures for multicolumn subtraction that others have presented to them.[9]

Thus, learning how to add and subtract multidigit numbers does not have to involve entirely new and unrelated ideas. The same observation can be made for multiplication and division.

Conceptual understanding helps students avoid many critical errors in solving problems, particularly errors of magnitude. For example, if they are multiplying 9.83 and 7.65 and get 7519.95 for the answer, they can immediately decide that it cannot be right. They know that 10×8 is only 80, so multiplying two numbers less than 10 and 8 must give a product less than 80. They might then suspect that the decimal point is incorrectly placed and check that possibility.

Conceptual understanding frequently results in students having less to learn because they can see the deeper similarities between superficially unrelated situations. Their understanding has been encapsulated into compact clusters of interrelated facts and principles. The contents of a given cluster may be summarized by a short sentence or phrase like "properties of multiplication," which is sufficient for use in many situations. If necessary, however, the cluster can be unpacked if the student needs to explain a principle, wants to reflect on a concept, or is learning new ideas. Often, the structure of students' understanding is hierarchical, with simpler clusters of ideas packed into larger, more complex ones. A good example of a knowledge cluster for mathematically proficient older students is the number line. In one easily visualized picture, the student can grasp relations between all the number systems described in chapter 3, along with geometric interpretations for the operations of arithmetic. It connects arithmetic to geometry and later in schooling serves as a link to more advanced mathematics.

As an example of how a knowledge cluster can make learning easier, consider the cluster students might develop for adding whole numbers. If students understand that addition is commutative (e.g., $3 + 5 = 5 + 3$), their learning of basic addition combinations is reduced by almost half. By exploiting their knowledge of other relationships such as that between the doubles (e.g., $5 + 5$ and $6 + 6$) and other sums, they can reduce still further the number of addition combinations they need to learn. Because young children tend to learn the doubles fairly early, they can use them to produce closely related sums.[10] For example, they may see that $6 + 7$ is just one more than $6 + 6$. These relations make it easier for students to learn the new addition combinations because they are generating new knowledge rather than relying on rote memorization. Conceptual understanding, therefore, is a wise investment that pays off for students in many ways.

Procedural Fluency

Procedural fluency refers to knowledge of procedures, knowledge of when and how to use them appropriately, and skill in performing them flexibly, accurately, and efficiently. In the domain of number, procedural fluency is especially needed to support conceptual understanding of place value and the meanings of rational numbers. It also supports the analysis of similarities and differences between methods of calculating. These methods include, in addition to written procedures, mental methods for finding certain sums, differences, products, or quotients, as well as methods that use calculators, computers, or manipulative materials such as blocks, counters, or beads.

Students need to be efficient and accurate in performing basic computations with whole numbers (6 + 7, 17 − 9, 8 × 4, and so on) without always having to refer to tables or other aids. They also need to know reasonably efficient and accurate ways to add, subtract, multiply, and divide multidigit numbers, both mentally and with pencil and paper. A good conceptual understanding of place value in the base-10 system supports the development of fluency in multidigit computation.[11] Such understanding also supports simplified but accurate mental arithmetic and more flexible ways of dealing with numbers than many students ultimately achieve.

Connected with procedural fluency is knowledge of ways to estimate the result of a procedure. It is not as critical as it once was, for example, that students develop speed or efficiency in calculating with large numbers by hand, and there appears to be little value in drilling students to achieve such a goal. But many tasks involving mathematics in everyday life require facility with algorithms for performing computations either mentally or in writing.

In addition to providing tools for computing, some algorithms are important as concepts in their own right, which again illustrates the link between conceptual understanding and procedural fluency. Students need to see that procedures can be developed that will solve entire classes of problems, not just individual problems. By studying algorithms as "general procedures," students can gain insight into the fact that mathematics is well structured (highly organized, filled with patterns, predictable) and that a carefully developed procedure can be a powerful tool for completing routine tasks.

It is important for computational procedures to be efficient, to be used accurately, and to result in correct answers. Both accuracy and efficiency can be improved with practice, which can also help students maintain fluency. Students also need to be able to apply procedures flexibly. Not all computational situations are alike. For example, applying a standard pencil-and-paper algorithm to find the result of every multiplication problem is neither neces-

Procedural fluency refers to knowledge of procedures, knowledge of when and how to use them appropriately, and skill in performing them flexibly, accurately, and efficiently.

sary nor efficient. Students should be able to use a variety of mental strategies to multiply by 10, 20, or 300 (or any power of 10 or multiple of 10). Also, students should be able to perform such operations as finding the sum of 199 and 67 or the product of 4 and 26 by using quick mental strategies rather than relying on paper and pencil. Further, situations vary in their need for exact answers. Sometimes an estimate is good enough, as in calculating a tip on a bill at a restaurant. Sometimes using a calculator or computer is more appropriate than using paper and pencil, as in completing a complicated tax form. Hence, students need facility with a variety of computational tools, and they need to know how to select the appropriate tool for a given situation.

Procedural fluency and conceptual understanding are often seen as competing for attention in school mathematics. But pitting skill against understanding creates a false dichotomy.[12] As we noted earlier, the two are interwoven. Understanding makes learning skills easier, less susceptible to common errors, and less prone to forgetting. By the same token, a certain level of skill is required to learn many mathematical concepts with understanding, and using procedures can help strengthen and develop that understanding. For example, it is difficult for students to understand multidigit calculations if they have not attained some reasonable level of skill in single-digit calculations. On the other hand, once students have learned procedures without understanding, it can be difficult to get them to engage in activities to help them understand the reasons underlying the procedure.[13] In an experimental study, fifth-grade students who first received instruction on procedures for calculating area and perimeter followed by instruction on understanding those procedures did not perform as well as students who received instruction focused only on understanding.[14]

Without sufficient procedural fluency, students have trouble deepening their understanding of mathematical ideas or solving mathematics problems. The attention they devote to working out results they should recall or compute easily prevents them from seeing important relationships. Students need well-timed practice of the skills they are learning so that they are not handicapped in developing the other strands of proficiency.

When students practice procedures they do not understand, there is a danger they will practice incorrect procedures, thereby making it more difficult to learn correct ones. For example, on one standardized test, the grade 2 national norms for two-digit subtraction problems requiring borrowing, such as $62 - 48 = ?$, are 38% correct. Many children subtract the smaller from the larger digit in each column to get 26 as the difference between 62 and 48 (see Box 4-2). If students learn to subtract with understanding, they rarely make

Box 4-2

A common error in multidigit subtraction

$$\begin{array}{r} 62 \\ -\ 48 \\ \hline 26 \end{array}$$

this error.[15] Further, when students learn a procedure without understanding, they need extensive practice so as not to forget the steps. If students do understand, they are less likely to forget critical steps and are more likely to be able to reconstruct them when they do. Shifting the emphasis to learning with understanding, therefore, can in the long run lead to higher levels of skill than can be attained by practice alone.

If students have been using incorrect procedures for several years, then instruction emphasizing understanding may be less effective.[16] When children learn a new, correct procedure, they do not always drop the old one. Rather, they use either the old procedure or the new one depending on the situation. Only with time and practice do they stop using incorrect or inefficient methods.[17] Hence initial learning with understanding can make learning more efficient.

When skills are learned without understanding, they are learned as isolated bits of knowledge.[18] Learning new topics then becomes harder since there is no network of previously learned concepts and skills to link a new topic to. This practice leads to a compartmentalization of procedures that can become quite extreme, so that students believe that even slightly different problems require different procedures. That belief can arise among children in the early grades when, for example, they learn one procedure for subtraction problems without regrouping and another for subtraction problems with regrouping. Another consequence when children learn without understanding is that they separate what happens in school from what happens outside.[19] They have one set of procedures for solving problems outside of school and another they learned and use in school—without seeing the relation between the two. This separation limits children's ability to apply what they learn in school to solve real problems.

Also, students who learn procedures without understanding can typically do no more than apply the learned procedures, whereas students who learn with understanding can modify or adapt procedures to make them easier to use. For example, students with limited understanding of addition would ordinarily need paper and pencil to add 598 and 647. Students with more understanding would recognize that 598 is only 2 less than 600, so they might add 600 and 647 and then subtract 2 from that sum.[20]

Strategic Competence

Strategic competence refers to the ability to formulate mathematical problems, represent them, and solve them. This strand is similar to what has been called problem solving and problem formulation in the literature of mathematics education and cognitive science, and mathematical problem solving, in particular, has been studied extensively.[21]

Although in school, students are often presented with clearly specified problems to solve, outside of school they encounter situations in which part of the difficulty is to figure out exactly what the problem is. Then they need to formulate the problem so that they can use mathematics to solve it. Consequently, they are likely to need experience and practice in problem formulating as well as in problem solving. They should know a variety of solution strategies as well as which strategies might be useful for solving a specific problem. For example, sixth graders might be asked to pose a problem on the topic of the school cafeteria.[22] Some might ask whether the lunches are too expensive or what the most and least favorite lunches are. Others might ask how many trays are used or how many cartons of milk are sold. Still others might ask how the layout of the cafeteria might be improved.

With a formulated problem in hand, the student's first step in solving it is to represent it mathematically in some fashion, whether numerically, symbolically, verbally, or graphically. Fifth graders solving problems about getting from home to school might describe verbally the route they take or draw a scale map of the neighborhood. Representing a problem situation requires, first, that the student build a mental image of its essential components. Becoming strategically competent involves an avoidance of "number grabbing" methods (in which the student selects numbers and prepares to perform arithmetic operations on them)[23] in favor of methods that generate problem models (in which the student constructs a mental model of the variables and relations described in the problem). To represent a problem accurately, students must first understand the situation, including its key features. They then need to generate a mathematical representation of the problem that captures the core mathematical elements and ignores the irrelevant features. This step may be facilitated by making a drawing, writing an equation, or creating some other tangible representation. Consider the following two-step problem:

> *At ARCO, gas sells for $1.13 per gallon.*
> *This is 5 cents less per gallon than gas at Chevron.*
> *How much does 5 gallons of gas cost at Chevron?*

In a common superficial method for representing this problem, students focus on the numbers in the problem and use so-called keywords to cue appropriate arithmetic operations.[24] For example, the quantities *$1.83* and *5 cents* are followed by the keyword *less*, suggesting that the student should subtract 5 cents from $1.13 to get $1.08. Then the keywords *how much* and *5 gallons* suggest that 5 should be multiplied by the result, yielding $5.40.

In contrast, a more proficient approach is to construct a problem model— that is, a mental model of the situation described in the problem. A problem model is not a visual picture per se; rather, it is any form of mental representation that maintains the structural relations among the variables in the problem. One way to understand the first two sentences, for example, might be for a student to envision a number line and locate each cost per gallon on it to solve the problem.

In building a problem model, students need to be alert to the quantities in the problem. It is particularly important that students represent the quantities mentally, distinguishing what is known from what is to be found. Analyses of students' eye fixations reveal that successful solvers of the two-step problem above are likely to focus on terms such as *ARCO*, *Chevron*, and *this*, the principal known and unknown quantities in the problem. Less successful problem solvers tend to focus on specific numbers and keywords such as *$1.13*, *5 cents*, *less*, and *5 gallons* rather than the relationships among the quantities.[25]

Not only do students need to be able to build representations of individual situations, but they also need to see that some representations share common mathematical structures. Novice problem solvers are inclined to notice similarities in surface features of problems, such as the characters or scenarios described in the problem. More expert problem solvers focus more on the structural relationships within problems, relationships that provide the clues for how problems might be solved.[26] For example, one problem might ask students to determine how many different stacks of five blocks can be made using red and green blocks, and another might ask how many different ways hamburgers can be ordered with or without each of the following:

catsup, onions, pickles, lettuce, and tomato. Novices would see these problems as unrelated; experts would see both as involving five choices between two things: red and green, or with and without.[27]

In becoming proficient problem solvers, students learn how to form mental representations of problems, detect mathematical relationships, and devise novel solution methods when needed. A fundamental characteristic needed throughout the problem-solving process is flexibility. Flexibility develops through the broadening of knowledge required for solving nonroutine problems rather than just routine problems.

Routine problems are problems that the learner knows how to solve based on past experience.[28] When confronted with a routine problem, the learner knows a correct solution method and is able to apply it. Routine problems require reproductive thinking; the learner needs only to reproduce and apply a known solution procedure. For example, finding the product of 567 and 46 is a routine problem for most adults because they know what to do and how to do it.

In contrast, nonroutine problems are problems for which the learner does not immediately know a usable solution method. Nonroutine problems require productive thinking because the learner needs to invent a way to understand and solve the problem. For example, for most adults a nonroutine problem of the sort often found in newspaper or magazine puzzle columns is the following:

> *A cycle shop has a total of 36 bicycles and tricycles in stock.*
> *Collectively there are 80 wheels.*
> *How many bikes and how many tricycles are there?*

One solution approach is to reason that all 36 have at least two wheels for a total of $36 \times 2 = 72$ wheels. Since there are 80 wheels in all, the eight additional wheels ($80 - 72$) must belong to 8 tricycles. So there are $36 - 8 = 28$ bikes.

A less sophisticated approach would be to "guess and check": If there were 20 bikes and 16 tricycles, that would give $(20 \times 2) + (16 \times 3) = 88$ wheels, which is too many. Reducing the number of tricycles, a guess of 24 bikes and 12 tricycles gives $(24 \times 2) + (12 \times 3) = 84$ wheels—still too many. Another reduction of the number of tricycles by 4 gives 28 bikes, 8 tricycles, and the 80 wheels needed.

A more sophisticated, algebraic approach would be to let b be the number of bikes and t the number of tricycles. Then $b + t = 36$ and $2b + 3t = 80$. The solution to this system of equations also yields 28 bikes and 8 tricycles.

A student with strategic competence could not only come up with several approaches to a nonroutine problem such as this one but could also choose flexibly among reasoning, guess-and-check, algebraic, or other methods to suit the demands presented by the problem and the situation in which it was posed.

Flexibility of approach is the major cognitive requirement for solving nonroutine problems. It can be seen when a method is created or adjusted to fit the requirements of a novel situation, such as being able to use general principles about proportions to determine the best buy. For example, when the choice is between a 4-ounce can of peanuts for 45 cents and a 10-ounce can for 90 cents, most people use a ratio strategy: the larger can costs twice as much as the smaller can but contains more than twice as many ounces, so it is a better buy. When the choice is between a 14-ounce jar of sauce for 79 cents and an 18-ounce jar for 81 cents, most people use a difference strategy: the larger jar costs just 2 cents more but gets you 4 more ounces, so it is the better buy. When the choice is between a 3-ounce bag of sunflower seeds for 30 cents and a 4-ounce bag for 44 cents, the most common strategy is unit-cost: The smaller bag costs 10 cents per ounce, whereas the larger costs 11 cents per ounce, so the smaller one is the better buy.

There are mutually supportive relations between strategic competence and both conceptual understanding and procedural fluency, as the various approaches to the cycle shop problem illustrate. The development of strategies for solving nonroutine problems depends on understanding the quantities involved in the problems and their relationships as well as on fluency in solving routine problems. Similarly, developing competence in solving nonroutine problems provides a context and motivation for learning to solve routine problems and for understanding concepts such as *given, unknown, condition*, and *solution*.

Strategic competence comes into play at every step in developing procedural fluency in computation. As students learn how to carry out an operation such as two-digit subtraction (for example, 86 – 59), they typically progress from conceptually transparent and effortful procedures to compact and more efficient ones (as discussed in detail in chapter 6). For example, an initial procedure for 86 – 59 might be to use bundles of sticks (see Box 4-3). A compact procedure involves applying a written numerical algorithm that carries out the same steps without the bundles of sticks. Part of developing strategic competence involves learning to replace by more concise and efficient procedures those cumbersome procedures that might at first have been helpful in understanding the operation.

> There are mutually supportive relations between strategic competence and both conceptual understanding and procedural fluency,

Box 4-3

Subtraction Using Sticks: Modeling 86 – 59 = ?

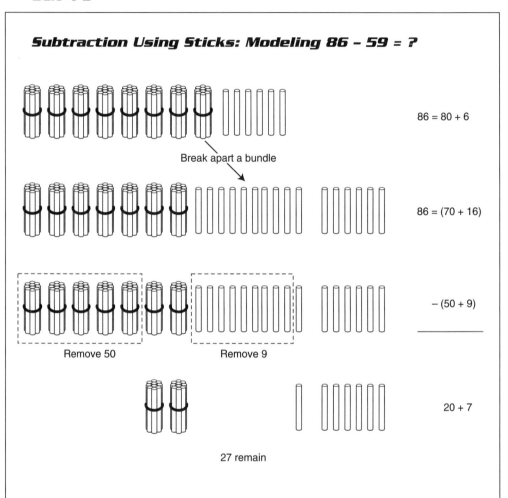

86 = 80 + 6

Break apart a bundle

86 = (70 + 16)

Remove 50   Remove 9

– (50 + 9)
_____

20 + 7

27 remain

Begin with 8 bundles of 10 sticks along with 6 individual sticks. Because you cannot take away 9 individual sticks, open one bundle, creating 7 bundles of 10 sticks and 16 individual sticks. Take away 5 of the bundles (corresponding to subtracting 50), and take away 9 individual sticks (corresponding to subtracting 9). The number of remaining sticks—2 bundles and 7 individual sticks, or 27—is the answer.

Students develop procedural fluency as they use their strategic competence to choose among effective procedures. They also learn that solving challenging mathematics problems depends on the ability to carry out procedures readily and, conversely, that problem-solving experience helps them acquire new concepts and skills. Interestingly, very young children use a variety of strategies to solve problems and will tend to select strategies that are well suited to particular problems.[29] They thereby show the rudiments of adaptive reasoning, the next strand to be discussed.

Adaptive Reasoning

Adaptive reasoning refers to the capacity to think logically about the relationships among concepts and situations. Such reasoning is correct and valid, stems from careful consideration of alternatives, and includes knowledge of how to justify the conclusions. In mathematics, adaptive reasoning is the glue that holds everything together, the lodestar that guides learning. One uses it to navigate through the many facts, procedures, concepts, and solution methods and to see that they all fit together in some way, that they make sense. In mathematics, deductive reasoning is used to settle disputes and disagreements. Answers are right because they follow from some agreed-upon assumptions through series of logical steps. Students who disagree about a mathematical answer need not rely on checking with the teacher, collecting opinions from their classmates, or gathering data from outside the classroom. In principle, they need only check that their reasoning is valid.

Adaptive reasoning refers to the capacity to think logically about the relationships among concepts and situations.

Many conceptions of mathematical reasoning have been confined to formal proof and other forms of deductive reasoning. Our notion of adaptive reasoning is much broader, including not only informal explanation and justification but also intuitive and inductive reasoning based on pattern, analogy, and metaphor. As one researcher put it, "The human ability to find analogical correspondences is a powerful reasoning mechanism."[30] Analogical reasoning, metaphors, and mental and physical representations are "tools to think with," often serving as sources of hypotheses, sources of problem-solving operations and techniques, and aids to learning and transfer.[31]

Some researchers have concluded that children's reasoning ability is quite limited until they are about 12 years old.[32] Yet when asked to talk about how they arrived at their solutions to problems, children as young as 4 and 5 display evidence of encoding and inference and are resistant to counter suggestion.[33] With the help of representation-building experiences, children can demonstrate sophisticated reasoning abilities. After working in pairs and reflecting on their activity, for example, kindergartners can "prove" theorems about sums of even and odd numbers.[34] Through a carefully constructed sequence of activities about adding and removing marbles from a bag containing many marbles,[35] second graders can reason that 5 + (-6) = -1. In the context of cutting short bows from a 12-meter package of ribbon and using physical models to calculate that 12 divided by $\frac{1}{3}$ is 36, fifth graders can reason that 12 divided by $\frac{2}{3}$ cannot be 72 because that would mean getting *more* bows from a package when the individual bow is *larger*, which does not make sense.[36] Research suggests that students are able to display reasoning ability when three conditions are met: They have a sufficient knowledge base, the task is understandable and motivating, and the context is familiar and comfortable.[37]

One manifestation of adaptive reasoning is the ability to justify one's work. We use *justify* in the sense of "provide sufficient reason for." Proof is a form of justification, but not all justifications are proofs. Proofs (both formal and informal) must be logically complete, but a justification may be more telegraphic, merely suggesting the source of the reasoning. Justification and proof are a hallmark of formal mathematics, often seen as the province of older students. However, as pointed out above, students can start learning to justify their mathematical ideas in the earliest grades in elementary school.[38] Kindergarten and first-grade students can be given regular opportunities to talk about the concepts and procedures they are using and to provide good reasons for what they are doing. Classroom norms can be established in which students are expected to justify their mathematical claims and make them clear to others. Students need to be able to justify and explain ideas in order to make their reasoning clear, hone their reasoning skills, and improve their conceptual understanding.[39]

It is not sufficient to justify a procedure just once. As we discuss below, the development of proficiency occurs over an extended period of time. Students need to use new concepts and procedures for some time and to explain and justify them by relating them to concepts and procedures that they already understand. For example, it is not sufficient for students to do only practice problems on adding fractions after the procedure has been developed. If students are to understand the algorithm, they also need experience in explaining and justifying it themselves with many different problems.

Adaptive reasoning interacts with the other strands of proficiency, particularly during problem solving. Learners draw on their strategic competence to formulate and represent a problem, using heuristic approaches that may provide a solution strategy, but adaptive reasoning must take over when they are determining the legitimacy of a proposed strategy. Conceptual understanding provides metaphors and representations that can serve as a source of adaptive reasoning, which, taking into account the limitations of the representations, learners use to determine whether a solution is justifiable and then to justify it. Often a solution strategy will require fluent use of procedures for calculation, measurement, or display, but adaptive reasoning should be used to determine whether the procedure is appropriate. And while carrying out a solution plan, learners use their strategic competence to monitor their progress toward a solution and to generate alternative plans if the current plan seems ineffective. This approach both depends upon productive disposition and supports it.

Productive Disposition

Productive disposition refers to the tendency to see sense in mathematics, to perceive it as both useful and worthwhile, to believe that steady effort in learning mathematics pays off, and to see oneself as an effective learner and doer of mathematics.[40] If students are to develop conceptual understanding, procedural fluency, strategic competence, and adaptive reasoning abilities, they must believe that mathematics is understandable, not arbitrary; that, with diligent effort, it can be learned and used; and that they are capable of figuring it out. Developing a productive disposition requires frequent opportunities to make sense of mathematics, to recognize the benefits of perseverance, and to experience the rewards of sense making in mathematics.

A productive disposition develops when the other strands do and helps each of them develop. For example, as students build strategic competence in solving nonroutine problems, their attitudes and beliefs about themselves as mathematics learners become more positive. The more mathematical concepts they understand, the more sensible mathematics becomes. In contrast, when students are seldom given challenging mathematical problems to solve, they come to expect that memorizing rather than sense making paves the road to learning mathematics,[41] and they begin to lose confidence in themselves as learners. Similarly, when students see themselves as capable of learning mathematics and using it to solve problems, they become able to develop further their procedural fluency or their adaptive reasoning abilities. Students' disposition toward mathematics is a major factor in determining their educational success. Students who view their mathematical ability as fixed and test questions as measuring their ability rather than providing opportunities to learn are likely to avoid challenging problems and be easily dis-

Productive disposition refers to the tendency to see sense in mathematics, to perceive it as both useful and worthwhile, to believe that steady effort in learning mathematics pays off, and to see oneself as an effective learner and doer of mathematics.

couraged by failure.[42] Students who view ability as expandable in response to experience and training are more likely to seek out challenging situations and learn from them. Cross-cultural research studies have found that U.S. children are more likely to attribute success in school to ability rather than effort when compared with students in East Asian countries.[43]

Most U.S. children enter school eager to learn and with positive attitudes toward mathematics. It is critical that they encounter good mathematics teaching in the early grades. Otherwise, those positive attitudes may turn sour as they come to see themselves as poor learners and mathematics as nonsensical, arbitrary, and impossible to learn except by rote memorization.[44] Such views, once adopted, can be extremely difficult to change.[45]

The teacher of mathematics plays a critical role in encouraging students to maintain positive attitudes toward mathematics. How a teacher views mathematics and its learning affects that teacher's teaching practice,[46] which ultimately affects not only what the students learn but how they view themselves as mathematics learners. Teachers and students inevitably negotiate among themselves the norms of conduct in the class, and when those norms allow students to be comfortable in doing mathematics and sharing their ideas with others, they see themselves as capable of understanding.[47] In chapter 9 we discuss some of the ways in which teachers' expectations and the teaching strategies they use can help students maintain a positive attitude toward mathematics, and in chapter 10 we discuss some programs of teacher development that may help teachers in that endeavor.

An earlier report from the National Research Council identified the cause of much poor performance in school mathematics in the United States:

> The unrestricted power of peer pressure often makes good performance in mathematics socially unacceptable. This environment of negative expectation is strongest among minorities and women— those most at risk—during the high school years when students first exercise choice in curricular goals.[48]

Some of the most important consequences of students' failure to develop a productive disposition toward mathematics occur in high school, when they have the opportunity to avoid challenging mathematics courses. Avoiding such courses may eliminate the need to face up to peer pressure and other sources of discouragement, but it does so at the expense of precluding careers in science, technology, medicine, and other fields that require a high level of mathematical proficiency.

Research with older students and adults suggests that a phenomenon termed *stereotype threat* might account for much of the observed differences in mathematics performance between ethnic groups and between male and female students.[49] In this phenomenon, good students who care about their performance in mathematics and who belong to groups stereotyped as being poor at mathematics perform poorly on difficult mathematics problems under conditions in which they feel pressure to conform to the stereotype. So-called wise educational environments[50] can reduce the harmful effects of stereotype threat. These environments emphasize optimistic teacher-student relationships, give challenging work to all students, and stress the expandability of ability, among other factors.

Students who have developed a productive disposition are confident in their knowledge and ability. They see that mathematics is both reasonable and intelligible and believe that, with appropriate effort and experience, they can learn. It is counterproductive for students to believe that there is some mysterious "math gene" that determines their success in mathematics.

Hence, our view of mathematical proficiency goes beyond being able to understand, compute, solve, and reason. It includes a disposition toward mathematics that is personal. Mathematically proficient people believe that mathematics should make sense, that they can figure it out, that they can solve mathematical problems by working hard on them, and that becoming mathematically proficient is worth the effort.

Properties of Mathematical Proficiency

Now that we have looked at each strand separately, let us consider mathematical proficiency as a whole. As we indicated earlier and as the preceding discussion illustrates, the five strands are interconnected and must work together if students are to learn successfully. Learning is not an all-or-none phenomenon, and as it proceeds, each strand of mathematical proficiency should be developed in synchrony with the others. That development takes time. One of the most challenging tasks faced by teachers in pre-kindergarten to grade 8 is to see that children are making progress along every strand and not just one or two.

The Strands of Proficiency Are Interwoven

How the strands of mathematical proficiency interweave and support one another can be seen in the case of conceptual understanding and procedural fluency. Current research indicates that these two strands of proficiency con-

Learning is not an all-or-none phenomenon, and as it proceeds, each strand of mathematical proficiency should be developed in synchrony with the others.

tinually interact.[51] As a child gains conceptual understanding, computational procedures are remembered better and used more flexibly to solve new problems. In turn, as a procedure becomes more automatic, the child is enabled to think about other aspects of a problem and to tackle new kinds of problems, which leads to new understanding. When using a procedure, a child may reflect on why the procedure works, which may in turn strengthen existing conceptual understanding.[52] Indeed, it is not always necessary, useful, or even possible to distinguish concepts from procedures because understanding and doing are interconnected in such complex ways.

Consider, for instance, the multiplication of multidigit whole numbers. Many algorithms for computing 47×268 use one basic meaning of multiplication as 47 groups of 268, together with place-value knowledge of 47 as $40 + 7$, to break the problem into two simpler ones: 40×268 and 7×268. For example, a common algorithm for computing 47×268 is written the following way, with the two so-called partial products, 10720 and 1876, coming from the two simpler problems:

$$
\begin{array}{r}
268 \\
\times\ 47 \\
\hline
1876 \\
1072 \\
\hline
12596
\end{array}
$$

Familiarity with this algorithm may make it hard for adults to see how much knowledge is needed for it. It requires knowing that 40×268 is $4 \times 10 \times 268$; knowing that in the product of 268 and 10, each digit of 268 is one place to the left; having enough fluency with basic multiplication combinations to find 7×8, 7×60, 7×200, and 4×8, 4×60, 4×200; and having enough fluency with multidigit addition to add the partial products. As students learn to execute a multidigit multiplication procedure such as this one, they should develop a deeper understanding of multiplication and its properties. On the other hand, as they deepen their conceptual understanding, they should become more fluent in computation. A beginner who happens to forget the algorithm but who understands the role of the distributive law can reconstruct the process by writing $268 \times 47 = 268 \times (40 + 7) = (268 \times 40) + (268 \times 7)$ and working from there. A beginner who has simply memorized the algorithm without understanding much about how it works can be lost later when memory fails.

Proficiency Is Not All or Nothing

Mathematical proficiency cannot be characterized as simply present or absent. Every important mathematical idea can be understood at many levels and in many ways. For example, even seemingly simple concepts such as even and odd require an integration of several ways of thinking: choosing alternate points on the number line, grouping items by twos, grouping items into two groups, and looking at only the last digit of the number. When children are first learning about even and odd, they may know one or two of these interpretations.[53]   But at an older age, a deep understanding of even and odd means all four interpretations are connected and can be justified one based on the others.

The research cited in chapter 5 shows that schoolchildren are never complete mathematical novices. They bring important mathematical concepts and skills with them to school as well as misconceptions that must be taken into account in planning instruction. Obviously, a first grader's understanding of addition is not the same as that of a mathematician or even a lay adult. It is still reasonable, however, to talk about a first grader as being proficient with single-digit addition, as long as the student's thinking in that realm incorporates all five strands of proficiency. Students should not be thought of as having proficiency when one or more strands are undeveloped.

Proficiency Develops Over Time

Proficiency in mathematics is acquired over time. Each year they are in school, students ought to become increasingly proficient. For example, third graders should be more proficient with the addition of whole numbers than they were in the first grade.

Acquiring proficiency takes time in another sense. Students need enough time to engage in activities around a specific mathematical topic if they are to become proficient with it. When they are provided with only one or two examples to illustrate why a procedure works or what a concept means and then move on to practice in carrying out the procedure or identifying the concept, they may easily fail to learn. To become proficient, they need to spend sustained periods of time doing mathematics—solving problems, reasoning, developing understanding, practicing skills—and building connections between their previous knowledge and new knowledge.

How Mathematically Proficient Are U.S. Students Today?

One question that warrants an immediate answer is whether students in U.S. elementary and middle schools today are becoming mathematically proficient. The answer is important because it influences what might be recommended for the future. If students are failing to develop proficiency, the question of how to improve school mathematics takes on a different cast than if students are already developing high levels of proficiency.

The best source of information about student performance in the United States is, as we noted in chapter 2, the National Assessment of Educational Progress (NAEP), a regular assessment of students' knowledge and skills in the school subjects. NAEP includes a large and representative sample of U.S. students at about ages 9, 13, and 17, so the results provide a good picture of students' mathematical performance. We sketched some of that performance in chapter 2, but now we look at it through the frame of mathematical proficiency.

Although the items in the NAEP assessments were not constructed to measure directly the five strands of mathematical proficiency, they provide some useful information about these strands. As in chapter 2, the data reported here are from the 1996 main NAEP assessment except when we refer explicitly to the long-term trend assessment. In general, the performance of 13-year-olds over the past 25 years tells the following story: Given traditional curricula and methods of instruction, students develop proficiency among the five strands in a very uneven way. They are most proficient in aspects of procedural fluency and less proficient in conceptual understanding, strategic competence, adaptive reasoning, and productive disposition. Many students show few connections among these strands. Examples from each strand illustrate the current situation.[54]

Conceptual Understanding

Students' conceptual understanding of number can be assessed in part by asking them about properties of the number systems. Although about 90% of U.S. 13-year-olds could add and subtract multidigit numbers, only 60% of them could construct a number given its digits and their place values (e.g., in the number 57, the digit 5 should represent five tens).[55] That is a common finding: More students can calculate successfully with numbers than can work with the properties of the same numbers.

The same is true for rational numbers. Only 35% of 13-year-olds correctly ordered three fractions, all in reduced form,[56] and only 35%, asked for a number between .03 and .04, chose the correct response.[57] These findings suggest that students may be calculating with numbers that they do not really understand.

Procedural Fluency

An overall picture of procedural fluency is provided by the NAEP long-term trend mathematics assessment,[58] which indicates that U.S. students' performance has remained quite steady over the past 25 years (see Box 4-4). A closer look reveals that the picture of procedural fluency is one of high levels of proficiency in the easiest contexts. Questions in which students are asked to add or subtract two- and three-digit whole numbers presented numerically in the standard format are answered correctly by about 90% of 13-year-olds, with almost as good performance among 9-year-olds.[59] Performance is slightly lower among 13-year-olds for division.[60]

Box 4-4

NAEP Scale Scores, Long-Term Trend Assessment, 1973-1999

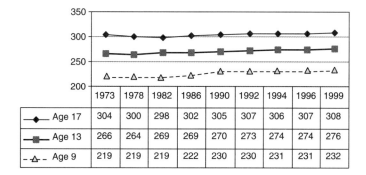

	1973	1978	1982	1986	1990	1992	1994	1996	1999
Age 17	304	300	298	302	305	307	306	307	308
Age 13	266	264	269	269	270	273	274	274	276
Age 9	219	219	219	222	230	230	231	231	232

SOURCE: Campbell, Hombo, and Mazzeo, 2000, p. 9. These scale scores include all content areas: number, geometry, algebra, and so on.

Students are less fluent in operating with rational numbers, both common and decimal fractions. The most recent NAEP in 1996 contained few computation items, but earlier assessments showed that about 50% of 13-year-olds correctly completed problems like $3\frac{1}{2} - 3\frac{1}{3}$, $4 \times 2\frac{1}{2}$, and $4.3 - 0.53$. Again, this level of performance has remained quite steady since the advent of NAEP. One conclusion that can be drawn is that by age 13 many students have not fully developed procedural fluency. Although most can compute well with whole numbers in simple contexts, many still have difficulties computing with rational numbers.

Strategic Competence

Results from NAEP dating back over 25 years have continually documented the fact that one of the greatest deficits in U.S. students' learning of mathematics is in their ability to solve problems. In the 1996 NAEP, students in the fourth, eighth, and twelfth grades did well on questions about basic whole number operations and concepts in numerical and simple applied contexts. However, students, especially those in the fourth and eighth grades, had difficulty with more complex problem-solving situations. For example, asked to add or subtract two- and three-digit numbers, 73% of fourth graders and 86% of eighth graders gave correct answers. But on a multistep addition and subtraction word problem involving similar numbers, only 33% of fourth graders gave a correct answer (although 76% of eighth graders did). On the 23 problem-solving tasks given as part of the 1996 NAEP in which students had to construct an extended response, the incidence of satisfactory or better responses was less than 10% on about half of the tasks. The incidence of satisfactory responses was greater than 25% on only two tasks.[61]

Performance on word problems declines dramatically when additional features are included, such as more than one step or extraneous information. Small changes in problem wording, context, or presentation can yield dramatic changes in students' success,[62] perhaps indicating how fragile students' problem-solving abilities typically are.

Adaptive Reasoning

Several kinds of items measure students' proficiency in adaptive reasoning, though often in conjunction with other strands. One kind of item asks students to reason about numbers and their properties and also assesses their conceptual understanding. For example,

If 49 + 83 = 132 is true, which of the following is true?

> *49 = 83 + 132*
> *49 + 132 = 83*
> *132 – 49 = 83*
> *83 – 132 = 49*

Only 61% of 13-year-olds chose the right answer, which again is considerably lower than the percentage of students who can actually compute the result.

Another example is a multiple-choice problem in which students were asked to estimate $\frac{12}{13} + \frac{7}{8}$. The choices were 1, 2, 19, and 21. Fifty-five percent of the 13-year-olds chose either 19 or 21 as the correct response.[63] Even modest levels of reasoning should have prevented these errors. Simply observing that $\frac{12}{13}$ and $\frac{7}{8}$ are numbers less than one and that the sum of two numbers less than one is less than two would have made it apparent that 19 and 21 were unreasonable answers. This level of performance is especially striking because this kind of reasoning does not require procedural fluency *plus* additional proficiency. In many ways it is less demanding than the computational task and requires only that basic understanding and reasoning be connected. It is clear that for many students that connection is not being made.

A second kind of item that measures adaptive reasoning is one that asks students to justify and explain their solutions. One such item (Box 4-5) required that students use subtraction and division to justify claims about the population growth in two towns. Only 1% of eighth graders in 1996 provided a satisfactory response for both claims, and only another 21% provided a partially correct response. The results were only slightly better at grade 12. In this item, Darlene's claim is stated somewhat cryptically, and students may not have understood that they needed to think about population growth not additively—as in the case of Brian's claim—but multiplicatively so as to conclude that Town A actually had the larger rate of growth. But given the low levels of performance on the item, we conclude that Darlene's enigmatic claim was not the only source of difficulty. Students apparently have trouble justifying their answers even in relatively simple cases.

Productive Disposition

Research related to productive disposition has not examined many aspects of the strand as we have defined it. Such research has focused on attitudes

Box 4-5

Population Growth in Two Towns

In 1980 the populations of Town A and Town B were 5,000 and 6,000, respectively. The 1990 populations of Town A and Town B were 8,000 and 9,000, respectively.

Brian claims that from 1980 to 1990 the populations of the two towns grew by the same amount. Use mathematics to explain how Brian might have justified his claim.

Darlene claims that from 1980 to 1990 the population of Town A grew more. Use mathematics to explain how Darlene might have justified her claim.

NAEP Results	Grade 8	Grade 12
Correct response for both claims	1%	3%
Partial response	21%	24%
Incorrect response	60%	56%
Omitted	16%	16%

SOURCE: 1996 NAEP assessment. Cited in Wearne and Kouba, 2000, p. 186. Used by permission of National Council of Teachers of Mathematics.

toward mathematics, beliefs about one's own ability, and beliefs about the nature of mathematics. In general, U.S. boys have more positive attitudes toward mathematics than U.S. girls do, even though differences in achievement between boys and girls are, in general, not as pronounced today as they were some decades ago.[64] Girls' attitudes toward mathematics also decline more sharply through the grades than those of boys.[65] Differences in mathematics achievement remain larger across groups that differ in such factors as race, ethnicity, and social class, but differences in attitudes toward mathematics across these groups are not clearly associated with achievement differences.[66]

The complex relationship between attitudes and achievement is well illustrated in recent international studies. Although within most countries, positive attitudes toward mathematics are associated with high achievement, eighth graders in some East Asian countries, whose average achievement in mathematics is among the highest in the world, have tended to have, on average, among the most negative attitudes toward mathematics. U.S. eighth graders, whose achievement is around the international average, have tended to be about average in their attitudes.[67] Similarly, within a country, students who perceive themselves as good at mathematics tend to have high levels of achievement, but that relationship does not hold across countries. In Asian countries, perhaps because of cultural traditions encouraging humility or because of the challenging curriculum they face, eighth graders tend to perceive themselves as not very good at mathematics. In the United States, in contrast, eighth graders tend to believe that mathematics is not especially difficult for them and that they are good at it.[68]

Data from the NAEP student questionnaire show that many U.S. students develop a variety of counterproductive beliefs about mathematics and about themselves as learners of mathematics. For example, 54% of the fourth graders and 40% of the eighth graders in the 1996 NAEP assessment thought that mathematics is mostly a set of rules and that learning mathematics means memorizing the rules. On the other hand, approximately 75% of the fourth graders and 75% of the eighth graders sampled reported that they understand most of what goes on in mathematics class. The data do not indicate, however, whether the students thought they could make sense out of the mathematics themselves or depended on others for explanations.

Despite the finding that many students associate mathematics with memorization, students at all grade levels appear to view mathematics as useful. The 1996 NAEP revealed that 69% of the fourth graders and 70% of the eighth graders agreed that mathematics is useful for solving everyday problems. Although students appear to think mathematics is useful for everyday problems or important to society in general, it is not clear that they think it is important for them as individuals to know a lot of mathematics.[69]

Proficiency in Other Domains of Mathematics

Although our discussion of mathematical proficiency in this report is focused on the domain of number, the five strands apply equally well to other domains of mathematics such as geometry, measurement, probability, and statistics. Regardless of the domain of mathematics, conceptual understanding refers to an integrated and functional grasp of the mathematical ideas. These may be ideas about shape and space, measure, pattern, function, uncertainty, or change. When applied to other domains of mathematics, procedural fluency refers to skill in performing flexibly, accurately, and efficiently such procedures as constructing shapes, measuring space, computing probabilities, and describing data. It also refers to knowing when and how to use

The five strands apply equally well to other domains of mathematics such as geometry, measurement, probability, and statistics.

those procedures. Strategic competence refers to the ability to formulate mathematical problems, represent them, and solve them whether the problems arise in the context of number, algebra, geometry, measurement, probability, or statistics. Similarly, the capacity to think logically about the relationships among concepts and situations and to reason adaptively applies to every domain of mathematics, not just number, as does the notion of a productive disposition. The tendency to see sense in mathematics, to perceive it as both useful and worthwhile, to believe that steady effort in learning mathematics pays off, and to see oneself as an effective learner and doer of mathematics applies equally to all domains of mathematics. We believe that proficiency in any domain of mathematics means the development of the five strands, that the strands of proficiency are interwoven, and that they develop over time. Further, the strands are interwoven across domains of mathematics in such a way that conceptual understanding in one domain, say geometry, supports conceptual understanding in another, say number.

All Students Should Be Mathematically Proficient

Becoming mathematically proficient is necessary and appropriate for all students. People sometimes assume that only the brightest students who are the most attuned to school can achieve mathematical proficiency. Those students are the ones who have traditionally tended to achieve no matter what kind of instruction they have encountered. But perhaps surprisingly, it is students who have historically been less successful in school who have the most potential to benefit from instruction designed to achieve proficiency.[70] All will benefit from a program in which mathematical proficiency is the goal.

Historically, the prevailing ethos in mathematics and mathematics education in the United States has been that mathematics is a discipline for a select group of learners. The continuing failure of some groups to master mathematics—including disproportionate numbers of minorities and poor students—has served to confirm that assumption. More recently, mathematics educators have highlighted the universal aspects of mathematics and have insisted on mathematics for *all* students, but with little attention to the differential access that some students have to high-quality mathematics teaching.[71]

One concern has been that too few girls, relative to boys, are developing mathematical proficiency and continuing their study of mathematics. That situation appears to be improving, although perhaps not uniformly across grades. The 1990 and 1992 NAEP assessments indicated that the few gender differences in mathematics performance that did appear favored male students at grade 12 but not before. These differences were only partly explained by the historical tendency of male students to take more high school mathematics courses than female students do, since that gap had largely closed by 1992. In the 1996 NAEP mathematics assessment, the average scores for male and female students were not significantly different at either grade 8 or grade 12, but the average score for fourth-grade boys was 2% higher than the score for fourth-grade girls.[72]

With regard to differences among racial and ethnic groups, the situation is rather different. The racial/ethnic diversity of the United States is much greater now than at any previous period in history and promises to become progressively more so for some time to come. The strong connection between economic advantage, school funding, and achievement in the United States has meant that groups of students whose mathematics achievement is low have tended to be disproportionately African American, Hispanic, Native American, students acquiring English, or students located in urban or rural school districts.[73] In the NAEP assessments from 1990 to 1996, white students recorded increases in their average mathematics scores at all grades. Over the same period, African American and Hispanic students recorded increases at grades 4 and 12, but not at grade 8.[74] Scores for African American, Hispanic, and American Indian students remained below scale scores for white students. The mathematics achievement gaps between average scores for these subgroups did not decrease in 1996.[75] The gap appears to be widening for African American students, particularly among students of the best-educated parents, which suggests that the problem is not one solely of poverty and disadvantage.[76]

Students identified as being of middle and high socioeconomic status (SES) enter school with higher achievement levels in mathematics than low-SES students, and students reporting higher levels of parental education tend to have higher average scores on NAEP assessments. At all three grades, in contrast, students eligible for free or reduced-price lunch programs score lower than those not eligible.[77] Such SES-based differences in mathematics achievement are greater among whites than among other racial or ethnic groups.[78] Some studies have suggested that the basis for the differences resides in the opportunities available to students, including opportunities to attend effective schools,[79] opportunities afforded by social and economic factors of the home and school community,[80] and opportunities to get encouragement to continue the study of mathematics.[81]

Goals for mathematics instruction like those outlined in our discussion of mathematical proficiency need to be set in full recognition of the differential access students have to high-quality mathematics teaching and the differential performance they show. Those goals should never be set low, however, in the mistaken belief that some students do not need or cannot achieve proficiency. In this day of rapidly changing technologies, no one can anticipate all the skills that students will need over their lifetimes or the problems they will encounter. Proficiency in mathematics is therefore an important foundation for further instruction in mathematics as well as for further education in fields that require mathematical competence. Schools need to prepare students to acquire new skills and knowledge and to adapt their knowledge to solve new problems.

The currency of value in the job market today is more than computational competence. It is the ability to apply knowledge to solve problems.[82] For students to be able to compete in today's and tomorrow's economy, they need to be able to adapt the knowledge they are acquiring. They need to be able to learn new concepts and skills. They need to be able to apply mathematical reasoning to problems. They need to view mathematics as a useful tool that must constantly be sharpened. In short, they need to be mathematically proficient.

Students who have learned only procedural skills and have little understanding of mathematics will have limited access to advanced schooling, better jobs, and other opportunities. If any group of students is deprived of the opportunity to learn with understanding, they are condemned to second-class status in society, or worse.

A Broader, Deeper View

Many people in the United States consider procedural fluency to be the heart of the elementary school mathematics curriculum. They remember school mathematics as being devoted primarily to learning and practicing computational procedures. In this report, we present a much broader view of elementary and middle school mathematics. We also raise the standard for success in learning mathematics and being able to use it. In a significant and fortuitous twist, raising the standard by requiring development across all five strands of mathematical proficiency makes the development of any one strand more feasible. Because the strands interact and boost each other, students who have opportunities to develop all strands of proficiency are more likely to become truly competent with each.

We conclude that during the past 25 years mathematics instruction in U.S. schools has not sufficiently developed mathematical proficiency in the sense we have defined it. It has developed some procedural fluency, but it clearly has not helped students develop the other strands very far, nor has it helped them connect the strands. Consequently, all strands have suffered. In the next four chapters, we look again at students' learning. We consider not just performance levels but also the nature of the learning process itself. We describe what students are capable of, what the big obstacles are for them, and what knowledge and intuition they have that might be helpful in designing effective learning experiences. This information, we believe, reveals how to improve current efforts to help students become mathematically proficient.

Notes

1. Brownell, 1935.
2. National Assessment Governing Board, 2000.
3. See Hiebert and Carpenter, 1992, for a discussion of the ways that cognitive science informs mathematics education on the nature of conceptual understanding. For views about learning in general, see Bransford, Brown, and Cocking, 1999; Donovan, Bransford, and Pellegrino, 1999. For discussion of learning in early childhood, see Bowman, Donovan, and Burns, 2001.
4. Bransford, Brown, and Cocking, 1999; Carpenter and Lehrer, 1999; Greeno, Pearson, and Schoenfeld, 1997; Hiebert, 1986; Hiebert and Carpenter, 1992. For a broader perspective on classrooms that promote understanding, see Fennema and Romberg, 1999.
5. See, for example, Hiebert and Carpenter, 1992, pp. 74–75; Hiebert and Wearne, 1996. For work in psychology, see Baddeley, 1976; Bruner, 1960, pp. 24–25; Druckman and Bjork, 1991, pp. 30–33; Hilgard, 1957; Katona, 1940; Mayer, 1999; Wertheimer, 1959.
6. Geary, 1995.
7. Hiebert and Wearne, 1986; Kilpatrick, 1985.
8. Bransford, Brown, and Cocking, 1999.
9. Hiebert and Wearne, 1996.
10. Steinberg, 1985; Thornton and Toohey, 1985.
11. Fuson, 1990, 1992b; Fuson and Briars, 1990; Fuson and Burghardt, 1993; Hiebert, Carpenter, Fennema, Fuson, Wearne, Murray, Olivier, and Human, 1997; Hiebert and Wearne, 1996; Resnick and Omanson, 1987.
12. Brownell, 1956/1987; Wu, 1999.
13. Brownell, 1935; Carpenter, Franke, Jacobs, Fennema, and Empson, 1998; Hatano, 1988; Wearne and Hiebert, 1988; Mack, 1995; Rittle-Johnson and Alibali, 1999.
14. Pesek and Kirshner, 2000.
15. Fuson and Briars, 1990; Fuson, Carroll, and Landis, 1996.
16. Resnick and Omanson, 1987.

17. Alibali, 1999; Lemaire and Siegler, 1995; Siegler and Jenkins, 1989.
18. Researchers have shown clear disconnections between students' "street mathematics" and school mathematics, implying that skills learned without understanding are learned as isolated bits of knowledge. See, for example, Nunes, 1992a, 1992b; Saxe, 1990. It should be emphasized that, as discussed above, conceptual understanding requires that knowledge be connected. See Bransford, Brown, and Cocking, 1999; Hiebert and Carpenter, 1992.
19. Saxe, 1990.
20. Carpenter, Franke, Jacobs, Fennema, and Empson, 1998.
21. See Schoenfeld, 1992; and Mayer and Wittrock, 1996, for reviews.
22. Wiest, 2000.
23. Such methods are discussed by Schoenfeld, 1988.
24. Mayer and Hegarty, 1996.
25. Hagarty, Mayer, and Monk, 1995.
26. Bransford, Brown, and Cocking, 1999, pp. 19-38. See also Krutetskii, 1968/1976, ch. 13.
27. For each of the five levels in the stack of blocks, there are two options: red or green. Similarly, for each of the five toppings on the hamburger, there are two options: include the topping or exclude it. The connection might be made explicit as follows: Let each level in the stack of blocks denote a particular topping (e.g., 1, catsup; 2, onions; 3, pickles; 4, lettuce; 5, tomato) and let the color signify whether the topping is to be included (e.g., green, include; red, exclude). Such a scheme establishes a correspondence between the $2 \times 2 \times 2 \times 2 \times 2 = 32$ stacks of blocks and the 32 kinds of hamburgers.
28. Pólya, 1945, defined such problems as follows: "In general, a problem is called a 'routine problem' if it can be solved either by substituting special data into a formerly solved general problem, or by following step by step, without any trace of originality, some well-worn conspicuous example" (p. 171).
29. Siegler and Jenkins, 1989.
30. English, 1997a, p. 4.
31. English, 1997a, p. 4. See English, 1997b, for an extended discussion of these ideas.
32. For example, Inhelder and Piaget, 1958; Sternberg and Rifkin, 1979.
33. Alexander, White, and Daugherty, 1997, p. 122.
34. Davis and Maher, 1997, p. 94.
35. Davis and Maher, 1997, pp. 99–100.
36. Davis and Maher, 1997, pp. 101–102.
37. Alexander, White, and Daugherty, 1997, propose these three conditions for reasoning in young children. There is reason to believe that the conditions apply more generally.
38. Carpenter and Levi, 1999; Hiebert, Carpenter, Fennema, Fuson, Wearne, Murray, Olivier, and Human, 1997; Schifter, 1999; Yaffee, 1999.
39. Maher and Martino, 1996.
40. There is a precedent for this term: "Students come to think of themselves as capable of engaging in independent thinking and of exercising control over their learning process [contributing] to what can best be called the disposition to higher order

thinking. The term *disposition* should not be taken to imply a biological or inherited trait. As used here, it is more akin to a *habit* of thought, one that can be learned and, therefore, taught" (Resnick, 1987, p. 41).

41. Schoenfeld, 1989.

42. Dweck, 1986.

43. See, for example, Stevenson and Stigler, 1992. Other researchers claim that Asian children are significantly more oriented toward ability than their U.S. peers and that in both groups attributing success to ability is connected with high achievement (Bempechat and Drago-Severson, 1999).

44. For evidence that U.S. students' attitudes toward mathematics decline as they proceed through the grades, see Silver, Strutchens, and Zawojewski, 1997; Strutchens and Silver, 2000; Ansell and Doerr, 2000.

45. McLeod, 1992.

46. Thompson, 1992.

47. Cobb, Yackel, and Wood, 1989, 1995. For a more general discussion of classroom norms, see Cobb and Bauersfeld, 1995; and Fennema and Romberg, 1999.

48. National Research Council, 1989, p. 10.

49. Steele, 1997; and Steele and Aronson, 1995, show the effect of stereotype threat in regard to subsets of the GRE (Graduate Record Examination) verbal exam, and it seems this phenomenon may carry across disciplines.

50. Steele, 1997.

51. Fuson 1992a, 1992b; Hiebert, 1986; Hiebert, Carpenter, Fennema, Fuson, Wearne, Murray, Olivier, and Human, 1997. A recent synthesis by Rittle-Johnson and Siegler, 1998, on the relationship between conceptual and procedural knowledge in mathematics concludes that they are highly correlated and that the order of development depends upon the mathematical content and upon the students and their instructional experiences, particularly for multidigit arithmetic.

52. Hiebert and Wearne, 1996.

53. Ball and Bass, 2000.

54. The NAEP data reported on the five strands are drawn from chapters in Silver and Kenney, 2000.

55. Kouba and Wearne, 2000.

56. Wearne and Kouba, 2000.

57. Kouba, Carpenter, and Swafford, 1989, p. 83.

58. The NAEP long-term trend mathematics assessment "is more heavily weighted [than the main NAEP] toward students' knowledge of basic facts and the ability to carry out numerical algorithms using paper and pencil, exhibit knowledge of basic measurement formulas as they are applied in geometric settings, and complete questions reflecting the direct application of mathematics to daily-living skills (such as those related to time and money)" (Campbell, Voelkl, and Donahue, 2000, p. 50).

59. Kouba and Wearne, 2000, p. 150.

60. Kouba and Wearne, 2000, p. 155.

61. Silver, Alacaci, and Stylianou, 2000.

62. Shannon, 1999.

63. Carpenter, Corbitt, Kepner, Lindquist, and Reys, 1981.
64. See Leder, 1992, and Fennema, 1995, for summaries of the research. In NAEP, gender differences may have increased slightly at grade 4 in the past decade, although they are still quite small; see Ansell and Doerr, 2000.
65. Ansell and Doerr, 2000.
66. For a review of the literature on race, ethnicity, social class, and language in mathematics, see Secada, 1992. Relevant findings from NAEP can be found in Silver, Strutchens, and Zawojewski, 1997; and Strutchens and Silver, 2000.
67. Beaton, Mullis, Martin, Gonzalez, Kelly, and Smith, 1996, pp. 124–125, 128; Mullis, Martin, Gonzalez, Gregory, Garden, O'Connor, Chrostowski, and Smith, 2000, pp. 137–144.
68. Mullis, Martin, Gonzalez, Gregory, Garden, O'Connor, Chrostowski, and Smith, 2000, pp. 132–136.
69. Swafford and Brown, 1989, p. 112.
70. Knapp, Shields, and Turnbull, 1995; Mason, Schroeter, Combs, and Washington, 1992; Steele, 1997.
71. Ladson-Billings, 1999, p. 1.
72. Reese, Miller, Mazzeo, and Dossey, 1997.
73. Tate, 1997.
74. Reese, Miller, Mazzeo, and Dossey, 1997, p. 31.
75. Reese, Miller, Mazzeo, and Dossey, 1997.
76. Zernike, 2000.
77. Reese, Miller, Mazzeo, and Dossey, 1997.
78. Secada, 1992.
79. Mullis, Jenkins, and Johnson, 1994.
80. Oakes, 1990.
81. Backer and Akin, 1993.
82. Committee for Economic Development, 1995; National Research Council, 1989, 1998; U.S. Department of Labor, Secretary's Commission on Achieving Necessary Skills, 1991.

References

Alexander, P. A., White, C. S., & Daugherty, M. (1997). Analogical reasoning and early mathematics learning. In L. D. English (Ed.), *Mathematical reasoning: Analogies, metaphors, and images* (pp. 117–147). Mahwah, NJ: Erlbaum.

Alibali, M. W. (1999). How children change their minds: Strategy change can be gradual or abrupt. *Developmental Psychology, 35,* 127–145.

Ansell, E., & Doerr, H. M. (2000). NAEP findings regarding gender: Achievement, affect, and instructional experiences. In E. A. Silver & P. A. Kenney (Eds.), *Results from the seventh mathematics assessment of the National Assessment of Educational Progress* (pp. 73–106). Reston, VA, National Council of Teachers of Mathematics.

Backer, A., & Akin, S. (Eds.). (1993). *Every child can succeed: Reading for school improvement.* Bloomington, IN: Agency for Instructional Television.

Baddeley, A. D. (1976). *The psychology of memory.* New York: Basic Books.

Ball, D. L., & Bass, H. (2000). Making believe: The collective construction of public mathematical knowledge in the elementary classroom. In D. Phillips (Ed.), *Constructivism in education: Opinions and second opinions on controversial issues* (Ninety-ninth Yearbook of the National Society for the Study of Education, Part 1, pp. 193–224). Chicago: University of Chicago Press.

Beaton, A. E., Mullis, I. V. S., Martin, M. O., Gonzalez, E. J., Kelly, D. L., & Smith, T. A. (1996). *Mathematics achievement in the middle school years: IEA's Third International Mathematics and Science Study.* Chestnut Hill, MA: Boston College, Center for the Study of Testing, Evaluation, and Educational Policy. Available: http://www.timss.org/timss1995i/MathB.html.

Bempechat, J. & Drago-Severson, E. (1999). Cross-national differences in academic achievement: Beyond etic conceptions of children's understanding. *Review of Educational Research, 69*(3), 287–314.

Bowman, B. T., Donovan, M. S., Burns, M. S. (Eds.). (2001). *Eager to learn: Educating our preschoolers.* Washington, DC: National Academy Press. Available: http://books.nap.edu/catalog/9745.html. [July 10, 2001].

Bransford, J. D., Brown, A. L., & Cocking, R. R. (Eds.). (1999). *How people learn: Brain, mind, experience, and school.* Washington, DC: National Academy Press. Available: http://books.nap.edu/catalog/6160.html. [July 10, 2001].

Brownell, W. A. (1935). Psychological considerations in the learning and the teaching of arithmetic. In W. D. Reeve (Ed.), *The teaching of arithmetic* (Tenth Yearbook of the National Council of Teachers of Mathematics, pp. 1–31). New York: Columbia University, Teachers College, Bureau of Publications.

Brownell, W. A. (1987). AT classic: Meaning and skill—maintaining the balance. *Arithmetic Teacher, 34*(8), 18–25. (Original work published 1956).

Bruner, J. S. (1960). *The process of education.* New York: Vintage Books.

Campbell, J. R., Hombo, C. M., & Mazzeo, J. (2000). *NAEP 1999 trends in academic progress: Three decades of student performance,* NCES 2000-469. Washington, DC: National Center for Education Statistics. Available: http://nces.ed.gov/spider/webspider/2000469.shtml. [July 10, 2001].

Campbell, J. R., Voelkl, K. E., & Donahue, P. L. (2000). *NAEP 1996 trends in academic progress* (NCES 97-985r). Washington, DC: National Center for Education Statistics. Available: http://nces.ed.gov/spider/webspider/97985r.shtml. [July 10, 2001].

Carpenter, T. P., Corbitt, M. K., Kepner, H. S., Jr., Lindquist, M. M., & Reys, R. E. (1981). *Results from the second mathematics assessment of the National Assessment of Educational Progress.* Reston, VA: National Council of Teachers of Mathematics.

Carpenter, T. P., Franke, M. L., Jacobs, V. R., Fennema, E., & Empson, S. B. (1998). A longitudinal study of invention and understanding in children's multidigit addition and subtraction. *Journal for Research in Mathematics Education 29,* 3–20.

Carpenter, T. P., & Lehrer, R. (1999). Teaching and learning mathematics with understanding. In E. Fennema & T. A. Romberg (Eds.), *Mathematics classrooms that promote understanding* (pp. 19–32). Mahway, NJ: Erlbaum.

Carpenter, T. P., & Levi, L. (1999, April). Developing conceptions of algebraic reasoning in the primary grades. Paper presented at the annual meeting of the American Educational Research Association, Montreal.

Cobb, P., & Bauersfeld, H. (Eds.). (1995). *The emergence of mathematical meaning: Interaction in classroom cultures.* Hillsdale, NJ: Erlbaum.

Cobb, P., Yackel, E., & Wood, T. (1989). Young children's emotional acts during mathematical problem solving. In D. B. McLeod & V. M. Adams (Eds.), *Affect and mathematical problem solving: A new perspective* (pp. 117–148). New York: Springer-Verlag.

Cobb, P., Yackel, E., & Wood, T. (1995). The teaching experiment classroom. In P. Cobb & H. Bauersfeld (Eds.), *The emergence of mathematical meaning: Interaction in classroom cultures* (pp. 17–24). Hillsdale, NJ: Erlbaum.

Committee for Economic Development, Research and Policy Committee. (1995). *Connecting students to a changing world: A technology strategy for improving mathematics and science education: A statement.* New York: Author.

Davis, R. B., & Maher, C. A. (1997). How students think: The role of representations. In L. D. English (Ed.), *Mathematical reasoning: Analogies, metaphors, and images* (pp. 93–115). Mahwah, NJ: Erlbaum.

Donovan, M. S., Bransford, J. D., & Pellegrino, J. W. (Eds.). (1999). *How people learn: Bridging research and practice.* Washington, DC: National Academy Press. Available: http://books.nap.edu/catalog/9457.html. [July 10, 2001].

Druckman, D., & Bjork, R. A. (Eds.). (1991). *In the mind's eye: Enhancing human performance.* Washington, DC: National Academy Press. Available: http://books.nap.edu/catalog/1580.html. [July 10, 2001].

Dweck, C. (1986). Motivational processes affecting learning. *American Psychologist, 41,* 1040–1048.

English, L. D. (1997a). Analogies, metaphors, and images: Vehicles for mathematical reasoning. In L. D. English (Ed.), *Mathematical reasoning: Analogies, metaphors, and images* (pp. 3–18). Mahwah, NJ: Erlbaum.

English, L. D. (Ed.). (1997b). *Mathematical reasoning: Analogies, metaphors, and images.* Mahwah, NJ: Erlbaum.

Fennema, E. (1995). Mathematics, gender and research. In B. Grevholm & G. Hanna (Eds.), *Gender and mathematics education* (pp. 21–38). Lund, Sweden: Lund University Press.

Fennema, E., & Romberg, T. A. (Eds.). (1999). *Mathematics classroom that promote understanding.* Mahwah, NJ: Erlbaum.

Fuson, K. C. (1990). Conceptual structures for multiunit numbers: Implications for learning and teaching multidigit addition, subtraction, and place value. *Cognition and Instruction 7,* 343–403.

Fuson, K. C. (1992a). Research on learning and teaching addition and subtraction of whole numbers. In G. Leinhardt, R. T. Putnam, & R. A. Hattrup (Eds.), *The analysis of arithmetic for mathematics teaching* (pp. 53–187). Hillsdale, NJ: Erlbaum.

Fuson, K. C. (1992b). Research on whole number addition and subtraction. In D. Grouws (Ed.), *Handbook of research on mathematics teaching and learning* (pp. 243–275). New York: Macmillan.

Fuson, K. C., & Briars, D. J. (1990). Using a base-ten blocks learning/teaching approach for first- and second-grade place-value and multidigit addition and subtraction. *Journal for Research in Mathematics Education 21,* 180–206.

Fuson, K. C., & Burghardt, B. H. (1993). Group case studies of second graders inventing multidigit addition procedures for base-ten blocks and written marks. In J. R. Becker & B. J. Pence (Eds.), *Proceedings of the fifteenth annual meeting of the North American Chapter of the International Group for the Psychology of Mathematics Education* (pp. 240–246). San Jose, CA: San Jose State University. (ERIC Document Reproduction Service No. ED 372 917).

Fuson, K. C., Carroll, W. M., & Landis, J. (1996). Levels in conceptualization and solving addition and subtraction compare word problems. *Cognition and Instruction, 14*, 345–371.

Geary, D. C. (1995). Reflections of evolution and culture in children's cognition. *American Psychologist, 50*(1), 24–37.

Greeno, J. G., Pearson, P. D., & Schoenfeld, A. H. (1997). Implications for the NAEP of research on learning and cognition. In R. Linn, R. Glaser, & G. Bohrnstedt (Eds.), *Assessment in transition: Monitoring the nation's educational progress* (Background Studies, pp. 151-215). Stanford, CA: National Academy of Education.

Hagarty, M., Mayer, R. E., & Monk, C. A. (1995). Comprehension of arithmetic word problems: A comparison of successful and unsuccessful problem solvers. *Journal of Educational Psychology, 87*, 18–32.

Hatano, G. (1988, Fall). Social and motivational bases for mathematical understanding. *New Directions for Child Development, 41*, 55–70.

Hiebert, J. (Ed.). (1986). *Conceptual and procedural knowledge: The case of mathematics.* Hillsdale, NJ: Erlbaum.

Hiebert, J., & Carpenter, T. P. (1992). Learning and teaching with understanding. In D. A. Grouws (Ed.), *Handbook of research on mathematics teaching and learning* (pp. 65–97). New York: Macmillan.

Hiebert, J., Carpenter, T. P., Fennema, E., Fuson, K. C., Wearne, D., Murray, H., Olivier, A., & Human, P. (1997). *Making sense: Teaching and learning mathematics with understanding.* Portsmouth, NH: Heinemann.

Hiebert, J., & Wearne, D. (1986). Procedures over concepts: The acquisition of decimal number knowledge. In J. Hiebert (Ed.), *Conceptual and procedural knowledge: The case of mathematics* (pp. 199–223). Hillsdale, NJ: Erlbaum.

Hiebert, J., & Wearne, D. (1996). Instruction, understanding, and skill in multidigit addition and subtraction. *Cognition and Instruction, 14*, 251–283.

Hilgard, E. R. (1957). *Introduction to psychology* (2nd ed.). New York: Harcourt Brace.

Inhelder, B., & Piaget, J. (1958). *The growth of logical thinking from childhood to adolescence.* New York: Basic Books.

Katona, G. (1940). *Organizing and memorizing.* New York: Columbia University Press.

Kilpatrick, J. (1985). Doing mathematics without understanding it: A commentary on Higbee and Kunihira. *Educational Psychologist, 20*(2), 65–68.

Knapp, M. S., Shields, P. M., & Turnbull, B. J. (1995). Academic challenge in high-poverty classrooms. *Phi Delta Kappan, 76*, 770–776.

Kouba, V. L., Carpenter, T. P., & Swafford, J. O. (1989). Number and operations. In M. M. Lindquist (Ed.), *Results from the fourth mathematics assessment of the National Assessment of Educational Progress* (pp. 64–93). Reston, VA: National Council of Teachers of Mathematics.

Kouba, V. L., & Wearne, D. (2000). Whole number properties and operations. In E. A. Silver & P. A. Kenney (Eds.), *Results from the seventh mathematics assessment of the National Assessment of Educational Progress* (pp. 141–161). Reston, VA: National Council of Teachers of Mathematics.

Krutetskii, V. A. (1976). *The psychology of mathematical abilities in schoolchildren* (J. Kilpatrick & I. Wirszup, Eds.; J. Teller, Trans.). Chicago: University of Chicago Press. (Original work published 1968).

Ladson-Billings, G. (1999). Mathematics for all? Perspectives on the mathematics achievement gap. Paper prepared for the Mathematics Learning Study Committee, National Research Council, Washington, DC.

Leder, G. C. (1992). Mathematics and gender: Changing perspectives. In D. Grouws (Ed.), *Handbook of research on mathematics teaching and learning* (pp. 597–622). New York: Macmillan.

Lemaire, P., & Siegler, R. S. (1995). Four aspects of strategic change: Contributions to children's learning of multiplication. *Journal of Experimental Psychology: General, 124,* 83–97.

Mack, N. K. (1995). Confounding whole-number and fraction concepts when building on informal knowledge. *Journal for Research in Mathematics Education, 26,* 422–441.

Maher, C. A., & Martino, A. M. (1996). The development of the idea of mathematical proof: A 5-year case study. *Journal for Research in Mathematics Education, 27,* 194–214.

Mason, D., Schroeter, D., Combs, R., & Washington, K. (1992). Assigning average achieving eighth graders to advanced mathematics classes in an urban junior high. *Elementary School Journal, 92,* 587–599.

Mayer, R. E. (1999). *The promise of educational psychology.* Upper Saddle River, NJ: Prentice Hall.

Mayer, R. E., & Hegarty, M. (1996). The process of understanding mathematical problems. In R. J. Sternberg & T. Ben-Zee (Eds.), *The nature of mathematical thinking* (Studies in Mathematical Thinking and Learning Series, pp. 29–53). Mahwah, NJ: Erlbaum.

Mayer, R. E., & Wittrock, M. C. (1996). Problem-solving transfer. In D. C. Berliner & R. C. Calfee (Eds.), *Handbook of educational psychology* (pp. 47–62). New York: Macmillan.

McLeod, D. B. (1992). Research on affect in mathematics education: A reconceptualization. In D. A. Grouws (Ed.), *Handbook of research on mathematics teaching and learning* (pp. 575–596). New York: Macmillan.

Mullis, I. V. S., Jenkins, F., & Johnson, E. G. (1994). *Effective schools in mathematics.* Washington, DC: National Center for Education Statistics.

Mullis, I. V. S., Martin, M. O., Gonzalez, E. J., Gregory, K. D., Garden, R. A., O'Connor, K. M., Chrostowski, S. J., & Smith, T. A. (2000). *TIMSS 1999 international mathematics report: Findings from IEA's repeat of the Third International Mathematics and Science Study at the eighth grade.* Chestnut Hill, MA: Boston College, Lynch School of Education, International Study Center. Available: http://www.timss.org/timss1999i/math_achievement_report.html. [July 10, 2001].

National Assessment Governing Board. (2000). *Mathematics framework for the 1996 and 2000 National Assessment of Educational Progress.* Washington, DC: Author. Available: http://www.nagb.org/pubs/96-2000math/toc.html. [July 10, 2001].

National Research Council. (1989). *Everybody counts: A report to the nation on the future of mathematics education*. Washington, DC: National Academy Press. Available: http://books.nap.edu/catalog/1199.html. [July 10, 2001].

National Research Council. (1998). *High school mathematics at work: Essays and Examples for the education of all students*. Washington, DC: National Academy Press. Available: http://books.nap.edu/catalog/5777.html. [July 10, 2001].

Nunes, T. (1992a). Cognitive invariants and cultural variation in mathematical concepts. *International Journal of Behavioral Development, 15*, 433–453.

Nunes, T. (1992b). Ethnomathematics and everyday cognition. In D. A. Grouws (Ed.), *Handbook of research on mathematics teaching and learning* (pp. 557–574). New York: Macmillan.

Oakes, J. (1990). *Multiplying inequalities: The effects of race, social class, and tracking on opportunities to learn mathematics and science*. Santa Monica: CA: RAND Corporation.

Pólya, G. (1945). *How to solve it: A new aspect of mathematical method*. Princeton, NJ: Princeton University Press.

Pesek, D. D., & Kirshner, D. (2000). Interference of instrumental instruction in subsequent relational learning. *Journal for Research in Mathematics Education, 31*, 524–540.

Reese, C. M., Miller, K. E., Mazzeo, J., & Dossey, J. A. (1997). *NAEP 1996 mathematics report card for the nation and the states*. Washington, DC: National Center for Education Statistics. Available: http://nces.ed.gov/spider/webspider/97488.shtml. [July 10, 2001].

Resnick, L. B. (1987). *Education and learning to think*. Washington, DC: National Academy Press. Available: http://books.nap.edu/catalog/1032.html. [July 10, 2001].

Resnick, L. B., & Omanson, S. F. (1987). Learning to understand arithmetic. In R. Glaser (Ed.), *Advances in instructional psychology* (vol. 3, pp. 41–95). Hillsdale, NJ: Erlbaum.

Rittle-Johnson, B., & Alibali, M. W. (1999). Conceptual and procedural knowledge of mathematics: Does one lead to the other? *Journal of Educational Psychology, 91*, 175–189.

Rittle-Johnson, B., & Siegler, R. S. (1998). The relation between conceptual and procedural knowledge in learning mathematics: A review. In C. Donlan (Ed.), *The development of mathematical skills* (pp. 75–110). East Sussex, UK: Psychology Press.

Saxe, G. (1990). *Culture and cognitive development*. Hillsdale, NJ: Erlbaum.

Schifter, D. (1999). Reasoning about operations: Early algebraic thinking in grades K-6. In L. V. Stiff (Ed.), *Developing mathematical reasoning in grades K-12* (1999 Yearbook of the National Council of Teachers of Mathematics, pp. 62-81). Reston, VA: NCTM.

Schoenfeld, A. H. (1988). Problem solving in context(s). In R. I. Charles & E. A. Silver (Eds.), *The teaching and assessing of mathematical problem solving* (Research Agenda for Mathematics Education, vol. 3, pp. 82–92). Reston, VA: National Council of Teachers of Mathematics.

Schoenfeld, A. H. (1989). Explorations of students' mathematical beliefs and behavior. *Journal for Research in Mathematics Education, 20*, 338–355.

Schoenfeld, A. H. (1992). Learning to think mathematically: Problem solving, metacognition, and sense making in mathematics. In D. Grouws (Ed.), *Handbook of research on mathematics teaching and learning* (pp. 334–370). New York: Macmillan.

Secada, W. G. (1992). Race, ethnicity, social class, language, and achievement in mathematics. In D. Grouws (Ed.), *Handbook of research on mathematics teaching and learning* (pp. 623–660). New York: Macmillan.

Shannon, A. (1999). *Keeping score*. Washington, DC: National Academy Press. Available: http://books.nap.edu/catalog/9635.html. [July 10, 2001].

Siegler, R. S., & Jenkins, E. A. (1989). *How children discover new strategies*. Hillsdale, NJ: Erlbaum.

Silver, E. A., Alacaci, C., & Stylianou, D. A. (2000). Students' performance on extended constructed-response tasks. In E. A. Silver & P. A. Kenney (Eds.), *Results from the seventh mathematics assessment of the National Assessment of Educational Progress* (pp. 301–341). Reston, VA: National Council of Teachers of Mathematics.

Silver, E. A., & Kenney, P. A. (2000). *Results from the seventh mathematics assessment of the National Assessment of Educational Progress*. Reston, VA: National Council of Teachers of Mathematics.

Silver, E. A., Strutchens, M. E., & Zawojewski, J. S. (1997). NAEP findings regarding race/ethnicity and gender: Affective issues, mathematics performance, and instructional context. In E. A. Silver & P. A. Kenney (Eds.), *Results from the sixth mathematics assessment of the National Assessment of Educational Progress* (pp. 33–59). Reston, VA: National Council of Teachers of Mathematics.

Steele, C. M. (1997). A threat in the air: How stereotypes shape intellectual identity and performance. *American Psychologist, 52*, 613–629.

Steele, C. M., & Aronson, J. (1995). Stereotype threat and the intellectual test performance of African-Americans. *Journal of Personality and Social Psychology, 69*, 797–811.

Steinberg, R. M. (1985). Instruction on derived facts strategies in addition and subtraction. *Journal for Research in Mathematics Education, 16*, 337–355.

Sternberg, R. J., & Rifkin, B. (1979). The development of analogical reasoning processes. *Journal of Experimental Child Psychology, 27*, 195–232.

Stevenson, H. W., & Stigler, J. W. (1992). *The learning gap: Why our schools are failing and what we can learn from Japanese and Chinese education*. New York: Simon & Schuster.

Strutchens, M. E., & Silver, E. A. (2000). NAEP findings regarding race/ethnicity: Students' performance, school experiences, and attitudes and beliefs. In E. A. Silver & P. A. Kenney (Eds.), *Results from the seventh mathematics assessment of the National Assessment of Educational Progress* (pp. 45–72). Reston, VA: National Council of Teachers of Mathematics.

Swafford, J. O., & Brown, C. A. (1989). Attitudes. In M. M. Lindquist (Ed.), *Results from the fourth mathematics assessment of the National Assessment of Educational Progress* (pp. 106–116). Reston, VA: National Council of Teachers of Mathematics.

Tate, W. F. (1997). Race, ethnicity, SES, gender, and language proficiency trends in mathematics achievement: An update. *Journal for Research in Mathematics Education, 28*, 652–679.

Thompson, A. G. (1992). Teachers' beliefs and conceptions: A synthesis of the research. In D. Grouws (Ed.), *Handbook of research on mathematics teaching and learning* (pp. 127–146). New York: Macmillan.

Thornton, C. A., & Toohey, M. A. (1985). Basic math facts: Guidelines for teaching and learning. *Learning Disabilities Focus, 1*(1), 44–57.

U.S. Department of Labor, Secretary's Commission on Achieving Necessary Skills. (1991). *What work requires of schools: A SCANS report for America 2000.* Washington, DC: Author. (ERIC Document Reproduction Service No. ED 332 054).

Wearne, D., & Hiebert, J. (1988). A cognitive approach to meaningful mathematics instruction: Testing a local theory using decimal numbers. *Journal for Research in Mathematics Education, 19,* 371–384.

Wearne, D., & Kouba, V. L. (2000). Rational numbers. In E. A. Silver & P. A. Kenney (Eds.), *Results from the seventh mathematics assessment of the National Assessment of Educational Progress* (pp. 163–191). Reston, VA: National Council of Teachers of Mathematics.

Wertheimer, M. (1959). *Productive thinking.* New York: Harper & Row.

Wiest, L. R. (2000). Mathematics that whets the appetite: Student-posed projects problems. *Mathematics Teaching in the Middle School, 5,* 286–291.

Wu, H. (1999, Fall). Basic skills versus conceptual understanding: A bogus dichotomy in mathematics education. *American Educator,* 14-19, 50–52.

Yaffee, L. (1999). Highlights of related research. In D. Schifter, V. Bastable, & S. J. Russell with L. Yaffee, J. B. Lester, & S. Cohen, *Number and operations: Making meaning for operations. Casebook* (pp. 127–149). Parsippany, NJ: Dale Seymour.

Zernike, K. (2000, August 25). Gap widens again on tests given to blacks and whites: Disparity widest among the best educated. *The New York Times,* p. A14.

5

THE MATHEMATICAL KNOWLEDGE CHILDREN BRING TO SCHOOL

Children begin learning mathematics well before they enter elementary school. Starting from infancy and continuing throughout the preschool period, they develop a base of skills, concepts, and misconceptions about numbers and mathematics. The state of children's mathematical development as they begin school both determines what they must learn to achieve mathematical proficiency and points toward how that proficiency can be acquired.

Chapter 4 laid out a framework for describing mathematical proficiency in terms of a set of interwoven strands. That framework is useful in thinking about the skills and knowledge that children bring to school, as well as the limitations of preschoolers' mathematical competence. Applying the framework to research on preschoolers' mathematical thinking also provides a good example of the way in which the strands of proficiency are interwoven and interdependent. Preschoolers' mathematical thinking rests on a combination of conceptual understanding, procedural fluency, strategic competence, adaptive reasoning, and productive disposition. During the last 25 years, developmental psychologists and mathematics educators have made substantial progress in understanding the ways in which these strands interact. In this chapter we describe the current state of knowledge concerning the proficiency that children bring to school, some of the factors that account for limitations in their mathematical competence, and current understanding about what can be done to ensure that all children enter school prepared for the mathematical demands of formal education.

Preschoolers' Mathematical Proficiency
Conceptual Understanding

The most fundamental concept in elementary school mathematics is that of *number*, specifically whole number. To get a sense of both the difficulty of the concept and how much of it is taken for granted, try to define what a whole number is.

One common conception of whole number says that two sets have the same numerosity (same number of members) if and only if each member of one set can be paired with exactly one member of the other (with no members left over from either set). If one set has members left over after this pairing, then that set has a greater numerosity (more items in it) than the other does.

This definition allows one to decide whether two sets have the same number of items without knowing how many there are in either set. The Swiss psychologist Jean Piaget developed a task based in part on this definition that has been widely used to assess whether children understand the critical importance of this one-to-one correspondence in defining numerosity.[1] In this task, children are shown an array like the one below, which might represent candies. They are then asked a question like the following: Are there more light candies, the same number of dark and light candies, or more dark candies?

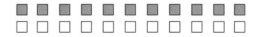

Most preschoolers recognize that the sets have the same amount of candy, based on the one-to-one alignment of the individual pieces. Next, the child watches the experimenter spread out the items in one set, which alters the spatial alignment of the pieces:

Shown this diagram, many children younger than 5 years assert that there are more of whichever kind of candy is in the longer row (the light candies in this example). Piaget argued that a true understanding of number requires an ability to reason about the effects of transformations that is beyond the capacity of preschool children. It was not uncommon several decades ago for educators aware of Piaget's findings and his claims to make assertions such as the following: "Children at different stages cannot learn the same content. They cannot learn about number, for example, until they reach the concrete operational stage [roughly ages 7 to 11, according to Piaget]."[2]

Research over the last 25 years, however, suggests that preschool children in fact know quite a bit about number before they enter school. Much of that knowledge is tied up with their understanding of counting. Even for preschoolers, the act of counting a set of objects is not entirely a rote activity but is guided by their mathematical understanding.

Preschool children in fact know quite a bit about number before they enter school.

Counting and the Origins of the Number Concept

Babies show numerical competence almost from the day they are born,[3] and some infants younger than six months have shown they can perform a rudimentary kind of addition and subtraction.[4] These abilities suggest that number is a fundamental component of the world children know. Whether and how this early sensitivity to number affects later mathematical development remains to be shown, but children enter the world prepared to notice number as a feature of their environment.

Much of what preschool children know about number is bound up in their developing understanding and mastery of counting. Counting a set of objects is a complex task involving thinking, perception, and movement, with much of its complexity obscured by familiarity. Consider what you need to do to count a set of objects: The items to be counted must be identified and distinguished from items not to be counted, as well as from those that have already been counted. Items are counted by pairing each one with some sort of verbal representation (typically a number name). An indicating act is needed that pairs each object in space with a word said in time. Finally, you need to understand that counting results in a number that represents how many things are in the set that was counted.

Competent counting requires mastery of a symbolic system, facility with a complicated set of procedures that require pointing at objects and designating them with symbols, and understanding that some aspects of counting are merely conventional, while others lie at the heart of its mathematical usefulness. We discuss issues related to competent counting, including the learning of number names, in the section on procedural fluency below. In this section, we discuss children's understanding of the conceptual aspects of counting. This separation is somewhat artificial because counting is a good example of the way in which the different strands of mathematical proficiency are interwoven.

As children learn to count, their thinking changes in a way that shapes their concept of number. Counting is not simply reciting the number word sequence. There must be items to count; and there must be a procedure to make each utterance of a number word correspond with one of the items to be counted.[5] At first, these items are perceptual; they might be, for example, beads, marbles, fingers, taps, steps, or drumbeats. The child must not only be able to perceive the items but also to conceive of them as individual things to be counted. Later, children become able to count sets of things (e.g., "how many different colors of buttons are there?") as well as items that may not be readily perceivable.[6] The counter must always create a mental representation of the items that are counted. This process of creation is clearly demonstrated when a child appears to count specific items in a situation where no such items are visible, audible, or tangible. Counting in the absence of perceivable objects is the culmination of a rather intricate developmental process. The process includes the progressive development of an ability to create unit items to be counted, first on the basis of conscious perception of external objects and then on the basis of internal representations.[7]

Early research on children's understanding of the mathematical basis for counting focused on five principles their thinking must follow if their counting is to be mathematically useful:[8]

1. *One-to-one:* there must be a one-to-one relation between counting words and objects;

2. *Stable order* (of the counting words): these counting words must be recited in a consistent, reproducible order;

3. *Cardinal:* the last counting word spoken indicates how many objects are in the set as a whole (rather than being a property of a particular object in the set);

4. *Abstraction:* any kinds of objects can be collected together for purposes of a count; and

5. *Order irrelevance* (for the objects counted): objects can be counted in any sequence without altering the outcome.

The first three principles define rules for how one ought to go about counting; the last two define circumstances under which such counting procedures should apply.

Understanding Counting and Mastering It

The relation between children's conceptual understanding of counting and their mastery of conventional counting remains controversial. According to one viewpoint,[9] children's emerging understanding of these counting principles organizes and motivates their acquisition of conventional counting procedures. Other studies indicate that much of children's conceptual understanding of counting follows (and may be based on) an initial mastery of conventional counting procedures.[10] An intermediate view is that conceptual and procedural knowledge of counting develop interactively, with small changes in one contributing to small changes in the other.[11]

One reason it has been hard to resolve contrasting claims about how children come to understand the conceptual basis for counting is that preschoolers' performance when they count is often quite variable, as it is with most other tasks.[12] The many errors preschoolers make when counting could indicate that they fail to understand the importance of the counting principles. The variability of their performance makes fundamentally ambiguous the task of inferring their knowledge of principles from their behavior. A child's difficulty in managing the complex processes involved in counting could mask a real understanding of its conceptual basis.

One way of circumventing the ambiguity of children's counting behavior involves asking them to judge the adequacy someone else's counting rather than perform the activity themselves. For example, asked to judge the accuracy of counting by a puppet who counted either correctly, incorrectly, or unconventionally (e.g., starting from an unusual starting point but counting all of a set of items), 3- to 5-year-olds demonstrated very good performance. Three-year-olds showed perfect acceptance of correct counting, 96% acceptance of unconventional but correct counting, and 67% rejection of real errors. Four-year-olds were better than 3-year-olds at rejecting true errors.[13]

Presented with a larger set of counting strategies to judge, children in a later study did not perform quite as well.[14] In fact, 3-year-olds' acceptance of unconventional correct counting was actually higher than that of 4-year-olds, suggesting that some of the acceptance of unconventional correct counting came from a blanket acceptance of the puppet's performance. Finally, and most relevant to the relation between counting skill and judgment of another's counting, the only children who failed to meet a criterion of 75% correct in rejecting the puppet's counting errors also failed to meet the same criterion in their own counting. Thus, children's own counting activity might form the basis for their judgments of what constitutes successful counting.

There are also important limits on children's ability to use counting in problem solving. Several studies have found that children 3 years and younger have a great deal of difficulty in using counting to produce sets of a given numerosity, even when that numerosity is well within their counting range.[15]

Taken as a whole, these studies indicate that variations in the context in which children are asked to judge another's counting can have a great effect on their acceptance of deviations from conventional counting and of errors that violate the counting principles. The ability of young preschool children to follow counting principles in their own counting and to focus on them in evaluating the counting of others is also quite vulnerable to situational variations.[16]

The controversy about the relation between how understanding of counting principles develops and how conventional counting ability is acquired echoes issues that emerge throughout children's later mathematics learning. Nevertheless, two points are clear. First, both aspects of counting are important developmental acquisitions. Second, by the time they enter kindergarten, most U.S. children understand the rules that underlie counting, can perform conventional counting correctly with sets of objects greater than 10, and can use counting to solve some simple mathematical problems.

Procedural Fluency

Procedural fluency refers to the ability to perform procedures flexibly, accurately, and efficiently. As we noted in Chapter 4, procedural fluency makes it possible for children to use mathematics reliably to solve problems and generate examples to test their mathematical ideas.

Procedural Fluency and Counting

In the case of counting, the difficulties young children have in fluently performing the complex activities required to count a set of objects accurately are a major obstacle to their mathematical development. For example, when asked to count increasingly longer row of up to 30 objects, 90% of $3\frac{1}{2}$- to $4\frac{1}{2}$-year-olds made some kind of violation of the one-to-one correspondence between pointing and objects or between pointing and saying the number words, although these errors were made on only 6% of the sets of objects counted.[17] Directives to "try hard" or "be careful" decreased errors substantially. Thus, effort and concentration are important aspects of accurate counting.

The difficulty preschoolers have in coordinating the process of keeping track of objects and counting them seems to be a universal characteristic of learning to count, with children in different cultures showing comparable rates of recounting or skipping objects.[18] Large differences across languages have been found in a second key aspect of procedural fluency in the preschool period, the mastery of the set of number names used in the child's native language.

Language and Early Mathematical Development

One aspect of counting that preschool children find particularly difficult is learning the number names. Learning a list of number names up to 100 is a challenging task for young children. Furthermore, the structure of the number names in a language is a major influence on the difficulties children have in learning to count correctly. These difficulties have important implications for the initial learning of mathematics in elementary school.

The number names used in a language provide children with a readymade representation for number. Counting principles are universal and so do not differ between languages, but number names do differ in sound and structure across languages and influence children's learning to count.

Linguistic structure of number names. Names for numbers have been generated according to a bewildering variety of systems.[19] The Hindu-Arabic system for representing the whole numbers is clearly a base-10 system, with 10 basic symbols (the digits 0–9). These may be freely combined, with the place of a digit indicating the power of 10 that it represents.[20] The Hindu-Arabic system is a useful reference point in describing number-naming schemes for two reasons. First, it is a widely used system for writing numbers. Second, it is as consistent and concise as a base-10 system could be.

Box 5-1 shows how spoken names for numbers are formed in three languages: English, Spanish, and Chinese. All of these languages use a base-10 system, but the languages differ in the clarity and consistency with which the base-10 structure is reflected in the number names.

As the first section of the figure shows, representations for numbers from 1 to 9 consist of an unsystematically organized list. There is no way to predict that 5 or *five* or *wu* come after 4, *four*, and *si*, respectively, in the Arabic numeral, English, and Chinese systems.

Box 5-1

Number Names in Chinese, English, and Spanish

a. One to ten

Arabic numeral	1	2	3	4	5
Chinese (spoken)	*yi*	*er*	*san*	*si*	*wu*
English	*one*	*two*	*three*	*four*	*five*
Spanish	*uno*	*dos*	*tres*	*cuatro*	*cinco*

b. Eleven to twenty

Arabic numeral	11	12	13	14	15
Chinese (spoken)	*shi yi*	*shi er*	*shi san*	*shi si*	*shi wu*
English	*eleven*	*twelve*	*thirteen*	*fourteen*	*fifteen*
Spanish	*once*	*doce*	*trece*	*catorce*	*quince*

c. Twenty to ninety-nine

Language	Rule
Chinese (spoken)	Decade name (unit name + *shi*) + unit name
English	Decade name [(*twen, thir, for, fif, six, seven, eight, nine*) + *-ty*] + unit name
Spanish	Decade name (*veinte, treinta, cuarenta, cincuenta, sesenta, setenta, ochenta, noventa*) + and (*y*) + unit name

6	7	8	9	10
liu	*qi*	*ba*	*jiu*	*shi*
six	*seven*	*eight*	*nine*	*ten*
seis	*siete*	*ocho*	*nueve*	*diez*

16	17	18	19	20
shi liu	*shi qi*	*shi ba*	*shi jiu*	*er shi*
sixteen	*seventeen*	*eighteen*	*nineteen*	*twenty*
diez y seis	*diez y siete*	*diez y ocho*	*diez y nueve*	*veinte*

Example

san shi qi

thirty-seven

trenta y siete

Names for numbers above 10 diverge in interesting ways among these different languages, as the second part of Box 5-1 demonstrates. The Chinese number-naming system maps directly onto the Hindu-Arabic number system used to write numerals. For example, a word-for-word translation of *shi qi* (17) into English produces *ten-seven*. English has unpredictable names for 11 and 12 that bear only a historical relation to *one* and *two*.[21] Whether the boundary between 10 and 11 is marked in some way can be very significant because this boundary can offer the first clue that number names are organized according to a base-10 system. The English names for numbers in the teens beyond 12 do have an internal structure, but it is obscured by phonetic modifications of many of the elements used in the first 10 numbers (e.g., *ten* becomes *-teen*, *three* becomes *thir-*, and *five* becomes *fif-*). Furthermore, the order of word formation reverses the place value, unlike the Hindu-Arabic and Chinese systems (and the English system above 20), naming the smaller value before the larger value. Spanish follows the same basic pattern for English to begin the teens, although there may be a clearer parallel between *uno, dos, tres* and *once, doce, trece* than between *one, two, three* and *eleven, twelve, thirteen*. The biggest difference between Spanish and English is that after 15 the number names in Spanish abruptly take on a different structure. Thus the name for 16 in Spanish, *diez y seis* (literally *ten and six*), follows the same basic structure as Arabic numerals and Chinese number names (starting with the tens value and then naming the ones value), rather than the structures of the number names in English from 13 to 19 and the names in Spanish from 11 to 15 (starting with the ones value and then naming the tens value).

Above 20, all these number-naming systems converge on the Chinese structure of naming the larger value before the smaller one. Despite this convergence, the systems continue to differ in the clarity of the connection between the decade names and the corresponding unit values. Chinese numbers are consistent in forming decade names by combining a unit value and the base (ten). Decade names in English and Spanish generally can be derived from the name for the corresponding unit value, with varying degrees of phonetic modification (e.g., *five* becomes *fif-* in English, *cinco* becomes *cincuenta* in Spanish) and with some notable exceptions, primarily the special name for 20 used in Spanish.

Psychological consequences of number names. Although all the number-naming systems being reviewed are essentially base-10 systems, they differ in the consistency and transparency with which that structure is reflected in the number names. Several studies comparing English-

and Chinese-speaking children demonstrate that the organization of number names does indeed play a significant role in mediating children's mastery of this symbolic system.[22] These studies have reported that (a) differences in performance on counting-related tasks do not emerge until children in both the United States and China begin learning the second decade of number names, sometime between 3 and 4 years of age; (b) those differences are generally limited to the verbal aspect of counting, rather than affecting children's ability to use counting in problem solving or their understanding of basic counting principles; and (c) differences in the patterns of mistakes that children make in learning to count reflect the structure of the systems they are learning.

Research on children's acquisition of number names suggests that U.S. children learn to recite the list of English number names through at least the teens as essentially a rote-learning task,[23] though occasional errors such as "fiveteen" suggest that some children notice the structure of the counting words for 13 through 19 that is partially obscured by linguistic modifications.[24] When first counting above 20, American preschoolers often produce idiosyncratic number names, indicating that they fail to understand the base-10 structure underlying larger number names; for instance, they might count "twenty-eight, twenty-nine, twenty-ten, twenty-eleven, twenty-twelve." This kind of mistake is extremely rare for Chinese children and indicates that the base-10 structure of number names is more accessible for learners of Chinese than it is for children learning to count in English.

The relative complexity of English number names has other cognitive consequences. Speakers of English and other European languages face a complex task in learning to write Arabic numerals, one that is more difficult than that faced by speakers of Chinese.[25] (For example, compare the mapping between name and numeral for *twenty-four* with that for *fourteen* in the two languages.) Speakers of languages whose number names are patterned after Chinese (including Korean and Japanese) are better able than speakers of English and other European languages to represent numbers using base-10 blocks and to perform other place-value tasks.[26] Because school arithmetic algorithms are largely structured around place value, the finding of a relationship between the complexity of number names and the ease with which children learn to count has important educational implications.

When learning to count, children must acquire a combination of conventional knowledge of number names, conceptual understanding of the mathematical principles that underlie counting, and ability to apply that knowledge in solving mathematical problems. Language differences during preschool appear to be limited to the first aspect of learning to count. In one study, for example, Chinese and American preschoolers did not differ in the extent to which they violated the previously discussed counting principles or in their ability to use counting to produce sets of a given size in the course of a game.[27] The effects of differences in number name structure on children's early mathematical development appear to be very specific to those aspects of mathematics that require the learning and use of these symbol systems. Nevertheless, these effects have implications for learning Arabic numerals and thus for understanding the principal symbol system used in school mathematics.

As with other aspects of mathematics, counting requires combining a conceptual understanding of the nature of number with a fluent mastery of procedures that allow one to determine how many objects there are. When children can count consistently to figure out how many objects there are, they are ready to use counting to solve problems. It also helps support their learning of conventional arithmetic procedures, such as those involved in computation with whole numbers.

Preschool children bring a variety of procedures to the task of learning simple arithmetic. Most of these procedures begin with strategic application of counting to arithmetic situations, and they are described in the next section. As with the distinction between conceptual understanding and procedural fluency, this categorization is somewhat arbitrary, but it provides a good example of how children can build on procedures such as counting in extending their mathematical competence to include new concepts and procedures.

Strategic Competence

Strategic competence refers to the ability to formulate mathematical problems, represent them, and solve them. An important feature of mathematical development is the way in which situations that involve extended problem solving at one point can later be handled fluently with known procedures.

Simple arithmetic tasks provide a good example. Most preschoolers show that they can understand and perform simple addition and subtraction by at least 3 years of age, often by modeling with real objects or thinking about sets of objects. In one study, children were presented with a set of objects of a given size that were then hidden in a box, followed by another set of objects that were also placed in the box.[28] The children were asked to produce a set of objects corresponding to the total number contained in the box. The majority of children around age 3 were able to solve such problems when they involved adding and subtracting a single item, although their performance decreased quickly as the size of the second set increased.

Preschool arithmetic: A wealth of strategies. Much research has described the diversity of strategies that children show in performing simple arithmetic, from preschool well into elementary school.[29] Strategies for solving a problem such as "What is 3 + 5?" include counting all ("1, 2, 3, . . . 4, 5, 6, 7, 8"), counting on from the larger addend ("5, . . . 6, 7, 8"), deriving the sum ("3 + 5 is like 4 + 4, so it's 8"), and recall. Some children will model the problem using available object or fingers; others will do it verbally. (These strategies are discussed in detail in Chapter 6.)

Kindergartners use all of these strategies, and second graders use all of them except for counting all.[30] What changes with age is the distribution of strategies, not the use of completely new ones. When 5-year-olds were given four individual sessions over 11 weeks in which they solved more than 100 addition problems, most of them discovered the counting-on-from-larger strategy, which saves effort by requiring them to do less counting.[31] The children typically first identified this strategy when they were working with small numbers, where it does not save much effort. They then were most likely to apply it to problems (e.g., "What is 2 + 9?") in which it makes a big difference in the amount of work needed.

The diversity of strategies that children show in early arithmetic is a feature of their later mathematical development as well. In some circumstances the number of different strategies children show predicts their later learning.[32] The fact that children are inventing their own diverse strategies for doing arithmetic creates its own educational issues, however, as teachers need to be able to help children understand why some strategies work and others do not and to help them move on to advanced strategies.

Solving word problems. Young children are able to make sense of the relationships between quantities and to come up with appropriate counting strategies when asked to solve simple word, or story, problems. Word problems are often thought to be more difficult than simple number sentences or equations. Young children, however, find them easier. If the problems pose simple relationships and are phrased clearly, preschool and kindergarten children can solve word problems involving addition, subtraction, multiplication, or division.[33] Young children are extremely sensitive to context, however, so the way in which the problem is posed can make a big difference in their performance. For example, if a picture of five birds and four worms is shown to preschoolers, most of them can answer the following: "Suppose the birds all race over and each one tries to get a worm. Will every bird get a worm? How many birds won't get a worm?" But fewer of them can answer the question, "How many more birds than worms are there?"[34]

In addition to using counting to solve simple arithmetic problems, preschool children show understanding at an early age that written marks on paper can preserve and communicate information about quantity.[35] For example, 3- and 4-year-olds can invent informal marks on paper, such as tally marks and diagrams, to show how many objects are in a set. But they are less able to represent changes in sets or relationships between sets, in part because they fail to realize that the order of their actions is not automatically preserved on paper.

Adaptive Reasoning

Adaptive reasoning refers to the capacity to think logically about the relationships among concepts and situations and to justify and ultimately prove the correctness of a mathematical procedure or assertion. Adaptive reasoning also includes reasoning based on pattern, analogy, or metaphor. Research suggests that young children are able to display reasoning ability if they have a sufficient knowledge base, if the task is understandable and motivating, and if the context is familiar and comfortable.[36] In particular, preschool children can generate solutions to problems and can explain their thinking.

Situations that require preschoolers to use their mathematical concepts and procedures in unconventional ways often cause them difficulty. For example, when preschool children are asked to count features of objects (e.g., the tines of forks) or subsets of objects (e.g., just the red buttons in a mixed set), they often cannot overcome their tendency to count all the separate objects.[37]

Another example of the limitations on preschoolers' ability to generalize their mathematics is that they perform better in situations that require them to think about adding or subtracting actual objects (even if those objects are hidden from view in a box) than they do when simply asked an equivalent question (e.g., "What's 3 and 5?").[38] Four- and 5-year-olds do begin to use their knowledge to answer correctly the Piagetian number task presented above involving equivalent sets of candies, and later they recognize without counting that the sets have the same number of candies.[39]

Most preschool children enter school with an initial understanding of procedures (e.g., counting, addition, subtraction) that forms the basis for much of their later mathematics learning, although they have limited ability to generalize that knowledge and to understand its importance. A major challenge of formal education is to build on the initial and often fragile understanding that children bring to school and to make it more reliable, flexible, and general.[40]

A major challenge of formal education is to build on the initial and often fragile understanding that children bring to school and to make it more reliable, flexible, and general.

Productive Disposition

In addition to the concepts and skills that underlie mathematical proficiency, children who are successful in mathematics have a set of attitudes and beliefs that support their learning. They see mathematics as a meaningful, interesting, and worthwhile activity; believe that they are capable of learning it; and are motivated to put in the effort required to learn. Reports on the attitudes of preschoolers toward learning in general and learning mathematics in particular suggest that most children enter school eager to become competent at mathematics. In a survey that examined a number of personality and motivational features relevant to success in mathematics, teachers and parents reported that kindergarteners have high levels of persistence and eagerness to learn (although teachers differed in their perceptions of children from different ethnic groups, as we discuss below).[41] Children enter school viewing mathematics as important and themselves as being competent to master it. In one study, first graders rated their interest in mathematics on average at approximately 6 on a scale from 1 to 7 (with 7 being the highest).[42] Children gave similar ratings to their competence in mathematics, with boys giving somewhat higher ratings for their mathematics competence than girls did, the opposite of the pattern for reading.

One important factor in attaining a productive disposition toward mathematics and maintaining the motivation required to learn it is the extent to which children perceive achievement as the product of effort as opposed to fixed ability. Extensive research in the learning of mathematics and other domains has shown that children who attribute success to a relatively fixed ability are likely to approach new tasks with a *performance* rather than a *learning* orientation, which causes them to show less interest in putting themselves in challenging situations that result in them (at least initially) performing poorly.[43] Preschoolers generally enter school with a learning orientation, but already by first grade a sizable minority react to criticism of their performance by inferring that they are not smart rather than that they just need to work harder.[44]

Most preschoolers enter school interested in mathematics and motivated to learn it. The challenge to parents and educators is to help them maintain a productive disposition toward mathematics as they develop the other strands of their mathematical proficiency.

Limitations of Preschoolers' Mathematical Proficiency

In some circumstances, preschool children show impressive mathematical abilities that can provide the basis for their later learning of school mathematics. These abilities are, however, limited in a number of important ways.

One of the most important limitations is that much of preschoolers' understanding of number is constrained to sets of a certain size. Because the algorithms that preschoolers develop are based on counting and on their experience with sets of objects, they do not generalize to larger numbers. For example, preschool children can show a mastery of the concepts of addition and subtraction for very small numbers.[45] But being able to predict the results of adding one to a number does not imply that children will be able to predict the results of adding two to the same number. This limitation is an important feature of preschool mathematical thinking and is an important way in which preschool mathematical proficiency differs from adult proficiency.

Another important limitation is that preschoolers' thinking about arithmetic is influenced heavily by the context of the problem. As stated above, the way in which a word problem is phrased can be the difference between success and failure. Furthermore, if children succeed, the strategy they use is a direct model of the story; they, in effect, act out the story to find the answer. They will need to make several advances in development before they realize that a few basic counting strategies can be used to solve a wide variety of word problems, that stories can be represented by written number sentences of the form $a + b = c$ or $a - b = c$, and that many different stories can be represented by the same sentence.

Equity and Remediation

Most U.S. children enter school with mathematical abilities that provide a strong base for formal instruction in mathematics. These abilities include understanding the magnitudes of small numbers, being able to count and to use counting to solve simple mathematical problems, and understanding many of the basic concepts underlying measurement. For example, a large survey of U.S. kindergartners found that 94% of first-time kindergartners passed their Level 1 test (counting to 10 and recognizing numerals and shapes) and 58% passed their Level 2 test (reading numerals, counting beyond 10, sequencing patterns, and using nonstandard units of length to compare objects).[46]

A number of children, however, particularly those from low socioeconomic groups, enter school with specific gaps in their mathematical proficiency. For example, the survey of kindergartners found that while 79% of children whose mother had a bachelor's degree passed the Level 2 test described above, only 32% of those whose mother had less than a high school degree could do so.[47] The same survey found large differences between ethnic groups on the more difficult tests (but not on the Level 1 tasks) with 70% of Asian and 66% of non-Hispanic white children passing the Level 2 tasks, but only 42% of African American, 44% of Hispanic, 48% of Hawaiian Native or Pacific Islander, and 34% of American Indian or Alaska Native participants doing so.[48] Other research has shown that children from lower socioeconomic backgrounds have particular difficulty understanding the relative magnitudes of single-digit whole numbers[49] and solving addition and subtraction problems verbally rather than using objects.[50] Overall, the research shows that poor and minority children entering school do possess some informal mathematical abilities but that many of these abilities have developed at a slower rate than in middle-class children.[51] This immaturity of their mathematical development may account for the problems poor and minority children have understanding the basis for simple arithmetic and solving simple word problems.[52]

Several promising approaches have been developed to deal with this developmental immaturity in mathematical knowledge. For example, the Rightstart program consists of a set of games and number-line activities aimed at providing children needing remedial assistance with an understanding of the relative magnitudes of numbers. Twenty minutes a day over a three- to four-month period in kindergarten was successful in bringing these children's mathematical knowledge up to a level commensurate with their peers, gains that persisted through the end of first grade.[53]

Another intervention is aimed at ensuring that Latino children understand the base-10 structure of number names, something that, as noted above, U.S. children in general find confusing.[54] Performance at the end of a yearlong intervention was at levels comparable to those reported for Asian children and substantially above those typically reported for nonminority children. Taken together, these results suggest that relatively simple interventions may yield substantial payoffs in ensuring that all children enter or leave first grade ready to profit from mathematics instruction.

The kindergarten survey cited above reported smaller ethnic differences in factors related to productive disposition (persistence, eagerness to learn, and ability to pay attention) than in mathematical knowledge. There were, however, some noteworthy differences between the reports of teachers and parents for different ethnic groups. Parents reported high levels of eagerness to learn (e.g., 93% for non-Hispanic whites, 90% for non-Hispanic African Americans, and 90% for Hispanics), but teachers differed in their judgments of eagerness (judging 78% of non-Hispanic whites, 66% of non-Hispanic African Americans, and 70% of Hispanics as eager to learn). Teachers and parents are, of course, judging children against different comparison groups, but the data at least raise the possibility that kindergarten teachers may be underestimating the eagerness of their students to learn mathematics.

Preschool Children's Proficiency

For preschool children, the strands of mathematical proficiency are particularly closely intertwined. Although their conceptual understanding is limited, as their understanding of number emerges they become able to count and solve simple problems. It is only when they move beyond what they informally understand—to the base-10 system for teens and larger numbers, for example—that their fluency and strategic competencies falter. Young children also show a remarkable ability to formulate, represent, and solve simple mathematical problems and to reason and explain their mathematical activities. The desire to quantify the world around them seems to be a natural one for young children. They are positively disposed to do and understand mathematics when they first encounter it.

Most U.S. children enter school with a basic understanding of number and number concepts that can form the foundation for learning school mathematics, but their knowledge is limited in some very important ways. Preschool children generally show a much more sophisticated understanding of small numbers than they do of larger numbers. They also have a great deal of difficulty in moving from the number names in languages such as English and Spanish to understanding the base-10 structure of number names and mastering the Arabic numerals used in school mathematics. Furthermore, not all children enter school with the intuitive understanding of number described above and assumed by the elementary school curriculum. Recent research suggests that effective methods exist for providing this basic understanding of number.

Notes

1. Piaget, 1941/1965.
2. Copeland, 1984, p. 12. In Piaget's theory, children typically enter the concrete operational stage from about 7 to 11 years of age, when they can think in a logical way about the characteristics of real objects.
3. Antell and Keating, 1983.
4. Wynn, 1992a, 1992b.

5. Steffe, von Glasersfeld, Richard, and Cobb, 1983, p. 24.

6. Steffe, Cobb, and von Glasersfeld, 1988.

7. Steffe, 1994.

8. Gelman and Gallistel, 1978.

9. Gelman, Meck, and Merkin, 1986; Gelman, 1990, 1993.

10. Briars and Siegler, 1984; Frye, Braisby, Lowe, Maroudas, and Nicholls, 1989; Fuson, 1988; Fuson and Hall, 1983, Siegler, 1991, Sophian, 1988; Wynn, 1990.

11. Baroody, 1992a; Baroody and Ginsburg, 1986; Rittle-Johnson and Siegler, 1998.

12. Siegler, 1994.

13. Gelman and Meck, 1983.

14. Briars and Siegler, 1984.

15. Frye, Braisby, Lowe, Maroudas, and Nicholls, 1989; Miller, Smith, Zhu, and Zhang, 1995; Wynn, 1990.

16. Similar suggestions have been made by Baroody, 1992a, 1992b; Fuson, 1988, 1992; and Siegler, 1991.

17. Fuson, 1988, p. 73.

18. Miller, Smith, Zhu, and Zhang, 1995.

19. See Ifrah, 1985; and Menninger, 1969.

20. The so-called Hindu-Arabic numeration system is in some sense a misnomer because the Chinese numeration system has been a decimal one from the time of the earliest historical records. Because of the frequent contact between the Chinese and the Indians since the time of antiquity, there has always been some question of whether the Indians got their decimal system from the Chinese. Language has to be the product of its culture. So the fact that the names for numbers in Chinese, especially for the teens, reflect a base-10 system indicates that the decimal system has been in place in China all along. By contrast, the Hindu-Arabic system did not take root in the West until the sixteenth century, long after the names for numbers in the various Western languages had been set. The irregularities in the English and Spanish number names may perhaps be understood better in this light.

21. Menninger, 1969.

22. Miller, Smith, Zhu, and Zhang, 1995; Miller and Stigler, 1987.

23. Fuson, Richards, and Briars, 1982; Miller and Stigler, 1987; Siegler and Robinson, 1982.

24. Baroody, 1987a.

25. Fuson, Fraivillig, and Burghardt, 1992; Séron, Deloche, and Noël, 1992.

26. Miura, 1987; Miura, Kim, Chang, and Okamoto, 1988; Miura and Okamoto, 1989; Miura, Okamoto, Kim, Steere, and Fayol, 1993.

27. Miller, Smith, Zhu, and Zhang, 1995.

28. Huttenlocher, Jordan, and Levine, 1994.

29. Carpenter and Moser, 1984; Siegler, 1996; Siegler and Jenkins, 1989; Siegler and Robinson, 1982; see also Baroody, 1987b, 1989; and Fuson, 1992.

30. Siegler, 1987.

31. Siegler and Jenkins, 1989.

32. Siegler, 1995. Alibali and Goldin-Meadow, 1993, showed that in learning to solve problems involving mathematical equivalence, students were most successful when they had passed through a stage of considering multiple solution strategies.
33. Carpenter, Ansell, Franke, Fennema, and Weisbeck, 1993; Riley, Greeno, and Heller, 1983; see also Fuson, 1992.
34. Riley, Greeno, and Heller, 1983.
35. Allardice, 1977; Ginsburg, 1989.
36. Alexander, White, and Daugherty, 1997, propose these three conditions for reasoning in young children. There is reason to believe that the conditions apply more generally.
37. Shipley and Shepperson, 1990.
38. Hughes, 1986; Jordan, Huttenlocher, and Levine, 1992.
39. Fuson, Secada, and Hall, 1983.
40. See Bowman, Donovan, and Burns, 2001, for a discussion of these ideas.
41. National Center for Education Statistics, 2000.
42. Wigfield, Eccles, Yoon, Harold, Arbreton, Freedman-Doan, and Blumenfeld, 1997.
43. Dweck, 1999; Heyman and Dweck, 1998.
44. Heyman, Dweck, and Cain, 1992.
45. For example, Jordan, Huttenlocher, and Levine, 1992.
46. National Center for Education Statistics, 2000.
47. National Center for Education Statistics, 2000.
48. National Center for Education Statistics, 2000.
49. Griffin, Case, and Siegler, 1994.
50. Jordan, Huttenlocher, and Levine, 1992.
51. Ginsburg, Klein, and Starkey, 1998.
52. Jordan, Levine, and Huttenlocher, 1995.
53. Griffin, Case, and Siegler, 1994.
54. Fuson, Smith, and Lo Cicero, 1997.

References

Alexander, P. A., White, C. S., & Daugherty, M. (1997). Analogical reasoning and early mathematics learning. In L. D. English (Ed.), *Mathematical reasoning: Analogies, metaphors, and images* (pp. 117–147). Mahwah, NJ: Erlbaum.

Allardice, B. (1977). The development of written representations for some mathematical concepts. *Journal of Children's Mathematical Behavior, 1*(4), 135–148.

Alibali, M. W., & Goldin-Meadow, S. (1993). Gesture-speech mismatch and mechanisms of learning: What the hands reveal about a child's state of mind. *Cognitive Psychology, 25*, 468–573.

Antell, S. E., & Keating, D. P. (1983). Perception of numerical invariance in neonates. *Child Development, 54*, 695–701.

Baroody, A. J. (1987a). *Children's mathematical thinking: A developmental framework for preschool, primary, and special education teachers*. New York: Teachers College Press.

Baroody, A. J. (1987b). The development of counting strategies for single-digit addition. *Journal for Research in Mathematics Education, 18*, 141–157.

Baroody, A. J. (1989). Kindergartners' mental addition with single-digit combinations. *Journal for Research in Mathematics Education, 20*, 159–172.

Baroody, A. J. (1992a). The development of preschoolers' counting skills and principles. In J. Bideaud & C. Meljac (Eds.), *Pathways to number: Children's developing numerical abilities* (pp. 99–126). Hillsdale, NJ: Erlbaum.

Baroody, A. J. (1992b). Remedying common counting difficulties. In J. Bideaud & C. Meljac (Eds.), *Pathways to number: Children's developing numerical abilities* (pp. 307–323). Hillsdale, NJ: Erlbaum.

Baroody, A. J., & Ginsburg, H. P. (1986). The relationship between initial meaningful and mechanical knowledge of arithmetic. In J. Hiebert (Ed.), *Conceptual and procedural knowledge: The case of mathematics* (pp. 75–112). Hillsdale, NJ: Erlbaum.

Bowman, B. T., Donovan, M. S., & Burns, M. S. (Eds.). (2001). *Eager to learn: Educating our preschoolers*. Washington, DC: National Academy Press. Available: http://books.nap.edu/catalog/9745.html. [July 10, 2001].

Briars, D., & Siegler, R. S. (1984). A featural analysis of preschoolers' counting knowledge. *Developmental Psychology, 20*, 607–618.

Carpenter, T. P., Ansell, E., Franke, M. L., Fennema, E., & Weisbeck, L. (1993). Models of problem solving: A study of kindergarten children's problem-solving processes. *Journal for Research in Mathematics Education, 24*, 428–441.

Carpenter, T. P., & Moser, J. M. (1984). The acquisition of addition and subtraction concepts in grades one through three. *Journal for Research in Mathematics Education, 15*(3), 179–202.

Copeland, R. W. (1984). *How children learn mathematics* (4th ed.). New York: Macmillan.

Dweck, C. S. (1999). *Self-theories: Their role in motivation, personality, and development*. Philadelphia: Taylor & Francis.

Frye, D., Braisby, N., Lowe, J., Maroudas, C., & Nicholls, J. (1989). Young children's understanding of counting and cardinality. *Child Development, 60*, 1158–1171.

Fuson, K. C. (1988). *Children's counting and concepts of number*. New York: Springer-Verlag.

Fuson, K. C. (1992). Research on whole number addition and subtraction. In D. Grouws (Ed.), *Handbook of research on mathematics teaching and learning* (pp. 243–275). New York: Macmillan.

Fuson, K. C., Fraivillig, J. L., & Burghardt, B. H. (1992). Relationships children construct among English number words, multiunit base-ten blocks, and written multidigit addition. In J. I. D. Campbell (Ed.), *Advances in psychology: Vol. 91. The nature and origins of mathematical skills* (pp. 39–112). Amsterdam: North-Holland.

Fuson, K. C., & Hall, J. W. (1983). The acquisition of early number work meanings. In H. Ginsburg (Ed.), *The development of children's mathematical thinking* (pp. 49–107). New York: Academic Press.

Fuson, K. C., Richards, J., & Briars, D. J. (1982). The acquisition and elaboration of the number work sequence. In C. Brainerd (Ed.), *Progress in cognitive development research: Vol. 1. Children's logical and mathematical cognition* (pp. 33–92). New York: Springer-Verlag.

Fuson, K. C., Secada, W. G., & Hall, J. W. (1983). Matching, counting, and conservation of numerical equivalence. *Child Development, 54*, 91–97.

Fuson, K. C., Smith, S. T., & Lo Cicero, A. M. (1997). Supporting Latino first graders' ten-structured thinking in urban classrooms. *Journal for Research in Mathematics Education, 28*, 738–766.

Gelman, R. (1990). First principles organize attention to and learning about relevant data: Number and the animate-inanimate distinction as examples. *Cognitive Science, 14*, 79–106.

Gelman, R. (1993). A rational-constructivist account of early learning about numbers and objects. In D. L. Medin (Ed.), *The psychology of learning and motivation: Vol. 30. Advances in research and theory* (pp. 61–96). San Diego: Academic Press.

Gelman, R., & Gallistel, C. R. (1978). *The child's understanding of number.* Cambridge, MA: Harvard University Press.

Gelman, R., & Meck, E. (1983). Preschoolers' counting: Principles before skill. *Cognition, 13*, 343–359.

Gelman, R., Meck, E., & Merkin, S. (1986). Young children's numerical competence. *Cognitive Development, 1*, 1–29.

Ginsburg, H. (1989). *Children's arithmetic* (2nd ed.). Austin, TX: Pro-Ed.

Ginsburg, H. P., Klein, A., & Starkey, P. (1998). The development of children's mathematical thinking: Connecting research with practice. In I. Sigel & A. Renninger (Eds.), *Handbook of child psychology: Vol. 4. Child psychology and practice* (5th ed., pp. 401–476). New York: Wiley.

Griffin, S., Case, R., & Siegler, R. S. (1994). Rightstart: Providing the central conceptual prerequisites for first formal learning of arithmetic to students at risk for school failure. In K. McGilly (Ed.), *Classroom lessons: Integrating cognitive theory and classroom practice* (pp. 25–49). Cambridge, MA: MIT Press/Bradford Books.

Heyman, G. D., & Dweck, C. S. (1998). Children's thinking about traits: Implications for judgments of the self and others. *Child Development, 69*, 391–403.

Heyman, G. D., Dweck, C. S., & Cain, K. M. (1992). Young children's vulnerability to self-blame and helplessness: Relationship to beliefs about goodness. *Child Development, 63*, 401–415.

Hughes, M. (1986). *Children and number.* Oxford: Blackwell.

Huttenlocher, J., Jordan, N. C., & Levine, S. C. (1994). A mental model for early arithmetic. *Journal of Experimental Psychology: General, 123*, 284–296.

Ifrah, G. (1985). *From one to zero: A universal history of numbers.* New York: Viking.

Jordan, N. C., Huttenlocher, J., and Levine, S. C. (1992). Differential calculation abilities in young children from middle- and low-income families. *Developmental Psychology, 28*, 644–653.

Jordan, N. C., Levine, S. C., & Huttenlocher, J. (1995). Calculation abilities in young children with different patterns of cognitive functioning. *Journal of Learning Disabilities, 28*, 53–64.

Menninger, K. (1969). *Number words and number symbols: A cultural history of numbers* (P. Broneer, Trans.). Cambridge, MA: MIT Press. (Original work published 1958).

Miller, K. F., Smith, C. M., Zhu, J., & Zhang, H. (1995). Preschool origins of cross-national differences in mathematical competence: The role of number-naming systems. *Psychological Science, 6*, 56–60.

Miller, K. F., & Stigler, J. W. (1987). Counting in Chinese: Cultural variation in a basic cognitive skill. *Cognitive Development, 2*, 279–305.

Miura, I. T. (1987). Mathematics achievement as a function of language. *Journal of Educational Psychology, 79*, 79–82.

Miura, I. T., Kim, C. C., Chang, C. M., & Okamoto, Y. (1988). Effects of language characteristics on children's cognitive representation of number: Cross-national comparisons. *Child Development, 59*, 1445–1450.

Miura, I. T., & Okamoto, Y. (1989). Comparisons of U.S. and Japanese first graders' cognitive representation of number and understanding of place value. *Journal of Educational Psychology, 81*, 109–114.

Miura, I. T., Okamoto, Y., Kim, C. C., Steere, M., & Fayol, M. (1993). First graders' cognitive representation of number and understanding of place value: Cross-national comparisons: France, Japan, Korea, Sweden, and the United States. *Journal of Educational Psychology, 85*, 24–30.

National Center for Education Statistics. (2000). *America's kindergartners* (NCES 2000-070). Washington, DC: U.S. Government Printing Office. Available: http://nces.ed.gov/spider/webspider/2000070.shtml. [July 10, 2001].

Piaget, J. (1965). *The child's conception of number.* New York: Norton. (Original work published 1941)

Riley, M. S., Greeno, J. G., & Heller, J. I. (1983). Development of children's problem-solving ability in arithmetic. In H. Ginsburg (Ed.), *The development of mathematical thinking* (pp. 153–196). New York: Academic Press.

Rittle-Johnson, B., & Siegler, R. S. (1998). The relation between conceptual and procedural knowledge in learning mathematics: A review. In C. Donlan (Ed.), *The development of mathematical skills* (pp. 75–110). East Sussex, UK: Psychology Press.

Séron, X., Deloche, G., & Noël, M. P. (1992). Number transcribing by children: Writing Arabic numbers under dictation. In J. Bideaud, C. Meljac, & J.-P. Fischer (Eds.), *Pathways to number: Children's developing numerical abilities* (pp. 245–264). Hillsdale, NJ: Erlbaum.

Shipley, E. F., & Shepperson, B. (1990). *Countable entities: Developmental changes.* Cognition, 34, 109–136.

Siegler, R. S. (1987). The perils of averaging data over strategies: An example from children's addition. *Journal of Experimental Psychology: General, 116*, 250–264.

Siegler, R. S. (1991). In young children's counting, procedures precede principles. *Educational Psychology Review, 3*(2), 127–135.

Siegler, R. S. (1994). Cognitive variability: A key to understanding cognitive development. *Current Directions in Psychological Science, 3*(1), 1–5.

Siegler, R. S. (1995). How does change occur: A microgenetic study of number conservation. *Cognitive Psychology, 28*, 255–273.

Siegler, R. S. (1996). *Emerging minds: The process of change in children's thinking.* New York: Oxford University Press.

Siegler, R. S., & Jenkins, E. A. (1989). *How children discover new strategies.* Hillsdale, NJ: Erlbaum.

Siegler, R. S., & Robinson, M. (1982). The development of numerical understandings. In H. W. Reese & L. P. Lipsitt (Eds.), *Advances in child development and behavior* (vol. 16, pp. 242–312). New York: Academic Press.

Sophian, C. (1988). Early developments in children's understanding of number: Inferences about numerosity and one-to-one correspondence. *Child Development, 59*, 1397–1414.

Steffe, L. P. (1994). Children's construction of meaning for number words: A curriculum problem. In D. Tirosh (Ed.), *Implicit and explicit knowledge: An educational approach* (pp. 131–168). Westport, CT: Ablex.

Steffe, L. P., Cobb, P., & von Glasersfeld, E. (1988). *Construction of arithmetical meanings and strategies.* New York: Springer-Verlag.

Steffe, L. P., von Glasersfeld, E., Richards, J., & Cobb, P. (1983). *Children's counting types: Philosophy, theory, and application.* New York: Praeger Scientific.

Wigfield, A., Eccles, J. S., Yoon, K. S., Harold, R. D., Arbreton, A. J. A., Freedman-Doan, C., & Blumenfeld, P. C. (1997). Change in children's competence beliefs and subjective task values across the elementary school years: A 3-year study. *Journal of Educational Psychology, 89*, 451–469.

Wynn, K. (1990). Children's understanding of counting. *Cognition, 36*, 155–193.

Wynn, K. (1992a). Addition and subtraction by human infants. *Nature, 358*, 749–750.

Wynn, K. (1992b). Addition and subtraction by human infants: Erratum. *Nature, 360*, 768.

6

DEVELOPING PROFICIENCY WITH WHOLE NUMBERS

Whole numbers are the easiest numbers to understand and use. As we described in the previous chapter, most children learn to count at a young age and understand many of the principles of number on which counting is based. Even if children begin school with an unusually limited facility with number, intensive instructional activities can be designed to help them reach similar levels as their peers.[1] Children's facility with counting provides a basis for them to solve simple addition, subtraction, multiplication, and division problems with whole numbers. Although there still is much for them to work out during the first few years of school, children begin with substantial knowledge on which they can build.

In this chapter, we examine the development of proficiency with whole numbers. We show that students move from methods of solving numerical problems that are intuitive, concrete, and based on modeling the problem situation directly to methods that are more problem independent, mathematically sophisticated, and reliant on standard symbolic notation. Some form of this progression is seen in each operation for both single-digit and multidigit numbers.

We focus on computation with whole numbers because learning to compute can provide young children the opportunity to work through many number concepts and to integrate the five strands of mathematical proficiency. This learning can provide the foundation for their later mathematical development. Computation with whole numbers occupies much of the curriculum in the early grades, and appropriate learning experiences in these grades improve children's chances for later success.

Whole number computation also provides an instructive example of how routine-appearing procedural skills can be intertwined with the other strands of proficiency to increase the fluency with which the skills are used. For years, learning to compute has been viewed as a matter of following the teacher's directions and practicing until speedy execution is achieved. Changes in career demands and the tasks of daily life, as well as the availability of new computing tools, mean that more is now demanded from the study of computation. More than just a means to produce answers, computation is increasingly seen as a window on the deep structure of the number system. Fortunately, research is demonstrating that both skilled performance and conceptual understanding are generated by the same kinds of activities. No tradeoffs are needed. As we detail below, the activities that provide this powerful result are those that integrate the strands of proficiency.

Operations with Single-Digit Whole Numbers

As students begin school, much of their number activity is designed to help them become proficient with single-digit arithmetic. By *single-digit arithmetic*, we mean the sums and products of single-digit numbers and their companion differences and quotients (e.g., $5 + 7 = 12$, $12 - 5 = 7$, $12 - 7 = 5$ and $5 \times 7 = 35$, $35 \div 5 = 7$, $35 \div 7 = 5$). For most of a century, learning single-digit arithmetic has been characterized in the United States as "learning basic facts," and the emphasis has been on memorizing those facts. We use the term *basic number combinations* to emphasize that the knowledge is relational and need not be memorized mechanically. Adults and "expert" children use a variety of strategies, including automatic or semiautomatic rules and reasoning processes to efficiently produce the basic number combinations.[2] Relational knowledge, such as knowledge of commutativity, not only promotes learning the basic number combinations but also may underlie or affect the mental representation of this basic knowledge.[3]

The domain of early number, including children's initial learning of single-digit arithmetic, is undoubtedly the most thoroughly investigated area of school mathematics. A large body of research now exists about how children in many countries actually learn single-digit operations with whole numbers. Although some educators once believed that children memorize their "basic facts" as conditioned responses, research shows that children do *not* move from knowing nothing about the sums and differences of numbers to having the basic number combinations memorized. Instead, they move through a series of progressively more advanced and abstract methods for working out the answers to simple arithmetic problems. Furthermore, as children get older, they use the procedures more and more efficiently.[4] Recent evidence indicates children can use such procedures quite quickly.[5] Not all children follow the same path, but all children develop some intermediate and temporary procedures.

Most children continue to use those procedures occasionally and for some computations. Recall eventually becomes the predominant method for some children, but current research methods cannot adequately distinguish between answers produced by recall and those generated by fast (nonrecall) procedures. This chapter describes the complex processes by which children learn to compute with whole numbers. Because the research on whole numbers reveals how much can be understood about children's mathematical development through sustained and interdisciplinary inquiry, we give more details in this chapter than in subsequent chapters.

Word Problems: A Meaningful Context

One of the most meaningful contexts in which young children begin to develop proficiency with whole numbers is provided by so-called word problems. This assertion probably comes as a surprise to many, especially mathematics teachers in middle and secondary school whose students have special difficulties with such problems. But extensive research shows that if children can count, they can begin to use their counting skills to solve simple word problems. Furthermore, they can advance those counting skills as they solve more problems.[6] In fact, it is in solving word problems that young children have opportunities to display their most advanced levels of counting performance and to build a repertoire of procedures for computation.

Most children entering school can count to solve word problems that involve adding, subtracting, multiplying, and dividing.[7] Their performance increases if the problems are phrased simply, use small numbers, and are accompanied by physical counters for the children to use. The exact procedures children are likely to use have been well documented. Consider the following problems:

Sally had 6 toy cars. She gave 4 to Bill. How many did she have left?

Sally had 4 toy cars. How many more does she need to have 6?

Most young children solve the first problem by counting a set of 6, removing 4, and counting the remaining cars to find the answer. In contrast, they solve the second problem by counting a set of 4, adding in more as they count "five, six," and then counting those added in to find the answer.

Children solve these problems by "acting out" the situation—that is, by modeling it. They invent a procedure that mirrors the actions or relationships described in the problem. This simple but powerful approach keeps procedural fluency closely connected to conceptual understanding and strategic competence. Children initially solve only those problems that they understand, that they can represent or model using physical objects, and that involve numbers within their counting range. Although this approach limits the kinds of problems with which children are successful, it also enables them to solve a remarkable range of problems, including those that involve multiplying and dividing.

Since children intuitively solve word problems by modeling the actions and relations described in them, it is important to distinguish among the different types of problems that can be represented by adding or subtracting, and among those represented by multiplying or dividing. One useful way of classifying problems is to heed the children's approach and examine the actions and relations described. This examination produces a taxonomy of problem types distinguished by the solution method children use and provides a framework to explain the relative difficulty of problems.

Four basic classes of addition and subtraction problems can be identified: problems involving (a) joining, (b) separating, (c) part-part-whole relations, and (d) comparison relations. Problems within a class involve the same type of action or relation, but within each class several distinct types of problems can be identified depending on which quantity is the unknown (see Table 6-1). Students' procedures for solving the entire array of addition and subtraction problems and the relative difficulty of the problems have been well documented.[8]

For multiplication and division, the simplest kinds of problems are grouping situations that involve three components: the number of sets, the number in each set, and the total number. For example:

> *Jose made 4 piles of marbles with 3 marbles in each pile. How many marbles did Jose have?*

In this problem, the number and size of the sets is known and the total is unknown. There are two types of corresponding division situations depending on whether one must find the number of sets or the number in each set. For example:

Table 6-1

Addition and Subtraction Problem Types

Problem Type			
Join	(Result Unknown)	(Change Unknown)	(Start Unknown)
	Connie had 5 marbles. Juan gave her 8 more marbles. How many marbles does Connie have altogether?	Connie has 5 marbles. How many more marbles does she need to have 13 marbles altogether?	Connie had some marbles. Juan gave her 5 more. Now she has 13 marbles. How many marbles did Connie have to start with?
Separate	(Result Unknown)	(Change Unknown)	(Start Unknown)
	Connie had 13 marbles. She gave 5 to Juan. How many marbles does Connie have left?	Connie had 13 marbles. She gave some to Juan. Now she has 5 marbles left. How many marbles did Connie give to Juan?	Connie had some marbles. She gave 5 to Juan. Now she has 8 marbles left. How many marbles did Connie have to start with?
Part-Part-Whole	(Whole Unknown)		(Part Unknown)
	Connie has 5 red marbles and 8 blue marbles. How many marbles does she have altogether?		Connie has 13 marbles. 5 are red and the rest are blue. How many blue marbles does Connie have?
Compare	(Difference Unknown)	(Compare Quantity Unknown)	(Referent Unknown)
	Connie has 13 marbles. Juan has 5 marbles. How many more marbles does Connie have than Juan?	Juan has 5 marbles. Connie has 8 more than Juan. How many marbles does Connie have?	Connie has 13 marbles. She has 5 more marbles than Juan. How many marbles does Juan have?

SOURCE: Carpenter, Fennema, Franke, Levi, and Empson, 1999, p. 12. Used by permission of Heinemann. All rights reserved.

Jose has 12 marbles and puts them into piles of 3. How many piles does he have?

Jose has 12 marbles and divides them equally into 3 piles. How many marbles are in each pile?

Additional types of multiplication and division problems are introduced later in the curriculum. These include rate problems, multiplicative comparison problems, array and area problems, and Cartesian products.[9]

As with addition and subtraction problems, children initially solve multiplication and division problems by modeling directly the action and relations in the problems.[10] For the above multiplication problem with marbles, they form four piles with three in each and count the total to find the answer. For the first division problem, they make groups of the specified size of three and count the number of groups to find the answer. For the other problem, they make the three groups by dealing out (as in cards) and count the number in one of the groups. Although adults may recognize both problems as 12 divided by 3, children initially think of them in terms of the actions or relations portrayed. Over time, these direct modeling procedures are replaced by more efficient methods based on counting, repeated adding or subtracting, or deriving an answer from a known number combination.[11]

The observation that children use different methods to solve problems that describe different situations has important implications. On the one hand, directly modeling the action in the problem is a highly sensible approach. On the other hand, as numbers in problems get larger, it becomes inefficient to carry out direct modeling procedures that involve counting all of the objects.

Children's proficiency gradually develops in two significant directions. One is from having a different solution method for each type of problem to developing a single general method that can be used for classes of problems with a similar mathematical structure. Another direction is toward more efficient calculation procedures. Direct-modeling procedures evolve into the more advanced counting procedures described in the next section. For word problems, these procedures are essentially abstractions of direct modeling that continue to reflect the actions and relations in the problems.

The method children might use to solve a class of problems is not necessarily the method traditionally taught. For example, many children come to solve the "subtraction" problems described above by counting, adding up, or thinking of a related addition combination because any of these methods is easier and more accurate than counting backwards. The method traditionally presented in textbooks, however, is to solve both of these problems by subtracting, which moves students toward the more difficult and error-prone procedure of counting down. Ultimately, most children begin to use recall or a rapid mental procedure to solve these problems, and they come to recognize that the same general method can be used to solve a variety of problems.

Single-Digit Addition

Children come to understand the meaning of addition in the context of word problems. As we noted in the previous section, children move from counting to more general methods to solve different classes of problems. As they do, they also develop greater fluency with each specific method. We call these specific counting methods *procedures*. Although educators have long recognized that children use a variety of procedures to solve single-digit addition problems,[12] substantial research from all over the world now indicates that children move through a progression of different procedures to find the sum of single-digit numbers.[13]

This progression is depicted in Box 6-1. First, children count out objects for the first addend, count out objects for the second addend, and count all of the objects (count all). This general counting-all procedure then becomes abbreviated, internalized, and abstracted as children become more experienced with it. Next, they notice that they do not have to count the objects for the first addend but can start with the number in the first or the larger addend and count on the objects in the other addend (count on). As children count

Box 6-1

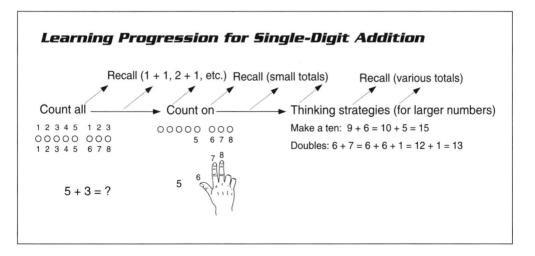

Learning Progression for Single-Digit Addition

Recall (1 + 1, 2 + 1, etc.) Recall (small totals)   Recall (various totals)

Count all ⟶ Count on ⟶ Thinking strategies (for larger numbers)

```
1 2 3 4 5   1 2 3          o o o o o   o o o        Make a ten: 9 + 6 = 10 + 5 = 15
o o o o o   o o o              5       6 7 8
1 2 3 4 5   6 7 8                                    Doubles: 6 + 7 = 6 + 6 + 1 = 12 + 1 = 13
```

5 + 3 = ?

on with objects, they begin to use the counting words themselves as countable objects and keep track of how many words have been counted on by using fingers or auditory patterns. The counting list has become a representational tool. With time, children recompose numbers into other numbers (4 is recomposed into 3 + 1) and use thinking strategies in which they turn an addition combination they do not know into one they do know (3 + 4 becomes 3 + 3 + 1). In the United States, these strategies for *derived number combinations* often use a so-called double (2 + 2, 3 + 3, etc.). These doubles are learned very quickly.

As Box 6-1 shows, throughout this learning progression, specific sums move into the category of being rapidly recalled rather than solved in one of the other ways described above. Children vary in the sums they first recall readily, though doubles, adding one (the sum is the next counting word), and small totals are the most readily recalled. Several procedures for single-digit addition typically coexist for several years; they are used for different numbers and in different problem situations. Experience with figuring out the answer to addition problems provides the basis both for understanding what it means to say "5 + 3 = 8" and for eventually recalling that sum without the use of any conscious strategy.

Children in many countries often follow this progression of procedures, a natural progression of embedding and abbreviating. Some of these procedures can be taught, which accelerates their use,[14] although direct teaching of these strategies must be done conceptually rather than simply by using imitation and repetition.[15] In some countries, children learn a general procedure known as "make a 10" (see Box 6-2).[16] In this procedure the solver makes a 10 out of one addend by taking a number from the other addend. Educators in some countries that use this approach believe this first instance of regrouping by making a 10 provides a crucial foundation for later multidigit arithmetic. In some Asian countries this procedure is presumably facilitated by the number words.[17] It has also been taught in some European countries in which the number names are more similar to those of English, suggesting that the procedure can be used with a variety of number-naming systems. The procedure is now beginning to appear in U.S. textbooks,[18] although so little space may be devoted to it that some children may not have adequate time and opportunity to understand and learn it well.

There is notable variation in the procedures children use to solve simple addition problems.[19] Confronted with that variation, teachers can take various steps to support children's movement toward more advanced procedures. One technique is to talk about slightly more advanced procedures *and* why

Box 6-2

Make a Ten: 8 + 6 = ?

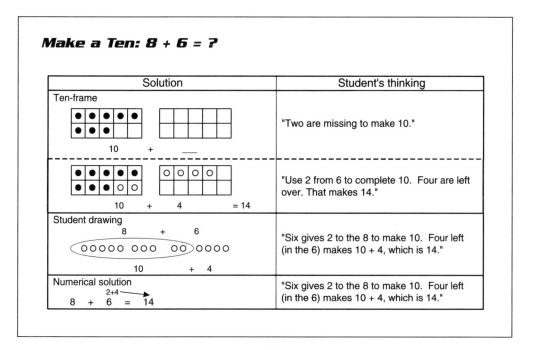

Solution	Student's thinking
Ten-frame	"Two are missing to make 10."
10 + ___	
10 + 4 = 14	"Use 2 from 6 to complete 10. Four are left over. That makes 14."
Student drawing 8 + 6 10 + 4	"Six gives 2 to the 8 to make 10. Four left (in the 6) makes 10 + 4, which is 14."
Numerical solution 2+4 8 + 6 = 14	"Six gives 2 to the 8 to make 10. Four left (in the 6) makes 10 + 4, which is 14."

they work.[20] The teacher can stimulate class discussion about the procedures that various students are using. Students can be given opportunities to present their procedures and discuss them. Others can then be encouraged to try the procedure. Drawings or concrete materials can be used to reveal how the procedures work. The advantages and disadvantages of different procedures can also be examined. For a particular procedure, problems can be created for which it might work well or for which it is inefficient.

Other techniques that encourage students to use more efficient procedures are using large numbers in problems so that inefficient counting procedures cannot easily be used and hiding one of the sets to stimulate a new way of thinking about the problem. Intervention studies indicate that teaching counting-on procedures in a conceptual way makes all single-digit sums accessible to U.S. first graders, including children who are learning disabled and those who do not speak English as their first language.[21] Providing support for children to improve their own procedures does *not* mean, however, that every child is taught to use all the procedures that other children develop. Nor does it mean that the teacher needs to provide every child in a class with support and justification for different procedures. Rather, the research provides evidence that, at any one time, most children use a small number of procedures and that teachers can learn to identify them and help children learn procedures that are conceptually more efficient (such as counting on from the larger addend rather than counting all).[22]

Mathematical proficiency with respect to single-digit addition encompasses not only the fluent performance of the operation but also conceptual understanding and the ability to identify and accurately represent situations in which addition is required. Providing word problems as contexts for adding and discussing the advantages and disadvantages of different addition procedures are ways of facilitating students' adaptive reasoning and improving their understanding of addition processes.

Single-Digit Subtraction

Subtraction follows a progression that generally parallels that for addition (see Box 6-3). Some U.S. children also invent counting-down methods that model the taking away of numbers by counting back from the total. But counting down and counting backward are difficult for many children.[23]

Box 6-3

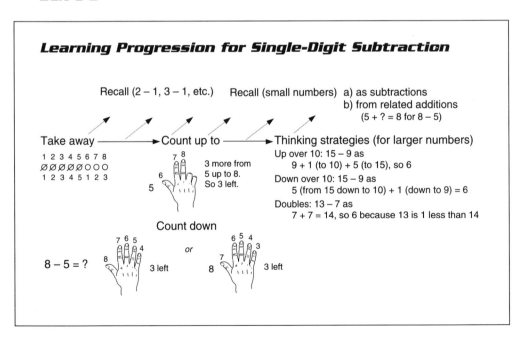

Learning Progression for Single-Digit Subtraction

Recall (2 – 1, 3 – 1, etc.)   Recall (small numbers) a) as subtractions
b) from related additions
(5 + ? = 8 for 8 – 5)

Take away ──────► Count up to ──────► Thinking strategies (for larger numbers)

1 2 3 4 5 6 7 8
Ø Ø Ø Ø Ø 0 0 0
1 2 3 4 5 1 2 3

3 more from
5 up to 8.
So 3 left.

Up over 10: 15 – 9 as
9 + 1 (to 10) + 5 (to 15), so 6
Down over 10: 15 – 9 as
5 (from 15 down to 10) + 1 (down to 9) = 6
Doubles: 13 – 7 as
7 + 7 = 14, so 6 because 13 is 1 less than 14

Count down

8 – 5 = ?   or

3 left   3 left

A considerable number of children invent counting-up procedures for situations in which an unknown quantity is added to a known quantity.[24] Many of these children later count up in taking-away subtraction situations (13 − 8 = ? becomes 8 + ? = 13). When counting up is not introduced, many children may not invent it until the second or third grade, if at all. Intervention studies with U.S. first graders that helped them see subtraction situations as taking away the first x objects enabled them to learn and understand counting-up-to procedures for subtraction. Their subtraction accuracy became as high as that for addition.[25]

Experiences that focus on part-part-whole relations have also been shown to help students develop more efficient thinking strategies, especially for subtraction.[26] Students examine a join or separate situation and identify which number represents the whole quantity and which numbers represent the parts. These experiences help students see how addition and subtraction are related and help them recognize when to add and when to subtract. For students in grades K to 2, learning to see the part-whole relations in addition and subtraction situations is one of their most important accomplishments in arithmetic.[27]

Examining the relationships between addition and subtraction and seeing subtraction as involving a known and an unknown addend are examples of adaptive reasoning. By providing experiences for young students to develop adaptive reasoning in addition and subtraction situations, teachers are also anticipating algebra as students begin to appreciate the inverse relationships between the two operations.[28]

> For students in grades K to 2, learning to see the part-whole relations in addition and subtraction situations is one of their most important accomplishments in arithmetic.

Single-Digit Multiplication

Much less research is available on single-digit multiplication and division than on single-digit addition and subtraction. U.S. children progress through a sequence of multiplication procedures that are somewhat similar to those for addition.[29] They make equal groups and count them all. They learn skip-count lists for different multipliers (e.g., they count 4, 8, 12, 16, 20, . . . to multiply by four). They then count on and count down these lists using their fingers to keep track of different products. They invent thinking strategies in which they derive related products from products they know.

As with addition and subtraction, children invent many of the procedures they use for multiplication. They find patterns and use skip counting (e.g., multiplying 4×3 by counting "3, 6, 9, 12"). Finding and using patterns and other thinking strategies greatly simplifies the task of learning multiplication tables (see Box 6-4 for some examples).[30] Moreover, finding and describing

Box 6-4

Thinking Strategies for Single-Digit Multiplication

In single-digit arithmetic, there are 100 multiplication combinations that students must learn. Commutativity reduces that number by about half. Multiplication by 0 and by 1 may quickly be deduced from the meaning of multiplication. Multiplication by 2 consists of the "doubles" from addition. Single-digit multiplication by 9 is simplified by a pattern: in the product, the sum of the digits is 9. (For example, $9 \times 7 = 63$ and $6 + 3 = 9$.) Multiplication by 5 may also be deduced through patterns or by first multiplying by 10 and then dividing by 2, since 5 is half of 10.

The remaining 15 multiplication combinations (and their commutative counterparts) may be computed by skip counting or by building on known combinations. For example, 3×6 must be 6 more than 2×6, which is 12. So 3×6 is 18. Similarly, 4×7 must be twice 2×7, which is 14. So 4×7 is 28. (Note that these strategies require proficiency with addition.) To compute multiples of 6, one can build on the multiples of 5. So, for example, 6×8 must be 8 more than 5×8, which is 40. So 6×8 is 48. If students are comfortable with such strategies for multiplication by 3, 4, and 6, only three multiplication combinations remain: 7×7, 7×8, and 8×8. These can be derived from known combinations in many creative ways.

patterns are a hallmark of mathematics. Thus, treating multiplication learning as pattern finding both simplifies the task and uses a core mathematical idea.

After children identify patterns, they still need much experience to produce skip-count lists and individual products rapidly. Little is known about how children acquire this fluency or what experiences might be of most help. A good deal of research remains to be done, in the United States and in other countries, to understand more about this process.

Single-Digit Division

Division arises from the two splitting situations described above. A collection is split into groups of a specified size or into a specified number of groups. Just as subtraction can be thought of using a part-part-whole relation, division can be thought of as splitting a number into two factors. Hence, divisions can also be approached as finding a missing factor in multiplication. For example, $72 \div 9 = ?$ can be thought of as $9 \times ? = 72$. But there is little research concerning how best to introduce and use this relationship, or whether it is helpful to learn a division combination at the same time as the corresponding multiplication combination. Further, there is little research about how to help children learn and use easily all of the different symbols for division, such as $\frac{15}{3}$, $15 \div 3$, and $3\overline{)15}$.

Practicing Single-Digit Calculations

Practicing single-digit calculations is essential for developing fluency with them. This practice can occur in many different contexts, including solving word problems.[31] Drill alone does not develop mastery of single-digit combinations.[32] Practice that follows substantial initial experiences that support understanding and emphasize "thinking strategies" has been shown to improve student achievement with single-digit calculations.[33] This approach allows computation and understanding to develop together and facilitate each other. Explaining how procedures work and examining their benefits, as part of instruction, support retention and yield higher levels of performance.[34] In this way, computation practice remains integrated with the other strands of proficiency such as strategic competence and adaptive reasoning.

It is helpful for some practice to be targeted at recent learning. After students discuss a new procedure, they can benefit from practicing it. For example, if they have just discussed the make-a-10 procedure (see Box 6-2), solving problems involving 8 or 9 in which the procedure can easily be used provides beneficial practice. It also is helpful for some practice to be cumulative, occurring well after initial learning and reviewing the more advanced procedures that have been learned.

Many U.S. students have had the experience of taking a timed test that might be a page of mixed addition, subtraction, multiplication, and division problems. This scattershot form of practice is, in our opinion, rarely the best use of practice time. Early in learning it can be discouraging for students who have learned only primitive, inefficient procedures. The experience can adversely affect students' disposition toward mathematics, especially if the tests are used to compare their performance.[35] If appropriately delayed, timed tests can benefit some students, but targeted forms of practice, with particular combinations that have yet to be mastered or on which efficient procedures can be used, are usually more effective.[36]

> Practicing single-digit calculations is essential for developing fluency with them.

Summary of Findings on Learning Single-Digit Arithmetic

For addition and subtraction, there is a well-documented progression of procedures used worldwide[37] by many children that stems from the sequential nature of the list of number words. This list is first used as a counting tool; then it becomes a representational tool in which the number words themselves are the objects that are counted.[38] Counting becomes abbreviated and rapid, and students begin to develop procedures that take advantage of properties of arithmetic to simplify computation. During this progression, individual children use a range of different procedures on different problems and even on the same problem encountered at different times.[39] Even adults have been found to use a range of different procedures for simple addition problems.[40] Further, it takes an extended period of time before new and better strategies replace previously used strategies.[41] Learning-disabled children and others having difficulty with mathematics do not use procedures that differ from this progression. They are just slower than others in moving through it.[42]

Instruction can help students progress.[43] Counting on is accessible to first graders; it makes possible the rapid and accurate addition of all single-digit numbers. Single-digit subtraction is usually more difficult than addition for U.S. children. If children understand the relationship between addition and subtraction, perhaps by thinking of the problem in terms of part-part-whole, then they recognize that counting up can be used to solve subtraction problems. This recognition makes subtraction more accessible.[44]

The procedures of counting on for addition and counting up for subtraction can be learned with relative ease. Multiplication and division are somewhat more difficult. Even adults might not have quick ways of reconstructing the answers to problems like $6 \times 8 = ?$ or $\frac{72}{8} = ?$ if they have forgotten the answers. Learning these combinations seems to require much specific pattern-based knowledge that needs to be orchestrated into accessible and rapid-enough products and quotients. As with addition and subtraction, children derive some multiplication and division combinations from others; for example, they recall that $6 \times 6 = 36$ and use that combination to conclude that $6 \times 7 = 42$. Research into ways to support such pattern finding, along with the necessary follow-up thinking and practice, is needed if all U.S. children are to acquire higher levels of proficiency in single-digit arithmetic.

Acquiring proficiency with single-digit computations involves much more than rote memorization. This domain of number demonstrates how the different strands of proficiency contribute to each other. At this early point in development, many of the linkages among strands result from children's natural inclination to make sense of things and to engage in actions that they understand. Children begin with conceptual understanding of number and the meanings of the operations. They develop increasingly sophisticated representations of the operations such as counting-on or counting-up procedures as they gain greater fluency. They also lean heavily on reasoning to use known answers such as doubles to generate unknown answers. Even in the early grades, students choose adaptively among different procedures and methods depending on the numbers involved or the context.[45] As long as the focus in the classroom is on sense making, they rarely make nonsensical errors, such as adding to find the answer when they should subtract. Proficiency comes from making progress within each strand and building connections among the strands. A productive disposition is generated by and supports this kind of learning because students recognize their competence at making sense of quantitative situations and solving arithmetic problems.

Multidigit Whole Number Calculations

Step-by-step procedures for adding, subtracting, multiplying, or dividing numbers are called algorithms. For example, the first step in one algorithm for multiplying a three-digit number by a two-digit number is to write the three-digit number above the two-digit number and to begin by multiplying the one's digit in the top number by the one's digit in the bottom number (see Box 6-5).

In the past, algorithms different from those taught today for addition, subtraction, multiplication, and division have been taught in U.S. schools. Also, algorithms different from those taught in the United States today are currently being taught in other countries.[46] Each algorithm has advantages

Box 6-5

Beginning a multiplication algorithm

$$\begin{array}{r} 752 \\ \times\ 23 \\ \hline 6 \end{array}$$

and disadvantages. Therefore, it is important to think about which algorithms are taught and the reasons for teaching them.

Learning to use algorithms for computation with multidigit numbers is an important part of developing proficiency with numbers. Algorithms are procedures that can be executed in the same way to solve a variety of problems arising from different situations and involving different numbers. This feature has three important implications. First, it means that algorithms are useful tools—different procedures do not need to be invented for each problem. Second, algorithms illustrate a significant feature of mathematics: The structure of problems can be abstracted from their immediate context and compared to see whether different-looking problems can be solved in similar ways. Finally, the process of developing fluency with arithmetic algorithms in elementary school can contribute to progress in developing the other strands of proficiency if time is spent examining why algorithms work and comparing their advantages and disadvantages. Such analyses can boost conceptual understanding by revealing much about the structure of the number system itself and can facilitate understanding of place-value representations.

Research findings about learning algorithms for whole numbers can be summarized with seven important observations. First, the linkages among the strands of mathematical proficiency that are possible when children develop proficiency with single-digit arithmetic can be continued with multidigit arithmetic. For example, there can be a close connection between understanding and fluency. Conceptual knowledge that comes with understanding is important for the development of procedural fluency, while fluent procedural knowledge supports the development of further understanding and learning. When students fail to grasp the concepts that underlie procedures or cannot connect the concepts to the procedures, they frequently generate flawed procedures that result in systematic patterns of errors.[47] These so-called buggy algorithms are signs that the strands are not well connected.[48] When the initial computational procedures that students use to solve multidigit problems reflect their understanding of numbers, understanding and fluency develop together.

A second observation is that understanding and fluency are related. For multidigit addition and subtraction, given conventional instruction that emphasizes practicing procedures, a substantial percentage of children gain understanding of multidigit concepts before using a correct procedure, but another substantial minority do the opposite.[49] In contrast, instructional programs that emphasize understanding algorithms before using them have been shown to lead to increases in both conceptual and procedural knowledge.[50]

So there is some evidence that understanding is the basis for developing procedural fluency.[51]

A third observation is that proficiency with multidigit computation is more heavily influenced by instruction than single-digit computation is. Many features of multidigit procedures (e.g., the base-10 elements and how they are represented by place-value notation) are not part of children's everyday experience and need to be learned in the classroom. In fact, many students are likely to need help learning efficient forms of multidigit procedures. This means that students in different classrooms and receiving different instruction might follow different learning progressions use different procedures.[52] For single-digit addition and subtraction, the same learning progression occurs for many children in many countries regardless of the nature and extent of instruction.[53] But multidigit procedures, even those for addition and subtraction, depend much more on what is taught.

A fourth observation is that children can and do devise or invent algorithms for carrying out multidigit computations.[54] Opportunities to construct their own procedures provide students with opportunities to make connections between the strands of proficiency. Procedural fluency is built directly on their understanding. The invention itself is a kind of problem solving, and they must use reasoning to justify their invented procedure. Students who have invented their own correct procedures also approach mathematics with confidence rather than fear and hesitation.[55] Students invent many different computational procedures for solving problems with large numbers. For addition, they eventually develop a procedure that is consistent with the thinking that is used with standard algorithms. That thinking enables them to make sense of the algorithm as a record on paper of what they have already been thinking. For subtraction, many students can develop adding-up procedures and, if using concrete materials like base-10 blocks, can also develop ways of thinking that parallel algorithms usually taught today.[56] Some students need help to develop efficient algorithms, however, especially for multiplication and division. Consequently, for these students the process of learning algorithms involves listening to someone else explain an algorithm and trying it out, all the while trying to make sense of it. Research suggests that students are capable of listening to their peers and to the teacher and of making sense of an algorithm if it is explained and if the students have diagrams or concrete materials that support their understanding of the quantities involved.[57]

Fifth, research has shown that students can learn well from a variety of different instructional approaches, including those that use physical materials to represent hundreds, tens, and ones, those that emphasize special counting activities (e.g., count by tens beginning with any number), and those that focus on developing mental computation methods.[58] Although the data do not point to a single preferred instructional approach, they do suggest that effective approaches share some key features: The multidigit procedures that students use are easily understood; students are encouraged to use algorithms that they understand; instructional supports (classroom discussions, physical materials, etc.) are available to focus students' attention on the base-10 structure of the number system and on how that structure is used in the algorithm; and students are helped to progress to using reasonably efficient but still comprehensible algorithms.[59]

Sixth, research on symbolic learning argues that, to be helpful, manipulatives or other physical models used in teaching must be represented by a learner both as the objects that they are and as symbols that stand for something else.[60] The physical characteristics of these materials can be initially distracting to children, and it takes time for them to develop mathematical meaning for any kind of physical model and to use it effectively. These findings suggest that sustained experience with any physical models that students are expected to use may be more effective than limited experience with a variety of different models.[61]

In view of the attention given to the use of concrete models in U.S. school mathematics classes, we offer a special note regarding their effective use in multidigit arithmetic. Research indicates that students' experiences using physical models to represent hundreds, tens, and ones can be effective *if* the materials help them think about how to combine quantities and, eventually, how these processes connect with written procedures. The models, however, are not automatically meaningful for students; the meaning must be constructed as they work with the materials. Given time to develop meaning for a model and connect it with the written procedure, students have shown high levels of performance using the written procedure and the ability to give good explanations for how they got their answers.[62] In order to support understanding, however, the physical models need to show tens to be collections of ten ones and to show hundreds to be simultaneously 10 tens and 100 ones. For example, base-10 blocks have that quality, but chips all of the same size but with different colors for hundreds, tens, and ones do not.

A seventh and final observation is that the English number words and the Hindu-Arabic base-10 place-value system for writing numbers complicate the teaching and learning of multidigit algorithms in much the same way, as discussed in Chapter 5, that they complicate the learning of early number concepts.[63] Closely related to the difficulties posed by the irregularities with number words are difficulties posed by the complexity of the system for writing numbers. As we said in chapter 3, the base-10 place-value system is very efficient. It allows one to write very large numbers using only 10 symbols, the digits 0 through 9. The same digit has a different meaning depending on its place in the numeral. Although this system is familiar and seems obvious to adults, its intricacies are not so obvious to children. These intricacies are important because research has shown that it is difficult to develop procedural fluency with multidigit arithmetic without an understanding of the base-10 system.[64] If such understanding is missing, students make many different errors in multidigit computations.[65]

This conclusion does not imply that students must master place value before they can begin computing with multidigit numbers. In fact, the evidence shows that students can develop an understanding of both the base-10 system and computation procedures when they have opportunities to explore how and why the procedures work.[66] That should not be surprising; it simply confirms the thesis of this report and the claim we made near the beginning of this chapter. Proficiency develops as the strands connect and interact.

The six observations can be illustrated and supported by examining briefly each of the arithmetic operations. As is the case for single-digit operations, research provides a more complete picture for addition and subtraction than for multiplication and division.

Addition Algorithms

The progression followed by students who construct their own procedures is similar in some ways to the progression that can be used to help students learn a standard algorithm with understanding. To illustrate the nature of these progressions, it is useful to examine some specific procedures in detail.

The episode in Box 6-6 from a third-grade class illustrates both how physical materials can support the development of thinking strategies about multidigit algorithms and one type of procedure commonly invented by children.[67] The episode comes from a discussion of students' solutions to a word problem involving the sum 54 + 48.

The episode suggests that students' invented procedures can be constructed through progressive abstraction of their modeling strategies with blocks. First, the objects in the problem were represented directly with the blocks. Then, the quantity representing the first set was abstracted, and only the blocks representing the second set were counted. Finally, the counting words were themselves counted by keeping track of the counts on fingers.

Box 6-6

A Third-Grade Class Finds 54 + 48

The students had worked on the problem at their desks for about 15 minutes and were sharing their procedures with the class. The teacher, Ms. G., called everyone over to look at Ellen's solution strategy.

Ellen: [Makes 54 and 48 with tens and ones blocks.] I knew this was 54, so I went 64, 74, 84, 94, ... [She moves one 10 block for each count. Then she counts the single cubes, moving a cube with each count.] Ninety-five, 96, . . . , 102.

Ms. G: Now class, what question am I going to ask her? Norman?

Norman: You didn't use the 54. Did you have to make it?

Ms. G: Good, Norman, that's just what I was going to ask her. Ellen, did you need to make that 54?

Ellen: No.

Ms. G: [Pulls the 54 away and covers it with her hand.] OK, now show me how you can solve the problem without the 54.

Ellen: Sixty-four, 74, ... [She repeats the above strategy, counting on without the 54.]

Ms. G: OK, now you told me that you could do this without us moving to your desk. How would you have done that?

Ellen: OK, I just put 54 in my head, and then I go 48 more. I go 54 [slight pause], 64, 74, 84, 94. [She puts up a finger with each count to keep track of the four tens in 48. At this point she has four fingers up. She puts down her fingers and puts them up again with each count as she continues counting by ones.] Ninety-five, 96, 97, . . . , 102.

SOURCE: Adapted from Carpenter, Fennema, and Franke, 1996, p. 11.

Ellen's final solution was for all intents and purposes a verbal description of what she did with the blocks. But it was more than that. It represented a solution that could actually be carried out without the blocks as explicit referents. Other invented procedures share some of the same features.

Boxes 6-7 through 6-10 illustrate procedures for multidigit addition and subtraction. Method C in Box 6-7 captures, in written form, the thinking strategies that many students use as they continue constructing procedures for adding multidigit numbers.[68] They usually begin by combining the larger units first and then combining the subtotals to find the sum. They invent a variety of mental and written techniques to keep track of the subtotals until they can combine them. The important observation is that students who construct these methods understand that ones are combined with ones, tens with tens, and hundreds with hundreds, and they understand that 10 of each unit compose one unit of the next higher magnitude (e.g., 10 tens make 100). Fundamental properties of the number system, like the associative and distributive properties, are used in decomposing and recombining numbers. In other words, the procedures children construct on their own build directly on the foundational number concepts, and these underlying concepts often are quite visible when one examines the steps in the procedures.

Standard algorithms, in contrast to children's constructed algorithms, are quite far removed from their conceptual underpinnings. They have evolved over centuries for efficiency and compactness. They can be executed quickly, but they can be difficult to learn with understanding.

Method A in Box 6-7 is an addition algorithm currently appearing in many U.S. textbooks. Learning this procedure with understanding poses three difficulties for many students. First, it moves from right to left, in contrast to reading and in contrast to most methods invented by children. Many children initially, and some children for a long time, have difficulty remembering to start on the right and move to the left.[69] Second, for some children, putting the little 1's above the top number changes the problem (it actually does change the problem, but that does not change the answer). This change can be a source of confusion. Third, adding the numbers in a given column is difficult with this method. You must add the 1 to the top number, remember the sum without writing it down, and add that remembered number you cannot see to the bottom number while you ignore the number you can see in the top row. If children instead add the two numbers they see (a much easier method), many of them then forget to add the extra 10 (or extra hundred).

> The procedures children construct on their own build directly on the foundational number concepts, and these underlying concepts often are quite visible when one examines the steps in the procedures.

Box 6-7

Three Methods for Multidigit Addition

A Common U.S. Algorithm

Method A

```
  1 1
  568
+ 876
------
 1444
```

(a) right to left

(b) add, carry to left

(c) add carry to top number, remember new number while adding it to bottom number

Accessible Generalizable Methods

Method B

```
  568        568        568
+ 876   →  + 876   →  + 876
------     ------     ------
    1         11         11
    4         44        1444
```

(a) right to left

(b) carry goes below in answer space, keeping total together

(c) add 2 numbers you see, then increase that number by 1 for previous carry

Method C

```
  568
+ 876
------
 1300
  130
   14
------
 1444
```

(a) can be done in either direction

(b) add each kind of unit first, then add those totals

Method B is a variation of Method A that addresses two of these three problems (it also moves from right to left). Method B is taught in China and has been invented by students in the United States.[70] In this method the new 1 or regrouped 10 (or new hundred) is recorded on the line separating the problem from the answer. This arrangement makes it easier to see the 14 that generated the regrouped 10 than when the 1 is written above the problem. Because the new 1 sits below in the answer space, it does not change the top number. Adding is easy: You just add the two numbers you see and then increase that total by one.

Methods A and B both require that children understand what to do when they get 10 or more in a given column. Because they can only write 9 or less of a given grouping in a column, they must make a group of 10 ones (or tens or hundreds, etc.) and give that group to the next left place. This conceptual trouble spot for students is called *carrying* or *regrouping* or *trading*. Method C, reflecting more closely many students' invented procedures, reduces the problem by writing the total for each kind of unit on a new line. The carrying-regrouping-trading is done as part of the adding of each kind of unit. Also, Method C can be done in either direction (Box 6-7 shows the left-to-right version). Because you write out the whole value of each partial sum (e.g., 500 + 800 = 1300), this method also facilitates children's thinking about and explaining how and what they are adding. Accessibility studies indicate that young children can solve multidigit addition problems using methods like B and C and some other methods also.[71]

Drawings like that in Box 6-8 can be used to support children's understanding of the quantities in the problem and how those quantities are grouped to make new tens, hundreds, or thousands. Such drawings can be used with any of the three methods (or with other methods). Whether drawings or objects are used to support understanding of an addition method, it is vital that they be linked to the numbers in the algorithm until the student can perform it with understanding. If the drawings (or physical models like base-10 blocks) are used simply to calculate answers, they lose their ability to help connect understanding to procedures. The benefits of using the materials come from seeing that the actions performed on the drawings or objects to get answers are the very actions that are used in carrying out the algorithm. Learning the algorithm then becomes a matter of students recording with numbers on paper the actions and thinking they did with the drawings or objects. This linking process takes time. Asking students to explain their procedure as if the numbers were the drawings or physical models can facilitate the linking process.

Box 6-8

A Model for Multidigit Addition: 568 + 876 = ?

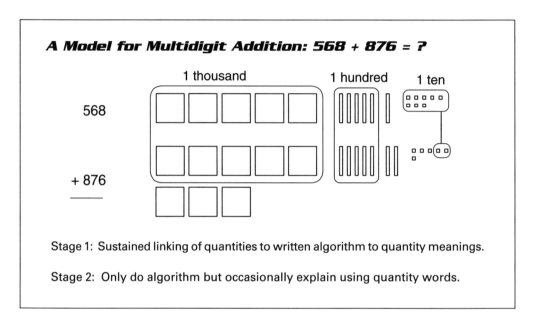

Stage 1: Sustained linking of quantities to written algorithm to quantity meanings.

Stage 2: Only do algorithm but occasionally explain using quantity words.

Subtraction Algorithms

Students can construct multidigit subtraction procedures, though often these procedures are less similar to standard algorithms than is the case for addition. Still, as with addition, research has shown that students can learn a subtraction algorithm meaningfully if provided with appropriate experiences. In most cases, subtraction algorithms require more time and support than addition algorithms, but students can learn to execute them accurately and to explain why they work.[72]

Two subtraction procedures are shown in Box 6-9. Method A is an algorithm commonly taught in the United States. It moves from right to left and alternates between the two major subtraction steps. Step 1 involves regrouping (or borrowing or trading) to get 10 or more in the top position. Step 2 is subtracting after the top number has been fixed. Alternating between these two steps presents three kinds of potential difficulties for students. The first is learning this alternation and the reasons for it. The second is remembering to alternate the steps. The third is that the alternation renders students susceptible to a very common subtracting error: subtracting a smaller top digit from a larger bottom digit. In the example, after subtracting bottom digit in

Box 6-9

Three Methods for Multidigit Subtraction

A Common U.S. Algorithm

Method A

```
   3 13
 1 4 4 4
-  5 6 8
 ─────────
   8 7 6
```

(a) right to left

(b) alternate ungrouping and subtracting

Accessible Generalizable Methods

Method B

```
      13
   13 14 14
  1 4 4 4
 -  5 6 8
 ─────────
    8 7 6
```

left-to-right ungrouping

Method C

```
      13
   13 3 14
  1 4 4 4
 -  5 6 8
 ─────────
    8 7 6
```

right-to-left ungrouping

Do all ungrouping, in any order, until every top number is larger than the bottom number. Then subtract each kind of multiunit, in any order.

the ones place to get 6, a student moves to the left and sees 3 on the top and 6 on the bottom. The answer 3 is generated spontaneously as a subtraction answer, given 6 and 3. It takes extra effort to suppress this answer and think about the direction in which one is subtracting.

Methods B and C are slight variations of Method A in which Step 1 (regrouping) is done for all columns first. For each column in either direction, the student asks the regrouping (borrowing) question, "Can I subtract in this column? Is the top digit as big as or bigger than the bottom digit?"

Box 6-10

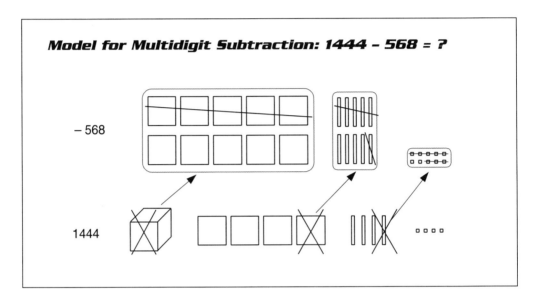

Model for Multidigit Subtraction: 1444 – 568 = ?

The goal is to fix the top number so that every top digit is larger than the corresponding bottom digit. The second major step is then to subtract in every column. This subtraction can also be done in any direction. Methods B and C clarify that the top number is a single number that must be rewritten in a form equivalent in value but ready for subtraction in every column. This rewriting can reduce the otherwise frequent "top from bottom" error.[73]

The drawing in Box 6-10 shows how students can make a quantity drawing to show both aspects of multidigit subtracting. Making such drawings initially can help students develop their own procedures or help them make sense of an algorithm presented by someone else. Again, such drawings should, when used, be linked to a numerical method and not just used to calculate an answer.

Multiplication Algorithms

There is much less research on children's understanding of multidigit multiplication (and division) than of addition and subtraction. Sample conceptual teaching lessons have been published for multiplication, and some alternative methods of instruction have been explored.[74] A preliminary learning progression of multidigit procedures that fosters children's invention of

Box 6-11

A Common U.S. Algorithm for Multidigit Multiplication

$$
\begin{array}{r}
\overset{3}{}\\[-2pt]
\overset{4}{}\\[-2pt]
46\\
\times\ 68\\
\hline
\overset{1}{3}68\\
\overset{1}{2}76\\
\hline
3128
\end{array}
$$

---

algorithms has also been reported.[75] The data are still insufficient, however, to permit firm conclusions about students' learning progressions in multidigit multiplication.

Nevertheless, it is useful to examine algorithms students are expected to learn and to consider alternatives that might facilitate understanding. Standard multiplication and division algorithms used in the United States are complex procedures in which multiplying alternates with adding or subtracting (see Box 6-11). In these algorithms the meaning and scaffolding provided by substeps have been sacrificed for efficiency. The algorithms use alignment of place value to keep the steps organized without requiring the student to understand what is actually happening with the ones, tens, hundreds, and so on. Algorithms that might be more accessible to students, and still generalizable and fairly efficient, are presented and discussed below.

Arrays are powerful representations of multiplication. An array or area model is shown on the left in Box 6-12. Such a model provides initial support for the crucial understanding of the effects of multiplying by 1, 10, and 100 (shown by arrows and products around the array). It also shows clearly how all of the tens and ones digits in 46 and 68 are multiplied by each other and then added. The sizes of the resulting rectangles indicate the sizes of these various products (sometimes referred to as *partial products*). The abbreviated array model (shown on the right in Box 6-12) can be drawn later when the students clearly understand the effects of multiplying by tens and by ones. This abbreviated model summarizes the steps in multidigit multiplication, and the separation into tens and ones facilitates finding the partial products.

Box 6-12

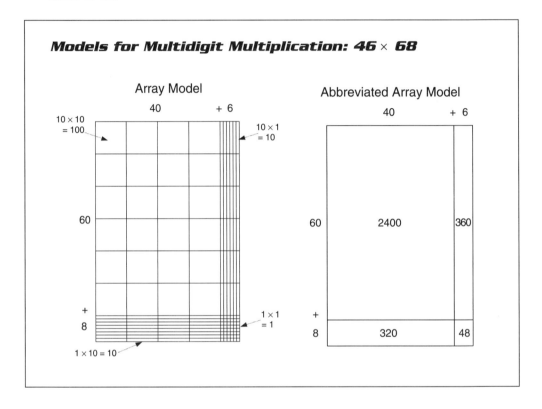

Models for Multidigit Multiplication: 46 × 68

The multiplication algorithm shown in Box 6-13 is an expanded form in which all possible products are written. As students come to understand each aspect of multiplication, some of the written supports can be dropped, resulting in a streamlined version that is a simple expanded form of typical U.S. algorithms. Although this algorithm has been proposed as an alternative for some time, and variations of it have been used in some textbooks,[76] algorithms currently used in the United States are substantially different. They typically start at the right and multiply ones first. The expanded algorithm begins at the left, as students are naturally inclined to do. That also has the advantage that the first product written is the largest, which permits all of the smaller products to be aligned easily under it in their correct places. Writing the factors beside each product emphasizes what one is actually doing in each step and permits an easy check. In this variation the complex alternation of multiplying and adding is not necessary. Students who understand and wish

Box 6-13

Expanded Algorithm for Multidigit Multiplication

$$
\begin{array}{rl}
46 = & 40 + 6 \\
\times\, 68 = & 60 + 8 \\
\hline
2400 = & 60 \times 40 \\
360 = & 60 \times\ \ 6 \\
320 = & \ \ 8 \times 40 \\
48 = & \ \ 8 \times\ \ 6 \\
\hline
3128 &
\end{array}
$$

Note: Steps can be dropped when they are no longer needed.

---

to drop steps in this algorithm can do so readily, with a result looking something like the common algorithm in Box 6-11, except that it has, in this case, four instead of two partial products to be added. These four can even be collapsed into two for those students who wish to do so. Therefore, the expanded model permits students to function at their own level of competence and is likely to help them understand what they are doing. The key point is that regardless of the algorithm that students use, they should be able to explain what they are doing and why it works.

Multiplying by a three-digit number is an extension of the two-digit version that requires the development of new understanding about multiplying by hundreds. The expanded algorithm for these larger numbers is relatively easy to carry out because the necessary steps are visible, although the number of partial products more than doubles. Given the accessibility of calculators, it might not be wise for students to spend a great deal of valuable school learning time becoming efficient at multiplication with three-digit or larger numbers. There is no research on how much pencil-and-paper computation is necessary or the impact of experiences with calculating with larger numbers on other mathematical understanding. Having some experience working with larger numbers, however, seems essential if students are to extend their conceptual understanding of multiplication and develop their ability to estimate the results of calculating with large numbers. Both of these skills are important even when children use calculators.

At present, many students have not achieved procedural fluency with single-digit multiplication when they begin work on multidigit multiplication. A proper balance in instruction among the strands of mathematical proficiency would serve to diminish the number of such students. Until that balance is achieved, however, such students need help in working simultaneously on a multiplication algorithm and obtaining fluency with single-digit multiplication. Using a table to look up some single-digit products can permit students to participate in classwork on algorithms while perhaps motivating as well as supporting their continued learning of single-digit arithmetic.

Division Algorithms

As we indicated earlier, relatively little research is available to shed light on how students think about multidigit division or what learning activities might be of most help to them. Sample teaching lessons have been proposed, and preliminary results suggest that students can construct their own procedures that, over time, approximate standard algorithms.[77] As with multiplication, however, the best that educators can do at this point is to examine some alternative algorithms that are likely to support students' efforts to develop proficiency with multidigit division.

Common U.S. division algorithms have two aspects that can create difficulties for students. First, the algorithms require students to determine *exactly* the maximum copies of the divisor that can be taken from successive parts of the dividend. For example, in the problem $3129 \div 46 = ?$, one must first determine exactly how many 46s can be subtracted from 312. That determination is not always easy. Second, the algorithms creates no sense of the size of the answers one is writing, in part because one is always multiplying by what looks like a single-digit number written above the dividend. In the example in Box 6-14, to begin the division process, the student just writes a 6 above the line as the first digit in the quotient. There is no sense of 60, because the student will be multiplying 46 by 6.

The accessible division method shown in Box 6-15 facilitates safe underestimating. Rather than trying to determine the largest number of 46s that can be subtracted from 312, the student can just keep subtracting multiples of 46s until the remainder is less than 46. This method builds experience with estimating (as well as accurate assessment of calculator answers) because students multiply by the correct number (e.g., 50, not 5). It is procedurally easy for those students still mastering multiplication combinations because it

Box 6-14

A Common Algorithm for Multidigit Division

$$
\begin{array}{r}
68 \\
46\overline{)3129} \\
-276 \\
\hline
369 \\
-\ 368 \\
\hline
1
\end{array}
$$

Box 6-15

Expanded Algorithm and Model for Multidigit Division

Accessible Division Algorithm:
Take away copies of 46 until no more remain

Abbreviated Model:
Build up copies of 46

$$
\begin{array}{r}
46\overline{)3129} \\
-2300 \quad | \quad 50 \\
\hline
829 \\
-\ 460 \quad | \quad 10 \\
\hline
369 \\
-\ 230 \quad | \quad 5 \\
\hline
139 \\
-\ 92 \quad | \quad 2 \\
\hline
47 \\
-\ 46 \quad | \quad 1 \\
\hline
\text{R } 1 \quad | \quad 68
\end{array}
$$

50 (5s are easy: take half of 10 × 46)

10

5 (I already did it)

2 (doubling is easy)

1

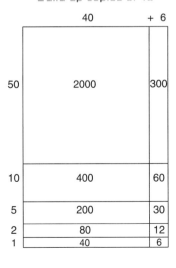

Box 6-16

Expanded Algorithm for Multidigit Division with Fewer Steps

$$
\begin{array}{r|l}
46\,\overline{)3129} & \\
-2760 & 60 \\
\hline
369 & \\
-\,276 & 6 \\
\hline
93 & \\
-\,92 & 2 \\
\hline
R\,1 & 68 \\
\end{array}
$$

---

permits the use of products likely to be known. It can be made as brief as the current standard algorithm for those who can manage the abbreviation. This accessible division algorithm has been proposed as an alternative for some time and since at least the 1950s has been used in some textbooks.[78]

The example of the accessible method given in Box 6-15 shows a solution that might be produced by a student very early in learning division. Box 6-15 also gives a model that supports accessible methods. The student builds up copies of the divisor until the dividend is reached and then reads off the quotient. A later version of the procedure by the same student is given in Box 6-16. At this point the student no longer needs the drawing to give meaning to the steps. This version can readily be related to the more common method in Box 6-14.

Summary of Findings on Multidigit Calculations

Research indicates that U.S. children can understand and explain procedures for calculating with multidigit numbers rather than just executing them mechanically. This conclusion, which is especially well established for addition and subtraction,[79] means that mathematical proficiency with multidigit arithmetic is achievable by students even at early grades. In fact, a higher level of performance can be achieved at earlier grades than is currently expected.[80]

Students acquire proficiency with multidigit algorithms by moving through a progression of experiences. Although there is relatively little research on students' learning of multiplication and division algorithms, it is likely that their learning trajectories are similar to the ones documented for addition and subtraction. The progression might begin with problem modeling and the use of easily understood concrete representations and algorithms and move toward more efficient methods that are less transparent and more problem independent. Or it might begin by learning with understanding some method that easily makes sense when connected to the quantities involved. Some students invent their own methods for performing multidigit computations, and some learn by listening to others—another student or the teacher—explain a method. Whatever avenue students take, their procedural fluency is intertwined with their conceptual understanding and adaptive reasoning. The many kinds of errors students make when multidigit methods are not connected to place-value meanings are well documented.[81]

Research on addition and subtraction algorithms clearly indicates that helping students keep the strands of proficiency connected means providing supports for their efforts to make sense of written algorithms. The use of easily understood versions of algorithms can facilitate procedural fluency. Discussing and comparing different methods, including those that students bring from home, can provide opportunities to extend their understanding of place value and its uses. Teachers need to ensure that children who are less proficient have a relatively advanced method they understand and can use. The focus of instruction, however, should be on their understanding and explaining and not just on routine use. Comparing methods through classroom discussion is a means of facilitating reflection by all children on the conceptual and notational features of arithmetic algorithms.

Physical materials or drawings that show the different sizes of ones, tens, and hundreds can support the development of understanding if those supports are used to develop thinking strategies for combining quantities and if they are linked to written algorithms. What appears to be essential is that sufficient time and support are provided at the outset for children to develop meaning for the algorithms. That development hinges on certain prerequisite understanding (which may be developed alongside methods), and children also need to negotiate and become more skilled with the complexities of multistep, multidigit methods.[82]

How much of the precious time available for school mathematics should be spent on written algorithms with large numbers is a question that will need to be continually revisited during the twenty-first century. New goals will arise to compete with the goal of fluency with written algorithms, as they already have. At present, it seems worthwhile to spend some time on written algorithms that facilitate students' understanding of how multidigit procedures can be built from key concepts of place value and properties of the number system, such as the distributive property. Because calculating activities with large numbers incorporate calculations with single-digit numbers, such activities can also buttress children's mastery of basic arithmetic. However, drilling for long periods on problems involving large numbers seems a goal more appropriate to the twentieth century than the twenty-first.

Mental Arithmetic and Estimation

Written procedures for adding, subtracting, multiplying, and dividing are the major focus of mathematics in the elementary school curriculum, and we have discussed how they can be integrated into the other strands of children's developing mathematical proficiency. We end this chapter by considering two other kinds of calculation methods and the roles they can play in fostering the development of mathematical proficiency.

Mental Arithmetic

A number of researchers have argued that mental arithmetic—calculating the solution to multidigit arithmetic problems mentally without the use of pencil and paper—can lead to deeper insights into the number system.[83] For example, a student might calculate 198×12 mentally by adding 2 to 198, multiplying 200 by 12 to get 2400, and then subtracting two 12s from the product, $2400 - 24 = 2376$. Mental arithmetic, or mental math, can provide opportunities for students to practice and use numbers and operations in ways that promote making sense of the mathematics and reveal further insights into the properties of numbers and operations.

In the United States, mental calculation has not been emphasized in school mathematics in recent decades.

Beliefs about the contribution of mental arithmetic to the development of mathematical proficiency have changed over time and differ across countries. In nineteenth-century America, the ability to perform mental arithmetic was held in high esteem.[84] Mental arithmetic, particularly as performed using a mental representation of the abacus, remains a popular activity in East Asian countries, with international competitions and a formalized system for rating calculation skill.[85] In the United States, however, mental calculation has not been emphasized in school mathematics in recent decades.[86]

Mental arithmetic places a premium on flexible procedures that take advantage of mathematical structure and rely on well-known operations. Students who have developed the ability to calculate mentally use a variety of procedures that take advantage of their knowledge of numbers, including working from left to right, using distributivity and other properties of arithmetic, and factoring numbers to simplify their work.[87] These procedures can increase students' awareness that typically there are multiple ways of solving any calculation problem.

Children entering school have already begun developing mental procedures for performing simple arithmetic, procedures that are eventually channeled into the pencil-and-paper algorithms that they can use for most computational work. If they are not encouraged to continue developing mental computation procedures, most will be inclined to view the new algorithms as the preferred, possibly the only, methods for computing and will discontinue use of mental procedures even when they are easier.[88] There is evidence, though, that some instruction on mental arithmetic in upper elementary grades, if it is focused on understanding and uses number and operation properties, can move students away from the clumsy and error-prone mental use of written algorithms toward use of a variety of mental procedures better adapted to particular number combinations.[89]

Beyond its many practical uses in the modern world, mental arithmetic can promote mathematical proficiency by bringing together the various strands. Mental arithmetic should be taught to encourage children to reason about the problem situation and the numbers involved, to take advantage of their conceptual understanding of the properties and rules of arithmetic, and to strategically select and adapt procedures to simplify a computation and calculate the answer.

Estimation

Making estimates of exact answers is another form of computation that has its own special properties and uses in developing mathematical proficiency. Estimating before solving a problem can facilitate number sense and place-value understanding by encouraging students to use number and notational properties to generate an approximate result. Estimating is also a practical skill. It can guide students' use of calculators, especially in identifying implausible answers, and is a valuable part of the mathematics used in everyday life.

Estimating the result of a computation is a complex skill in itself. It may require reformulating numbers, compensating for errors, and sometimes restructuring a problem.[90] For example, the sum 261 + 242 + 235 could be estimated by reformulating (in this case, rounding) each number as 250. In this form the simplest way of estimating the sum would be multiplying 250 by 3 and then compensating for the fact that the sum will be somewhat less than 750. Computational estimation takes advantage of important properties of numbers and notational systems, including powers of ten, place value, and relations among different operations. It also requires recognizing that the appropriateness of an estimate is related to the problem and its context.[91] Estimation requires a flexibility of calculation that emphasizes adaptive reasoning and strategic competence, guided by children's conceptual understanding of both the problem situation and the mathematics underlying the calculation.

Research on estimation shows how difficult it is for students who receive conventional instruction, with its frequent overemphasis on routine paper-and-pencil calculation, to move from calculating exact answers to estimating wisely. For example, one study[92] reported that many students' fear of being wrong led them to find the exact answer first and then round it to obtain a close estimate, with this tendency increasing from grades 5 to 9. Children also had difficulty using powers of 10 to identify the order of magnitude of a calculation (e.g., $4.638 \times 87,325$), and failed to understand that rounding can lead to systematic errors that need to be taken into account.

Estimating the results of a computation is a complex activity that should integrate all strands of mathematical proficiency. Its potential benefit is lost, however, if it is treated as a separate skill and taught as a set of isolated rules and techniques. Its benefit is realized when students are allowed to draw on other strands to find ways to simplify calculations and compensate for that simplification. For example, the representation students make of the mathematical situation enables them to make simple, appropriate estimates. Both fluency with computational procedures and awareness of the kinds of calculations that are easy to perform contribute to successful estimation. Finally, estimation is a good indicator of students' productive disposition—in this case, their propensity to make sense of mathematical situations so that they understand that estimates are not wild guesses but informed, approximate solutions.

Developmental Themes

Becoming proficient with whole numbers is more complicated than many people realize. It is not simply moving quickly from ignorance to competence. Nor is it a matter of students following the teacher's directions and explanations and then practicing until they get it right. Rather, it involves students—with support from learning materials, teachers, and peers—inventing, understanding, and practicing methods; trying to learn and use concepts that look easy to adults but are challenging for children (e.g., place value); and gradually increasing their mathematical proficiency by continually seeking to make sense of number and numerical operations.

A few basic themes are critical. First, students' progress viewed from a distance is marked by a kind of gradualness and continuity, but viewed up close it appears uneven and varied. At any given moment, students know and use a range of computation methods that may vary according to the numbers in the problem, the problem situation, and other individual and classroom variables. A student may use different methods even on very similar problems, and any new method competes for a long time with older methods and may not be used consistently. In general, however, students steadily extend methods they understand to solve a larger variety of problems, and they shape current methods into more efficient ones.

A second theme is the many ways in which the strands of proficiency can be interwoven. Initially, in classrooms focused on understanding, students' conceptual understanding and procedural fluency are tightly connected—students use only methods they understand. Later, their learning in one strand boosts their progress in the others. As students become more fluent with multidigit algorithms, their understanding and use of the place-value notational system become more robust. As their reasoning about multidigit numbers and place-value concepts improves, they make sense of more efficient multidigit algorithms. Students also actively choose among different procedures and representations. In so doing, they strengthen their strategic knowledge and their conceptual understanding of the procedures and the representations. Not only is mathematical proficiency multidimensional, but also the path to proficient performance requires progress along each strand interactively.

A third and final theme is that there are some identifiable patterns in the development of students' proficiency as long as the strands are allowed to develop together in mutual dependence. Students begin their study of number situations by modeling problems directly, using the context to shape their concrete and often cumbersome methods. They gradually move toward representing problems more abstractly. They apply methods that are less transparent and more embedded, abbreviated, and independent of the problem. These methods are more sophisticated mathematically, use structural properties such as commutativity, and use the place-value symbolic notation in productive ways. As students begin multidigit arithmetic, it is vital that teachers and classrooms provide support for all to build understanding of multidigit quantities that can enable their calculation methods to become personally meaningful. Mathematical proficiency with whole numbers depends on all five strands developing together.

Notes

1. Griffin, Case, and Siegler, 1994; Fuson, Smith, and Lo Cicero, 1997.
2. Baroody, 1984b, 1985; LeFevre, Bisanz, Daley, Buffone, Greenham, and Sadesky, 1996; LeFevre, Sadesky, and Bisanz, 1996.
3. Baroody, 1985, 1994. Basic number combinations may be represented not as a table of facts but as a network of facts and interconnecting relations (e.g., Baroody, 1985, 1987b, 1992). This idea is consistent with research in cognitive science, which says that expert knowledge is organized and connected (Bransford, Brown, and Cocking, 1999).
4. This observation was suggested by Jerman, 1970, and later verified by the work of Baroody, 1999a, 1999b, and many others.
5. Baroody, 1999a, 1999b.
6. Carpenter, Ansell, Franke, Fennema, Weisbeck, 1993; Carpenter and Moser, 1984; Carpenter, Moser, and Romberg, 1982; Fuson, 1992a, 1992b; Riley and Greeno, 1988; Siegler, in press; Verschaffel and De Corte, 1993.
7. Carpenter, Ansell, Franke, Fennema, and Weisbeck, 1993.
8. Carpenter, 1985; Fuson, 1992a, 1992b.
9. For a detailed analysis of multiplication and division problems, see Greer, 1992; Nesher, 1992; Vergnaud, 1983; Harel and Confrey, 1994.
10. Carpenter, Ansell, Franke, Fennema, and Weisbeck, 1993; Kouba, 1989.
11. Kouba, 1989.
12. For example, Brownell, 1956/1987.
13. Fuson, 1992b.
14. Fuson and Secada, 1986; Leutzinger, 1979; Steinberg, 1985; Thornton, 1978.
15. Baroody, 1996; Resnick and Ford, 1981.
16. Fuson and Kwon, 1992b; Fuson, Stigler, and Bartsch, 1988; Geary, 1994; Matsushita, 1994. Hatano, 1988, discusses a "complementary number-to-10" strategy used by Japanese students on an abacus. When there are not enough beads available to add 8, for example, the student adds 10 and subtracts 2.
17. Fuson and Kwon, 1991.
18. See, for example, the 1999 edition of *Scott Foresman-Addison Wesley Math, Grade 1.*
19. Carpenter and Moser, 1984; Fuson, 1992a, 1992b.
20. See reviews in Fuson, 1992a, 1992b.
21. Fuson and Secada, 1986; Fuson and Fuson, 1992. Both studies included students with learning disabilities and English-language learners (K. C. Fuson, personal communication, Northwestern University, 2000).
22. Carpenter, Ansell, Franke, Fennema, and Weisbeck, 1993; Carpenter, Moser, and Romberg, 1982; Fuson, 1992a; Riley and Greeno, 1988; Siegler, in press.
23. See, for example, Baroody, 1984a.

24. Carpenter and Moser, 1984.
25. Fuson, 1986b; Fuson and Fuson, 1992.
26. Armstrong, 1990/1991; Huinker, 1990/1991; Rathmell and Huinker, 1989.
27. Resnick, 1983.
28. Baroody, 1999a.
29. Mulligan and Mitchelmore, 1997; Steffe, 1994. Lemaire and Siegler, 1995, found similar results with French second graders. Brownell, 1944, showed that, from grades 3 to 5, students became faster at multiplication combinations because they progressively used more efficient strategies.
30. Thornton, 1978; Baroody, 1987a, 1999b.
31. Carpenter, Fennema, Peterson, Chiang, and Loef, 1989, found that when instruction focused on problem solving, children not only became better problem solvers but also mastered more combinations than did children whose instruction focused on drill and practice of basic facts.
32. Brownell and Chazal, 1935, found that drill on arithmetic facts does not necessarily lead to recall. In spite of drill, children tend to maintain whatever procedures have satisfied their number needs. Drill does not supply children with more mature ways of dealing with number combinations. Brownell and Chazal argue that drill must be preceded by sound instruction.
33. Carnine and Stein, 1981; Cook and Dossey, 1982; Rathmell, 1978; Thornton, 1978.
34. See Rathmell, 1978.
35. Bergeron and Herscovics, 1990.
36. Brownell and Chazal, 1935.
37. Davydov and Andronov, 1981; Fuson and Kwon, 1992b; Saxe, 1982.
38. Bergeron and Herscovics, 1990; Fuson, 1988; Steffe, Cobb, and von Glasersfeld, 1988.
39. Geary and Brown 1991; Siegler, 1996, pp. 61–71.
40. Siegler, 1996, p. 97.
41. Siegler and Jenkins, 1989.
42. Geary, 1994; Ginsburg and Allardice, 1984.
43. Carnine and Stein, 1981; Cook and Dossey, 1982; Thornton, 1978.
44. Fuson, 1986b; Fuson and Fuson, 1992; Fuson and Willis, 1988.
45. Siegler and Jenkins, 1989; Siegler, 1996, pp. 61–71.
46. For example, see Ron, 1998, for a discussion of a European-Latino subtraction algorithm; Fuson and Kwon, 1992a, for a Korean subtraction algorithm; and Chapter 3 of this volume for various multiplication algorithms learned by teachers in this country.
47. Siegler, in press.
48. Brown and Van Lehn, 1980.
49. For a synthesis on the relationship between conceptual and procedural knowledge for multidigit addition and subtraction, see Rittle-Johnson and Siegler, 1998. For a specific study, see Hiebert and Wearne, 1996.
50. Fuson and Briars, 1990; Fuson, Wearne, Hiebert, Murray, Human, Olivier, Carpenter, Fennema, 1997; Hiebert and Wearne, 1996.

51. On the basis of these results for multidigit addition and subtraction, Siegler, in press, suggests, as a broad principle, that conceptual instruction should occur prior to teaching of procedures. Rittle-Johnson and Alibali, 1999, reported similar results with respect to mathematical equivalence.

52. Beishuizen, 1993; Beishuizen, Van Putten, and Van Mulken, 1997; Hiebert, Carpenter, Fennema, Fuson, Wearne, Murray, Olivier, Human, 1997; Hiebert and Wearne, 1993, 1996.

53. Fuson, 1992a, 1992b.

54. Carpenter, Franke, Jacobs, Fennema, Empson, 1998; Carraher, Carraher, and Schliemann, 1987; Cobb and Wheatley, 1988; Fuson and Burghardt, 1993; Hiebert, Carpenter, Fennema, Fuson, Wearne, Murray, Olivier, and Human, 1997; Hiebert and Wearne, 1996; Kamii, 1989; Labinowicz, 1985; Nunes, 1992; Olivier, Murray, and Human, 1990; Saxe, 1988; Ambrose, Baek, and Carpenter, in press.

55. Kamii and Dominick, 1998.

56. Hiebert and Wearne, 1993, 1996.

57. Carpenter, Franke, Jacobs, Fennema, and Empson, 1998; Fuson and Briars, 1990; Hiebert and Wearne, 1993, 1996.

58. Cobb and Bauersfeld, 1995; Fuson, 1992a, 1992b; Hiebert, Carpenter, Fennema, Fuson, Wearne, Murray, Olivier, and Human, 1997; Kamii, 1989.

59. Carpenter, Franke, Jacobs, Fennema, and Empson, 1998; Fuson and Briars, 1990; Hiebert and Wearne, 1993, 1996. See Carroll and Porter, 1998, for some alternative algorithms. For a discussion of principles for creating classroom environments that incorporate these features of effective teaching, see Fuson, De La Cruz, Smith, Lo Cicero, Hudson, Ron, and Steeby, 2000.

60. Uttal, Scudder, DeLoache, 1997.

61. Hiebert and Wearne, 1996.

62. Beishuizen, Gravemeijer, and van Lieshout, 1997; Bowers, Cobb, and McClain, 1999; Fuson and Burghardt, 1993, in press; Carpenter, Franke, Jacobs, Fennema, and Empson, 1998; McClain, Cobb, and Bowers, 1998; Fuson and Briars, 1990.

63. Fuson, 1990.

64. Cauley, 1988; Fuson and Burghardt, 1993, 1997, in press; Hiebert and Wearne, 1996.

65. VanLehn, 1986.

66. Fuson and Briars, 1990; Hiebert and Wearne, 1993, 1996. For examples of student difficulties with numeration and the base-10 system, see Bednarz and Janvier, 1982.

67. Student-invented procedures are sometimes not really algorithms because the steps are not precisely specified but instead follow a path that emerges through the process—and that path may be slightly different if the same problem is posed again. Because such procedures can often be made into algorithms by deliberate specification of the steps, the distinction between algorithms and ad hoc procedures is seldom maintained in the literature. (See, e.g., the articles in Morrow and Kenney, 1998.)

68. Carpenter, Franke, Jacobs, Fennema, Empson, 1998; Fuson and Burghardt, 1993; Hiebert, Carpenter, Fennema, Fuson, Wearne, Murray, Olivier, and Human, 1997.

69. Fuson, Wearne, Hiebert, Murray, Human, Olivier, Carpenter, and Fennema, 1997.

70. Fuson and Burghardt, 1993, in press.

71. Bowers, Cobb, and McClain, 1999; Hiebert and Wearne, 1996; Kamii, 1989.
72. Carpenter, Franke, Jacobs, Fennema, and Empson, 1998; Fuson, 1986a; Fuson and Briars, 1990; Hiebert and Wearne, 1993, 1996; Kamii, 1989.
73. Fuson, 1986a; Fuson and Briars, 1990.
74. For example, Carroll and Porter, 1998; Kamii, 1994; Lampert, 1986a, 1986b.
75. Baek, 1998; Ambrose, Baek, and Carpenter, in press.
76. See, for example, the 1999 edition of *Scott Foresman-Addison Wesley Math, Grade 4*.
77. Lampert, 1992; Murray, Olivier, and Human, 1992.
78. See, for example, Scott Foresman's *Seeing Through Arithmetic*, Grade 4 (Hartung, Van Engen, and Knowles, 1955).
79. For example, Bowers, Cobb, and McClain, 1999, and Carpenter, Franke, Jacobs, Fennema, and Empson, 1998; Fuson and Burghardt, in press; Hiebert and Wearne, 1996; Kamii, 1994. In a comparison study, Hiebert and Wearne, 1993, showed that students who spent more time on fewer problems and were asked to explain their procedures outperformed their more traditionally taught peers.
80. Fuson, 1986a; Fuson, Smith, Lo Cicero, 1997.
81. For example, VanLehn, 1986, and Fuson and Burghardt, in press.
82. For example, Bowers, Cobb, and McClain, 1999; Carpenter, Franke, Jacobs, Fennema, and Empson, 1998; Fuson, 1986a; Fuson and Burghardt, in press; Hiebert and Wearne, 1993, 1996; Kamii, 1994.
83. Beberman, 1959; Rathmell and Trafton, 1990. For a similar discussion about estimation, see Buchanan, 1978. Beishuizen, 1993, discusses students connecting mental arithmetic procedures to using base-10 blocks and hundreds squares.
84. Cohen, 1982.
85. Stigler, 1984; Hatano, 1988.
86. Sowder, 1992.
87. Hope and Sherrill, 1987.
88. Davis, 1984
89. Markovits and Sowder, 1988.
90. Reys, Rybolt, Bestgen, and Wyatt, 1982.
91. Markovits and Sowder, 1994; Rubenstein, 1985.
92. Sowder and Wheeler, 1989.

References

Ambrose, R., Baek, J., & Carpenter, T. P. (in press). Children's construction of multiplication and division algorithms. In A. J. Baroody & A. Dowker (Eds.), *The development of arithmetic concepts and skills: Constructing adaptive expertise*. Mahwah, NJ: Erlbaum.

Armstrong, G. A. (1991). Use of the part-whole concept for teaching word problems to grade three children (Doctoral dissertation, National College of Education, 1990). *Dissertation Abstracts International, 52*(03), 833A.

Baek, J.-M. (1998). Children's invented algorithms for multidigit multiplication problems. In L. J. Morrow & M. J. Kenney (Eds.), *The teaching and learning of algorithms in school mathematics* (1998 Yearbook of the National Council of Teachers of Mathematics, pp. 151–160). Reston, VA: NCTM.

Baroody, A. J. (1984a). Children's difficulties in subtraction: Some causes and cures. *Arithmetic Teacher, 32*(3), 14–19.

Baroody, A. J. (1984b). The case of Felicia: A young child's strategies for reducing memory demands during mental addition. *Cognition and Instruction, 1*, 109–116.

Baroody, A. J. (1985). Mastery of the basic number combinations: Internalization of relationships or facts? *Journal of Research in Mathematics Education, 16*, 83–98.

Baroody, A. J. (1987a). *Children's mathematical thinking: A developmental framework for preschool, primary, and special education teachers.* New York: Teachers College Press.

Baroody, A. J. (1987b). The development of counting strategies for single-digit addition. *Journal for Research in Mathematics Education, 18*, 141–157.

Baroody, A. J. (1992). The development of kindergartners' mental-addition strategies. *Learning and Individual Differences, 4*, 215–235.

Baroody, A. J. (1994). An evaluation of evidence supporting fact-retrieval models. *Learning and Individual Differences, 6*, 1–36.

Baroody, A. J. (1996). Self-invented addition strategies by children classified as mentally handicapped. *American Journal of Mental Retardation, 101*, 72–89.

Baroody, A. J. (1999a). Children's relational knowledge of addition and subtraction. *Cognition and Instruction, 17*, 137–175.

Baroody, A. J. (1999b). The roles of estimation and the commutativity principle in the development of third-graders' mental multiplication. *Journal of Experimental Child Psychology, 74* [Special issue on mathematical cognition], 157–193.

Beberman, M. (1959). Introduction. In C. H. Shutter & R. L. Spreckelmeyer (Eds.), *Teaching the third R.* Washington, DC: Council for Basic Education.

Bednarz, N., & Janvier, B. (1982). The understanding of numeration in primary school. *Educational Studies in Mathematics, 13*, 33–57.

Beishuizen, M. (1993). Mental procedures and materials or models for addition and subtraction up to 100 in Dutch second grades. *Journal for Research in Mathematics Education, 24*, 294–323.

Beishuizen, M., Gravemeijer, K. P. E., & van Lieshout, E. C. D. M. (Eds.). (1997). *The role of contexts and models in the development of mathematical strategies and procedures* (pp. 163–198). Utrecht: CD-B Press/Freudenthal Institute.

Beishuizen, M., Van Putten, C. M., & Van Mulken, F. (1997). Mental arithmetic and strategy use with indirect number problems up to one hundred. *Learning and Instruction, 7*, 87–106.

Bergeron, J. C., & Herscovics, N. (1990). Psychological aspects of learning early arithmetic. In P. Nesher & J. Kilpatrick (Eds.), *Mathematics and cognition: A research synthesis by the International Group for the Psychology of Mathematics Education. ICMI study series* (pp. 31–52). Cambridge, UK: Cambridge University Press.

Bowers, J., Cobb, P., & McClain, K. (1999). The evolution of mathematical practices: A case study. *Cognition and Instruction, 17*, 25–64.

Bransford, J. D., Brown, A. L., & Cocking, R. R. (Eds.). (1999). *How people learn: Brain, mind, experience, and school.* Washington, DC: National Academy Press. Available: http://books.nap.edu/catalog/6160.html. [July 10, 2001].

Brown, J. S., & Van Lehn, K. (1980). Repair theory: A generative theory of bugs in procedural skills. *Cognitive Science, 4*, 379–426.

Brownell, W. A. (1944). Rate accuracy and process in learning. *Journal of Educational Psychology, 35*, 321–337.

Brownell, W. A. (1987). AT classic: Meaning and skill—maintaining the balance. *Arithmetic Teacher, 34*(8), 18–25. (Original work published 1956)

Brownell, W. A., & Chazal, C. B. (1935). The effects of premature drill in third-grade arithmetic. *Journal of Educational Research, 29*, 17–28.

Buchanan, A. D. (1978). *Estimation as an essential mathematical skill* (Professional Paper No. 39, SWRL-PP-39). Los Alamitos, CA: Southwest Regional Laboratory for Educational Research and Development. (ERIC Document Reproduction Service No. ED 167 385)

Carnine, D. W., & Stein, M. (1981). Organizational strategies and practice procedures for teaching basic facts. *Journal for Research in Mathematics Education, 12*, 65–69.

Carpenter, T. P. (1985). Learning to add and subtract: An exercise in problem solving. In E. A. Silver (Ed.), *Teaching and learning mathematical problem solving: Multiple research perspectives* (pp. 17–40). Hillsdale, NJ: Erlbaum.

Carpenter, T. P., Ansell, E., Franke, M. L., Fennema, E., & Weisbeck, L. (1993). Models of problem solving: A study of kindergarten children's problem-solving processes. *Journal for Research in Mathematics Education, 24*, 428–441.

Carpenter, T. P., Fennema, E., & Franke, M. L. (1996). Cognitively guided instruction: A knowledge base for reform in primary mathematics instruction. *Elementary School Journal, 97*, 3–20.

Carpenter, T. P., Fennema, E., Franke, M. L., Empson, S. B., & Levi, L. W. (1999). *Children's mathematics: Cognitively guided instruction.* Portsmouth, NH: Heinemann.

Carpenter, T. P., Fennema, E., Peterson, P. L., Chiang, C. P., & Loef, M. (1989). Using knowledge of children's mathematics thinking in classroom teaching: An experimental study. *American Educational Research Journal, 26*, 499–531.

Carpenter, T. P., Franke, M. L., Jacobs, V. R., Fennema, E., & Empson, S. B. (1998). A longitudinal study of invention and understanding in children's multidigit addition and subtraction. *Journal for Research in Mathematics Education, 29*, 3–20.

Carpenter, T. P., & Moser, J. M. (1984). The acquisition of addition and subtraction concepts in grades one through three. *Journal for Research in Mathematics Education, 15*, 179–202.

Carpenter, T. P., Moser, M. J., & Romberg, T. A. (Eds.). (1982). *Addition and subtraction: A cognitive perspective.* Hillsdale, NJ: Erlbaum.

Carraher, T. N., Carraher, D. W., & Schliemann, A. D. (1987). Written and oral mathematics. *Journal for Research in Mathematics Education, 18*, 83–97.

Carroll, W. M., & Porter, D. (1997). Invented procedures can develop meaningful mathematical procedures. *Teaching Children Mathematics, 3*, 370–74.

Carroll, W. M., & Porter, D. (1998). Alternative algorithms for whole-number operations. In L. J. Morrow & M. J. Kenney (Eds.), *The teaching and learning of algorithms in school mathematics* (1998 Yearbook of the National Council of Teachers of Mathematics, pp.

106–114). Reston, VA: NCTM.

Cauley, K. M. (1988). Construction of logical knowledge: Study of borrowing in subtraction. *Journal of Educational Psychology, 80*, 202–205.

Cobb, P., & Bauersfeld, H. (Eds.). (1995). *The emergence of mathematical thinking: Interaction in classroom cultures.* Hillsdale, NJ: Erlbaum.

Cobb, P., & Wheatley, G. (1988). Children's initial understandings of ten. *Focus on Learning Problems in Mathematics, 10*(3), 1–28.

Cohen, P. C. (1982). *A calculating people: The spread of numeracy in early America.* Chicago: University of Chicago Press.

Cook, C. J., & Dossey, J. A. (1982). Basic facts thinking strategies for multiplication— revisited. *Journal for Research in Mathematics Education, 13*, 163–171.

Davis, R. B. (1984). *Learning mathematics: The cognitive science approach to mathematics education.* Norwood, NJ: Ablex.

Davydov, V. V., & Andronov, V. P. (1981). *Psychological conditions of the origination of ideal actions* (Project Paper No. 81–2). Madison: University of Wisconsin, Research and Development Center for Individualized Schooling.

Fuson, K. C. (1986a). Roles of representation and verbalization in the teaching of multi-digit addition and subtraction. *European Journal of Psychology of Education, 1*, 35–56.

Fuson, K. C. (1986b). Teaching children to subtract by counting up. *Journal for Research in Mathematics Education, 17*, 172–189.

Fuson, K. C. (1988). *Children's counting and concepts of number.* New York: Springer-Verlag.

Fuson, K. C. (1990). Conceptual structures for multiunit numbers: Implications for learning and teaching multidigit addition, subtraction, and place value. *Cognition and Instruction, 7*, 343–403.

Fuson, K. C. (1992a). Research on learning and teaching addition and subtraction of whole numbers. In G. Leinhardt, R. T. Putnam, & R. A. Hattrup (Eds.), *The analysis of arithmetic for mathematics teaching* (pp. 53–187). Hillsdale, NJ: Erlbaum.

Fuson, K. C. (1992b). Research on whole number addition and subtraction. In D. Grouws (Ed.), *Handbook of research on mathematics teaching and learning* (pp. 243–275). New York: Macmillan.

Fuson, K. C., & Briars, D. J. (1990). Using a base-ten blocks learning/teaching approach for first- and second-grade place-value and multidigit addition and subtraction. *Journal for Research in Mathematics Education, 21*, 180–206.

Fuson, K. C., & Burghardt, B. H. (1993). Group case studies of second graders inventing multidigit addition procedures for base-ten blocks and written marks. In J. R. Becker & B. J. Pence (Eds.), *Proceedings of the fifteenth annual meeting of the North American Chapter of the International Group for the Psychology of Mathematics Education* (pp. 240–246). San Jose, CA: San Jose State University. (ERIC Document Reproduction Service No. ED 372 917).

Fuson, K. C., & Burghardt, B. H. (1997). Group case studies of second graders inventing multidigit subtraction methods. In J. A. Dossey, J. O. Swafford, M. Parmantie, & A. E. Dossey (Eds.), *Proceedings of the nineteenth annual meeting of the North American Chapter of the International Group for the Psychology of Mathematics Education* (Vol. 1, pp. 291–298). Columbus, OH: ERIC Clearinghouse for Science, Mathematics, and Environmental Education. (ERIC Document Reproduction Service No. ED 420 494).

Fuson, K. C., & Burghardt, B. H. (in press). Multi-digit addition and subtraction methods invented in small groups and teacher support of problem solving and reflection. In A. Baroody & A. Dowker (Eds.), *The development of arithmetic concepts and skills: Constructing adaptive expertise.* Hillsdale, NJ: Erlbaum.

Fuson, K. C., De La Cruz, Y., Smith, S., Lo Cicero, A., Hudson, K., Ron, P., & Steeby, R. (2000). Blending the best of the twentieth century to achieve a mathematics equity pedagogy in the twenty-first century. In M. J. Burke (Ed.), *Learning mathematics for a new century* (2000 Yearbook of the National Council of Teachers of Mathematics, pp. 197–212). Reston, VA: NCTM.

Fuson, K. C., & Fuson, A. M. (1992). Instruction to support children's counting on for addition and counting up for subtraction. *Journal for Research in Mathematics Education, 23,* 72–78.

Fuson, K. C., & Kwon, Y. (1991). Chinese-based regular and European irregular systems of number words: The disadvantages for English-speaking children. In K. Durkin & B. Shire (Eds.), *Language and mathematical education* (pp. 211–226). Milton Keynes, UK: Open University Press.

Fuson, K. C., & Kwon, Y. (1992a). Korean children's understanding of multidigit addition and subtraction. *Child Development, 63,* 491–506.

Fuson, K. C., & Kwon, Y. (1992b). Korean children's single-digit addition and subtraction: Numbers structured by ten. *Journal for Research in Mathematics Education, 23,* 148–165.

Fuson, K. C., & Secada, W. G. (1986). Teaching children to add by counting-on with one-handed finger patterns. *Cognition and Instruction, 3,* 229–260.

Fuson, K. C., Smith, S. T., & Lo Cicero, A. M. (1997). Supporting Latino first graders' ten-structured thinking in urban classrooms. *Journal for Research in Mathematics Education, 28,* 738–766.

Fuson, K. C., Stigler, J., & Bartsch, K. (1988). Brief report: Grade placement of addition and subtraction topics in Japan, mainland China, the Soviet Union, Taiwan, and the United States. *Journal for Research in Mathematics Education, 19,* 449–456.

Fuson, K. C., Wearne, D., Hiebert, J. C., Murray, H. G., Human, P. G., Olivier, A. I., Carpenter, T. P., & Fennema, E. (1997). Children's conceptual structures for multidigit numbers and methods of multidigit addition and subtraction. *Journal for Research in Mathematics Education, 28,* 130–162.

Fuson, K. C., & Willis, G. B. (1988). Subtracting by counting up: More evidence. *Journal for Research in Mathematics Education, 19,* 402–420.

Geary, D. C. (1994). *Children's mathematical development: Research and practical applications.* Washington, DC: American Psychological Association.

Geary, D. C., & Brown, S. C. (1991). Cognitive addition: Strategy choice and speed-of-processing differences in gifted, normal and mathematically disabled children. *Developmental Psychology, 27,* 298–406.

Ginsburg, H. P., & Allardice, B. S. (1984). Children's difficulties with school mathematics. In B. Rogoff & J. Lave (Eds.), *Everyday cognition: Its development in social contexts* (pp. 194–219). Cambridge, MA: Harvard University Press.

Greer, F. (1992). Multiplication and division as models of situations. In D. Grouws (Ed.), *Handbook of research on mathematics teaching and learning* (pp. 276–295). New York: Macmillan.

Griffin, S. A., Case, R., & Siegler, R. S. (1994). Rightstart: Providing the central conceptual prerequisites for first formal learning of arithmetic to students at risk for school failure. In K. McGilly (Ed.), _Classroom lessons: Integrating cognitive theory and classroom practice_ (pp. 25–49). Cambridge, MA: MIT Press.

Harel, G., & Confrey, J. (1994). _The development of multiplicative reasoning in the learning of mathematics_. Albany: State University of New York Press.

Hartung, M. L., Van Engen, H., & Knowles, L. (1955). _Seeing through arithmetic_. Chicago: Scott Foresman.

Hatano, G. (1988, Fall). Social and motivational bases for mathematical understanding. _New Directions for Child Development, 41_, 55–70.

Hiebert, J., Carpenter, T., Fennema, E., Fuson, K. C., Wearne, D., Murray, H., Olivier, A., & Human, P. (1997). _Making sense: Teaching and learning mathematics with understanding_. Portsmouth, NH: Heinemann.

Hiebert, J., & Wearne, D. (1993). Instructional tasks, classroom discourse, and student learning in second grade. _American Educational Research Journal, 30_, 393–425.

Hiebert, J., & Wearne, D. (1996). Instruction, understanding, and skill in multidigit addition and subtraction. _Cognition and Instruction, 14_, 251–83.

Hope, J. A., & Sherrill, J. M. (1987). Characteristics of unskilled and skilled mental calculators. _Journal for Research in Mathematics Education, 18_(2), 98–111.

Huinker, D. M. (1991). Effects of instruction using part-whole concepts with one-step and two-step word problems in grade four (Doctoral dissertation University of Michigan, 1990). _Dissertation Abstracts International, 52_(01), 103A.

Jerman, M. (1970). Some strategies for solving simple multiplication combinations. _Journal for Research in Mathematics Education, 1_, 95–128.

Kamii, C. (1989). _Young children continue to reinvent arithmetic—2nd grade: Implications of Piaget's theory_. New York: Teachers College Press.

Kamii, C. (1994). _Young children continue to reinvent arithmetic—3rd grade: Implications of Piaget's theory_. New York: Teachers College Press.

Kamii, C. & Dominick, A. (1998). The harmful effects of algorithms in grades 1-4. In L. J. Morrow & M. J. Kenney (Eds.), _The teaching and learning of algorithms in school mathematics_ (1998 Yearbook of the National Council of Teachers of Mathematics, pp. 130–140). Reston VA: NCTM.

Kouba, V. (1989). Children's solution procedures for equivalent set multiplication and division word problems. _Journal for Research in Mathematics Education, 20_, 147–158.

Labinowicz, E. (1985). _Learning from children: New beginnings for teaching numerical thinking_. Menlo Park, CA: Addison-Wesley.

Lampert, M. (1986a). Knowing, doing, and teaching multiplication. _Cognition and Instruction, 3_, 305–342.

Lampert, M. (1986b). Teaching multiplication. _Journal of Mathematical Behavior, 5_, 241–280.

Lampert, M. (1992). Teaching and learning long division for understanding in school. In G. Leinhardt, R. T. Putnam, & R. A. Hattrup (Eds.), _The analysis of arithmetic for mathematics teaching_ (pp. 221–282). Hillsdale, NJ: Erlbaum.

LeFevre, J., Bisanz, J., Daley, K. E., Buffone, L., Greenham, S. L., & Sadesky, G. S. (1996). Multiple routes to solution of single-digit multiplication problems. _Journal of Experimental Psychology: General, 125_, 284–306.

LeFevre, J., Sadesky, G. S., & Bisanz, J. (1996). Selection of procedures in mental addition: Reassessing the problem-size effect in adults. *Journal of Experimental Psychology: Learning, Memory, and Cognition, 22*, 216–230.

Lemaire, P., & Siegler, R. S. (1995). Four aspects of strategic change: Contributions to children's learning of multiplication. *Journal of Experimental Psychology: General, 124*, 83–97.

Leutzinger, L. P. (1979). The effects of counting on the acquisition of addition facts in grade one (Doctoral dissertation, University of Iowa, 1979). *Dissertation Abstracts International, 40*(07), 3765A.

Markovits, Z., & Sowder, J. (1988). Mental computation and number sense. In M. J. Behr, C. B. Lacampagne, & M. M. Wheeler (Eds.), *Proceedings of the tenth annual meeting of the North American Chapter of the International Group for the Psychology of Mathematics Education* (pp. 58–64). DeKalb: Northern Illinois University. (ERIC Document Reproduction Service No. ED 411 126).

Markovits, Z., & Sowder, J. (1994). Developing number sense: An intervention study in grade 7. *Journal for Research in Mathematics Education, 25*, 4–29.

Matsushita, K. (1994). Acquiring mathematical knowledge through semantic and pragmatic problem solving. *Human Development, 37*, 220–232.

McClain, K., Cobb, P., & Bowers, J. (1998). A contextual investigation of three-digit addition and subtraction. In L. J. Morrow & M. J. Kenney (Eds.), *The teaching and learning of algorithms in school mathematics* (1998 Yearbook of the National Council of Teachers of Mathematics, pp. 141–150). Reston, VA: NCTM.

Morrow, L. J., & Kenney, M. J. (Eds.). (1998). *The teaching and learning of algorithms in school mathematics* (1998 Yearbook of the National Council of Teachers of Mathematics). Reston, VA: NCTM.

Mulligan, J., & Mitchelmore, M. (1997). Young children's intuitive models of multiplication and division. *Journal for Research in Mathematics Education, 28*, 309–330.

Murray, H., Olivier, A. & Human, P. (1992). The development of young children's division strategies. In W. Geeslin & K. Graham (Eds.), *Proceedings of the Sixteenth International Conference for the Psychology of Mathematics Education* (vol. 2, pp. 152–159). Durham, NH: PME Program Committee. (ERIC Document Reproduction Service No. ED 383 538).

Nesher, P. (1992). Solving multiplication word problems. In G. Leinhardt, R. T. Putnam, & R. A. Hattrup (Eds.), *The analysis of arithmetic for mathematics teaching* (pp. 189–220). Hillsdale, NJ: Erlbaum.

Nunes, T. (1992). Ethnomathematics and everyday cognition. In D. A. Grouws (Ed.), *Handbook of research on mathematics teaching and learning* (pp. 557–574). New York: Macmillan.

Olivier, A., Murray, H. & Human, P. (1990). Building on young children's informal mathematical knowledge. In G. Booker, P. Cobb, & T. N. Mendicuti (Eds.), *Proceedings of the Fourteenth International Conference for the Psychology of Mathematics Education* (vol. 3, pp. 297–304). Oaxtepec, Mexico: PME Program Committee. (ERIC Document Reproduction Service No. ED 411 139).

Rathmell, E. C. (1978). Using thinking procedures to learn basic facts. In M. Suydam (Ed.), *Developing computational skills* (1978 Yearbook of the National Council of Teachers of Mathematics, pp. 13-38). Reston, VA: NCTM.

Rathmell, E., & Huinker, D. (1989). Using "part-whole" language to help children represent and solve word problems. In P. R. Trafton (Ed.), *New directions for elementary school mathematics* (1989 Yearbook of the National Council of Teachers of Mathematics, pp. 99–110). Reston, VA: NCTM.

Rathmell, E. C., & Trafton, P. R. (1990). Whole number computation. In J. R. Payne (Ed.), *Mathematics for the young child* (pp. 153-172). Reston, VA: National Council of Teachers of Mathematics.

Resnick, L. B. (1983). A developmental theory of number understanding. In H. P. Ginsburg (Ed.), *The development of mathematical thinking* (pp. 110–152). Hillsdale, NJ: Erlbaum.

Resnick, L. B., & Ford, W. W. (1981). *The psychology of mathematics for instruction.* Hillsdale, NJ: Erlbaum.

Reys, R. E., Rybolt, J. F., Bestgen, B. J., & Wyatt, J. W. (1982). Processes used by good computational estimators. *Journal for Research in Mathematics Education, 13,* 183–201.

Riley, M. S., & Greeno, J. G. (1988). Developmental analysis of understanding language about quantities and of solving problems. *Cognition and Instruction, 5,* 49–101.

Rittle-Johnson, B., & Alibali, M. W. (1999). Conceptual and procedural knowledge of mathematics: Does one lead to the other? *Journal of Educational Psychology, 91,* 175–189.

Rittle-Johnson, B., & Siegler, R. S. (1998). The relation between conceptual and procedural knowledge in learning mathematics: A review. In C. Donlan (Ed.), *The development of mathematical skills* (pp. 75–110). East Sussex, UK: Psychology Press.

Ron, P. (1998). My family taught me this way. In L. J. Morrow & M. J. Kenney (Eds.), *The teaching and learning of algorithms in school mathematics* (1998 Yearbook of the National Council of Teachers of Mathematics, pp. 115–119). Reston, VA: NCTM.

Rubenstein, R. N. (1985). Computational estimation and related mathematical skills. *Journal for Research in Mathematics Education, 16,* 106–119.

Saxe, G. B. (1982). Culture and the development of numerical cognition: Studies among the Oksapmin of Papua New Guinea. In C. J. Brainerd (Ed.), *Progress in cognitive development research: Vol. 1: Children's logical and mathematical cognition* (pp. 157–176). New York: Springer-Verlag.

Saxe, G. B. (1988). The mathematics of child street vendors. *Child Development, 59,* 1415–1425.

Siegler, R. S. (1996). *Emerging minds: The process of change in children's thinking.* New York: Oxford University Press.

Siegler, R. S. (in press). *Implications for cognitive science research for mathematics education.* In J. Kilpatrick, W. G. Martin, & D. E. Schifter (Eds.), *A research companion to principles and standards for school mathematics.* Reston, VA: National Council of Teachers of Mathematics.

Siegler, R. S., & Jenkins, E. (1989). *How children discover new strategies.* Hillsdale, NJ: Erlbaum.

Sowder, J. T. (1992). Making sense of numbers in school mathematics. In G. Leinhardt, R. Putnam, & R. A. Hattrup (Eds.), *Analysis of arithmetic for mathematics teaching* (pp. 1–51). Hillsdale, NJ: Erlbaum.

Sowder, J. T., & Wheeler, M. M. (1989). The development of concepts and procedures used in computational estimation. *Journal for Research in Mathematics Education, 20,* 130–146.

Steffe, L. (1994). Children's multiplying schemes. In G. Harel & J. Confrey (Eds.), *The development of multiplicative reasoning in the learning of mathematics* (pp. 3–39). Albany: State University of New York Press.

Steffe, L. P., Cobb, P., & von Glasersfeld, E. (1988). *Construction of arithmetical meanings and procedures*. New York: Springer-Verlag.

Stigler, J. W. (1984). "Mental abacus": The effect of abacus training on Chinese children's mental calculation. *Cognitive Psychology, 16*, 145–176.

Steinberg, R. (1985). Instruction on derived facts strategies in addition and subtraction. *Journal for Research in Mathematics Education, 16*, 337–355.

Thornton, C. A. (1978). Emphasizing thinking strategies in basic fact instruction. *Journal for Research in Mathematics Education, 9*, 214–227.

Uttal, D. H., Scudder, K. V., & DeLoache, J. S. (1997). Manipulatives as symbols: A new perspective on the use of concrete objects to teach mathematics. *Journal of Applied Developmental Psychology, 18*, 37–54.

VanLehn, K. (1986). Arithmetic procedures are induced from examples. In J. Hiebert (Ed.), *Conceptual and procedural knowledge: The case of mathematics* (pp. 133–179). Hillsdale, NJ: Erlbaum.

Vergnaud, G. (1983). Multiplicative structures. In R. Lesh & M. Landau (Eds.), *Acquisition of mathematics concepts and processes* (pp. 127–174). New York: Academic Press.

Verschaffel, L., & De Corte, E. (1993). A decade of research on word-problem solving in Leuven: Theoretical, methodological, and practical outcomes. *Educational Psychology Review, 5*(3), 1–18.

7

DEVELOPING PROFICIENCY
WITH OTHER NUMBERS

In this chapter, we look beyond the whole numbers at other numbers that are included in school mathematics in grades pre-K to 8, particularly in the upper grades. We first look at the rational numbers, which constitute what is undoubtedly the most challenging number system of elementary and middle school mathematics. Then we consider proportional reasoning, which builds on the ratio use of rational numbers. Finally, we examine the integers, a stepping stone to algebra.

Rational Numbers

Learning about rational numbers is more complicated and difficult than learning about whole numbers. Rational numbers are more complex than whole numbers, in part because they are represented in several ways (e.g., common fractions and decimal fractions) and used in many ways (e.g., as parts of regions and sets, as ratios, as quotients). There are numerous properties for students to learn, including the significant fact that the two numbers that compose a common fraction (numerator and denominator) are related through multiplication and division, not addition.[1] This feature often causes misunderstanding when students first encounter rational numbers. Further, students are likely to have less out-of-school experience with rational numbers than with whole numbers. The result is a number system that presents great challenges to students and teachers.

Moreover, how students become proficient with rational numbers is not as well understood as with whole numbers. Significant work has been done, however, on the teaching and learning of rational numbers, and several points can be made about developing proficiency with them. First, students do have informal notions of sharing, partitioning sets, and measuring on which instruction can build. Second, in conventional instructional programs, the proficiency with rational numbers that many students develop is uneven across the five strands, and the strands are often disconnected from each other. Third, developing proficiency with rational numbers depends on well-designed classroom instruction that allows extended periods of time for students to construct and sustain close connections among the strands. We discuss each of these points below. Then we examine how students learn to represent and operate with rational numbers.

Using Informal Knowledge

In some ways, sharing can play the role for rational numbers that counting does for whole numbers.

Students' informal notions of partitioning, sharing, and measuring provide a starting point for developing the concept of rational number.[2] Young children appreciate the idea of "fair shares," and they can use that understanding to partition quantities into equal parts. Their experience in sharing equal amounts can provide an entrance into the study of rational numbers. In some ways, sharing can play the role for rational numbers that counting does for whole numbers.

In view of the preschooler's attention to counting and number that we noted in chapter 5, it is not surprising that initially many children are concerned more that each person gets an equal *number* of things than with the size of each thing.[3] As they move through the early grades of school, they become more sensitive to the *size* of the parts as well.[4] Soon after entering school, many students can partition quantities into equal shares corresponding to halves, fourths, and eighths. These fractions can be generated by successively partitioning by half, which is an especially fruitful procedure since one half can play a useful role in learning about other fractions.[5] Accompanying their actions of partitioning in half, many students develop the language of "one half" to describe the actions. Not long after, many can partition quantities into thirds or fifths in order to share quantities fairly among three or five people.

An informal understanding of rational number, which is built mostly on the notion of sharing, is a good starting point for instruction. The notion of sharing quantities and comparing sizes of shares can provide an entry point that takes students into the world of rational numbers.[6] Equal shares, for example, opens the concept of equivalent fractions (e.g., If there are 6 children sharing 4 pizzas, how many pizzas would be needed for 12 children to receive the same amount?).

It is likely, however, that an informal understanding of rational numbers is less robust and widespread than the corresponding informal understanding of whole numbers. For whole numbers, many young children enter school with sufficient proficiency to invent their own procedures for adding, subtracting, multiplying, and dividing. For rational numbers, in contrast, teachers need to play a more active and direct role in providing relevant experiences to enhance students' informal understanding and in helping them elaborate their informal understanding into a more formal network of concepts and procedures. The evidence suggests that carefully designed instructional programs can serve both of these functions quite well, laying the foundation for further progress.[7]

Discontinuities in Proficiency

Proficiency with rational numbers, as with all mathematical topics, is signaled most clearly by the close intertwining of the five strands. Large-scale surveys of U.S. students' knowledge of rational number indicate that many students are developing some proficiency within individual strands.[8] Often, however, these strands are not connected. Furthermore, the knowledge students acquire *within* strands is also disconnected. A considerable body of research describes this separation of knowledge.[9]

As we said at the beginning of the chapter, rational numbers can be expressed in various forms (e.g., common fractions, decimal fractions, percents), and each form has many common uses in daily life (e.g., a part of a region, a part of a set, a quotient, a rate, a ratio).[10] One way of describing this complexity is to observe that, from the student's point of view, a rational number is not a single entity but has multiple personalities. The scheme that has guided research on rational number over the past two decades[11] identifies the following interpretations for any rational number, say $\frac{3}{4}$: (a) a part-whole relation (3 out of 4 equal-sized shares); (b) a quotient (3 divided by 4); (c) a measure ($\frac{3}{4}$ of the way from the beginning of the unit to the end); (d) a ratio (3 red cars for every 4 green cars); and (e) an operation that enlarges or reduces the size of something ($\frac{3}{4}$ of 12). The task for students is to recognize these distinctions and, at the same time, to construct relations among them that generate a coherent concept of rational number.[12] Clearly, this process is lengthy and multifaceted.

Instructional practices that tend toward premature abstraction and extensive symbolic manipulation lead students to have severe difficulty in representing rational numbers with standard written symbols and using the symbols appropriately.[13] This outcome is not surprising, because a single rational number can be represented with many different written symbols (e.g., $\frac{3}{5}$, $\frac{12}{20}$, 0.6, 0.60, 60%). Instructional programs have often treated this complexity as simply a "syntactic" translation problem: One written symbol had to be translated into another according to a sequence of rules. Different rules have often been taught for each translation situation. For example, "To change a common fraction to a decimal fraction, divide the numerator by the denominator."

But the symbolic representation of rational numbers poses a "semantic" problem—a problem of meaning—as well. Each symbol representation *means* something. Current instruction often gives insufficient attention to developing the meanings of different rational number representations and the connections among them. The evidence for this neglect is that a majority of U.S. students have learned rules for translating between forms but understand very little about what quantities the symbols represent and consequently make frequent and nonsensical errors.[14] This is a clear example of the *lack* of proficiency that results from pushing ahead within one strand but failing to connect what is being learned with other strands. Rules for manipulating symbols are being memorized, but students are not connecting those rules to their conceptual understanding, nor are they reasoning about the rules.

Another example of disconnection among the strands of proficiency is students' tendency to compute with written symbols in a mechanical way without considering what the symbols mean. Two simple examples illustrate the point. First, recall (from chapter 4) the result from the National Assessment of Educational Progress (NAEP)[15] showing that more than half of U.S. eighth graders chose 19 or 21 as the best estimate of $\frac{12}{13} + \frac{7}{8}$. These choices do not make sense if students understand what the symbols mean and are reasoning about the quantities represented by the symbols. Another survey of students' performance showed that the most common error for the addition problem 4 + .3 = ? is .7, which is given by 68% of sixth graders and 51% of fifth and seventh graders.[16] Again, the errors show that many students have learned rules for manipulating symbols without understanding what those symbols mean or why the rules work. Many students are unable to reason appropriately about symbols for rational numbers and do not have the strategic competence that would allow them to catch their mistakes.

Supporting Connections

Of all the ways in which rational numbers can be interpreted and used, the most basic is the simplest—rational numbers are numbers. That fact is so fundamental that it is easily overlooked. A rational number like $\frac{3}{4}$ is a single entity just as the number 5 is a single entity. Each rational number holds a unique place (or is a unique length) on the number line (see chapter 3). As a result, the entire set of rational numbers can be ordered by size, just as the whole numbers can. This ordering is possible even though between any two rational numbers there are infinitely many rational numbers, in drastic contrast to the whole numbers.

It may be surprising that, for most students, to think of a rational number as a number—as an individual entity or a single point on a number line—is a novel idea.[17] Students are more familiar with rational numbers in contexts like parts of a pizza or ratios of hits to at-bats in baseball. These everyday interpretations, although helpful for building knowledge of some aspects of rational number, are an inadequate foundation for building proficiency. The difficulty is not just due to children's limited experience. Even the interpretations ordinarily given by adults to various forms of rational numbers, such as percent, do not lead easily to the conclusion that rational numbers are numbers.[18] Further, the way common fractions are written (e.g., $\frac{3}{4}$) does not help students see a rational number as a distinct number. After all, $\frac{3}{4}$ looks just like one whole number over another, and many students initially think of it as two different numbers, a 3 and a 4.

Research has verified what many teachers have observed, that students continue to use properties they learned from operating with whole numbers even though many whole number properties do not apply to rational numbers. With common fractions,[19] for example, students may reason that $\frac{1}{8}$ is larger than $\frac{1}{7}$ because 8 is larger than 7. Or they may believe that $\frac{3}{4}$ equals $\frac{4}{5}$ because in both fractions the difference between numerator and denominator is 1. With decimal fractions,[20] students may say .25 is larger than .7 because 25 is larger than 7. Such inappropriate extensions of whole number relationships, many based on addition, can be a continuing source of trouble when students are learning to work with fractions and their multiplicative relationships.[21]

The task for instruction is to use, rather than to ignore, the informal knowledge of rational numbers that students bring with them and to provide them with appropriate experiences and sufficient time to develop meaning for these new numbers and meaningful ways of operating with them. Systematic errors can best be regarded as useful diagnostic tools for instruction since they more often represent incomplete rather than incorrect knowledge.[22] From the current research base, we can make several observations about the kinds of learning opportunities that instruction must provide students if they are to develop proficiency with rational numbers. These observations address both representing rational numbers and computing with them.

Representing Rational Numbers

As with whole numbers, the written notations and spoken words used for decimal and common fractions contribute to—or at least do not help correct—the many kinds of errors students make with them. Both decimals and common fractions use whole numbers in their notations. Nothing in the notation or the words used conveys their meaning as fractured parts. The English words used for fractions are the same words used to tell order in a line: *fifth* in line and *three fifths* (for $\frac{3}{5}$). In contrast, in Chinese, $\frac{3}{5}$ is read "out of 5 parts (take) 3." Providing students with many experiences in partitioning quantities into equal parts using concrete models, pictures, and meaningful contexts can help them create meaning for fraction notations. Introducing the standard notation for common fractions and decimals must be done with care, ensuring that students are able to connect the meanings already developed for the numbers with the symbols that represent them.

Research does not prescribe a one best set of learning activities or one best instructional method for rational numbers. But some sequences of activities do seem to be more effective than others for helping students develop a conceptual understanding of symbolic representations and connect it with the other strands of proficiency.[23] The sequences that have been shown to promote mathematical proficiency differ from each other in a number of ways, but they share some similarities. All of them spend time at the outset helping students develop meaning for the different forms of representation. Typically, students work with multiple physical models for rational numbers as well as with other supports such as pictures, realistic contexts, and verbal descriptions. Time is spent helping students connect these supports with the written symbols for rational numbers.

In one such instructional sequence, fourth graders received 20 lessons introducing them to rational numbers.[24] Almost all the lessons focused on helping the students connect the various representations of rational number with concepts of rational number that they were developing. Unique to this program was the sequence in which the forms were introduced: percents, then decimal fractions, and then common fractions. Because many children in the fourth grade have considerable informal knowledge of percents, percents were used as the starting point. Students were asked to judge, for example, the relative fullness of a beaker (e.g., 75%), and the relative height of a tube of liquid (e.g., 30%). After a variety of similar activities, the percent representations were used to introduce the decimal fractions and, later, the common fractions. Compared with students in a conventional program, who spent less time developing meaning for the representations and more time practicing computation, students in the experimental program demonstrated higher levels of adaptive reasoning, conceptual understanding, and strategic competence, with no loss of computational skill. This finding illustrates one of our major themes: Progress can be made along all strands if they remain connected.

Another common feature of learning activities that help students understand and use the standard written symbols is the careful attention the activities devote to the concept of unit.[25] Many conventional curricula introduce rational numbers as common fractions that stand for part of a whole, but little attention is given to the whole from which the rational number extracts its meaning. For example, many students first see a fraction as, say, $\frac{3}{4}$ of a pizza. In this interpretation the amount of pizza is determined by the fractional part ($\frac{3}{4}$) *and* by the size of the pizza. Hence, three fourths of a medium pizza is not the same amount of pizza as three fourths of a large pizza, although it may be the same number of pieces. Lack of attention to the nature of the unit or whole may explain many of the misconceptions that students exhibit.

A sequence of learning activities that focus directly on the whole unit in representing rational numbers comes from an experimental curriculum in Russia.[26] In this sequence, rational numbers are introduced in the early grades as ratios of quantities to the unit of measure. For example, a piece of string is measured by a small piece of tape and found to be equivalent to five copies of the tape. Children express the result as "string/tape = 5." Rational numbers appear quite naturally when the quantity is not measured by the unit an exact number of times. The leftover part is then represented, first informally and then as a fraction of the unit. With this approach, the size of the unit always is in the foreground. The evidence suggests that students who engage in these experiences develop coherent meanings for common fractions, meanings that allow them to reason sensibly about fractions.[27]

Computing with Rational Numbers

As with representing rational numbers, many students need instructional support to operate appropriately with rational numbers. Adding, subtracting, multiplying, and dividing rational numbers require that they be seen as *numbers* because in elementary school these operations are defined only for numbers. That is, the principles on which computation is based make sense only if common fractions and decimal fractions are understood as representing numbers. Students may think of a fraction as part of a pizza or as a batting average, but such interpretations are not enough for them to understand what is happening when computations are carried out. The trouble is that many students have not developed a meaning for the symbols before they are asked to compute with rational numbers.

Proficiency in computing with rational numbers requires operating with at least two different representations: common fractions and finite decimal fractions. There are important conceptual similarities between the rules for computing with both of these forms (e.g., combine those terms measured with the same unit when adding and subtracting). However, students must learn how those conceptual similarities play out in each of the written symbol systems. Procedural fluency for arithmetic with rational numbers thus requires that students understand the meaning of the written symbols for both common fractions and finite decimal fractions.

What can be learned from students' errors? Research reveals the kinds of errors that students are likely to make as they begin computing with common fractions and finite decimals. Whether the errors are the consequence of impoverished learning of whole numbers or insufficiently developed meaning for rational numbers, effective instruction with rational numbers needs to take these common errors into account.

Some of the errors occur when students apply to fractions poorly understood rules for calculating with whole numbers. For example, they learn to "line up the numbers on the right" when they are adding and subtracting whole numbers. Later, they may try to apply this rule to decimal fractions, probably because they did not understand why the rule worked in the first place and because decimal fractions look a lot like whole numbers. This confusion leads many students to get .61 when adding 1.5 and .46, for example.[28]

It is worth pursuing the above example a bit further. Notice that the rule "line up the numbers on the right" and the new rule for decimal fractions "line up the decimal points" are, on the surface, very different rules. They prescribe movements of digits in different-sounding ways. At a deeper level, however, they are exactly the same. Both versions of the rule result in aligning digits measured with the same unit—digits with the same place value (tens, ones, tenths, etc.). This deeper level of interpretation is, of course, the one that is more useful. When students know a rule only at a superficial level, they are working with symbols, rules, and procedures in a routine way, disconnected from strands such as adaptive reasoning and conceptual understanding. But when students see the deeper level of meaning for a procedure, they have connected the strands together. In fact, seeing the second level is a consequence of connecting the strands. This example illustrates once more why connecting the strands is the key to developing proficiency.

A second example of a common error and one that also can be traced to previous experience with whole numbers is that "multiplying makes larger" and "dividing makes smaller."[29] These generalizations are not true for the full set of rational numbers. Multiplying by a rational number less than 1 means taking only a part of the quantity being multiplied, so the result is less than the original quantity (e.g., $\frac{2}{3} \times 12 = 8$, which is less than 12). Likewise, dividing by a rational number less than 1 produces a quantity larger than either quantity in the original problem (e.g., $6 \div \frac{2}{3} = 9$).

As with the addition and subtraction of rational numbers, there are important conceptual similarities between whole numbers and rational numbers when students learn to multiply and divide. These similarities are often revealed by probing the deeper meaning of the operations. In the division example above, notice that to find the answer to $6 \div 2 = ?$ and $6 \div \frac{2}{3} = ?$, the same question can be asked: How many [2s or $\frac{2}{3}$s] are in 6? The similarities are not apparent in the algorithms for manipulating the symbols. Therefore, if students are to connect what they are learning about rational numbers with what they already understand about whole numbers, they will need to do so through other kinds of activities.

One helpful approach is to embed the calculation in a realistic problem. Students can then use the context to connect their previous work with whole numbers to the new situations with rational numbers. An example is the following problem:

> *I have six cups of sugar. A recipe calls for $\frac{2}{3}$ of a cup of sugar. How many batches of the recipe can I make?*

Since the size of the parts is less than one whole, the number of batches will necessarily be larger than the six (there are nine $\frac{2}{3}$s in 6). Useful activities might include drawing pictures of the division calculation, describing solution methods, and explaining why the answer makes sense. Simply teaching the rule "invert and multiply" leads to the same sort of mechanical manipulation of symbols that results from just telling students to "line up the decimal points."

What can be learned from conventional and experimental instruction?

Conventional instruction on rational number computation tends to be rule based.[30] Classroom activities emphasize helping students become quick and accurate in executing written procedures by following rules. The activities often begin by stating a rule or algorithm (e.g., "to multiply two fractions, multiply the numerators and multiply the denominators"), showing how it works on several examples (sometimes just one), and asking students to practice it on many similar problems. Researchers express concern that this kind of learning can be "highly dependent on memory and subject to deterioration."[31] This "deterioration" results when symbol manipulation is emphasized to the relative exclusion of conceptual understanding and adaptive reasoning. Students learn that it is not important to understand why the procedure works but only to follow the prescribed steps to reach the correct answer. This approach breaks the incipient connections between the strands of proficiency, and, as the breaks increase, proficiency is thwarted.

A number of studies have documented the results of conventional instruction.[32] One study, for example, found that only 45% of a random sample of 20 sixth graders interviewed could add fractions correctly.[33] Equally disturbing was that fewer than 10% of them could *explain* how one adds fractions even though all had heard the rules for addition, had practiced the rules on many problems, and sometimes could execute the rules correctly. These results, according to the researchers, were representative of hundreds of interviews conducted with sixth, seventh, and ninth graders. The results point to the need for instructional materials that support teachers and students so that they can explain why a procedure works rather than treating it as a sequence of steps to be memorized.

Many researchers who have studied what students know about operations with fractions or decimals recommend that instruction emphasize conceptual understanding from the beginning.[34] More specifically, say these researchers, instruction should build on students' intuitive understanding of fractions and use objects or contexts that help students make sense of the operations. The rationale for that approach is that students need to under-

Margin note: Conventional instruction on rational number computation tends to be rule based.

stand the key ideas in order to have something to connect with procedural rules. For example, students need to understand why the sum of two fractions can be expressed as a single number only when the parts are of the same size. That understanding can lead them to see the need for constructing common denominators.

One of the most challenging tasks confronting those who design learning environments for students (e.g., curriculum developers, teachers) is to help students learn efficient written algorithms for computing with fractions and decimals. The most efficient algorithms often do not parallel students' informal knowledge or the meaning they create by drawing diagrams, manipulating objects, and so on. Several instructional programs have been devised that use problem situations and build on algorithms invented by students.[35] Students in these programs were able to develop meaningful and reasonably efficient algorithms for operating with fractions, even when the formal algorithms were not presented.[36] It is not yet clear, however, what sequence of activities can support students' meaningful learning of the less transparent but more efficient formal algorithms, such as "invert and multiply" for dividing fractions.

Although there is only limited research on instructional programs for developing proficiency with computations involving rational numbers, it seems clear that instruction focused solely on symbolic manipulation without understanding is ineffective for most students. It is necessary to correct that imbalance by paying more attention to conceptual understanding as well as the other strands of proficiency and by helping students connect them.

Proportional Reasoning

Proportions are statements that two ratios are equal. These statements play an important role in mathematics and are formally introduced in middle school. Understanding the underlying relationships in a proportional situation and working with these relationships has come to be called *proportional reasoning*.[37] Considerable research has been conducted on the features of proportional reasoning and how students develop it.[38]

Proportional reasoning is based, first, on an understanding of ratio. A ratio expresses a mathematical relationship that involves multiplication, as in $2 for 3 balloons or $\frac{2}{3}$ of a dollar for one balloon. A proportion, then, is a relationship between relationships. For example, a proportion expresses the fact that $2 for 3 balloons is in the same relationship as $6 for 9 balloons ($\frac{2}{3} = \frac{6}{9}$).

Ratios are often changed to unit ratios by dividing. For example, the unit ratio $\frac{2}{3}$ dollars per balloon is obtained by "dividing" $2 by 3 balloons. The ratio or rate, $\$\frac{2}{3}$ per balloon, is called the *unit rate* because it is the cost of one balloon. The unit rate may be useful to students when they think about real situations.[39] In this case it describes the precise manner by which any number of dollars can be compared with any number of balloons at the same price.

Proportional reasoning has been described as the capstone of elementary school arithmetic and the gateway to higher mathematics, including algebra, geometry, probability, statistics, and certain aspects of discrete mathematics.[40] Nevertheless, U.S. seventh and eighth graders have not performed well on even simple proportion problems such as finding the cost of 6 pieces of candy if 2 pieces cost 8 cents and if the price of the candy is the same no matter how many are sold.[41] On the 1996 NAEP, only 12% of eighth-grade students could solve a problem involving the comparison of two rates, 8 miles every 10 minutes and 20 miles every 25 minutes.[42]

Research tracing the development of proportional reasoning shows that children have some informal knowledge of proportions. Studies with second graders have suggested that their intuitive understanding is insufficient for solving certain proportion problems.[43] Proficiency grows as students connect different aspects of proportional reasoning.[44] Three aspects are especially important. First, students' reasoning is facilitated as they learn to make comparisons based on multiplication rather than just addition. For example, consider two marigolds that were 8 inches and 12 inches tall two weeks ago and 11 inches and 15 tall inches now. Which plant grew more? There are two different correct responses to this question. An additive or absolute comparison focuses on the difference and concludes that each plant grew the same, 3 inches. A multiplicative or relative comparison looks at the change relative to the original height; the shorter plant grew $\frac{3}{8}$ of its original height, while the larger plant grew less, just $\frac{3}{12}$ of its original height. Either answer is correct depending on whether "grew more" is interpreted in absolute or relative terms. The ability to reason about comparisons in relative terms is closely tied to reasoning proportionally.[45]

A second aspect is that students' reasoning is facilitated as they distinguish between those features of a proportion situation that can change and those that must stay the same.[46] In a proportion the quantities composing a ratio can change together in such a way that the relationship between them (the quotient) remains the same. Some students are inclined to take a more simplistic view, believing that if something changes, everything changes. In a proportion the numbers in the ratios can change but the multiplicative relationship must stay the same (e.g., $2 for 3 balloons expresses the same relationship as $4 for 6 balloons). The physical situation is not the same because the second ratio refers to twice as many dollars and balloons as the first. What is the same is the multiplicative relationship between the dollars and the balloons or, said another way, the cost of a single balloon (the unit rate). Written symbolically, without labels, the statement becomes $\frac{2}{3} = \frac{4}{6}$. But notice how the important contextual framework is lost with this abstract notation.

Proportional reasoning is further enhanced as the first two aspects are connected with a third: Students' reasoning is facilitated as they learn to build composite units, or units of units. The rate "$2 for 3 balloons" or "2-for-3" is a composite unit.[47] The ability to use composite units is one of the most obvious differences between students who reason well with proportions and those who do not.[48] Students who reason correctly about proportional situations often choose one ratio as a composite unit and use it as a comparative base. For example, they might use "2-for-3" to examine whether another ratio, such as 12-for-24, has the same relationship. By building up the 2-for-3 units (2-for-3, 4-for-6, 6-for-9, 8-for-12, 10-for-15, 12-for-18), the students realize 2-for-3 is not proportional to 12-for-24, because 12-for-24 cannot be generated with the 2-for-3 composite unit. There is a danger, of course, in using this essentially additive building-up process to generate equivalent ratios because students may not understand that the relationship is multiplicative. They need to see that 2-for-3 and 6-for-9, for example, express the same relationship or unit rate because 9 is the same multiple of 3 as 6 is of 2. But building from composite units does provide many students with a useful tool for working with proportional situations.

The conceptual aspects of proportional reasoning usually play out in three types of proportion problems. Missing value problems present three values and ask students to find the fourth or missing value (e.g., If 3 balloons cost $2, then how much do 24 balloons cost?). Numerical comparison problems ask students to determine which of two given ratios represents more or less (e.g., Which is the better value: 3 balloons for $2 or 24 balloons for $12?). Qualitative comparison problems ask students to evaluate the effect on a ratio of a qualitative change in one or both of the quantities involved (e.g., What happens to the price of a balloon if you get more balloons for the same amount of money?). Traditionally, instruction has focused on missing-value problems, with some attention to numerical comparisons. For both kinds of problems, traditional textbooks tend to emphasize formal strategies from the beginning[49]—setting up a correct equation ($3:2 = 24:x$), using a variable for the missing value, and using a "cross-multiplication" algorithm ($3x = 48$ or $x = 16$).

It should be clear from the previous analysis that moving directly to the cross-multiplication algorithm, without attending to the conceptual aspects of proportional reasoning, can create difficulties for students. The aspects of proportional reasoning that must be developed can be supported through exploring proportional (and nonproportional) situations in a variety of problem contexts using concrete materials or situations in which students collect data, build tables, and determine the relationships between the number pairs (ratios) in the tables.[50] When 187 seventh-grade students with different curricular experiences were presented with a sequence of realistic rate problems, the students in the reform curricula considerably outperformed a comparison group of students 53% versus 28% in providing correct answers with correct support work.[51] These students were part of the field trials for a new middle school curriculum in which they were encouraged to develop their own procedures through collaborative problem-solving activities. The comparison students had more traditional, teacher-directed instructional experiences.

Proportional reasoning is complex and clearly needs to be developed over several years.[52] One simple implication from the research suggests that presenting the cross-multiplication algorithm before students understand proportions and can reason about them leads to the same kind of separation between the strands of proficiency that we described earlier for other topics. But more research is needed to identify the sequences of activities that are most helpful for moving from well-understood but less efficient procedures to those that are more efficient.

Ratios and proportions, like fractions, decimals, and percents, are aspects of what have been called multiplicative structures.[53] These are closely related ideas that no doubt develop together, although they are often treated as separate topics in the typical school curriculum. Reasoning about these ideas likely interacts, but it is not well understood how this interaction develops. Much more work needs to be done on helping students integrate their knowledge of these components of multiplicative structures.

Integers

The set of integers comprises the positive and negative whole numbers and zero or, expressed another way, the whole numbers and their inverses, often called their opposites (see Chapter 3). The set of integers, like the set of whole numbers, is a subset of the rational numbers. Compared with the research on whole numbers and even on noninteger rational numbers, there has been relatively little research on how students acquire an understanding of negative numbers and develop proficiency in operating with them.

A half-century ago students did not encounter negative numbers until they took high school algebra. Since then, integers have been introduced in the middle grades and even in the elementary grades. Some educators have argued that integers are easier for students than fractions and decimals and therefore should be introduced first. This approach has been tried, but there is very little research on the long-term effects of this alternative sequencing of topics.

Concept of Negative Numbers

Even young children have intuitive or informal knowledge of nonpositive quantities prior to formal instruction.[54] These notions often involve action-based concepts like those associated with temperature, game moves, or other spatial and quantitative situations. For example, in some games there are moves that result in points being lost, which can lead to scores below zero or "in the hole."

Various metaphors have been suggested as approaches for introducing negative numbers, including elevators, thermometers, debts and assets, losses and gains, hot air balloons, postman stories, pebbles in a bag, and directed arrows on a number line.[55] Many of the physical metaphors for introducing integers have been criticized because they do not easily support students' understanding of the operations on integers (other than addition).[56] But some studies have demonstrated the value of using these metaphors, especially for introducing negative numbers.[57]

Students do appear to be capable of understanding negative numbers far earlier than was once thought. Although more research is needed on the metaphors and models that best support students' conceptual understanding of negative numbers, there already is enough information to suggest that a variety of metaphors and models can be used effectively.

Operations with Integers

Research on learning to add, subtract, multiply, and divide integers is limited. In the past, students often learned the "rules of signs" (e.g., the product of a positive and negative number is negative) without much understanding. In part, perhaps, because instruction has not found ways to make the learning meaningful, some secondary and college students still have difficulty working with negative numbers.[58]

Alternative approaches, using the models mentioned earlier, have been tried with various degrees of success.[59] A complete set of appropriate learning activities with integers has not been identified, but there are some promising elements that should be explored further. Students generally perform better on problems posed in the context of a story (debts and assets, scores and forfeits) or through movements on a number line than on the same problems presented solely as formal equations.[60] This result suggests, as for other number domains, that stories and other conceptual structures such as a number line can be used effectively as the context in which students begin their work and develop meaning for the operations. Furthermore, there are some approaches that seem to minimize commonly reported errors.[61] In general, approaches that use an appropriate model of integers and operations on integers, and that spend time developing these and linking them to the symbols, offer the most promise.

Beyond Whole Numbers

Although the research provides a less complete picture of students' developing proficiency with rational numbers and integers than with whole numbers, several important points can be made. First, developing proficiency is a gradual and prolonged process. Many students acquire useful informal knowledge of fractions, decimals, ratios, percents, and integers through activities and experiences outside of school, but that knowledge needs to be made more explicit and extended through carefully designed instruction. Given current learning patterns, effective instruction must prepare for interferences arising from students' superficial knowledge of whole numbers. The unevenness many students show in developing proficiency that we noted with whole numbers seems especially pronounced with rational numbers, where progress is made on different fronts at different rates. The challenge is to engage students throughout the middle grades in learning activities that support the integration of the strands of proficiency.

A second observation is that doing just that—integrating the strands of proficiency—is an even greater challenge for rational numbers than for whole numbers. Currently, many students learn different aspects of rational numbers as separate and isolated pieces of knowledge. For example, they fail to see the relationships between decimals, fractions, and percents, on the one hand, and whole numbers, on the other, or between integers and whole numbers. Also, connections among the strands of proficiency are often not made. Numerous studies show that with common fractions and decimals, especially, conceptual understanding and computational procedures are not appropriately linked. Further, students can use their informal knowledge of proportionality or rational numbers strategically to solve problems but are unable to represent and solve the same problem formally. These discontinuities are of great concern because the research we have reviewed indicates that real progress along each strand and within any single topic is exceedingly difficult without building connections between them.

A third issue concerns the level of procedural fluency that should be required for arithmetic with decimals and common fractions. Decimal fractions are crucial in science, in metric measurement, and in more advanced mathematics, so it is important for students to be computationally fluent—to understand how and why computational procedures work, including being able to judge the order-of-magnitude accuracy of calculator-produced answers. Some educators have argued that common fractions are no longer essential in school mathematics because digital electronics have transformed almost all numerical transactions into decimal fractions. Technological developments certainly have increased the importance of decimals, but common fractions are still important in daily life and in their own right as mathematical objects, and they play a central role in the development of more advanced mathematical ideas. For example, computing with common fractions sets the stage for computing with rational expressions in algebra. It is important, therefore, for students to develop sound meanings for common fractions and to be fluent with ordering fractions, finding equivalent fractions, and using unit rates. Students should also develop procedural fluency for computations with "manageable" fractions. However, the rapid execution of paper-and-pencil computation algorithms for less frequently used fractions (e.g., $\frac{7}{24} + \frac{11}{54}$) is unnecessary today.

Finally, we cannot emphasize too strongly the simple fact that students need to be fully proficient with rational numbers and integers. This proficiency forms the basis for much of advanced mathematical thinking, as well as the understanding and interpretation of daily events. The level at which many U.S. students function with rational numbers and integers is unacceptable. The disconnections that many students exhibit among their conceptual understanding, procedural fluency, strategic competence, and adaptive reasoning pose serious barriers to their progress in learning and using mathematics. Evidence from experimental programs in the United States and from the performance of students in other countries suggests that U.S. middle school students are capable of learning more about rational numbers and integers, with deeper levels of understanding.

Notes

1. See Harel and Confrey, 1994. Rational numbers, ratios, and proportions, which on the surface are about division, are called *multiplicative* concepts because any division problem can be rephrased as multiplication. See Chapter 3.
2. Behr, Lesh, Post, and Silver, 1983; Confrey, 1994, 1995; Empson, 1999; Kieren, 1992; Mack, 1990, 1995; Pothier and Sawada, 1983; Streefland, 1991, 1993.
3. Hiebert and Tonnessen, 1978; Pothier and Sawada, 1983.
4. Empson, 1999; Pothier and Sawada, 1983.
5. Confrey, 1994; Pothier and Sawada 1989.
6. Confrey, 1994; Streefland, 1991, 1993.
7. Cramer, Behr, Post, and Lesh, 1997; Empson, 1999; Mack, 1995; Morris, in press; Moss and Case, 1999; Streefland, 1991, 1993.
8. Kouba, Zawojewski, and Strutchens, 1997; Wearne and Kouba, 2000.
9. Behr, Lesh, Post, and Silver, 1983; Behr, Wachsmuth, Post, and Lesh, 1984; Bezuk and Bieck, 1993; Hiebert and Wearne, 1985; Mack, 1990, 1995; Post, Wachsmuth, Lesh, and Behr, 1985; Streefland, 1991, 1993.
10. Kieren, 1976.
11. Kieren, 1976, 1980, 1988.
12. Students not only should "construct relations among them" but should also eventually have some grasp of what is entailed in these relations—for example, that Interpretation D is a contextual instance of E—namely, you multiply the number of green cars by $\frac{3}{4}$ to get the number of red cars, while thinking of $\frac{3}{4}$ as three times $\frac{1}{4}$ (Interpretation A), and thinking of it as 3 divided by 4, is the equation $\frac{(3 \times 1)}{4} = \frac{3}{4}$, which is basically the associative law for multiplication.
13. Behr, Wachsmuth, Post, and Lesh, 1984; Hiebert and Wearne, 1986.
14. Hiebert and Wearne, 1986; Resnick, Nesher, Leonard, Magone, Omanson, and Peled, 1989.
15. Carpenter, Corbitt, Kepner, Lindquist, and Reys, 1981.
16. Hiebert and Wearne, 1986.
17. Behr, Lesh, Post, and Silver, 1983.
18. Davis, 1988.
19. Behr, Wachsmuth, Post, and Lesh, 1984.
20. Resnick, Nesher, Leonard, Magone, Omanson, and Peled, 1989.
21. Behr, Wachsmuth, Post, and Lesh, 1984.
22. Resnick, Nesher, Leonard, Magone, Omanson, and Peled, 1989.
23. Cramer, Post, Henry, and Jeffers-Ruff, in press; Hiebert and Wearne, 1988; Hunting, 1983; Mack, 1990, 1995; Morris, in press; Moss and Case, 1999; Hiebert, Wearne, and Taber, 1991.
24. Moss and Case, 1999.
25. Behr, Harel, Post, and Lesh, 1992.
26. Davydov and Tsvetkovich, 1991; Morris, in press; Schmittau, 1993.
27. Morris, in press.

28. Hiebert and Wearne, 1986.
29. Bell, Fischbein, and Greer, 1984; Fischbein, Deri, Nello, and Marino, 1985.
30. Hiebert and Wearne, 1985.
31. Kieren, 1988, p. 178.
32. Mack, 1990; Peck and Jencks, 1981; Wearne and Kouba, 2000.
33. Peck and Jencks, 1981.
34. Behr, Lest, Post, and Silver, 1983; Bezuk and Bieck, 1993; Bezuk and Cramer, 1989; Hiebert and Wearne, 1986; Kieren, 1988; Mack, 1990; Peck and Jencks, 1981; Streefland, 1991, 1993.
35. Cramer, Behr, Post, and Lesh, 1997; Huinker, 1998; Lappan, Fey, Fitzgerald, Friel, and Phillips, 1996; Streefland, 1991.
36. Huinker, 1998; Lappan and Bouck, 1998.
37. Lesh, Post, and Behr, 1988.
38. Tourniaire and Pulos, 1985.
39. Behr, Harel, Post, and Lesh, 1992; Cramer, Behr, and Bezuk, 1989.
40. Post, Behr, and Lesh, 1988.
41. Lesh, Post, and Behr, 1988.
42. Wearne and Kouba, 2000.
43. Ahl, Moore, and Dixon, 1992; Dixon and Moore, 1996.
44. Lamon, 1993, 1995.
45. Lamon, 1993.
46. Lamon, 1995.
47. The term *composite unit* refers to thinking of 3 balloons (and hence $2) as a single entity. The related term *compound unit* is used in science to refer to units such as "miles/hour," or in this case "dollars per balloon."
48. Lamon, 1993, 1994.
49. Heller, Ahlgren, Post, Behr, and Lesh, 1989; Langrall and Swafford, 2000.
50. Cramer, Post, and Currier, 1993; Kaput and West, 1994.
51. Ben-Chaim, Fey, Fitzgerald, Benedetto, and Miller, 1998; Heller, Ahlgren, Post, Behr, and Lesh, 1989.
52. Behr, Harel, Post, and Lesh, 1992; Karplus, Pulas, and Stage, 1983.
53. Vergnaud, 1983.
54. Hativa and Cohen, 1995.
55. English, 1997. See also Crowley and Dunn, 1985.
56. Fischbein, 1987, ch. 8.
57. Duncan and Sanders, 1980; Moreno and Mayer, 1999; Thompson, 1988.
58. Bruno, Espinel, Martinon, 1997; Kuchemann, 1980.
59. Arcavi and Bruckheimer, 1981; Carson and Day, 1995; Davis, 1990; Liebeck, 1990; Human and Murray, 1987.
60. Moreno and Mayer, 1999; Mukhopadhyay, Resnick, and Schauble, 1990.
61. Duncan and Saunders, 1980; Thompson, 1988; Thompson and Dreyfus, 1988.

References

Ahl, V. A., Moore, C. F., & Dixon, J. A. (1992). Development of intuitive and numerical proportional reasoning. *Cognitive Development, 7*, 81–108.

Arcavi, A., & Bruckheimer, M. (1981). How shall we teach the multiplication of negative numbers? *Mathematics in School, 10*, 31–33.

Behr, M., Harel, G., Post, T., & Lesh, R. (1992). Rational number, ratio, and proportion. In D. Grouws (Ed.), *Handbook of research on mathematics teaching and learning* (pp. 296–333). New York: Macmillan.

Behr, M. J., Lesh, R., Post, T. R., & Silver, E. A. (1983). Rational number concepts. In R. Lesh & M. Landau (Eds.), *Acquisition of mathematics concepts and processes* (pp. 91–126). New York: Academic Press.

Behr, M. J., Wachsmuth, I., Post, T. R., & Lesh, R. (1984). Order and equivalence of rational numbers: A clinical teaching experiment. *Journal for Research in Mathematics Education, 15*, 323–341.

Bell, A. W., Fischbein, E., & Greer, B. (1984). Choice of operation in verbal arithmetic problems: The effects of number size, problem structure and content. *Educational Studies in Mathematics, 15*, 129–147.

Ben-Chaim, D., Fey, J. T., Fitzgerald, W. M., Benedetto, C., & Miller, J. (1998). Proportional reasoning among 7th grade students with different curricular experiences. *Educational Studies in Mathematics, 36*, 247–273.

Bezuk, N. D., & Bieck, M. (1993). Current research on rational numbers and common fractions: Summary and implications for teachers. In D. T. Owens (Ed.), *Research ideas for the classroom: Middle grades mathematics* (pp. 118–136). New York: Macmillan.

Bezuk, N., & Cramer, K. (1989). Teaching about fractions: What, when, and how? In P. Trafton (Ed.), *New directions for elementary school mathematics* (1989 Yearbook of the National Council of Teachers of Mathematics, pp. 156–167). Reston VA: NCTM.

Bruno, A., Espinel, M. C., Martinon, A. (1997). Prospective teachers solve additive problems with negative numbers. *Focus on Learning Problems in Mathematics, 19*, 36–55.

Carpenter, T. P., Corbitt, M. K., Kepner, H. S., Jr., Lindquist, M. M., & Reys, R. E. (1981). *Results from the second mathematics assessment of the National Assessment of Educational Progress.* Reston, VA: National Council of Teachers of Mathematics.

Carson, C. L., & Day, J. (1995). *Annual report on promising practices: How the algebra project eliminates the "game of signs" with negative numbers.* San Francisco: Far West Lab for Educational Research and Development. (ERIC Document Reproduction Service No. ED 394 828).

Confrey, J. (1994). Splitting, similarity, and the rate of change: New approaches to multiplication and exponential functions. In G. Harel & J. Confrey (Eds.), *The development of multiplicative reasoning in the learning of mathematics* (pp. 293–332). Albany: State University of New York Press.

Confrey, J. (1995). Student voice in examining "splitting" as an approach to ratio, proportion, and fractions. In L. Meira & D. Carraher (Eds.), *Proceedings of the nineteenth international conference for the Psychology of Mathematics Education* (Vol. 1, pp. 3–29). Recife, Brazil: Federal University of Pernambuco. (ERIC Document Reproduction Service No. ED 411 134).

Cramer, K., Behr, M., & Bezuk, N. (1989). Proportional relationships and unit rates. *Mathematics Teacher, 82*, 537–544.

Cramer, K., Behr, M., Post, T., & Lesh, R. (1997). *Rational Numbers Project: Fraction lessons for the middle grades, level 1 and level 2.* Dubuque, IA: Kendall Hunt.

Cramer, K., Post, T., & Currier, S. (1993). Learning and teaching ratio and proportion: Research implications. In D. T. Owens (Ed.), *Research ideas for the classroom: Middle grades mathematics* (pp. 159–178). New York: Macmillan.

Cramer, K., Post, T., Henry, A., & Jeffers-Ruff, L. (in press). Initial fraction learning of fourth and fifth graders using a commercial textbook or the Rational Number Project Curriculum. *Journal for Research in Mathematics Education.*

Crowley, M. L., & Dunn, K. A. (1985). On multiplying negative numbers. *Mathematics Teacher, 78,* 252–256.

Davydov, V. V., & Tsvetkovich, A. H. (1991). On the objective origin of the concept of fractions. *Focus on Learning Problems in Mathematics, 13,* 13–64.

Davis, R. B. (1988). Is a "percent" a number?" *Journal of Mathematical Behavior, 7*(1), 299–302.

Davis, R. B. (1990). Discovery learning and constructivism. In R. B. Davis, C. A. Maher, & N. Noddings, (Eds.), *Constructivist views on the teaching and learning of mathematics* (Journal for Research in Mathematics Education Monograph No. 4, pp. 93–106). Reston, VA: National Council of Teachers of Mathematics.

Dixon, J. A., & Moore, C. F. (1996). The developmental role of intuitive principles in choosing mathematical strategies. *Developmental Psychology, 32,* 241–253.

Duncan, R. K., & Saunders, W. J. (1980). Introduction to integers. *Instructor, 90*(3), 152–154.

Empson, S. B. (1999). Equal sharing and shared meaning: The development of fraction concepts in a first-grade classroom. *Cognition and Instruction, 17,* 283–342.

English, L. D. (Ed.). (1997). *Mathematical reasoning: Analogies, metaphors, and images.* Mahwah, NJ: Erlbaum.

Fischbein, E. (1987). *Intuition in science and mathematics.* Dordrecht, The Netherlands: Reidel.

Fischbein, E., Deri, M., Nello, M. S., & Marino, M. S. (1985). The role of implicit models in solving problems in multiplication and division. *Journal for Research in Mathematics Education, 16,* 3–17.

Harel, G., & Confrey, J. (1994). *The development of multiplicative reasoning in the learning of mathematics.* Albany: State University of New York Press.

Hativa, N., & Cohen, D. (1995). Self learning of negative number concepts by lower division elementary students through solving computer-provided numerical problems. *Educational Studies in Mathematics, 28,* 401–431.

Heller, P., Ahlgren, A., Post, T., Behr, M., & Lesh, R. (1989). Proportional reasoning: The effect of two concept variables, rate type and problem setting. *Journal for Research in Science Teaching, 26,* 205–220.

Hiebert, J., & Tonnessen, L. H. (1978). Development of the fraction concept in two physical contexts: An exploratory investigation. *Journal for Research in Mathematics Education, 9,* 374–378.

Hiebert, J., & Wearne, D. (1985). A model of students' decimal computation procedures. *Cognition and Instruction, 2,* 175–205.

Hiebert, J., & Wearne, D. (1986). Procedures over concepts: The acquisition of decimal number knowledge. In J. Hiebert (Ed.), *Conceptual and procedural knowledge: The case of mathematics* (pp. 199–223). Hillsdale, NJ: Erlbaum.

Hiebert, J., & Wearne, D. (1988). Instruction and cognitive change in mathematics. *Educational Psychologist, 23*, 105–117.

Hiebert, J., Wearne, D., & Taber, S. (1991). Fourth graders' gradual construction of decimal fractions during instruction using different physical representations. *Elementary School Journal, 91*, 321–341.

Huinker, D. (1998). Letting fraction algorithms emerge through problem solving. In L. J. Morrow & M. J. Kenney (Eds.), *The teaching and learning of algorithms in school mathematics* (1998 Yearbook of the National Council of Teachers of Mathematics, pp. 170–182). Reston, VA: NCTM.

Human, P., & Murray, H. (1987). Non-concrete approaches to integer arithmetic. In J. C. Bergeron, N. Herscovics, & C. Kieran (Eds.), *Proceedings of the Eleventh International Conference for the Psychology of Mathematics Education* (vol. 2, pp. 437–443). Montreal: University of Montreal. (ERIC Document Reproduction Service No. ED 383 532)

Hunting, R. P. (1983). Alan: A case study of knowledge of units and performance with fractions. *Journal for Research in Mathematics Education, 14*, 182–197.

Kaput, J. J., & West, M. M. (1994). Missing-value proportional reasoning problems: Factors affecting informal reasoning patterns. In G. Harel & J. Confrey (Eds.), *The development of multiplicative reasoning in the learning of mathematics* (pp. 235–287). Albany: State University of New York Press.

Karplus, R., Pulas S., & Stage E. (1983). Proportional reasoning and early adolescents. In R. Lesh & M. Landau (Eds.), *Acquisition of mathematics concepts and processes* (pp. 45–91). New York: Academic Press.

Kieren, T. E. (1976). On the mathematical, cognitive and institutional foundations of rational numbers. In R. Lesh & D. Bradbard (Eds.), *Number and measurement: Papers from a research workshop* (pp. 104–144). Columbus OH: ERIC/SMEAC. (ERIC Document Reproduction Service No. ED 120 027).

Kieren, T. E. (1980). The rational number construct—Its elements and mechanisms. In T. E. Kieren (Ed.), *Recent research on number learning* (pp. 125–149). Columbus, OH: ERIC/SMEAC. (ERIC Document Reproduction Service No. ED 212 463).

Kieren, T. E. (1988). Personal knowledge of rational numbers: Its intuitive and formal development. In J. Hiebert & M. Behr (Eds.), *Number concepts and operations in the middles grades* (pp. 162–181). Reston, VA: National Council of Teachers of Mathematics.

Kieren, T. E. (1992). Rational and fractional numbers as mathematical and personal knowledge; Implications for curriculum and instruction. In G. Leinhardt & R. T. Putnam (Eds.), *Analysis of arithmetic for mathematics teaching* (pp. 323–371). Hillsdale, NJ: Erlbaum.

Kouba, V. L., Zawojewski, J. S., & Strutchens, M. E. (1997). What do students know about numbers and operations? In P. A. Kenney & E. A. Silver (Eds.), *Results from the sixth mathematics assessment of the National Assessment of Educational Progress* (pp. 33–60). Reston, VA: National Council of Teachers of Mathematics.

Kuchemann, D. (1980). Children's understanding of integers. *Mathematics in School, 9*, 31–32.

Lamon, S. J. (1993). Ratio and proportion: Connecting content and children's thinking. *Journal for Research in Mathematics Education, 24*, 41–61.

Lamon, S. J. (1994). Ratio and proportion: Cognitive foundations in unitizing and norming. In G. Harel & J. Confrey (Eds.), *The development of multiplicative reasoning in the learning of mathematics* (pp. 89–120). Albany: State University of New York Press.

Lamon, S. J. (1995). Ratio and proportion: Elementary didactical phenomenology. In J. T. Sowder & B. P Schappell (Eds.), *Providing a foundation for teaching mathematics in the middle grades* (pp. 167–198). Albany: State University of New York Press.

Langrall, C. W., & Swafford, J. O. (2000). Three balloons for two dollars: Developing proportional reasoning. *Mathematics Teaching in the Middle School, 6*, 254–261.

Lappan, G., & Bouck, M. K. (1998). Developing algorithms for adding and subtracting fractions. In L. J. Morrow & M. J. Kenney (Eds.), *The teaching and learning of algorithms in school mathematics* (1998 Yearbook of the National Council of Teachers of Mathematics, pp. 183–197). Reston, VA: NCTM.

Lappan, G., Fey, J. Fitzgerald, W., Friel, S., & Phillips E. (1996). *Bits and pieces 2: Using rational numbers.* Palo Alto, CA: Dale Seymour.

Lesh, R., Post, T. R., & Behr, M. (1988). Proportional reasoning. In J. Hiebert & M. Behr (Eds.), *Number concepts and operations in the middle grades* (pp. 93–118). Reston, VA: National Council of Teachers of Mathematics.

Liebeck, P. (1990). Scores and forfeits: An intuitive model for integer arithmetic. *Educational Studies in Mathematics, 21*, 221–239.

Mack, N. K. (1990). Learning fractions with understanding: Building on informal knowledge. *Journal for Research in Mathematics Education, 21*, 16–32.

Mack, N. K. (1995). Confounding whole-number and fraction concepts when building on informal knowledge. *Journal for Research in Mathematics Education, 26*, 422–441.

Moreno, R., & Mayer, R. E. (1999). Multimedia-supported metaphors for meaning making in mathematics. *Cognition and Instruction, 17*, 215–248.

Morris, A. L. (in press). A teaching experiment: Introducing fourth graders to fractions from the viewpoint of measuring quantities using Davydov's mathematics curriculum. *Focus on Learning Problems in Mathematics.*

Moss, J., & Case, R. (1999). Developing children's understanding of the rational numbers: A new model and an experimental curriculum. *Journal for Research in Mathematics Education, 30*, 122–147.

Mukhopadhyay, S., Resnick, L. B., & Schauble, L. (1990). *Social sense-making in mathematics; Children's ideas of negative numbers.* Pittsburgh: University of Pittsburgh, Learning Research and Development Center. (ERIC Document Reproduction Service No. ED 342 632).

Peck, D. M., & Jencks, S. M. (1981). Conceptual issues in the teaching and learning of fractions. *Journal for Research in Mathematics Education, 12*, 339–348.

Post, T., Behr, M., & Lesh, R. (1988). Proportionality and the development of pre-algebra understanding. In A. F. Coxford & A. P. Schulte (Eds.), *The ideas of algebra, K–12* (1988 Yearbook of the National Council of Teachers of Mathematics, pp. 78–90). Reston, VA: NCTM.

Post, T. P., Wachsmuth, I., Lesh, R., & Behr, M. J. (1985). Order and equivalence of rational numbers: A cognitive analysis. *Journal for Research in Mathematics Education, 16*, 18–36.

Pothier, Y., & Sawada, D. (1983). Partitioning: The emergence of rational number ideas in young children. *Journal for Research in Mathematics Education, 14,* 307–317.

Pothier, Y., & Sawada, D. (1989). Children's interpretation of equality in early fraction activities. *Focus on Learning Problems in Mathematics, 11*(3), 27–38.

Resnick, L. B., Nesher, P., Leonard, F., Magone, M., Omanson, S., & Peled, I. (1989). Conceptual bases of arithmetic errors: The case of decimal fractions. *Journal for Research in Mathematics Education, 20,* 8–27.

Schmittau, J. (1993). Connecting mathematical knowledge: A dialectical perspective. *Journal of Mathematical Behavior, 12,* 179–201.

Streefland, L. (1991). *Fractions in realistic mathematics education: A paradigm of developmental research.* Dordrecht, The Netherlands: Kluwer.

Streefland, L. (1993). Fractions: A realistic approach. In T. P. Carpenter, E. Fennema, & T. A. Romberg (Eds.), *Rational numbers: An integration of research* (pp. 289–325). Hillsdale, NJ: Erlbaum.

Thompson, F. M. (1988). Algebraic instruction for the younger child. In A. F. Coxford & A. P. Shulte (Eds.), *The ideas of algebra, K-12* (1988 Yearbook of the National Council of Teachers of Mathematics, pp. 69–77). Reston, VA: NCTM.

Thompson, P. W., & Dreyfus, T. (1988). Integers as transformations. *Journal for Research in Mathematics Education, 19,* 115–133.

Tourniaire, F., & Pulos, S. (1985). Proportional reasoning: A review of the literature. *Educational Studies in Mathematics, 16,* 181–204.

Vergnaud, G. (1983). Multiplicative structures. In D. Lesh & M. Landau (Eds.), *Acquisition of mathematics concepts and processes* (pp. 127–174). New York: Academic Press.

Wearne, D., & Kouba, V. L. (2000). Rational numbers. In E. A. Silver & P. A. Kenney (Eds.), *Results from the seventh mathematics assessment of the National Assessment of Educational Progress* (pp. 163–191). Reston, VA: National Council of Teachers of Mathematics.

DEVELOPING MATHEMATICAL PROFICIENCY BEYOND NUMBER

In this chapter, we go beyond number to examine other domains of school mathematics in grades pre-K to 8. Because a great deal of the curriculum dealing with number leads naturally to algebra and because whether and how to teach algebra to all children is a hotly debated topic in many schools, we devote the bulk of the chapter to issues of beginning algebra. The first section is organized according to the algebraic activities of representing, transforming, and generalizing and justifying, which allows us to survey the literature relevant to learning algebra in grades pre-K to 8. We close the chapter with two briefer sections: one on measurement and geometry, the other on statistics and probability. As we noted in Chapters 1 and 3, these domains are intimately related to number. Measurement is one of the most common uses of number, and the geometry studied in elementary and middle school uses lengths, areas, and volumes usually expressed as numerical quantities. Statistics and probability involve the quantification of phenomena dealing with data and chance. Throughout the last two sections we emphasize the strands of conceptual understanding and adaptive reasoning because these have been the focus of much recent research and because traditional instruction has tended to emphasize the development of procedural fluency instead.

Beginning Algebra

For most students, school algebra—with its symbolism, equation solving, and emphasis on relationships among quantities—seems in many ways to signal a break with number and arithmetic. In fact, algebra builds on the proficiency that students have been developing in arithmetic and develops it

Algebra builds on the proficiency that students have been developing in arithmetic and develops it further.

further. In particular, the place-value numeration system used for arithmetic implicitly incorporates some of the basic concepts of algebra, and the algorithms of arithmetic rely heavily on the "laws of algebra." Nevertheless, for many students, learning algebra is an entirely different experience from learning arithmetic, and they find the transition difficult.

The difficulties associated with the transition from the activities typically associated with school arithmetic to those typically associated with school algebra have been extensively studied.[1] In this chapter, we review in some detail the research that examines these difficulties and describe new lines of research and development on ways that concepts and symbol use in elementary school mathematics can be made to support the development of algebraic reasoning. These recent efforts have been prompted in part by the difficulties exposed by prior research and in part by widespread dissatisfaction with student learning of mathematics in secondary school and beyond. The efforts attempt to avoid the difficulties many students now experience and to lay the foundation for a deeper set of mathematical experiences in secondary school. Before reviewing the research, we first describe and illustrate the main activities of school algebra.

Previous chapters have shown how the five strands of conceptual understanding, procedural fluency, strategic competence, adaptive reasoning, and productive disposition are interwoven in achieving mathematical proficiency with number and its operations. These components of proficiency are equally important and similarly entwined in successful approaches to school algebra.

The Main Activities of Algebra

What is school algebra? Various authors have given different definitions, including, with "tongue in cheek, the study of the 24th letter of the alphabet [x]."[2] To understand more fully the connections between elementary school mathematics and algebra, it is useful to distinguish two aspects of algebra that underlie all others: (a) algebra as a systematic way of expressing generality and abstraction, including algebra as generalized arithmetic; and (b) algebra as syntactically guided transformations of symbols.[3] These two main aspects of algebra have led to various activities in school algebra, including representational activities, transformational (rule-based) activities, and generalizing and justifying activities.[4]

The *representational* activities of algebra involve translating verbal information into symbolic expressions and equations that often, but not always, involve functions. Typical examples include generating (a) equations that represent quantitative problem situations in which one or more of the quantities are unknown, (b) functions describing geometric patterns or numerical sequences, and (c) expressions of the rules governing numerical relationships (see Box 8-1 for an example of each).

Proficiency with representational activities involves conceptual understanding of the mathematical concepts, operations, and relations expressed in the verbal information, and it involves strategic competence to formulate and represent that information with algebraic equations and expressions. Hence, facility with generating expressions and equations combines two of the strands of mathematics proficiency.

The second kind of algebraic activities—the *transformational* or rule-based activities—includes, for instance, collecting like terms, factoring, expanding, substituting, solving equations, and simplifying expressions. These activities are largely concerned with changing the form of an expression or equation to an equivalent one using the rules for manipulating algebraic symbols. For example, in solving the equation $4(x + 3) = 2x + 19$, you can replace the expression $4(x + 3)$ by the equivalent expression $4x + 12$. Subsequently, by subtracting $2x$ and then 12 from both sides, the equation $4x + 12 = 2x + 19$ can be replaced by the equivalent equation $2x = 7$; finally, dividing both sides by

Box 8-1

Representational Activities of Algebra

1.   There are 3 piles of stones; the first has 5 less than the third, and the second has 15 more than the third. There are 31 altogether. Find the number in each pile.

2.   Say to yourself what you see in the picture sequence. Then state a rule for extending the sequence of pictures indefinitely.

3.   The sum of two consecutive numbers is always an odd number. Can you show why, using algebra?

SOURCES: Bell, 1995, p. 61; Lee and Wheeler, 1987, p. 160; Mason, 1996, p. 84. Used by permission of Elsevier Science and of Kluwer Academic Publishers.

2 yields the solution $x = 3\frac{1}{2}$. Facility with symbolic computation in algebra has an obvious parallel with, and indeed draws upon, procedural fluency in the domain of number. Just as in arithmetic, aspects of conceptual understanding and strategic competence interact with each other and with procedural fluency in transformational activities in algebra.

Lastly, there are the *generalizing and justifying* activities. These include problem solving, modeling, noting structure, justifying, proving, and predicting. These activities are not exclusive to algebra, but they often use its language and tools. For example, the consecutive numbers problem (show that the sum of two consecutive numbers is always an odd number) illustrates how algebra is used to generalize and justify.[5] Arithmetic can be used to generate many instances to show that the sum of two consecutive numbers is odd: $3 + 4 = 7$, $12 + 13 = 25$, and so on. But the representational and transformational aspects of algebra make it possible to justify that the sum is *always* odd. The sum of two consecutive integers can be represented with algebra as $x + (x + 1)$, where the key is the recognition that x represents *any* whole number. This expression can be transformed into the equivalent expression $2x + 1$, which is the general form of any odd number. This example illustrates the power of algebra, as against arithmetic, as a tool for making generalizations and providing justifications, at least for those learners who understand how statements using variables express generality.

Generalizing and justifying activities typically involve examining and interpreting representations that have previously been generated or manipulated. Such activities can provide insight into, for example, the underlying mathematical structure of a situation, or they can yield answers to specific questions or conjectures. They encourage students to develop an awareness of the role that algebra can play in mathematical thinking. All of the strands of algebraic proficiency come together in these activities, especially adaptive reasoning.

One of the great strengths of algebra is that, for experts, a great deal of its transformational activity can be carried out in what appears to be a rather automated manner. Once a student makes the transformation rules his or her own, the algorithms of algebra can be executed, in a sense, without thinking. The student needs to be thinking, for example, not of what the letters in the expressions refer to or of the operations he or she is carrying out, but only that the actions on the symbolic objects are allowable. In fact, once an expression or equation has been generated (or provided) and the goal is known, it seems to be treated in an almost mindless fashion. But is that possible?

Every algebraic manipulation involves an anticipatory element, a sense of the direction in which you want to be going and of what the desired expression will look like once you get there.[6] The development of this sense of anticipation provides an alternative to the "blind" manipulation that is so often performed by beginning algebra students.[7] Research suggests, however, that such anticipatory thinking is not acquired without effort. Even students with extensive algebra experience can make poor strategic decisions that leave them "going round in circles" because they cannot seem to "see" the right thing in algebraic expressions.[8]

The transformational aspects of algebra have traditionally been emphasized in U.S. textbooks, which have tended to pay more attention to the rules to be followed in manipulating symbolic expressions and equations than to the concepts that support those rules or give meaning to the expressions or equations being manipulated. Although few experimental comparisons have been conducted, research has shown that rule-based instructional approaches that do not give students opportunities to create meaning for the rules or to learn when to use them can lead to forgetting,[9] unsystematic errors,[10] reliance on visual clues,[11] and poor strategic decisions.[12] For example, experienced algebra students were found to choose inappropriate strategies when deciding what to do next in the simplification of an algebraic expression and would often end up with an expression that was more difficult to deal with, even though they had performed legal transformations.[13] Beginning algebra students were found to be quite haphazard in their approach; they might simplify $4(6x - 3y) + 5x$ as $4(6x - 3y - 5x)$ on one occasion and do something else on another.[14] When the consecutive numbers problem was given to 113 high school students who had studied algebra, only 8 worked the problem correctly.[15] The rest made a variety of errors, including substituting a few values for x to show the sum's "oddness," using different letters for each number (x and y), representing the consecutive numbers as $1x$ and $2x$, and setting the expression $x + (x + 1)$ equal to a fixed odd number and then solving for x. In one of the few experimental studies of rule-based instruction, students who were taught an estimate-and-test sense-making strategy performed better in solving systems of equalities and inequalities than students taught rule-based equation solving.[16]

Data from the National Assessment of Educational Progress (NAEP) further reveal the shortcomings of traditional school algebra. For example, one of the NAEP tasks from the second mathematics assessment involved completing the table shown in Box 8-2. Most of the students with one or two years of algebra could recognize the pattern—adding 7—from the given nu-

Box 8-2

Table Completion Task from NAEP

Give the values of _y_ when _x_ = 3 and when _x_ = _n_.

_x_	1	3	4	7	_n_
_y_	8		11	14	

SOURCE: Carpenter, Corbitt, Kepner, Lindquist, and Reys, 1981. Used by permission of the National Council of Teachers of Mathematics.

---

merical values and use it when $x = 3$ (with success rates of 69% and 81% for the two groups of students, respectively). They were less successful, however, when asked to derive from the same table the value of y when $x = n$ (correct response: $y = n + 7$; success rates: 41% and 58%, respectively).

The next three sections of the chapter present representative findings from the large body of research on algebra learning and teaching for the three types of algebraic activity sketched above. Since much of this research has been carried out with students making the transition from arithmetic to algebra, it casts light on the kinds of thinking that students bring with them to algebra from the traditional arithmetic curriculum centered on algorithmic computation that has been predominant in U.S. schools.[17] Indeed, many studies have been oriented toward either developing approaches to teaching algebra that take this arithmetic thinking into account or, more recently, developing approaches to elementary school mathematics that build foundations of algebraic reasoning earlier.

Much research also has focused on linear relations and linear functions, perhaps because these are considered the easiest and are the first ones encountered by students making the transition from arithmetic to algebra. Although the domain of algebra is far richer than linear relations, much of the research at the cusp of arithmetic and algebra focuses on them.[18] Some of the newer curriculum programs, however, introduce nonlinear relations along with linear relations in the middle grades. In particular, exponential growth relations (e.g., doubling) have been shown to be an accessible topic for middle school students.[19]

Several of the teaching approaches discussed in the following sections have profitably used computer technologies, especially graphics, as a means of making algebraic symbolism more meaningful. These studies provide evidence of the positive role that computer-supported approaches can play in the learning of algebra, as well as suggesting that technology can be a means for making algebra accessible to all students, including those who, for whatever reason, lack skill in pencil-and-paper computation.[20] Thus, these examples suggest that some version of "algebra for all" may be viable.

The Representational Activities of Algebra
What the Number-Proficient Student Brings

Traditional representational activities of algebra center on the formation of algebraic expressions and equations. Creating these expressions and equations involves understanding the mathematical operations and relations and representing them through the use of letters and—for equations—the equal sign. It also requires thinking that proceeds in rather different ways from the thinking that develops in traditional arithmetic.

In the transition from arithmetic to algebra, students need to make many adjustments, even those students who are quite proficient in arithmetic. At present, for example, elementary school arithmetic tends to be heavily answer oriented and does not focus on the representation of relations.[21] Students beginning algebra, for whom a sum such as 8 + 5 is a signal to compute, will typically want to evaluate it and then, for example, write 13 for the box in the equation $8 + 5 = \Box + 9$ instead of the correct value of 4. When an equal sign is present, they treat it as a separator between the problem and the solution, taking it as a signal to write the result of performing the operations indicated to the left of the sign.[22] Or, when doing a sequence of computations, students often treat the equal sign as a left-to-right directional signal. For example, consider the following problem:

Daniel went to visit his grandmother, who gave him $1.50. Then he bought a book for $3.20. If he has $2.30 left, how much money did he have before visiting his grandmother?

In solving this problem, sixth graders will often write 2.30 + 3.20 = 5.50 – 1.50 = 4.00, tacking the second computation onto the result of the first.[23] Since 2.30 + 3.20 equals 5.50, not 5.50 – 1.50, the string of equations they have written violates the definition of equality. To modify their interpretation of the equality sign in algebra, students must come to respect the true meaning of equality as a statement that the two sides of an equation are equal to each other.

Students oriented toward computation are also perplexed by an expression such as $x + 3$; they think they should be able to do something with it, but are unsure as to what that might be. They are not disposed to think about the expression itself as being the subject of attention. Similarly, they need to rethink their approach to problems. In solving a problem such as "When 3 is added to 5 times a certain number, the sum is 38; find the number," students emerging from arithmetic will subtract 3 from 38 and then divide by 5—undoing in reverse order, as they have been taught, the operations stated in the problem text. In contrast, they will be taught in algebra classes first to represent the relationships in the situation by using those operations and not reversing them: $3 + 5x = 38$.

Although most students beginning algebra have had some experience with the use of letters in arithmetic, such as finding the number n such that $n + 12 = 37$, rarely have they worked with more general problem situations in which the letter can take on any of an infinite set of values. In a third-grade class,[24] the students were presented with the problem, "Who can make up a number sentence that equals 10 but has more than two numbers adding up to 10?" Most students started with examples like $5 + 2 + 3 = 10$ and $8 + 1 + 1 = 10$, but the class went on to generate a variety of equations, including $200 - 200 + 10 = 10$ and $1,000,000 - 1,000,000 + 10 = 10$. With the teacher's help, they soon were able to formulate the equation $x - x + 10 = 10$, for any number x. This use of a letter as variable, where the letter can take on a range of values, is seldom seen in typical elementary school mathematics. More often, the letter, or some placeholder, represents an unknown, and only one numerical value will make the equation true. In algebra, both of these conceptions of literal terms (or letters) are important.

A number of recent intervention studies have shown how selected modifications of elementary school mathematics might support the development of algebraic reasoning. One approach infuses elementary mathematics with a systematic use of problems requiring students to generalize, to determine values of a literal term that satisfy quantitative constraints (with or without equations), or to treat numbers in algebraic ways. For example, students might be asked to determine how many ways the number 4 can be written using a given number of 1s and the four basic operations. Since each expression must equal 4, students must distinguish among the different possibilities on the basis of their symbolic form rather than their value when evaluated.[25]

Another approach is to assist elementary school teachers in modifying their instructional materials and classroom practices to emphasize generalizing and expressing generality in elementary mathematics, particularly using patterns, functions, and the notions of variable. Third graders whose teachers were given such assistance showed substantial increases in their understanding of variable and equality compared with traditionally instructed students in the same grade and school. Further, these third graders outperformed fourth graders on items testing number sense from a mandated statewide assessment.[26]

A third approach to modifying elementary school mathematics focuses on helping teachers understand their students' thinking when the students are asked to generalize operations and properties from arithmetic. In one combination first-and-second-grade class, the teacher focused on number sentences twice a week during the school year. Instruction started with true and false number sentences and progressed to increasingly complex forms of open sentences. Number sentences were also used to help the children articulate and represent conjectures about properties of numbers and operations. By the end of the year most of the students (13 of 17) developed a relational concept of equality and operations, along with an ability to form and express general relations among number sentences.[27] In particular, the majority of these students no longer made mistakes like writing 13 for the box in $8 + 5 = \Box + 9$.

Much of the difficulty that students experience when they first encounter algebra is symptomatic of the cognitive challenges inherent in moving from one mode of thinking to another, from arithmetic reasoning to algebraic reasoning. Research on algebra learning has sought to uncover the ways in which beginning algebra students think, thus helping ease their transition into algebra. In the examples cited above of research on more algebraic approaches to elementary school mathematics that are intended to avoid transition problems, the approaches are in their early stages. Although the long-term impact of these approaches is still unknown, they offer considerable promise for avoiding the difficulties many students now experience.

Developing Meaning

Much of the algebra research in the 1970s and early 1980s yielded evidence that incoming algebra students have trouble interpreting letters as variables.[28] Building on these findings, recent work has focused on how students learn to use algebraic letters to represent a range of values.

One investigator studied an approach designed to address students' difficulties with thinking about and symbolizing algebraic expressions.[29] Students were asked to give instructions to an "idealized mathematics machine": for example, "I want the machine to add 5 to any number I give it; how will I write the instructions?" or "I want the machine to add any two numbers I give it" or "Have the machine find the area of any square, given a side." The students easily made sense of the idea of employing letters to write rules that would enable the machine to solve whole classes of problems. In the examples above, the rules would be expressed using $(x + 5)$, $(x + y)$, and x^2, respectively. This approach addresses two issues related to the introduction of algebra: the usefulness or purpose of learning algebra, and the difficulty of new algebraic concepts. The investigator emphasized that "children who are not persuaded on the former point will make little effort to try and come to terms with the latter" and added that "certainly the evidence . . . clearly indicated this to be the case."[30] The majority of the students in the study made significant gains in thinking about the letters in algebraic expressions as taking on multiple values (from 23% correct on the pretest to 85% correct on the delayed posttest) and in improving their attitude toward algebra (at the beginning of the study, they "hated algebra, didn't understand it" and complained that "letters are stupid; they don't mean anything").[31] Later research in which students used actual computers confirmed these results, both with respect to increasing the students' motivation and developing their understanding of algebraic expressions as general computational procedures.[32]

Representational activities of algebra can interact with well-established natural-language-based habits. These interactions are particularly clear in the well-studied class of tasks exemplified by the so-called students-and-professors problem:[33]

> *At a certain university, there are six times as many students as professors. Using S for the number of students and P for the number of professors, write an equation that gives the relation between the number of students and the number of professors.*

A robust reversal error is committed by a majority of students, ranging from first-year algebra students to college freshmen, who write "$6S = P$" and treat the "6" as an adjective modifying the "S" as if it were a noun.[34] This error occurs across different versions of the problem and is resistant to easy correction.[35] The error, while of intrinsic interest, has an especially important connection to the instruction that students receive prior to studying algebra. In particular, detailed correlational analyses have shown that the error's robust-

Representational activities of algebra can interact with well-established natural-language-based habits.

ness is strongly associated with students' understanding of rates and ratios—the worse their understanding, the more robust the error.[36] Such findings could signal the connections between building proficiency in using algebra as a representational tool and building conceptual understanding of number ideas—in this case, multiplicative ideas. Interestingly, related findings show that a procedural perspective that treats the variables in the equation as input-output pairs leads to improved equation-writing performance,[37] which is consistent with the results described above using the idealized machine and the computer.

A series of teaching experiments conducted over three years during the late 1980s in Mexico and the United Kingdom demonstrated the potential of computer spreadsheets to help students grasp the meaning of variables and algebraic expressions, including students who had been having difficulty with traditional approaches to algebraic symbolism.[38] Further, spreadsheets can provide a vehicle for introducing students to formal symbolism.[39] For an example of how a student can profit from the use of a spreadsheet, see Box 8-3. This student was a tenth grader in a low mathematics track of a school in England who had little previous experience with algebra.

Experimental studies involving spreadsheets have also shown enhanced student learning relative to traditional instruction.[40] Studies of the use of spreadsheets have found that it is relatively easy for students to pass from a mixture of spreadsheet and algebraic notation to traditional algebraic symbolism.[41] It should be noted that the spreadsheet approach involves creating a range of values for the expressions that represent the various relationships in the problem statement. Thus, a spreadsheet column of the values that are generated provides an explicit representation of sample values of each variable. Moreover, the particular value of X that solves the problem is often found in one line of the spreadsheet array (if the situation is linear). In the spreadsheet approach, therefore, the unknown is viewed simply as that particular value that satisfies the constraints of the problem.

In general, the use of spreadsheets has been found to be an effective way to develop several notions involved in the representational activities of algebra. It encourages discussion of the role of a letter as both a variable and an unknown; it provides meaningful experience in creating algebraic expressions; and it puts the focus squarely on the representation of quantitative relationships. Research from both small-group instruction[42] and broad-based implementations involving several schools[43] provides support for these claims.

Closely related to spreadsheets are intelligent tutors in which students label spreadsheet-like worksheets and fill in calculated results for specific

Box 8-3

Building on Spreadsheet Experiences

Jo, like several of her 14- and 15-year-old peers, had some previous experience with algebra. But she disliked mathematics and had performed very poorly on the algebra test given at the beginning of the study. She viewed algebraic symbols as no more than letters of the alphabet whose numerical values corresponded to their position in the alphabet. During a four-month study (with one lesson per week), Jo learned how to use a spreadsheet to solve various kinds of word problems. At the end of the study, she was given the following problem to solve (with no computer available):

> One hundred chocolates were distributed to three groups of children. The second group received four times as many chocolates as the first group. The third group received 10 chocolates more than the second group. How many chocolates did the first, second, and third groups receive?

Jo drew a spreadsheet on paper and showed in her written solution how the spreadsheet code was beginning to play a role in her thinking processes. Interviewed subsequently, she was asked,

> "If we call this cell x, what could you write down for the number of chocolates in the other groups?"

She wrote the following, which shows that she was now able to represent the problem using the literal symbols of algebra (note that the syntax of many spreadsheets requires the entry of an equal sign before the algebraic expression):

$$= x \qquad\qquad = x \times 4 \qquad\qquad = x \times 4 + 10$$

SOURCE: Sutherland, 1993, p. 22. Used by permission of *Micromath*.

---

values of the variable.[44] For example, given the situation that a plumbing company charges $42 per hour plus $35 for the service call, students are asked to find the cost of a 3-hour service call and of a 4.5-hour service call. This inductive-support strategy has students provide an arithmetic representation for the problem before being asked to give the algebraic representation. Such an intelligent tutor has been made part of an experimental ninth-grade algebra curriculum that focuses on the mathematical analysis of realistic situations.

When the curriculum was tested in three urban schools, students in the experimental classes significantly outperformed students in comparison classes on standardized tests (42% correct vs. 37% correct) and on tests targeting the curriculum's objectives (38% correct vs. 18% correct).[45]

Recent research in algebra learning also has examined coordinate graphs as a means of representing the relationships of problem situations and providing visual support for symbolic expressions. This use of graphs has usually been done with families of functions; that is, linear functions, quadratic functions, exponential functions, and so on. The wide assortment of computer graphing packages on the market that not only generate coordinate graphs but also link operations on them to updated tabular and symbolic representations have made it feasible for mathematics teachers to use innovative approaches involving these representations.[46]

One research group that has worked extensively with multirepresentational approaches to the teaching of elementary algebra has developed a computer-intensive, function-based algebra curriculum focused on problem solving that has been tested in first-year algebra classes, as well as college algebra classes.[47] The curriculum uses several kinds of software to "develop students' understanding of algebra concepts and their ability to solve problems requiring algebra, before they master symbol manipulation techniques."[48] An adaptation of a sample problem from the curriculum is presented in Box 8-4.

Even though this curriculum was not intended as an alternative curriculum to be compared to a traditional one, members of the research team carried out a few such evaluations. Interviews and tests of one cohort of students at the end of their first year of algebra showed that the experimental group did significantly better than their counterparts from conventional classes in improving their problem-solving abilities and in comprehending the notion of variable. For example, in constructing mathematical representations, the success rates were 48% versus 21%; in interpreting mathematical representations, 78% versus 28%; and in planning solutions and solving problems, 77% versus 66%, respectively.[49]

A similar approach to teaching algebra that involves graphing calculators has been implemented in a three-year high school mathematics curriculum used in several states.[50] When students from three schools at the end of their third year in this curriculum were compared with students nearing the end of their high school algebra experience in advanced algebra classes in three other schools, the students in the new curriculum did better than the comparison group on algebraic tasks that were embedded in applied problem contexts when graphing calculators were available (43% correct for the project group

Box 8-4

Weather Balloon Problem

Situation. Summer weather in Maryland and Pennsylvania brings heavy clouds and thunderstorms on many late afternoons. As warm, moist air rises, it cools. When the air has cooled to the condensation temperature, it forms water drops. These data were recorded by a weather balloon sent up on a warm day.

Data

Altitude in meters	Temperature in degrees centigrade
0	32
500	27
1000	23
1500	18
2000	14.5
2500	9
3000	3.5
3500	-3

1. Use a function-fitting program to find a linear function that describes the data well. Record the rule relating temperature, $t(a)$, to altitude, a, rounding the coefficient and constant term appropriately.

$$t(a) = \underline{\quad\quad}.$$

2. Explain what the slope and constant term reveal about the temperature as it is related to altitude.

3. Look at a plot of your data and the fitted function to see how well the rule matches the experimental data. Can you see any reason that the altitude and temperature data are not exactly linear? How well does the fitted function represent a reasonable range of values for the altitude?

SOURCE: Heid, 1990, p. 195. A later version of this problem appears in Fey, Heid, et al., 1999, p. 171. Used by permission of the National Council of Teachers of Mathematics.

vs. 34% for the comparison group). On transformation tasks involving equation solving and expression simplification without any context and for which calculators were not permitted, however, the comparison group scored higher (38% correct vs. 29%). This finding did not surprise the researchers because the new curriculum had not emphasized symbolic manipulation with paper and pencil, whereas the curriculum for the comparison group had consisted almost exclusively of such manipulation. In fact, when the equation-solving tasks were presented in a contextualized form, such as the example shown in Box 8-5, the students in the new curriculum were more successful than the comparison students (61% correct vs. 45%).[51]

The ways that graphing calculator use can produce improved student performance were examined more deeply in a recent study.[52] The study used a three-condition pretest-posttest design to study the impact of prolonged use of the graphing calculator throughout the entire school year for all topics of the mathematics curriculum (i.e., functions and graphs, change, exponential and periodic functions). Three experimental classes used the graphing calculator throughout the year; a second set of five experimental classes used the graphing calculator with only one topic for six weeks; and four classes, which served as the control group, covered the same subject matter throughout the year but without the graphing calculator. The students who used the calculator throughout the year had enriched solution reper-

Box 8-5

Water Business Problem

The Turtle Mountain Springs Company made plans for growth in its share of the water business. They predicted that annual income from the sale of its bottled water B and filters F would change over time according to the following formulas. Time, t, is in years since 1990, and income is in millions of dollars per year.

Bottled Water Income: $B = 20 + 5t$

Filtering Devices Income: $F = 28 + 3t$

Question: When does the Turtle Mountain Springs Company expect the two water products to give the same annual income?

SOURCE: Huntley, Rasmussen, Villarubi, Sangtong, and Fey, 2000, p. 347. Used by permission of the author.

toires and a better understanding of functions. The students who used the graphing calculator for only a short period of time did no better on the posttest than the students in the control group. They merely replaced their algebraic and guess-and-test procedures with graphing methods. Unlike the students who spent more time using the graphing calculator, they were not able to enrich their conceptual understanding of functions.

The widespread availability of computer and graphing-calculator technologies has dramatically affected the kinds of representational activities that have been developed and studied since the 1980s. Today's graphing programs, curve fitters, spreadsheets, and spreadsheet-like generators of tables of values and so on have been found to provide more effective environments than pencil and paper for introducing students to variables, algebraic expressions, and equations in a problem-solving context. Research has documented that the visual and numerical supports provided for symbolic expressions by digital representations of graphs and tables help students create meaning for expressions and equations in ways difficult to manage in learning environments not supported by computers or calculators. More research is needed into the ways that computers and graphing calculators are being used and can be used effectively in the early grades.

The Transformational Activities of Algebra
What the Number-Proficient Child Brings

In the previous section, we discussed some of the perspectives brought to the study of algebra by students emerging from traditional elementary school arithmetic. These perspectives included the following:

- An orientation to execute operations rather than to use them to represent relationships; which leads to
- Use of the equal sign to announce a result rather than signify an equality;
- Use of inverse or undoing operations to solve a problem and the corresponding absence of a notion of describing a situation with the stated operations of a problem; and
- A perception of letters as representing unknowns but not variables.

In this section, we discuss additional features of arithmetic thinking that must be addressed when students encounter the transformational activities of algebra.

Students who are proficient with arithmetic are generally assumed to have facility with the arithmetic operations of addition and multiplication and their inverses (subtraction and division), with computations written in a horizontal form, and with the equivalence of numerical expressions. These notions, however, are not always as well cultivated in elementary school mathematics as they should be if they are to serve as a basis for algebraic reasoning.

Students emerging from six or seven years of elementary school mathematics are ordinarily aware of the close relationship between addition and subtraction. After all, they check subtraction written vertically by adding the answer (the difference) to the number above it (the subtrahend) to see if it gives the number in the top line of the subtraction (the minuend). But they seem less comfortable with moving among the written forms of this relationship—for example, from an addition statement written horizontally to its equivalent subtraction (e.g., writing $35 + 42 = 77$ as $35 = 77 - 42$). Thus, these students seem somewhat bewildered when asked in initial algebra instruction to express, say, $x + 42 = 77$ as $x = 77 - 42$. The same confusion over the written notation for the inverse relationship between addition and subtraction is seen in the errors students make in solving equations[53] when they judge, say, $x + 37 = 150$ to be equivalent to $x = 37 + 150$ and $x + 37 = 150$ to be equivalent to $x + 37 - 10 = 150 + 10$.

Solving equations and simplifying expressions require the ability to reason about operations as expressions of quantitative relationships rather than just procedures. Researchers have found that sixth graders lack adequate experience in developing this ability. Students were asked to judge the equivalence (without computing the totals) of three-term arithmetic expressions with a subtraction and an addition operation;[54] for example, $685 - 492 + 947$, $947 + 492 - 685$, $947 - 685 + 492$, and $947 - 492 + 685$. The typical answer was that you needed to calculate to decide whether the expressions were equivalent. Similar results were found in another study[55] when students of the same age were presented with the task of stating the value of $\square$ in the expression $(235 + \square) + (679 - 122) = 235 + 679$. Findings such as these illustrate that traditionally instructed students who are proficient with numbers need to shift from thinking about "finding the answer" to thinking about the "numerical relationships" underlying the calculations they perform and the nature of the methods they use.

Students' experience with equivalence in earlier grades is often restricted to their study of equivalent fractions. For example, $\frac{1}{2}$ is equivalent to $\frac{2}{4}$, which is equivalent to $\frac{3}{6}$, and so on. But this equivalence is one of numbers, not of operations or expressions. There are few opportunities in the present

> Traditionally instructed students who are proficient with numbers need to shift from thinking about "finding the answer" to thinking about the "numerical relationships" underlying the calculations they perform and the nature of the methods they use.

elementary school number curriculum for students to gain experience with these more abstract forms of equivalence. It would be helpful, for example, if the curriculum included perimeter problems in which students were asked to calculate the perimeter of a 7-by-4 rectangle in three ways that yield equivalent expressions: $2(7 + 4)$, $(2 \times 7) + (2 \times 4)$, and $7 + 7 + 4 + 4$. Such situations are ideal for initiating discussions of the equivalence of arithmetic expressions and of the properties underlying that equivalence. Because such occasions are currently quite rare in the part of the curriculum dealing with number, however, notions of equivalence generally have to be further developed when arithmetic is extended to algebra.

Developing Meaning

Students' notions of equality and equivalence, as well as their deepening understanding of the relationship between operations and their inverses, are developed through the transformational activities of algebra, especially those related to simplifying expressions and solving equations. A great deal of research has been carried out on this sphere of algebraic activity.

Performing the same operation on both sides of the equation is an important formal equation-solving procedure. This method, however, is often not the first one taught to students. Trial-and-error substitution of values for the unknown and other informal techniques such as the cover-up method and working backwards (undoing) are used to introduce equation solving (see Box 8-6).

In one comparison of the cover-up method with the formal procedure of performing the same operation on both sides of the equation in six seventh-grade classes, the students who learned to solve equations by means of the cover-up method performed better than those who learned both methods in close proximity.[56] The students who learned to solve equations using only the formal method performed worse than those who learned both methods. These findings suggest that students learning formal methods of equation solving may benefit from well-timed prior instruction in the informal technique of "cover up."

Another study found that students who were entering their first algebra course showed one of two preferences when solving simple linear equations in which there was only one operation: Some used trial-and-error substitution; the others used undoing.[57] For two-step equations involving two operations such as $2x - 5 = 11$, the latter group of students spontaneously extended their right-to-left undoing technique: Take 11, add 5 to it, then divide by 2.

Box 8-6

Two Methods for Solving Equations

Cover-Up Method	*Work Backward (Undoing) Method*
$2x + 9 = 5x$	$2x + 5 = 11$
Cover up 9.	Undo adding 5; subtract 5 from 11;
Since $2x +$ (cover up) $= 5x$,	$2x = 6$
$9 = 3x$.	Undo multiplying by 2; divide 6 by 2;
Cover up x.	$x = 3$.
Since 3 times (cover up) equals 9,	
$x = 3$.	

For equations involving multiple operations, such as $3x + 4 - 2x = 8$, they erroneously generalized their method and simply undid each operation as they came to it. For example, they would take 8, divide it by 2, add 4, and then subtract 3. (They had to ignore the last operation of multiplication because they had run out of operands.) A preference for the undoing method of equation solving seemed to work against the students when they were later taught the procedure of performing the same operation on both sides of an equation. The students who preferred the undoing method were, in general, unable to make sense of "performing the same operation on both sides." The instruction seemed to have its greatest impact on those students who had an initial preference for the informal method of substitution and who viewed the equation as a balance between left and right sides. This observation suggests that learning to operate on the structure of a linear equation by performing the same operation on both sides may be easier for students who already view equations as entities with symmetric balance and not as statements about a calculation on the left side and the answer on the right.

Despite the considerable body of research on creating meaning for the transformational activities of algebra, few researchers have been able to shed light on the long-term acquisition and retention of transformational fluency. In one study, students were able to produce a meaningful justification for equivalence transformations, but soon afterwards most remembered only the rules, and some did not even remember that much.[58] According to another study, recency of experience seems to account best for students' ability to carry out certain transformational activities.[59] Regardless of the teaching approach used, whether reform-based or traditional (i.e., oriented toward symbol manipulation), students' ability to carry out successfully the transformational activities of algebra by the end of their high school career appears to be severely limited. This result has been found repeatedly, even in recent studies: "Few students [can] do the kinds of basic symbolic calculation that are common fare on college-admission and placement tests."[60]

The Role of Technology

Transformational activities of algebra have benefited substantially less than representational activities from the use of computer technology to help develop meaning and skill. Nevertheless, a few researchers have used graphing technology as a means of providing a foundation for simplifying expressions and solving equations.[61] This research is based on the idea that an important aspect of students' mathematical development is their ability to support the symbolic transformations of algebraic objects by means of visual representations. For instance, the graphs of two functions can be added geometrically to arrive at a third graph whose expression is their algebraic sum. Equations also can be solved by graphing the functional expressions on each side of an equation on a computer or graphing calculator, zooming in on the point of intersection, and finding the approximate value of x for which the two functions are equal.

In one study the students had become so skilled at graphing linear functions by focusing on the y-intercept and slope that they could do it mentally (see Box 8-7). Although most teachers of algebra would be happy if a student could solve equations mentally by visualizing graphs, they would not be satisfied with solutions found by such informal methods. The issue is not, however, simply being able to produce a more accurate solution than one obtained by examining a graph. If it were, computer software and calculators that can do symbol manipulation could be called on to generate solutions that are as accurate as desired. The issue is the role the process plays in learning:

> When symbol manipulators become widely available, we will probably take the same view with equation solving that we do with graphing. That is, we will continue to teach students paper-and-pencil means for solving linear equations *because the idea is important and the process*

Box 8-7

Mentally Graphing to Find the Solution to an Equation

Toward the end of a study of equation solving by means of a graphical representation, a seventh grader was asked to solve the equation $7x + 4 = 5x + 8$ (an equation whose solution is $x = 2$). Rather than graph the two expressions, the student took a "shortcut."

Interviewer: Can you solve $7x + 4 = 5x + 8$?

Jer: Well, you could, see, it would be like start at 4 and 8, this one would go up by 7, hold on, 8, 8 and 7, hold on, no, 4 and 7, 4 and 7 is 11. They'd be equal, like, 2 or 3 or something like that.

Interviewer: How are you getting that 2 or 3?

Jer: I'm just like graphing it in my head.

SOURCE: Kieran and Sfard, 1999, p. 15. Used by permission of the author.

---

is generalizable, but we will also teach how to use symbol manipulators to solve these and more-complicated equations [emphasis added].[62]

Thus, most teachers—for the time being, at least—remain insistent that students learn to do by hand the various algebraic transformations of expressions and equations. In 1989 one mathematics educator noted that "the unanswered question standing in the way of reducing the manipulative skills agenda of secondary school algebra is whether students can learn to plan and interpret manipulations of symbolic forms without being themselves proficient in the execution of those transformations."[63] Very little research has been conducted since then to help resolve the question; however, the research that has been done is quite telling. A recent study investigated the impact on algebra achievement of a three-year integrated mathematics curriculum in which technology was used to perform symbolic manipulations as well as to link various representations of problem situations.[64] In this study, which involved over 300 high school students in 12 schools, some support was found for the notion that learning how to interpret results of algebraic calculations is not highly dependent on the ability to perform the calculations themselves.

Furthermore, skill in algebraic symbol manipulation was not a prerequisite for the students' success in problem solving, and as the researchers emphasized, "when those students had access to the kind of technological tools that are becoming standard mathematical tools, they could overcome limited personal calculation skills."[65]

Although researchers have made notable advances in finding ways to make representing and interpreting algebraic expressions and equations more meaningful for students with the help of computer and calculator technology, similar efforts in the realm of transforming expressions and equations have been less abundant. As inexpensive symbol manipulators continue to become available for the algebra classroom, it may be feasible to develop and evaluate programs that incorporate their use. At present, despite the occasional use of calculator- and computer-supported approaches to the transformational activities of algebra, the traditional rule-based methods for developing manipulative skills tend to dominate. However, few people at any level in education are satisfied that the traditional approach leads to sufficient proficiency in algebra for most students.

Generalizing and Justifying Activities of Algebra

In this section, we consider activities such as solving problems, modeling situations, noting mathematical structure, justifying, proving, and predicting. None of these activities is exclusive to algebra, but in all of them algebra is often used as a tool. Several of these activities require a certain level of skill in representing and transforming algebraic expressions, as well as in adaptive reasoning. Two problems from the research literature help illustrate the issues (see Box 8-8).

Justifying Generalizations

Students given Problem A in Box 8-8 tended to give a strictly numerical justification in Part 1. The explicit demand of Part 2 to use algebra, however, requires translating the nonspecific number and the sequence of operations into algebraic notation and then manipulating that notation to obtain an expression that can be interpreted in terms of the problem's conditions. If x is the number, that translation yields

$$\left(5x + 12 - x\right)/4 \Rightarrow \left(4x + 12\right)/4$$
$$\Rightarrow 4\left(x + 3\right)/4$$
$$\Rightarrow x + 3.$$

Box 8-8

Problems That Involve Generalizing and Justifying Activities

Problem A

Part 1. A girl multiplies a number by 5 and then adds 12. She then subtracts the original number and divides the result by 4. She notices that the answer she gets is 3 more than the number she started with. She says, "I think that would happen, whatever number I started with."

Part 2. Using algebra, show that she is right.

Problem B

Triangular numbers can be built with dots as shown below. The first four triangular numbers are 1, 3, 6, and 10.
Part 1. Predict the number of dots in the 20th triangle.

Part 2. Give a rule for predicting the number of dots in any triangle.

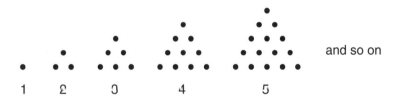

SOURCES: Arzarello, 1992; Lee and Wheeler, 1987. Used by permission of Springer-Verlag and by the authors.

More specifically, the major conceptual demands of Problem A are the following: (a) translating from a verbal representation to a symbolic representation through the use of a letter as a variable to represent "any number," (b) manipulating the algebraic expression to yield simpler equivalent expressions with the underlying aim of arriving at an expression indicating "3 more than the number she started with," and (c) being aware that the algebraic result—the expression $x + 3$—constitutes a proof or justification of the result that one obtains empirically by trying several particular numbers. Note that the only conceptual demand that is somewhat independent of the context is manipulating the algebraic expression to yield simpler algebraic expressions. That activity is very important, however, since it allows the student to see at a glance why the result for the above problem is always $x + 3$, whatever the value of x. The evolving sequence of simplified algebraic expressions can permit a perception of "$x + 3$-ness" in a way that is not so readily available from simply reading the problem. Thus, the algebraic representation can induce an awareness of structure that is much more difficult, if not impossible, to achieve using everyday language.

One hundred eighteen algebra students who had already taken algebra for a year were given Problem A. Only nine set up the expression $(5x + 12 - x)/4$ and then reduced it algebraically to $x + 3$. Four of them went on to "demonstrate further" by substituting a couple of numerical values for x. Thirty-four others set up the equation $(5x + 12 - x)/4 = x + 3$ and then proceeded to simplify the left side, yet they did not base their conclusions on their algebraic work. Instead, they worked numerical examples and drew conclusions from them.

For the great majority of students, therefore, this task posed enormous problems both in representing a general statement and in using that statement to justify numerical arguments. According to the researchers, these students seemed completely lost when asked to use algebra. "Formulating the algebraic generalization was not a major problem for the [few] students who chose to do so; using it and appreciating it as a general statement was where these students failed."[66] Therefore, for the students who responded to the request to use algebra, their difficulties were related not to the simplification of the expression but to the third of the conceptual demands outlined above: being aware that the algebraic result constitutes a proof or justification of the arithmetical result that one obtains empirically by trying several numbers. This research also suggests that even when students are successfully taught symbolic manipulation, they may fail to see the power of algebra as a tool for representing the general structure of a situation. Without some skill with symbolic manipulations, however, students are unlikely to use algebra to justify generalizations.

> Even when students are successfully taught symbolic manipulation, they may fail to see the power of algebra as a tool for representing the general structure of a situation.

Predicting Patterns

Tasks involving geometric and numerical patterns are a frequent means of introducing students to the use of algebra for predicting. Problem B in Box 8-8 is typical. To help students find a pattern in the arrangement of dots in the problem, they might be asked to use a table of values in which the first column points to a position in the sequence and the second column gives the corresponding number of dots.[67]

Sequential position (x) of the triangular number	Number of dots (y) in the triangular number
1	1
2	3
3	6
4	10
⋮	⋮

Two kinds of rules describe this table. One, the *recursive rule*, is based on an analysis of the growth occurring in the right-hand column. For the nth triangle, add n dots to the number of dots in the previous triangle. But this right-hand regularity, which is not too difficult to detect, is easier to say in words than to symbolize algebraically. The other kind of rule, the *closed form*, requires analyzing both columns together to try to determine a relationship between a member of the left-hand column and the corresponding member in the right-hand column. Algebra students have more difficulty deriving the latter rule, $y = x(x + 1)/2$, than the former.[68]

The use of computer technology can enable students to engage in activities like those above without having to generate or transform algebraic equations on their own.[69] But students have to learn how to use the equations produced by the technology to make predictions, even if they do not actually generate them by hand.

Through an emphasis on generalization, justification, and prediction, students can learn to use and appreciate algebraic expressions as general statements. More research is needed on how students develop such awareness. At the same time, more attention needs to be paid to including activities in the curriculum on identifying structure and justifying. Their absence is an obstacle to developing the "symbol sense"[70] that constitutes the power of algebra.

Algebra for All

Because of advancements in the use of technology and its prevalence today, a greater understanding of the fundamentals of algebra and algebraic reasoning is viewed as necessary for all members of society, including those who are low achieving or underserved.[71] The U.S. eighth-grade curriculum is not as advanced as those of other countries. In the Third International Mathematics and Science (TIMSS) Video Study, for example, whereas 40% of U.S. eighth-grade lessons included topics from arithmetic, German and Japanese eighth-grade lessons were more likely to cover algebra and geometry.[72] Over the past decade, however, more and more U.S. schools have started to offer first-year algebra in the eighth grade. According to data collected by NAEP, 25% of eighth-grade students were enrolled in algebra in 1996 compared with 16% in 1990.[73] Further, all but 3% of the twelfth-grade students reported that they had taken first-year algebra, the majority in grade 9. Although the goal of "algebra for all" has essentially been achieved by the time students reach the end of high school, many of these students experience difficulties in their first course in algebra.

The study of algebra need not begin with a formal course in the subject. Recent research and development efforts have been encouraging. By focusing on ways to use the elementary and middle school curriculum to support the development of algebraic reasoning, these efforts attempt to avoid the difficulties many students now experience and to lay a better foundation for secondary school mathematics.[74] From the earliest grades of elementary school, students can be acquiring the rudiments of algebra, particularly its representational aspects. They can observe that over time and across different circumstances, numerical quantities may vary in principled ways—the essence of the concept of variable. They can learn about functions by studying how a change in one variable is reflected in the behavior of another. As students encounter algebraic ideas, they discover the value of precise language and of working with clear definitions.

Once students are familiar with the laws of arithmetic, they can learn to see them as a convenient summary of arithmetic practice and as a valuable guide to methods that work. Students can learn to express the laws algebraically and can use them to support their reasoning and to justify their claims about numbers. It is important that they become aware of the role played by general statements expressed in algebraic symbols when justifying numerical arguments or discussing classes of situations. Little is known, however, about the relative effectiveness of strategies for helping students learn to justify their claims. With the development of new approaches to algebra and the infusion of the rudiments of algebra in the elementary and middle grades, an algebra-proficient population might become a reality.

Measurement and Geometry

In elementary and middle school mathematics, the closely related domains of measurement and geometry are often referred to as measure and space. Geometry, as its Greek origin as "earth measure" indicates, is a route for developing an understanding of two- and three-dimensional space. Measurement, too, is a process that links mathematics with the world, and with science in particular. Measure is a diverse topic, built on the need to quantify particular attributes of an object or phenomenon. By learning about how length, area, and volume are measured, students mentally structure and revise their construction of space, both large-scale and small-scale. When they study science, they need to know about other measures, such as time, density, and speed, and they need to know about choosing a measurement scale and considering the precision of their measurements. Although measurement and the theory behind it can be treated as distinct from geometry, there is much pedagogical value in returning geometry to its roots in spatial measure. Our discussion focuses on the measurement of length, area, and volume, three measures that are the basis for the connection between geometry and number, as shown in chapter 3 through the geometric interpretations of the operations of addition and multiplication.

> There is much pedagogical value in returning geometry to its roots in spatial measure.

Acquiring Measure Concepts

The early work of Piaget and his collaborators[75] focused on showing that understanding measure entails successive mental restructurings of space. The idea of a unit of measure is fundamental, as is the notion that measurement involves the organized accumulation of standard units. Further, *conservation* of length, area, and volume (understanding that these quantities do not change under transformations such as reflection or other rigid motion) was considered both a hallmark of, and a constraint on, children's development in each domain of spatial measure. Studies conducted in the last two decades, however, have generally failed to support the contention that there is a tight coupling between understanding a spatial measure and knowing when it is conserved.[76]

Length Measure

Length needs to be understood from several perspectives: for example, as magnitude, as a span, as the distance traveled, or as motion.[77] Proficiency in the measurement of length requires the learner to restructure space so that he or she "sees" a count of n adjacent unit lengths as representing a distance of n units. Children need to recognize the need for identical units, and they need to understand that a unit can be partitioned into smaller units.[78]

Children's first understanding of length measure involves the direct comparison of objects.[79] They observe that two congruent objects can be put side by side and shown to have the same length. As early as first grade, children typically understand that the lengths of two objects can be compared by representing them with a string or paper strip. First graders can also use given units to find the length of different objects, and they associate higher counts with longer objects.[80] This apparent ease of counting, however, need not imply understanding of length measure as a distance. First and second graders, for example, often fail to see the point of having identical units of length measure. They freely mix units such as inches and centimeters, counting them all to "measure" a length.[81]

Given a measuring device such as a ruler, very few young children understand that any point on the scale can serve as the starting point or origin, and even many older children (e.g., fifth graders) respond to measurement with a nonzero origin by simply reading off whatever number on a ruler aligns with the other end of the object.[82] These difficulties young children have in understanding length indicate that teachers cannot assume that their students understand various aspects of the number line. When the number line is used as a pedagogical tool, efforts must be made to be sure that students understand that they are counting lengths, not the endpoints where the numbers are. In a recent teaching experiment on measuring length, children used computer tools that provided them experience with a unit and the repetition of units to get a measurement. The tools helped the children mentally restructure lengths into units.[83] In other studies, researchers have placed a premium on transitions from active forms of length measure, like pacing, to recording and symbolizing these forms as "foot strips" and other kinds of measurement tools.[84] Tools like foot strips help children reason about the mathematically important components of activity (e.g., pacing) so that invariants like unit are represented physically and then mentally.[85] Although constructing and using tools have a long tradition in teaching practice, recent teaching experiments have shown ways in which these practices can contribute to conceptual change.[86]

Area Measure

The basic idea of measuring area is that of *covering* a region by units that "just fit" (an idea that is sometimes called tiling). In many ways the development of area measure parallels that of length, but it lags behind. First and second graders often treat length measure as a surrogate for area measure. For example, some children will measure the area of a square by measuring the length of one side, moving the ruler parallel to itself a bit and measuring the length again, and so on, treating length as a space-filling attribute.[87] When provided with geometric manipulatives (squares, right triangles, circles, and rectangles) for use in finding the area measure of a variety of shapes, most students in grades 1 to 3 freely mix units and then report the total count of those units.

As they progress through the elementary grades, students usually begin to differentiate area measure from length measure, and the space-filling (tiling) requirement of the unit becomes more apparent to most of them. Other aspects of area measure, however, remain problematic. Students find it very difficult to decompose and then recompose shapes or even to see one shape as a composition of others, an idea that is fundamental to conservation.[88] For example, students in grades 1 to 3 often cannot think of a rectangle as an array of units.[89]

By the end of the elementary grades, students typically understand core concepts like using identical units and covering the object for length measure but not for area measure. Younger children often employ resemblance as the prime criterion for selecting a unit of area measure, suggesting the need for attention to the qualities of a unit that make it suitable for measuring area. The common instructional practice of declaring that the square is *the* unit of area measure may lead to procedural competence but may violate students' preconceptions about what makes a unit suitable.

Teaching experiments with area measure have revealed that second graders could develop a comprehensive understanding of area measure when they began by solving problems involving partitioning and redistributing areas without measuring.[90] It is worth emphasizing that this approach makes conservation of area a fundamental construct rather than an afterthought. Later, when the children explored the suitability of different units (e.g., beans) for finding the areas of irregular shapes like handprints, they found that units like squares had desirable properties of space filling and identity. By the end of the school year, these children had little difficulty creating two-dimensional arrays of units for rectangles and even for irregular (nonpolygonal) shapes.

Volume Measure

The measurement of volume presents some additional complexities for reasoning about the structure of space, primarily because the units of measure must be defined and coordinated in three dimensions. Although the evolution of children's conceptions of units of volume measure is not well understood, an emerging body of work addresses strategies that children use to measure a volume when given a unit.[91]

In one study, fifth graders who had a wide range of experience with representations of volume and its measurement typically organized space into three-dimensional arrays, and most could conceive of volume as a product of area and height.[92] Thus, traditional notions about how volume concepts develop may need to be revised in light of the results from recent teaching experiments.

Developing Geometric Reasoning

Early work on geometric reasoning suggested that proficiency in geometry develops in a sequence of stages associated with age[93] and that children can be assisted, through appropriate activities, to move to more advanced levels of reasoning.[94] Recent work has confirmed the effectiveness of appropriate activities even as it has called into question the notion of a stage-like sequence.[95]

Reasoning About Shape and Form

Children enter school with a great deal of knowledge about shapes. They can identify circles quite accurately and squares fairly well as early as age four.[96] They are less accurate at recognizing triangles (about 60% correct) and rectangles (about 50% correct). Given conventional instruction, which tends to elicit and verify this prior knowledge, children generally fail to make much improvement in their knowledge of shapes from preschool through the elementary grades.[97]

Instruction needs to build on students' informal knowledge and move beyond it. For example, in one experiment, first graders were given a 10-day instructional sequence to help them identify specific classes of quadrilaterals and understand the relationships among the classes.[98] They learned to arrange the figures from the most to the least general members of the class (e.g., from quadrilaterals to squares), to embed hierarchies in the names they gave to shapes (e.g., "square-rectangles"), and to examine characteristics of the figures.

Encouraged to reflect on and articulate their developing knowledge, the children subsequently demonstrated levels of reasoning well beyond their earlier performance, both in their precision of language and in their use of arguments based on the properties of shapes rather than on visual comparison to some prototypical shape.

In another study, fourth graders were encouraged to reflect on and articulate their ideas about concepts such as angle and line and also about relational concepts, such as class inclusion among quadrilaterals. One group of 16 students received instruction with Logo, a computer programming language with a feature called Turtle Geometry that allows children to instruct a turtle on the screen to move, tracing a geometric path as it goes. A second group of 16 students used traditional tools like protractors and rulers. On a set of geometry items from NAEP,[99] the performance of both groups well exceeded the performance by the high school students in NAEP. Moreover, on measures of abstracting and applying geometric properties for reasoning, the fourth graders who had used Logo as a construction tool significantly outperformed their contemporaries.[100]

Although previous work had suggested that children's reasoning about geometric figures is based on global appearances, primary school children in one study[101] routinely used a variety of attributes of shape and form to describe how two shapes, in either two or three dimensions, were alike yet different from a third shape. Their judgments about shape and form revealed distinctions that appeared to involve several distinct forms of mental operation, ranging from simple feature detection ("it has four sides"), to comparison to known prototypes ("it's squarish"), to mental representation of the action-based embodiment of transforming one form into another ("if you push the top of this one [a parallelogram] to the side, it makes a rectangle"). Mixture across levels of reasoning was the rule, not the exception.

Concepts about shapes begin forming in the preschool years and stabilize as early as age 6.[102] Hence, if preschool provides sufficient opportunities for children to learn about geometric figures, by the end of second grade they should be able to "identify a wide range of examples and non-examples of a wide range of geometric figures; classify, describe, draw, and visualize shapes; and describe and compare shapes based on their attributes."[103]

Although they have considerable experience with three-dimensional objects, students are less proficient with three-dimensional geometric shapes than they are with two-dimensional ones. Even intermediate-grade students have difficulty naming solids, using names of plane figures instead.[104] In reasoning about solids, they refer to a variety of characteristics, such as "pointyness" or slenderness.[105] Studying only plane figures in the early grades may be responsible for some of the difficulty students have in discriminating between the terms for two- and three-dimensional figures. Construction activities involving foldout shapes of solids may help students make such discriminations.[106] Other promising activities need to be developed and investigated.

An important and difficult geometric figure for students to understand and be able to use is the angle. In the course of schooling, students need to encounter multiple mathematical conceptions of angle,[107] including: (a) angle as movement, as in rotation or sweep; (b) angle as a geometric shape, a delineation of space by two intersecting lines; and (c) angle as a measure, a perspective that encompasses the other two.[108] Although as preschoolers, they encounter and use angles intuitively in their play, children have many misconceptions about angles. They typically believe that angle measures are influenced by the lengths of the intersecting lines or by the angle's orientation in space.[109] The latter conception decreases with age, but the former is robust at every age.[110] Some researchers have suggested that students in the elementary grades should develop separate mental models of angle as movement and angle as shape.[111]

There is some research on instructional approaches that attempt to develop the two models of angles. With appropriate instruction, Logo's Turtle Geometry can support the development of measures of rotations.[112] The students, however, rarely connected these rotations to models of the space in the interior of figures traced by the turtle.[113] Simple modifications to Logo helped students perceive the relationship between turns and traces (the path made by Logo's turtle), and the students could then use turns to measure static intersections of lines.[114] Another approach used multiple concrete analogies such as turns, slopes, meetings, bends, directions, corners, and openings to help children develop general angle concepts by recognizing common features of these situations.[115] Other research took as the starting point children's experience with physical rotations, especially rotations of their own bodies.[116] In time, students were able to assign numbers to certain turns and integrate turn-as-body-motion with turn-as-number.

An understanding of angle requires novel forms of mental structuring, the coordination of several potential models, and an integration of those models. The long developmental process is best begun in the early grades. Common admonitions to teach angles as turns run the risk of students developing only one concept of angle since they rarely spontaneously relate situations involving rotations to those involving shape and form.

In several studies of instruction in space and geometry,[117] teachers have posed challenging tasks (e.g., design a playground), engaged students in mathematical explanation and justification, and provided computer tools (e.g., Sketchpad,[118] Logo) and related means (e.g., Polydrons[119]) for reasoning about space. The emerging portrait of mathematical reasoning in these contexts suggests that children's conceptions of shape and form can encompass fairly sophisticated mathematical understanding.

Reasoning About More Advanced Concepts

During the last decade, studies of geometry learning have focused less exclusively on shape and form, although conceptions of form are still a prominent topic. Related ideas like congruence, symmetry, similarity, and transformation have received more systematic attention in recent studies. Beginning as early as age 4, children can create and use strategies for judging whether two figures are the same size and shape.[120] By about first grade they can develop sophisticated and accurate mathematical procedures for determining congruence.

Children also have intuitive notions of symmetry from a very early age, preferring symmetric figures over asymmetrical ones.[121] Vertical bilateral symmetry, in particular, seems to be easier for children to identify than horizontal symmetry.[122] Young children can identify similar shapes in certain situations. They can verify their identifications using an overhead projector,[123] and they can use computers to create similar figures.[124]

The findings are mixed regarding children's ability with geometric motions. In one study, second graders could perform transformations manually but not mentally.[125] In contrast, other researchers found that children do learn something about these motions and appear to internalize them.[126] Slides appear to be the easiest motion, followed by flips and turns, although the difficulty depends on the specific task.[127] Computer environments can be particularly useful in helping students develop proficiency with congruence, similarity, symmetry, and transformations.[128]

Several researchers have looked at the effects of introducing children to ideas about modeling space. In these studies, middle school students made significant progress in developing their conceptions of proportion and scale when they used a computer-assisted-drawing (CAD) tool to map their classroom[129] or designed a playground and its equipment.[130] Modeling of space can be done by primary grade children as well. For example, first graders learned about properties of shapes as they searched for a configuration of players (ultimately a circle) that would be "fair" (equidistant) in a classroom game of tag.[131]

Some research has focused on relationships between spatial models and learning about science. For example, middle school students' understanding of area and volume measure was found to make a significant contribution to their understanding of concepts like buoyancy,[132] and the idea of similarity in substance helped in developing their understanding of similarity of shapes.[133] Engineering problems involving stability have also been employed to help middle school students understand the relationship between geometry and the success or failure of architectural structures.[134]

Collectively, research on geometry points the way to a significant expansion of what is meant by the study of shape and form in school mathematics. Children enter school with much informal knowledge of geometry that can be developed throughout the grades. Given children's affinity toward, knowledge of, and ability to gain geometric knowledge, it is important that this domain of mathematics not be neglected. Instruction in geometry needs to complement the study of number and operation in grades pre-K to 8.

Statistics and Probability

In the elementary and middle grades, the domains of statistics and probability are often referred to as the study of data and chance. Research in these two domains is less extensive than that in number and operation, in algebra, or in measurement and geometry. But like measurement and geometry, many of the central conceptual structures of statistics and probability have been identified, especially with respect to school mathematics in grades pre-K to 8. [135]

Learning to Use Data

Although the graphing of data is a common activity in grades pre-K to 8 and has been the focus of some investigations, recent research into students' statistical thinking at the elementary and middle school grades has adopted a broader perspective. Four key processes have been studied: describing, organizing, representing, and analyzing data.[136] We consider research on each of these processes in turn, starting with a definition of the process.

Describing Data

Describing data involves reading displays of data (e.g., tables, lists, graphs); that is, finding information explicitly stated in the display, recognizing graphical conventions, and making direct connections between the original data and the display. The process is essentially what has been called *reading the data*,[137] and researchers have found that the majority of students in the elementary and middle school grades can read data displays accurately.[138] Although children in the primary grades often give idiosyncratic descriptions of data, explorations with categorical and numerical data in instruction that incorporates technology produce more focused and less idiosyncratic descriptions.[139]

Organizing Data

The process of organizing, and reducing, data incorporates mental actions such as ordering, grouping, and summarizing.[140]   Data reduction also includes the use of representative measures of center (often termed *measures of central tendency*) such as mean, mode, or median, and measures of spread such as range or standard deviation. Research on organizing data at grades pre-K to 8 is quite limited.

Most of the available research on data reduction by elementary school students has focused on their understanding of measures of center, particularly the mean. The most familiar measure of center is the mean, which is computed by adding up all the data values and dividing by the number of values. The median is the middle value when the data are sorted (or the mean of the two middle values). The mode is the most common data value. All of these measures of center are called "averages" for some kinds of data. With housing prices and incomes, for example, the preferred average is the median because the mean is easily skewed by a few very high incomes, giving a false impression of income for an "average" or typical family. With clothing sizes, the preferred average is the mode because it gives the best impression of the typical buyer.

First and second graders have informal conceptions of mode and median as measures of center, and they also have some conception of spread.[141] Most elementary school students understand that the mean is located between extreme values.[142] Nearly all realize that the mean is influenced by values in the data set and that the mean does not necessarily equal one of the actual data values. In a study of fourth, sixth, and eighth graders' concept of average, the younger students interpreted the average as the mode.[143] Although the researchers claimed that these students did not see the data set as an entity that can be represented by a single value, an alternative interpretation is that the students used the mode because it is so easily identified in a graph.[144] Some students consider the average to be a data point roughly centered within the data, that is, they conceptualize average as median.[145] Students in the primary grades seem not to have the idea of center as a mathematical point of balance, a vital characteristic of the mean. They cannot use an algorithmic procedure to find the mean, let alone create a data set given the mean.[146] Different measures of center appear to be important for different students; all need eventually to understand the different measures and their purposes.

Representing Data

Representing data in visual displays requires the generation of different organizations of data according to certain conventions. Many elementary students have difficulty creating visual displays of data.[147] First and second graders' knowledge of how to represent data appears to be constrained by difficulties in sorting and organizing data, and technology has been found to be helpful in overcoming those difficulties.[148]

Studies of middle school students have revealed substantial gaps in their abilities to construct graphs from given data.[149] Processes like organizing data and conventions like labeling and scaling are crucial to data representation and are strongly connected to the concepts and processes of measurement. Given the difficulties students experience, instruction might need to differentiate these processes and conventions more sharply and utilize the potential of technology to make them more accessible to students.

Analyzing Data

The process of analyzing, and interpreting, data incorporates recognizing patterns and trends in data and making inferences and predictions from the data. It includes what has been referred to as *reading between the data* and *reading beyond the data*.[150] Reading between the data requires students to compare quantities and use mathematical operations to combine and integrate data and to identify mathematical relationships expressed in the data or in visual representations of the data. Reading beyond the data requires students to make predictions or inferences from the data that are neither explicitly nor implicitly stated in the visual representation.

Elementary school students have difficulty analyzing and interpreting data. In one study, 80% of the first and second graders interviewed gave idiosyncratic or incomplete responses when they attempted to analyze data from a line plot and a bar graph.[151]   In another study, almost all the fourth and sixth graders could describe bar graphs, but fewer could interpret them, and many fewer still could use the graphs to predict.[152]

Learning About Chance

Although there has been substantial research on students' probabilistic thinking over the past 50 years by both psychologists[153] and mathematics educators,[154] only recently has students' learning about chance been examined with a view toward informing instruction. In this section, we examine what is known about students' probabilistic thinking about five key concepts: sample space, probability of an event, probability comparisons, conditional probability, and independence.[155]

Sample Space

Students exhibit an understanding of sample space when they are able to identify the complete set of possible outcomes in a random experiment, an experiment in which the actual outcome cannot be determined ahead of time even though the set of possible outcomes can be determined. When two coins are flipped, for example, the possible outcomes may be represented as HH, HT, TH, and TT.

Several studies have addressed children's thinking about sample space.[156] Recent research has concluded that a substantial number of students in grades 1 through 3 are not able to list the outcomes of a one-dimensional experiment (such as rolling a single die) even after instruction.[157]   The students in these studies adopted a deterministic posture, maintaining that it was "always" possible to predict a particular outcome. The situation with respect to two-dimensional experiments (such as rolling two dice) is also problematic. Although some children as young as seven years can use efficient procedures for listing all outcomes,[158] other children in grades 4 through 6 are reluctant or unable to list them all.[159]

Probability of an Event

Although probability tasks used in research with elementary and middle school students have typically involved equally likely outcomes, a number of

Comparisons
of event
probabilities
are difficult for
students and
seem to be
linked to their
proficiency with
rational
numbers.

researchers have investigated children's probabilistic thinking about unequally likely events.[160] In comparing event probabilities, students commit them- selves to one of three strategies: (a) a numerator strategy in which they only examine the part that corresponds to the event; (b) an "incomplete" denomi- nator strategy in which they examine the part that corresponds to the comple- ment of the event; and (c) an integrating strategy in which they recognize the moderating effect that each part has on the other.[161] In a recent study that incorporated instruction, the kind of reasoning that third graders used was fundamental to their quantifying probability situations in a meaningful way.[162] Overall, comparisons of event probabilities are difficult for students and seem to be linked to their proficiency with rational numbers.

Probability Comparisons Across Sample Spaces

Students' understanding of probability comparisons is measured by their ability to determine and justify which of two probability situations is more likely to generate the target event in a random draw. For example, given a bag with 2 red and 2 blue bears and another with 3 red and 4 blue, they might be asked, "Which bag would give the better chance of getting a red bear?" Researchers have found that elementary and middle school students use both intuitive and informal quantitative strategies for comparing the probabilities of the target event.[163] In one seminal study the three incorrect strategies used by students in grades 1 through 5 involved choosing the probability situation with: (a) more instances corresponding to the target event; (b) fewer instances corresponding to the nontarget event; and (c) a greater difference (as opposed to greater ratio) of instances favoring the target event.[164]

Conditional Probability

A number of studies have addressed elementary and middle school stu- dents' thinking in conditional probability situations—their ability to recog- nize when the probability of an event is or is not changed by the occurrence of another event.[165] For example, the conditional probability of drawing a white ball, given that you have already drawn and not replaced a white ball from a bag containing three white balls and three red balls, is 0.4, not 0.5. When fifth, sixth, and seventh graders were asked to determine conditional probabilities, the performance of the sixth and seventh graders was dramati- cally lower when the tasks involved selection without replacement compared with selection with replacement.[166] Similar results were found in a study[167] with students in grades 6 through 8. In a study with third graders, several levels of thinking in conditional probability were identified, with few children being able to recognize that the probabilities changed in situations of selection without replacement. Following instruction, 51% were able to recognize that conditional probabilities changed in these situations.[168] Children have difficulty determining the conditioning event and may be confused about the context of a conditional probability problem.

Independence

Students' intuitive understanding of independence is measured by their ability to recognize and justify when the occurrence of one event has no influence on the occurrence of another. In one study, students in grades 4 through 8 were asked to determine which event was more likely: obtaining 3 heads by tossing one coin 3 times, or by tossing 3 coins simultaneously.[169] Some 38% of fourth and fifth graders and 30% of seventh and eighth graders with no prior instruction in probability responded that the probabilities were not equal. Follow-up interviews revealed that these students harbored the pervasive misconception that the outcomes of a coin toss can be controlled. Similar misconceptions were evident in other studies of middle school students.[170] Misconceptions of the kind illustrated above have been characterized more generally as *representativeness*—a belief that a sample or sequence of outcomes should reflect the whole population.[171]

From Arithmetic to Mathematics

As children move from number to other domains of mathematics, they both use their proficiency with number and develop it further. The school mathematics curriculum, although separated into domains for the purposes of this report, needs to be experienced by the learner as a unified whole.

In general, the arithmetic thinking of number-proficient students emerging from the typical elementary school mathematics program is different from the thinking that is central to algebra. Some of the conceptual understanding of the arithmetic thinker requires an adjustment when the student engages in the main types of activities in algebra. Whereas arithmetic focuses on number and numerical answers, school algebra focuses on relations. Algebra remains, however, a natural extension of arithmetic. Students' numerical thinking can therefore continue to grow and develop into algebraic thinking, but their numerical thinking habits must be taken into account.

Just as current research has influenced conceptions of algebra in the early grades, the nature of school algebra in higher grades has likewise been evolving. Over the past two decades, computational tools have increasingly influenced the kinds of transformations that are important to learn, the kinds of representations, especially graphical ones, that are readily accessible, and the kinds of applications of mathematics that are appropriate to address. One of the biggest shifts has been to emphasize the ideas of pattern, function, and variation.[172] This new focus is particularly amenable to approaches that begin in the elementary grades and continue through middle school, and a sizable body of instructional materials has been developed that reflects this emphasis.[173] But the long-term impact of these materials is as yet unknown.

Recent research on measurement and geometry suggests that children's development of geometric reasoning can be greatly enhanced in instructional environments that are specifically designed to promote such understanding and that children's thinking may fluctuate across stages identified by earlier researchers. Furthermore, computer technologies offer the promise of being able to support developing understanding in ways not available before.

Unlike the domains of measurement and geometry, research on the development of concepts of statistics and probability indicates that, especially for probability, very young children are capable of less than developmental theories might predict. Fundamental concepts in both domains, such as the conventions of scaling in graphs and the makeup of the sample space, need more careful attention in initial instruction. As in the areas of measurement and geometry, technology offers promise for helping to support and link students' developing conceptions of data and chance. It is still an open question when and how many of the central conceptual structures of probability and statistics should be introduced in the elementary and middle grades.

Notes

1. Kieran, 1992.
2. Mason, Graham, Pimm, and Gowar, 1985, p. 38.
3. Bochner, 1966.
4. This characterization of the main activities of school algebra is based on a categorization by Kieran, 1996. A number of different characterizations of algebra can be found in the literature. For example, Usiskin, 1988, listed four conceptions of algebra: generalized arithmetic, study of procedures for solving certain kinds of problems, study of relationships among quantities, and study of structures. The National Council of Teachers of Mathematics, 1997, offers four organizing themes for school algebra: functions and relations, modeling, structure, and language and representation. Kaput, 1995, identified five aspects of algebra: generalization and formalization; syntactically guided manipulations; study of structure; study of

functions, relations, and joint variation; and modeling language. Any one of these characterizations would have led to a somewhat different organization of the research we review.

5. Lee and Wheeler, 1987.
6. Boero, 1993.
7. Pimm, 1995.
8. Wenger, 1987.
9. For example, Kirshner and Awtry, in press.
10. For example, Booth, 1984, and Greeno, 1982.
11. Kirshner, 1989.
12. Carry, Lewis, and Bernard, 1980; Wenger, 1987.
13. Wenger, 1987.
14. Greeno, 1982.
15. Lee and Wheeler, 1987.
16. Nhouyvanisvong, 2001.
17. Thompson, Philipp, Thompson, and Boyd, 1994.
18. See Swafford and Langrall, 2000, for research using exponential and inverse variation functions with sixth graders; Rojano, 1996, for research involving systems of linear equations; and Bednarz, Radford, and Janvier, 1995, and Radford, 1994, for research using situations with more than one unknown.
19. Phillips, Smith, Star, and Herbel-Eisenmann, 1998. For a rationale, see Confrey, 1994, and Confrey and Smith, 1994, 1995.
20. For example, Heid, 1990. In an historical and theoretical discussion, Kaput, 1994, goes further to argue that, with technology, many of the ideas of calculus are accessible without relying on traditional algebraic skills.
21. Thompson, Philipp, Thompson, and Boyd, 1994.
22. Behr, Erlwanger, and Nichols, 1980; Kieran, 1981; Saenz-Ludlow and Walgamuth, 1998.
23. Vergnaud, Benhadj, and Dussouet, 1979.
24. Ball and Bass, 1999. See also Ball and Bass, 2001.
25. Carraher, Brizuela, and Schliemann, 2000; Schliemann, Carraher, and Brizuela, 2000.
26. Blanton and Kaput, 2000.
27. Carpenter and Levi, 1999.
28. For example, Küchemann, 1978, 1981; Kieran, 1983; Wagner, Rachlin, and Jensen, 1984.
29. Booth, 1984.
30. Booth, 1984, p. 45.
31. Booth, 1984, p. 44.
32. Noss, Hoyles, and Healy, 1997.
33. Clement, 1982; Clement, Lochhead, and Monk, 1981; Fisher, 1988; Kaput and Sims-Knight, 1983; Lochhead, 1980; MacGregor and Stacey, 1993; Rosnick, 1981; Rosnick and Clement, 1980; Sims-Knight and Kaput, 1983.
34. By analyzing interview transcripts, Clement, Lockhead, and Monk, 1981, found that some students simply translated the words of the problem directly into mathematical

symbols. Other students who gave the same incorrect answer drew a diagram showing six students and one professor and seemed to think of S and P as units of measure rather than variables. They thought it just as sensible to write $6S = P$ as to write 12 in. = 1 ft.

35. Rosnick and Clement, 1980.
36. Kaput and Sims-Knight, 1983.
37. Soloway, Lochhead, and Clement, 1982.
38. Sutherland and Rojano, 1993.
39. Sutherland, 1993.
40. Kalchman, Moss, and Cass, 2001; Koedinger, Anderson, Hadley, and Mark, 1997.
41. Sutherland, 1993.
42. For example, Davis and Pobjoy, 1995; Sutherland, Jinich, Mochón, Molyneux, and Rojano, 1996.
43. Koedinger, Anderson, Hadley, and Mark, 1997; Moreno, Rojano, Bonilla, and Perrusquia, 1999; Rojano, 1999.
44. Koedinger and Anderson, 1998.
45. Koedinger, Anderson, Hadley, and Mark, 1997.
46. For example, Borba and Confrey, 1996.
47. Fey, 1989b; Heid, 1988; Heid, Sheets, Matras, and Menasian, 1988; O'Callaghan, 1998.
48. Heid, Sheets, Matras, and Menasian, 1988, p. 2.
49. Heid, 1988.
50. Huntley, Rasmussen, Villarubi, Sangtong, and Fey, 2000.
51. Huntley, Rasmussen, Villarubi, Sangtong, and Fey, 2000.
52. Streun, Harskamp, and Suhre, 2000.
53. Kieran, 1982, 1984.
54. Chaiklin and Lesgold, 1984.
55. Collis, 1975.
56. Whitman, 1976.
57. Kieran, 1988.
58. Kieran and Sfard, 1999.
59. Linchevski and Vinner, 1990.
60. Huntley, Rasmussen, Villarubi, Sangtong, and Fey, 2000, p. 357.
61. Kieran and Sfard, 1999; Thompson and Thompson, 1987.
62. Usiskin, 1998, pp. 17–18.
63. Fey, 1989a, pp. 206–207.
64. Huntley, Rasmussen, Villarubi, Sangtong, and Fey, 2000.
65. Huntley, Rasmussen, Villarubi, Sangtong, and Fey, 2000, p. 357.
66. Lee and Wheeler, 1987, p. 149.
67. See "Building Blocks" in Chapter 3 for several other approaches to this problem.
68. Arzarello, 1992; Swafford and Langrall, 2000.
69. See, for example, Heid, Sheets, Matras, and Menasian, 1988.
70. Arcavi, 1994.
71. Edwards, 1990.

72. Peak, 1996, p. 38.
73. Mitchell, Hawkins, Jakwerth, Stancavage, and Dossey, 1999, p. 216.
74. Blanton and Kaput, 2000; Carpenter and Levi, 1999; Carraher, Brizuela, and Schliemann, 2000; Schliemann, Carraher, and Brizuela, 2000.
75. Piaget and Inhelder, 1956; Piaget, Inhelder, and Szeminska, 1960.
76. E.g., Hiebert, 1981a, 1984.
77. See Freudenthal, 1983, pp. 1–27, for an extended discussion of conceptual issues in understanding length.
78. Carpenter, 1975; Carpenter and Lewis, 1976; Hiebert, 1981b.
79. Lindquist, 1989; Miller and Baillargeon, 1990.
80. Hiebert, 1981a, 1984.
81. Lehrer, Jenkins, and Osana, 1998.
82. Lehrer, Jacobson, Thoyre, Demeny, Strom, Horvath, Gance, and Koehler, 1998. For further discussion of measure see Lehrer, Jacobson, Kemeny, and Strom, 1999.
83. Clements, Battista, and Sarama, 1998.
84. Lehrer, Jacobson, Kemeny, and Strom, 1999; McClain, Cobb, Gravemeijer, and Estes, 1999.
85. Lehrer and Schauble, 2000b, 2000c.
86. Wertsch, 1998.
87. Lehrer, Jenkins, and Osana, 1998.
88. Lehrer, Jenkins, and Osana, 1998.
89. Battista, Clements, Arnoff, Battista, Van Auken Borrow, 1998. For similar work in three dimensions see Battista, 1999.
90. Lehrer, Jacobson, Thoyre, Demeny, Strom, Horvath, Gance, and Koehler, 1998.
91. Battista, 1999; Battista and Clements, 1998.
92. Lehrer and Schauble, 2000a.
93. Van Hiele, 1957/1984b, 1959/1984a; Van Hiele-Geldof, 1957/1984. See also Burger and Shaughnessy, 1986.
94. Fuys, Geddes, and Tischler, 1988.
95. Lehrer, Jenkins, and Osana, 1998. See also Gutiérrez, Jaime, and Fortuny, 1991.
96. Clements, Swaminathan, Hannibal, and Sarama, 1999.
97. Clements and Battista, in press.
98. Kay, 1986/1987.
99. Carpenter, Corbitt, Kepner, Lindquist, and Reys, 1981.
100. Lehrer, Randle, and Sancilio, 1989.
101. Lehrer, Jenkins, and Osana; 1998.
102. Gagatsis and Patronis, 1990.
103. Clements, 2000, pp. 24–25.
104. Carpenter, Coburn, Reys, and Wilson, 1976.
105. Lehrer, Jenkins, and Osana, 1998.
106. Nieuwoudt and van Niekerk, 1997.
107. Freudenthal, 1973. See Matos, 1999, for a discussion of seven metaphoric models of angle.
108. Henderson, 1996.

109. Clements and Battista, 1989.
110. Lehrer, Jacobson, Thoyre, Demeny, Strom, Horvath, Gance, and Koehler, 1998.
111. Mitchelmore, 1998; Lehrer, Jacobson, Thoyre, Demeny, Strom, Horvath, Gance, and Koehler, 1998.
112. Clements and Battista, 1989, 1990; Lehrer, Randle, and Sancilio, 1989.
113. See, for example, Clements, Battista, Sarama, and Swaminathan, 1996.
114. Lehrer, Randle, and Sancilio, 1989.
115. Mitchelmore, 1993; Mitchelmore and White, 2000.
116. Clements, Battista, Sarama, and Swaminathan, 1996.
117. Lehrer and Chazan, 1998.
118. The Geometer's Sketchpad, Cabri, and other "dynamic geometry" software allow students to construct geometric figures on the computer screen just as students and mathematicians for centuries have used a ruler (or straightedge) and a compass to construct figures on paper. A significant advantage of such software is that when points, lines, and circles are changed (through dragging with the computer's mouse), all dependent figures change automatically.
119. Polydrons are rigid plastic geometric figures such as triangles, squares, and pentagons that click together in ways that allow students to create three-dimensional figures such as cubes, pyramids, and octahedrons.
120. Vurpillot, 1976.
121. Vurpillot, 1976.
122. Genkins, 1975.
123. Confrey, 1992.
124. Sophian and Crosby, 1998.
125. Williford, 1972.
126. Clements, Battista, Sarama, and Swaminathan, 1997; Del Grande, 1986/1987.
127. Perham, 1978; Schultz and Austin, 1983; Rosser, Ensing, Glider, and Lane, 1984.
128. Clements and Battista, in press; Jacobson and Lehrer, 2000.
129. Watt, 1998.
130. Zech, Vye, Bransford, Goldman, Barron, Schwartz, Kisst-Hackett, Mayfield-Stewart, and the Cognition and Technology Group, 1998.
131. Penner and Lehrer, 2000.
132. Raghavan, Sartoris, and Glaser, 1998.
133. Lehrer, Schauble, Strom, and Pligge, 2001.
134. Middleton and Corbett, 1998.
135. Friel, Bright, Frierson, and Kader, 1997; Jones, Langrall, Thornton, and Mogill, 1997; Jones, Thornton, Langrall, and Tarr, 1999; Metz, 1997, 1998; Mooney, 1999; Piaget and Inhelder, 1951/1975; Watson, 1997; Watson, Collis, and Moritz, 1997.
136. Jones, Thornton, Langrall, Mooney, Perry, and Putt, 2000; Mooney, 1992.
137. Curcio, 1987.
138. Beaton, Mullis, Martin, Gonzalez, Kelly, and Smith, 1996; Bright and Friel, 1998; Jones, Thornton, Langrall, Mooney, Wares, Perry, and Putt, 1999; Jones, Thornton, Langrall, Mooney, Perry, and Putt, 2000; Pereira-Mendoza and Mellor, 1991.

139. Jones, Thornton, Langrall, Mooney, Wares, Perry, and Putt, 1999; Jones, Thornton, Langrall, Mooney, Perry, and Putt, 2000.
140. Moore, 1997.
141. Jones, Thornton, Langrall, Mooney, Wares, Perry, and Putt, 1999; Jones, Thornton, Langrall, Mooney, Perry, and Putt, 2000.
142. Strauss and Bichler, 1988.
143. Mokros and Russell, 1995.
144. Bright and Friel, 1998.
145. Strauss and Bichler, 1988.
146. Mokros and Russell, 1995.
147. Mullis, Martin, Beaton, Gonzalez, Kelly, and Smith, 1997, pp. 96–97; Zawojewski and Heckman, 1997.
148. Jones, Thornton, Langrall, Mooney, Wares, Perry, and Putt, 1999.
149. Berg and Phillips, 1994; Mevarech and Kramarsky, 1997.
150. Curcio, 1987, 1989.
151. Putt, Jones, Thornton, Perry, Langrall, and Mooney, 1999.
152. Pereira-Mendoza and Mellor, 1991. For further discussion of children's construction, use, and interpretation of graphs, see Zawojewski and Heckman, 1997.
153. For example, Piaget and Inhelder, 1951/1975, and Tversky and Kahneman, 1974.
154. For example, Amir and Williams, 1999; Fischbein, Barbat, and Minzat, 1971; and Fischbein and Schnarch, 1997.
155. For a synthesis of research in probability and statistics, see Shaughnessy, 1992.
156. Borovcnik and Bentz, 1991; English, 1991, 1993; Jones, 1974/1975; Jones, Langrall, Thornton, and Mogill, 1997, 1999; Piaget and Inhelder, 1951/1975.
157. Jones, Langrall, Thornton, and Mogill, 1997, 1999. For older students, see also Borovcnik and Bentz, 1991, commenting on data from Green, 1982.
158. English, 1991, 1993.
159. Schroeder, 1988.
160. For example, Acredolo, O'Conner, Banks, and Horobin, 1989; Jones, Langrall, Thornton, and Mogill, 1997, 1999; Perner, 1979; Piaget and Inhelder, 1951/1975.
161. Acredolo, O'Conner, Banks, and Horobin, 1989.
162. Jones, Langrall, Thornton, and Mogill, 1999.
163. For example, Falk, 1983; Fischbein, Nello, and Marino, 1991; Jones, Langrall, Thornton, and Mogill, 1997, 1999.
164. Falk, 1983.
165. Fischbein and Gazit, 1984; Jones, Langrall, Thornton, and Mogill, 1997, 1999; Tarr and Jones, 1997.
166. Fischbein and Gazit, 1984.
167. Tarr and Jones, 1997.
168. Jones, Langrall, Thornton, and Mogill, 1997, 1999.
169. Fischbein, Nello, and Marino, 1991.
170. Brown, Carpenter, Kouba, Lindquist, Silver, and Swafford, 1988; Green, 1983; Tarr and Jones, 1997.

171. Tversky and Kahneman, 1974. See Shaughnessy, 1992, pp. 470–473, for a discussion.
172. Fey, 1989a, 1989b.
173. See, for example, Phillips, Gardella, Kelly, and Stewart, 1994.

References

Acredolo, C., O'Connor, J., Banks, L., & Horobin, K. (1989). Students' ability to make probability estimates: Skills revealed through application of Anderson's functional measurement methodology. *Student Development, 60*, 933–945.

Amir, G. S., & Williams, J. S. (1999). Cultural influences on children's probabilistic thinking. *Journal of Mathematical Behavior, 18*, 85–107.

Arcavi, A. (1994). Symbol sense: Informal sense-making in formal mathematics. *For the Learning of Mathematics, 14*(3), 24–35.

Arzarello, F. (1992). Pre-algebraic problem solving. In J. P. Ponte, J. F. Matos, J. M. Matos, & D. Fernandes (Eds.), *Mathematical problem solving and new information technologies* (NATO ASI Series, vol. 89, pp. 155–166). Berlin: Springer-Verlag.

Ball, D. L., & Bass, H. (1999, June). What counts as an explanation in math class? Interdisciplinary analysis of teaching. Paper presented at the mathematics education seminar series of the Weizmann Institute of Science, Rehovot, Israel.

Ball, D. L., & Bass, H. (2001). What mathematical knowledge is entailed in teaching children to reason mathematically? In National Research Council, *Knowing and learning mathematics for teaching: Proceedings of a workshop* (pp. 26–34). Washington, DC: National Academy Press. Available: http://books.nap.edu/catalog/10050.html. [July 10, 2001].

Battista, M. T. (1999). Fifth graders' enumeration of cubes in 3D arrays: Conceptual progress in an inquiry classroom. *Journal for Research in Mathematics Education, 30*, 417–448.

Battista, M. T., & Clements, D. H. (1998). Students' understanding of three-dimensional cube arrays: Findings from a research and curriculum development project. In R. Lehrer & D. Chazan (Eds.), *Designing learning environments for developing understanding of geometry and space* (pp. 227–248). Mahwah, NJ: Erlbaum.

Battista, M. T., Clements, D. H., Arnoff, J., Battista, K., & Van Auken Borrow, C. (1998). Students' spatial structuring of 2D arrays of squares. *Journal for Research in Mathematics Education, 29*, 503–532.

Beaton, A. E., Mullis, I. V. S., Martin, M. O., Gonzalez, E. J., Kelly, D. L., & Smith, T. A. (1996). *Mathematics achievement in the middle school years: IEA's Third International Mathematics and Science Study (TIMSS)*. Chestnut Hill, MA: Boston College, Center for the Study of Testing, Evaluation, and Educational Policy. Available: http://www.timss.org/timss1995i/MathB.html. [July 10, 2001].

Bednarz, N., Radford, L., & Janvier, B. (1995). Algebra as a problem-solving tool: One unknown or several unknowns? In L. Meira & D. Carraher (Eds.), *Proceedings of the nineteenth international conference for the Psychology of Mathematics Education* (vol. 3, pp. 160–167). Recife, Brazil: Federal University of Pernambuco. (ERIC Document Reproduction Service No. ED 411 136).

Behr, M., Erlwanger, S., & Nichols, E. (1980). How children view the equal sign. *Mathematics Teaching, 92*, 13–15.

Bell, A. (1995). Purpose in school algebra. In C. Kieran (Ed.), New perspectives on school algebra: Papers and discussions of the ICME-7 Algebra Working Group [Special issue]. *Journal of Mathematical Behavior, 14,* 41–73.

Berg, C. A., & Phillips, D. G. (1994). An investigation of the relationship between logical thinking structures and the ability to construct and interpret line graphs. *Journal of Research in Science Teaching, 31,* 323–344.

Blanton, M., & Kaput, J. (2000). Characterizing generative and self-sustaining teacher change in a classroom practice that promotes students' algebraic thinking. In T. Nakahara & M. Koyama (Eds.), *Proceedings of the Twenty-fourth International Conference for the Psychology of Mathematics Education* (vol. 1, p. 144). Hiroshima, Japan: PME Program Committee.

Bochner, S. (1966). *The role of mathematics in the rise of science.* Princeton, NJ: Princeton University Press.

Boero, P. (1993). About the transformation function of the algebraic code. In R. Sutherland (Ed.), *Algebraic processes and the role of symbolism* (pp. 55–62). London: University of London, Institute of Education.

Booth, L. R. (1984). *Algebra: Children's strategies and errors.* Windsor, UK: NFER-Nelson.

Borba, M. C., & Confrey, J. (1996). A student's construction of transformations of functions in a multiple representational environment. *Educational Studies in Mathematics, 31,* 319–337.

Borovcnik, M. G., & Bentz, H. J. (1991). Empirical research in understanding probability. In R. Kapadia & M. Borovcnik (Eds.), *Chance encounters: Probability in education* (pp. 73–105). Dordrecht, The Netherlands: Kluwer.

Bright, G. W., & Friel, S. N. (1998). Graphical representations: Helping students interpret data. In S. P. Lajoie (Ed.), *Reflections on statistics: Learning, teaching, and assessment in grades K-12* (pp. 63–88). Mahwah, NJ: Erlbaum.

Brown, C. A., Carpenter, T. P., Kouba, V. L., Lindquist, M. M., Silver, E. A., & Swafford, J. O. (1988). Secondary school results for the fourth NAEP mathematics assessment: Discrete mathematics, data organization and interpretation, measurement, number and operations. *Mathematics Teacher, 81,* 241–248.

Burger, W., & Shaughnessy, M. (1986). Characterizing the van Hiele levels of development in geometry. *Journal for Research in Mathematics Education, 17,* 31–48.

Carpenter, T. P. (1975). Measurement concepts of first- and second-grade students. *Journal for Research in Mathematics Education, 6,* 3–13.

Carpenter, T. P., Coburn, T., Reys, R., & Wilson, J. (1976). Notes from National Assessment: Recognizing and naming solids. *Arithmetic Teacher, 23,* 62–66.

Carpenter, T. P., Corbitt, M. K., Kepner, H. S., Jr., Lindquist, M. M., & Reys, R. E. (1981). *Results from the second mathematics assessment of the National Assessment of Educational Progress.* Reston, VA: National Council of Teachers of Mathematics.

Carpenter, T. P., & Levi, L. (1999, April). Developing conceptions of algebraic reasoning in the primary grades. Paper presented at the meeting of the American Educational Research Association, Montreal.

Carpenter, T. P., & Lewis, R. (1976). The development of the concept of a standard unit of measure in young children. *Journal for Research in Mathematics Education, 7,* 53–64.

Carraher, D., Brizuela, B., & Schliemann, A. (2000). Bringing out the algebraic character of arithmetic: Instantiating variables in addition and subtraction. In T. Nakahara &

M. Koyama (Eds.), *Proceedings of the Twenty-fourth International Conference for the Psychology of Mathematics Education* (vol. 2, pp. 145–152). Hiroshima, Japan: PME Program Committee.

Carry, L. R., Lewis, C., & Bernard, J. (1980). *Psychology of equation solving: An information processing study* (Final Technical Report). Austin: University of Texas at Austin, Department of Curriculum and Instruction. (ERIC Document Reproduction Service No. ED 186 243).

Chaiklin, S., & Lesgold, S. (1984, April). Prealgebra students' knowledge of algebraic tasks with arithmetic expressions. Paper presented at the meeting of the American Educational Research Association, New Orleans. (ERIC Document Reproduction Service No. ED 247 147).

Clement, J. (1982). Algebra word problem solutions: Thought processes underlying a common misconception. *Journal for Research in Mathematics Education, 13,* 16–30.

Clement, J., Lochhead, J., & Monk, G. (1981). Translation difficulties in learning mathematics. *American Mathematical Monthly, 88,* 286–290.

Clements, D. H. (2000). *Geometric and spatial thinking in early childhood education.* Paper presented at the meeting of the National Council of Teachers of Mathematics, San Francisco.

Clements, D. H., & Battista, M. T. (in press). *Logo and geometry* (Journal for Research in Mathematics Education Monograph Series). Reston, VA: National Council of Teachers of Mathematics.

Clements, D. H, & Battista, M.T. (1990). The effects of Logo on children's conceptualizations of angle and polygons. *Journal for Research in Mathematics Education, 21,* 356–371.

Clements, D. H., & Battista, M. T. (1989). Learning of geometric concepts in a Logo environment. *Journal for Research in Mathematics Education, 20,* 450–467.

Clements, D. H., Battista, M. T., & Sarama, J. (1998). Development of geometric and measurement ideas. In R. Lehrer & D. Chazan (Eds.), *Designing learning environments for developing understanding of geometry and space* (pp. 201–225). Mahwah, NJ: Erlbaum.

Clements, D. H., Battista, M. T., Sarama, J., & Swaminathan, S. (1996). Development of turn and turn measurement concepts in a computer-based instructional unit. *Educational Studies in Mathematics, 30,* 313–337.

Clements, D. H., Battista, M. T., Sarama, J., & Swaminathan, S. (1997). Development of students' spatial thinking in a unit on geometric motions and area. *Elementary School Journal, 98,* 171–186.

Clements, D. H., Swaminathan, S., Hannibal, M. A. Z., & Sarama, J. (1999). Young children's concepts of shape. *Journal for Research in Mathematics Education, 30,* 192–212.

Collis, K. F. (1975). *The development of formal reasoning.* Newcastle, Australia: University of Newcastle.

Confrey, J. (1992, April). First graders' understanding of similarity. Paper presented at the meeting of the American Educational Research Association, San Francisco.

Confrey, J. (1994). Splitting, similarity, and the rate of change: New approaches to multiplication and exponential functions. In G. Harel & J. Confrey (Eds.), *The development of multiplicative reasoning in the learning of mathematics* (pp. 291–330). Albany: State University of New York Press.

Confrey, J., & Smith, E. (1994). Exponential functions, rates of change, and the multiplicative unit. *Educational Studies in Mathematics, 26,* 135–164.

Confrey, J., & Smith, E. (1995). Splitting, covariation, and their role in the development of exponential functions. *Journal for Research in Mathematics Education, 26,* 66–86.

Crosby, A. W. (1997). *The measure of reality.* Cambridge: Cambridge University Press.

Curcio, F. R. (1987). Comprehension of mathematical relationships expressed in graphs. *Journal for Research in Mathematics Education, 18,* 382–393.

Curcio, F. R. (1989). *Developing graph comprehension.* Reston, VA: National Council of Teachers of Mathematics.

Davis, G. E., & Pobjoy, M. (1995). Spreadsheets as constructivist tools for the learning and teaching of mathematics. In O. P. Ahuja (Ed.), *Quality mathematics education in developing countries* (pp. 25–56). New Delhi: UBSPD.

Del Grande, J. J. (1987). Can grade two children's spatial perception be improved by inserting a transformation geometry component into their mathematics program? (Doctoral dissertation, University of Toronto, 1986). *Dissertation Abstracts International, 47*(10), 3689A.

Edwards, E. L., Jr. (Ed.). (1990). *Algebra for everyone.* Reston, VA: National Council of Teachers of Mathematics.

Ellis, S., Siegler, R. S., & Van Voorhis, F. E. (in preparation). Developmental changes in children's understanding of measurement procedures and principles.

English, L. D. (1991). Young children's combinatoric strategies. *Educational Studies in Mathematics, 22,* 451–474.

English, L. D. (1993). Children's strategies for solving two- and three-stage combinatorial problems. *Journal for Research in Mathematics Education, 24,* 255–273.

Falk, R. (1983). Children's choice behaviour in probabilistic situations. In D. R. Grey, P. Holmes, V. Barnett, & G. M. Constable (Eds.), *Proceedings of the First International Conference on Teaching Statistics* (vol. 2, pp. 714–716). Sheffield, UK: University of Sheffield. (ERIC Document Reproduction Service No. ED 262 977).

Fey, J. (1989a). Technology and mathematics education: A survey of recent developments and important problems. *Educational Studies in Mathematics, 20,* 237–272.

Fey, J. T. (1989b). School algebra for the year 2000. In S. Wagner & C. Kieran (Eds.), *Research issues in the learning and teaching of algebra* (pp. 199–213). Reston, VA: National Council of Teachers of Mathematics; Hillsdale, NJ: Erlbaum.

Fey, J. T., Heid, M. K., with Good, R.A., Sheets, C., Blume, G. W., & Zbiek, R. M. (1999). *Concepts in algebra: A technological approach.* Chicago: Everyday Learning.

Fischbein, E., & Gazit, A. (1984). Does the teaching of probability improve probabilistic intuitions? *Educational Studies in Mathematics, 15,* 1–24.

Fischbein, E., & Schnarch, D. (1997). The evolution with age of probabilistic intuitively based misconceptions. *Journal for Research in Mathematics Education, 28,* 96–105.

Fischbein, E., Barbat, I., & Minzat, I. (1971). Intuitions primaires et intuitions secondaires dans l'initiation aux probabilités [Primary and secondary intuitions in introductory probability]. *Educational Studies in Mathematics, 4,* 264–280.

Fischbein, E., Nello, M. S., & Marino, M. S. (1991). Factors affecting probabilistic judgments in students and adolescents. *Educational Studies in Mathematics, 22,* 523–549.

Fisher, K. M. (1988). The students and professors problem revisited. *Journal for Research in Mathematics Education, 19*, 260–262.

Freudenthal, H. (1973). *Mathematics as an educational task.* Dordrecht, The Netherlands: Reidel.

Freudenthal, H. (1983). *Didactical phenomenology of mathematical structures.* Dordrecht, The Netherlands: Reidel.

Friel, S. N., Bright, G. W., Frierson, D., & Kader, G. (1997). A framework for assessing knowledge and learning in statistics (K–8). In I. Gal & J B. Garfield (Eds.), *The assessment challenge in statistics education* (pp. 55–64). Amsterdam, The Netherlands: International Statistical Institute.

Fuys, D., Geddes, D., & Tischler, R. (1988). *The van Hiele model of thinking in geometry among adolescents* (Journal for Research in Mathematics Education Monograph No. 3). Reston, VA: National Council of Teachers of Mathematics.

Gagatsis, A., & Patronis, T. (1990). Using geometrical models in a process of reflective thinking in learning and teaching mathematics. *Educational Studies in Mathematics, 21*, 29–54.

Genkins, E. F. (1975). The concept of bilateral symmetry in young children. In M. F. Rosskopf (Ed.), *Children's mathematical concepts: Six Piagetian studies in mathematics education* (pp 5–43). New York: Teachers College Press.

Gravemeijer, K. P. (1998). From a different perspective: Building on students' informal knowledge. In R. Lehrer & D. Chazan (Eds.), *Designing learning environments for developing understanding of geometry and space* (pp. 45–66). Mahwah, NJ: Erlbaum.

Green, D. R. (1983). A survey of probability concepts in 3000 pupils aged 11–16 years. In D. R. Grey, P. Holmes, V. Barnett, & G. M. Constable (Eds.), *Proceedings of the First International Conference on Teaching Statistics* (vol. 2, pp. 766–783). Sheffield, UK: University of Sheffield. (ERIC Document Reproduction Service No. ED 262 977).

Greeno, J. G. (1982, March). A cognitive learning analysis of algebra. Paper presented at the meeting of the American Educational Research Association, Boston.

Gutiérrez, A., Jaime, A., & Fortuny, J. M. (1991). An alternative paradigm to evaluate the acquisition of the van Hiele levels. *Journal for Research in Mathematics Education, 22*, 237–251.

Heid, M. K. (1988). *"Algebra with Computers": A description and an evaluation of student performance and attitudes* (Report submitted to the State College Area School District Board of Education). State College: Pennsylvania State University.

Heid, M. K. (1990). Uses of technology in prealgebra and beginning algebra. *Mathematics Teacher, 83*, 194–198.

Heid, M. K., Sheets, C., Matras, M. A., & Menasian, J. (1988, April). Classroom and computer lab interaction in a computer-intensive algebra curriculum. Paper presented at the meeting of the American Educational Research Association, New Orleans.

Henderson, D. W. (1996). *Experiencing geometry on plane and sphere.* Upper Saddle River, NJ: Prentice Hall.

Hiebert, J. (1981a). Cognitive development and learning linear measurement. *Journal for Research in Mathematics Education, 12*, 197–211.

Hiebert, J. (1981b). Units of measure: Results and implications from national assessment. *Arithmetic Teacher, 28*, 38–43.

Hiebert, J. (1984). Why do some children have trouble learning measurement concepts? *Arithmetic Teacher, 31,* 19–24.

Huntley, M. A., Rasmussen, C. L., Villarubi, R. S., Sangtong, J., & Fey, J. T. (2000). Effects of standards-based mathematics education: A study of the Core-Plus Mathematics Project algebra and functions strand. *Journal for Research in Mathematics Education, 31,* 328–361.

Jacobson, C., & Lehrer, R. (2000). Teacher appropriation and student learning of geometry through design. *Journal for Research in Mathematics Education, 31,* 71–88.

Jones, G. A. (1975). The performances of first, second, and third grade children on five concepts of probability and the effects of grade, I.Q., and embodiments on their performances (Doctoral dissertation, Indiana University, 1974). *Dissertation Abstracts International, 35*(07), 4272A–4273A.

Jones, G. A., Langrall, C. W., Thornton, C. A., & Mogill, A. T. (1997). A framework for assessing and nurturing young children's thinking in probability. *Educational Studies in Mathematics, 32,* 101–125.

Jones, G. A., Langrall, C. W., Thornton, C. A., & Mogill, A. T. (1999). Students' probabilistic thinking in instruction. *Journal for Research in Mathematics Education, 30,* 487–519.

Jones, G. A., Thornton, C. A., Langrall, C. W., & Tarr, J. E. (1999). Understanding students' probability reasoning. In L. V. Stiff & F. R. Curcio (Eds.), *Developing mathematical reasoning in grades K-12* (1999 Yearbook of the National Council of Teachers of Mathematics, pp. 146–155). Reston, VA: NCTM.

Jones, G. A., Thornton, C. A., Langrall, C. W., Mooney, E. S., Perry, B., & Putt, I. J. (2000). A framework for characterizing children's statistical thinking. *Mathematical Thinking and Learning, 2,* 269–307.

Jones, G. A., Thornton, C. A., Langrall, C. W., Mooney, E. S., Wares, A., Perry, B., & Putt, I. A. (1999). *Using students' statistical thinking to inform instruction.* Paper presented at the research presession of the meeting of the National Council of Teachers of Mathematics, San Francisco.

Kalchman, N., Moss, J., & Case, R. (2001). Psychological models for the development of mathematical understanding: Rational numbers and functions. In S. Carver & D. Klahr (Eds.), *Cognition and instruction: Twenty-five years of progress* (pp. 1–38). Mahwah, NJ: Erlbaum.

Kaput, J. J. (1994). Democratizing access to calculus: New roads to old roots. In A. H. Schoenfeld (Ed.), *Mathematical thinking and problem solving* (pp. 77–156). Hillsdale, NJ: Erlbaum.

Kaput, J. J. (1995). A research base supporting long term algebra reform? In D. T. Owens, M. K. Reed, & G. M. Millsaps (Eds.), *Proceedings of the Seventeenth Annual Meeting of the North American Chapter of the International Group for the Psychology of Mathematics Education* (vol. 1, pp. 71–94). Columbus, OH: ERIC Clearinghouse for Science, Mathematics, and Environmental Education. (ERIC Document Reproduction Service No. ED 389 539).

Kaput, J., & Sims-Knight, J. (1983). Errors in translations to algebraic equations: Roots and implications. *Focus on Learning Problems in Mathematics, 5*(3), 63–78.

Kay, C. S. (1987). Is a square a rectangle? The development of first-grade students' understanding of quadrilaterals with implications for the Van Hiele theory of the development of geometric thought (Doctoral dissertation, University of Georgia, 1986). *Dissertation Abstracts International, 47*(08), 2934A.

Kieran, C. (1981). Concepts associated with the equality symbol. *Educational Studies in Mathematics, 12*, 317–326.

Kieran, C. (1982, March). The learning of algebra: A teaching experiment. Paper presented at the meeting of the American Educational Research Association, New York. (ERIC Document Reproduction Service No. ED 216 884).

Kieran, C. (1983). Relationships between novices' views of algebraic letters and their use of symmetric and asymmetric equation-solving procedures. In J. C. Bergeron & N. Herscovics (Eds.), *Proceedings of the Fifth Annual Meeting of the North American Chapter of the International Group for the Psychology of Mathematics Education* (vol. 1, pp. 161–168). Montreal: University of Montreal. (ERIC Document Reproduction Service No. ED 289 688).

Kieran, C. (1984). A comparison between novice and more-expert algebra students on tasks dealing with the equivalence of equations. In J. M. Moser (Ed.), *Proceedings of the Sixth Annual Meeting of the North American Chapter of the International Group for the Psychology of Mathematics Education* (pp. 83–91). Madison: University of Wisconsin. (ERIC Document Reproduction Service No. ED 253 432).

Kieran, C. (1988). Two different approaches among algebra learners. In A. F. Coxford (Ed.), *The ideas of algebra, K-12* (1988 Yearbook of the National Council of Teachers of Mathematics, pp. 91–96). Reston, VA: NCTM.

Kieran, C. (1992). The learning and teaching of school algebra. In D. A. Grouws (Ed.), *Handbook of research on mathematics teaching and learning* (pp. 390–419). New York: Macmillan.

Kieran, C. (1996). The changing face of school algebra. In C. Alsina, J. Alvarez, B. Hodgson, C. Laborde, & A. Pérez (Eds.), *Eighth International Congress on Mathematical Education: Selected lectures* (pp. 271–290). Seville: S.A.E.M. Thales.

Kieran, C., & Sfard, A. (1999). Seeing through symbols: The case of equivalent expressions. *Focus on Learning Problems in Mathematics, 21*(1), 1–17.

Kirshner, D. (1989). The visual syntax of algebra. *Journal for Research in Mathematics Education, 20*, 274–287.

Kirshner, D., & Awtry, T. (in press). The visual salience of algebra transformational rules.

Koedinger, K. R., & Anderson, J. R. (1998). Illustrating principled design: The early evolution of a cognitive tutor for algebra symbolization. *Interactive Learning Environments, 5*, 161–180.

Koedinger, K. R., Anderson, J. R., Hadley, W. H., & Mark, M. A. (1997). Intelligent tutoring goes to school in the big city. *International Journal of Artificial Intelligence in Education, 8*, 30–43.

Küchemann, D. (1978). Children's understanding of numerical variables. *Mathematics in School, 7*(4), 23–26.

Küchemann, D. (1981). Algebra. In K. M. Hart (Ed.), *Children's understanding of mathematics: 11–16* (pp. 102–119). London: John Murray.

Lee, L., & Wheeler, D. (1987). *Algebraic thinking in high school students: Their conceptions of generalisation and justification* (Research report). Montreal: Concordia University, Mathematics Department.

Lehrer, R., & Chazan, D. (Eds.). (1998). *Designing learning environments for developing understanding of geometry and space.* Mahwah, NJ: Erlbaum.

Lehrer, R., Jacobson, C., Kemeny, V., & Strom, D. (1999). Building on children's intuitions to develop mathematical understanding of space. In E. Fennema & T. R. Romberg (Eds.), *Classrooms that promote understanding* (pp. 63–87). Mahwah, NJ: Erlbaum.

Lehrer, R., Jacobson, C., Thoyre, G., Demeny, V., Strom, D., Horvath, J., Gance, S., & Koehler, M. (1998). Developing understanding of geometry and space in the primary grades. In R. Lehrer & D. Chazan (Eds.), *Designing learning environments for developing understanding of geometry and space* (pp. 169–200). Mahwah, NJ: Erlbaum.

Lehrer, R., Jenkins, M., & Osana, H. (1998). Longitudinal study of children's reasoning about space and geometry. In R. Lehrer & D. Chazan (Eds.), *Designing learning environments for developing understanding of geometry and space* (pp. 137–167). Mahwah, NJ: Erlbaum.

Lehrer, R., Randle, L., & Sancilio, L. (1989). Learning pre-proof geometry with Logo. *Cognition and Instruction, 6,* 159–184.

Lehrer, R., & Schauble, L. (2000a). Inventing data structures for representational purposes: Elementary grade students' classification models. *Mathematical Thinking and Learning, 2,* 49–72.

Lehrer, R., & Schauble, L. (2000b). Modeling in mathematics and science. In R. Glaser (Ed.), *Advances in instructional psychology* (vol. 5, pp. 101–159). Mahwah, NJ: Erlbaum.

Lehrer, R., & Schauble, L. (2000c). The development of model-based reasoning. *Journal of Applied Developmental Psychology, 21*(1), 39–48.

Lehrer, R., Schauble, L., Strom, D., & Pligge, M. (2001). Similarity of form and substance: Modeling material kind. In S. Carver & D. Klahr (Eds.), *Cognition and instruction: Twenty-five years of progress* (pp. 39–74). Mahwah, NJ: Erlbaum.

Linchevski, L., & Vinner, S. (1990). Embedded figures and the structures of algebraic expressions. In G. Booker, P. Cobb, & T. N. de Mendicuti (Eds.), *Proceedings of the Fourteenth International Conference for the Psychology of Mathematics Education* (vol. 2, pp. 85–92). Oaxtepec, Mexico: PME Program Committee. (ERIC Document Reproduction Service No. ED 411 138).

Lindquist, M. (1989). The measurement standards. *Arithmetic Teacher, 37,* 22–26.

Lochhead, J. (1980). Faculty interpretations of simple algebraic statements: The professor's side of the equation. *Journal of Mathematical Behavior, 3,* 29–37.

MacGregor, M., & Stacey, K. (1993). Cognitive models underlying students' formulation of simple linear equations. *Journal for Research in Mathematics Education, 24,* 217–232.

Mason, J. (1996). Expressing generality and roots of algebra. In N. Bednarz, C. Kieran, & L. Lee (Eds.), *Approaches to algebra: Perspectives for research and teaching* (pp. 65–86). Dordrecht, The Netherlands: Kluwer.

Mason, J., Graham, A., Pimm, D., & Gowar, N. (1985). *Routes to/roots of algebra.* Milton Keynes, UK: Open University Press.

Matos, J. M. L. de. (1999). Cognitive models for the concept of angle (Unpublished doctoral dissertation, University of Georgia, 1999). *Dissertation Abstracts International, 60*(05), 1491A. Abstract available: http://wwwlib.umi.com/dissertations/fullcit/9928965. [July 10, 2001].

McClain, K., Cobb, P., Gravemeijer, K., & Estes, B. (1999). Developing mathematical reasoning within the context of measurement. In L. V. Stiff & F. R. Curcio (Eds.),

Developing mathematical reasoning in grades K-12 (1999 Yearbook of the National Council of Teachers of Mathematics, pp. 93–106). Reston, VA: NCTM.

Metz, K. E. (1997). Dimensions in the assessment of students' understanding and application of chance. In I. Gal & J. B. Garfield (Eds.), *The assessment challenge in statistics education* (pp. 223–238). Amsterdam, The Netherlands: International Statistical Institute.

Metz, K. E. (1998). Emergent ideas of chance and probability in primary grade children. In S. P. Lajoie (Ed.) *Reflections on statistics: Learning, teaching, and assessment in grades K-12* (pp. 149–174). Mahwah, NJ: Erlbaum.

Mevarech, Z. R., & Kramarsky, B. (1997). From verbal descriptions to graphic representations: Stability and change in students' alternative conceptions. *Educational Studies in Mathematics, 32,* 229–263.

Middleton, J., & Corbett, R. (1998). Sixth-grade students' conceptions of stability in engineering contexts. In R. Lehrer & D. Chazan (Eds.), *Designing learning environments for developing understanding of geometry and space* (pp. 249–265). Mahwah, NJ: Erlbaum.

Miller, K. F., & Baillargeon, R. (1990). Length and distance: Do preschoolers think that occlusion brings things together? *Developmental Psychology, 26,* 103–114.

Mitchell, J. H., Hawkins, E. F., Jakwerth, P. M., Stancavage, R. B., & Dossey, J. A. (1999). *Student work and teacher practices in mathematics* (NCES 1999-453). Washington, DC: National Center for Education Statistics. Available: http://nces.ed.gov/spider/webspider/1999453.shtml. [July 10, 2001].

Mitchelmore, M. C. (1993). The development of pre-angle concepts. In A. Baturo & L. Harris (Eds.), *New directions in geometry education: Proceedings of the third annual conference on Mathematics Teaching and Learning* (pp. 87–93). Brisbane, Australia: Centre for Mathematics and Science Education, Queensland University of Technology.

Mitchelmore, M. C. (1998). Young students' concepts of turning and angle. *Cognition and Instruction, 16,* 265–284.

Mitchelmore, M. C., & White, P. (2000). Development of angle concepts by progressive abstraction and generalisation. *Educational Studies in Mathematics, 41,* 209–238.

Mokros, J., & Russell, S. J. (1995). Children's concepts of average and representativeness. *Journal for Research in Mathematics Education, 26,* 20–39.

Mooney, E. S. (1992). Development of a middle school statistical thinking framework (Doctoral dissertation, Illinois State University, 1992). *Dissertation Abstracts International, 60*(04), 1056A.

Moore, D. S. (1997). *Statistics: Concepts and controversies* (4th ed.). New York: Freeman.

Moreno, L., Rojano, T., Bonilla, E., & Perrusquia, E. (1999). The incorporation of new technologies to school culture: The teaching of mathematics in secondary school. In F. Hitt & M. Santos (Eds.), *Proceedings of the Twenty-first Annual Meeting of the North American Chapter of the International Group for the Psychology of Mathematics Education* (vol. 2, pp. 827–832). Columbus, OH: ERIC Clearinghouse for Science, Mathematics, and Environmental Education. (ERIC Document Reproduction Service No. ED 433 998)

Mullis, I. V. S., Martin, M. O., Beaton, A. E., Gonzalez, E. J., Kelly, D. L., & Smith, T. A. (1997). Mathematics achievement in the primary school years: IEA's Third International Mathematics and Science Study (TIMSS). Chestnut Hill, MA: Boston College. Available: http://www.timss.org/timss1995i/Achievement.html. [July 10, 2001].

National Council of Teachers of Mathematics. (1997). *A framework for constructing a vision of algebra: A discussion document.* Reston, VA: National Council of Teachers of Mathematics.

Nhouyvanisvong, A. (2001). Enhancing mathematical competence and understanding: Using open-ended problems and informal strategies (Unpublished doctoral dissertation, Carnegie Mellon University, 1999). *Dissertation Abstracts International, 61*, 5010B.

Nieuwoudt, H. D., & van Niekerk, R. (1997, March). The spatial competence of young children through the development of solids. Paper presented at the meeting of the American Educational Research Association, Chicago.

Noss, R., Hoyles, C., & Healy, L. (1997). The construction of mathematical meanings: Connecting the visual with the symbolic. *Educational Studies in Mathematics, 33,* 203–233.

O'Callaghan, B. R. (1998). Computer-intensive algebra and students' conceptual knowledge of functions. *Journal for Research in Mathematics Education, 29,* 21–40.

Peak, L. (1996). *Pursuing excellence: A study of U.S. eighth-grade mathematics and science teaching, learning, curriculum, and achievement in an international context.* Washington, DC: National Center for Educational Statistics. Available: http://nces.ed.gov/spider/webspider/ 97198.shtml. [July 10, 2001].

Penner, E., & Lehrer, R. (2000). The shape of fairness. *Teaching Children Mathematics, 7,* 210–214.

Pereira-Mendoza, L., & Mellor, J. (1991). Students' concepts of bar graphs: Some preliminary findings. In D. Vere-Jones (Ed.), *Proceedings of the Third International Conference on Teaching Statistics* (vol. 1, pp. 150–157). Amsterdam, The Netherlands: International Statistical Institute.

Perham, F. (1978). An investigation into the effect of instruction on the acquisition of transformation geometry concepts in first grade children and subsequent transfer to general spatial ability. In R. Lesh & D. Mierkiewicz (Eds.), *Concerning the development of spatial and geometric concepts* (pp. 229–241). Columbus, OH: ERIC Clearinghouse for Science, Mathematics, and Environmental Education. (ERIC Document Reproduction Service No. ED 159 062).

Perner, J. (1979). Discrepant results in experimental studies of young children's understanding of probability. *Child Development, 50,* 1121–1127.

Phillips, E., with Gardella, T., Kelly, C., & Stewart, J. (1994). *Patterns and functions* (Curriculum and Evaluation Standards for School Mathematics Addenda Series, Grades 5-8, F. R. Curcio, Series Ed.). Reston, VA: National Council of Teachers of Mathematics.

Phillips, E.A., Smith, J.P., III, Star, J., & Herbel-Eisenmann, B. (1998). Algebra in the middle grades. *New England Mathematics Journal, 30*(2), 48–60.

Piaget, J., & Inhelder, B. (1956). *The child's conception of space.* London: Routledge & Kegan Paul. (Original work published 1948).

Piaget, J., & Inhelder, B. (1975). *The origin of the idea of chance in the child.* London: Routledge & Kegan Paul. (Original work published 1951).

Piaget, J., Inhelder, B., & Szeminska, A. (1960). *The child's conception of geometry.* New York: Basic Books.

Pimm, D. (1995). *Symbols and meanings in school mathematics.* London: Routledge.

Putt, I. J., Jones, G. A., Thornton, C.A., Perry, B., Langrall, C. W., & Mooney, E. S. (1999). Young students' informal statistical knowledge. *Teaching Statistics, 21,* 74–77.

Radford, L. (1994). Moving through systems of mathematical knowledge: From algebra with a single unknown to algebra with two unknowns. In J. P. da Ponte & J. F. Matos (Eds.), *Proceedings of the eighteenth international conference for the Psychology of Mathematics Education* (vol. 4, pp.73–80). Lisbon, Portugal: PME Program Committee. (ERIC Document Reproduction Service No. ED 383 537).

Raghavan, K., Sartoris, M. L., & Glaser, R. (1998). Interconnecting science and mathematics concepts. In R. Lehrer & D. Chazan (Eds.), *Designing learning environments for developing understanding of geometry and space* (pp. 267–295). Mahwah, NJ: Erlbaum.

Rojano, T. (1996). Developing algebraic aspects of problem solving within a spreadsheet environment. In N. Bednarz, C. Kieran, & L. Lee (Eds.), *Approaches to algebra: Perspectives for research and teaching* (pp. 137–145). Dordrecht, The Netherlands: Kluwer.

Rojano, T. (1999, April). The potential of spreadsheets in the learning of algebra. Paper presented at the meeting of the American Educational Research Association, Montreal.

Rosnick, P. (1981). Some misconceptions concerning the concept of variable. *Mathematics Teacher, 74, 418–420.*

Rosnick, P., & Clement, J. (1980). Learning without understanding: The effect of tutoring strategies on algebra misconceptions. *Journal of Mathematical Behavior, 3,* 3–27.

Rosser, R. A., Ensing, S. S., Glider, P. J., & Lane, S. (1984). An information-processing analysis of children's accuracy in predicting the appearance of rotated stimuli. *Child Psychology Monographs, 110,* 21–41.

Saenz-Ludlow, A., & Walgamuth, C. (1998). Third graders' interpretations of equality and the equal symbol. *Educational Studies in Mathematics, 35,* 153–187.

Schliemann, A. D., Carraher, D. W., & Brizuela, B. (2000, April). From quantities to ratio, functions, and algebraic relations. Paper presented at the meeting of the American Educational Research Association, New Orleans.

Schroeder, T. L. (1988). Elementary school children's use of strategy in playing microcomputer probability games. In R. Davidson & J. Swift (Eds.), *Proceedings of the Second International Conference on Teaching Statistics* (pp. 51–56). Victoria, BC: University of Victoria.

Schultz, K. A., & Austin, J. D. (1983). Directional effects in transformational tasks. *Journal for Research in Mathematics Education, 14,* 95–101.

Shaughnessy, J. M. (1992). Research in probability and statistics: Reflections and directions. In D. A. Grouws (Ed.), *Handbook of research on mathematics teaching and learning* (pp. 465–494). New York: Macmillan.

Sims-Knight, J., & Kaput, J. J. (1983). Exploring difficulties in transformations between natural language and image-based representations and abstract symbols systems of mathematics. In D. Rogers & J. Sloboda (Eds.), *The acquisition of symbolic skills* (pp. 561–569). New York: Plenum.

Soloway, E., Lochhead, J., & Clement, J. 1982). Does computer programming enhance problem solving ability? Some positive evidence on algebra word problems. In R. J. Seidel, R. E. Anderson, & B. Hunter (Eds.), *Computer literacy* (pp. 171–185). New York: Academic Press.

Sophian, C., & Crosby, M. E. (1998, August). Ratios that even young children understand: The case of spatial proportions. Paper presented at the meeting of the Cognitive Science Society of Ireland, Dublin, Ireland.

Strauss, S., & Bichler, E. (1988). The development of children's concepts of the arithmetic average. *Journal for Research in Mathematics Education, 19*, 64–80.

Streun, A. V., Harskamp, E., & Suhre, C. (2000). The effect of the graphic calculator on students' solution approaches: A secondary analysis. *Hiroshima Journal of Mathematics Education, 8*, 27–40.

Sutherland, R. (1993). Symbolising through spreadsheets. *Micromath, 10*(1), 20–22.

Sutherland, R., & Rojano, T. (1993). A spreadsheet approach to solving algebra problems. *Journal of Mathematical Behavior, 12*, 353–383.

Sutherland, R., Jinich, E., Mochón, S., Molyneux, S., & Rojano, T. (1996). *Mexican/British project on the role of spreadsheets within school-based mathematical practices* (Final report to the Spencer Foundation, Grant No. B-1493). Chicago: Spencer Foundation.

Swafford, J.O., & Langrall, C. (2000). Grade-six students' preinstructional use of equations to describe and represent problem situations. *Journal for Research in Mathematics Education, 31*, 89–112.

Tarr, J. E., & Jones, G. A. (1997). A framework for assessing middle school students' thinking in conditional probability and independence. *Mathematics Education Research Journal, 9*, 39–59.

Thompson, A. G., Philipp, R. A., Thompson, P. W., & Boyd, B. A. (1994). Calculational and conceptual orientations in teaching mathematics. In D. B. Aichele & A. F. Coxford (Eds.), *Professional development of teachers of mathematics* (1994 Yearbook of the National Council of Teachers of Mathematics, pp. 79–92). Reston, VA: NCTM.

Thompson, P., & Thompson, A. (1987). Computer presentations of structure in algebra. In J. C. Bergeron, N. Herscovics, & C. Kieran (Eds.), *Proceedings of the Eleventh International Conference for the Psychology of Mathematics Education* (vol. 1, pp. 248–254). Montreal: University of Montreal. (ERIC Document Reproduction Service No. ED 383 532)

Tversky, A., & Kahneman, D. (1974). Judgment under uncertainty: Heuristics and biases. *Science, 185*, 1124–1131.

Usiskin, Z. (1988). Conceptions of school algebra and uses of variable. In A. F. Coxford & A. P. Shulte (Eds.) *The ideas of algebra, K-12* (1988 Yearbook of the National Council of Teachers of Mathematics, pp. 8–19). Reston, VA: NCTM.

Usiskin, Z. (1998). Paper-and-pencil algorithms in a calculator-and-computer age. In L. J. Morrow & M. J. Kenney (Eds.), *The teaching and learning of algorithms in school mathematics* (1998 Yearbook of the National Council of Teachers of Mathematics, pp. 7–20). Reston, VA: NCTM.

Van Hiele, P. M. (1984a). A child's thought and geometry. In D. Fuys, D. Geddes, & R. Tischler, *English translation of selected writings of Dina van Hiele-Geldof and P. M. van Hiele* (pp 243–252). Brooklyn: Brooklyn College. (Original work published 1959).

Van Hiele, P. M. (1984b). The problem of insight in connection with school children's insight into the subject matter of geometry. In D. Fuys, D. Geddes, & R. Tischler, *English translation of selected writings of Dina van Hiele-Geldof and P. M. van Hiele* (pp. 237–241). Brooklyn: Brooklyn College. (Original work published 1957).

Van Hiele-Geldof, D. (1984). The didactics of geometry in the lowest class of secondary school. In D. Fuys, D. Geddes, & R. Tischler, *English translation of selected writings of Dina Van Hiele-Geldof and P. M. Van Hiele* (pp. 1–214). Brooklyn: Brooklyn College. (Original work published 1957).

Vergnaud, G., Benhadj, J., & Dussouet, A. (1979). *La coordination de l'enseignement des mathématiques entre le cours moyen 2e année et la classe de sixième* [The coordination of the teaching of mathematics between the fifth and sixth grades]. Paris: Institut National de Recherche Pédagogique.

Vurpillot, E. (1976). *The visual world of the child.* New York: International Universities Press.

Wagner, S., Rachlin, S. L., & Jensen, R. J. (1984). *Algebra Learning Project: Final report.* Athens: University of Georgia, Department of Mathematics Education.

Watson, J. M. (1997). Assessing statistical thinking using the media. In I. Gal & J. B. Garfield (Eds.), *The assessment challenge in statistics education* (pp. 123–138). Amsterdam, The Netherlands: International Statistical Institute.

Watson, J. M., Collis, K. F., & Moritz, J. B. (1997). The development of chance measurement. *Mathematics Education Research Journal, 9,* 60–82.

Watt, D. L. (1998). Mapping the classroom using a CAD program: Geometry as applied mathematics. In R. Lehrer & D. Chazan (Eds.), *Designing learning environments for developing understanding of geometry and space* (pp. 419–438). Mahwah, NJ: Erlbaum.

Wenger, R. H. (1987). Cognitive science and algebra learning. In A. H. Schoenfeld (Ed.), *Cognitive science and mathematics education* (pp. 217–251). Hillsdale: NJ: Erlbaum.

Wertsch, J. V. (1998). *Mind as action.* New York: Oxford University Press.

Whitman, B. S. (1976). Intuitive equation solving skills and the effects on them of formal techniques of equation solving (Doctoral dissertation, Florida State University, 1975). *Dissertation Abstracts International, 36*(08), 5180A. (University Microfilms No. 76-2720)

Williford, H. J. (1972). A study of transformational geometry instruction in the primary grades. *Journal for Research in Mathematics Education, 3,* 260–271.

Zawojewski, J. S., & Heckman, D. S. (1997). What do students know about data analysis, statistics, and probability? In P. A. Kenney & E. A. Silver (Eds.), *Results from the sixth mathematics assessment of the National Assessment of Educational Progress* (pp. 195–223). Reston, VA: National Council of Teachers of Mathematics.

Zech, L., Vye, N. J., Bransford, J., Goldman, S., Barron, B. J., Schwartz, D. L., Kisst-Hackett, R., Mayfield-Stewart, C., & the Cognition and Technology Group. (1998). An introduction to geometry through anchored instruction. In R. Lehrer & D. Chazan (Eds.), *Designing learning environments for developing understanding of geometry and space* (pp. 439–463). Mahwah, NJ: Erlbaum.

9

TEACHING FOR MATHEMATICAL PROFICIENCY

Previous chapters have described mathematical proficiency as the integrated attainment of conceptual understanding, procedural fluency, strategic competence, adaptive reasoning, and productive disposition. Effective forms of instruction attend to all these strands of mathematical proficiency. In this chapter we turn from considering what there is to learn and what is known about learning to an examination of teaching that promotes learning over time so that it yields mathematical proficiency.

Instruction as Interaction

Our examination of teaching focuses not just on what teachers do but also on the *interactions among teachers and students around content*.[1] Rather than considering only the *teacher* and what the *teacher* does as a source of teaching and learning, we view the teaching and learning of mathematics as the product of interactions among the teacher, the students, and the mathematics in an *instructional triangle* (see Box 9-1).

Certainly the knowledge, beliefs, decisions, and actions of teachers affect what is taught and ultimately learned. But students' expectations, knowledge, interests, and responses also play a crucial role in shaping what is taught and learned. For instruction to be effective, students must have, perceive, and use their opportunities to learn. The particular mathematical content and its representation in instructional tasks and curriculum materials also matter for teachers' and students' work, but teachers and students vary in their interpretations and uses of the same content and of the same curricular resources. Students interpret and respond differently to the same mathemati-

We view the teaching and learning of mathematics as the product of interactions among the teacher, the students, and the mathematics.

Box 9-1

The Instructional Triangle:
Instruction as the Interaction Among Teachers,
Students, and Mathematics, in Contexts

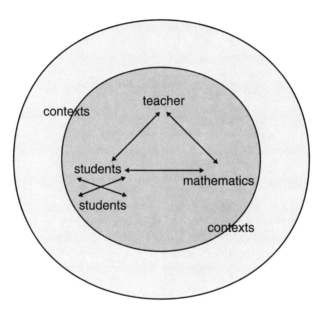

SOURCE: Adapted from Cohen and Ball, 1999, 2000, in press.

cal task, ask different questions, and complete the work in different ways. Their interpretations and actions affect what becomes the enacted lesson. Teachers' attention and responses to students further shape the course of instruction. Some teachers may not notice how students are interpreting the content, others may notice but not investigate further, and still others may notice and respond by reiterating their own interpretation.

Moreover, instruction takes place in contexts. By *contexts* we mean the wide range of environmental and situational elements that bear on instruction—for instance, educational policies, assessments of students and teachers, school organizational structures, school leadership characteristics, the nature and organization of teachers' work, and the social matrix in which the school is embedded. These matter principally as they permeate instruction—that is, whether and how they enter into the interactions among teachers, students, and content.[2] Hence, what goes on in classrooms to promote the development of mathematical proficiency is best understood through an examination of how these elements—teachers, students, content—interact in contexts to produce teaching and learning.

Much debate centers on forms and approaches to teaching: "direct instruction" versus "inquiry," "teacher centered" versus "student centered," "traditional" versus "reform." These labels make rhetorical distinctions that often miss the point regarding the quality of instruction. Our review of the research makes plain that the effectiveness of mathematics teaching and learning does not rest in simple labels. Rather, the quality of instruction is a function of teachers' knowledge and use of mathematical content, teachers' attention to and handling of students, and students' engagement in and use of mathematical tasks. Moreover, effective teaching—teaching that fosters the development of mathematical proficiency over time—can take a variety of forms. To highlight this point, we use excerpts from four classroom lessons and analyze what we see going on in them in light of what we know from research on teaching.

Four Classroom Vignettes

The pedagogical challenge for teachers is to manage instruction in ways that help particular students develop mathematical proficiency. High-quality instruction, in whatever form it comes, focuses on important mathematical content, represented and developed with integrity. It takes sensitive account of students' current knowledge and ways of thinking as well as ways in which those develop. Such instruction is effective with a range of students and over time develops the knowledge, skills, abilities, and inclinations that we term mathematical proficiency.

The four classroom vignettes we present below offer four distinct images of what mathematics instruction can look like. Each vignette configures differently the mathematical content and the roles and work of teachers and students in contexts; hence, each produces different opportunities for mathematics teaching and learning. Two points are important to interpreting and using these vignettes. First, to provide a close view, each vignette zooms in on an individual lesson. Effective instruction, however, depends on the coherent connection over time among lessons designed collectively to achieve important mathematical goals. For example, some of these teachers may be attempting to develop students' productive disposition toward mathematics and as mathematics learners, but it is difficult to pinpoint isolated attempts in a single lesson since that development takes place gradually—over months rather than minutes. Second, rather than seeking to argue that one of these lessons is "right," our analysis probes the possibilities and the risks each affords. The instructional challenge in any approach to teaching and learning is to capitalize on its opportunities and ward off its pitfalls.

The first example (Box 9-2) is typical of much teaching that many American adults remember from their own experience in mathematics classes.[3] Note how the teacher, Mr. Angelo, constructs the lesson in a way that structures the students' path through the mathematics by tightly constraining both the content and his students' encounters with it. The approach used by Mr. Angelo structures and focuses students' attention on a specific aspect of the topic: multiplying by powers of 10. He has distilled the content into an integrated "rule" that his students can use for all instances of multiplication by powers of 10.

Box 9-2

> ### Mr. Angelo—
> ### Teaching Eighth Graders About Multiplying
> ### by Powers of 10
>
> After a conducting a short warm-up activity and checking a homework assignment that focused on multiplying by 10, Mr. Angelo announces that the class is going to work on multiplying by powers of 10. He is concerned that students tend to perform poorly on this topic on the spring tests given by the school district, and he wants to make sure that his students know what to do. He reviews briefly the idea of *powers of 10* by showing that 100 equals 10^2, 1000 equals 10^3, and so on. Going to the overhead projector, he writes the following:
>
> $$4 \times 10 = \qquad 45 \times 100 = \qquad 450 \times 100 =$$
>
> "Who knows the first one?" Mr. Angelo asks. "Luis?" "Forty," replies Luis. Nodding, Mr. Angelo points to the second, "And this one?" Sonja near the front offers, "Forty-five hundred." "That's right—forty-five hundred," affirms Mr. Angelo, and he writes the number on the overhead transparency. "And what about the last one?" he asks. "Forty-five *thousand*," call out several students.

Writing "45,000," Mr. Angelo says, "Good, you are all seeing the trick. What is it? Who can say it?"

Several hands shoot into the air. Ethel says, "You just add the same number of zeros as are all together in the number and in the number you are multiplying by. Easy." "Right," says Mr. Angelo. "Let's try some more and see if you are getting it."

He writes three more examples:

$$30 \times 70 = \qquad 40 \times 600 = \qquad 45 \times 6000 =$$

"So who can do these?" he asks, looking over the students. "What's the first one?" "Three hundred!" announces Robert, confidently. Mr. Angelo pauses and looks at the other students. "Who can tell Robert what he did wrong?"

There is a moment of silence and then Susan raises her hand, a bit hesitantly. "I think it should be twenty-one hundred," she says. "You have to multiply both the 3 and the 7, too, in ones like this. So 3 times 7 is 21, and then add two zeros—one from the 30 and one from the 70." "Good!" replies Mr. Angelo. "Susan reminded us of something important for our trick. It's not just about adding the right number of zeros. You also have to look to see whether the number you are multiplying by begins with something other than a 1, and if it does, you have to multiply by that number first and then add the zeros." He writes 2100 after the equals sign and continues with the remaining examples.

Mr. Angelo writes another three examples on the overhead:

$$4.5 \times 0.1 = \qquad 4.5 \times 0.01 = \qquad 4.5 \times 0.001 =$$

"I wonder whether I can fool you. Now we are going to multiply by decimals that are also powers of 10: one tenth, one hundredth, one thousandth, and so on. We'll do easy ones to start." Who knows the first one?" he asks. "Luis?" "Point four five," replies Luis. Nodding, Mr. Angelo rephrases Luis's answer: "Forty-five hundredths." He then points to the second, "How about this one?" Nadya responds, "Point zero four five," almost inaudibly. "That's right. Forty-five thousandths," Mr. Angelo affirms, and he writes the number on the overhead. "And what about the last one?" "Point zero zero forty-five," responds the girl near the front again.

Mr. Angelo writes "0.0045" and says, "Good, does anyone see the rule. Who can say it?"

After a long pause, one hand in the back goes up. "You just move the decimal point."

continued

Box 9-2 Continued

"Right," says Mr. Angelo. "You move the decimal point to the left as many places as there are in the multiplier.* But think now. What did we decide happens to the product when we multiply a decimal by 10, 100, or 1,000? These are the powers of 10 that are greater than one, right?"

This time several hands go up.

"You just add the same number of zeros to the end of the number as are in the number you are multiplying by."

"Okay, that *is* what we said. But now we are ready for a better rule now that we have looked at some powers of 10 that are less than one. They are numbers like one tenth, one hundredth, one thousandth, and so on. Instead of having two completely different rules, it is better to have one good rule. And here it is. Listen carefully:

"When you multiply by a power of 10 that is greater than one, you move the decimal point to the *right* as many places as the number of zeros in the multiplier. When you multiply by a power of 10 that is less than one, you move the decimal point to the *left* as many places as there are in the multiplier."

Mr. Angelo illustrates the movement of the decimal point with a colored pen. He explains, "You can remember which way to move the decimal point if you remember that multiplying by a number greater than one makes the product bigger and multiplying by a number less than one makes the product smaller. Right makes bigger, left makes smaller."

"Let's practice this a bit now and get it under our belts." Mr. Angelo passes out a worksheet with 40 exercises that resemble what was done in class. He goes over the first exercise to make sure his students remember what to do. While the students work, Mr. Angelo circulates around the room, answering questions and giving hints. The students make a variety of computational errors, but most seem able to use the rule correctly. Mr. Angelo is pleased with the outcome of his lesson.

―――――――――――――――

* Mr. Angelo is referring to the number of places between the decimal point and the last nonzero digit in the multiplier. Strictly speaking the first factor in a product is the multiplier. But because of the commutative property, Mr. Angelo uses the term for whichever factor he wishes to focus on.

This lesson focuses on mathematical procedures for multiplying by powers of 10. Mr. Angelo designs the work to progress from simple examples (multiplying by 10, 100, and 1,000), to more complex ones (multiplying by multiples of powers of 10), to multiplying by powers of 10 less than one.[4] He stages the examples so that the procedure he is trying to teach covers more and more cases, thus leading to a more general rule usable for multiplication by any power of 10 other than $10^0 = 1$.

Mr. Angelo asks brief questions to engage students in the steps he is taking. By giving the students a rule, he simplifies their learning, heading off frustration and making getting the right answer the point—and likely to be attained. Concerned about the spring testing, he attempts to ensure that his students develop a solid grasp of the procedure and can use it reliably. He is careful to connect what are often two disjointed fragments: a rule for adding zeros when multiplying by powers of 10 greater than one and a different rule for moving the decimal point when multiplying by powers of 10 less than one.

Although Mr. Angelo integrates these two "rules," he does not work in the underlying conceptual territory. He does not, for example, explain why, for problems such as $30 \times 70 = ?$, students multiply the 3 and the 7. He might have shown them that $30 \times 70 = 3 \times 10 \times 7 \times 10$ and that, using associativity and commutativity, one can multiply 3 by 7 and then multiply that product by 10 times 10, or 100. Instead, he skips this opportunity to help the procedure make sense and instead adds an extra twist to the rule. He also does not show his students what they are doing when they "move the decimal point." In fact, of course, one does not "move" the decimal point. Instead, when a number is multiplied by a power of 10 other than one, each digit can be thought of as shifting into a new decimal place. For example, since .05 is *one tenth* times .5, in $.5 \times 10^{-1} = ?$, the 5 can be thought of as shifting one place to the right—to the hundredths place, which is one tenth of one tenth. If a 5 is in the tens place, then multiplying by 10 shifts it to the left one place, to the hundreds place: What was 50 is now 500. Describing these changes in terms of "adding zeros" or "moving the decimal point" stays at the surface level of changes in written symbols and does not go beneath to the numbers themselves and what it means to multiply them. Students miss an opportunity to see and use the power of place-value notation: that the placement of digits in a numeral determines their value. A 5 in the tens place equals 50; in the hundredths place, 0.05; and in the ones place, 5. Mr. Angelo offers his students an effective and mathematically justifiable rule, but he does so without exploring its conceptual underpinnings.

In lessons such as Mr. Angelo's, mathematics entails following rules and practicing procedures, often with little attention to the underlying concepts.[5] Procedural fluency is given central attention. Adaptive reasoning is not Mr. Angelo's goal: He does not offer a justification for the rule he is teaching, nor does he engage students in reasoning about the structure of the place-value notation system that is its foundation. He focuses instead on ensuring that they can use it correctly. Other aspects of mathematical proficiency are also not on his agenda. Instead, Mr. Angelo has a clear purpose for the lesson, and to accomplish that purpose he controls its pace and content. Students speak only in response to closed questions calling for a short answer, and students do not interact with one another. When a student gets an answer wrong, Mr. Angelo signals that immediately and asks someone else to provide the correct answer. The lesson is paced quickly.

We turn now to our second teacher, Ms. Lawrence, who is working with her fifth graders on adding fractions (Box 9-3). Ms. Lawrence's goals are different from Mr. Angelo's. Although she also structures the lesson to accomplish her goals, unlike Mr. Angelo, she emphasizes explanation and reasoning along with procedures. The pace of the lesson is carefully controlled to allow students time to think but with enough momentum to engage and maintain their interest.

Box 9-3

Ms. Lawrence—
Teaching Fifth Graders About Adding Fractions

After a few minutes in which the class does mental computation to warm up, Ms. Lawrence reviews equivalent fractions by asking the students to provide other names for $\frac{3}{5}$. She asks the class what fractions are called that "name the same number." On the chalkboard she writes a problem involving the addition of fractions with like denominators:

$$\frac{3}{8} + \frac{4}{8} =$$

She asks the students how to find the sum. One student, Betsy, volunteers that you just add the numerators and write the sum over the denominator. "Why does this work?" Ms. Lawrence asks. She asks Betsy to go to the board and explain. Confidently, Betsy draws two pie diagrams, one for each fraction, and explains that the denominator tells the size of the pieces and the numerators how many pieces all together:

$$\frac{3}{8} \qquad\qquad \frac{4}{8}$$

In response, Ms. Lawrence poses another problem, this time involving unlike denominators: $\frac{2}{3} + \frac{1}{4} = ?$ "How would we find the sum of *these* two?" she asks. Stepping back, she gives the students a chance to think. She then asks whether the sum would be less than or greater than 1. Several students raised their hands, eager to respond. Ms. Lawrence calls on Susan, who explains that the sum would be less than 1 because $\frac{1}{4}$ is less than $\frac{1}{3}$ and $\frac{2}{3} + \frac{1}{3}$ equals exactly 1.

Ms. Lawrence then asks how you could find the exact sum. Jim raises his hand and offers $\frac{8}{12}$ and $\frac{3}{12}$ as equivalent fractions with a common denominator. Ms. Lawrence writes on the chalkboard as Jim dictates:

$$\frac{2}{3} + \frac{1}{4} = \frac{8}{12} + \frac{3}{12} = \frac{(8+3)}{12} = \frac{11}{12}$$

$$\frac{8}{12} + \frac{3}{12} = \frac{11}{12}$$

She asks Jim why he chose 12 as the common denominator. "Twelve is the smallest number that both 3 and 4 go into," replies Jim. "How did you come up with that?" Ms. Lawrence asks. "By multiplying 3 and 4," he answers

Ms. Lawrence turns to the class. "Let's take a closer look. Jim got the equivalent fractions by multiplying the numerator and denominator of each fraction by the denominator of the other fraction. So if we show all the steps, it looks like this." She then reworks the problem to make her point, justifying each step by giving a property of the rational numbers:

$$\frac{2}{3} + \frac{1}{4} = \frac{(2\times 4)}{(3\times 4)} + \frac{(1\times 3)}{(4\times 3)} = \frac{(2\times 4)+(1\times 3)}{(3\times 4)} = \frac{(8+3)}{12} = \frac{11}{12}$$

Ms. Lawrence stops and looks at the students. "How do we know that what Jim did makes sense? How do we know that he is adding the same fractions as in the original problem: $\frac{2}{3}$ and $\frac{1}{4}$? This is really important. Maybe he has just added two *other* fractions."

continued

Box 9-3 Continued

"Oh!" exclaims Lucia. "I know! Two thirds is *equivalent to* eight twelfths. We could show that with a picture like what Betsy drew for three eighths and four eighths. If we draw two thirds on a pie that has three pieces, those two pieces will actually make *eight* pieces on that same pie if it's divided into 12. But the eight pieces, eight *twelfths,* will equal the same total amount of pie as two pieces that are each one third of the pie." She pauses, and beams, looking at Ms. Lawrence expectantly. "Is that right?"

"Yes, you explained it well," says Ms. Lawrence. "Can someone come up and make pictures to show what Lucia just said?"

Several hands go up, and Ms. Lawrence picks Nicole, who comes to the board and represents accurately what Lucia said. Ms. Lawrence makes a few additional remarks to make sure that all the students understand.

Ms. Lawrence continues with three more examples, showing all the steps in each. She then asks the students to generalize the process by writing "a rule that would work for any two fractions." Several students volunteer a verbal rule. "Let's try this out on a couple of less obvious examples," she says, writing on the overhead projector:

$$\frac{3}{8} + \frac{4}{15} = \qquad\qquad \frac{7}{16} + \frac{11}{24} =$$

Ms. Lawrence asks the students to work on these problems in pairs. As the students work, she walks around, listening, observing, and answering questions. Satisfied that the students seem to understand and are able to carry out the procedure, she assigns a page from their textbook for practice. The assignment contains a mixture of problems in adding fractions, including some fractions that already have like denominators and many that do not, and in adding whole numbers as well as several word problems.

Ms. Lawrence wants the practice that she provides to require the students to think and not merely follow the algorithm blindly. She believes that this way of working will equip them well for the standardized test her district administers in April and the basic skills test they have to take at the beginning of sixth grade. She expects the students to remember the procedure because they have had opportunities to learn why it makes sense. She knows that this approach is understandable to her students' parents, while at the same time she is stretching them beyond what some have been demanding—a solid focus on basic skills. She feels comfortable with the balance she has struck on these issues.

SOURCE: This vignette was constructed to embody the principles from Good, Grouws, and Ebmeier, 1983.

In this lesson, Ms. Lawrence is trying to develop her students' ability to add fractions with like or unlike denominators. She wants them to understand how to convert fractions to fractions with the same denominator and add them, and to have a reliable procedure for doing so. She also wants them to understand why the procedure works. Her lesson is designed to engage the students actively in the conceptual and procedural development of the topic. She begins by reviewing equivalent fractions, a concept both familiar and necessary for the new work. She poses a variety of questions and expects the students to explain their reasoning. She does not stop with well-articulated statements of the procedure but demands explanation and connection to the underlying meaning. She seeks to make the procedure make sense by asking for and providing explanations.

In this lesson, time is spent in a variety of ways to address Ms. Lawrence's goals: The students spend time practicing mental computation, developing a general rule for adding fractions, explaining and making sense of others' explanations, and working with a partner to practice on more complex examples of what they were learning. The lesson proceeds at a steady pace, but one that affords time for developing the ideas. Ms. Lawrence checks to see whether the students are understanding before she assigns them independent work, and the assignment mixes familiar and extension problems to help strengthen students' proficient command of the content. Although the focus of the lesson is not on strategic competence, when she asks students to estimate the sum of two fractions, she is helping them become sensitive to strategies they might use.

Our third teacher, Mr. Hernandez, is working on making and linking different representations of rational numbers (Box 9-4). He works hard to engage all his students in active work on the mathematics. Toward that end, he asks challenging questions that allow for a variety of solutions, and he expects the students to push themselves. He is conscious of the district and state basic skills assessments, but he has concluded that if he invests in this sort of work with his students, it pays off in their preparedness for the test. Occasionally, he finds that the approach is not working for some of his students, and he seeks ways to build their skills more solidly. He worries a bit, since the parents have been quite vocal in his school, with much pressure about getting students to algebra in eighth grade. He takes a strong stand on the importance of developing a solid foundation with number and representation, particularly with rational numbers.

This lesson is different from either Mr. Angelo's or Ms. Lawrence's. Mr. Hernandez has selected a task that draws on students' past experience

Box 9-4

Mr. Hernandez—
Teaching Seventh Graders About Representations of
Rational Numbers

Mr. Hernandez presents his seventh graders with a set of rectangular grids of various sizes. He lists specified portions of these areas—as a percentage of the total, a fraction of the total, a decimal fraction of the total, or a specific number of squares—and the students are to shade that portion. For each region shaded, he asks them to give a fraction, a decimal, or a percent to represent the shaded part of the total area. After working on the problems alone, the students are expected to be able to explain their strategies to the rest of the class.

After the students have had a chance to work on the task for about 15 minutes, Mr. Hernandez calls on Michelle to do the first problem at the overhead projector:

Shade .725 of the area of an 8-by-10 grid

Drawing a grid on the transparency, Michelle incorrectly shades 72.5 of the 80 squares. Mr. Hernandez asks her to explain her thinking. "I'm not sure," she admits. He then asks her to reread the problem. He asks the class to think about what would happen if they tried to distribute 100% across the 80 squares. "Each square would represent more than 1%," responds Michelle, a glimmer of understanding on her face. "Wouldn't each square represent 1.25%?" asks Eric. Michelle thinks for a minute and then explains that after allocating 1 percent to each square there would be 20 left over and that 20 divided among 80 would give one quarter more for each square or 0.25. "Oh, I see!" exclaims Michelle excitedly, doing some calculations off to the side of the transparency. "Fifty-eight squares should be shaded for 72.5% of 80, because 58 times 1.25 equals 72.5! Is that it?"

In the discussion that follows, Louis says that he multiplied 0.725 by 80 to get 58 and explains that he obtained a fraction $\frac{58}{80}$ and reduced it to $\frac{29}{40}$. Jenny says that she divided 80 squares into 10 equal columns of eight squares each and then shaded seven columns (56 squares) and two more squares (because 2 is $\frac{1}{4}$ of 8, which equals 0.025 of 80) for a total of 58 squares. Lynn explains how she used a calculator to find her solution.

Throughout the lesson, Mr. Hernandez presses the students to make their reasoning explicit and to explain their solution processes. He requires them to say what the symbols and representations mean in the context of the problems they are solving. When the students arrive at a numerical answer, he asks questions such as "Can you explain what that number refers to?"

To wrap things up for today, Mr. Hernandez summarizes the different strategies presented. He then assigns a similar set of problems for homework and asks the students to experiment with the various strategies they had seen in class with an eye toward determining the one they thought "best." "What does it mean for a strategy to be 'best'?" asks Laura. "Good question!" says Mr. Hernandez. "That's part of what I want you to think about. What criteria *would* you use to decide whether one strategy was better than others?" Several hands shoot up, but he waves them down. "We'll discuss that tomorrow. I want everyone to work on this first."

SOURCE: Adapted from Henningsen and Stein, 1997.

with decimals, percents, and fractions—all of which they have modeled using multiple representations prior to this lesson—while also setting them up to extend their proficiency in this domain. He has used this same task many times and has discussed it with other teachers who have also used it with their students. He knows what students are likely to do and where they might stumble. He has prepared questions to help move the work firmly toward the mathematical goal. He is able to take advantage of students' questions as they arise. He appraises the mathematical value of their questions and makes careful decisions, on the spot, as to which are worth taking up in class, which might be better simply answered, and which merit individual work but do not seem worth bringing up in class for everyone's consideration.

The students have had considerable experience representing areas other than the usual 10×10 grid. At the same time, the task Mr. Hernandez presents is not yet routine for the students and is open to a variety of solution strategies. He does not tell them what to do; instead, he uses the task as the medium for the lesson development. Mr. Hernandez has given the discussion of multiple solution strategies a great deal of thought before making it part of the lesson, for he is aware that explicitly examining the correspondences among alternative representations is crucial. If students merely see different representations without explicit attention to their correspondences, the lesson he is teaching will not produce the learning that he is striving for. The discussion of multiple solution strategies at the overhead projector provides an opportunity for Mr. Hernandez and several of the students to model adaptive reasoning and conceptual understanding. He also knows how much he has to do to make sure that the productive work the students are doing comes together at the end. He has found this way of working valuable. He is sensitive to the critical role that he plays during the lesson, even though it seems that the students are doing a large amount of the talking and the work.

We have been looking at upper elementary and middle school classrooms. In the last sample lesson (Box 9-5), a fourth teacher, Ms. Kaye, is attempting to develop her first-grade students' understanding of subtraction as it is used to compare quantities. She wants the students to find and consider their own ways of making comparisons of two-digit whole numbers in which the larger number has the smaller digit in the ones place.

Box 9-5

Ms. Kaye—
Teaching First Graders About Comparing Prices

Ms. Kaye gives her first-grade class a problem that involves comparing prices on a menu. She reads the following problem several times and writes the numbers on the overhead projector:

> *At Wu's Dairy a single ice cream cone costs 59¢. A double costs 85¢. How much more does a double dip cost than a single dip?*

The children eagerly set to work on the problem at their desks. A number of tools— including counters of various kinds, plastic coins, and base-10 blocks—are available in the corner of the room. While the children work, Ms. Kaye talks with individual children about their solutions.

Ms. Kaye stops at Kurt's desk and asks him what he is doing. He explains that he is trying to find out how much more 85 is than 59 and proceeds to make 59 with base-10 blocks. Ms. Kaye asks him what he is going to do next. Without answering, Kurt makes 85, again with the blocks. Once more Ms. Kaye asks him what he is going to do next. Staring at the blocks, Kurt does not respond. Ms. Kaye asks what he is trying to figure out. "How much bigger 85 is than 59," he murmurs. He does not seem know how to proceed. Ms. Kaye focuses his attention on the base-10 blocks and asks whether they could help him figure it out. Saying that he wants find out how much more there is in the 85 set of blocks than the 59 set, Kurt proceeds to match the two sets, pairing block for block. He trades in a rod (a 10) from the 85 set for 10 ones to make possible the matching of the 5 ones and the 9 ones. After the matching is complete, Kurt counts the blocks left unmatched and gets

---

two rods (tens) and six units (ones). "That's 26 more," he announces, looking up and smiling at his accomplishment.

This interaction with Kurt takes about five minutes. Continuing to circulate around the class, Ms. Kaye works with five more students in a similar fashion, asking questions, watching, listening carefully, and guiding where needed.

After about 15 minutes of individual work by the students, Ms. Kaye gathers the class together for a discussion of the problem. Some of the students are asked to share their solutions with the rest of the class. As they do, Ms. Kaye asks them to explain what they are doing and why. She asks the children to compare solutions: "How is Mina's solution like the one Brian showed? How is it like Liona's? Are there differences?" Five children present their solutions. Two have counted up from 59 to 85, although using different approaches. Another counts with money from 59¢ to 85¢. One has subtracted 59 from 85, another 59¢ from 85¢. One child has 34¢ for an answer, and Ms. Kaye gently guides her to see where she made an error, which she corrects.

After each child finishes, Ms. Kaye tries to make sure that the presented solution is clear. She also keeps asking the class to compare the different strategies. Ms. Kaye presents a new problem, and the work begins again, following the same pattern as before. Again, she works with individual students. Over the course of the class period, she is able to work individually with almost half the class; the next day, while working on the next set of problems, she will try to get to the rest.

At the end of the lesson, Ms. Kaye asks the children to summarize what they did in class by writing in their math journals. She reads over their shoulders and notes how much more articulate they are becoming in speaking and in writing. She passes out a sheet of paper with a problem for homework, asks them to put the sheet in their backpacks, and sends them out for recess.

SOURCE: Adapted from Carpenter, Fennema, Fuson, Hiebert, Human, Murray, Olivier, and Wearne, 1999.

In this lesson, students work on contextualized problems—problems set in a realistic context—that are designed to develop their ability to model situations and use arithmetic operations to solve questions about comparing quantities. Developing the students' representational ability and adaptive reasoning is an explicit goal. In particular, Ms. Kaye is trying to develop in her students the inclination and skill to compare alternative representations for a problem situation and their solutions to the problem. She has been impressed by their developing capacity to work sensibly with numbers larger than she would have expected several years ago. Ms. Kaye is also deliberately working on helping the students develop language as a tool for doing mathematics: to pose and respond to questions, to give explanations, to reflect on their work. The lesson is structured in a way that enables Ms. Kaye, when the class is working independently, to deal individually with students, guiding their work in particular ways while remaining attuned to each student's efforts and progress.

The approach Ms. Kaye is using takes considerable planning: The task that the students are doing must be mathematically productive of the next step in the curriculum, and it must also be engaging and appropriately difficult for all the children, so that they are able to work without constant supervision. It also takes developing norms in the class whereby the teacher can work individually with students and be able to attend closely to the mathematical knowledge and ways of reasoning being used by each child. This approach is worth developing, Ms. Kaye believes, for it continually provides her with accurate information about what the students are learning, information she uses to shape how she continues the lesson. The lesson also provides students with time to work alone, uninterrupted by others' thinking, as well as with time to share and compare ideas, methods, and results. Ms. Kaye is aware of risks she runs with this approach. For example, when students share different methods, they may become confused. Students may end up wondering what the right answer to the problem is. However, she has seen the benefits of this approach and is committed to continuing to work on developing her skills in working with students in these ways. She knows that some parents are pleased and others worried about what she is doing. She works hard to keep the parents informed and frequently invites them in to observe and later talk with her about what she and the children are doing. She finds that this investment in parents' awareness and support has paid off in terms of her students' learning, as well as in communication between home and school.

Comparing the Lessons

The four classroom vignettes provide snapshots of different ways in which students, teachers, and content interact to produce different opportunities for student learning, teaching practice, and curriculum content to be manifested. With respect to developing the mathematical proficiency of the students in the class, each approach affords possibilities, and each holds risks.

Consider first the mathematical content and how each teacher selects, shapes, and represents it for learning. Mr. Angelo, for example, constrains the content topic of multiplying by powers of 10 in ways that make it likely that all students will be able to produce correct answers, at least as long as they remember the rule. He provides them with a single rule that consolidates two separate rules, adding zeros and moving decimal points. His role is to demonstrate, provide practice, and check on their progress. The focus of this lesson is not to explore different methods for solving problems or probe the underlying meanings. Rather, he is deeply concerned with helping every student in his class learn to multiply by powers of 10 efficiently and accurately.

Mr. Angelo recognizes that one risk he faces is that students will develop competence with the procedure and yet lack understanding of what they are doing or why. Should they forget the procedure, they would have no conceptual basis for reconstructing it. However, he has seen that when they learn rules solidly, they are able to demonstrate procedural fluency with routine mathematical procedures. One way in which he has tried to avoid that risk is to make sure that the rules his students do learn are not mere fragments (add zeros, move decimal points). More general rules have greater power; he knows that and works to avoid giving the students lots of bits and pieces. He also designs his work with them to stage the development of the procedure in a way that he thinks will help build a better platform for their capacity to multiply numbers by powers of 10.

Ms. Lawrence organizes her students' mathematical work to bring them to a general process for adding fractions, including an indication of its natural origins and why it works. She asks questions designed to take the lesson where she wants it to go; the students are expected to participate in that venture, answering questions and following the development of the ideas. What she makes mathematically central—a procedure for adding fractions together with its justification—melds conceptual understanding, procedural fluency, and adaptive reasoning. How she engages students requires active participation on their part, following closely her design for the lesson. Her students rarely produce unexpected ideas or solutions, for she tightly plans her lessons to anticipate what students will do and say, and their contributions typically fit her plan.

Again, Mr. Hernandez's lesson about different representations of rational numbers is different from either Mr. Angelo's or Ms. Lawrence's. Mr. Hernandez's approach involves less control of students' work as he seeks

> With respect to developing the mathematical proficiency of the students in the class, each approach affords possibilities, and each holds risks.

to develop their understanding and skill. He takes rational number—a topic often treated piecemeal in school mathematics—and works explicitly on connections: How do different representations of the same rational number map onto one another? The problems he offers students are not as straightforward as those provided by any of the other teachers: That is, the mathematical work is designed to challenge the students' thinking and to elicit specific variations in their strategies and solutions. The tasks and the ways in which Mr. Hernandez uses them are not designed to lead students directly to obvious conclusions. Instead, they set the stage for the work he intends. Students' solutions and explanations provide raw material for the lesson, and Mr. Hernandez expects the students to work on one another's solutions during the class discussion. He has seen that students will not automatically be able to engage in discussions of complex mathematical problems, especially in classrooms as diverse as his. Consequently, he has been working hard over the last few years to develop his own skills at getting all students involved, including challenging different students appropriately.

In Ms. Kaye's first-grade lesson on whole numbers, the students are not taught a procedure for solving comparison problems (e.g., When you see "how many more?" it means you should subtract). In fact, a major mathematical goal of her lesson goes well beyond comparison of two quantities. It is to generate and uncover different solution strategies, including modeling situations and using representations, to explore and justify those strategies, and then to find similarities and differences between different solutions. She wants to build on her students' mathematical understanding.

Ms. Kaye's lesson also illustrates that how the development of the mathematical content in instruction can rest on the teacher engaging students in solving mathematical problems. In her class the students' ideas and methods generate significant portions of the lesson's substance, and the students are expected to play a major role in the development of the lesson—sharing their solutions, providing explanations, analyzing options. Ms. Kaye's forays around the room give her detailed information about individual students' progress that she uses in directing their mathematical work toward her goals.

Because Ms. Kaye has designed a lesson that opens up space for a variety of student ideas and methods, her approach risks generating multiplicity without clarity, connection, or closure. Although it is not Ms. Kaye's intention, the students may conclude that mathematics is a subject in which everyone can devise his or her own equally valid concepts and methods. The students may fail to appreciate the need for analysis, comparison, and evaluation—for common knowledge—or may continue to use their own safe procedures rather than developing more sophisticated ones. These are serious risks, ones she has seen emerge both in her own teaching before she was as aware of this problem as she is now and in the classrooms and accounts of many of her colleagues. Consequently, she is now much more careful to see to it that the lesson is pulled together at the conclusion, so that the mathematical points are made plain for students. Ms. Kaye keeps a close eye on all the district's learning goals for first grade as she uses problems like the one in the lesson, being careful that she covers the curriculum for the year.

While Ms. Kaye poses a problem that invites a wide range of solution methods appropriate for students at different places in their understanding, Mr. Hernandez gives a problem strategically designed to elicit specific approaches, material to be used to advance students' understanding of the correspondences among representations of rational numbers. In both Mr. Hernandez's and Ms. Kaye's classes, the students hear, use, and interact with other students' ideas. In Mr. Angelo's and Ms. Lawrence's classes, the teacher is the source of the lesson substance, and the students engage less with one another as a source and medium of mathematical work.

These vignettes help to show that the mathematical content and how it is framed and formulated into instructional tasks make a difference for the learning opportunities provided in a lesson. How the teacher interprets and uses such tasks to develop a lesson also fundamentally shapes instruction. Moreover, the ways in which the students make sense of and engage with the tasks and the teacher significantly affect how the lesson proceeds. All teachers face the challenge of engaging students in the mathematical work, maintaining their focused involvement in it, and helping them take advantage of instruction to learn. Each of our four teachers manages this challenge differently, which has different consequences for students' opportunities to learn. Mr. Angelo constrains the mathematical content in ways that focus students' attention on the specific learning goals of the lesson, making divergence of method or result unlikely. Ms. Lawrence musters students' engagement by asking them to explain and justify what they are saying. Mr. Hernandez's approach relies on setting challenging tasks and using anticipated students' solutions—errors as well as correct solutions—as part of the lesson material. Ms. Kaye engages the students through thought-provoking, carefully chosen tasks that invite multiple representations and strategies, and then she works intensively with individual students. Whereas Mr. Angelo runs the risk of his students forgetting the procedure since they lack the conceptual foundation, Ms. Kaye risks confusing her students with a blizzard of solution methods. Ms. Lawrence maintains a tight focus and hence reduces the ambiguity for her students—ambiguity that in Mr. Hernandez's lesson may be leading to frustration or disengagement for his students.

Teachers vary in how they manage the content and the incentives for students to engage in and succeed with it, and their choices present different advantages and risks for learning. Although it may not seem obvious, teachers who teach in ways like Mr. Hernandez and Ms. Kaye must prepare in detail for class; many observers of teaching fail to appreciate the significance of design and preparation in making these sorts of lessons more effective in helping students learn. Teachers like Mr. Angelo and Ms. Lawrence, however, need to work hard to figure out what their students are actually taking from instruction and what that implies for their approach to teaching common mathematical procedures.

The four lessons make plain that instruction does not occur in a vacuum. Parents, administrators, policies, the expectations of other teachers all may affect teachers' conceptions and practices. Teachers are differentially sensitive to particular features of their environments and respond in different ways. Mr. Angelo is concerned about the pressures exerted by testing and tailors his approach to target the focus of these tests. Mr. Hernandez, in contrast, is sure that approaching the topic more conceptually and with more complexity will equip his students to do well even on relatively routine, skill-based tests. Just as teachers' perceptions of their environments affect instruction, so too do students' perceptions. For example, if students hear criticism at home or if parents are puzzled and concerned about the mathematics program, students' resulting unease will affect their interactions with their teachers.

These snapshots of four classrooms are no more than glimpses into a complex set of interactions happening over time. They are segments from single lessons and, as such, provide a nearsighted view of school mathematics instruction. Instruction is not self-contained in serial lessons but draws on what happened yesterday, last week, last fall. Ideas about decimal notation that were taken up in a previous unit are used as Mr. Hernandez's students grapple with correspondences among different ways to represent rational numbers. Ms. Kaye's work with her first graders early in the year, helping them learn to express mathematical ideas in speech and in writing, equips them to write better now. Later learning builds on earlier successful accomplishment; new ideas are constructed using those already known. For example, a teacher could not effectively define a prime number if her students did not already possess some understanding of factoring. That understanding might have been developed in a variety of ways, but without it teaching the concept of a prime number would require simultaneously teaching about factors.

Neither in one lesson nor over a year does any one of the core elements of instruction—mathematical content, teacher, students—alone determine what happens. Instead, it is in *enactment*—in their mutual and interdependent interaction—that instruction unfolds. The quality of instruction does not inhere in any single element, whether challenging, exemplary curriculum material; competent, enthusiastic teachers; or capable, eager students. What makes curriculum exemplary, teachers competent, and students capable is their skilled use of one another to produce teaching and learning. How well they can take advantage of the possibilities afforded by the lesson and how well they can avoid the pitfalls determine how well students are able to use instruction to learn and how well teachers are able to guide that learning.

We turn next to what research on teaching has to say about shaping the nature and quality of instructional interaction. Given the possibilities that are paramount in each of the episodes described above and the potential risks of each approach, what is known about how to take advantage of the possibilities and avoid the pitfalls?

Findings from Research on Teaching

The interactive perspective on instruction[6] that we take in this chapter shapes our discussion of the studies we review. Using the instructional triangle depiction of instruction in Box 9-1, we ask what is known about the impact on student learning of how teachers select and use content (the teacher-content side of the triangle), how teacher and students interact (the teacher-student side), and how students interact with content (the student-content side). Although we discuss each side of the instructional triangle separately, instruction is not about one side alone but is about the trilateral interaction among teacher, students, and content.

Teachers and Content

What is learned depends on what is taught. Choosing the content, deciding how to present it, and determining how much time to allocate to it are ways in which learning is affected by how the teacher interacts with the content. Furthermore, some decisions about the content are made not at the classroom level but at the school, district, or even state levels.

Opportunity to Learn

The circumstances that allow students to engage in and spend time on academic tasks such as working on problems, exploring situations and gathering data, listening to explanations, reading texts, or conjecturing and justifying have been labeled *opportunity to learn*. As might be expected, students' opportunity to learn affects their achievement. In fact, opportunity to learn is widely considered the single most important predictor of student achievement.[7] Opportunity to learn can be influenced by individual students, their teachers, their schools or school districts, or even the country's educational system.

Research at the local and national levels has identified the curriculum as a potent force in students' opportunity to learn. Students in different curriculum tracks receive differential opportunities to learn mathematics, which is then reflected in their achievement.[8] Some studies show that when students believed to be less capable academically are given an opportunity to learn, they can in fact do so.[9]

Many curriculum decisions are made at the school or district level and lie outside the province of the classroom teacher. Nevertheless, teachers still have considerable control over their students' opportunity to learn. U.S. elementary school teachers vary widely, for example, in how much instructional time they allocate to various school subjects. In one study of second-grade classes, the average time allocated to mathematics ranged dramatically from a low of 24 to a high of 61 minutes a day for different teachers.[10] In another study some "teachers spent as much as 40 percent of their time teaching mathematics; several others never taught mathematics in the twenty randomly chosen hours when our observers visited each classroom."[11] That sort of variation is not unusual across classrooms and even within an individual teacher's practice. Teachers also vary in how they manage the time they have, sometimes focusing on one strand of proficiency and ignoring others. For example, two fourth-grade teachers ostensibly following the same mathematics textbook were found to spend their time quite differently: One teacher focused on concepts, and the other emphasized drill and practice of computational skills.[12] Even when the amount of time and the textbook are uniform, therefore, students can encounter different content and have different opportunities to learn it.

Consider the lessons of Mr. Angelo and Ms. Lawrence in the vignettes presented above. These two teachers use about the same amount of instructional time. The crucial differences lie in how they use that time. Mr. Angelo works on developing fluency with the procedures without a focus on their underlying meanings or justification. Ms. Lawrence, in contrast, spends most of her time developing understanding of a procedure through structured interactions with her students. Mr. Angelo gives 40 practice problems, whereas Ms. Lawrence uses only four.

Task Selection and Use

Researchers have recently taken a closer look at instruction by investigating the choice and use of academic tasks. Tasks are central to students' learning, shaping not only their opportunity to learn but also their view of the subject matter. The cognitive demand of tasks can vary significantly. Moreover, the tasks typically assigned to students in many classrooms make only minimal demands on their thinking, relying primarily on memorization or use of procedures without connections to concepts. There is growing evidence that students learn best when they are presented with academically challenging work that focuses on sense making and problem solving as well as skill building.[13] Take a couple of the tasks from our lesson vignettes. The task presented by Mr. Hernandez, shading 0.725 of an 8×10 grid, is a cognitively demanding task for seventh graders. His students have had prior experience with decimals, percents, and fractions, all of which they have modeled using multiple representations. But they have not had to coordinate the three, a mathematical problem of considerably more sophistication. The task presented by Mr. Angelo is less cognitively demanding, for all that students have to do is recall the steps of the procedure and answer questions about them. Still, whatever task a teacher poses, its cognitive demand is shaped by the way students use it. In fact, tasks that are set up to engage students in cognitively demanding activities often degenerate into less demanding activities as teachers and students work together to help the student "understand."[14]

Several factors have been identified as influencing the decline in cognitive demand from task setup to task enactment. Chief among them is that the task is made routine in one of two ways: The students may start pressing the teacher to reduce the challenge by specifying explicit procedures or steps for them to perform, or the teacher may take over the demanding aspects of the task when the students encounter difficulty by either telling them or demonstrating what to do.

Similarly, factors have been identified that help to maintain student engagement at a high level.[15] One is choosing tasks that build on students' prior knowledge. In our vignettes both Ms. Lawrence and Ms. Kaye use students' prior knowledge to engage them in demanding cognitive tasks. Ms. Lawrence links what students already know about adding fractions to the new topic of adding fractions with unlike denominators. Rather than merely presenting the process, she guides them in formulating the process themselves, building on their existing knowledge. Ms. Kaye uses students' informal knowledge about numbers, money, and operations to pose a demanding two-digit subtraction problem to her first graders. She also provides so-called scaffolding to help Kurt stay engaged in the task without showing him how to do it.

The use of scaffolding is another factor that helps to maintain student engagement at a high level. By offering a subtle hint, posing a similar problem, or asking for ideas from other students, Mr. Hernandez provides some scaffolding to assist his students as they reason through the grid problems. He does so without reducing the complexity of the task at hand or specifying exactly how to proceed. He allows substantial time for discussion of the problem, thus affording the students an opportunity to learn by considering and discussing multiple solution strategies.

Allocating neither too much nor too little time for the task is another factor associated with keeping engagement and cognitive demand high. Recall how Ms. Lawrence steps back to give her students a chance to think. Had she not provided that opportunity, Jim might not have come up with his solution. Mr. Hernandez also allows ample time for discussing the problems, thus affording his students an opportunity to learn by considering and discussing multiple solution strategies. The discussion of multiple solution strategies at the overhead projector provides an opportunity for Mr. Hernandez as well as several students to model a high level of performance—another factor that helps maintain engagement in cognitively demanding tasks. Ms. Lawrence also models a high level of performance by justifying each step in the general procedure for adding fractions with unlike denominators.

A final factor in maintaining high levels of student engagement with demanding tasks is sustained pressure from the teacher on explanation and the development of meaning. Throughout their lesson, Ms. Lawrence and Mr. Hernandez press students to explain their solution processes and to attach meaning to the symbols they are using. Ms. Kaye does likewise, both as she talks with individual students and as she responds to individual students presenting their solutions to the class. Teachers must not only select and successfully launch a high-level mathematical task but must also actively and consistently support students' cognitive activity without reducing the complexity and cognitive demands of the task. In the classroom the teacher, the students, and the task clearly interact in a dynamic way to shape students' learning.

Planning

Given that the learning of mathematics develops interactively over time, effective teachers understand that teaching requires considerable effort at design. Such design is often termed *planning*, which many teachers think of as a core routine of teaching.

Studies of how U.S. teachers plan show that they tend to focus on the activities in which students will be engaged and how those activities will be organized.[16] Teachers' plans seldom elaborate the content that the students are to learn through their engagement with the proposed activities.[17] Other research suggests that teachers who make detailed plans can sometimes be relatively inflexible when students encounter difficulties or raise thoughtful questions. These teachers are committed to their plans and have difficulty making midcourse adjustments.

Some teacher educators have made planning a central objective of their teacher preparation programs. Most programs provide prospective teachers with model plans or rubrics to scaffold their planning. Derived from teacher educators' ideas about what would constitute helpful approaches to preparing lessons, these frameworks do not necessarily reflect what good teachers do.

Researchers have rarely explored what it might mean to prepare for teaching in ways that would elaborate content goals and simultaneously equip the teacher with good maps of the paths they might take to reach desired destinations. Because many curriculum materials seek to do this sort of preparation for teachers, an important area for research is how teachers use the highly elaborated teachers' guides often held up by educators as positive examples. What do teachers read when planning, how do they interpret and use what they read, and how do those uses affect their teaching?

Recent studies of Japanese professional development programs have revealed a practice termed *lesson study* that involves groups of teachers working together on single lessons, elaborating goals, investigating pupils' thinking and difficulties with particular content, and exploring different representations and tasks. The teachers make repeated trials of these lessons, improving them in light of their collective study of the effectiveness of the lesson designs. We discuss this approach to professional development in chapter 10. Here we highlight the idea of designing lessons to combine a significant elaboration of one's content goals with a dedicated and thorough anticipation of and preparation for a range of likely student responses. Planning can profitably be seen as a detailed form of instructional design aimed at reducing the uncertainties of one's practice, centered on the continual adjustment and improvement of instruction, and informed by a close scrutiny of what happens as the lesson unfolds.

Teachers and Students

Teacher Expectations

Teachers' selections of tasks and their interactions with students during instruction are guided by their beliefs about what students need to learn and are capable of learning.[18] Low expectations can lead a teacher to interact with certain students in ways that fail to support their development of mathematical proficiency. For example, in comparison with their treatment of high achievers, some teachers consistently wait less time for low achievers to answer a question before calling on someone else. They tend to give these students the answer rather than helping them improve their responses by rephrasing questions, they criticize them more frequently for failure and praise them less frequently for success, they call on them less often, and they give them less cognitively demanding questions and tasks.[19] Mr. Hernandez might easily have succumbed to such a temptation in responding to Michelle's wrong answer. Instead, he asked her to reread the problem and think about what would happen if 100% were to be distributed across the 80 squares. That is, he expected Michelle to be able to solve the problem if she persisted in working on it—and on her own and with assistance from her classmates, she did.

Closely related to teachers' expectations is their sense of efficacy, the feeling that they are effective in helping students learn. Successful teachers not only expect their students to succeed but also see themselves as capable of motivating and instructing students effectively. Less successful teachers lack confidence either in themselves as instructors (e.g., "I don't know the mathematics well enough to teach it effectively"; "I know what I want to teach, but I don't know how to give my students what they need to be able to learn it") or in their students' learning potential (e.g., "No teacher could be effective with these students because they lack ability, motivation, supportive home environments, and so on"). Studies have identified consistent relationships among teachers' sense of efficacy, the patterns of teacher-student interactions that occur in their classrooms, and their students' achievement. For example, teachers with a high sense of efficacy tend to appear more confident in the classroom, to be more positive and less critical with their students, to be better classroom managers, to be more accepting and effective in responding to challenges from students (e.g., "Why are we learning this?"), and to be more effective in supporting growth and achievement.[20]

> Successful teachers not only expect their students to succeed but also see themselves as capable of motivating and instructing students effectively.

These findings on teachers' sense of efficacy underscore the importance of preparing teachers so they possess sufficient knowledge to teach with confidence and effectiveness. They need to know the mathematics they will teach, their students' current mathematical thinking, and strategies for representing mathematics and meeting their students' learning needs. Helping teachers become proficient in understanding their students' reasoning, in choosing a good follow-up question, and otherwise providing scaffolding for their students can be particularly challenging because such techniques require high levels of all three types of knowledge and are different from the techniques emphasized in most teachers' prior experience.[21]

Motivation

To make consistent progress toward proficiency, students need to be motivated to engage productively in mathematics lessons and the learning activities in those lessons. Motivation for school mathematics learning depends primarily on the interaction of students with teachers and of students with mathematical tasks.[22] Traditional approaches to motivation typically either attempt to make learning fun or to rely on grades and other extrinsic rewards and punishments to pressure students to put forth the necessary effort. Recent research on students' motivation has moved well beyond these traditional conceptions to establish a richer, more balanced depiction of motivation, allowing the identification of effective motivational strategies that apply to the teaching of all subjects, including mathematics.[23]

Students' motivation depends on both expectation and value.[24] That is, students are motivated to engage in a learning task to the extent that they *expect* to be able to perform the task successfully if they apply themselves and the degree to which they *value* the task or the rewards that performing it successfully will bring. Therefore, teachers can motivate students to strive for mathematical proficiency both by supporting their expectations for achieving success through a reasonable investment of effort and by helping them appreciate the value of what they are learning.

Maintaining an expectation of success. To make steady progress toward proficiency, students need continued confidence that they can meet the challenges of school mathematics. The most basic strategy for supporting students' expectations of success (and their related perceptions and beliefs, such as a sense of efficacy) involves two basic elements. The first is to design for success by assigning tasks on which students can succeed if they invest reasonable effort. The second is to provide whatever scaffolding may be needed to help students acquire and apply concepts, skills, and abilities as they work on assignments. This strategy involves building on students' current knowledge, which in turn requires understanding what they already know and where they are headed.

Other strategies include helping students to commit themselves to goals that are near at hand, specific, and challenging and then following up by helping them assess their performance in terms of their progress toward those goals rather than by comparing their performance to that of their classmates. In modeling their own mathematical thinking, in communicating expectations to students, and in socializing students' attitudes and beliefs, teachers should continually emphasize that mathematical proficiency is built up through experiences in learning and applying what has been learned (and are not innately given and limited). They need to emphasize that students can meet daily challenges successfully and move toward higher levels of proficiency if they consistently put forth reasonable effort and that such effort results in a gradual but productive deepening of understanding and refinement of skill.[25]

Valuing learning activities. To be optimally motivated, students need not only confidence that they can achieve success but belief that what they are learning is worth learning. Traditional approaches to the value aspect of motivation have attempted not to help students see value in learning activities but instead to link their performance on these activities to something else that they do value, such as the prospect of earning rewards. Rewards can be useful, but they need to be handled carefully because they can undermine intrinsic motivation and distract students' attention from learning goals if they are overemphasized. Rewards can also have undesirable side effects if they are tied to competitions that create winners and losers.

Alternative strategies for addressing the value aspect of motivation involve taking advantage of students' existing intrinsic motivation by emphasizing topics they find interesting and tasks they find enjoyable. For example, students usually enjoy responding actively rather than merely listening; opportunities to interact with their peers; situations that invite thought by posing divergent questions; and activities with game-like features, such as puzzles and brainteasers.[26] These strategies for intrinsic motivation can be helpful, although teachers may find that their opportunities to use such strategies are limited by constraints of time and curriculum.

Moreover, although use of these strategies may increase students' enjoyment of a lesson, it does not directly stimulate their motivation to learn what the lesson is designed to teach. Motivation to learn includes the students' tendency to find mathematical activities meaningful and worthwhile, to try to get intended learning benefits by attempting to make sense of the activities, to relate the new knowledge or skills they are developing to their prior knowledge or skills, and to think about how they can apply the mathematics they are learning. Teachers create motivation to learn by modeling it in their own classroom discourse, communicating their expectations for success, assuming that their students are already motivated to learn, and molding their class into a coherent learning community. When teaching particular lessons or providing learning activities, teachers can spur students' motivation to learn by communicating enthusiasm for the content, stimulating curiosity or suspense, personalizing the content to make it more concrete or familiar, introducing it in ways that stimulate interest or an appreciation for its value, engaging the students in authentic applications of the content, and helping them to remain goal oriented and attuned to strategies as they work on applications.[27]

The lessons taught by our four teachers illustrate some of these principles. These teachers provide environments that support learning. Their students participate actively by answering questions, offering solutions, or providing explanations. Ms. Lawrence, Mr. Hernandez, and Ms. Kaye focus on students' understanding and sense making, and they try to connect the lesson to students' prior knowledge. Mr. Angelo gives his rule for multiplying by powers of 10 and relates it to the earlier "add zeros" rule for multiplying by powers of 10 greater than one. His approach of giving explicit rules to follow helps to assure success on the tasks, provided that students can remember the rule. Mr. Angelo relies for motivation on the personal engagement he shows with his students and on the extrinsic pressures built into the grading system. Rather than motivate students through interest or intrinsic aspects of the intellectual work, he inspires confidence because the goal seems attainable.

Teaching Students with Special Needs

Although existing research does not provide clear guidelines for teaching mathematics to children with severe learning difficulties, existing evidence and experience suggest that the same teaching and learning principles apply to all children, including special-needs children. It has long been assumed that children with moderate, mild, and borderline mental retardation or learning disabilities are not capable of meaningful or conceptual mathematical learning and, thus, unlike other children, have to be taught by rote. Researchers have found, however, that it useful not to prejudge them or to assume that they learn by means of different "laws of learning." Instead, it is in the best interest of special-needs children to assume that the following principles apply to all children: (a) learning with understanding involves connecting and organizing knowledge; (b) learning builds on what children already know; and (c) formal school instruction should take advantage of children's informal everyday knowledge of mathematics.[28]

Learning difficulties among special-needs children stem largely from instruction that violates one or more of these principles. Common mistakes in their instruction include (a) not assessing, fostering, or building on their informal knowledge; (b) overly abstract instruction that proceeds too quickly; and (c) instruction that relies on memorizing mathematics by rote. In other words, the learning difficulties of special-needs children and children in general are the same.

When special-needs children are taught mathematics in accordance with the above principles, many show significant improvement in learning concepts and skills and can exhibit considerable proficiency.[29] Furthermore, even within what are presumed to be homogeneous groups of children, there are significant individual differences in their readiness and capacity to learn particular mathematical skills and concepts. Together, these findings imply that many, if not all, special-needs children can benefit from meaningful instruction that addresses the development of all five strands of proficiency and that gives attention to both the students' thinking and the mathematics.

Note that it does not follow from the above principles that special children should be treated identically to their same-age peers. For children with mental retardation, for example, it may take several years to help them construct the number or arithmetic concepts that other children do in a much shorter span of time. Moreover, applying these principles to teaching special-needs children may require creative adaptations. With children who are blind, for example, computer-based instruction may not be helpful or may need to be adapted in imaginative ways. Likewise, for children with communication disorders, creative solutions may be required to enable them to benefit from small-group work.[30] Again, good instruction of special-needs children will depend on reflective, knowledgeable, and flexible teachers.

Special-needs children can benefit from careful and thoughtful use of both mainstreaming and segregated instruction. Mainstreaming is an instructional tool that can be used wisely or not. Currently, it is all too often used inflexibly and ineffectively. Consider the case of Ann, a Down syndrome child, who is placed in a regular eighth-grade mathematics class along with children the same chronological age. Ann sits through class after class with little or no comprehension of the instruction. The assigned aide tries to discuss the instruction afterward, but with little success. The aide also provides simplified or watered-down worksheets (e.g., asking Ann what half of various amounts are instead of worksheets on operations on fractions). In brief, Ann's integration into the class is in name only and does almost nothing to foster her mathematical proficiency or even rote learning of mathematics.

It is worth noting that Alfred Binet devised the IQ test and advocated segregated instruction for low-ability students for the most humane of reasons. As the case of Ann illustrates, he saw that such children were often utterly lost in regular classrooms and suffered terribly there. Because segregated instruction was implemented poorly or abused, it has now largely been abandoned. Now educators advocate mainstreaming for the most humane of reasons. Unfortunately, this approach is all too frequently being implemented poorly. In the end there is no substitute for providing adequate support for all children. This support includes providing sufficient staff who are both well trained and caring. Real improvement in the education of special-needs children will also require moving past dogmatic positions and taking a reflective approach that takes into account the best interests of each child.

Interactions with Different Students

In the mathematics class the teacher naturally interacts differently with different students. Sometimes, however, differential interactions are associated not with differences in mathematical ability or accomplishment but with differences in students' social class, ethnicity, language, or gender. For example, studies have shown that boys have a larger number of academic interactions with teachers in mathematics class than girls do. Not only is the quantity of interactions different, but the quality differs also. Studies have documented that girls often receive simpler, more routine questions than boys, who then receive more difficult and challenging questions.[31] As noted earlier, some teachers interact differently with lower achieving students than higher achieving students, giving them less time to respond, asking them less demanding questions, criticizing them more often, and calling on them less. And lower achieving students are disproportionately children of color, from poverty, or from households without native speakers of English. Not only is there substantial evidence that teachers interact differently with students, but students from marginalized groups are also more vulnerable than other students are to self-fulfilling prophecies of low expectations.[32]

Interactions between teacher and student need to be appropriate to the student and the content, regardless of the student's social class, ethnicity, language, or gender. Effective teachers often make use of their students' interests to engage them in academic tasks. Effective teachers of urban African American students do so by making use of the culture of their students. They demonstrate an understanding of their students' backgrounds and experiences, link classroom content to those experiences, use familiar cultural patterns, and focus on the child.[33] High expectations for all students without regard to their social class, ethnicity, or gender can also pay high dividends. For example, low-achieving minority students can do as well as other students when placed in more demanding programs.[34] Also, in a study of teachers in schools serving children of poverty, higher achievement results were obtained when teachers placed more emphasis on meaning in their mathematics classrooms.[35] Because the quality of the interaction of teacher and student around the content is so critical to the success of instruction, the most successful teachers are not merely sensitive to the cultural diversity of their students but use that diversity to enrich the learning experiences they provide to the class as a whole.[36]

Communities of Learners

Creating classrooms that function as communities of learners has been the focus of much recent research and scholarship in mathematics education.[37] In the research on teaching and learning mathematics with understanding, four features of the social culture of the classroom have been identified.[38] The first is that ideas and methods are valued. Ideas expressed by any student warrant respect and response and have the potential to contribute to everyone's learning.

A second feature of a classroom community of learners is that students have autonomy in choosing and sharing their methods of solving problems. Students recognize that many strategies are likely to exist for solving a problem, they respect the methods used by others and that others need to understand their own methods, and they are given the freedom to explore alternatives and to share their thinking with the rest of the class. Notice how Mr. Hernandez has three other students besides Michelle share their solutions to the grid problem. Ms. Kaye has five students present their solution methods. She also engages the class in a discussion of the similarities and differences between the various methods. In contrast, Ms. Lawrence and Mr. Angelo, although they call on students to answer questions, are more interested in presenting a correct solution method than in soliciting multiple methods.

A third feature of classrooms that function as communities of learners is an appreciation of the value of mistakes as sites of learning for everyone. Mistakes are not covered up; rather, they are used as opportunities to examine reasoning and to deepen everyone's analysis. The appreciation of mistakes is a fundamental aspect of mathematical work outside the classroom; inside, it helps build the community. When Michelle makes a mistake on the grid problem, Mr. Hernandez does not tell her it is wrong and then call on someone else. He uses it instead to push her thinking.

Finally, a core feature of these classrooms is the recognition that the authority for whether something is both correct and sensible lies in the logic and structure of the subject rather than the status of the teacher or the popularity of the person making the argument. The resolution of disagreements resides in mathematical argument. Both Mr. Hernandez and Ms. Kaye have their students justify their solution strategies. Although Ms. Lawrence frequently asks her students to justify their work, when she presents the procedure for adding fractions with unlike denominators, she provides the justification. She does use mathematical properties to explain the procedure, however, rather than simply present the rule as Mr. Angelo did. Hence, in addition to selecting tasks with goals in mind and sharing essential information, the teacher's primary role is to establish a classroom culture that supports learning with understanding, thereby serving to motivate students to learn.

Managing Discourse

An important part of classroom instruction is to manage the discourse around the mathematical tasks in which teachers and students engage. Teachers must make judgments about when to tell, when to question, and when to correct. They must decide when to guide with prompting and when to let students grapple with a mathematical issue. Their decisions do not simply rest with the mathematical task at issue. They also need to decide who should get the floor in whole-group discussions and how turns should be allocated. Teachers have responsibility for moving the mathematics along while affording students opportunities to offer solutions, make claims, answer questions, and provide explanations to their colleagues. The point of classroom discourse is to develop students' understanding of key ideas. But it also provides opportunities to emphasize and model mathematical reasoning and problem solving and to enhance students' disposition toward mathematics. Therefore, discourse needs to be planned with these goals in mind, not merely as a "checking for understanding" form of recitation.

Teachers are often inclined to call on students who have the correct or desired solutions. This practice makes managing the discourse less complex, since less complicated or confusing ideas get the floor. It also shapes both the task and students' opportunities to learn from it.

Our four teachers manage the discourse in their classrooms in very different ways. In Mr. Angelo's lesson, for instance, he does virtually all the talking, opening only a few constrained entry points for students to offer their answers. Ms. Kaye, in contrast, deliberately elicits five disparate solutions from a range of students. The group discussion forms the content of the lesson, so individual students' ideas contribute directly to the enacted curriculum of the class. Ms. Lawrence controls students' contributions to the lesson but proffers complex questions so that the discourse requires substantial work from students. She manages by planning strategic questions to move the lesson to its goal. Mr. Hernandez incorporates students' ideas into his design, deliberately sowing questions that will get particular issues and ideas on the table for the class to hear and learn from. Managing the discourse is both one of the most complex tasks of teaching and the least thoroughly studied. Research needs to make visible teachers' considerations as they handle classroom discourse and the consequences of their moves for students' learning.

Grouping

Students are sometimes grouped for instruction either by curriculum path or achievement level. Grouping by curriculum, often called *tracking*, is more common in high school, where different curriculum tracks exist for students with different goals for the future: college, business, or trades. Grouping by achievement level is more common in elementary and middle schools. At those grades, homogeneously grouped classes are usually taught essentially the same content, but the higher the level, the greater the depth and breadth of mathematical ideas and the more rapid the pace.

Grouping by achievement level is especially relevant in grades pre-K to 8. We make two points about such grouping. First, it is in fact grouping by achievement and not ability grouping, as it is so often called. The test scores (and in some cases school grades) that provide the basis for such grouping are measures of mathematical knowledge and skills that students have accumulated to date; they are not measures of some underlying (presumably fixed, stable, and possibly innate) substrate of mathematical ability. What is known about neural capacity and brain functioning with respect to mathematical abilities is limited and largely speculative. The evidence does not support any practice of grouping pre-K to grade 8 students according to their supposed mathematical abilities. Meanwhile, data from international comparisons (especially studies of Asian countries) support proceeding on the assumption that all students can achieve important mathematical learning goals and working within heterogeneously grouped classes to see that students do.

In the United States, interest in grouping students by achievement for mathematics instruction has waxed and waned over the years. Proponents of homogeneous grouping claim that reducing the range of achievement levels within a class or group enables the teacher to meet that group's needs more consistently. Opponents of such grouping claim that the advantages to high achievers are overstated. Instead of providing low achievers with ideal instruction that helps them make rapid gains in proficiency, homogenous grouping typically results in low achievers being taught a barren curriculum by less capable teachers in classes that lack strong peer role models. Any gains that might accrue to the high achievers are more than offset by losses to the low achievers and by the resultant perpetuation of social class, racial, and ethnic inequities in schooling.[39]

This controversy highlights a second point about grouping: Many studies on grouping have been conducted over the years (including studies on grouping for mathematics instruction), but the results concerning effects on achievement have been both weak and mixed.[40] The findings indicate that overall mathematical achievement is likely to be similar whether students are grouped homogeneously or heterogeneously, especially if the same curriculum is provided to all groups. When the curriculum is altered, tracking appears to benefit students in high-track classes.[41] At the same time, there is evidence that heterogeneous classes may help students whose earlier performance was low, with little effect on other students' performance.[42] An analysis of data from the National Education Longitudinal Study (NELS), however, found that the estimated achievement of average and high-achieving students would be depressed in heterogeneous eighth-grade mathematics classes.[43] If one were to look only at these achievement data, one might conclude that it makes little difference whether students are grouped homogeneously or heterogeneously. However, concerns raised about undesirable side effects of homogeneous grouping in grades pre-K–8 in the United States, as well as international comparison data indicating that some countries with the most impressive mathematical achievement scores practice heterogeneous grouping, suggest that heterogeneous grouping is the wiser course in the elementary and middle school grades.

Significant improvements in students' mathematical achievement are more likely to result from adjustments in curriculum and instruction than from adjustments in how students are assigned to classes. The snapshot of Ms. Kaye's class illustrates how a teacher can work effectively with a heterogeneous group of students. All of her first graders are given the same problem, but she encourages the use of different solution strategies depending on the level of the student. Mr. Hernandez provides another example. He allows students to present both more and less sophisticated procedures, provided the students can explain them. In each case the key is the interaction of the teacher and the students around a challenging problem, rather than some particular instructional organization.

Cooperative Groups

Cooperative grouping of students in a class is a teaching practice that has become popular in recent years. Because it has also been a target of concern and criticism, we devote specific attention to it and to the warrants for and conditions of its use. First, important to realize is that there is no single practice or structure that can be identified as "cooperative groups." Cooperative groups are usually groups of three, four, or five students who have been given a task to work on together, with some effort by the teacher to specify the role each child is to play in the group's work. The several different models for organizing and conducting cooperative groups generally share common goals. One goal is to specify the social processes of the groups so as to accommodate students' lack of experience with collective work and to provide them with support. A second is a commitment to distributing classroom talk more widely, encouraging all students to talk, to share their ideas, and to become more actively engaged intellectually. A third is to help students develop their social and collaborative skills and not just support their learning of content. Like most such techniques and tools, whether cooperative groups contribute to the development of mathematical proficiency depends primarily on how they are used.

Several models of cooperative grouping have been extensively studied. The research indicates that these cooperative group methods are likely to have positive effects on achievement and on other social and psychological characteristics.[44] The effects on achievement appear to be related to the use of specific rewards for a group based on its members' performance rather than on the particular cooperative method used. Ensuring the accountability of individual group members for the collective work can prevent one or two students from doing it all while the others simply copy or sit passively. The most effective methods combine group goals with individual accountability.

Effects of such grouping on outcomes other than achievement are more impressive. Cooperative grouping arrangements promote friendship and positive social interaction among students who differ in achievement, gender, race, or ethnicity, and they promote acceptance of handicapped students who have been placed in regular classes. Although there may be disadvantages to using cooperative groups, their judicious use may have potential nonacademic benefits.

For cooperative groups to be effective, students need to be taught how to work in this mode. Simply telling students to push their desks together and work on a task together does not ensure cooperative learning. Skills for working cooperatively have to be taught directly, and students need to be prepared for both the social and the cognitive demands of such work. Further, there is evidence that children's collaborative interactions vary across social and cultural groups.[45] For teachers to use cooperative groups effectively, they also need to select, organize, and present tasks that are well suited both to collaborative work and to the curriculum.

Cooperative grouping is one of many instructional practices that teachers may choose to use at times. It is neither a wholesale replacement for whole-class instruction nor a disastrous technique to be avoided at all costs. Further, the cooperative methods that have been found to produce positive learning outcomes take knowledge and skill to implement. Like any practice, cooperative groups can be used effectively or not.

Assessment

Information about students is crucial to a teacher's ability to calibrate tasks and lessons to students' current understanding and skills. Mr. Hernandez and Ms. Kaye have each designed the lesson to afford them critical information about their students' progress. The tasks they frame create a strategic space for students' work and for gaining insight into students' thinking. Ms. Lawrence gets some of the same sort of information from her probing of Jim's solution. Although Mr. Angelo and Ms. Lawrence get some idea of how students are doing by circulating around the room, they use the questions they ask during class as their primary mode of assessment during the lesson.

In addition to tasks that reveal what students know and can do, the quality of instruction depends on how teachers interpret and use that information. Teachers' understanding of their students' work and the progress they are making relies on the teachers' own understanding of the mathematics and their ability to use that understanding to make sense of what the students are doing. Moreover, after interpreting students' work, teachers need to be able to use their interpretations productively in making specific instructional decisions: what questions to ask, tasks to pose, homework to assign. Studies show that when teachers learn to see and hear students' work during a lesson and to use that information to shape their instruction, their instruction becomes clearer, more focused, and more effective.[46]

More formal sources of assessment information can also help improve the quality of instruction, including homework, project reports, notebooks, journals, quizzes, tests, and examinations. The more precise and detailed the information and the better coordinated it is with curricular goals, the better a resource it is for instruction. Teachers' ability to interpret and make judicious strategic use of assessment information from many sources is a critical factor in their instructional effectiveness.

Students and Content
Students and Tasks

How well a mathematical task works to support students' learning is a function both of its quality—that is, of its potential for stimulating mathematics learning—and of the ways students interpret and use it. The tasks Mr. Hernandez designed offer sufficient complexity to be challenging because he has varied the grid from the familiar 10×10 to other configurations. His students can make sense of these tasks and are able to work on them, coming up with solutions that open opportunities for instruction. Had the tasks been either too difficult or too trivial for these students, the tasks might not have worked. One important consideration in designing mathematical tasks, therefore, is that they must take account of what the students already know and must maximize the possibility for the students to make progress in learning the content. This process entails judgments about design so that the tasks anticipate students' responses and are built on appropriate-sized mathematical steps. All four of our teachers were able to choose and pose problems that engaged their students in addressing the mathematical goals for the lesson. Where the lessons differed was in the mathematical significance of the tasks and in the challenge they posed to students' thinking and learning.

Practice

Role of practice. To many students, practice is as much a part of studying mathematics as of playing a sport or a musical instrument. The role of practice in mathematics, as in sports or music, is to be able to execute procedures automatically without conscious thought. That is, a procedure is practiced over and over until so-called *automaticity* is attained.[47]

There are cognitive benefits to automatization. The more automatically a procedure can be executed, the less mental effort is required. Since each person has a limited amount of mental effort that he or she can expend at any one time, more complex tasks can be done well only when some of the subtasks are automatic.[48] Hence, the automatization of mathematical procedures is justifiable when those procedures are regularly required to complete other tasks. For example, basic multiplication combinations such as $4 \times 6 = 24$ and $6 \times 7 = 42$ are needed for estimation, multidigit multiplication, single-digit division, multidigit division, and addition and multiplication of fractions, to name a few. Therefore, multiplication combinations need to be practiced until they can be produced quickly and effortlessly. The availability of calculators and computers raises the question of which mathematical procedures today need to be practiced to the point of automatization. Single-digit whole number addition, subtraction, multiplication, and division certainly need to be automatic, since they are used in almost all other numerical procedures. Opinions vary, however, as to which other procedures should be made automatic.

Kinds of practice. Textbook and worksheet exercises offer the most common kinds of practice used in U.S. mathematics classrooms. Such exercises are used to provide students frequent and repeated opportunities to practice what they have learned. Often the practice is directly associated with the topic of the lesson, with the teacher or other students providing assistance until the student can perform independently. Another approach distributes the practice over a longer period: On any one day, only a few of the exercises assigned might address the lesson topic, and the rest would address topics studied earlier in the year. Such distributed practice is based on the principle that mastery is achieved gradually and once achieved is maintained through regular practice. A number of studies of the U.S. curriculum have concluded that it is too repetitive.[49] These criticisms are about topics being retaught year after year, not about students practicing learned concepts and procedures throughout the year to improve efficiency and retention. Ms. Lawrence's assignment of a mixture of problems is presumably no acci-

The role of practice in mathematics, as in sports or music, is to be able to execute procedures automatically without conscious thought.

dent. Notice that she has even included problems on whole-number addition to help her students maintain their skill with that operation.

Sites for practice that often go unrecognized are problem solving and the learning of new content.[50] When a group of primary teachers in several studies shifted their emphasis from skills to problem solving, for example, there was no overall change in their students' computational performance.[51] Their students were still getting ample opportunity to practice computations. Ms. Kaye's lesson is an example of how practice can be embedded in problem-solving activity. Students can also practice previously learned skills while they are learning new material. Consider how much practice students get with single-digit addition while learning how to add multidigit numbers.

Homework

Homework is widely viewed as a useful supplement to classroom instruction. Little is known, however, about how much or what kinds of homework to assign for learning to be optimal. The limited research on homework has been confined to investigations of the relation between the quantity of homework assigned and students' achievement test scores. Neither the quality nor the function of homework has been considered.[52] In fact, even the definition of homework—done in school or not and with what assistance, if any— has not always been clear. Several useful purposes that homework can serve have been identified, including providing practice, preparing students for the next class, fostering traits such as responsibility and independence, and communicating with the home. Assigning homework for punishment, however, is always inappropriate.[53]

As a site for practice, homework can be used to increase procedural fluency and to maintain skill. Homework can provide for both focused and distributed practice. When used for practice, homework assignments should be realistic in length and difficulty if students are to complete them independently and successfully. Students, however, need to be able to perform procedures correctly before they undertake practice without supervision. Otherwise, the practice can automatize incorrect procedures, which are then difficult to correct. Further, homework must be monitored and followed up if it is to have instructional value.[54] In making her homework assignment, Ms. Lawrence first determines that the students understand the new procedure and can perform it correctly. The next day she will follow up on the assignment by asking the students to check one another's work on selected problems.

Students can be assigned tasks for homework that might be used to launch the next day's lesson or to engage the class in an enrichment activity. For example, Mr. Angelo uses the homework to introduce the rule for multiplying by powers of 10. In Mr. Hernandez's class, students are asked to try the various strategies that have been presented and to think about which one they thought was "best" in preparation for the next day's discussion.

Homework also provides a means to communicate with parents about the importance of schoolwork and learning. Many opportunities exist to send home assignments that call for relatively little parental involvement. They may require no specialized knowledge, or relatively simple guidelines may be provided. For example, parents or other caregivers can supervise practice on the basic number combinations. Homework support needs to be provided, however, when home environments may make doing homework difficult.

Manipulatives

The use of concrete materials, sometimes termed *manipulatives*, for teaching mathematics is widely accepted, particularly in the elementary grades. Manipulatives should always be seen as a means and not an end in themselves. They require careful use over sufficient time to allow students to build meaning and make connections. Beginning in the 1960s, manipulatives gained popularity in U.S. elementary school mathematics with the introduction of a variety of concrete materials, including base-10 blocks, Cuisenaire rods, chips for trading, logic blocks, fraction pieces, and Unifix cubes, to name a few.

Manipulatives have had their advocates and critics. Both sides agree, however, that simply putting concrete materials on desks or suggesting to students that they might use manipulatives is not enough to guarantee that students will learn appropriate mathematics from them. The relationship between learning and the use of manipulatives is far more complex than many mathematics educators have thought. Recent research has explored how students interact with manipulatives. Students may not look at these objects the same way adults do, and it can be a challenge for students to see mathematical ideas in them. When students use a manipulative, they need to be helped to see its relevant aspects and to link those aspects to appropriate symbolism and mathematical concepts and operations.[55] Observational studies have documented cases in which students were taught to use manipulatives in a prescribed way to perform "wooden algorithms."[56] If students do not see the connections among object, symbol, language, and idea, using a manipulative becomes just one more thing to learn rather than a process leading to a larger mathematical learning goal.[57]

When used well, manipulatives can enhance student understanding. They can, for example, enable teachers and students to have a conversation that is grounded in a common referential medium, and they can provide material on which students can act productively provided they reflect on their actions in relation to the mathematics being taught.[58] The base-10 blocks that Kurt is using in Ms. Kaye's class provide both student and teacher with a way to discuss the problem that would have been more difficult without the blocks. Research on four successful projects aimed at teaching multidigit number concepts and operations through a problem-solving approach found that, although different in approach, the projects treated the use of conceptual supports, whether manipulatives or diagrams, in similar ways.[59] Each project provided sustained opportunities for students to construct connections between the conceptual support, the written symbols, and the number words and to use the object-word-symbol triad in solving multidigit addition and subtraction problems. Manipulatives also help students correct their own errors.[60] The evidence indicates, in short, that manipulatives can provide valuable support for student learning when teachers interact over time with the students to help them build links between the object, the symbol, and the mathematical idea both represent.

Calculators

Although calculators are used more frequently than manipulatives in grades 4 and 8, the use of calculators is more controversial in mathematics lessons in grades pre-K-8 than are manipulatives, particularly in the elementary grades. Although mathematics educators have advocated the appropriate use of calculators since the 1970s, persistent concerns have been expressed that an extensive use of calculators in mathematics instruction interferes with students' mastery of basic skills and the understanding they need for more advanced mathematics.[61]

A large number of empirical studies of calculator use, including long-term studies,[62] have generally shown that the use of calculators does not threaten the development of basic skills and that it can enhance conceptual understanding, strategic competence, and disposition toward mathematics. A meta-analysis of 79 research studies on the effects of calculator was conducted in 1986 and extended in 1992 with nine additional studies.[63] This analysis found that with the exception of the fourth grade, students at all grade levels who used calculators together with traditional instruction maintained their computational skills. For average-ability students, a small negative effect at fourth grade suggested that sustained use of calculators at that grade might hamper the acquisition of basic skills. On the other hand, use of calculators enhanced basic skills acquisition by average-ability students at all other grade levels, so the negative effect at fourth grade might have been an artifact of conditions specific to those studies that included fourth graders. For all ability groups at all grades, problem solving was improved by the use of calculators. The positive effects were found when calculator use was permitted in testing; the effects were weak or absent, but never negative, when testing was conducted without calculators. Students using calculators were also found to possess a better attitude toward mathematics and a better self-concept in mathematics. This meta-analysis of calculator use has been widely cited to support efforts to introduce calculators into mathematics instruction in grades K to 8. Meta-analysis as a procedure for synthesizing research results, however, has not been without its critics.[64] Studies included in such meta-analyses often vary in quality and use a variety of different treatments labeled with a single term, in this case "calculator use."

Long-term studies of calculator use, however, support the findings of the meta-analysis. A study in Sweden found that students in grades 4–6 who used calculators improved in conceptual understanding, the ability to choose the correct operation, and proficiency with estimation and mental arithmetic but did not lose skill in pencil-and-paper calculations when compared with students in traditional classes.[65] The students in the experimental classes continued to study algorithms, but they spent relatively less time on algorithms and more on problem solving than students in the traditional classes. In an Australian project involving over 60 teachers and 1,000 students, students who had been given unrestricted access to a calculator beginning in kindergarten were familiar with a wider range of numbers, were better with mental calculations and estimation, and were better able to tackle real-world problems than students who had not had access to calculators. Their pattern of use of standard algorithms, left-to-right algorithms, and invented methods did not vary greatly from that of the children who did not have access to calculators. Further, they did not become reliant on calculators at the expense of other methods of calculations. In sum, no detrimental effects of calculator use were observed.[66] These findings are consistent with those from England in which six-year-olds in a calculator awareness project, compared with children in a regular program, demonstrated knowledge of a wider range of numbers, including decimals and negative numbers. Project children also performed better than traditionally taught children with respect to understanding and mental computations and were more enthusiastic and persistent.[67]

Calculator use has been increasing in the United States since 1980. In the 1996 NAEP, teachers of 80% of both fourth graders and eighth graders reported that their students had access to calculators at school. Only 33% of the fourth graders were reported to use calculators as frequently as once a week, whereas 76% of the eighth graders reportedly used calculators daily or weekly. These percentages were up from 16% and 56%, respectively, in 1992. Concomitantly, the percentage of students who never or hardly ever used calculators in class was down from 51% to 26% at the fourth grade and from 24% to 9% at the eighth grade.[68] On TIMSS similar percentages for calculator use were reported by U.S. teachers. In some countries, including some high-achieving countries (such as Japan and Korea) as well as in some low-achieving countries, mathematics teachers rarely had students use calculators.[69] Internationally, there does not appear to be a correlation between calculator use and achievement in mathematics.

The question, therefore, is not whether but how calculators should be used. There is very little empirical research, however, on the effectiveness of various uses of calculators. Issues just beginning to be investigated include when calculators should be introduced, how young children should use them, and how much time needs to be spent on written algorithms when calculators are available. In the experimental projects described above, calculator use was accompanied by instruction on number combinations and traditional written algorithms and by an emphasis on mental calculations. These projects also demonstrate how instructional emphasis in a calculator-inclusive environment can shift from computational procedures to problem solving and mental arithmetic. Although there is substantial support for the use of calculators in school mathematics, their role and place remain open to debate and experimentation.

Issues in Improving Instruction

Research on teaching mathematics offers useful direction for developing instructional practices that lead to mathematical proficiency. The studies we have cited, as well as others too numerous to include, offer a set of recurrent findings worthy of attention. Although these findings are presented in broad strokes, they matter for the finer-grained questions of concern to practitioners and policy makers, parents, and the public. Unless these findings are understood, efforts to improve instructional quality and consequent learning are likely to founder.

First, no instructional practice, commodity, or material exists independently of context and participants as a durable and reliable resource for developing mathematical proficiency. How teachers and students interpret, value, and use such matters as time, curriculum, books, tasks, and calculators shapes whether and how these affect instruction.

Second, effectiveness depends on enactment. The effectiveness of a curriculum, for example, depends not only on its mathematical integrity and organizational design, but also on how usefully it guides instruction. Although analyses of the content of instructional materials are crucial, so too are analyses of how those materials actually play out in lessons day by day across units of instruction: what is taught, in what ways, and what students learn. The same can be said of tools and techniques such as manipulatives, calculators, small-group work, and homework.

Third, teachers and students' interactions about mathematics iteratively shape the effectiveness of their instructional work. Teachers' expectations of students can shape the nature of the tasks the teachers pose, what they ask, how long they wait, how and how much encouragement they provide— elements that together compose students' opportunities to learn as well as their motivation and confidence to learn. The students' responses, in turn, affect teachers' estimates of their capacity and progress, shaping their next moves with students.

Although much is known about effective instruction, many questions merit close study if teachers and researchers are to develop the kind of knowledge needed to improve instruction. We conclude with some core issues crucial to building the knowledge base on teaching and learning for mathematical proficiency.

The first issues center on our myopia in examining the research. The research on teaching that we reviewed was almost entirely U.S. based. Closer probes of practice in other social, political, and cultural settings may challenge many current assumptions about effective instruction in mathematics. Despite an intense and appropriate interest in practices in other countries, Americans know too little about instruction or its effects in other systems. The interactive framework in this chapter offers a perspective that could be used to design studies to look across systems. Comparative research that affords opportunities to learn about key elements of teaching and learning, as well as examining both practice and the environments that shape it, would be enormously helpful in developing a greater knowledge of teaching and learning for mathematical proficiency. Researchers need to address not just what the curriculum is but how it is used and what teachers and students do with it, not just how much time is allocated for mathematics but how that time is spent. They need to investigate not just whether calculators or other resources are used, but how they are used.[70] Research that looks across countries can provide a sharper picture of what matters in instruction aimed at developing proficiency.

A second set of issues concerns instruction over time. Although learning is fundamentally temporal, too little research has addressed the ways in which instruction develops over time. Many studies are restricted to isolated fragments of teaching and learning, providing little understanding of how the interactions of teachers, students, and content emerge over time, and how earlier interactions shape later ones. How do ideas developed in class affect later work, and what affects teachers' and students' ability and inclination to make such links, as well as their use of such connections over time? How is time used, and how does its use by teachers and students affect the quality of instruction?

A third arena concerns students and how their diversity affects instruction. Too little research offers insight into the experience of students and how the instruction offered, together with their responses to it, affects their learning. Still more important, there are too few well-designed studies that would offer insight into how instruction might be developed to work effectively for all students. Too often, research on classroom teaching and learning either studies faceless, colorless students and teachers out of context, or it is situated in particular contexts but lacks a design that permits analyses that could provide the knowledge needed for effective instruction in mathematics.

Fourth, too little research has addressed what it takes for students to learn mathematics in class. What do students need to do, and know how to do, in order to profit from the instruction offered by each of our four teachers? A cursory glance at any mathematics class makes plain that the skills, abilities, knowledge, and dispositions displayed by students are not the same, and yet teachers and researchers rarely attend to what students need to know and be able to do in order to use instruction effectively. People seem to assume implicitly that instruction acts on students and that opportunities to learn are actually moments of learning. Research that examined both what students have to know and do in mathematics instruction and what teachers can do to enable all students to make use of that instruction would add significantly to the knowledge base on teaching and learning mathematics.

A fifth set of issues has to do with reconnecting research on teacher knowledge with instructional effectiveness. Although most people believe that teachers' knowledge of mathematics and of students makes a difference for the quality of teaching, little empirical confirmation of this belief can be found. Moreover, too little is known about the mathematical knowledge that teachers need and how it is used in instruction. We discuss this point more in chapter 10, but it is important to the discussion in this chapter, too. Every time we reiterate that how teachers *use* texts, manipulatives, and calculators makes the difference, we are hovering around questions concerning what teachers know and how they make use of that knowledge in teaching.

Finally, too little of the extant research probes the work of teaching at a sufficiently fine grain to contribute to the development of a conceptual and practical language of practice. Much of the interactive work in instruction remains unexamined, which leaves to teachers the unnecessary challenge of reinventing their practice from scratch, armed with only general advice. Suggestions that a class "discuss the solutions to a problem" provides little specificity about what constitutes a productive discussion and runs the risk of a free-for-all session that resembles sharing more than instruction. Research needs to be designed to illuminate what is entailed in a "discussion" and to probe the specific moves that teachers and students engage in that lead to productive rather than an unproductive discussions.

Instruction that develops mathematical proficiency is neither simple, common, nor well understood. It comes in many forms and can follow a variety of paths. As this chapter demonstrates, such instruction offers numerous fertile sites for research that could make a profound difference in teachers' practice and their students' learning.

Notes

1. An interactive perspective on teaching and learning has been discussed by a number of people, including Piaget, Vygotsky, Bauersfeld, Steier, Voigt, Hawkins, Gravemeijer, Easley, Cobb, and von Glaserfeld. The particular version employed here is based on the work of Cohen and Ball, 1999, 2000, in press.
2. Cohen and Ball, 1999, 2000, in press.
3. This lesson is typical of lessons observed in many U.S. classrooms during the past half-century. See, for example, the report by Fey, 1979, or the more recent TIMSS video study (Stigler and Hiebert, 1999).
4. Note that Mr. Angelo has avoided 10^0, partly because the rule is stated in terms of moving the decimal point, and multiplying by $10^0 = 1$ leaves the number unchanged.
5. U.S. eighth-grade lessons from the TIMSS video study were characterized the same way. See Stigler and Hiebert, 1999.
6. Cohen and Ball, 2000.

7. Berliner and Biddle, 1995. Opportunity to learn was also studied in what is now called the First International Mathematics Study (Husén, 1967), although there it was based on teachers' perceptions of students' opportunity to learn.

8. McKnight, Crosswhite, Dossey, Kifer, Swafford, Travers, and Cooney, 1987.

9. Knapp, Shields, and Turnbull, 1995; Mason, Schroeter, Combs, and Washington, 1992; Steele, 1992.

10. Berliner, 1979.

11. Stevenson and Stigler, 1992, p. 150.

12. Freeman and Porter, 1989; Porter, 1993.

13. See, for example, Campbell, 1996; Carpenter, Fennema, Peterson, Chiang, and Loef, 1989; Hiebert, Carpenter, Fennema, Fuson, Wearne, Murray, Olivier, and Human, 1997; Knapp, 1995; Silver and Stein, 1996.

14. Doyle, 1983, 1988; Stein, Grover, and Henningsen, 1996.

15. Henningsen and Stein, 1997; Stein, Grover, and Henningsen, 1996.

16. Clark and Yinger, 1979.

17. Shavelson and Stern, 1981.

18. Boaler, 1997.

19. Good and Brophy, 2000.

20. Good and Brophy, 2000.

21. Smith, 1996.

22. For example, Hatano, 1988, suggests that students are motivated to learn with understanding when they encounter novel problems regularly, are encouraged to seek comprehension over efficiency, and engage in dialogue.

23. National Research Council, 1999b, pp. 29–38.

24. Feather, 1982.

25. Bandura, 1997; Bandura and Schunk, 1981; Dweck and Elliott, 1983.

26. Good and Brophy, 2000.

27. Brophy, 1998, Brophy and Kher, 1986; Good and Brophy, 2000.

28. These principles and the discussion that follows are based largely on a synthesis by Baroody, 1999. For related research and syntheses, see also Baroody, 1987, 1996; Cawley, 1985; and Geary, 1993. For practical advice for teaching, see Thornton and Bley, 1994.

29. Baroody, 1999.

30. See Donlan, 1998, for example, for a discussion of students with speech deficiencies. See Nunes and Moreno, 1998, for a discussion of hearing impairment.

31. Becker, 1981; Leder, 1987. See also Leder, 1992.

32. Ladson-Billings, 1999.

33. Foster, 1995.

34. Steele, 1992.

35. Knapp, 1995.

36. Good and Brophy, 2000.

37. See, for example, Ball and Bass, 2000; Cobb, Boufi, McClain, and Whitenack, 1997; Hiebert and Wearne, 1993; Lampert, 1990; Wood, 1999.

38. Hiebert, Carpenter, Fennema, Fuson, Wearne, Murray, Olivier, and Human, 1997.

39. Oakes, 1985: Oakes, Gamoran, and Page, 1992.
40. Kulik, 1992; Linchevski and Kutsher, 1998; Mason and Good, 1993; Mosteller, Light, and Sachs, 1996; Slavin, 1987, 1993.
41. Loveless, 1998.
42. Linchevski and Kutscher, 1998.
43. Argys, Rees, and Brewer, 1996.
44. Druckman and Bjork, 1994, pp. 83-111; Johnson, Johnson, and Maruyama, 1983; Sharan, 1980; Slavin, 1980, 1983, 1995.
45. Ellis and Gauvain, 1992.
46. Fennema, Carpenter, Franke, Levi, Jacobs, and Empson, 1996; Thompson and Briars, 1989.
47. Hiebert, 1990.
48. Case, 1985.
49. Flanders, 1987; McKnight, Crosswhite, Dossey, Kifer, Swafford, Travers, and Cooney, 1987; Schmidt, McKnight, and Raizen, 1997.
50. Siegler and Stern, in press; Sophian, 1997.
51. Carpenter, Fennema, Peterson, Chiang, and Loef, 1989; Cobb, Wood, Yackel, Nicholls, Wheatley, Trigatti, and Perlwitz, 1991; Fennema, Carpenter, Franke, Levi, Jacobs, and Empson, 1996; Hiebert and Wearne, 1993.
52. Cooper, 1989; Epstein, 1988; Miller and Kelley, 1991.
53. Epstein, 1998; Good and Brophy, 2000.
54. Good and Brophy, 2000.
55. Fuson, 1986; Fuson and Briars, 1990; Wearne and Hiebert, 1988.
56. Cohen, 1990; Hart, 1996; Resnick and Omanson, 1987.
57. Ball, 1992a, 1992b.
58. Thompson and Lambden, 1994.
59. Fuson, Wearne, Hiebert, Murray, Human, Olivier, Carpenter, and Fennema, 1997; Hiebert, Carpenter, Fennema, Fuson, Wearne, Murray, Olivier, and Human, 1997.
60. Fuson, 1986.
61. Fey, 1989; NCTM, 1974.
62. Brolin and Björk, 1992; Groves 1993, 1994a, 1994b; Hembree and Dessart, 1986, 1992; Ruthven, 1996, 1998; Shuard, 1992.
63. Hembree and Dessart, 1986, 1992.
64. Ruthven, 1996.
65. Brolin and Björk, 1992.
66. Groves, 1993, 1994a, 1994b.
67. Shuard, 1992.
68. Mitchell, Hawkins, Jakwerth, Stancavage, and Dossey, 1999.
69. National Research Council, 1999a, p. 48.
70. Stigler and Hiebert, 1999.

References

Argys, L. M., Rees, D. I., & Brewer, D. J. (1996). Detracking America's schools: Equity at zero cost? *Journal of Policy Analysis and Management, 15,* 623–645.

Ball, D. L. (1992a). Constructing new forms of teaching: Subject matter knowledge in inservice teacher education. *Journal of Teacher Education, 43,* 347–356.

Ball, D. L. (1992b). Magical hopes: Manipulatives and the reform of math education. *American Educator, 14,* 46–47.

Ball, D. L., & Bass, H. (2000). Making believe: The collective construction of public mathematical knowledge in the elementary classroom. In D. Phillips (Ed.), *Constructivism in education* (Ninety-ninth Yearbook of the National Society for the Study of Education, Part 1, pp. 193–224). Chicago: University of Chicago Press.

Bandura, A. (1997). *Self-efficacy: The exercise of control.* New York: Freeman.

Bandura, A., & Schunk, D. (1981). Cultivating competence, self-efficacy, and intrinsic interest through proximal self-motivation. *Journal of Personality and Social Psychology, 41,* 586–598.

Baroody, A. J. (1987). *Children's mathematical thinking: A developmental framework for preschool, primary, and special education teachers.* New York: Teachers College Press.

Baroody, A. J. (1996). An investigative approach to teaching children labeled learning disabled. In D. K. Reid, W. P. Hresko, & H. L. Swanson (Eds.), *Cognitive approaches to learning disabilities* (3rd ed., pp. 545–615). Austin, TX: Pro-Ed.

Baroody, A. J. (1999). The development of basic number and arithmetic knowledge among children classified as mentally retarded. In L. M. Glidden (Ed.), *International review of research in mental retardation* (vol. 22, pp. 51–103). New York: Academic Press.

Becker, J. (1981). Differential treatment of females and males in mathematics class. *Journal for Research in Mathematics Education, 12,* 40–53.

Berliner, D. (1979). Tempus educare. In P. Peterson & H. Walberg (Eds.), *Research on teaching: Concepts, findings, and implications.* Berkeley, CA: McCutchan.

Berliner, D., & Biddle, B. (1995). *The manufactured crisis: Myth, fraud, and the attack on America's public schools.* New York: Addison-Wesley.

Boaler, J. (1997). *Experiencing school mathematics: Teaching styles, sex and setting.* Buckingham, UK: Open University Press.

Brolin, H., & Björk, L-E. (1992). Introducing calculators in Swedish schools. In J. T. Fey and C. R. Hirsch (Eds.), *Calculators in mathematics education* (1992 Yearbook of the National Council of Teachers of Mathematics, pp. 226–232). Reston, VA: NCTM.

Brophy, J. (1998). *Motivating students to learn.* Boston: McGraw-Hill.

Brophy, J., & Kher, N. (1986). Teacher socialization as a mechanism for developing student motivation to learn. In R. Feldman (Ed.), *Social psychology applied to education* (pp. 256–288). New York: Cambridge University Press.

Campbell, P. F. (1996). Empowering children and teachers in the elementary mathematics classrooms of urban schools. *Urban Education, 30,* 449–475.

Case, R. (1985). *Intellectual development: Birth to adulthood.* New York: Academic Press.

Carpenter, T. P., Fennema, E., Fuson, K., Hiebert, J. Human, P., Murray, H., Olivier, A., & Wearne, D. (1999). Learning basic number concepts and skills as problem solving. In E. Fennema & T. A. Romberg, *Mathematics classrooms that promote understanding* (pp. 45–61). Mahwah, NJ: Erlbaum.

Carpenter, T. P., Fennema, E., Peterson, P. L., Chiang, C. P., & Loef, M. (1989). Using knowledge of children's mathematics thinking in classroom teaching: An experimental study. *American Educational Research Journal, 26,* 499–531.

Cawley, J. F. (1985). Cognition and the learning disabled. In J. F. Cawley (Ed.), *Cognitive strategies and mathematics for the learning disabled* (pp. 1–32). Rockville, MD: Aspen.

Clark, C., & Yinger, R. (1979). Teachers' thinking. In P. L. Peterson & H. J. Walberg (Eds.), *Research on teaching: Concepts, findings, and implications* (pp. 231–263). Berkeley, CA: McCutchan.

Cobb, P., Boufi, A., McClain, K., & Whitenack, J. (1997). Reflective discourse and collective reflection. *Journal for Research in Mathematics Education, 28,* 258–277.

Cobb, P., Wood, T., Yackel, E., Nicholls, J., Wheatley, G., Trigatti, B., & Perlwitz, M. (1991). Assessment of a problem-centered second-grade mathematics project. *Journal for Research in Mathematics Education, 22,* 3–29.

Cohen, D. K. (1990). Revolution in one classroom: The case of Mrs. Oublier. *Education Evaluation and Policy Analysis, 12,* 311–329.

Cohen, D. K., & Ball, D. L. (1999). *Instruction, capacity, and improvement* (CPRE Research Report No. RR-043). Philadelphia: University of Pennsylvania, Consortium for Policy Research in Education. Available: http://www.gse.upenn.edu/cpre/docs/pubs/rr43.pdf. [July 10, 2001].

Cohen, D. K., & Ball, D. L. (2000, April). Instructional innovation: Reconsidering the story. Paper presented at the meeting of the American Educational Research Association, New Orleans.

Cohen, D. K., & Ball, D. L. (in press). Making change: Instruction and its improvement. *Phi Delta Kappan.*

Cooper, H. (1989). *Homework.* New York: Longman.

Donlan, C. (1998). Number without language? Studies of children with specific language impairments. In C. Donlan (Ed.), *The development of mathematical skills* (pp. 255–274). East Sussex, UK: Psychology Press.

Doyle, W. (1983). Academic work. *Review of Educational Research, 53,* 159–199.

Doyle, W. (1988). Work in mathematics classes: The context of students' thinking during instruction. *Educational Psychologist, 23,* 167–180.

Druckman, D., & Bjork, R. A. (Eds). (1994). *Learning, remembering, believing: Enhancing human performance.* Washington, DC: National Academy Press. Available: http://books.nap.edu/catalog/2303.html. [July 10, 2001].

Dweck, C., & Elliott, E. (1983). Achievement motivation. In E. M. Heatherington (Ed.), P. H. Mussen (Series Ed.), *Handbook of child psychology: Vol. 4. Socialization, personality, and social development* (4th ed., pp. 643–691). New York: Wiley.

Ellis, S. A., & Gauvain, M. (1992). Social cultural influences on children's collaborative interactions. In L. T. Winegar & J. Valsiner (Eds.), *Children's development within social context* (pp. 155–180). Hillsdale, NJ: Erlbaum.

Epstein, J. (1988). Homework practices, achievements, and behaviors of elementary school students (Report No. 26). Baltimore: Johns Hopkins University, Center for Research on Elementary and Middle Schools. (ERIC Document Reproduction Service No. ED 301 322).

Epstein, J. (1998, April). *Interactive homework: Effective strategies to connect home and school.* Paper presented at the meeting of the American Educational Research Association, San Diego, CA.

Feather, N. (Ed.). (1982). *Expectations and actions.* Hillsdale, NJ: Erlbaum.

Fennema, E., Carpenter, T. P., Franke, M. L., Levi, L., Jacobs, V. R., & Empson, S. B. (1996). A longitudinal study of learning to use children's thinking in mathematics instruction. *Journal for Research in Mathematics Education, 27,* 403–434.

Fey, J. T. (1979). Mathematics teaching today: Perspectives from three national surveys. *Mathematics Teacher, 72,* 490–504.

Fey, J. T. (1989). Technology and mathematics education: A survey of recent developments and important problems. *Educational Studies in Mathematics, 20,* 237–272.

Flanders, J. R. (1987, September). How much of the content in mathematics textbooks is new? *Arithmetic Teacher, 35,* 1, 18–23.

Foster, M. (1995). African American teachers and culturally relevant pedagogy. In J. A. Banks & C. M. Banks (Eds.), *Handbook of research on multicultural education* (pp. 570–581). New York: Macmillan.

Freeman, D., & Porter, A. (1989). Do textbooks dictate the content of mathematics instruction in elementary schools? *American Educational Research Journal, 26,* 403–421.

Fuson, K. C. (1986). Roles of representation and verbalization in the teaching of multi-digit addition and subtraction. *European Journal of Psychology of Education, 1,* 35–56.

Fuson, K. C., Wearne, D., Hiebert, J. C., Murray, H. G., Human, P. G., Olivier, A. I, Carpenter, T. P., & Fennema E. (1997). Children's conceptual structures for multidigit numbers and methods of multidigit addition and subtraction. *Journal for Research in Mathematics Education, 28,* 130–162.

Fuson, K. C., & Briars, D. J. (1990). Using a base-ten block learning/teaching approach for first and second grade place-value and multidigit addition and subtraction. *Journal for Research in Mathematics Education 21,* 180–206.

Geary, D. C. (1993). Mathematical disabilities: Cognitive, neuropsychological, and genetic components. *Psychological Bulletin, 114,* 345–362.

Geary, D. C. (1994). *Children's mathematical development: Research and practical applications.* Washington, DC: American Psychological Association.

Good, T. L., & Brophy, J. E. (2000). *Looking in classrooms* (8th ed.). New York: Longman.

Good, T. L., Grouws, D. A., & Ebmeier, H. (1983). *Active teaching.* New York: Longman.

Groves, S. (1993). The effect of calculator use on third graders' solutions of real world division and multiplication problems. In I. Hirabayashi, N. Nodha, K. Shigematsu, & F. L. Lin (Eds.), *Proceedings of the Seventeenth International Conference for the Psychology of Mathematics Education,* (vol. 2, pp. 9–16). Tsukuba, Japan: PME Program Committee. (ERIC Document Reproduction Service No. ED 383 536).

Groves, S. (1994a). Calculators: A learning environment to promote number sense. Paper presented at the meeting of the American Educational Research Association, New Orleans. (ERIC Document Reproduction Service No. ED 373 969).

Groves, S. (1994b). The effect of calculator use on third and fourth graders' computation and choice of calculating device. In J. da Ponte & J. F. Matos (Eds.), *Proceedings of the Eighteenth International Conference for the Psychology of Mathematics Education* (vol. 3, pp. 33–40). Lisbon, Portugal: PME Program Committee. (ERIC Document Reproduction Service No. ED 383 537).

Hatano, G. (1988). Social and motivational bases for mathematical understanding. In G. B. Saxe & M. Gearhart (Eds.), *Children's mathematics* (pp. 55–70). San Francisco: Jossey-Bass.

Hart, K. (1996). What responsibility do researchers have to mathematics teachers and children? In C. Alsina, J. M. Alvarez, B. Hodgson, C. Laborde, & A. Perez (Eds.), *8th International Congress on Mathematics Education: Selected lectures* (pp. 251–256). Seville, Spain: S.A.E.M. Thales.

Hembree, R., & Dessart, D. J. (1986). Effects of hand-held calculators in precollege mathematics education: A meta-analysis. *Journal for Research in Mathematics Education, 17*, 83–99.

Hembree R., & Dessart, D. J. (1992). Research on calculators in mathematics education. In J. Fey & C. Hirsch (Eds.), *Calculators in mathematics education* (pp. 23–32). Reston, VA: National Council of Teachers of Mathematics.

Henningsen, M., & Stein, M. K. (1997). Mathematical tasks and student cognition: Classroom-based factors that support and inhibit high-level mathematical thinking and reasoning. *Journal for Research in Mathematics Education, 28*, 524–549.

Hiebert, J. (1990). The role of routine procedures in the development of mathematical competence. In T. J. Cooney & C. R. Hirsch (Eds.), *Teaching and learning mathematics in the 1990s* (1990 Yearbook of the National Council of Teachers of Mathematics, pp. 31–40). Reston, VA: NCTM.

Hiebert, J., & Wearne, D. (1993). Instructional tasks, classroom discourse, and student learning in second grade. *American Educational Research Journal, 30*, 393–425.

Hiebert, J., Carpenter, T. P., Fennema, E., Fuson, K. C., Wearne, D., Murray, H., Olivier, A., & Human, P. (1997). *Making sense: Teaching and learning mathematics with understanding.* Portsmouth, NH: Heinemann.

Husén, T. (Ed.). (1967). *International study of achievement in mathematics: A comparative study of twelve countries* (vol. 2). New York: Wiley.

Johnson, D., Johnson, R., & Maruyama, G. (1983). Interdependence and interpersonal attraction among heterogeneous and homogeneous individuals: A theoretical formulation and a meta-analysis of the research. *Review of Educational Research, 53*, 5–54.

Knapp M. S., Shields, P. M., Turnbull, B. J. (1995). Academic challenge in high-poverty classrooms. *Phi Delta Kappan, 76*, 770–776.

Knapp, M. S. (1995). *Teaching for meaning in high poverty classrooms.* New York: Teachers College Press.

Kulik, J. A. (1992). *An analysis of the research on ability grouping: Historical and contemporary perspectives* (Ability Grouping Research-Based Decision Making Series, No. 9204). Ann Arbor: University of Michigan.

Ladson-Billings, G. (1999). *Mathematics for all? Perspectives on the mathematics achievement gap.* Unpublished paper prepared for the National Research Council, Washington, DC.

Lampert, M. (1990). When the problem is not the question and the solution is not the answer: Mathematical knowing and teaching. *American Educational Research Journal, 27*, 29–63.

Leder, G. C. (1987). Teacher student interaction: A case study. *Educational Studies in Mathematics, 18*, 255–271.

Leder, G. C. (1992). Mathematics and gender: Changing perspectives. In D. Grouws (Ed.), *Handbook of research on mathematics teaching and learning* (pp. 597–622). New York: Macmillan.

Linchevski, L., & Kutscher, F. (1998). Tell me with whom you're learning, and I'll tell you how much you've learned: Mixed-ability versus same-ability grouping in mathematics. *Journal for Research in Mathematics Education, 29*, 533–554.

Loveless, T. (1998). The tracking and ability grouping debate. *Fordham Report, 2*(8), 1–27. Available: http://www.edexcellence.net/library/track.html. [July 10, 2001].

Mason, D. A., & Good, T. L. (1993). Effects of two-group and whole-class teaching on regrouped elementary students' mathematics achievement. *American Educational Research Journal, 30*, 328–360.

Mason, D., Schroeter, D., Combs, R., & Washington, K. (1992). Assigning average achieving eighth graders to advanced mathematics classes in an urban junior high. *Elementary School Journal, 92*, 587–599.

McKnight, C. C., Crosswhite, F. J., Dossey, J. A., Kifer, E., Swafford, J. O., Travers, K. J., & Cooney, T. J. (1987). *The underachieving curriculum: Assessing U.S. schools mathematics from an international perspective.* Champaign, IL: Stipes.

Mitchell, J. H., Hawkins, E. F., Jakwerth, P. M,. Stancavage, F. B., & Dossey, J. A. (1999). *Student work and teacher practices in mathematics* (NCES 1999-453). Washington, DC: National Center for Educational Statistics. Available: http://nces.ed.gov/spider/webspider/1999453.shtml. [July 10, 2001].

Miller, D., & Kelley, M. (1991). Interventions for improving homework performance: A critical review. *School Psychology Quarterly, 6*, 174–185.

Mosteller, F., Light, R. J., & Sachs, J. A. (1996). Sustained inquiry in education: Lessons from skill grouping and class size. *Harvard Educational Review, 66*, 797–842.

National Council of Teachers of Mathematics. (1974, December). NCTM Board approves policy statement on the use of minicalculators in the mathematics classroom. *NCTM Newsletter, 11*, 3.

National Research Council. (1999a). *Global perspectives for local action: Using TIMSS to improve U.S. mathematics and science education.* Washington, DC: National Academy Press. Available: http://books.nap.edu/catalog/9605.html. [July 10, 2001].

National Research Council. (1999b). *Improving student learning: A strategic plan for education research and its utilization.* Washington, DC: National Academy Press. Available: http://books.nap.edu/catalog/6488.html. [July 10, 2001].

Nunes, T., & Moreno, C. (1998). Is hearing impairment a cause of difficulties in learning mathematics? In C. Donlan (Ed.), *The development of mathematical skills* (pp. 227–254). East Sussex, UK: Psychology Press.

Oakes, J. (1985). *Keeping track: How schools structure inequality.* New Haven: Yale University Press.

Oakes, J., Gamoran, A., & Page, R. N. (1992). Curriculum differentiation: Opportunities, outcomes, and meanings. In P. W. Jackson (Ed.), *Handbook of research on curriculum* (pp. 570–608). New York: Macmillan.

Porter, A. (1993). School delivery standards. *Educational Research, 22*, 24–30.

Resnick, L., & Omanson, S. (1987). Learning to understand arithmetic. In R. Glaser (Ed.), *Advances in instructional psychology* (vol. 3, pp. 41–95). Hillsdale, NJ: Erlbaum.

Ruthven, K. (1996). Calculators in mathematics curriculum: The scope of personal computational technology. In A. J. Bishop, K Clements, C. Keitel, J. Kilpatrick, & C. Laborde (Eds.), *International handbook of mathematics education* (pp. 435–468). Dordrecht, The Netherlands: Kluwer.

Ruthven, K. (1998). The use of mental, written and calculator strategies of numerical computation by upper primary pupils within a "calculator-aware" curriculum. *British Educational Research Journal, 24*, 21–42.

Schmidt, W. H., McKnight, C. C., & Raizen, S. A. (1997). *A splintered vision: An investigation of U.S. science and mathematics education.* Dordrecht, The Netherlands: Kluwer.

Sharan S. (1980). Cooperative learning in small groups: Recent methods and effects on achievement, attitudes, and ethnic relations. *Review of Education Research, 50*, 241–271.

Shavelson, R. J., & Stern, P. (1981). Research on teachers' pedagogical thoughts, judgments, decisions, and behavior. *Review of Educational Research, 51*, 455–498.

Shuard, H. (1992). CAN: Calculator use in the primary grades in England and Wales. In J. T. Fey and C. R. Hirsch (Eds.), *Calculators in mathematics education* (1992 Yearbook of the National Council of Teachers of Mathematics, pp. 33–45). Reston, VA: NCTM.

Siegler, R. S., & Stern, E. (in press). Conscious and unconscious strategy discoveries: A microgenetic analysis. *Journal of Experimental Psychology: General.*

Silver, E. A., & Stein, M. (1996). The QUASAR Project: The "revolution of the possible" in mathematics instructional reform in urban middle schools. *Urban Education, 30*, 476–521.

Slavin, R. E. (1980). Cooperative learning. *Review of Educational Research, 50*, 315–342.

Slavin, R. E. (1983). *Cooperative learning.* New York: Longman.

Slavin, R. E. (1987). Ability grouping and student achievement in elementary schools: A best-evidence synthesis. *Review of Educational Research, 57*, 293–336.

Slavin, R. E. (1993). Ability grouping in the middle grades: Achievement effects and alternatives. *Elementary School Journal, 93*, 535–552.

Slavin, R. E. (1995). *Cooperative learning: Theory, research, and practice* (2nd ed.). Boston: Allyn & Bacon.

Smith, J. P., III. (1996). Efficacy and teaching mathematics by telling: A challenge for reform. *Journal for Research in Mathematics Education, 27*, 387–402.

Sophian, C. (1997). Beyond competence: The significance of performance for conceptual development. *Cognitive Development, 12*, 281–303.

Steele, C. (1992, April). Race and the schooling of black Americans. *Atlantic Monthly*, pp. 68–78.

Stein, M. K., Grover, B. W., & Henningsen, M. (1996). Building student capacity for mathematical thinking and reasoning: An analysis of mathematical tasks used in reform classrooms. *American Educational Research Journal, 33*, 455–488.

Stevenson, H. W., & Stigler, J. W. (1992). *The learning gap: Why our schools are failing and what we can learn from Japanese and Chinese education.* New York: Simon & Schuster.

Stigler, J. W., & Hiebert, J. (1999). *The teaching gap: Best ideas from the world's teachers for improving education in the classroom.* New York: Free Press.

Thompson, A. G., & Briars, D. J. (1989). Assessing students' learning to inform teaching: The message in NCTM's Evaluation Standards. *Arithmetic Teacher, 37* (4), 22–26.

Thompson, P. W., & Lambdin, D. (1994). Research into practice: Concrete materials and teaching for mathematical understanding. *Arithmetic Teacher, 41*, 556–558.

Thornton, C. A., & Bley, N. S. (1994). *Windows of opportunity: Mathematics for students with special needs*. Reston, VA: National Council of Teachers of Mathematics.

Wood, T. (1999). Creating a context for argument in mathematics class. *Journal for Research in Mathematics Education, 30*, 171–191.

Wearne, D., & Hiebert, J. (1988). A cognitive approach to meaningful mathematics instruction: Testing a local theory using decimal numbers. *Journal for Research in Mathematics Education, 19*, 371–384.

10

DEVELOPING PROFICIENCY IN TEACHING MATHEMATICS

In the previous chapter, we examined teaching for mathematical proficiency. We now turn our attention to what it takes to develop *proficiency in teaching mathematics*. Proficiency in teaching is related to effectiveness: consistently helping students learn worthwhile mathematical content. Proficiency also entails versatility: being able to work effectively with a wide variety of students in different environments and across a range of mathematical content.

What Does It Take to Teach for Mathematical Proficiency?

Teaching in the ways portrayed in chapter 9 is a complex practice that draws on a broad range of resources. Despite the common myth that teaching is little more than common sense or that some people are just born teachers, effective teaching practice can be learned. In this chapter, we consider what teachers need to learn and how they can learn it.

First, what does it take to be proficient at mathematics teaching? If their students are to develop mathematical proficiency, teachers must have a clear vision of the goals of instruction and what proficiency means for the specific mathematical content they are teaching. They need to know the mathematics they teach as well as the horizons of that mathematics—where it can lead and where their students are headed with it. They need to be able to use their knowledge flexibly in practice to appraise and adapt instructional materials, to represent the content in honest and accessible ways, to plan and conduct instruction, and to assess what students are learning. Teachers need to be able to hear and see expressions of students' mathematical ideas and to design

> Despite the common myth that teaching is little more than common sense or that some people are just born teachers, effective teaching practice can be learned.

A Chinese teacher on how a profound understanding of fundamental mathematics is attained

One thing is to study whom you are teaching, the other thing is to study the knowledge you are teaching. If you can interweave the two things together nicely, you will succeed. . . . Believe me, it seems to be simple when I talk about it, but when you really do it, it is very complicated, subtle, and takes a lot of time. It is easy to be an elementary school teacher, but it is difficult to be a good elementary school teacher.

SOURCE: Ma, 1999, p. 136. Used by permission from Lawrence Erlbaum Associates.

---

appropriate ways to respond. A teacher must interpret students' written work, analyze their reasoning, and respond to the different methods they might use in solving a problem. Teaching requires the ability to see the mathematical possibilities in a task, sizing it up and adapting it for a specific group of students. Familiarity with the trajectories along which fundamental mathematical ideas develop is crucial if a teacher is to promote students' movement along those trajectories. In short, teachers need to muster and deploy a wide range of resources to support the acquisition of mathematical proficiency.

In the next two sections, we first discuss the knowledge base needed for teaching mathematics and then offer a framework for looking at proficient teaching of mathematics. In the last two sections, we discuss four programs for developing proficient teaching and then consider how teachers might develop communities of practice.

The Knowledge Base for Teaching Mathematics

Three kinds of knowledge are crucial for teaching school mathematics: knowledge of mathematics, knowledge of students, and knowledge of instructional practices.[1] These can be seen in the instructional triangle (Box 9-1 in chapter 9 and below).[2] Mathematics and students are two of the triangle's vertices, and instructional practices are the interactions portrayed by the arrows.

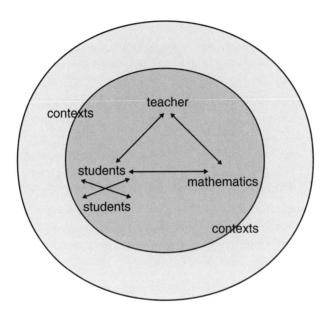

Mathematical knowledge includes knowledge of mathematical facts, concepts, procedures, and the relationships among them; knowledge of the ways that mathematical ideas can be represented; and knowledge of mathematics as a discipline—in particular, how mathematical knowledge is produced, the nature of discourse in mathematics, and the norms and standards of evidence that guide argument and proof. In our use of the term, *knowledge of mathematics* includes consideration of the goals of mathematics instruction and provides a basis for discriminating and prioritizing those goals. Knowing mathematics for teaching also entails more than knowing mathematics for oneself. Teachers certainly need to be able to understand concepts correctly and perform procedures accurately, but they also must be able to understand the conceptual foundations of that knowledge. In the course of their work as teachers, they must understand mathematics in ways that allow them to explain and unpack ideas in ways not needed in ordinary adult life. The mathematical sensibilities they hold matter in guiding their decisions and interpretations of students' mathematical efforts.

Knowledge of students and how they learn mathematics includes general knowledge of how various mathematical ideas develop in children over time as well as specific knowledge of how to determine where in a developmental trajectory a child might be. It includes familiarity with the common difficulties that students have with certain mathematical concepts and procedures, and it encompasses knowledge about learning and about the sorts of experiences, designs, and approaches that influence students' thinking and learning.

Knowledge of instructional practice includes knowledge of curriculum, knowledge of tasks and tools for teaching important mathematical ideas, knowledge of how to design and manage classroom discourse, and knowledge of classroom norms that support the development of mathematical proficiency. Teaching entails more than knowledge, however. Teachers need to do as well as to know. For example, knowledge of what makes a good instructional task is one thing; being able to use a task effectively in class with a group of sixth graders is another. Understanding norms that support productive classroom activity is different from being able to develop and use such norms with a diverse class.

Knowledge of Mathematics

Because knowledge of the content to be taught is the cornerstone of teaching for proficiency, we begin with it. There is a substantial body of research on teachers' mathematical knowledge, and teachers' knowledge of mathematics is prominent in discussions of how to improve mathematics instruction. Improving teachers' mathematical knowledge and their capacity to use it to do the work of teaching is crucial in developing students' mathematical proficiency.

Many recent studies have revealed that U.S. elementary and middle school teachers possess a limited knowledge of mathematics, including the mathematics they teach. The mathematical education they received, both as K-12 students and in teacher preparation, has not provided them with appropriate or sufficient opportunities to learn mathematics. As a result of that education, teachers may know the facts and procedures that they teach but often have a relatively weak understanding of the conceptual basis for that knowledge. Many have difficulty clarifying mathematical ideas or solving problems that involve more than routine calculations.[3] For example, virtually all teachers can multiply multidigit numbers, but several researchers have found that many prospective and practicing elementary school teachers cannot explain the basis for multidigit multiplication using place-value concepts and the underlying properties for adding and multiplying.[4] In another study,[5] teachers of fourth through sixth graders scored over 90% on items testing common decimal calculations, but fewer than half could find a number between 3.1 and 3.11.

Teachers frequently regard mathematics as a fixed body of facts and procedures that are learned by memorization, and that view carries over into their instruction. Many have little appreciation of the ways in which mathematical knowledge is generated or justified. Preservice teachers, for example, have repeatedly been shown to be quite willing to accept a series of instances as proving a mathematical generalization.[6] Nowhere in their education have they had opportunities to study and experience the nature and role of justification in mathematics, a notion central to developing mathematical knowledge.

Although teachers may understand the mathematics they teach in only a superficial way, simply taking more of the standard college mathematics courses does not appear to help matters. The evidence on this score has been consistent, although the reasons have not been adequately explored. For example, a study of prospective secondary mathematics teachers at three major institutions showed that, although they had completed the upper-division college mathematics courses required for the mathematics major, they had only a cursory understanding of the concepts underlying elementary mathematics.[7] The mathematics of the elementary and middle school curriculum is not trivial, and the underlying concepts and structures are worthy of serious, sustained study by teachers. To develop prospective teachers' understanding of the mathematics they will teach, careful attention must be given to identifying the mathematics that teachers need in order to teach effectively, articulating the ways in which they must use it in practice and what that implies for their opportunities to learn mathematics. This sort of attention to teachers' mathematical knowledge and its central role in practice is crucial to ensure that their study of mathematics provides teachers with mathematical knowledge useful to teaching well.

Teachers' mathematical knowledge and student achievement. Conventional wisdom asserts that student achievement must be related to teachers' knowledge of their subject. That wisdom is contained in adages such as "You cannot teach what you don't know." For the better part of a century, researchers have attempted to find a positive relation between teacher content knowledge and student achievement. For the most part, the results have been disappointing: Most studies have failed to find a strong relationship between the two.

Many studies, however, have relied on crude measures of these variables. The measure of teacher knowledge, for example, has often been the number of mathematics courses taken or other easily documented data from college transcripts. Such measures do not provide an accurate index of the specific mathematics that teachers know or of how they hold that knowledge. Teachers may have completed their courses successfully without achieving mathematical proficiency. Or they may have learned the mathematics but not know how to use it in their teaching to help students learn. They may have learned mathematics that is not well connected to what they teach or may not know how to connect it. Similarly, many of the measures of student achievement used in research on teacher knowledge have been standardized tests that focus primarily on students' procedural skills. Some evidence suggests that there is a positive relationship between teachers' mathematical knowledge and their students' learning of advanced mathematical concepts.[8] There seems to be no association, however, between how many advanced mathematics courses a teacher takes and how well that teacher's students achieve overall in mathematics.[9] In general, empirical evidence regarding the effects of teachers' knowledge of mathematics content on student learning is still rather sparse.

In the National Longitudinal Study of Mathematical Abilities (NLSMA), conducted during the 1960s and still today the largest study of its kind, there was essentially no association between students' achievement and the number of credits a teacher had in mathematics at the level of calculus or beyond.[10] Commenting on the findings from NLSMA and a number of other studies of teacher knowledge, the director of NLSMA later said,

> It is widely believed that the more a teacher knows about his subject matter, the more effective he will be as a teacher. The empirical literature suggests that this belief needs drastic modification and in fact suggests that once a teacher reaches a certain level of understanding of the subject matter, then further understanding contributes nothing to student achievement.[11]

The notion that there is a threshold of necessary content knowledge for teaching is supported by the findings of another study in 1994 that used data from the Longitudinal Study of American Youth (LSAY).[12] There was a notable increase in student performance for each additional mathematics course their teachers had taken, yet after the fifth course there was little additional benefit.[13]

Data from the 1996 NAEP on teachers' college major rather than the number of courses they had taken provide a contrast to the general trend of this line of research. The NAEP data revealed that eighth graders taught by teachers who majored in mathematics outperformed those whose teachers majored in education or some other field. Fourth graders taught by teachers who majored in mathematics education or in education tended to outperform those whose teachers majored in a field other than education.[14]

Although studies of teachers' mathematical knowledge have not demonstrated a strong relationship between teachers' mathematical knowledge and their students' achievement, teachers' knowledge is still likely a significant factor in students' achievement. That crude measures of teacher knowledge, such as the number of mathematics courses taken, do not correlate positively with student performance data, supports the need to study more closely the nature of the mathematical knowledge needed to teach and to measure it more sensitively.

The persistent failure of the many efforts to show strong, definitive relations between teachers' mathematical knowledge and their effectiveness does not imply that mathematical knowledge makes no difference in teaching. The research, however, does suggest that proposals to improve mathematics instruction by simply increasing the number of mathematics courses required of teachers are not likely to be successful. As we discuss in the sections that follow, courses that reflect a serious examination of the nature of the mathematics that teachers use in the practice of teaching do have some promise of improving student performance.

Teachers need to know mathematics in ways that enable them to help students learn. The specialized knowledge of mathematics that they need is different from the mathematical content contained in most college mathematics courses, which are principally designed for those whose professional uses of mathematics will be in mathematics, science, and other technical fields. Why does this difference matter in considering the mathematical education of teachers? First, the topics taught in upper-level mathematics courses are often remote from the core content of the K-12 curriculum. Although the abstract mathematical ideas are connected, of course, basic algebraic concepts or elementary geometry are not what prospective teachers study in a course in advanced calculus or linear algebra. Second, college mathematics courses do not provide students with opportunities to learn either multiple representations of mathematical ideas or the ways in which different representations relate to one another. Advanced courses do not emphasize the conceptual underpinnings of ideas needed by teachers whose uses of mathematics are to help others learn mathematics.[15] Instead, the study of college mathematics involves the increasing compression of elementary ideas into the more and more powerful and abstract forms needed by those whose professional uses of mathematics will be in scientific domains. Third, advanced mathematical study entails using elementary concepts and procedures without much conscious attention to their meanings or implications, thus reinforcing the making of prior learning routine in the service of more advanced work. While this approach is important for the education of mathematicians and scientists, it is at odds with the kind of mathematical study needed by teachers.

Consider the proficiency teachers need with algorithms. The power of computational algorithms is that they allow learners to calculate without having to think deeply about the steps in the calculation or why the calculations work. That frees up the learners' thinking so that they can concentrate on the problem they are trying to use the calculation to solve rather than having to worry about the details of the calculation. Over time, people tend to forget the reasons a procedure works or what is entailed in understanding or justifying a particular algorithm. Because the algorithm has become so automatic, it is difficult to step back and consider what is needed to explain it to someone who does not understand. Consequently, appreciating children's difficulties in learning an algorithm can be very difficult for adults who are fluent with that algorithm.

The necessary compression of ideas in the course of mathematical study also shortchanges teachers' mathematical needs. Most advanced mathematics classes engage students in taking ideas they have already learned and using them to construct increasingly powerful and abstract concepts and methods. Once theorems have been proved, they can be used to prove other theorems. It is not necessary to go back to foundational concepts to learn more advanced ideas. Teaching, however, entails reversing the direction followed in learning advanced mathematics. In helping students learn, teachers must take abstract ideas and unpack them in ways that make the basic underlying concepts visible.[16] For example, most adults have lost sight of the fact that there are different interpretations of division. For adults, division is an operation on numbers. Division, however, is rooted in quite different physical situations, and distinctions among those situations are important for understanding children's thinking, developing their understanding of the meaning of division, and helping them apply that understanding to solve problems.[17] For example, although both of the following problems can be represented as dividing 24 by 6, young children think about them in very different ways and use quite different strategies to solve them:[18]

Jane has 24 cookies. She wants to put 6 cookies on each plate. How many plates will she need?

Jeremy has 24 cookies. He wants to put all the cookies on 6 plates. If he puts the same number of cookies on each plate, how many cookies will he put on each plate?

These two problems correspond to the measurement and sharing models of division, respectively, that were discussed in chapter 3. Young children using counters solve the first problem by putting 24 counters in piles of 6 counters each. They solve the second by partitioning the 24 counters into 6 groups. In the first case the answer is the number of groups; in the second, it is the number in each group. Until the children are much older, they are not aware that, abstractly, the two solutions are equivalent. Teachers need to see that equivalence so that they can understand and anticipate the difficulties children may have with division.

To understand the sense that children are making of arithmetic problems, teachers must understand the distinctions children are making among those problems and how the distinctions might be reflected in how the children think about the problems. The different semantic contexts for each of the operations of arithmetic is not a common topic in college mathematics courses, yet it is essential for teachers to know those contexts and be able to use their knowledge in instruction. The division example illustrates a different way of thinking about the content of courses for teachers—a way that can make those courses more relevant to the teaching of school mathematics.

A recent study indicates that teachers' performance on mathematical tasks that have been set in the context of teaching practice is positively related to student achievement.[19] In the study, teachers' ability to interpret four student responses to a ratio problem and to determine which were correct was strongly related to their students' mathematics achievement.

Teachers' mathematical knowledge and their teaching practice. Conventional wisdom holds that a teacher's knowledge of mathematics is linked to how the teacher teaches. Teachers are unlikely to be able to provide an adequate explanation of concepts they do not understand, and they can hardly engage their students in productive conversations about multiple ways to solve a problem if they themselves can only solve it in a single way.

In the last 15 years, researchers have investigated how teachers' mathematical knowledge shapes the way they teach. Most of the investigations have been case studies, almost all involving fewer than 10 teachers, and most only one to three teachers. In general, the researchers found that teachers with a relatively weak conceptual knowledge of mathematics tended to demonstrate a procedure and then give students opportunities to practice it. Not surprisingly, these teachers gave the students little assistance in developing an understanding of what they were doing.[20] When the teachers did try to provide a clear explanation and justification, they were not able to do so.[21] In some cases, their inadequate conceptual knowledge resulted in their presenting incorrect procedures.[22]

Some of the same studies contrasted the teaching practices of teachers with low levels of mathematical knowledge with the teaching practices of teachers who had a better command of mathematics. These studies indicate that a strong grasp of mathematics made it possible for teachers to understand and use constructively students' mathematical solutions, explanations, and questions.[23] Several researchers found, however, that some teachers with strong conceptual knowledge did not necessarily use that knowledge to understand their students' mathematical explanations, preferring instead to impose their own explanations.[24]

Knowledge of Students

Knowledge of students includes both knowledge of the particular students being taught and knowledge of students' learning in general. Knowing one's own students includes knowing who they are, what they know, and how they view learning, mathematics, and themselves. The teacher needs to know something of each student's personal and educational background, especially the mathematical skills, abilities, and dispositions that the student brings to the lesson. The teacher also needs to be sensitive to the unique ways of learning, thinking about, and doing mathematics that the student has developed. Each student can be seen as located on a path through school mathematics, equipped with strengths and weaknesses, having developed his or her own approaches to mathematical tasks, and capable of contributing to and profiting from each lesson in a distinctive way.

Teachers also need a general knowledge of how students think—the approaches that are typical for students of a given age and background, their common conceptions and misconceptions, and the likely sources of those ideas. Over the last decade, researchers have produced an impressive body of evidence about how children's thinking about various mathematical concepts progresses over time. We have described some of those progressions in chapters 6 through 8. Using that body of evidence, researchers have also studied how teachers' knowledge of students' mathematical thinking is related to how they teach and to how well their students achieve.

From the many examples of misconceptions to which teachers need to be sensitive, we have chosen one: An important mathematical notion that poses a major stumbling block when students are moving from arithmetic to algebra is the role played by "=," the sign for equality.[25] As we discussed in chapter 8, many if not most elementary school children have the misconception that the equality sign is a signal to do something, to carry out the calculation that precedes it.[26] The number immediately after the equal sign is seen as the answer to the calculation. For example, in the number sentence $8 + 4 = \square + 5$, many students would put 12 in the box. Children can develop this impression because that is how the notation is often described in the elementary school curriculum and most of their practice exercises fit that pattern. Few teachers realize the degree of their students' misunderstanding of such sentences.[27] Moreover, although most teachers have some idea that equality is a relation between two numbers, few realize how important it is that students understand equality as a relation, and few consider this need for understanding when they use the equals sign.

Knowledge of Classroom Practice

Knowing classroom practice means knowing what is to be taught and how to plan, conduct, and assess effective lessons on that mathematical content. It includes a knowledge of learning goals as expressed in the curriculum and a knowledge of the resources at one's disposal for helping students reach those goals. It also includes skill in organizing one's class to create a community of learners and in managing classroom discourse and learning activities so that everyone is engaged in substantive mathematical work. We have discussed these matters in chapter 9. This type of knowledge is gained through experience in classrooms and through analyzing and reflecting on one's own practice and that of others.

In the sections that follow, we consider how to develop an integrated corpus of knowledge of the types discussed in this section. First, however, we need to clarify our stance on the relation between knowledge and practice. We have discussed the kinds of knowledge teachers need if they are to teach for mathematical proficiency. Although we have used the term *knowledge* throughout, we do not mean it exclusively in the sense of *knowing about*. Teachers must also *know how* to use their knowledge in practice. Teachers' knowledge is of value only if they can apply it to their teaching; it cannot be divorced from practice. Effective programs of teacher preparation and professional development cannot stop at simply engaging teachers in acquiring knowledge; they must challenge teachers to develop, apply, and analyze that knowledge in the context of their own classrooms so that knowledge and practice are integrated.

Proficient Teaching of Mathematics

In chapter 4 we identified five components or strands of mathematical proficiency. From that perspective, successful learning is characterized by comprehension of ideas; ready access to skills and procedures; an ability to formulate and solve problems; a capacity to reflect on, evaluate, and adapt one's knowledge; the ability to reason from what is known to what is wanted; and a habitual inclination to make sense of and value what is being learned. Teaching is a complex activity and, like other complex activities, can be conceived in terms of similar components. Just as mathematical proficiency itself involves interwoven strands, teaching for mathematical proficiency requires similarly interrelated components. In the context of teaching, proficiency requires:

- *conceptual understanding* of the core knowledge required in the practice of teaching;
- *fluency* in carrying out basic instructional routines;
- *strategic competence* in planning effective instruction and solving problems that arise during instruction;
- *adaptive reasoning* in justifying and explaining one's instructional practices and in reflecting on those practices so as to improve them; and a
- *productive disposition* toward mathematics, teaching, learning, and the improvement of practice.

Like the strands of mathematical proficiency, these components of mathematical teaching proficiency are interrelated. In this chapter we discuss the problems entailed in developing a proficient command of teaching. In the previous section we discussed issues relative to the knowledge base needed to develop proficiency across all components. Now we turn to specific issues that arise in the context of the components.

Understanding of Core Knowledge

It is not sufficient that teachers possess the kinds of core knowledge delineated in the previous section. One of the defining features of conceptual understanding is that knowledge must be connected so that it can be used intelligently. Teachers need to make connections within and among their knowledge of mathematics, students, and pedagogy.

The kinds of knowledge that make a difference in teaching practice and in students' learning are an elaborated, integrated knowledge of mathematics, a knowledge of how students' mathematical understanding develops, and a repertoire of pedagogical practices that take into account the mathematics being taught and how students learn it. The implications for teacher preparation and professional development are that teachers need to acquire these forms of knowledge in ways that forge connections between them. For teachers who have already achieved some mathematical proficiency, separate courses or professional development programs that focus exclusively on mathematics, on the psychology of learning, or on methods of teaching provide limited opportunities to make these connections. Unfortunately, most university teacher preparation programs offer separate courses in mathematics, psychology, and methods of teaching that are taught in different departments. The difficulty of integrating such courses is compounded when they are located in different administrative units.

The professional development programs we discuss later in this chapter all situate their portrayals of mathematics and children's thinking in contexts directly relevant to the problems teachers face daily in teaching mathematics.[28] This grounding in reality allows knowledge of mathematics and knowledge of students to be connected in ways that make a difference for instruction and for learning. It is not enough, however, for mathematical knowledge and knowledge of students to be connected; both need to be connected to classroom practice. Teachers may know mathematics, and they may know their students and how they learn. But they also have to know how to use both kinds of knowledge effectively in the context of their work if they are to help their students develop mathematical proficiency.

Similarly, many inservice workshops, presentations at professional meetings, publications for teachers, and other opportunities for teacher learning focus almost exclusively on activities or methods of teaching and seldom attempt to help teachers develop their own conceptual understanding of the underlying mathematical ideas, what students understand about those ideas, or how they learn them. Alternative forms of teacher education and professional development that attempt to teach mathematical content, psychology of learning, and methods of teaching need to be developed and evaluated to see whether prospective and practicing teachers from such programs can draw appropriate connections and apply the knowledge they have acquired to teach mathematics effectively.

Instructional Routines

The second basic component of teaching proficiency is the development of instructional routines. Just as students who have acquired procedural fluency can perform calculations with numbers efficiently, accurately, and flexibly with minimal effort, teachers who have acquired a repertoire of instructional routines can readily draw upon them as they interact with students in teaching mathematics. Some routines concern classroom management, such as how to get the class started each day and procedures for correcting and collecting homework. Other routines are more grounded in mathematical activity. For example, teachers need to know how to respond to a student who gives an answer the teacher does not understand or who demonstrates a serious misconception. They need to know how to deal with students who lack critical prerequisite skills for the day's lesson. Teachers need business-like ways of dealing with situations like these that occur on a regular basis so that they can devote more of their attention to the more serious issues facing them. When teachers have several ways of approaching teaching problems, they can try a different approach if one does not work.

Researchers have shown that expert teachers have a large repertoire of routines at their disposal.[29] They can choose among a number of approaches for teaching a given topic or responding to a situation that arises in their classes. Novice teachers, in contrast, have a limited range of routines and often cannot respond appropriately to situations. Expert teachers not only have access to a range of routines, they also can apply them flexibly, know when they are appropriate, and can adapt them to fit different situations.

Strategic Competence

The third component of teaching proficiency is strategic competence. Although teachers need a range of routines, teaching is very much a problem-solving activity.[30] Like other professionals, teachers are constantly faced with decisions in planning instruction, implementing those plans, and interacting with students.[31] Useful guidelines are seldom available for figuring out what to teach when, how to teach it, how to adapt material so that it is appropriate for a given group of students, or how much time to allow for an activity. On the spot, teachers need to find out what a student knows, choose how to respond to a student's question or statement, and decide whether to follow a student's idea. These are problems that every teacher faces every day, and most do not have readymade solutions.

Conceptual understanding of the knowledge required to teach for proficiency can help equip teachers to deal intelligently with these problems. It is misleading to claim that teachers actually *solve* such problems in the sense of *solving* a mathematical problem. There is never an ideal solution to the more difficult problems of teaching, but teachers can learn to contend with these problems in reasonable ways that take into account the mathematics that students are to learn; what their students understand and how they may best learn it; and representations, activities, and teaching practices that have proven most effective in teaching the mathematics in question or that have been effective in teaching related topics.

Teacher education and professional development programs that take into account the strategic decision making in teaching can help prepare teachers to be more effective in solving instructional problems. Rather than being designed to resolve teachers' problems, programs of teacher education and professional development can engage prospective and practicing teachers in the analysis of instructional problems and potential ways of dealing with them. Teachers can learn to recognize that teaching involves solving problems and that they can address these problems in reasonable and intelligent ways.

Adaptive Reasoning

The fourth component of teaching proficiency is adaptive reasoning. Teachers can learn from their teaching by analyzing it: the difficulties their students have encountered in learning a particular topic; what the students have learned; how the students responded to particular representations, questions, and activities; and the like.[32] Teachers can become reflective practitioners, and reflection is essential in improving their practice. The focus of teachers' reflection and the tools they use shape the nature of that reflection and affect whether, what, and how they learn from it. Many successful programs of teacher education and professional development engage teachers in reflection, but the reflection, or perhaps more appropriately the analysis, is grounded in specific examples. In those programs, teachers engage in analyses in which they are asked to provide evidence to justify claims and assertions. As with other complex activities, teacher learning can be enhanced by making more visible the goals, assumptions, and decisions involved in the practice of teaching.[33] The implications for teacher education and professional development is that teachers engage not only in learning methods of teaching but also in reflecting on them and justifying and explaining them in relation to such matters as the mathematics being taught, the goals for students, the conceptions and misconceptions that students have about the mathematics, the difficulties they have in learning it, and the representations that are most effective in communicating essential ideas.

One of the ways that the professional development programs described below foster teachers' ability to justify and explain classroom practices is that teachers examine familiar artifacts from practice, and those artifacts help them focus their attention and develop a common language for discussion. In some cases the program leaders provide the artifacts; in others the artifacts come from the teachers' classrooms. Teachers are often asked to pose a particular mathematical problem to their classes and to discuss the mathematical thinking that they observe.

Productive Disposition

The final component of teaching proficiency is a productive disposition about one's own knowledge, practice, and learning. Just as students must develop a productive disposition toward mathematics such that they believe that mathematics makes sense and that they can figure it out, so too must teachers develop a similar productive disposition. Teachers should think that mathematics, their understanding of children's thinking, and their teaching practices fit together to make sense and that they are capable of learning about mathematics, student mathematical thinking, and their own practice themselves by analyzing what goes on in their classes. Teachers whose learning becomes generative perceive themselves as in control of their own learning.[34] They learn by listening to their students and by analyzing their teaching practices. Not only do they develop more elaborated conceptions of how students' mathematical thinking develops by listening to their students, but they also learn mathematical concepts and strategies from their interactions with students. The teachers become more comfortable with mathematical ideas and ripe for a more systematic view of the subject.

Teachers whose learning becomes generative see themselves as lifelong learners who can learn from studying curriculum materials[35] and from analyzing their practice and their interactions with students. Programs of teacher education and professional development that portray to the participants that they are in control of their own learning help teachers develop a productive disposition toward learning about mathematics, student mathematical thinking, and teaching practice. Programs that provide readymade, worked-out solutions to teaching problems should not expect that teachers will see themselves as in control of their own learning.

Programs to Develop Proficient Teaching

In a teacher preparation program, teachers clearly cannot learn all they need to know about the mathematics they will teach, how students learn that mathematics, and how to teach it effectively. Consequently, some authorities have recommended that teacher education be seen as a professional continuum, a career-long process.[36] Hence, teachers need a basis for ongoing learning. They need to be able to adapt to new curriculum frameworks, new materials, advances in technology, and advances in research on student thinking and teaching practice. They have to learn how to learn, whether they are learning about mathematics, students, or teaching. Teachers can continue to learn by participating in various forms of professional development. But formal professional development programs represent only one source for continued learning. Teachers' schools and classrooms can also become places for teachers as well as students to learn.[37] Professional development programs that engage teachers in inquiry in their classrooms can provide the basis for teachers' learning to become generative so that their knowledge, conceptions, and practice continue to grow and evolve.[38]

Programs of teacher education and professional development based on research integrate the study of mathematics and the study of students' learning so that teachers will forge connections between the two. Some of these programs begin with mathematical ideas from the school curriculum and ask teachers to analyze those ideas from the learners' perspective. Other programs use students' mathematical thinking as a springboard to motivate teachers' learning of mathematics. Still others begin with teaching practice and move toward a consideration of mathematics and students' thinking. We consider below examples of four such program types that represent an array of alternative approaches to developing integrated proficiency in teaching mathematics.[39]

Focus on Mathematics

Some teacher preparation and professional development programs attempt to enhance prospective and practicing teachers' knowledge of mathematics by having them probe more deeply fundamental ideas from elementary school mathematics, often through problem solving. For example, prospective elementary school teachers may take a mathematics course that focuses, in part, on rational numbers or proportionality rather than the usual college algebra or calculus. Such courses are offered in many universities, but they are seldom linked to instructional practice. The lesson depicted in Box 10-1 comes from a course in which connections to practice are being made.

Box 10-1

Investigating Division of Fractions in a Mathematics Course

The prospective teachers stare at the board, trying to figure out what the instructor is asking them to do. After calculating the answer to a simple problem in the division of fractions ($1\frac{3}{4} \div \frac{1}{2} = ?$) and recalling the old algorithm—invert and multiply—most of them have come up with the answer, $3\frac{1}{2}$. It is familiar content, and although they have not had occasion to divide fractions recently, they feel comfortable, remembering their own experiences in school mathematics and what they learned. But now, what are they being asked? The instructor has challenged them to consider why they are getting what seems to be an answer ($3\frac{1}{2}$) that is larger than either of the numbers in the original problem ($1\frac{3}{4}$ and $\frac{1}{2}$). "Doesn't dividing make numbers smaller?" she asks. Confused, they are suddenly stuck. None of them noticed this fact before.

The instructor proposes a new task: "See if you can make up a story problem, devise a real-world context, or draw a picture that will go with one and three fourths divided by a half. Can you come up with an example or a model that shows what is going on with dividing one and three fourths by one half?"

The prospective teachers set to work, some in pairs, some alone. The instructor walks around, watching them work, and occasionally asking a question. Most have drawn pictures like those below:

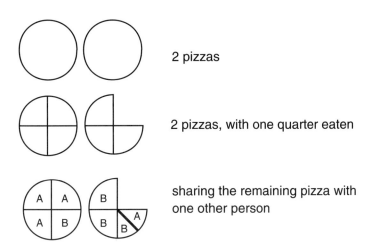

2 pizzas

2 pizzas, with one quarter eaten

sharing the remaining pizza with one other person

They have written problems like the following:

> I have two pizzas. My little brother eats one quarter of one of them and then I have one and three quarters pizzas left. My sister is very hungry, so we decide to split the remaining pizza between us. We each get $3\frac{1}{2}$ pieces of pizza.

One pair of students has a different problem:

> I have $1\frac{3}{4}$ cups of sugar. Each batch of sesame crackers takes $\frac{1}{2}$ cup of sugar. How many batches of crackers can I make?

And another pair has envisioned filling $\frac{1}{2}$-liter containers, starting with $1\frac{3}{4}$ liters of water.

After about 10 minutes, the instructor invites students to share their problems with the rest of the class. One student presents the pizza situation above. Most students nod appreciatively. When a second student offers the sesame cracker problem, most nod again, not noticing the difference. The instructor poses a question: How does each problem we heard connect with the original computation? Are these two problems similar or different, and does it matter?

Through discussion the students gradually come to recognize that, in the pizza problem, the pizza has been divided *in half* and that the answer is in terms of *fourths*—that is, that the $3\frac{1}{2}$ pieces are fourths of pizzas. In the case of the sesame cracker problem, the answer of $3\frac{1}{2}$ batches is in terms of *half cups* of sugar. In the first instance, they have represented division *in half,* which is actually division by two; in the second they have represented division *by one half.*

continued

Box 10-1 Continued

The instructor moves into a discussion of different interpretations of division: sharing and measurement. After the students observe that the successful problems—involving the sesame crackers and the liters of water—are measurement problems, she asks them to try to develop a problem situation for $1\frac{3}{4} \div \frac{1}{2}$ that represents a sharing division. In other words, could they make a sensible problem in which the $\frac{1}{2}$ is not the unit by which the whole is being measured, but instead is the number of units into which the whole has been divided?

For homework, the instructor asks the students to try making representations for several other division situations, which she chooses strategically, and finally asks them to select two numbers to divide that they think are particularly good choices and to say why. She also asks them to try to connect what they have done in class today with the familiar algorithm of "invert and multiply."

In this excerpt from a university mathematics course, the prospective teachers are being asked to unpack familiar arithmetic content, to make explicit the ideas underlying the procedures they remember and can perform. Repeatedly throughout the course, the instructor poses problems that have been strategically designed to expose concepts on which familiar procedures rest.

One principle behind the instructor's efforts is to engage the prospective teachers in a kind of mathematical work that focuses on developing their proficiency with the mathematical content of the elementary school curriculum. A second principle is to link that work with larger mathematical ideas and structures. For example, the lesson on the division of fractions is part of a larger agenda that includes understanding division, its relationship to fractions and to multiplication, and the meaning and representation of operations. Moreover, throughout the development of these ideas and connections, the prospective teachers work with whole and rational numbers, considering how the mathematical world looks inside these nested systems.

The overriding purpose of a course like this is to provide prospective teachers with ample opportunities to learn fundamental ideas of school mathematics, how they are related, and how students come to learn them. The ways in which the prospective teachers' opportunities to learn are designed may at times situate the mathematical questions within apparently pedagogical contexts (e.g., make a story problem), so that the kind of mathematical work they do in the course helps them develop mathematical proficiency in ways they can use in teaching. But the course is not about how to teach, nor about how children learn. It is explicitly and deliberately a sustained opportunity for prospective teachers to learn mathematical ideas in ways that will equip them with mathematical resources needed in teaching.

Focus on Student Thinking

The successful programs that focus on mathematics and children's thinking are programs grounded in practice. Teachers do not learn abstract concepts about mathematics and children. In the programs, teachers look at problem-solving strategies of real students, artifacts of student work, cases of real classrooms, and the like. Furthermore, the teachers in these programs are challenged to relate what they learn to their own students and their own instructional practices. They learn about mathematics and students both in workshops and by interacting with their own students. Specific opportunity is provided for the teachers to discuss with one another how the ideas they are encountering influence their practice and how their practice influences what they are learning. Discussions in these programs are conducted in a spirit of supporting the teachers' inquiry. The analysis of children's thinking is not presented as a fixed body of knowledge, and the teachers engage not only in inquiry about how to apply knowledge about students' thinking in planning and implementing instruction but also in inquiry to deepen their understanding of students' thinking.[40]

The workshop described in Box 10-2 forms part of a professional development program designed to help teachers develop a deeper understanding of some critical mathematical ideas, including the equality sign. The program, modeled after Cognitively Guided Instruction (CGI), which has proven to be a highly effective approach,[41] assists teachers in understanding how to help their students reason about number operations and relations in ways that enhance the learning of arithmetic and promote a smoother transition from arithmetic to algebra.[42] This particular workshop was directed at illuminating students' misconceptions about equality and considering how those misconceptions might be addressed.

Several features of this example of professional development are worth noting. The teachers focus on children's thinking about a critical mathematical idea. Although they begin by considering how children think, the teachers

Box 10-2

Investigating the Concept of Equality in a Professional Development Group

Before attending the workshop, participating teachers ask their students to find the number that they could put in the box to make the following open-number sentence a true number sentence: $8 + 4 = \square + 5$. At the workshop, the teachers share their findings with the other participants. Fewer than 10% of the students in any teacher's class solved the problem correctly.* The majority of the incorrect responses were 12, with a number of responses of 17. These findings, which surprised most teachers, have led them to begin to listen to their students, and a number of teachers have engaged their students in a discussion of the reasons for their responses. The teachers' experiences have precipitated a discussion in the workshop of how students are thinking about equality and how these misconceptions might have been acquired. The discussion generates insights about how children are thinking and what teachers can learn by listening to their students. Although the teachers recognize the students' errors on this problem, however, they do not have a good idea of how they would address the misconception.

The workshop leader introduces several true and false number sentences as a context to challenge children's incorrect notions of equality. Examples include $8 = 3 + 5$, $17 + 9 = 36$, $23 = 23$, $17 + 26 = 27 + 16$, and $76 + 7 = 76$. The task is to decide whether the sentence is true or false. Sometimes the decision requires calculation (e.g., $74 - 57 = 17$), and sometimes it does not (e.g., $67 + 96 = 96 + 67$). The teachers work in small groups to construct true and false number sentences they might use to elicit various views of equality. Using these sentences, their students could engage in explorations that might lead to understanding equality as a relation. The sentences could also provide opportunities for discussions about how to resolve disagreement and develop a mathematical argument. The teachers work together to consider how their students might respond to different number sentences and which number sentences might produce the most fruitful discussion.

---

* These responses and this level of success are typical for classes ranging from grade 1 to 6.

SOURCE: Falkner, Levi, and Carpenter, 1999. Used by permission of the authors.

---

must also examine their own conceptions. Properties of equality that the teachers have not usually examined carefully before emerge in their discussions of students' conceptions and misconceptions in using the equals sign. The teachers also begin to ponder how notation is used and how ideas are justified in mathematics. A central feature of their discussion is that mathematics and children's thinking are set in a context that relates to their practice. The mathematical ideas and how children think about them are seen in classroom interactions. The problems discussed in the workshop are problems that the teachers can and do use in their classes; the interactions about mathematics that occur in the teachers' classes provide a setting for workshop discussion of mathematical ideas and children's thinking. The activities taking place in the workshop and in the teachers' classrooms have the same goals. In both places the teachers engage in inquiry to gain a deeper understanding of mathematics, students' thinking about that mathematics, and how to plan their instruction so as to foster the development of students' mathematical thinking.

Before beginning a professional development program similar to the one described above, teachers participating in the program found that fewer than 10% of their students at any grade demonstrated a relational concept of equality. After one year of the program, the percentage of students in their classes who demonstrated a relational concept of equality ranged from 66% in first and second grades to 84% in sixth grade.[43]

Although these programs place a heavy emphasis on children's thinking, understanding children's mathematical thinking depends upon understanding the mathematics with which that thinking is engaged. The programs do not deal with general theories of learning. They concentrate instead on understanding children's thinking in specific domains of mathematical content. Understanding the mathematics of the domain being studied is a prerequisite to understanding children's thinking in that domain. For example, to understand the different strategies that children use to solve different problems, teachers must understand the semantic differences between problems represented by the same operation, as illustrated by the sharing and measurement examples of dividing cookies described above in Box 10-1. In programs focusing on children's mathematical thinking, teachers learn to recognize and appreciate the mathematical significance of children's informal methods for solving problems, how these methods evolve into more abstract and more powerful methods, and how the informal methods could serve as a basis for students to learn formal concepts and procedures with understanding.

Professional development programs focusing on helping teachers understand both the mathematics of specific content domains and students' mathematical thinking in that domain have consistently been found to contribute to major changes in teachers' instructional practices that have resulted in significant gains in students' achievement.[44] For example, in an experimental study of CGI with first-grade teachers, teachers who had taken a month-long workshop on children's development of addition and subtraction concepts taught problem solving significantly more and number facts significantly less than did teachers who had instead taken two 2-hour workshops on nonroutine problem solving. Students in the CGI teachers' classes performed as well as students in the comparison teachers' classes on a standardized computation test and outperformed students in the comparison teachers' classes on complex addition and subtraction word problems.[45] After teachers have studied the development of children's mathematical thinking, they tend to place a greater emphasis on problem solving, listen to their students more and know more about their students' abilities, and provide greater opportunity for their students to use a variety of solution methods. Gains in student achievement generally have been in the areas of understanding and problem solving, but none of the programs has led to a decline in computational skills, despite their greater emphasis on higher levels of thinking.

Focus on Cases

Case examples are yet another way to build the connections between knowledge of mathematics, knowledge of students, and knowledge of practice. Although the cases focus on classroom episodes, the discussions the teachers engage in as they reflect on the cases emphasize mathematics content and student thinking. The cases involve instruction in specific mathematical topics, and teachers analyze the cases in terms of the mathematics content being taught and the mathematical thinking reflected in the work the children produce and the interactions they engage in. Cases can be presented in writing or using multiple media such as videotapes and transcriptions of lessons. The episode in Box 10-3 is taken from a case discussion in which the case is presented through video recordings of lessons from an entire year that were captured on computer disks, together with the teacher's plans and reflections and with samples of student work.

Notable in this example is how the teachers' opportunities to consider mathematical ideas—in this case, functions—are set in the context of the use of those ideas in teaching. These teachers are probing the concept of functions from several overlapping perspectives. They dig into the mathematics through close work on and analysis of the task that the teacher posed. They also explore the ideas by investigating students' work on the problem. And they revisit the mathematical ideas by looking carefully at how the teacher deals with the mathematics during the lesson.

Box 10-3

Investigating Mathematical Tasks Using Cases from Real Practice

A dozen teachers are gathered around a table. They have read a case of a teacher teaching a lesson on functions. The written case includes the task the teacher used and a detailed narrative account of what happened in the class as students worked on the problem. The teacher used the following task:

> Sara has made several purchases from a mail-order company. She has found that the company charges $12.90 to ship an 8-kg package, $6.40 to ship a 3-kg package, and $9.00 to ship a 5-kg package. Sara decides that the company must be using a simple rule to determine how much to charge for shipping. Help her figure out how much it would most likely cost to ship a 1-kg package and how much each additional kilogram would cost.

Photocopies of students' work are available, as are pages from the curriculum materials being used. Before the teachers studied the case and the accompanying materials, they solved the mathematical problem themselves.

To begin the discussion, the workshop leader asks the teachers to look closely at one segment of the lesson in which two students are presenting solutions to the problem. She asks them to interpret what each student did and to compare the two solutions. This request precipitates an animated discussion in which the teachers probe the students' representations and explanations. One teacher notes that a third student has a method that is similar to the first student's, but several others argue that the method is not similar. The teachers continue to analyze the students' thinking, with repeated careful use of the reproductions of the students' work. At one point one teacher raises a mathematical point, asking whether there might be something particularly significant in one student's idea.

The teachers launch into a discussion of the mathematics for several minutes. They note that if the given values (weight, cost) are graphed, the points lie on the same straight line. Reading the graph provides a solution. Also, by asking how much each additional kilogram would cost, the problem suggests there is a constant difference that can be used in solving it. Since the 2-kg difference between 5 kg and 3 kg is $2.60, and the 3-kg difference between 8 kg and 5 kg is $3.90, the simplest rule would be that each additional kilogram costs $1.30. A linear function ($y = 1.30x + 2.50$) fits the three values, and one can use constant differences or a graph to find this function (although that is not necessary to answer the two questions).

After a much-needed break, the leader refocuses the discussion on the teacher's moves throughout the episode that they have been discussing. At first, several

continued

Box 10-3 Continued

teachers comment that the teacher doesn't seem to be doing much. "She is more of a guide," one teacher remarks. "It is really a student-centered class." "Is it?" asks the leader. She asks them to analyze the text closely and try to categorize what the teacher is doing.

This discussion yields surprises for most of the teachers. Suddenly the intricate work that the teacher is doing becomes visible. They see her posing strategic questions, using particular aspects of the students' solutions to focus the class discussion, providing direction at some moments and letting the students struggle a bit at others. They begin to describe and name the different moves she makes. One teacher becomes intrigued with how the teacher helps students express their ideas by asking questions to support their explanations before she asks other students to comment. It is quite clear that this is no generic skill, for the mathematical sensitivity and knowledge entailed are quite visible throughout. Another teacher notices how the teacher's own mathematical knowledge seems to shape her skilled questioning. The teachers become fascinated with what looks like an important missed opportunity to unpack a common misconception about function. Speculating about why that happened leads them to a productive conversation about what one might do to seize and capitalize on the opportunity.

The session ends with the teachers agreeing to bring back one mathematical task from their own work on functions and compare it with the task used in the case. Several are overheard to be discussing features of this problem that seem particularly fruitful and that have them thinking about how they frame problems for their students. The group briefly discusses some ways to vary the problem to make it either simpler or more complex. The leader then closes by summarizing some of the mathematical issues embedded in the task. She points out that it is not obvious what the value of 2.50 means in the algebraic expression of the function. It is the cost of sending a package of zero weight, an idea that does not appear anywhere in the problem itself or in real life. She also says that it is important to understand that x refers to whole numbers only. Finally, she notes that with a different function, the differences might not be constant. The assumption of constant differences is one suggested by the problem and common in situations like those involving shipping costs, but it is not necessarily always warranted.

Studies of teachers' learning in professional development programs that have used classroom cases show that the teachers learned mathematics from studying such cases. They gained a greater repertoire of ways to represent mathematical ideas, were able to articulate connections among mathematical ideas, and developed a deeper understanding of mathematical structures.[46]

As a result of their work in this program, the teachers became more likely to bring out students' reasoning in discussions and to invite both public and private reflection on the students' ideas. At least some of the teachers continued the process of learning mathematics by examining the mathematical work of their own students in their own classrooms.

The case-based programs that focus on classroom instruction treat the cases as problematic situations that serve as a basis for discussion and inquiry rather than as models of instruction for the teachers to emulate. Teachers analyze classes not to figure out how they can do what the teacher in the case example did; instead, the case discussions provide models for inquiry that teachers may apply to analyze their own students' mathematical thinking and their own teaching practices.

Focus on Lesson Study

A somewhat different approach to professional development is represented by so-called lesson study groups, which are used in Japan (see Box 10-4). These study groups focus on the development and refinement of one specific mathematical lesson, called a "research lesson." Teachers work together to consider a specific difficulty entailed in teaching some important piece of mathematics. They design a lesson, and one member of the group teaches it while the others watch. Afterwards they discuss what happened in light of their anticipations and goals. Based on this experience, the group revises the lesson and someone else teaches it. The cycle continues of trying the lesson, discussing and analyzing how it worked, and revising it. Through such lesson study groups, teachers engage in very detailed analyses of mathematics, of students' mathematical thinking and skill, of teaching and learning. Although the process results in a well-crafted lesson, in the process of developing and refining the lesson, teachers work on analyzing students' responses and learn from and revise their own teaching practices. Their knowledge becomes a basis for further learning through the study of a lesson.[47]

Lesson study groups might follow somewhat different formats and schedules than the one described above, but most meet regularly during the year and focus on improving a very few lessons with clear learning goals. Using the lesson as the unit of analysis and improvement, the teachers are encouraged to improve their knowledge of all aspects of teaching within the context of their own classrooms—knowledge of mathematics, of students' thinking, of pedagogy, of curriculum, and of assessment. Although the year's activity yields a collective product that can be shared with other teachers (the group's written report), Japanese teachers say that the primary value of lesson study

Box 10-4

The Japanese Lesson Study

Small groups of teachers form within the school around areas of common teaching interests or responsibilities (e.g., grade-level groups in mathematics or in science). Each group begins by formulating a goal for the year. Sometimes the goal is adapted from national-level recommendations (e.g., improve students' problem-solving skills) and is translated into a more specific goal (e.g., improve students' understanding of problems involving ratios). The more specific goal might focus on a curriculum topic that has been problematic for students in their classrooms. A few lessons then are identified that ordinarily deal with that topic, and the group begins its yearlong task to improve those lessons.

Lesson study groups meet regularly, often once a week after school (e.g., 3:00 to 5:00 pm), to develop, test, and refine the improved lessons. Some groups divide their work into three major phases, each taking about one third of the school year. During the first phase, teachers do research on the topic, reading and sharing relevant research reports and collecting information from other teachers on effective approaches for teaching the topic. During the second phase, teachers design the targeted lessons (often just one, two, or perhaps three lessons). Important parts of the design include (a) the problems that will be presented to students, (b) the teachers' predictions about how students will solve the problems, and (c) how these different solution methods are to be integrated into a productive class discussion.

During the third phase, the lessons are tested and refined. The first test often involves one of the group members teaching a lesson to his or her class while the other group members observe and take notes. After the group refines the lesson, it might be tested with another class in front of all the teachers in the school. In this case, a follow-up session is scheduled, and the lesson study group engages their colleagues in a discussion about the lesson, receiving feedback about its effectiveness.

The final task for the group is to prepare a report of the year's work, including a rationale for the approach used and a detailed plan of the lesson, complete with descriptions of the different solution methods students are likely to present and the ways in which these can be orchestrated into a constructive discussion.

is teacher development. Working directly on improving teaching is their means of becoming better teachers.

Communities of Practice

Learning in ways that continue to be generative over time is best done in a community of fellow practitioners and learners, as illustrated by the Japanese lesson study groups. The foregoing discussion of teacher proficiency focused on individual teachers' knowledge, but teaching proficiency does not easily develop and is not generally sustained in isolation. Studies of school reform efforts suggest that professional development is most effective when it extends beyond the individual teacher.[48] Collaboration among teachers provides support for them to engage in the kinds of inquiry that are needed to develop teaching proficiency. Professional development can create contexts for teacher collaboration, provide a focus for the collaboration, and provide a common frame for interacting with other teachers around common problems. When teachers have opportunities to continue to participate in communities of practice that support their inquiry, instructional practices that foster the development of mathematical proficiency can more easily be sustained.

The focus of teacher groups matters for what teachers learn from their interactions with others. When sustained work is focused on mathematics, on students' thinking about specific mathematical topics, or on the detailed work of designing and enacting instruction, the resources generated for teachers' own practice are greater than when there is less concrete focus. For example, general sharing, or discussion of approaches, ungrounded in the particulars of classroom artifacts, while possibly enjoyable, less often produces usable knowledge that can make a difference for teachers' work.

> Professional development can create contexts for teacher collaboration, provide a focus for the collaboration, and provide a common frame for interacting with other teachers around common problems.

Mathematics Specialists

Because of the specialized knowledge required to teach mathematics, there has been increased discussion recently of the use of mathematics specialists, particularly in the upper elementary and middle school grades. The Learning First Alliance, comprising 12 major education groups, recommends that mathematics teachers from grades 5 through 9 have "a solid grounding in the coursework of grades K-12 and the teaching of middle grades mathematics."[49] The Conference Board of the Mathematical Sciences recommends in its draft report that mathematics in middle grades should be taught by mathematics specialists, starting at least in the fifth grade.[50] They further recommend that teachers of middle school mathematics have taken 21 semester hours of mathematics, 12 of which are on fundamental ideas of school mathematics appropriate for middle school teachers.

Implicit in the recommendations for mathematics specialists is the notion of the mathematics specialist in a departmental arrangement. In such arrangements, teachers with a strong background in mathematics teach mathematics and sometimes another subject, depending on the student population, while other teachers in the building teach other subject areas. Departmentalization is most often found in the upper elementary grades (4 to 6). Other models of mathematics specialists are used, particularly in elementary schools, which rarely are departmentalized. Rather than a specialist for all mathematics instruction, a single school-level mathematics specialist is sometimes used. This person, who has a deep knowledge of mathematics and how students learn it, acts as a resource for other teachers in the school. The specialist may consult with other teachers about specific issues, teach demonstration lessons, observe and offer suggestions, or provide special training sessions during the year. School-level mathematics specialists can also take the lead in establishing communities of practice, as discussed in the previous section. Because many districts do not have enough teachers with strong backgrounds in mathematics to provide at least one specialist in every school, districts instead identify district-level mathematics coaches who are responsible for several schools. Whereas a school-level specialist usually has a regular or reduced teaching assignment, district-level specialists often have no classroom teaching assignment during their tenure as a district coach. The constraint on all of the models for mathematics specialists is the limited number of teachers, especially at the elementary level, with strong backgrounds in mathematics. For this reason, summer leadership training programs have been used to develop mathematics specialists.

Effective Professional Development

Perhaps the central goal of all the teacher preparation and professional development programs is in helping teachers *understand* the mathematics they teach, how their students learn that mathematics, and how to facilitate that learning. Many of the innovative programs described in this chapter make serious efforts to help teachers connect these strands of knowledge so that they can be applied in practice. Teachers are expected to explain and justify their ideas and conclusions. Teachers' ideas are respected, and they are encouraged to engage in inquiry. They have opportunities to develop a productive disposition toward their own learning about teaching that contributes to their learning becoming generative. Teachers are not given readymade solutions to teaching problems or prescriptions for practice. Instead, they adapt what they are learning and engage in problem solving to deal with the situations that arise when they attempt to use what they learn.

Professional development beyond initial preparation is critical for developing proficiency in teaching mathematics. However, such professional development requires the marshalling of substantial resources. One of the critical resources is time. If teachers are going engage in inquiry, they need repeated opportunities to try out ideas and approaches with their students and continuing opportunities to discuss their experiences with specialists in mathematics, staff developers, and other teachers. These opportunities should not be limited to a period of a few weeks or months; instead, they should be part of the ongoing culture of professional practice. Through inquiry into teaching, teacher learning can become generative, and teachers can continue to learn and grow as professionals.

Notes

1. Shulman, 1987.
2. Cohen and Ball, 1999, 2000.
3. Ball, 1991; Ma, 1999; Post, Harel, Behr, and Lesh, 1991; Tirosh, Fischbein, Graeber, and Wilson, 1999.
4. Ball, 1991; Ma, 1999.
5. Post, Harel, Behr, and Lesh, 1991.
6. Ball, 1988; Martin and Harel, 1989; Simon and Blume, 1996.
7. Ball, 1990, 1991.
8. Mullens, Murnane, and Willet, 1996; but see Begle, 1972.
9. Monk, 1994.
10. Begle, 1979.
11. Begle, 1979, p. 51.
12. The Longitudinal Study of American Youth (LSAY) was conducted in the late 1980s and early 1990s with high school sophomores and juniors. Student achievement data were based on items developed for NAEP.
13. Monk, 1994, p. 130.
14. Hawkins, Stancavage, and Dossey, 1998.
15. In fact, it appears that sometimes content knowledge by itself may be detrimental to good teaching. In one study, more knowledgeable teachers sometimes overestimated the accessibility of symbol-based representations and procedures (Nathan and Koedinger, 2000).
16. Ball and Bass, 2000; Ma, 1999.
17. Carpenter, Fennema, and Franke, 1996; Carpenter, Fennema, Franke, Empson, and Levi, 1999; Greer, 1992.

18. Carpenter, Fennema, Franke, Empson, and Levi, 1999.

19. Rowan, Chiang, and Miller, 1997.

20. Ball, 1991; Leinhardt and Smith, 1985.

21. Borko, Eisenhart, Brown, Underhill, Jones, Agard, 1992.

22. Leinhardt and Smith, 1985; Putnam, Heaton, Prawat, and Remillard, 1992.

23. Ball, 1991; Fernandez, 1997.

24. Lubinski, Otto, Rich, and Jaberg, 1998; Thompson and Thompson, 1994, 1996.

25. Kieran, 1981; Matz, 1982.

26. Behr, Erlwanger, and Nichols,1976, 1980; Erlwanger and Berlanger, 1983; Kieran, 1981; Saenz-Ludlow and Walgamuth, 1998.

27. Falkner, Levi, and Carpenter, 1999.

28. Ball and Bass, 2000; Putnam and Borko, 2000.

29. Leinhardt and Smith, 1985; Schoenfeld, 1998.

30. Carpenter, 1988.

31. Clark and Peterson, 1986.

32. Schon, 1987.

33. Brown, Collins, and Duguid, 1989; Lewis and Ball, 2000; Schon, 1987.

34. Franke, Carpenter, Fennema, Ansell, and Behrent, 1998; Franke, Carpenter, Levi, and Fennema, in press.

35. For an example of how such study might be conducted, see Ma, 1999.

36. National Research Council, 2000.

37. Franke, Carpenter, Fennema, Ansell, and Behrend, 1998; Franke, Carpenter, Levi, and Fennema, in press; Little, 1993; Sarason, 1990, 1996.

38. Franke, Carpenter, Levi, and Fennema, in press.

39. These programs share the idea that professional development should be based upon the mathematical work of teaching. For more examples, see National Research Council, 2001. A comprehensive guide for designing professional development programs can be found in Loucks-Horsley, Hewson, Love, Stiles, 1998.

40. Franke, Carpenter, Levi, and Fennema, in press.

41. Cognitively Guided Instruction (CGI) is a professional development program for teachers that focuses on helping them construct explicit models of the development of children's mathematical thinking in well-defined content domains. No instructional materials or specifications for practice are provided in CGI; teachers develop their own instructional materials and practices from watching and listening to their students solve problems. Although the program focuses on children's mathematical thinking, teachers acquire a knowledge of mathematics as they are learning about children's thinking by analyzing structural features of the problems children solve and the mathematical principles underlying their solutions. A major thesis of CGI is that children bring to school informal or intuitive knowledge of mathematics that can serve as the basis for developing much of the formal mathematics of the primary school mathematics curriculum. The development of children's mathematical thinking is portrayed as the progressive abstraction and formalization of children's informal attempts to solve problems by constructing models of problem situations.

42. Carpenter and Levi, 1999.

43. Falkner, Levi, and Carpenter, 1999.
44. Campbell, 1996; Carpenter, Fennema, Peterson, Chiang, and Loef, 1989; Cobb, Wood, Yackel, Nicholls, Wheatley, Tragatti, and Perlwitz, 1991; Fennema, Carpenter, Franke, Levi, Jacobs, and Empson, 1996; Silver and Stein, 1996; Villasenor and Kepner, 1993.
45. Carpenter, Fennema, Peterson, Chiang, and Loef, 1989; Fennema, Carpenter, Franke, Levi, Jacobs, and Empson, 1996.
46. Barnett, 1991, 1998; Davenport, in press; Gordon and Heller, 1995.
47. Lewis and Tsuchida, 1998; Shimahara, 1998; Stigler and Hiebert, 1999.
48. Hargreaves, 1994; Little, 1993; Tharp and Gallimore, 1988.
49. Learning First Alliance, 1998, p. 5.
50. Conference Board of the Mathematical Sciences, 2000.

References

Ball, D. L. (1988). *The subject matter preparation of prospective mathematics teachers: Challenging the myths* (Research Report 88-3). East Lansing: Michigan State University, National Center for Research on Teacher Learning. Available: http://ncrtl.msu.edu/http/rreports/html/rr883.htm. [July 10, 2001].

Ball, D. L. (1990). The mathematical understandings that prospective teachers bring to teacher education. *Elementary School Journal, 90,* 449–466.

Ball, D. L. (1991). Research on teaching mathematics: Making subject matter knowledge part of the equation. In J. Brophy (Ed.), *Advances in research on teaching, Vol. 2: Teachers' knowledge of subject matter as it relates to their teaching practice* (pp. 1–48). Greenwich, CT: JAI Press.

Ball, D. L., & Bass, H. (2000). Interweaving content and pedagogy in teaching and learning to teach: Knowing and using mathematics. In J. Boaler (Ed.), *Multiple perspectives on the teaching and learning of mathematics* (pp. 83–104). Westport, CT: JAI/Ablex.

Barnett, C. (1991). Building a case-based curriculum to enhance the pedagogical content knowledge of mathematics teachers. *Journal of Teacher Education, 42,* 263–272.

Barnett, C. (1998). Mathematics teaching cases as a catalyst for informed strategic inquiry. *Teaching and Teacher Education, 14*(1), 81–93.

Begle, E. G. (1972). *Teacher knowledge and student achievement in algebra* (SMSG Reports No. 9). Stanford, CA: Stanford University, School Mathematics Study Group.

Begle, E. G. (1979). *Critical variables in mathematics education: Findings from a survey of the empirical literature.* Washington, DC: Mathematical Association of America and National Council of Teachers of Mathematics.

Behr, M., Erlwanger, S., & Nichols, E. (1976). *How children view equality sentences* (PMDC Technical Report No. 3). Tallahassee: Florida State University. (ERIC Document Reproduction Service No. ED 144 802).

Behr, M., Erlwanger, S., & Nichols, E. (1980). How children view the equals sign. *Mathematics Teaching, 92,* 13–15.

Borko, H., Eisenhart, M., Brown, C. A., Underhill, R. G., Jones, D. & Agard, P. C. (1992). Learning to teach hard mathematics: Do novice teachers and their instructors give up too easily? *Journal for Research in Mathematics Education, 23,* 194–222.

Brown, J. S., Collins, A., & Duguid, P. (1989). Situated cognition and the culture of learning. *Educational Researcher, 18*(1), 32–42.

Campbell, P. F. (1996). Empowering children and teachers in the elementary mathematics classrooms of urban schools. *Urban Education, 30,* 449–475.

Carpenter, T. P. (1988). Teaching as problem solving. In R. I. Charles & E. A. Silver (Eds.), *The teaching and assessing of mathematical problem solving* (pp. 187–202). Reston, VA: National Council of Teachers of Mathematics.

Carpenter, T. P., Fennema, E., & Franke, M. L. (1996). Cognitively Guided Instruction: A knowledge base for reform in primary mathematics instruction. *Elementary School Journal, 97,* 3–20.

Carpenter, T. P., Fennema, E., Franke, M. L., Empson, S. B., & Levi, L. W. (1999). *Children's mathematics: Cognitively guided instruction.* Portsmouth, NH: Heinemann.

Carpenter, T. P., Fennema, E., Peterson, P. L., Chiang, C. P., & Loef, M. (1989). Using knowledge of children's mathematics thinking in classroom teaching: An experimental study. *American Educational Research Journal, 26,* 499–531.

Carpenter, T. P., & Levi, L. (1999, April). Developing conceptions of algebraic reasoning in the primary grades. Paper presented at the meeting of the American Educational Research Association, Montreal.

Clark, C. M., & Peterson, P. L. (1986). Teachers' thought processes. In M. C. Wittrock (Ed.), *Handbook of research on teaching* (3rd ed., pp 225–296). New York: Macmillan.

Cobb, P., Wood, T., Yackel, E. Nicholls, J., Wheatley, G., Trigatti, B., & Perlwitz, M. (1991). Assessment of a problem-centered second-grade mathematics project. *Journal for Research in Mathematics Education, 22,* 3–29.

Cohen, D. K., & Ball, D. L. (1999). *Instruction, capacity, and improvement* (CPRE Research Report No. RR-043). Philadelphia: University of Pennsylvania, Consortium for Policy Research in Education.

Cohen, D. K., & Ball, D. L. (2000, April). Instructional innovation: Reconsidering the story. Paper presented at the meeting of the American Educational Research Association, New Orleans.

Conference Board of the Mathematical Sciences. (2000, September). *CBMS Mathematical Education of Teachers Project draft report* [On-line]. Available: http://www.maa.org/cbms/metdraft/index.htm. [January 3, 2001].

Davenport, L. (in press). Elementary mathematics curricula as a tool for mathematics education reform: Challenges of implementation and implications for professional development. In P. Smith, A. Morse, & L. Davenport (Eds.), *Teacher learning and curriculum implementation.* Newton, MA: Education Development Center, Center for the Development of Teaching.

Erlwanger, S., & Berlanger, M. (1983). Interpretations of the equal sign among elementary school children. In J. C. Bergeron & N. Herscovics (Eds.), *Proceedings of the Fifth Annual Meeting of the North American Chapter of the International Group for the Psychology of Mathematics Education* (vol. 1, pp. 250–258). Montreal: University of Montreal. (ERIC Document Reproduction Service No. ED 289 688).

Falkner, K. P., Levi, L., & Carpenter, T. P. (1999). Children's understanding of equality: A foundation for algebra. *Teaching Children Mathematics, 6,* 232–236.

Fennema, E., Carpenter, T. P., Franke, M. L., Levi, L., Jacobs, V., & Empson, B. (1996). A longitudinal study of learning to use children's thinking in mathematics instruction. *Journal for Research in Mathematics Education, 27,* 403–434.

Fernández, E. (1997). The "'Standards'-like" role of teachers' mathematical knowledge in responding to unanticipated student observations. Paper presented at the meeting of the American Educational Research Association, Chicago. (ERIC Document Reproduction Service No. ED 412 261).

Franke, M. L., Carpenter, T. P., Fennema, E., Ansell, E., & Behrent, J. (1998). Understanding teachers' self-sustaining, generative change in the context of professional development. *Teaching and Teacher Education, 14*(1), 67–80.

Franke, M. L., Carpenter, T. P., Levi, L. & Fennema, E. (in press). Capturing teachers' generative change: A follow up study of teachers' professional development in mathematics. *American Educational Research Journal.*

Gordon, A., & Heller, J. (1995, April). Traversing the web: Pedagogical reasoning among new and continuing case methods participants. Paper presented at the meeting of the American Educational Research Association, San Francisco.

Greer, B. (1992). Multiplication and division as models of situations. In D. Grouws (Ed.), *Handbook of research on mathematics teaching and learning* (pp. 276–295). New York: Macmillan.

Hargreaves, A. (1994). *Changing teachers, changing times: Teacher work and culture in the postnuclear age.* New York: Teachers College Press.

Hawkins, E. F., Stancavage, F. B., & Dossey, J. A. (1998). *School policies and practices affecting instruction in mathematics* (NCES 98-495). Washington, DC: National Center for Education Statistics. Available: http://nces.ed.gov/spider/webspider/98495.shtml. [July 10, 2001].

Kieran, C. (1981). Concepts associated with the equality symbol. *Educational Studies in Mathematics, 12,* 317–326.

Learning First Alliance. (1998). *Every child mathematically proficient: An action plan.* Washington, DC: Author. Available: http://www.learningfirst.org/publications.html. [July 10, 2001].

Leinhardt, G., & Smith, D. A. (1985). Expertise in mathematics instruction: Subject matter knowledge. *Journal of Educational Psychology, 77,* 247–271.

Lewis, C., & Tsuchida, I. (1998). A lesson is like a swiftly flowing river: How research lessons improve Japanese education. *American Educator, 22*(4), 12–17, 50–52.

Lewis, J. M., & Ball, D. L. (2000, April). Making teaching visible. Paper presented at the meeting of the American Educational Research Association, New Orleans.

Little, J. W. (1993). Teachers' professional development in a climate of educational reform. *Educational Evaluation and Policy Analysis, 15,* 129–151.

Loucks-Horsley, S., Hewson, P. W., Love, N., & Stiles, K. E. (1998). *Designing professional development for teachers of science and mathematics.* Thousand Oaks, CA: Corwin Press.

Lubinski, C. A., Otto, A. D., Rich, B. S., & Jaberg, P. A. (1998). An analysis of two novice K-8 teachers using a model of teaching-in-context. In S. Berenson, K. Dawkins, M. Blanton, W. Coulombe, J. Kolb, K. Norwood, & L. Stiff (Eds.), *Proceedings of the Twentieth Annual Meeting of the North American Chapter of the International Group for the Psychology of Mathematics Education* (vol. 2, pp. 704–709). Columbus, OH: ERIC Clearinghouse for Science, Mathematics, and Environmental Education. (ERIC Document Reproduction Service No. ED 430 776).

Ma, L. (1999). *Knowing and teaching elementary mathematics: Teachers' understanding of fundamental mathematics in China and the United States.* Mahwah, NJ: Erlbaum.

Matz, M. (1982). Towards a process model for school algebra errors. In D. Sleeman & J. S. Brown (Eds.), *Intelligent tutoring systems* (pp. 25–50). New York: Academic Press.

Martin, W. G., & Harel, G. (1989). Proof frames of preservice elementary teachers. *Journal for Research in Mathematics Education, 20*, 41–51.

Monk, D. H. (1994). Subject area preparation of secondary mathematics and science teachers and student achievement. *Economics of Education Review, 13*, 125–145.

Mullens, J. E., Murnane, R. J., & Willett, J. B. (1996). The contribution of training and subject matter knowledge to teaching effectiveness: A multilevel analysis of longitudinal evidence from Belize. *Comparative Education Review, 40*, 139–157.

Nathan, M. J., & Koedinger, K. R. (2000). An investigation of teachers' beliefs of students' algebra development. *Cognition and Instruction, 18*, 209–237.

National Research Council. (2000). *Educating teachers of science, mathematics, and technology: New practices for the new millennium.* Washington, DC: National Academy Press. Available: http://books.nap.edu/catalog/9832.html. [July 10, 2001].

National Research Council. (2001). *Knowing and learning mathematics for teaching: Proceedings of a workshop.* Washington, DC: National Academy Press. Available: http://books.nap.edu/catalog/10050.html. [July 10, 2001].

Post, T. R., Harel, G., Behr, M. J. & Lesh, R. (1991). Intermediate teachers' knowledge of rational number concepts. In E. Fennema, T. P. Carpenter, & S. J. Lamon (Eds.), *Integrating research on teaching and learning mathematics* (pp. 194–217). Albany: State University of New York Press.

Putnam, R. T., & Borko, H. (2000, January-February). What do new views of knowledge and thinking have to say about research on teacher learning? *Educational Researcher, 29*(1), 4–15.

Putnam, R. T., Heaton, R. M., Prawat, R. S., & Remillard, J. (1992). Teaching mathematics for understanding: Discussing case studies of four fifth-grade teachers. *Elementary School Journal, 93*, 213–228.

Rowan, B., Chiang, F. S., & Miller, R. J. (1997). Using research on employee's performance to study the effects of teachers on student achievement. *Sociology of Education, 70*, 256–284.

Saenz-Ludlow, A., & Walgamuth, C. (1998). Third graders' interpretation of equality and the equal symbol. *Educational Studies in Mathematics, 35*, 153–187.

Sarason, S. B. (1990). *The predictable failure of educational reform: Can we change course before it's too late?* San Francisco: Jossey Bass.

Sarason, S. B. (1996). *Revisiting "The culture of school and the problem of change."* New York: Teachers College Press.

Schon, D. (1987). *Educating the reflective practitioner: Toward a new design for teaching and learning in the professions.* San Francisco: Jossey Bass.

Schoenfeld, A. H. (1998). Toward a theory of teaching-in-context. *Issues in Education, 4*(1), 1–94. Available: http://www-gse.berkeley.edu/faculty/aschoenfeld/TeachInContext/teaching-in-context.html. [July 10, 2001].

Shimahara, N. K. (1998). The Japanese model of professional development: Teaching as a craft. *Teaching and Teacher Education, 14*, 451–462.

Shulman, L. S. (1987). Knowledge and teaching: Foundations of the new reform. *Harvard Educational Review, 57*, 1–22.

Silver, E. A., & Stein, M. (1996). The QUASAR Project: The "revolution of the possible" in mathematics instructional reform in urban middle schools. *Urban Education, 30*, 476–521.

Simon, M. A., & Blume, G. W. 1996). Justification in the mathematics classroom: A study of prospective elementary teachers. *Journal of Mathematical Behavior, 15*(1), 3–31.

Stigler, J. W., & Hiebert, J. (1999). *The teaching gap: Best ideas from the world's teachers for improving education in the classroom.* New York: Free Press.

Tharp, R. G., & Gallimore, R. (1988). *Rousing minds to life: Teaching, learning, and schooling in a social context.* New York: Cambridge University Press.

Thompson, A. G., & Thompson, P. W. (1996). Talking about rates conceptually, Part 2: Mathematical knowledge for teaching. *Journal for Research in Mathematics Education, 27*, 2–24.

Thompson, P. W., & Thompson, A. G. (1994). Talking about rates conceptually, Part 1: A teacher's struggle. *Journal for Research in Mathematics Education, 2*5, 279–303.

Tirosh, D., Fischbein, E., Graeber, A. O. & Wilson, J. W. (1999). *Prospective elementary teachers' conceptions of rational numbers.* Available: http://jwilson.coe.uga.edu/Texts.Folder/tirosh/Pros.El.Tchrs.html. [July 10, 2001].

Villasenor, A., & Kepner, H. S. (1993). Arithmetic from a problem-solving perspective: An urban implementation. *Journal for Research in Mathematics Education, 24*, 62–69.

11

CONCLUSIONS AND RECOMMENDATIONS

To many people, school mathematics is virtually a phenomenon of nature. It seems timeless, set in stone—hard to change and perhaps not needing to change. But the school mathematics education of yesterday, which had a practical basis, is no longer viable. Rote learning of arithmetic procedures no longer has the clear value it once had. The widespread availability of technological tools for computation means that people are less dependent on their own powers of computation. At the same time, people are much more exposed to numbers and quantitative ideas and so need to deal with mathematics on a higher level than they did just 20 years ago. Too few U.S. students, however, leave elementary and middle school with adequate mathematical knowledge, skill, and confidence for anyone to be satisfied that all is well in school mathematics. Moreover, certain segments of the U.S. population are not well represented among those who succeed in learning mathematics. Widespread failure to learn mathematics limits individual possibilities and hampers national growth. Our experiences, discussions, and review of the literature have convinced us that school mathematics demands substantial change. We recognize that such change needs to be undertaken carefully and deliberately, so that every child has both the opportunity and support necessary to become proficient in mathematics.

In this chapter, we present conclusions and recommendations to help move the nation toward the change needed in school mathematics. In the preceding chapters, we have offered citations of research studies and of theoretical analyses, but we recognize that clear, unambiguous evidence is not available to address many of the important issues we have raised. It should

> Our experiences, discussions, and review of the literature have convinced us that school mathematics demands substantial change.

be obvious that much additional research will be needed to fill out the picture, and we have recommended some directions for that research to take. The remaining recommendations reflect our consensus that the relevant data and theory are sufficiently persuasive to warrant movement in the direction indicated, with the proviso that more evidence will need to be collected along the way.

Information is now becoming available as to the effects on students' learning in new curriculum programs in mathematics that are different from those programs common today. Over the coming years, the volume of that information is certain to increase. The community of people concerned with mathematics education will need to pay continued attention to studies of the effectiveness of new programs and will need to examine the available data carefully. In writing this report we were able to use few such studies because they were just beginning to be published. We expect them collectively to provide valuable information that will warrant careful review at a later date by a committee like ours.

Our report has concentrated on learning about numbers, their properties, and operations on them. Although number is the centerpiece of pre-K to grade 8 mathematics, it is not the whole story, as we have noted more than once. Our reading of the scholarly literature on number, together with our experience as teachers, creators, and users of mathematics, has yielded observations that might be applied to other components of school mathematics such as measurement, geometry, algebra, probability, and data analysis. Number is used in learning concepts and processes from all these domains.

Below we present some comprehensive recommendations concerning mathematical proficiency that cut across all domains of policy, practice, and research. Then we propose changes needed in the curriculum if students are to develop mathematical proficiency, and we offer some recommendations for instruction. Finally, we discuss teacher preparation and professional development related to mathematics teaching, setting out recommendations designed to help teachers be more proficient in their work.

Mathematical Proficiency

As a goal of instruction, mathematical proficiency provides a better way to think about mathematics learning than narrower views that leave out key features of what it means to know and be able to do mathematics. Mathematical proficiency, as defined in chapter 4, implies expertise in handling mathematical ideas. Students with mathematical proficiency understand basic concepts, are fluent in performing basic operations, exercise a repertoire of strategic knowledge, reason clearly and flexibly, and maintain a positive outlook toward mathematics. Moreover, they possess and use these strands of mathematical proficiency in an integrated manner, so that each reinforces the others. It takes time for proficiency to develop fully, but in every grade in school students can demonstrate mathematical proficiency in some form. In this report we have concentrated on those ideas about number that are developed in grades pre-K through 8. We must stress, however, that proficiency spans all parts of school mathematics and that it can and should be developed every year that students are in school.

> In every grade in school, students can demonstrate mathematical proficiency in some form.

All young Americans must learn to think mathematically, and they must think mathematically to learn. We have elaborated on what such learning and thinking entail by proposing five strands of mathematical proficiency to be developed in school. *The overriding premise of our work is that throughout the grades from pre-K through 8* **all students can and should be mathematically proficient.** That means they understand mathematical ideas, compute fluently, solve problems, and engage in logical reasoning. They believe they can make sense out of mathematics and can use it to make sense out of things in their world. For them mathematics is personal and is important to their future.

School mathematics in the United States does not now enable most students to develop the strands of mathematical proficiency in a sound fashion. Proficiency for all demands that fundamental changes be made concurrently in curriculum, instructional materials, classroom practice, teacher preparation, and professional development. These changes will require continuing, coordinated action on the part of policy makers, teacher educators, teachers, and parents. Although some readers may feel that substantial advances are already being made in reforming mathematics teaching and learning, we find real progress toward mathematical proficiency to be woefully inadequate. These observations led us to five general recommendations regarding mathematical proficiency that reflect our vision for school mathematics.

> School mathematics in the United States does not now enable most students to develop the strands of mathematical proficiency in a sound fashion.

• *The integrated and balanced development of all five strands of mathematical proficiency should guide the teaching and learning of school mathematics. Instruction should not be based on extreme positions that students learn, on the one hand, solely by internalizing what a teacher or book says or, on the other hand, solely by inventing mathematics on their own.*

• *Teachers' professional development should be high quality, sustained, and systematically designed and deployed to help all students develop math-*

*ematical proficiency. Schools should support, as a central part of teachers'
work, engagement in sustained efforts to improve their mathematics instruction. This support requires the provision of time and resources.*

- *The coordination of curriculum, instructional materials, assessment,
instruction, professional development, and school organization around the
development of mathematical proficiency should drive school improvement
efforts.*

- *Efforts to improve students' mathematics learning should be informed
by scientific evidence, and their effectiveness should be evaluated systematically. Such efforts should be coordinated, continual, and cumulative.*

- *Additional research should be undertaken on the nature, development, and assessment of mathematical proficiency.*

These recommendations are augmented in the discussion below. In that discussion we propose additional recommendations that detail some of the policies and practices needed if all children are to be mathematically proficient.

Curriculum

The balanced and integrated development of all five strands of mathematical proficiency requires that various elements of the school curriculum—
goals, core content, learning activities, and assessment efforts—be coordinated toward the same end. Achieving that coordination puts heavy demands
on instructional programs, on the materials used in instruction, and on the
way in which instructional time is managed. The curriculum has to be organized within and across grades so that time for learning is used effectively.
Instead of cursory and repeated treatments of a topic, the curriculum should
be focused on important ideas, allowing them to be developed thoroughly
and treated in depth. The unproductive recycling of mathematical content is
to be avoided, but students need ample opportunities to review and consoli-
date their knowledge.

> Instead of cursory and repeated treatments of a topic, the curriculum should be focused on important ideas, allowing them to be developed thoroughly and treated in depth.

Building on Informal Knowledge

Most children in the United States enter school with an extensive stock
of informal knowledge about numbers from the counting they have done,
from hearing number words and seeing number symbols used in everyday

life, and from various experiences in judging and comparing quantities. Many are also familiar with various patterns and some geometric shapes. This knowledge serves as a basis for developing mathematical proficiency in the early grades. The level of children's knowledge, however, varies greatly across socioeconomic and ethnic groups. Some children have not had the experiences necessary to build the informal knowledge they need before they enter school.

A number of interventions have demonstrated that any immaturity of mathematical development can be overcome with targeted instructional activities. Parents and other caregivers, through games, puzzles, and other activities in the home, can also help children develop their informal knowledge and can augment the school's efforts. Just as adults in the home can help children avoid reading difficulties through activities that promote language and literacy growth, so too can they help children avoid difficulties in mathematics by helping them develop their informal knowledge of number, pattern, shape, and space. Support from home and school can have a catalytic effect on children's mathematical development, and the sooner that support is provided, the better:

- *School and preschool programs should provide rich activities with numbers and operations from the very beginning, especially for children who enter without these experiences.*

- *Efforts should be made to educate parents and other caregivers as to why they should, and how they can, help their children develop a sense of number and shape.*

Learning Number Names

Research has shown that the English number names can inhibit children's understanding of base-10 properties of the decimal system and learning to use numerals meaningfully. Names such as "twelve" and "fifteen" do not make clear to children that $12 = 10 + 2$ and $15 = 10 + 5$. These connections are more obvious in some other languages.

U.S. children, therefore, often need extra help in understanding the base-ten organization underlying number names and in seeing quantities organized into hundreds, tens, and ones. Conceptual supports (objects or diagrams) that show the magnitude of the quantities and connect them to the number names and written numerals have been found to help children acquire insight into the base-10 number system. That insight is important to learning and understanding numerals and also to developing strategies for solving problems in arithmetic. So that number names will be understood and used correctly, we recommend the following:

• *Mathematics programs in the early grades should make extensive use of appropriate objects, diagrams, and other aids to ensure that all children understand and are able to use number words and the base-10 properties of numerals, that all children can use the language of quantity (hundreds, tens, and ones) in solving problems, and that all children can explain their reasoning in obtaining solutions.*

Learning About Numbers

The number systems of pre-K–8 mathematics—the whole numbers, integers, and rational numbers—form a coherent structure. For each of these systems, there are various ways to represent the numbers themselves and the operations on them. For example, a rational number might be represented by a decimal or in fractional form. It might be represented by a word, a symbol, a letter, a point or length on a line, or a portion of a figure. Proficiency with numbers in the elementary and middle grades implies that students can not only appreciate these different notations for a number but also can translate freely from one to another. It also means that they see connections among numbers and operations in the different number systems. As a consequence of many instructional programs, students have had severe difficulty representing, connecting, and using numbers other than whole numbers. Innovations that link various representations of numbers and situations in which numbers are used have been shown to produce learning with understanding. Creating this kind of learning will require changes in all parts of school mathematics to ensure that the following recommendations are implemented:

• *An integrated approach should be taken to the development of all five strands of proficiency with whole numbers, integers, and rational numbers to ensure that students in grades pre-K–8 can use the numbers fluently and flexibly to solve challenging but accessible problems. In particular, procedures for calculation should frequently be linked to various representations and to situations in which they are used so that all strands are brought into play.*

- *The conceptual bases for operations with numbers and how those operations relate to real situations should be a major focus of the curriculum. Addition, subtraction, multiplication, and division should be presented initially with real situations. Students should encounter a wide range of situations in which those operations are used.*

- *Different ways of representing numbers, when to use a specific representation, and how to translate from one representation to another should be included in the curriculum. Students should be given opportunities to use these different representations to carry out operations and to understand and explain these operations. Instructional materials should include visual and linguistic supports to help students develop this representational ability.*

Operating with Single-Digit Numbers

Learning to operate with single-digit numbers has long been characterized in the United States as "learning basic facts," and the emphasis has been on rote memorization of those facts, also known as basic number combinations. For adults the simplicity of calculating with single-digit numbers often masks the complexity of learning those combinations and the many different methods children can use in carrying out such calculations. Research has shown that children move through a fairly well-defined sequence of solution methods in learning to perform operations with single-digit numbers, particularly for addition and subtraction, where rapid general procedures exist. Children progress from using physical objects for representing problem situations to using more sophisticated counting and reasoning strategies, such as deriving one number combination from another (e.g., finding $7 + 8$ by knowing that it is 1 more than $7 + 7$ or, similarly, finding 7×6 as 7 more than 7×5). They know that addition and multiplication are commutative and that there is a relation between addition and subtraction and between multiplication and division. They use patterns in the multiplication table as the basis for learning the products of single-digit numbers. Instruction that takes such research into account is needed if students are to become proficient:

- *Children should learn single-digit number combinations with understanding.*

- *Instructional materials and classroom teaching should help students learn increasingly abbreviated procedures for producing number combinations rapidly and accurately without always having to refer to tables or other aids.*

Learning Numerical Algorithms

We believe that algorithms and their properties are important mathematical ideas that all students need to understand. An algorithm is a reliable step-by-step procedure for solving problems. To perform arithmetic calculations, children must learn how numerical algorithms work. Some algorithms have been well established through centuries of use; others may be invented by children on their own. The widespread availability of calculators for performing calculations has greatly reduced the level of skill people need to acquire in performing multidigit calculations with paper and pencil. Anyone who needs to perform such calculations routinely today will have a calculator, or even a computer, at hand. But the technology has not made obsolete the need to understand and be able to perform basic written algorithms for addition, subtraction, multiplication, and division of numbers, whether expressed as whole numbers, fractions, or decimals. Beyond providing tools for computation, algorithms can be analyzed and compared, which can help students understand the nature and properties of operations and of place-value notation for numbers. In our view, algorithms, when well understood, can serve as a valuable basis for reasoning about mathematics.

Students acquire proficiency with multidigit numerical algorithms through a progression of experiences that begin with the students modeling various problem situations. They then can learn algorithms that are easily understood because of obvious connections to the quantities involved. Eventually, students can learn and use methods that are more efficient and general, though perhaps less transparent. Proficiency with numerical algorithms is built on understanding and reasoning, as well as frequent opportunity for use.

Two recommendations reflect our view of the role of numerical algorithms in grades pre-K–8:

• *For addition, subtraction, multiplication, and division, all students should understand and be able to carry out an algorithm that is general and reasonably efficient.*

• *Students should be able to use adaptive reasoning to analyze and compare algorithms, to grasp their underlying principles, and to choose with discrimination algorithms for use in different contexts.*

Using Estimation and Mental Arithmetic

The accurate and efficient use of an algorithm rests on having a sense of the magnitude of the result. Estimation techniques enable students not only to check whether they are performing an operation correctly but also to decide whether that operation makes sense for the problem they are solving.

The base-10 structure of numerals allows certain sums, differences, products, and quotients to be computed mentally. Activities using mental arithmetic develop number sense and increase flexibility in using numbers. Mental arithmetic also simplifies other computations and estimations. For example, dividing by 0.25 is the same as multiplying by 4, which can be found by doubling twice. Whether or not students are performing a written algorithm, they can use mental arithmetic to simplify certain operations with numbers. Techniques of estimation and of mental arithmetic are particularly important when students are checking results obtained from a calculator or computer. If children are not encouraged to use the mental computational procedures they have when entering school, those procedures will erode. But when instruction emphasizes estimation and mental arithmetic, conceptual understanding and fluency with mental procedures can be enhanced. Our recommendation about estimation and computation, whether mental or written, is as follows:

> Whether or not students are performing a written algorithm, they can use mental arithmetic to simplify certain operations with numbers.

- *The curriculum should provide opportunities for students to develop and use techniques for mental arithmetic and estimation as a means of promoting a deeper number sense.*

Representing and Operating with Rational Numbers

Rational numbers provide the first number system in which all the operations of arithmetic, including division, are possible. These numbers pose a major challenge to young learners, in part because each rational number can represent so many different situations and because there are several different notational schemes for representing the same rational number, each with its own method of calculation.

An important part of learning about rational numbers is developing a clear sense of what they are. Children need to learn that rational numbers are numbers in the same way that whole numbers are numbers. For children to use rational numbers to solve problems, they need to learn that the same rational number may be represented in different ways, as a fraction, a decimal, or a percent. Fraction concepts and representations need to be related to those of division, measurement, and ratio. Decimal and fractional representations need to be connected and understood. Building these connections takes extensive experience with rational numbers over a substantial period of time. Researchers have documented that difficulties in working with rational numbers can often be traced to weak conceptual understanding. For example, the idea that a fraction gets smaller when its denominator becomes larger is difficult for children to accept when they do not understand what the fraction represents. Children may try to apply ideas they have about whole numbers to rational numbers and run into trouble. Instructional sequences in which more time is spent at the outset on developing meaning for the various representations of rational numbers and the concept of unit have been shown to promote mathematical proficiency.

Research reveals that the kinds of errors students make when beginning to operate with rational numbers often come because they have not yet developed meaning for these numbers and are applying poorly understood rules for whole numbers. Operations with rational numbers challenge students' naïve understanding of multiplication and division that multiplication "makes bigger" and division "makes smaller." Although there is limited research on instructional programs for developing proficiency with computations involving rational numbers, approaches that build on students' intuitive understanding and that use objects or contexts that help students make sense of the operations offer more promise than rule-based approaches.

We make the following recommendation concerning the rational numbers:

> • *The curriculum should provide opportunities for students to develop a thorough understanding of rational numbers, their various representations including common fractions, decimal fractions, and percents, and operations on rational numbers. These opportunities should involve connecting symbolic representations and operations with physical or pictorial representations, as well as translating between various symbolic representations.*

Extending the Place-Value System

The system of Hindu-Arabic numerals—in which there is a decimal point and each place to the right and the left is associated with a different power of 10—is one of humanity's greatest inventions for thinking about and operating with numbers. Mastery of that system does not come easily, however. Students need assistance not only in using the decimal system but also in understanding its structure and how it works.

Conceptual understanding and procedural fluency with multidigit numbers and decimal fractions require that students understand and use the base-10 quantities represented by number words and number notation. Research indicates that much of students' difficulty with decimal fractions stems from their failure to understand the base-10 representations. Decimal representations need to be connected to multidigit whole numbers as groups getting 10 times larger (to the left) and one tenth as large (to the right). Referents (diagrams or objects) showing the size of the quantities in different decimal places can be helpful in understanding decimal fractions and calculations with them. The following recommendation expresses our concern that the decimal system be given a central place in the curriculum:

• *The curriculum should devote substantial attention to developing an understanding of the decimal place-value system, to using its features in calculating and problem solving, and to explaining calculation and problem-solving methods with decimal fractions.*

Developing Proportional Reasoning

The concept of ratio is much more difficult than many people realize. *Proportional reasoning* is the term given to reasoning that involves the equality and manipulation of ratios. Children often have difficulty comparing ratios and using them to solve problems. Many school mathematics programs fail to develop children's understanding of ratio comparisons and move directly to formal procedures for solving missing-value proportion problems. Research tracing the development of proportional reasoning shows that proficiency grows as students develop and connect different aspects of proportional reasoning. Further, the development of proportional reasoning can be supported by having students explore proportional situations in a variety of problem contexts using concrete materials or through data collection activities. We see ratio and proportion as underdeveloped components of grades pre-K–8 mathematics:

• *The curriculum should provide extensive opportunities over time for students to explore proportional situations concretely, and these situations should be linked to formal procedures for solving proportion problems whenever such procedures are introduced.*

Using the Number Line

Students often view the study of whole numbers, decimal fractions, common fractions, and integers as disconnected topics. One tool that we believe may be useful in developing numerical understanding and in making connections across number systems is the number line, a geometric representation of numbers that gives each number a unique point on the line and an oriented distance from the origin, depicting its magnitude and direction. Although it may be difficult to learn, the number line gives a unified geometric representation of integers and rational numbers within the real number system, later to be encountered in geometry, algebra, and calculus. The geometric models of operations afforded by the number line apply uniformly to all real numbers, thus presenting one unified number system. The number line may become particularly useful as students are learning about integers and rational numbers, for it may help students develop a sense of the magnitudes and relationships of those numbers in a way that is less clear in other representations:

• *Because it can serve as a tool for simultaneously representing whole numbers, integers, and rational numbers, teachers and researchers should explore effective uses of the number line representation when students learn about operations with numbers, relations among number systems, and more formal symbolic representations of numbers.*

Expanding the Number Domain

Students currently encounter the expansion of the number domain by starting with whole numbers, gradually incorporating fractions, and only much later expanding the domain to include negative integers and irrational numbers. That sequence has a long history, but there are arguments for an alternative. For example, expanding the whole numbers to take in the negative integers in the early grades would allow students to do more with addition and subtraction before venturing into the rational number system, which requires multiplication and division. Systematic study of this alternative is needed:

• *Teachers, curriculum developers, and researchers should explore the possibility of introducing integers before rational numbers. Ways to engage younger children in meaningful uses of negative integers should be developed and tested.*

Developing Algebraic Thinking

The formal study of algebra is both the gateway into advanced mathematics and a stumbling block for many students. The transition from arithmetic to algebra is often not an easy one. The difficulties associated with the transition from the activities typically associated with school arithmetic to those typically associated with school algebra (representational activities, transformational activities, and generalizing and justifying activities) have been extensively studied. Research has documented that the visual and numerical supports provided for symbolic expressions by computers and graphing calculators help students create meaning for expressions and equations. The research, however, has shed less light on the long-term acquisition and retention of transformational fluency. Although through generalizing and justifying, students can learn to use and appreciate algebraic expressions as general statements, more research is need on how students develop such awareness.

The study of algebra, however, does not have to begin with a formal course in the subject. New lines of research and development are focusing on ways that the elementary and middle school curriculum can be used to support the development of algebraic reasoning. These efforts attempt to avoid the difficulties many students now experience and to lay a better foundation for secondary school mathematics. We believe that from the earliest grades of elementary school, students can be acquiring the rudiments of algebra, particularly its representational aspects and the notion of variable and function. By emphasizing both the relationships among quantities and ways of representing these relationships, instruction can introduce students to the basic ideas of algebra as a generalization of arithmetic. They can come to value the roles of definitions and see how the laws of arithmetic can be expressed algebraically and be used to support their reasoning. We recommend that algebra be explicitly connected to number in grades pre-K–8:

- *The basic ideas of algebra as generalized arithmetic should be anticipated by activities in the early elementary grades and learned by the end of middle school.*

- *Teachers and researchers should investigate the effectiveness of instructional strategies in grades pre-K–8 that would help students move from arithmetic to algebraic ways of thinking.*

> The formal study of algebra is both the gateway into advanced mathematics and a stumbling block for many students.

Promoting Algebra for All

In some countries by the end of eighth grade, all students have been studying algebra for several years, although not ordinarily in a separate course. "Algebra for all" is a worthwhile and attainable goal for middle school students. In the United States, however, some efforts to promote algebra for all have involved simply offering a standard first-year algebra course (algebra through quadratics) to everyone. We believe such efforts are virtually guaranteed to result in many students failing to develop proficiency in algebra, in part because the transition to algebra is so abrupt. Instead, a different curriculum is needed for algebra in middle school:

* *Teachers, researchers, and curriculum developers should explore ways to offer a middle school curriculum in which algebraic ideas are developed in a robust way and connected to the rest of mathematics.*

Using Technology to Learn Algebra

Research has shown that instruction that makes productive use of computer and calculator technology has beneficial effects on understanding and learning algebraic representation. It is not clear, however, what role the newer symbol manipulation technologies might play in developing proficiency with the transformational aspects of algebra. We recommend the following:

* *Research should be conducted on the effects on students' learning of using the symbol-manipulating capacities of calculators and computers to study algebraic concepts and to transform algebraic expressions and equations.*

Solving Problems as a Context for Learning

An important part of our conception of mathematical proficiency involves the ability to formulate and solve problems coming from daily life or other domains, including mathematics itself. That ability is not being developed well in U.S. pre-K to grade 8 classrooms. Studies in almost every domain of mathematics have demonstrated that problem solving provides an important context in which students can learn about number and other mathematical topics.

Problem-solving ability is enhanced when students have opportunities to solve problems themselves and to see problems being solved. Further, problem solving can provide the site for learning new concepts and for practicing learned skills. We believe problem solving is vital because it calls on all strands of proficiency, thus increasing the chances of students integrating them. Problem solving also provides opportunities for teachers to assess students' performance on all of the strands. Other activities, such as listening to an explanation or practicing solution methods, can help develop specific strands of proficiency, but too much emphasis on them, to the exclusion of solving problems, may give a one-sided character to learning and inhibit the formation of connections among the strands. We see problem solving as central to school mathematics:

> We see problem solving as central to school mathematics.

- *Problem solving should be the site in which all of the strands of mathematics proficiency converge. It should provide opportunities for students to weave together the strands of proficiency and for teachers to assess students' performance on all of the strands.*

Improving Materials for Instruction

Analyses of the U.S. curriculum reveal much repetition from grade to grade and many topics, few of which are treated in much depth. Further, instructional materials in pre-K to grade 8 mathematics seldom provide the guidance and assistance that teachers in other countries find helpful, such as discussions of children's typical misconceptions or alternative solution methods. How teachers might understand and use instructional materials to help students develop mathematical proficiency is not well understood. On the basis of our reasoned judgment, we offer the following recommendations for improving instructional materials in school mathematics:

- *Textbooks and other instructional materials should develop the core content of school mathematics in a focused way, in depth, and with continuity in and across grades, supporting all strands of mathematical proficiency.*

- *Textbooks and other instructional materials should support teacher understanding of mathematical concepts, of student thinking and student errors, and of effective pedagogical supports and techniques.*

- *Activities and strategies should be developed and incorporated into instructional materials to assist teachers in helping all students become proficient in mathematics, including students low in socio-economic status, English language learners, special education students, and students with a special interest or talent in mathematics.*

- *Efforts to develop textbooks and other instructional materials should include research into how teachers can understand and use those materials effectively.*

- *A government agency or research foundation should fund an independent group to analyze textbooks and other instructional materials for the extent to which they promote mathematical proficiency. The group should recommend how these materials might be modified to promote greater mathematical proficiency.*

Giving Time to Instruction

Research indicates that a key requirement for developing proficiency is the opportunity to learn. In many U.S. elementary and middle school classrooms, students are not engaged in sustained study of mathematics. On some days in some classes they are spending little or no time at all on the subject. Mathematical proficiency as we have defined it cannot be developed unless regular time (say, one hour each school day) is allocated to and used for mathematics instruction in every grade of elementary and middle school. Further, we believe the strands of proficiency will not develop in a coordinated fashion unless continual attention is given to every strand. The following recommendation expresses our concern that mathematics be given its rightful place in the curriculum:

> Mathematical proficiency as we have defined it cannot be developed unless regular time is allocated to and used for mathematics instruction in every grade of elementary and middle school.

- *Substantial time should be devoted to mathematics instruction each school day, with enough time devoted to each unit and topic to enable students to develop understanding of the concepts and procedures involved. Time should be apportioned so that all strands of mathematical proficiency together receive adequate attention.*

Giving Students Time to Practice

Practice is important in the development of mathematical proficiency. When students have multiple opportunities to use the computational procedures, reasoning processes, and problem-solving strategies they are learning, the methods they are using become smoother, more reliable, and better understood. Practice alone does not suffice; it needs to be built on understanding and accompanied by feedback. In fact, premature practice has been shown to be harmful. The following recommendation reflects our view of the role of practice:

- *Practice should be used with feedback to support all strands of mathematical proficiency and not just procedural fluency. In particular, practice on computational procedures should be designed to build on and extend understanding.*

Using Assessment Effectively

At present, substantial time every year is taken away from mathematics instruction in U.S. classrooms to prepare for and take externally mandated assessments, usually in the form of tests. Often, those tests are not well articulated with the mathematics curriculum, testing content that has not been taught during the year or that is not central to the development of mathematical proficiency. Preparation for such tests, moreover, does not ordinarily focus on the development of proficiency. Instead, much time is given to practicing calculation procedures and reviewing a multitude of topics. Teachers and students often waste valuable learning time because they are not informed about the content to be tested or the form that test items will take.

We believe that assessment, whether externally mandated or developed by the teacher, should support the development of students' mathematical proficiency. It needs to provide opportunities for students to learn rather than taking time away from their learning. Assessments in which students are learning as well as showing what they have already learned can provide valuable information to teachers, schools, districts, and states, as well as the students themselves. Such assessments help teachers modify their instruction to support better learning at each grade level.

Time and money spent on assessment need to be used more effectively so that students have the opportunity to show what they know and can do. Teachers need to receive timely and detailed information about students' performance on each external assessment. In that way, students and teachers alike can learn from assessments instead of having assessments used only to rank students, teachers, or schools. The following recommendations will help make assessment more effective in developing mathematical proficiency:

> Students and teachers alike can learn from assessments instead of having assessments used only to rank students, teachers, or schools.

- *Assessment, whether internal or external, should be focused on the development and achievement of mathematical proficiency. In particular, assessments used to determine qualification for state and federal funding should reflect the definition of mathematics proficiency presented in this report.*

- *Information about the content and form of each external assessment should be provided so that teachers and students can prepare appropriately and efficiently.*

- *The results of each external assessment should be reported so as to provide feedback useful for teachers and learners rather than simply a set of rankings.*

- *A government agency or research foundation should fund an independent group to analyze external assessment programs for the extent to which they promote mathematical proficiency. The group should recommend how programs might be modified to promote greater mathematical proficiency.*

Instruction

The development of mathematical proficiency requires thoughtful planning, careful execution, and continual improvement of instruction.

Effective teaching—teaching that fosters the development of mathematical proficiency over time—can take a variety of forms. Consequently, we endorse no single approach. All forms of instruction configure relations among teachers, students, and content. The quality of instruction is a function of teachers' knowledge and use of mathematical content, teachers' attention to and handling of students, and students' engagement in and use of mathematical tasks. The development of mathematical proficiency requires thoughtful planning, careful execution, and continual improvement of instruction. It depends critically on teachers who understand mathematics, how students learn, and the classroom practices that support that learning. They also need to know their students: who they are, what their backgrounds are, and what they know.

Planning for Instruction

Planning, whether for one lesson or a year, is often viewed as routine and straightforward. However, plans seldom elaborate the content that the students are to learn or develop good maps of paths to take to reach learning goals. We believe that planning needs to reflect a deep and thorough consideration of the mathematical content of a lesson and of students' thinking and learning. Instructional materials need to support teachers in their planning, and teachers need to have time to plan. Instruction needs to be planned with the development of mathematical proficiency in mind:

- *Content, representations, tasks, and materials should be chosen so as to develop all five strands of proficiency toward the big ideas of mathematics and the goals for instruction.*

- *Planning for instruction should take into account what students know, and instruction should provide ways of ascertaining what students know and think as well as their interests and needs.*

- *Rather than simply listing problems and exercises, teachers should plan for instruction by focusing on the learning goals for their students, keeping in mind how the goals for each lesson fit with those of past and future lessons. Their planning should anticipate the events in the lesson, the ways in which the students will respond, and how those responses can be used to further the lesson goals.*

Managing Classroom Discourse

Mathematics classrooms are more likely to be places in which mathematical proficiency develops when they are communities of learners and not collections of isolated individuals. Research on creating classrooms that function as communities of learners has identified several important features of these classrooms: ideas and methods are valued, students have autonomy in choosing and sharing solution methods, mistakes are valued as sites of learning for everyone, and the authority for correctness lies in logic and the structure of the subject, not in the teacher. In such classrooms the teacher plays a key role as the orchestrator of the discourse students engage in about mathematical ideas. Teachers are responsible for moving the mathematics along while affording students opportunities to offer solutions, make claims, answer questions, and provide explanations to their peers. Teachers need to help bring a mathematical discussion to a close, making sure that gaps have been filled and errors addressed. To develop mathematical proficiency, we believe that students require more than just the demonstration of procedures. They need experience in investigating mathematical properties, justifying solution methods, and analyzing problem situations. We recommend the following:

- *A significant amount of class time should be spent in developing mathematical ideas and methods rather than only practicing skills.*

- *Questioning and discussion should elicit students' thinking and solution strategies and should build on them, leading to greater clarity and precision.*

- *Discourse should not be confined to answers only but should include discussion of connections to other problems, alternative representations and solution methods, the nature of justification and argumentation, and the like.*

Linking Experience to Abstraction

Students acquire higher levels of mathematical proficiency when they have opportunities to use mathematics to solve significant problems as well as to learn the key concepts and procedures of that mathematics. Although mathematics gains power and generality through abstraction, it finds both its sources and applications in concrete settings, where it is made meaningful to the learner. There is an inevitable dialectic between concrete and abstract in which each helps shape the other. Exhortations to "begin with the concrete" need to consider carefully what is meant by *concrete*. Research reveals that various kinds of physical materials commonly used to help children learn mathematics are often no more concrete to them than symbols on paper might be. *Concrete* is not the same as *physical*. Learning begins with the concrete when meaningful items in the child's immediate experience are used as scaffolding with which to erect abstract ideas. To ensure that progress is made toward mathematical abstraction, we recommend the following:

- *Links among written and oral mathematical expressions, concrete problem settings, and students' solution methods should be continually and explicitly made during school mathematics instruction.*

Assigning Independent Work

Part of becoming proficient in mathematics is becoming an independent learner. For that purpose, many teachers give homework. The limited research on homework in mathematics has been confined to investigations of the relation between the quantity of homework assigned and students' achievement test scores. Neither the quality nor the function of homework has been studied. Homework can have different purposes. For example, it might be used to practice skills or to prepare the student for the next lesson. We believe that independent work serves several useful purposes. Regarding independence and homework, we make the following recommendations:

• *Students should be provided opportunities to work independently of the teacher both individually and in pairs or groups.*

• *When homework is assigned for the purpose of developing skill, students should be sufficiently familiar with the skill and the tasks so that they are not practicing incorrect procedures.*

Using Calculators and Computers

In the discussion above, we mention the special role that calculators and computers can play in learning algebra. But they have many other roles to play throughout instruction in grades pre-K–8. Using calculators and computers does not replace the need for fluency with other methods. Confronted with a complex arithmetic problem, students can use calculators and computers to see beyond tedious calculations to the strategies needed to solve the problem. Technology can relieve the computational burden and free working memory for higher-level thinking so that there can be a sharper focus on an important idea. Further, skillfully planned calculator investigations may reveal subtle or interesting mathematical ideas, such as the rules for order of operations.

A large number of empirical studies of calculator use, including long-term studies, have generally shown that the use of calculators does not threaten the development of basic skills and that it can enhance conceptual understanding, strategic competence, and disposition toward mathematics. For example, students who use calculators tend to show improved conceptual understanding, greater ability to choose the correct operation, and greater skill in estimation and mental arithmetic without a loss of basic computational skills. They are also familiar with a wider range of numbers than students who do not use calculators and are better able to tackle realistic mathematics problems.

Just like any instructional tool, calculators and computers can be used more or less effectively. Our concern is that, when computing technology is used, it needs to contribute positively:

> When computing technology is used, it needs to contribute positively.

• *In all grades of elementary and middle school, any use of calculators and computers should be done in ways that help develop all strands of students' mathematical proficiency.*

Teacher Preparation and Professional Development

One critical component of any plan to improve mathematics learning is the preparation and professional development of teachers. If the goal of mathematical proficiency as portrayed in this report is to be reached by all students in grades pre-K to 8, their teachers will need to understand and practice techniques of teaching for that proficiency. Our view of mathematics proficiency requires teachers to act in new ways and to have understanding that they once were not expected to have. In particular, it is not a teacher's fault that he or she does not know enough to teach in the way we are asking. It is a far from trivial task to acquire such understanding—something that cannot reasonably be expected to happen in one's spare time and something that will require major policy changes to support and promote. Teacher preparation and professional development programs will need to develop proficiency in mathematics teaching, which has many parallels to proficiency in mathematics.

Developing Specialized Knowledge

The knowledge required to teach mathematics well is specialized knowledge. It includes an integrated knowledge of mathematics, knowledge of the development of students' mathematical understanding, and a repertoire of pedagogical practices that take into account the mathematics being taught and the students learning it. The evidence indicates that these forms of knowledge are not acquired in conventional undergraduate mathematics courses, whether they are general survey courses or specialized courses for mathematics majors. The implications for teacher preparation and professional development are that teachers need to learn these forms of knowledge in ways that help them forge connections.

Mathematical knowledge is a critical resource for teaching. Therefore, teacher preparation and professional development must provide significant and continuing opportunities for teachers to develop profound and useful mathematical knowledge. Teachers need to know the mathematics of the curriculum and where the curriculum is headed. They need to understand the connections among mathematical ideas and how they develop. Teachers also need to be able to unpack mathematical content and make visible to students the ideas behind the concepts and procedures. Finally, teachers need not only mathematical proficiency but also the ability to use it in guiding discussions, modifying problems, and making decisions about what matters to pursue in class and what to let drop. Very few teachers currently have

> Very few teachers currently have the specialized knowledge needed to teach mathematics in the way envisioned in this report.

the specialized knowledge needed to teach mathematics in the way envisioned in this report. Although it is not reasonable in the short term to expect all teachers to acquire such knowledge, every school needs access to expertise in mathematics teaching.

Teachers' opportunities to learn can help them develop their own knowledge about mathematics, about children's thinking about mathematics, and about mathematics teaching. Such opportunities can also help teachers learn how to solve the sorts of problems that are central to the practice of teaching. The following recommendations reflect our judgment concerning the specialized knowledge that teachers need:

- *Teachers of grades pre-K–8 should have a deep understanding of the mathematics of the school curriculum and the principles behind it.*

- *Programs and courses that emphasize "classroom mathematical knowledge" should be established specifically to prepare teachers to teach mathematics to students in such grades as pre-K–2, 3–5, and 6–8.*

- *Teachers should learn how children's mathematical knowledge develops and what their students are likely to bring with them to school.*

- *To provide a basis for continued learning by teachers, their preparation to teach, their professional development activities, and the instructional materials they use should engage them, individually and collectively, in developing a greater understanding of mathematics and of student thinking and in finding ways to put that understanding into practice. All teachers, whether preservice or inservice, should engage in inquiry as part of their teaching practice (e.g., by interacting with students and analyzing their work).*

- *Through their preparation and professional development, teachers should develop a repertoire of pedagogical techniques and the ability to use those techniques to accomplish lesson goals.*

- *Mathematics specialists—teachers who have special training and interest in mathematics—should be available in every elementary school.*

Working Together

Elementary and middle school teachers in the United States report spending relatively little time, compared with their counterparts in other countries, discussing the mathematics they are teaching or the methods they are using. They seldom plan lessons together, observe one another teach, or analyze students' work collectively. Studies of programs that require teachers to teach mathematically demanding curricula suggest that success is greater when teachers help one another not only learn the mathematics and learn about student thinking but also practice new teaching strategies. Our recommendation concerning time is not just about how much is available but how it is used:

• *Teachers should be provided with more time for planning and conferring with each other on mathematics instruction with appropriate support and guidance.*

Capitalizing on Professional Meetings

Teachers need more mathematically focused opportunities to learn mathematics, and they need to be prepared to manage changes in the field. Mathematics teachers already come together at meetings of professional societies such as the National Council of Teachers of Mathematics (NCTM), its affiliated groups, or other organizations. These occasions can provide opportunities for professional development of the sort discussed above. For example, portions of national or regional meetings of the NCTM could be organized into minicourses or institutes, without competing sessions being held at the same time. Professional development needs to grow out of current activities:

• *Professional meetings and other occasions when teachers come together to work on their practice should be used as opportunities for more serious and substantive professional development than has commonly been available.*

Sustaining Professional Development

Preparing to teach is a career-long activity. Teachers need to continue to learn. But rather than being focused on isolated facts and skills, teacher learning needs to be generative. That is, what teachers learn needs to serve as a basis for them to continue to learn from their practice. They need to see that practice as demanding continual review, analysis, and improvement. Studies of teacher change indicate that short-term, fragmented professional development is ineffective for developing teaching proficiency.

More resources of all types—money, time, leadership, attention—need to be invested in professional development for teachers of mathematics, and those resources already available could be used more wisely and productively. Each year a substantial amount of money is invested in professional development programs for teachers. Individual schools and districts fund some programs locally. Others are sponsored and funded by state agencies, federal agencies, or professional organizations. Much of the time and money invested in such programs, however, is not used effectively. Sponsors generally fund short-term, even one-shot, activities such as daylong workshops or two-day institutes that collectively do not form a cohesive and cumulative program of professional development. Furthermore, these activities are often conducted by an array of professional developers with minimal qualifications in mathematics and mathematics teaching. Professional development in mathematics needs to be sustained over time that is measured in years, not weeks or months, and it needs to involve a substantial amount of time each year. Our recommendations to raise the level of professional development are as follows:

> *Professional development in mathematics needs to be sustained over time that is measured in years, not weeks or months.*

- *Local education authorities should give teachers support, including stipends and released time, for sustained professional development.*

- *Providers of professional development should know mathematics and should know about students' mathematical thinking, how mathematics is taught, and teachers' thinking about mathematics and their own practice.*

- *Organizations and agencies that fund professional development in mathematics should focus resources on multi-year, coherent programs. Resources of agencies at every level should be marshaled to support substantial and sustained professional development.*

Monitoring Progress Toward Mathematical Proficiency

In this report we have set forth a variety of observations, conclusions, and recommendations that are designed to bring greater coherence and balance to the learning and teaching of mathematics. In particular, we have described five strands of mathematical proficiency that should frame all efforts to improve school mathematics.

Over the past decades, various visions have been put forward for improving curriculum, instruction, and assessment in mathematics, and many of those ideas have been tried in schools. Unfortunately, new programs are tried but then abandoned before their effectiveness has been well tested, and lessons learned from program evaluations are often lost. Although aspects of mathematics proficiency have been studied, other aspects such as productive disposition have received less attention; and no one, including the National Assessment of Educational Progress (NAEP), has studied the integrated portrait of mathematics proficiency set forth in this report. In order that efforts to improve U.S. school mathematics might be more cumulative and coordinated, we make the following recommendation:

• *An independent group of recognized standing should be constituted to assess the progress made in meeting the goal of mathematical proficiency for all U.S. schoolchildren.*

Supporting the Development of Mathematical Proficiency

The mathematics students need to learn today is not the same mathematics that their parents and grandparents needed to learn. Moreover, mathematics is a domain no longer limited to a select few. *All* students need to be mathematically proficient to the levels discussed in this report. The mathematics of grades pre-K–8 today involves much more than speed in pencil-and-paper arithmetic. Students need to understand mathematics, use it to solve problems, reason logically, compute fluently, and use it to make sense of their world. For that to happen, each student will need to develop the strands of proficiency in an integrated fashion.

No country—not even those performing highest on international surveys of mathematics achievement—has attained the goal of mathematical proficiency for all its students. It is an extremely ambitious goal, and the United States will never reach it by continuing to tinker with the controls of educational policy, pushing one button at a time. Adopting mathematics textbooks from other countries, testing teachers, holding students back a grade, putting schools under state sanctions—none of these alone will advance school mathematics very far toward mathematical proficiency for all. Instead, coordinated, systematic, and sustained modifications will need to be made in how school mathematics instruction has commonly proceeded, and support of new and different kinds will be required. Leadership and attention to the teaching of mathematics are needed in the formulation and implementation of policies at all levels of the educational system.

BIOGRAPHICAL SKETCHES

Jeremy Kilpatrick, *Chair,* is Regents Professor of Mathematics Education at the University of Georgia. He is currently studying the process of changing the school mathematics curriculum, which includes documenting the history of reform efforts in the United States. He is a former vice president of the International Commission on Mathematical Instruction, was a charter member of the Mathematical Sciences Education Board (MSEB) of the National Research Council (NRC), was a member of the National Council of Teachers of Mathematics' Commission on the Future of the Standards, and currently serves on the NRC's Board on International Comparative Studies in Education. He also chaired the MSEB study that produced *Measuring What Counts* (NRC, 1993). Kilpatrick has published extensively on mathematics education issues, including "Confronting Reform," in the *American Mathematical Monthly*, and "Reflections on Verifying Change in School Mathematics," in the *Journal of Classroom Interaction*. He has engaged in numerous editorial activities, most recently with Anna Sierpinska editing *Mathematics Education as a Research Domain: A Search for Identity* (1998); and with George Stanic editing *A History of School Mathematics* (in preparation). He is the recipient of multiple awards and honors, including the John W. Wilson Memorial Award and several Fulbright lecturer and scholar awards. He holds an honorary doctorate from the University of Gothenburg. Kilpatrick received an A.A. in mathematics and science from Chaffey College; an A.B. in mathematics and an M.A. in education from the University of California, Berkeley; and an M.S. in mathematics and a Ph.D. in mathematics education from Stanford University.

Deborah Loewenberg Ball is Arthur F. Thurnau Professor of Mathematics Education and Teacher Education at the University of Michigan. An experienced elementary teacher, Ball conducts research on instruction and on the processes of learning to teach. She also investigates efforts to improve teaching through policy, curriculum, reform initiatives, and teacher education. Ball's publications include articles on teacher learning and teacher education; the role of subject matter knowledge in teaching and learning to teach; endemic challenges of teaching; and the relations of policy and practice in instructional improvement.

Hyman Bass is the Roger Lyndon Collegiate Professor of Mathematics and Professor of Mathematics Education at the University of Michigan. From 1959 to 1998, he was a member of the Mathematics Department at Columbia University. His mathematical research publications cover broad areas of algebra, with connections to geometry, topology, and number theory. He has received the Cole Prize in Algebra from the American Mathematical Society and the Van Amringe Book Award from Columbia University for a book that helped found the subject of algebraic K-theory. He has held visiting research and faculty positions at mathematical centers around the world, including Princeton, Paris, Bombay, Rio, Cambridge, Stockholm, Mexico, Rome, Trieste, Hong Kong, Berkeley, and Jerusalem. He has lectured widely, in particular as a Phi Beta Kappa National Visiting Scholar. He is a member of the National Academy of Sciences and the American Academy of Arts and Sciences. Bass currently serves as President of the American Mathematical Society. He formerly chaired the Mathematical Sciences Education Board of the National Research Council and the Committee on Education of the American Mathematical Society and is President of the International Commission on Mathematics Instruction.

Jere Brophy is University Distinguished Professor of Teacher Education and Educational Psychology and formerly Co-Director of the Institute for Research on Teaching at Michigan State University. He has done extensive research on teacher effectiveness, the interpersonal dynamics of teacher-student relationships, teacher expectation effects, classroom management, and student motivation. He received a Ph.D. in human development and clinical psychology from the University of Chicago.

Felix Browder is University Professor of Mathematics at Rutgers, The State University of New Jersey, and Max Mason Distinguished Service Professor

Emeritus of Mathematics at the University of Chicago, where he was a faculty member from 1963 to 1986. He also served as Vice President for Research at Rutgers University from 1986 to 1991. Browder is the immediate Past President of the American Mathematical Society and was awarded the Presidential National Medal of Science in 1999. He is a member of the National Academy of Sciences (NAS) and the American Academy of Arts and Sciences. He has served as a member of the Council of the NAS and its Committee on Science, Engineering, and Public Policy. His research interests include topological methods in analytical problems; history and philosophy of mathematics and science; problems of scientific organizations and institutions; and mathematics and science education.

Thomas Carpenter is Professor of Curriculum and Instruction at the University of Wisconsin–Madison. He is currently Director of the National Center for Improving Student Learning and Achievement in Mathematics and Sciences, and he is a former editor of the *Journal for Research in Mathematics Education*. Along with Elizabeth Fennema, Megan Franke, and others, he developed the Cognitively Guided Instruction research and professional development project. His research investigates the development of children's mathematical thinking, how teachers use specific knowledge about children's mathematical thinking in instruction, and how children's thinking can be used as a basis for professional development. He is currently focusing on the development of algebraic thinking in elementary school. Carpenter received a B.S. from Stanford University and a Ph.D. from the University of Wisconsin.

Carolyn Day is Associate Director for Elementary Mathematics and Science for the Dayton Public Schools in Ohio. She has been with the district for 28 years, first as an elementary teachers, then as a teacher of mathematics in grades 6 through 8, and for the past 10 years as a mathematics supervisor. Day has a B.S. in elementary education from Central State University in Wilberforce, Ohio, and an M.Ed. in curriculum, instruction, and administration from Wright State University. She currently serves on the board of the Ohio Mathematics Leadership Council, the Aullwood Audubon Center in Ohio, and the National Council of Supervisors of Mathematics as secretary.

Karen Fuson is Professor of Education and Psychology in the School of Education and Social Policy at Northwestern University. She received her B.A. in mathematics from Oberlin College and her M.A.T. and Ph.D. from the University of Chicago. Her research interests concern young children's mathematical understanding and the classroom and school conditions that can facilitate such understanding. She seeks to identify and describe developmental or experiential sequences in children's understanding of various mathematical domains, particularly for ages 2 through 11, and to use this understanding of children's thinking to build classroom teaching and learning experiences that will support children's thinking. She is the author of numerous research articles and review articles, including a chapter on addition and subtraction in the *Handbook of Research on Mathematics Teaching and Learning*. Her book *Children's Counting and Concepts of Number* focuses on understanding children's counting and their conceptual advances in using counting in various situations. She has done extensive work on children's multidigit addition and subtraction and on word problem solving and has more recently focused on various aspects of multiplication, division, and fractions at grades 3 through 6 as well as on aspects of geometry and measure. She is directing the Children's Math Worlds project, which focuses on research to design effective methods of teaching and learning in grade K–5 English-speaking and Spanish-speaking urban and suburban classrooms.

James Hiebert is H. Rodney Sharp Professor of Education at the University of Delaware, where he works with preservice and inservice teachers. His professional interests focus on mathematics teaching and learning in classrooms. He has edited books, including *Conceptual and Procedural Knowledge: The Case of Mathematics* and *Number Concepts and Operations in the Middle Grades*, and he co-authored the books *Making Sense: Teaching and Learning Mathematics with Understanding* and *The Teaching Gap: Best Ideas from the World's Teachers for Improving Education in the Classroom*. He currently serves as the mathematics content specialist on the Video Study of the Third International Mathematics and Science Study-Repeat. He received a B.A. in mathematics from Fresno Pacific College, an M.A. in mathematics from the University of Illinois, and a Ph.D. in mathematics education from University of Wisconsin.

Roger Howe is a Professor of Mathematics at Yale University where he has been since 1974. He received his Ph.D. from the University of California at Berkeley, and prior to joining the Yale faculty, spent five years at the State University of New York at Stony Brook. He has been a visiting professor at many universities, both in the United States and abroad. Howe's mathematical research focuses on symmetry and its consequences. He is a member of the Connecticut Academy of Science and Engineering, the American Academy of Arts and Sciences, and the National Academy of Sciences. He has served on Mathematical Sciences Education Board and on the board of directors of the Connecticut Academy for Education in Mathematics, Science, and Technology. He served as chair of the American Mathematical Society (AMS) Association Review Group for revision of the National Council of Teachers of Mathematics Standards and is currently chair of the AMS Committee on Education.

Carolyn Kieran is Professor of Mathematics Education at the University of Quebec, Montreal. Her research interests include the learning and teaching of school algebra, the use of technology in school mathematics, the role of collaboration in mathematical discourse, and the application of historical and psychological models to mathematics education research. Her publications include *Research Agenda for Mathematics Education: Research Issues in the Learning and Teaching of Algebra* with S. Wagner, *Approaches to Algebra: Perspectives for Research and Teaching* with N. Bednarz and L. Lee, and a chapter on "The Learning and Teaching of School Algebra" in the 1992 *Handbook of Research on Mathematics Teaching and Learning*. She has served as president of the International Group for the Psychology of Mathematics Education, vice president of the Canadian Mathematics Education Study Group, and chair of the editorial panel of the *Journal for Research in Mathematics Education*. Her degrees include a Ph.D. from the Department of Educational Psychology at McGill University and a Master's in the Teaching of Mathematics from Concordia University in Montreal. In addition to teaching mathematics and mathematics education courses to preservice and inservice teachers at both the graduate and undergraduate levels, Kieran has also taught mathematics at public school.

Richard E. Mayer is Professor of Psychology at the University of California, Santa Barbara (UCSB), where he has served since 1975. His major research interests are in educational psychology, with a focus on instructional methods that promote problem-solving transfer. He is a former president of the Division of Educational Psychology of the American Psychological Association and a former chair of the Department of Psychology at UCSB. In 2000 he received the American Psychological Association's E. L. Thorndike Award for lifetime achievement in educational psychology. He was editor of *Educational Psychologist and Instructional Science* and currently serves on the editorial boards of 12 journals. He has authored 13 books including *Thinking, Problem Solving, Cognition* (2nd edition) and *The Promise of Educational Psychology: Learning in the Content Areas*. He has authored more than 200 articles and chapters, mainly in the area of educational psychology.

Kevin Miller is Associate Professor in the departments of Psychology, Educational Psychology, and the Beckman Institute of the University of Illinois at Urbana-Champaign. His research focuses on how cognitive tools such as number-naming systems, writing systems, and other representational systems affect children's learning. Recent research involves cross-cultural comparisons of the learning of reading and mathematics by children in China and the United States and research on how videotaped representations of classroom teaching can be used to improve mathematics education in the United States. He received a Ph.D. in child psychology from the Institute of Child Development of the University of Minnesota and taught at Michigan State University and the University of Texas prior to coming to the University of Illinois.

Casilda Pardo has been a teacher for 18 years. She became a full-time mathematics resource teacher in 1998 at Valle Vista Elementary School in Albuquerque, New Mexico. From 1994 to 1998, she was a half-time classroom teacher and half-time mathematics resource teacher at Armijo Elementary School in Albuquerque. She is also a national trainer for the *Investigations in Number, Data, and Space* curriculum. From 1992 to 1994, she served as a clinical supervisor of student teachers, which included teaching mathematics and science methods courses. Among her professional activities, she has taught mathematical methods at the University of New Mexico (UNM), has been a teacher in the State Initiative in Math and Science Education summer institutes, and has taught Thinking Mathematics I and II at the Continuing Education division of UNM. Pardo received a B.A. from Marymount College and an M.A. from the University of Wisconsin.

Edgar Robinson was Vice President and Treasurer of the Exxon Corporation upon retirement in 1998. In that role he oversaw various financial activities of the Corporation. During his almost 40 years with Exxon he held many senior management positions in Texas, New York, and London. Robinson holds an A.B. in economics from Brown University and an M.B.A. from Harvard Business School. He served as member of President Reagan's Private Sector Survey on Cost Control (the Grace Commission). He has also been a member of the Conference Board's Council of Financial Executives (1990–1998). He is a trustee emeritus of Brown University and a past chairman and life member of the Dean's Advisory Council at Chicago Business School. Robinson is current Past President of the Dallas Zoological Society and the Vogel Alcove Childcare Center for the Homeless, a project of the Dallas Jewish Coalition. He is a member of the boards of the Dallas Symphony, the Dallas Theater

Center, the Greenwall Foundation, and the American Trust for the British Library.

Hung-Hsi Wu is Professor of Mathematics at the University of California, Berkeley. His area of expertise is real and complex geometry. He received his A.B. from Columbia University and his Ph.D. from the Massachusetts Institute of Technology. He has authored several articles on mathematics education and is also a technical reviewer of the 1999 California Mathematics Framework. Almost all his writings in education can be found on his homepage: <http://www.math.berkeley.edu/~wu/>.

INDEX

M